A HISTORY OF JAPAN

1334–1615

A HISTORY OF JAPAN
1334-1615

George Sansom

STANFORD UNIVERSITY PRESS
STANFORD, CALIFORNIA

Stanford University Press
Stanford, California
© 1961 by the Board of Trustees of the
Leland Stanford Junior University
Printed in the United States of America
Cloth ISBN 0-8047-0524-0
Paper ISBN 0-8047-0525-9
Original edition 1961
Last figure below indicates year of this printing:
83 82 81 80 79 78 77 76 75 74

PREFACE

This volume relates the course of events in a period of some two hundred and eighty years during which the whole of Japan was torn by factions and plagued by incessant civil war until late in the sixteenth century, when a process of national unification by force of arms was begun by a great general, Nobunaga, continued by his successor Hideyoshi, and completed by the victories of Ieyasu, the first Tokugawa Shōgun.

Examined in retrospect this prolonged achievement of the military power reveals a decline in the moral standards of its leaders. The rule of the Hōjō had been distinguished by prudent administration and a concern for justice until after the Mongol invasion of 1281, which threw a great strain upon the feudal economy. At the turn of the century the Hōjō were showing clear signs of weakness, and in 1334 (perhaps because any feudal system harbours an internal contradiction) they succumbed to the pressure of dangerous rivals. Kamakura fell, the Regency was destroyed, and the Throne, after a fruitless restoration, was subjected to the dominance of a new line of Shōguns, beginning with Ashikaga Takauji.

Takauji and his kinsmen and associates were men without scruple. They have been blamed for their ill-treatment of the Imperial House, although in this they were no more guilty than the Hōjō, who had banished an Emperor in 1221. Their real faults were their gross ambition and their ruthless greed. Yet the two centuries and more of Ashikaga rule (from 1336 to 1573) are the liveliest, the most varied and interesting period in Japanese history, whether military, political, or social. In the nineteenth century, because political orthodoxy regarded the Ashikaga Shōguns as traitors, Japanese historians tended to neglect this period; but today it is enthusiastically explored by specialists in almost every field bent upon tracing the evolution of the national life during the middle ages.

Some scholars describe the dynastic struggle of the fourteenth century and its sequels as a social revolution. Such a label seems to me misleading, for what took place was a redistribution of feudal privilege and power due to economic stresses rather than to conscious political design and affecting the lives of both warrior and peasant in unforeseen ways.

It is upon this aspect of Ashikaga history that I have mainly dwelt in the following chapters. I have paid comparatively little attention to the activities of Western missionaries and traders in Japan in the six-

teenth century because I regard their intrusion as an episode of secondary importance in the history of the nation. From the Western view-
point it has been amply treated by Murdoch.

Since warfare was almost incessant during the years treated here,
I have dealt at length and in what may seem tiresome detail with campaigns and the clash of arms. I wish I could have abbreviated these
chronicles, but they are a necessary part of any study of a society in
which the warriors compose the ruling class. Moreover, because development in the arts of war was rapid, the changing needs of armies
influenced the direction of the economic development of the whole
country and often dictated changes in its social and political structure.
Even the aesthetic climate of the fifteenth century reflects the taste of
successful fighting men.

G. S.

ACKNOWLEDGMENTS

I owe a great debt to many friends in Japan for continued assistance and encouragement.

Fukui Rikichirō (formerly Professor at Tōhoku Daigaku, Sendai), as well as reading critically parts of my manuscript, took pains to select and procure photographs for use as illustrations and gave me good advice out of his store of learning on mediaeval art and letters.

Yashiro Yukio (celebrated as an art historian and now Director of the Yamato Bunkakan Museum at Nara), whose friendship I have enjoyed for many years, never failed to give me generous help.

For several months in the spring and summer of 1959 I had the exceptional advantage of almost daily guidance by Toyoda Takeshi, of Tōhoku Daigaku, one of the leading Japanese historians, who was at that time a guest of Stanford University. Our collaboration was as fruitful and harmonious as he is erudite and kind. We worked at the same desk side by side, although metaphorically I sat at his feet, with great profit and enjoyment. I also owe thanks to his accomplished wife, Toyoda Yoshiko, a specimen of whose calligraphy adorns the page preceding the half title of this volume.

Sakamoto Tarō, the learned director of the Historiographical Institute of Tokyo University, supplied me with much valuable material in the shape of photographs of documents of historical importance.

Ishizawa Masao, of the Tokyo National Museum and a member of the Commission for the Protection of Cultural Property, also kindly furnished photographs of paintings and other articles under his care.

Here I must also acknowledge the permission granted to me by the above Commission (Bunkazai Hogo Iinkai) to publish photographs of materials under its protection.

At Stanford Dr. Joseph Williams, Professor of Geography, again generously gave time and care to the preparation of maps and diagrams.

I am indebted to Helen Craig McCullough of the University of California at Berkeley for research assistance, especially in regard to the first five chapters of this volume. Her translation of part of the *Taiheiki* covers some of the matters treated in those chapters.

Other friends here and at Berkeley, in particular the library staff of the East Asiatic collections, gave me valuable assistance. I am especially obliged to J. G. Bell and Linda Brownrigg, of the Stanford University Press, for highly skilled editorial work.

CONTENTS

DESCRIPTIVE LIST OF PLATES

FRONTISPIECE

Suigetsu Kannon. A sculpture of the late Kamakura period, foreshadowing the strong influence of Sung art during Ashikaga times. It is of wood, painted; 47 cm. in height. Now in the Kamakura Museum, it is the property of the Tōkeiji.

1. Ashikaga Takauji. An equestrian portrait bearing the cipher of Ashikaga Yoshiakira, Takauji's son. Formerly the property of the Moriya family. It has been questioned, but it is almost certainly authentic.

2. Musō Kokushi. A contemporary portrait, now owned by the Myōchi-In; the photograph was kindly furnished by Benridō. The Saihōji portrait is less flattering, but probably more revealing of the prelate's character.

3. A seascape by Sesson, ca. 1550.

4. Detail from the Long Scroll (Chōkan) of Sesshū, ca. 1470. Property of the Mōri family.

5. Portraits of the Emperor Go-Daigo and the retired Emperor Hanazono. Part of a scroll in the Imperial Collection (*Rekidai Tennō Shinyei Emaki*).

6. Four figures from the *Tōhoku-In Uta-awase,* a picture scroll portraying a verse-matching party for members of various occupations. It is ascribed —both script and drawings—to Hanazono. The figures are from left to right (1) a gambler, (2) a carpenter, (3) a sorceress, and (4) a moulder of pots and pans.

7. A portrait of the Emperor Hanazono in monastic dress, by Gōshin, a contemporary Court painter. It formerly belonged to the Chōfukuji. A contemporary writer described it as a very good likeness.

8. A portrait of Ashikaga Yoshimitsu. In the Rokuonji.

9. A portrait of Ashikaga Yoshimochi. In colour, on silk. It is the property of the Jingōji in Kyoto, and is thought to represent Yoshimochi at the age of about 21. The photograph was kindly furnished by Benridō.

10. Ashigaru destroying a building. From *Shinnyodō Engi Emaki,* a picture scroll belonging to the Kyoto Gokurakuji.

11. Detail from *Yūki Kassen Ekotoba,* a picture scroll showing episodes in the civil war of 1440, when Yūki Ujitomo revolted against the Bakufu. In colour, on paper. Property of the Hosomi family, Ōsaka.

12. Ritual dance at rice-planting time.

13. The market place at Fukuoka in Hizen. From the scroll *Ippen Shōnin E-den* ("Pictorial Life of Ippen").

LIST OF ILLUSTRATIONS IN TEXT

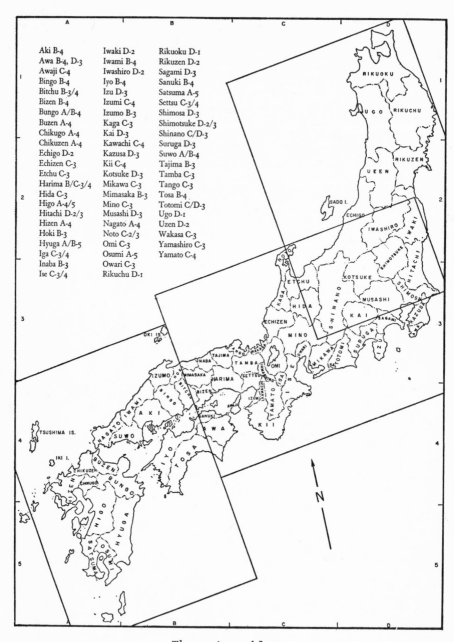

Aki B-4	Iwaki D-2	Rikuoku D-1
Awa B-4, D-3	Iwami B-4	Rikuzen D-2
Awaji C-4	Iwashiro D-2	Sagami D-3
Bingo B-4	Iyo B-4	Sanuki B-4
Bitchu B-3/4	Izu D-3	Satsuma A-5
Bizen B-4	Izumi C-4	Settsu C-3/4
Bungo A/B-4	Izumo B-3	Shimosa D-3
Buzen A-4	Kaga C-3	Shimotsuke D-2/3
Chikugo A-4	Kai D-3	Shinano C/D-3
Chikuzen A-4	Kawachi C-4	Suruga D-3
Echigo D-2	Kazusa D-3	Suwo A/B-4
Echizen C-3	Kii C-4	Tajima B-3
Etchu C-3	Kotsuke D-3	Tamba C-3
Harima B/C-3/4	Mikawa C-3	Tango C-3
Hida C-3	Mimasaka B-3	Tosa B-4
Higo A-4/5	Mino C-3	Totomi C/D-3
Hitachi D-2/3	Musashi D-3	Ugo D-1
Hizen A-4	Nagato A-4	Uzen D-2
Hoki B-3	Noto C-2/3	Wakasa C-3
Hyuga A/B-5	Omi C-3	Yamashiro C-3
Iga C-3/4	Osumi A-5	Yamato C-4
Inaba B-3	Owari C-3	
Ise C-3/4	Rikuchu D-1	

The provinces of Japan

The five northern provinces correspond to the earlier Mutsu and Dewa. There are two provinces named Awa; the names are written with different characters. The islands of Iki, Oki, Sado, and Tsushima are not provinces. The three small rectangles correspond to the enlarged maps on the following three pages.

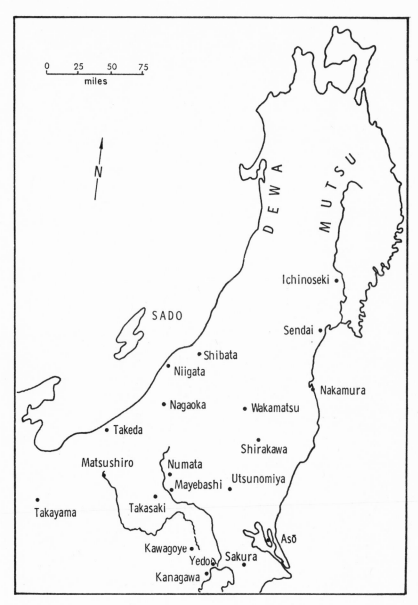

The northern and eastern provinces

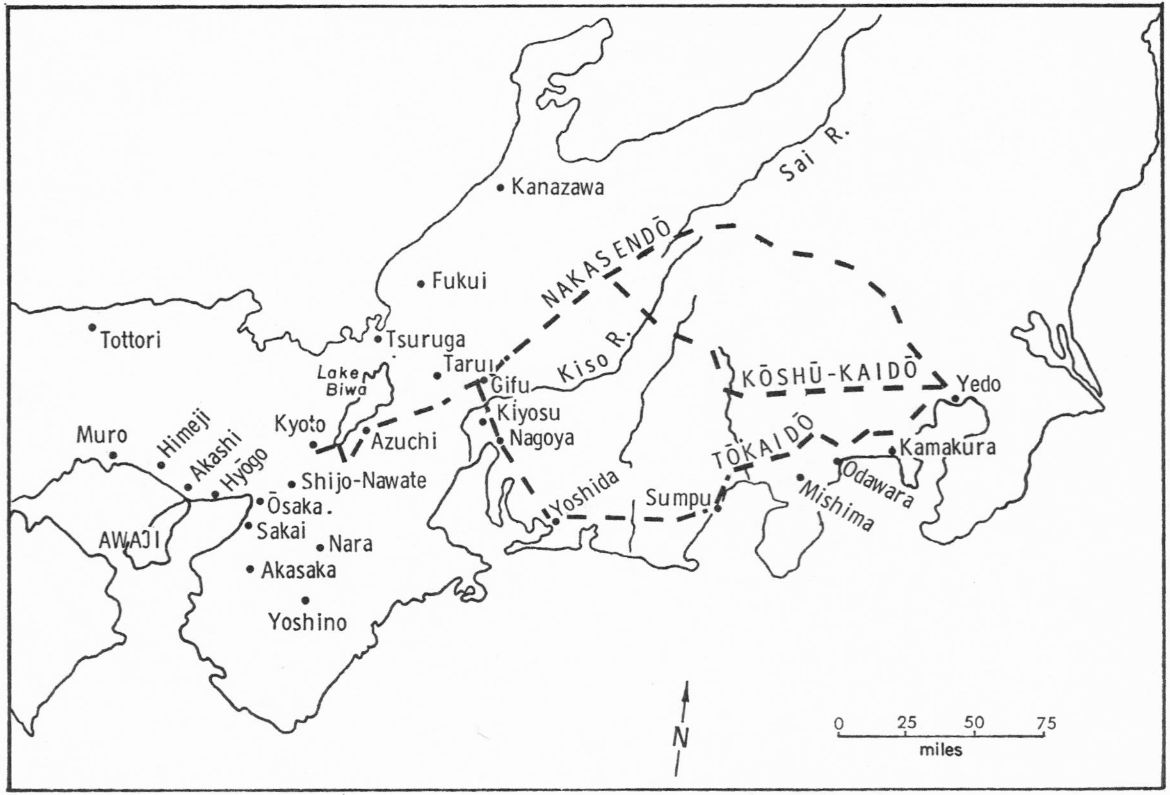

Kanazawa

Sai R.

KŌSHŪ-KAIDŌ

Yedo

Kamakura

Odawara

Mishima

TŌKAIDŌ

Sumpu

NAKASENDŌ

Kiso R.

Yoshida

Fukui

Tsuruga

Taruı

Gifu

Kiyosu

Nagoya

Azuchi

Lake Biwa

Shijo-Nawate

Kyoto

Ōsaka

Nara

Akasaka

Yoshino

Sakai

Hyōgo

Akashi

Himeji

AWAJI

Muro

Tottori

N

miles

0   25   50   75

The central provinces (Chūgoku) and the Home Provinces

xviii

The western provinces, Shikoku, and Kyūshū

THE SCRIPT ON THE OPPOSITE PAGE,
FROM THE ACCOMPLISHED BRUSH OF TOYODA YOSHIKO,
FORMS THE WORD *arasoi*, MEANING *strife*,
AND THAT IS THE MAIN THEME
OF THIS VOLUME.

> They around the flag
> Of each his faction, in their several Clans
> Light-arm'd or heavy, sharp, smooth, swift or slow,
> Swarm populous, unnumber'd as the Sands
>
> . . . .
>
> To whom these most adhere,
> Hee rules a moment; *Chaos* Umpire sits,
> And by decision more imbroiles the fray
> By which he Reigns. Next him high Arbiter
> *Chance* governs all.
>
> (*Paradise Lost*, II)

> The history upon which I am entering is rich
> in disasters, dreadful in its battles, rent by its
> seditions and cruel even in its peace.
>
> (TACITUS, *Histories*, I, ii)

A HISTORY OF JAPAN
1334–1615

1318	Accession of Go-Daigo
1321	Abolition of cloister government (Insei)
1324	Failure of Go-Daigo's plot against the Bakufu
1331	Failure of Go-Daigo's second plot against the Bakufu
1332	Go-Daigo banished to Oki
1333	Fall of the Hōjō Regency and the Kamakura Bakufu
1334	The Kemmu restoration
1335	Ashikaga Takauji rebels
1336	Minatogawa. Takauji enters Kyoto
1337	Go-Daigo escapes to Yoshino. The era of the two Courts begins
1338	Takauji appointed Shōgun. The foundation of the Muromachi Bakufu
1339	Kitabatake Chikafusa establishes headquarters in Hitachi. Go-Daigo dies
1340	Prince Kanenaga arrives in Kyūshū
1342	Chikafusa returns to Yoshino
1350	Ashikaga Tadayoshi quarrels with Takauji
1351	Tadayoshi attempts to effect a reconciliation between the Courts
1352	Tadayoshi killed by Takauji. The loyalists capture Kyoto
1353	Takauji recaptures Kamakura and Kyoto
1354	Chikafusa dies
1358	Takauji dies. Ashikaga Yoshiakira appointed Shōgun
1362	Southern army attacks Kyoto. Yoshiakira escapes
1365	Kanenaga gains control of all Kyūshū
1368	Ashikaga Yoshimitsu appointed Shōgun
1370	Imagawa Sadayo sent to Kyūshū
1372	Imagawa gains control of northern Kyūshū
1383	Kanenaga dies. Loyalist resistance at an end
1392	Union of the Northern and Southern Courts

CHAPTER I

THE REIGN OF GO-DAIGO

1. The Rival Dynasties. Go-Daigo's Accession, 1318

THE LONG-DRAWN-OUT succession dispute between the senior and junior lines of descent from the Emperor Go-Saga has been described in detail in the first volume of this work; but for the sake of clarity it is useful to recapitulate here some of its main features.

It began after the death of Go-Saga in 1272, and lasted until the accession of Go-Daigo in 1318, by which it was temporarily solved, only to be resumed in 1331 and to last for more than fifty years during which the whole country was disturbed by incessant civil war. In the period from 1272 to 1318 the rivalry between the two lines was so intense and continuous that the Kamakura Bakufu, though reluctant to take sides, felt obliged to intervene and to give its support to one candidate or another simply in order to prevent continuous wrangling and to preserve the peace. No choice of sovereign or heir-apparent was valid unless it had the approval of the Bakufu, and the Bakufu displayed a neutral attitude in this contentious matter, working out a plan by which succession alternated between the two lines. Its object was to please both sides, yet as might have been foreseen it ended by pleasing neither. But the decisions of Kamakura had to be accepted because the imperial Court had a lively memory of the fate of the abdicated emperor Go-Toba, whose resistance to the Bakufu in 1221 had brought a punitive force to the capital and led to his banishment.

Despite the strength of their position, the leaders in Kamakura were surprisingly patient in their treatment of the quarrelsome aspirants. Unlike the Regent Yoshitoki, who chastised Go-Toba for his insubordination, the deputies of the Shōgun in Kamakura two or three generations later seem to have lacked confidence in their own power to control the warrior class in the provinces and to direct the behaviour of princes and nobles in the capital. They were no doubt aware of a rising antagonism to themselves and their rule, in feudal society as well as in Court circles, but they were at a loss when it came to deciding how to deal with it.

It is true that their position had been weakened—and not through their own fault—by the awful ordeal of defending the country against invasion over a period of almost half a century. Their finances were dangerously weak, and the loyalty of their vassals was strained. But these facts are not enough to account for their decline, which was a deterioration in quality as well as a loss of wealth and power. There can be little doubt that the weakness of the Bakufu from the end of the thirteenth century was due in a large measure to the poor character of the Hōjō Regents after the death of Tokimune in 1284. Sadatoki (1284–1301) was able but indolent. Takatoki (1316–26) was dissolute and was described (in an unfriendly chronicle, it is true) as base and incorrigibly shameless; moreover, he was only a boy when he succeeded, a weak youth in the hands of corrupt advisers. It was these men whose management of the affairs of the Bakufu put into the minds of aggrieved or envious vassals ideas of destroying the Hōjō family, and emboldened the party at Court which desired to restore the power of the Throne.

That was no doubt a general desire in the capital. However, the Court was not united in support of one candidate, and on that account the position was weaker than it might have been had the two lines been able to reach even provisional agreement. Indeed the wrangling between them was most unseemly, as one of the contestants pointed out. This was the Emperor Hanazono, an acute and remarkably unbiassed observer, who was in 1318 obliged to abdicate and give place to Go-Daigo. In his diary, under dates in January 1325, he describes how in order to urge their respective claims, messengers and deputations from both parties had speeded to Kamakura in what the people in derision called a "horse race." The rivals competed also in prayers and incantations at the great shrines and monasteries, each condemning the other, doubtless to the confusion of the divinities addressed.

At the end of a long series of dynastic arguments Go-Daigo ascended the throne in the year 1318, and to the surprise—or at any rate the displeasure—of the Bakufu, he showed that he meant to break the pattern of accession and early abdication which had been followed since the death of Go-Saga. He made it clear that he would not abdicate to make way for an infant, or indeed for anybody. He was a man of thirty and he intended to govern the country as long as he lived. He had plans for reform which he was determined to execute, and he began to organize his government on new lines.

Quite early in his reign he had an experience which hardened his resentment against the Bakufu. He had been enthroned in April 1318, and had been carrying on the government under the direction of his father, the cloistered Go-Uda. Towards the end of the year the regular meeting was held to determine promotions and retirements, and shortly thereafter the Kampaku resigned and was replaced by Ichijō Uchitsune. The Bakufu apparently did not approve of this change, which had been arranged by Go-Daigo. Accordingly, when the installation of the new Kampaku was due to take place, it turned out that none of the Court nobles would attend because they feared the Bakufu's displeasure. The Emperor sent word of this to Go-Uda and asked his advice. Go-Uda was incensed and scrawled across the letter the words "This is outrageous" ("motte no hoka ni sōrō"). He suggested the name of a high official who might be summoned, but nothing came of his suggestion. The installation took place soon after, without the usual attendance. No doubt Go-Daigo's determination to resist the Bakufu was strengthened by this and similar instances of the intrusion of Kamakura upon the imperial prerogative.

It would be superflous to trace here in detail the steps by which Go-Daigo began the reforms which he had planned, since within a few years he was in exile while his supporters struggled against the military power of the Hōjō. But it is convenient to give a brief outline of his early measures, because some of them were followed up when he was able to resume his reign in 1333. His first important action was to abolish the practice of cloister government (Insei), which had been at the root of much political trouble since the days of its first great exponent, Shirakawa, who although abdicated was the de facto sovereign from 1086 to 1129. Go-Daigo took this important step in 1321,[1] with the consent of his father, Go-Uda-In, who resigned from his office as a demonstration of approval. News of this gesture was conveyed to the Bakufu and there accepted, although it must have been clear that a really crucial change had been accomplished to the advantage of the ruling sovereign.

Several changes in the organization of government became necessary after this move. The offices of the In—both the buildings and the functions—were transferred to new holders under the direction of the sovereign himself. Advisory councils were set up which were intended to make real decisions, and the former Record Office was revived and enlarged so that it constituted a court of law for the settlement not only of disputes about land but also of suits and complaints connected with public business in general. Some arrangement of this nature was essential, since during the long period of cloister government important official business tended to be handled (sometimes very summarily) in the In's secretariat (In no Fudono).

Contemporary notices speak well of Go-Daigo's reforms, praising his wisdom and devotion to kingly duty; but his new arrangements were not put to the severe test of time, since during the ten years from the abolition of cloister government to the break with the Bakufu, that is, from 1321 to 1331, he and his advisers must have devoted much

---

[1] It will be noticed that the era name was changed in the year 1321 to Genkō, signifying the start of a new regime. This was the fifty-eighth year in the current sexagenary cycle, and it had been the practice to make a change at this point since 901, when the era called Engi was opened to inaugurate a period of wise laws and good government. The successive eras of this sequence were as follows:

Engi	901	Eiji	1141
Ōwa	961	Kennin	1201
Jian	1021	Kōchō	1261
Eihō	1081	Genkō	1321

These changes did not preclude new era names for intervening years. That was a matter of choice. It should be noted that the imperial titles Go-Uda and Go-Daigo were chosen to express an intention to return to the ideals of Uda and Daigo, who reigned in the auspicious years of Kampyō (889–98) and Engi (901–22).

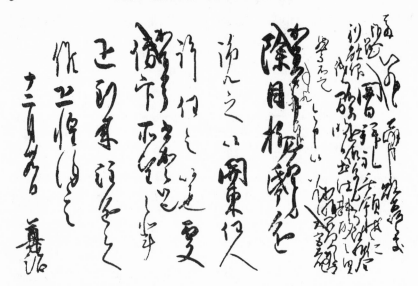

The letter from Go-Daigo to Go-Uda referred to on p. 4. Go-Uda's reply begins on the extreme right with the words "This is outrageous." The last line is overwritten on the large black characters to the right of centre.

if not most of their effort to the exacting task of planning and plotting a rising against the supreme military power. He knew that in order to carry out his design he would have to resist the Bakufu, and since there was no prospect of changing their policy by argument, he was obliged to contemplate the use of force. His thoughts seem to have followed that line even before his enthronement, and within a few years he was conspiring to overthrow the Shōgunate, encouraged by certain signs of weakness in Kamakura. The story of the conspiracies and the breath-taking risks they involved makes an exciting chapter of history and throws light on the nature of Kyoto life and its more engaging follies. Its most surprising feature is the failure of the Bakufu to see evidence that must have been staring them in the face. One incident will suffice as an example of the rashness of the conspirators and the short sight of the warriors, and perhaps it reveals a general rule that conspirators in all countries are men so proud of their undertaking that they cannot bear to keep it entirely secret.

In Kyoto in the year 1324 the main conspirators formed a secret society called the Free-and-Easy (Burei-kō or Harei-kō, meaning a gathering at which the rules of etiquette are suspended). Its members were of various ranks, and they used to meet at parties where, to put it mildly, all formality was banned. This had the advantage that persons of different social standing could talk to one another without reserve or circumspection. They would sit and drink in extreme dishabille, without their hats, their hair loose and their clothes rumpled—those who were monks discarded their robes and sat in their long shirts. They were waited upon by a score of beautiful girls of about seventeen, in diaphanous garments, serving delicacies of all kinds and pouring wine as if from a spring. All present enjoyed singing and dancing. But in the midst of these riotous pleasures only one thing was discussed—how to destroy "the savages in the East," the warriors of Kamakura.

The source of this anecdote is the *Taiheiki*, a great historical romance, but there is no reason to disbelieve it. One might suppose that such exceptional gatherings would not escape the attention of nocturnal passers-by, and it is clear that they did somehow come to the notice of the observant ex-Emperor Hanazono. In his diary he describes the goings-on of the Burei-kō as they had been told to him. He says that the members sit and drink half-naked, and by inviting certain scholars who are ignorant of their purpose they try to give the meetings an air of solemnity proper to the discussion of learned matters. He suggests that people in Kyoto have already guessed that these are not ordinary banquets. Yet there is no sign that the Bakufu's Rokuhara headquarters in Kyoto had got wind of them.

The Bakufu seems to have lost its traditional sense of proportion, its pragmatic wisdom; for its officers, even while they were failing as intelligence agents, were interfering with Kyoto in matters of no true importance and thereby enraging the Court.

But whatever the truth about the Burei-kō conspirators, in 1324 the Bakufu agents in Kyoto did uncover a rather well developed conspiracy against Kamakura, in which some of the Burei-kō members were involved. They acted promptly and arrested the ringleaders, but they accepted Go-Daigo's protestation and his emissary Fujiwara Nobufusa's plea that the Emperor had no knowledge of this plot, though they must have been pretty certain of his complicity. No doubt they tortured some of the suspects to get evidence, but they did not punish the persons they had arrested, except for one or two, and even these were not severely treated. This moderation is not easy to explain. It may be that the Bakufu, while strengthening their precautions in Kyoto, thought it prudent not to make a major issue of the conspiracy but to play it down, on the principle that it is a part of political wisdom not to make a second-class dispute into a first-class quarrel. It is more likely, however, that their decision was due not so much to good judgment as to lack of resolution.

However that may be, the Emperor, though for a time rather frightened, did not abandon hope of ousting the Bakufu, and he stood out firmly against attempts of the senior line to force his abdication. He continued to seek support for his plans, relying mainly upon the great religious bodies to furnish him with spiritual and some military aid. He could not count upon any powerful warrior families to declare in his favour, though he might hope after some early successes, however slight, to persuade one or more of the important vassals to join a movement against the Hōjō family. There were doubtless many chieftains who felt that a share in the spoils of a civil war might restore their fortunes. A strong temptation was offered by the great estates controlled by the Hōjō leaders, whom they no longer respected.

Accordingly Go-Daigo went on with his plans until the spring of 1331, when they were treacherously revealed by one of his three trusted advisers, Fujiwara Sadafusa. Shortly after this the Bakufu sent officers to Kyoto, where they caused the arrest of certain important monks and others party to the Court's intentions. These persons were sent to Kamakura for interrogation, and the nature of the conspiracy was made clear. Go-Daigo hastily endeavoured to collect a force strong enough to attack and hold the Rokuhara headquarters, but before this bold step could be taken, a force under commanders sent at speed from Kamakura arrested some of his leading supporters, including Hino Toshimoto, one of two courtiers named Hino who had been among those seized in 1324 for complicity in the "Burei-kō" plot.[2]

This was in June 1331, but still the Bakufu refrained from decisive measures, perhaps because of a disagreement between Takatoki and his chief adviser, an unscrupulous official named Nagasaki. They seem not to have recognized the dimensions of the revolt, and they may have supposed that the Hino suspects were of no importance, thinking that high treason was the business of men of high rank. There was certainly some internal rift that prevented a determined and unanimous policy towards Kyoto, and this no doubt encouraged Go-Daigo.

Slow as they were to act, the Bakufu did presently decide to send a strong expedition to the West, a demonstration in force. Go-Daigo heard of this intention from his eldest son, Prince Daitō (better known by his lay name of Morinaga), whom he had made an Abbot of Hiyeizan for military rather than ecclesiastical purposes. He had wisely foreseen that in a struggle with the feudal overlords it would be of great importance to have the most influential religious bodies on his side. Meanwhile, to add to these advantages, the Enryakuji and its chapels formed an immense receiving house for political news and gossip

---

[2] The two Hino (they were not related) were much trusted by Go-Daigo. He seems to have interceded with the Bakufu, but could not save Suketomo, who was exiled to Sado, where he was later (1332) killed. Toshimoto was released in 1324 and continued to serve Go-Daigo until 1331, when he was denounced by an enemy to Rokuhara leaders, arrested, and sent to Kamakura, where he was questioned and executed (1332). One of the most admired passages in the *Taiheiki* is the "Michi-yuki," an account of his sad journey to the East, not knowing whether he would be killed on the way or in prison at his destination. This is an imitation of similar passages in the *Heike Monogatari* which, when recited by itinerant monks, could be counted upon to draw tears from every listener.

from all quarters. The leading prelates had the entry into high places, and they generally knew what was afoot.

Go-Daigo's relationship with Buddhist institutions and Buddhist dignitaries is of some interest. The influence of the leading Zen masters in certain aspects of political affairs grew fast in this period. Among them perhaps the most capable was Musō Soseki (1275–1351), who came to be known as Musō Kokushi (National Teacher), a title awarded to him by the state. It was upon Musō's advice that an official embassy was sent to China in 1325, the first for nearly five centuries. Musō's close contacts with the Emperor did much to establish the strong position at Court which was enjoyed by later Zen masters.

2. Go-Daigo's Resistance and Exile

Towards the end of September 1331 the Emperor saw that there was no hope of holding the Palace against the Bakufu garrison. He hurriedly escaped with the Regalia and fled first to the Tōdaiji at Nara.[3] Thence he went on to Kasagi, an eminence of some six hundred feet which overlooks the beautiful Kizugawa. He was made welcome by soldier-monks of the monastery at the summit, who rapidly strengthened the position. The monastery was attacked by Bakufu troops who had come in pursuit, and though sturdily defended it fell to a determined assault. Go-Daigo escaped but was soon captured and taken to Rokuhara.

By this time orders had come from Kamakura to enthrone Prince Kazuhito (the son of Go-Fushimi), and an accession[4] ceremony took place about two weeks later. An attempt had been made to persuade Go-Daigo to enter holy orders and then to abdicate, but he refused. This meant that the junior line had lost the support of the Kamakura government. Go-Daigo had in fact been deposed. His prospects seemed bleak, but he had found some useful allies, mainly among local

[3] Great importance was attached to the Regalia, without which no succession was valid. The records do not state clearly what part of the Regalia was carried by Go-Daigo in his flight. The Mirror is not mentioned, since the true Mirror was kept in the Great Shrine at Ise and the one in the Naishi-dokoro at the Palace was a duplicate. The Sword was also a duplicate, the true Sword being enshrined at Atsuta. But Go-Daigo may have taken the duplicate Sword and the Seal with him. Since it would not be possible to conceal the Sword, he may have left it at the Tōdaiji or in some other safe place, but on escaping from Kasagi he might have concealed the Seal about his person. A seemingly contemporary document describes a ceremony at the Rokuhara headquarters in which the Sword and the Seal were handed over to the new sovereign's ministers on November 6, 1331; but subsequently Go-Daigo and his supporters always contended that any part of the Regalia produced by the "senior" line must be counterfeit. Interesting particulars are recorded by Hanazono in his diary for the same day.

[4] The accession was in the ninth month of Genkō (1331), but the enthronement was postponed until the end of the following year because the Bakufu hoped by then to have secured the genuine Regalia.

gentry in the central provinces who owed no allegiance to the Hōjō Regents. Chief among them was a warrior of modest standing in Kawachi named Kusunoki Masashige, who is celebrated in Japanese history as a scholar, a soldier, and a pattern of loyalty. But such men were few, and most of those who offered their services at this stage had only a small number of fighting men at their command.

Kusunoki, whom the Bakufu soon recognized as a dangerous enemy, held out in his own stronghold, at a place called Akasaka in Kawachi province, until about November 20, 1331, when it fell to a determined attack after less than a week of hard fighting. Kusunoki managed to escape with a few companions to build up a new force. Prince Morinaga had been with him but left separately and made his way to a Nara monastery, where he is said to have hidden in a great chest usually containing Buddhist scriptures. He was later able to reach Yoshino in safety. Go-Daigo had already been captured and taken to Rokuhara, where he was treated unceremoniously but not roughly.[5] He was confined in a shabby annex, because the best rooms were already occupied by distinguished guests, namely the former Emperors of the senior line Go-Fushimi and Hanazono, and the future Emperor Kōgon, then the Prince Kazuhito. Hanazono was an acute observer, and his diary gives some useful information about conditions in the capital at that time, with comments not unfriendly to Go-Daigo.

In April of the following year (1332), Go-Daigo with a few followers was banished to the island of Oki. The outlook for the junior line was dark, but there were a few encouraging prospects. Kusunoki was able to use guerrilla tactics in a rough country which he knew well, and he was in constant touch with Prince Morinaga, Go-Daigo's son, who had given up his prelacy on Hiyeizan and was now engaged in political activity and in recruiting supporters for the loyalist cause. While Kusunoki was giving Hōjō commanders great trouble by his raids, Morinaga was taking advantage of the discontent of many warriors who disliked the Hōjō rulers. From his protected base in the mountainous region of Yoshino he sent out appeals far and wide to warriors and in particular to religious bodies, inviting them to join in the revolt against Kamakura. He had some success in obtaining promises of help from warrior chieftains, and by the end of 1332, although he and Kusunoki had no lasting offensive strength, they were causing such anxiety to the Hōjō leaders that the Bakufu felt obliged to employ almost the whole of its strength against them.

By itself the gallant effort of Kusunoki and Morinaga was not a permanent reply to the superior numbers that could be brought against them. But it had an effect which perhaps they had not foreseen. To

---

[5] Hanazono quotes a report that Go-Daigo was in a wretched condition, exhausted, wearing a thin robe and quite dishevelled. "Abominable treatment," he notes.

deal with the uprising of loyalists in the Home Provinces the Bakufu
had been obliged to withdraw troops from the outer provinces, such
as Harima. There Norimura, the head of a family named Akamatsu
(of Murakami Genji stock), was emboldened by the absence of Bakufu
forces to take control of his own province and to march into Settsu,
next to the province of Yamashiro, in which the capital lay. He even
tried a coup de main in the capital itself. He was repulsed, but the
fact that a provincial chieftain of moderate standing could venture an
attack on the imperial city was a disconcerting sign of the times. The
Kamakura government could be challenged and even resisted; and
as the news reached remoter parts of the country other chieftains rose
against the Hōjō, among them Kikuchi in Kyūshū and Yūki in the
northern region of Mutsu.

These indications of the decline of the Hōjō power were of course
pleasing to the supporters of the cause of Go-Daigo. To be sure, they
did not prove that the country was in favour of restoring direct imperial
rule, but were rather expressions of dislike or envy of the Hōjō domination of feudal society. They were enough, however, to encourage
the Court party to plan the escape of Go-Daigo from his place of banishment on Oki. The time was not yet ripe for decided action, since
it was necessary to make sure that if he returned to the mainland the
loyalists would have enough military strength to take him to the capital
and protect him there. But thanks to a growing response to the call
to arms issued by Morinaga, the position was improving and the commanders in the Rokuhara headquarters were uneasy. The atmosphere
in the city was full of gloom.

When the Emperor had escaped to Kasagi in the autumn of 1331,
the Bakufu deputies in Kyoto (the North and South Tandai, Nakatoki
and Tokimasu) had thought fit to demonstrate their firmness by examining and punishing persons suspected of conspiring against the Bakufu.
Armed men poured into the streets and entered the houses of people
known to have been close to His Majesty. They arrested such eminent
persons as Madenokōji Nobufusa and numerous officials and monks.
Most of the men arrested were released, but the main conspirators
were severely punished. The unfortunate Hino Toshimoto lost his life,
certain monks were tortured, and a number of notables were banished.
By subjecting the Emperor and his followers to harsh treatment, the
Bakufu presumably sought to show the country that the pattern of the
Jōkyū affair of 1221 could be repeated. But in fact the prestige of the
Hōjō Regents was already waning, and many of the eastern warriors
whose forebears had hastened to the call of men like Tokimasa and
Yoshitoki had now lost faith in their successors.

With the capture of Go-Daigo the Bakufu had for a time restored
its political authority in Kyoto, but it had not brought back peace to

the city. The streets were full of robbers and cutthroats and the capital was under martial law, not only for the purpose of keeping order but also because Rokuhara feared sudden raids or attempts to rescue the imprisoned Emperor. After Go-Daigo was exiled the situation grew less tense in the capital, but anxiety now spread to the surrounding country, where it was known that emissaries of Kusunoki and Morinaga were more than ever active in stirring up warriors and circulating orders to join the imperial forces.

By the end of the year 1332 the garrison in Kyoto was showing signs of alarm. In the diary of the abdicated Hanazono, who was living in Kyoto under surveillance, there is an entry towards the end of November saying that Kusunoki had recovered from his losses and was about to take the offensive with the help of Morinaga; that the guards at the gates had suddenly been strengthened; and that the warriors were in full battle dress. Troops were coming in from the East, but meanwhile the position was alarming.

During the month of December 1332 Morinaga remained in his headquarters in Yoshino, while Kusunoki was very active in Kawachi. There was excitement in the capital when it was reported that he was advancing to the border of Yamashiro province, evidently with designs on the city. In January 1333 he was in control of Kawachi, where the local gentry were friendly, and he was able to advance upon Tennōji, well on the road to Kyoto. To meet this threat the Rokuhara commanders got together a force of 5,000 men and sent it to attack Kusunoki. There was a sharp engagement, lasting from morning until nightfall. Kusunoki had tricked the Bakufu force into crossing the Yodo River in pursuit and then turned upon them. They were taken by surprise and retreated, but he broke off the action and returned to Kawachi to rest, satisfied that the fighting men of the Hōjō had been shown to be vulnerable.

By the beginning of the 1333 there had been a plentiful response to the summonses[6] of Morinaga throughout most of the western prov-

---

[6] The official name for a summons of this nature was *ryōji*. It was a document transmitting a command from an Imperial Prince or other personage of the highest rank. A translation of one of the commands of Prince Morinaga reads as follows: "The incumbents and monks of the Kumeta monastery in the province of Izumi are requested to be zealous in performing their loyal duty of prayer for the Emperor and further to resist the entry of troops into their monastery or its domains. This order [ryōji] of the Prince Morinaga is conveyed by an officer to the Abbot Myōchi." Its purpose was to encourage the monks to keep soldiers of either side from entering and pillaging, and so to retain the good will of the Church.

One of the most interesting of these documents is a ryōji addressed to the strategically placed Ōyamadera in the province of Harima. It is dated in March 1333 and it opens by reciting the misdeeds of Hōjō Tokimasa and his descendants, describing them as "eastern barbarians who have presumed to take arms against the imperial Court and even to banish His Majesty. This reversal of the order of society, this attempt of the low to rise above the high, is unspeakable and must be put down. In all the fifteen western provinces along the coast large forces are gathering to hasten to the battlefront in support of the Throne."

This ryōji does not give a direct order, but suggests that the monastery should

inces of the main island, and orders had been issued to sympathizers in Kyūshū to attack the Bakufu deputies there—the Kyūshū Tandai. The degree of success that attended these efforts to raise armies is not exactly known, but the results were certainly enough to alarm the Bakufu. A council was held in Kamakura and it was decided that an overwhelming attack must be launched against the growing forces of the imperial party, whose banner was attracting more and more good fighting men in the West.

Late in January 1333 Nikaidō, a trusted servant of the Bakufu and a frequent emissary to the Court, entered the capital at the head of the vanguard of a great Bakufu army. This (apart from reinforcements for the Rokuhara garrison) was composed of three divisions, which were to attack the loyalist army of the South from three directions. They were under the command of sturdy kinsmen of the Hōjō family, Aso, Osaragi, and Nagoshi,[7] each leading a body of picked troops from the East, who were to be strengthened by the incorporation of local warriors owing fidelity to the Bakufu.

The first division, commanded by Aso, was to take in levies from Kawachi and adjacent provinces and to attack along the Kawachi road in the direction of Mount Kongō.

The second division, under Osaragi, was to be swelled by troops furnished by vassals in Yamato, Iga, Tamba, and other nearby provinces. It was also to incorporate troops composing the Ōban, or Great Watch, that is to say the warriors on the roster to protect the Home Provinces and safeguard the Throne. This division was to advance southward through Yamato in the direction of Yoshino.

The third division, under Nagoshi, was to take in levies from Owari, Echizen, and other provinces, eleven in all, and to attack along the Kii road.

The three divisions were ordered by the Bakufu to coordinate their movements, and they were assured that successes in the field would be richly rewarded. To any man, however low in rank, who could show proof that he had killed Kusunoki a rich estate would be granted. This was a sad departure from tradition, because in earlier days the Bakufu would have scorned to bribe their warriors in this open way; and to announce a reward for the murder of an Imperial Prince, as was done at the same time, was an offence against tradition unthinkable to the Bakufu in its prime.

The first action in which this army engaged was a siege of the now strengthened Akasaka castle by Aso's division early in March 1333. The assault was fierce and very costly to the attackers, but the castle

---

help the loyalist cause. In fact the Ōyamadera and the force raised by Akamatsu Norimura were between them able to hold the province of Harima against the Hōjō attacks and to use it as a base for raids upon the country round the capital.

[7] Nagoshi was the senior commander of the Bakufu army. The *Taiheiki* readings of the names Osaragi and Nagoshi are Daibutsu and Nagoya.

fell during the month. Nikaidō's contingent, part of Osaragi's division, made an onslaught upon Morinaga's position in Yoshino at about the same time, and succeeded in breaking down the stubborn resistance of the defenders whom he had assembled, including a number of monks from neighbouring monasteries. The Prince escaped to Kōyasan, where he remained in hiding. Nagoshi's division met with no resistance as it proceeded south along the Kii road.

The three divisions had thus accomplished the first part of their task. They now turned their attention to the Chihaya fortress on Mount Kongō, which had so far withstood prolonged attack. It held out and in fact was never reduced.[8]

This remarkable success of the loyalist arms was due to the skill and courage of Kusunoki Masashige. After the fall of Akasaka he had collected and trained a small body of first-class fighting men, and he made such clever use of the terrain when planning the defences of Chihaya that he was able to throw back repeated assaults first by Osaragi's force and then by the columns of Aso and Nagoshi. The position on which he took his stand was favourable to defensive fighting. Mount Kongō rises to 1,112 metres above the plains of Kawachi and Yamato. At or near its summit there are remains and traces of a number of ancient strongholds. Most of these cannot be identified or dated, but it is clear that the main defence works put up by Kusunoki were at Chihaya, while there were subsidiary works at several other points, intended only to delay and enfilade an attacking force.

Kusunoki's victory gave heart to the loyalists and brought new support to their cause.

[8] The size of this Bakufu army of three divisions is not known. The romantic war tales put it as high as one million, an absurd figure. Hakuseki, relying upon *Jōkyūki*, puts the total number of men mobilized for the attack upon Kyoto in 1221 at 190,000, of which the contingent based upon Kamakura accounts for 100,000. This is hard to believe. It is more likely that the force of mounted warriors sent from the Kamakura command area was a fast-moving body of about 10,000 picked men under Yasutoki. The main body, which left the eastern provinces by the mountain road (Tōsandō), may have numbered 50,000, and the troops from the North, which arrived from Echizen too late, were put at 40,000. The total number mobilized was probably about 100,000.

In the campaign of 1333 the force mobilized by the Bakufu is not likely to have much exceeded this total. The hard core of Kantō warriors furnished by Kamakura was probably not more than 10,000 in combatant strength. Local warriors recruited by Osaragi in or near the Home Provinces may have numbered 20,000, and his total strength perhaps reached 50,000. Nagoshi is not likely to have collected a larger force than this. The total combatant strength of the three divisions may have been over 100,000, but it would have been difficult to supply and manoeuvre a really great number in the wild Yoshino country. The opposing armies at Austerlitz each numbered 80,000.

For a further discussion of the numbers engaged in the civil wars, see pp. 120–21 below. The defence of Chihaya is discussed in detail on pp. 123–24.

3. Go-Daigo's Return

Some historians argue that Kusunoki had deliberately tempted the Bakufu army to concentrate upon the siege of Chihaya so that other parts of the country could be held by the loyalist volunteers. This may be an exaggerated view, but it is true that the Bakufu found it increasingly difficult to hold Kyoto in face of the rising fortunes of the loyalists, and that the levies of the three Bakufu generals on the vassals in and near the Home Provinces left wide areas open for the movement of adherents to the cause of Go-Daigo.

In these circumstances the banished Emperor, to whom news was regularly sent by fishing boat, began to see a prospect of victory, and as the spring of 1333 advanced he received messages from Morinaga and Kusunoki that encouraged him to take the risk of leaving the island. With the connivance of one or more of his guards he got away in a small craft, pursued but not overtaken by the dismayed governor. He reached the Izumo shore safely and made his way thence to Hōki province, where an escort was provided by a loyal warrior, Nawa Nagatoshi. He was lodged in a monastery near Nawa's house. There he established a temporary court while awaiting news from Morinaga or Kusunoki, and met with encouraging responses to a call for loyal supporters which he had issued soon after landing. The partisans of the imperial cause had now begun to dominate the western part of Japan, and even the Rokuhara garrison in the capital was sorely tried. It was able to beat off one attack after another, but was obliged to call for strong reinforcements from the East. The Bakufu responded by sending two divisions, which were put under the command of Nagoshi Takaiye and Ashikaga Takauji, respectively.

Both of these generals came from great feudal houses. Nagoshi was a member of the Hōjō clan. Takauji was the head of the Ashikaga, a family of Seiwa Minamoto stock that had stood by Yoritomo from the time of his rising in 1180 and was now one of the wealthiest and most respected families in the East. The Regent Takatoki placed great faith in Takauji, who had already been sent on military duty to the west in 1331 and had taken part in the attack upon Kasagi. Both divisions set out from Kyoto early in June 1333. Nagoshi was promptly killed in battle, leaving Takauji in sole command of all Bakufu forces in western Japan.[9] He was soon using them against the Bakufu.

Takauji had led his powerful army along the Sanindō in the direction of Hōki province, with the announced intention of attacking and capturing Go-Daigo and his now rapidly multiplying supporters. But

[9] Nagoshi's force had left Kyoto on the same day as Takauji. He was to march along the Sanyōdō by way of Harima and Bizen into the province of Hōki. But when he reached the environs of Yodo he encountered Akamatsu Norimura, the enterprising leader of guerrilla raids from Harima, and was defeated and slain. His troops fled back to Kyoto. It may be imagined what dismay this news caused in Kamakura.

he suddenly halted just after leaving Yamashiro province, turned round, and threw his weight on the side of the imperial cause. He forthwith attacked the Hōjō garrison in Kyoto and drove it out of the city. His decision to change sides was not sudden, but had been made before he reached Kyoto from the East, and (it seems) communicated secretly to Go-Daigo not long afterwards. He sent envoys to Hōki asking for a commission to attack the Bakufu, and the commission reached him while he was still in Ōmi province. He then (June 1333) sent word secretly to possible allies throughout the country from Ōshū to Kyūshū, on minute scraps of paper concealed in the topknots of messengers or in the seams of their garments.

Relieved of all fear of capture, Go-Daigo with the courtiers who had joined him in Hōki returned by an easy, indirect route to Kyoto and established himself in the Palace towards the end of July 1333. He reentered the capital as if returning from a journey. He had the Imperial Seal with him and there was no need for an accession ceremony. He treated the young Kazuhito (the Emperor Kōgon according to the Hōjō view) quite generously, according him the privileges of an ex-emperor and transferring to him and other royal personages of the senior line a fair share of the estates left by Go-Saga, including the rich Chōkōdō domain. He then set about the great task of government, upon lines that showed the best of intentions and the worst of qualifications—an ignorance of political realities. His efforts to introduce reforms will be described in the next chapter. Meanwhile it is important to understand what results in other parts of Japan followed from Takauji's action—what in fact were the conditions with which the restored Emperor had to deal.

Something should be said first about the situation in Kyoto after Takauji's intentions became clear. Although it was not to be expected that the Rokuhara garrison could hold out for long against the great army of Takauji, there is a certain tragic interest in the doom of the feudal headquarters that had for over a century dominated the imperial city.

Having assembled a great force in Tamba, Takauji began to move towards Kyoto on June 19. Late that night his vanguard had reached the suburbs and were beginning to stream into the city in seven lines converging upon Rokuhara. Street fighting began soon after daybreak and the defenders were forced back into their headquarters. At the same time Akamatsu and other western chieftains pressed on from Yamazaki and Yahata, setting fire to buildings as they fanned out and made their way into the city. The scene is described in the *Masukagami* as follows: "By afternoon the sky was full of smoke rising from Yahata, Yamazaki, Takeda, Uji, Seta, and the neighbourhood of the Hōjōji. There was no daylight. It was as if the scene had been rubbed over with ink." From these grim surroundings the two Hōjō deputies (Tandai) decided that they must somehow extricate the two ex-emperors and the young Kōgon. They contrived to escape under cover of night and reached Ōmi, whence they hoped to join one of the Bakufu armies still in the field. They were attacked on the way, and one of them (Tokimasu) was killed. Turning eastward, they were checked by loyalist soldiers and suffered heavy losses. The survivors rallied, but on the following morning they found their way east stopped by a royal prince in holy orders who had assembled a force near Ibukiyama. This was Itsutsuji Hyōbukyō Shinnō, who had doubtless been in touch with Go-Daigo. Loyalist supporters from Mino were also closing in, and Nakatoki, the second Tandai, saw that there was no hope of storming through to the Tōkaidō. He and his men went to a nearby chapel and there committed suicide. To this day there is preserved in a monastery called Rengeji a death roll of more than four hundred names. The royal fugitives were captured and led to safety.

Such was the end of the great establishment of the Kamakura Bakufu in the West. It had held down the capital and its neighbouring provinces, dictated to the Emperor and his nobles, and kept a watch on the vassals in the western provinces for over a century since the appointment of the first pair of Rokuhara Tandai, Yasutoki and Tokifusa, in 1221. Now it was utterly destroyed and there was no prospect of a revival of the Hōjō power. When news of the collapse of the Rokuhara troops reached the army that was still besieging Chihaya, its commanders raised the siege and withdrew. They moved southward, in the hope of later recovery, but they soon found that their position was impossible. They surrendered, and their troops went over to Takauji. Some of them were executed by Takauji's order.

One immediate sequel of the fall of the Bakufu was the end of the line of Kamakura Shōguns. It had begun with Yoritomo, who was followed by two Shōguns of Minamoto stock. After that the Bakufu had drawn upon the Fujiwara family for two successive Shōguns, and then came four princes of the blood royal. The last of these was Prince Morikuni, who held office from 1308 to 1333—longer than any of his royal predecessors—until his functions ceased with the collapse of his headquarters. A new line of Shōguns was to begin five years later, the first being Ashikaga Takauji.

In reviewing the success of the loyalist movement which led to the restoration of Go-Daigo, one cannot but be impressed by the important part played by Prince Morinaga. His skill, his courage, and his prestige combined to evoke a remarkable response to the appeals for support sent by him to warriors and to monasteries. In Kusunoki he had a perfect colleague, brave and resourceful and firm in his loyalty.

It is at first sight surprising that Go-Daigo was able to find so much support among warrior families who had no special feeling of loyalty

to the sovereign. Men like Kusunoki belonged to families which had
for generations been loyal tenants of Crown lands, and had therefore
suffered from the depredations of the Bakufu. But there were other
families not especially devoted to the Throne whose estates had been
confiscated or reduced by the Bakufu after the abortive rising of
Go-Toba in 1221, and they also were hostile to the Bakufu. A third
and very important element in the loyalist resistance was the animosity
of powerful rivals of the Ashikaga family, notably Nitta and Akamatsu.

The historical importance of the conflict lies in its character not
as a dynastic struggle but as an aspect of the emergence of a new
feudal society in which families hitherto of no great prominence play
a leading part. It will be shown in later chapters that the war between
the Courts was not confined to rivals for succession to the throne, but
was a national war among great houses throughout the country. It
would not have lasted fifty years had it been a mere quarrel of princes.

4. *The Fall of Kamakura*

While the fortunes of the Bakufu were rapidly declining in western
Japan, the outlook in Kamakura was becoming desperate. Many strong
feudal chieftains were ready to join in destroying the Hōjō family.
Apart from Ashikaga Takauji, whose change of front had undermined
their position in the capital and surrounding provinces, the Hōjō had
a dangerous enemy in the East. This was a warrior named Nitta
Yoshisada, who was soon to strike their death blow.

Nitta probably felt no need to justify attacking the Hōjō, but he
had some grounds for disliking them. His family were of the same
origin as the Ashikaga but ranked below them, although descended
from an elder son.[10] They were long settled in Kōtsuke province and

[10] The abbreviated pedigree is:

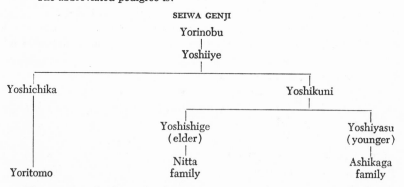

There was no absolute rule of primogeniture. The Ashikaga family was ranked
above the Nitta family partly, no doubt, because of its connexion by marriage with
the Hōjō family.

had not been prominent in Kamakura because their ancestor at the
time of Yoritomo's uprising was deaf to the Minamoto call. Thus
unable to reach the heights of feudal society, they tended to live
apart and nourish their grievances. They spread into Echigo and
other regions to the north, where they became moderately powerful
and (it is said) awaited the time when they could restore their family
fortunes by striking down the Hōjō leaders.

The opportunity did not come until some time after the fighting
started in Kyoto in 1331. Nitta as a vassal had been ordered by the
Bakufu to join the army investing the stronghold of Chihaya. He
disliked this errand, and found an excuse for returning to his fief
after accepting a summons (*ryōji*) from Prince Morinaga. He also
received a command (*rinji*) from Go-Daigo to join in destroying the
Hōjō, having doubtless got into touch secretly with agents of Morinaga. He found means of relaying the summons to other Minamoto
vassals in the provinces of Echigo, Kai, and Shinano. By the middle
of June 1333 he was able to raise his banner before the Ikushima
shrine in his home district, where he was soon joined by the warrior
chieftains he had summoned and others who also desired the downfall
of the Hōjō government.

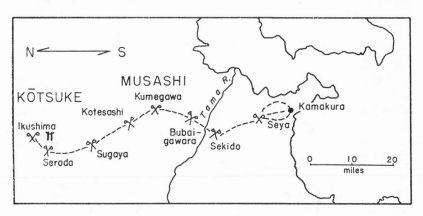

Nitta's march to Kamakura (1333)

These allies marched into Kōtsuke, ejected Nagasaki, the Constable
of that province, and with Nitta's clansmen crossed the Tonegawa
into Musashi. They came to the Tamagawa and engaged a force which
had been sent to meet them by Hōjō Takatoki. The fighting began at
a place in the river basin called Bubai-Kawara and on rising ground
at Sekido, these being points which since Yoritomo's day had been
regarded as the outer defences of Kamakura to the north, comparable
to the Hakone Pass to the west. Here the Hōjō force, after at first
throwing the invaders back, was taken unawares, routed, and then

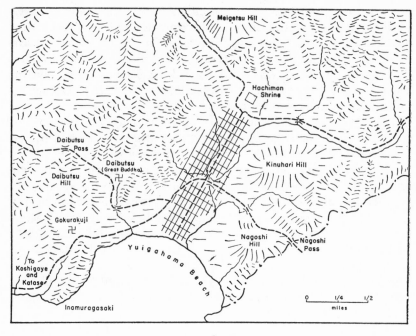

Kamakura

vigorously pursued by Nitta southward from the Tamagawa towards Kamakura.

After halting to regroup his army Nitta advanced upon the city in three divisions, right, left, and centre. The Kamakura garrison was rapidly organized in three bodies to hold the main roads of entry. By the evening of July 1 the attack had reached the outskirts of Kamakura. The fighting was heavy; the troops trying to enter the city through the cuttings and tunnels by which it is approached from the east and west sides were held back by the defenders and found themselves in great difficulties. One of the commanders withdrew and by a detour led his men to the hills, from which they came down on the rear of the defenders behind the Gokurakuji monastery. Ōdate with the right division had reached the southern fringe of the city along the short line but had been pressed back to Koshigoye, the point at which Yoshitsune had once been denied entrance by his brother Yoritomo. Ōdate rallied and advanced again, but his force was at last wiped out. Upon hearing this news, Nitta turned his main body to pass through Katase and Koshigoye to Inamuragasaki, and there, taking advantage of a very low tide, crossed the head of the bay along the sands and stormed the city from the south.[11]

[11] The legendary version of this exploit, as given in the *Taiheiki*, explains that the Sun Goddess held back the waters at the prayer of Yoshisada.

There was desperate fighting at all points, but the stubborn Kamakura defence was at last broken. The struggle went on in the streets. The chronicle in a customary hyperbole says: "The shouts of warriors, the whistling of arrows, the sound of the feet of armed men and the hoofs of the chargers did not cease for five days." On the last of those five days (July 5) Takatoki set fire to the Bakufu buildings and with several hundred men withdrew to a monastery called Tōshōji, where all committed suicide.

Although Nitta Yoshisada was the man who planned and carried out the defeat of the Hōjō in the East, and in fact brought about their destruction, there is no doubt that he had the moral support and encouragement of Ashikaga Takauji. Indeed it is doubtful whether he would have taken the risk of acting against Takauji's wishes. He had with him in his march upon Kamkura captains whose names figure prominently in later feudal history—Yamana, Satomi, Horiguchi, Ōdate, Iwamatsu, and Momonoi.

To complete the destruction of the Hōjō regime it was necessary to deal with their deputies in Kyūshū and Nagato. The Kyūshū Tandai, Hōjō Hidetoki, was taken and killed after some resistance at his headquarters near Hakata. His colleague at Nagato, not being a member of the Hōjō family, was spared. Thus by the end of 1333 the Kamakura Bakufu and all its organs were destroyed, the Hōjō family was swept away, and much of the city founded by Yoritomo was in ashes. But, as one chronicler observed, although several hundred of the descendants of Hōjō Tokimasa lost their lives, the laws which their family had made were unchanged. The feudal system had survived; but it was to suffer great vicissitudes.

CHAPTER II

THE KEMMU RESTORATION

1. *Go-Daigo's Policies*

ONCE Go-Daigo had ascended the throne in 1318, though respecting the views of his father Go-Uda, he made it clear that he had no intention of abdicating and that he meant to govern without interference from Kamakura. He had a definite policy, which was largely concerned with the tenure of land. He revived the Record Office (Kirokujo), which had been established by a previous sovereign in 1069 to investigate the claims of great landlords to the immunity of their estates. It had never been effective, and after a few years most of its functions had been assumed by the In's secretariat. It was all but obsolete at the time Go-Daigo chose to transform it into a court of law for the settlement of disputes. This broadening of its scope was a natural development, seeing that most suits and complaints had to do with that very contentious matter, the ownership of rights in the land and its product.

In Go-Daigo's discussions with his advisers it had been strongly urged upon him that the growth of immune estates had brought disorder to the country, and that such abuses must be remedied before good government could be restored. But in the years between his accession and his flight to Kasagi in 1331, he had neither time nor authority to govern; his urgent task was to make sure of his position against the Bakufu. While he was in exile (1332–33) he could do no more than reflect upon the duties of a monarch, and even when he had escaped from the island of Oki he had still to overthrow his enemies, the Hōjō Regents in Kamakura. At last, however, for a short space after his escape while he was in Kyoto, he was able to pay attention to the business of government and to introduce certain measures of reform which together made what is called the Kemmu Restoration or Revival, Kemmu being the era name for the years 1334–36.

From things Go-Daigo said and did at this time it seems that he seriously thought it possible to return to the ideals of a golden age. He even wrote a treatise (called *Kemmu Nenchū Gyōji*) for the purpose of reviving certain annual Court ceremonies which had fallen out of use; and in general he believed that he could summon back a vanished past. He and his advisers showed a curious blindness, for any impartial observer could see that the old ways were now of little more than antiquarian interest. It was idle to look up precedents, now that the prestige of the Throne and the ritual pattern of Court life had been changed beyond recovery by civil wars, fires, and other disasters. The great fire of 1177—which the citizens called Tarō, or Big Brother, by contrast with its successor Jirō, or Little Brother—alone had destroyed most of the public buildings in Kyoto, including the colleges, and caused the irreparable loss of tens or even hundreds of thousands of books and manuscripts. These calamities put the finishing touch to a decline of the old metropolitan culture; and once the centre of real power had moved to Kamakura, the Throne was too concerned with preserving itself from further humiliation to give much thought to elegance and decorum.

Of course the principal item of reform in the minds of Go-Daigo and his counsellors was the restoration of the imperial authority that had been usurped by the Bakufu. But it was inevitable that the subject of land ownership should claim attention, since it was at the base of the national economy. Kitabatake Chikafusa, a country gentleman of high character who was later to become Go-Daigo's chief adviser, discussed the problem of immune estates in his writings on the legitimate succession. He said that in the "middle" age the growth of the manor (shō) had brought disorder to the whole country ("rankoku ni nari"), and he went on to describe how the appointment of Constables (Shugo) and Stewards (Jitō) from about 1190 onwards had changed the traditional shape of things ("inishie no sugata"), with the result that the art of government was lost.[1]

It was true that the tax exemptions enjoyed by the great landholders impoverished the central government by depriving the Crown of revenue, and diminished its power by creating within the state wide areas of autonomy. Yet Chikafusa admitted that neither the military families nor the Court nobility had even dreamed of abolishing these immunities, so that the prospects of the so-called Kemmu Revival were poor indeed. The object of the reform in his mind was to do away with the agrarian system as it had developed under feudal rule, and this required the abolition of Stewards and Constables—and indeed of the whole apparatus of land tenure and tax collection upon which the Bakufu had depended.

What was to take its place is not clear, but it seems that Chikafusa contemplated a return to the ancient, pre-feudal rural administration by provincial and district governors laid down in the Taihō codes (702) and subsequent laws. Certainly he did not envisage any division of power between the Throne and the leaders of the military class; he hated the warriors as age-old enemies of the Throne (sūdai no chōteki).

[1] Chikafusa was right about the Stewards and Constables; but he might have added that their predecessors, the Governors of provinces and districts, were also grasping and land-hungry. It used to be said of such officials that if a Zuryō (the Governor or Deputy of a province) stumbled and fell, he always got up holding two handfuls of earth.

It is plain that Chikafusa was a man of immense courage and high but somewhat mistaken ideals. In calling for a return to the Engi and Enchō eras (901 to 930), which were celebrated for wise legislation and enlightened government, he supposed that restoration or revival was the same as reform, and generally that what was old was good and beautiful. Yet the truth is that the old system, though perhaps beautiful in its symmetry, had never worked in practice from the day of its introduction, and accordingly that its advocates in 1334 were guilty of either nonsense or sophistry.

There is no strong evidence that Go-Daigo intended to revert to the policies of those times. His purpose was to restore the personal rule of the sovereign, and his chief political concern was to restrict the power of the Bakufu. He had to deal with immediate problems and had no interest in elaborate schemes of revival. Indeed most of his Court nobles scoffed at the "Back to Engi" movement. The only measures of Go-Daigo which might be described as a return to early principles are his firm refusal to appoint a Shōgun with the full powers that had been granted to Yoritomo and his abolition of the office of Kampaku.

There is no doubt that the Constables and the Stewards abused their power deplorably; but in the programme of reform as it was worked out by Go-Daigo and his advisers there was no serious effort to regulate, far less to abolish, the manors. There was some attempt to control the activities of Constables and Stewards in specific cases, but not in general as a matter of principle. Moreover, to tamper with the shō—now a most intricate system of rights and obligations—was in most cases to deprive loyal warriors and officials of rewards for their services; and when it was tried it usually provoked violent resentment of a kind likely to affect the stability of the Throne. For all their animus against the Bakufu, Go-Daigo and Chikafusa, as well as Kusunòki and Prince Morinaga, could not forget that it was to warriors from manors in the western provinces that they owed their success against the Bakufu forces.

Since Go-Daigo's period of peaceful civil government was brief, it bore little fruit, and his policies need not be described in detail. But it is worth while to notice some of his actions which concerned the ownership of land, for even failures are instructive. When he returned from exile he first stayed briefly in the Tōji, an ancient and powerful Shingon monastery on the southern edge of the city. He then moved to a mansion known as the Tominokōji palace, from its position at the intersection of Nijō (Second Avenue) and Tominokōji (Fortune Lane). It had been repaired and enlarged for him. There he at once devoted his attention to the property of the senior line, which included the estates of Go-Fushimi, Hanazono, and Fushimi. Of these and other manors he took charge, meaning to see to their fair distribution. This he carried out, assigning for instance the tax revenue of Harima province to his rival Kōgon-In. He was also careful to confirm in their holdings such monasteries as the Tōji and the Daitokuji, as an act of piety and also in the hope of securing the continued support of powerful churchmen. He had made this his policy since his accession, thinking that the influence of the Church would counterbalance the force of the Bakufu; and the course of events during the year of his exile had shown the support of the great monasteries to be of much value to Morinaga and Kusunoki.

Although the land policy of Go-Daigo may have gained some approval among the great landowners, it made no favourable impression upon the lower grades of tenant and farm workers. The new regime removed none of their grievances, and the records kept by the monks of the Tōji show the Church to have been no less grasping a landlord than any avaricious layman. Complaints poured into the monastery about the treatment of tenants and workers by stewards and others. There is an interesting document in the Tōji archives, under a date in July 1334: a complaint by the farmers of a certain manor (the Tarashō), in which they say that when the estate reverted to the monastery they had expected to lead a peaceful life, but to their distress they had found that, far from reducing their burdens, the Tōji was levying heavier taxes than those of Hōjō times and was in general guilty of cruel oppression. Many other petitions made the same point, that things had been better when the Bakufu was in full command of the situation. Thus a Tōji document of September 1334 complains that in a manor of which the Tōji was the ultimate landlord, over six hundred men had been taken from the fields and put to work on the steward's own land. It is not likely that such an abuse of power by a delinquent vassal would have been tolerated by the Bakufu or the Regent as landlord-in-chief.

Moreover, the monks themselves proved to be harsh landlords, and petitions from farmers to the Tōji and similar foundations were rarely entertained. Thus in 1346, more than ten years after Go-Daigo's return to power, fifty-four farmers signed a complaint against the Tōji, and begged for the dismissal of two particularly dishonest monks. Their prayer was granted but the monks soon returned and resumed their malpractices. The truth is that feudal discipline had been replaced by anarchy. When Go-Daigo granted a certain manor to the Tōji in 1333, men were sent to take over the property. But they were ejected by the former steward, who with his armed bullies resisted even emissaries of the Court. It was not until 1335 that the Constable of the province was able to restore the estate to the monastery.

It will be seen that the farming population put no trust in the reforms. The small holders could not rely upon the Kyoto government for protection, and the peasants found their own condition no better

than before, or even worse. Sometimes they showed signs of revolt
and sometimes in despair they would abscond, as their ancestors had
done in the seventh century. They had no faith in the justice of their
landlords, as is clear from the words in a petition submitted during
the Kemmu era: "Even though your lordship should not consider us
to be human beings . . ." ("hito to oboshi-mesare sōrawazu to mo").
Nor did the landowners, large or small, desire or even in theory approve
any redistribution of rights in land. Most of them asked for more land,
more rights, as a reward for assisting the loyalist cause, which (it is
true) could not have triumphed without them.

It is doubtful whether Go-Daigo or even Chikafusa fully understood
the feelings of the military class or realized what the country owed to
them, although the Emperor seems to have thought that there was a
possibility of persuading warriors and the Court nobility to work together harmoniously in high office. In fact, the character of Go-Daigo
is something of a mystery, for his actions do not square with his reputation for learning and wisdom. Chikafusa said of him: "He rises early
and retires late. He listens to the complaints of the people and is
looked up to by all." Similarly the abdicated Hanazono (who might
have been spiteful) praised him for his conduct of affairs in difficult
times, going so far as to say that he had restored purity to government.
But there is little to justify that praise in the history of his reign after
his return from Oki, for it is a monotonous tale of well-intentioned folly
and misrule. He probably deserved his reputation for scholarship, and
it is on record that he was deeply interested in the new Confucian
philosophy of the Sung masters, which was at this time enthusiastically
studied by the young nobles at Court.

Perhaps his studies qualified him to discuss political theory, but
his knowledge of philosophy does not appear to have fitted him to
deal with the practical issues that had to be faced. The first of these
was the settlement of claims for rewards which poured in an endless
stream into the tribunals. The Hōjō Regents had found it impossible
to compensate their supporters because they had no property available
for that purpose, but Go-Daigo had at his disposal all the estates of
the Hōjō family, which he had confiscated upon their defeat. Yet of
such rich material he made the poorest use. Favouritism was rampant,
bribery was common, and rich estates fell to unworthy owners, while
the hardships of deserving applicants went unrelieved.

The story of these awards needs telling in some detail, for it is
essential to an understanding of the complicated politics of the next
few decades. After the first step, the lavish recompense made to
certain religious foundations in August 1333, preparations were made
to distribute the confiscated Hōjō estates, and as soon as this became
known, the warriors poured into Kyoto to present their claims—each
man treading on the heels of one in front, if we may believe the chron-

iclers. By the middle of September the awards to the leaders in the struggle had been made known. The principal appointments, some of which carried with them substantial revenues and other valuable prerogatives were as follows:

Kitabatake Akiiye, Governor of Mutsu
Ashikaga Takauji, Governor of Musashi and Constable of other eastern provinces
Nitta Yoshisada, Governor of Echigo and Vice-Governor of Kōtsuke and Harima
Kusunoki Masashige, Governor of Settsu and Kawachi
Nawa Nagatoshi, Governor of Hōki
Shōni Sadatsune, Constable of Chikuzen and Chikugo
Shimazu Sadahisa, Constable of Ōsumi

It will be seen from these appointments that it was the warriors, not the civil officials, who obtained the most powerful positions, including the office of Governor, traditionally filled by civil candidates. They were almost independent rulers of great areas, sometimes as many as three provinces.[2] Thus the first step in Go-Daigo's reform was a negation of any plan to restore the provinces to the civil authority. It must be said, however, that he made appointments of both Governor and Constable side by side in some provinces, without favouring either civil or military candidates in his choice.

Now followed the obligation to reward the lesser warriors who had supported the loyalist cause, a matter of the greatest urgency if the Court wished to retain their good will. It was here that Go-Daigo and his advisers made an irreparable blunder, for the cases dragged on indefinitely, partly because the tribunals that dealt with them were composed of persons without experience and partly because their task was difficult, if not impossible.

A month after his return to the capital from Hōki the Emperor had established an office for the determination of rewards for good service to the Crown. It was called the Onshō-gata (Office of Awards), and it was to commence operations after the awards to the great generals had been decided by the Emperor in council. This was early in September 1333, and by that time petitioners were pouring into the city and clamouring at the doors of the Office of Awards. Besides warriors in great numbers there were delegates from monasteries and shrines who claimed that they had contributed to the success of the loyalist cause by their prayers and by furnishing soldiers or supplies. There is no doubt that they had rendered such services and that the Court party had made promises which it could not fulfil.

[2] Chigusa Tadaaki received three great provinces and a great number of smaller fiefs; but he did not live long enough to enjoy them.

The confusion in the city is described in an entertaining miscellany (*Kemmu Nenkan Ki*) which includes a number of satirical gibes said to have been scribbled on walls by sharp-witted citizens. The first of these reads: "What is the fashion in the city today?—Night raids, robbery, and forged documents of title." Others make fun of country-bred warriors aping the dress and manners of the nobility, or of the struggles of petitioners to get a hearing in the courts. Others again deplore the breakdown of good breeding and the intrusion of vulgarity, in such words as: "No distinction between high and low in a world of license and disorder."

The Office of Awards and other bodies which had to deal with claims were elaborately organized. Their description on paper is impressive. But they were staffed mainly by men with no experience of official duties, who owed their appointments to patronage and were being rewarded by salaries which they were not qualified to earn, for, it must be remembered, the administrative offices in the capital had for long past exercised no real authority, whereas the Kamakura government had developed a highly efficient civil service.[3] Thus the machinery of adjudication was cumbrous and costly, while the property at the government's disposal was scarcely sufficient to meet even all reasonable claims. It is not surprising that the more strong-minded petitioners were enraged by the resulting blunders, and lost what loyalty to the government they may once have felt.

The incompetence of the administration was aggravated by a startling imprudence on the part of Go-Daigo. Soon after his return to Kyoto he planned a new palace, suitable to the majesty of the Throne. There was a real need for new buildings. The inner palace enclosure had been destroyed by fire in 1227 and not rebuilt, with the result that for more than a century the sovereign had lived either in a temporary palace, in one of the mansions of the high nobility, or in apartments within the precincts of a great monastery. Yet this was not a time for lavish ex-

---

[3] Perhaps an exception should be made of the tribunal for miscellaneous claims (Zasshō Ketsudansho), which dealt with minor suits. It met frequently for two years and was staffed by experienced officials. Recent researches indicate that its decisions were fairly prompt and that its orders were usually obeyed in the provinces where the claims arose. Documents announcing the tribunal's decisions have been preserved throughout the country. The following is a sample:

Zasshō Ketsudansho Order. (Date: 1334.x.12)
Regarding the claim of Saigo Yatarō Morimitsu:
    Buildings, wet and dry rice fields in Inuzuka village, Musashi
    Buildings, wet and dry rice fields in Higashi Ebukuro village
    Wet and dry fields of Amida monastery
The claimant's title is hereby confirmed and cannot be revoked.

This document is signed by the senior member of the Court, who was a nobleman of high rank, and four assessors.

penditure, and a wiser emperor would have delayed his projected extravagance. Go-Daigo pushed stubbornly ahead. Since the imperial treasury was empty, an order was sent to vassals and stewards of all estates to contribute to the Crown one-twentieth of their income from land, together with certain payments in kind. The whole tax revenue of two provinces was put aside for the same purpose, and new copper coins were minted.[4] Meanwhile the courts of enquiry made few awards to claimants.

So, while justly aggrieved petitioners were chafing at delays, news got round the country that the warriors not only must wait for what was due them, but also must pay for luxurious buildings in the capital. An ironic flavour is given to this situation by the issue in the same month of a decree in the sovereign's name, forbidding extravagance in dress.

This is one of several instances in which the Emperor and his advisers failed to understand the trend of feeling in the country. The Court still believed that the warriors had risen to destroy the Hōjō out of loyalty to the Throne rather than in the hope of sharing the spoils of civil war—to which many thought they had a just claim in advance, since they or their fathers had not been fully recompensed by Kamakura for their services in repelling the Mongols. The plain fact was that the Court had broken its promises, and strained such loyalty as did exist.

All loyal landholders were confirmed in their tenure, but few could so much as get a hearing for their individual claims. As we have seen, the officials assigned to appraising claims were largely inexperienced men. A few members of the tribunal were men of high standing, both civil and military, among them being Kusunoki and Nawa, who had been through all the fighting; and a few others had had administrative experience in Kamakura. The ordinary official, however, was overwhelmed by the amount of evidence presented to him, and had no idea what to do with it. Yet inexperience was only part of the difficulty. Even had the boards and tribunals been highly organized and staffed by capable men, they could not have satisfied more than a fraction of the total claims with the confiscated property available. And it should be added that to unravel the complexities of land tenure in Japan was a long and laborious business for even the most experienced investigator at the best of times.

It was to be expected, therefore, that many claimants would seek to gain their ends by bribery. It was easier to get the ear of a favourite mistress in the Palace than of a judge in the courts, and claimants who followed this irregular procedure could even purchase estates to which they had no right whatever. One Director after another resigned from the Office of Awards in despair, and a great part of the available con-

---

[4] Paper money was proposed, but there is no record of its being circulated.

fiscated lands came into the hands of courtiers or their friends and favourites. It is said that Go-Daigo's favourite consort, Renshi, acquired
the estates of the Hōjō general Osaragi in this way, and that petty officials, dancing girls, and the like became owners of valuable property.

The sources for these accounts are not entirely reliable, especially
since the writers of the *Taiheiki*, the principal historical romance of the
period, liked to give plenty of colour to a bald recital. But it is clear
that whether the officials were to blame or not, the system of allocation
by the appointed organs broke down, and the warriors began to take
matters into their own hands.

The imperial Court was certainly to blame in some cases, for there
is good evidence to show that courtiers and Palace ladies interfered in
the business of the tribunals by causing the issue of imperial grants of
estates under review or already awarded to claimants. Such grants by
a kind of order called *rinji*[5] were (according to one authority) so common as to be worthless, and became an object of derision among the
populace, especially since even forged rinji began to circulate.

Kitabatake Chikafusa, in his *Jinnō Shōtōki* (1339), admitted that the
government had been at fault in the matter of land distribution, but held
that the claimants were also to blame, since to sacrifice property and
even life was the duty of a warrior, and to scramble for rewards was not
the behaviour of a gentleman. He also said that the dynastic warfare
which followed Go-Daigo's reign was due to the claims of an unlimited
number of persons on a limited amount of land. In that statement, although he could not know it, Chikafusa was summarizing the whole of
Japanese history from the beginning down to modern times.

Discontent in Kyoto was so acute that as early as the end of August
1333 orders were sent to the provincial authorities to prevent both warriors and civilians from leaving their duty and going up to the capital
to prosecute their claims. But no argument or order could stem the flow
of petitioners up and down the streets of the capital or along the highroads from the east or the west; and before long the feelings of the warriors began to run strongly against the Court nobility, who were apt
to treat them with condescension. There was, however, one warrior
chieftain whom the courtiers could not afford to displease. In the first
distribution of honours Ashikaga Takauji had been made Governor of
Musashi and Constable of several eastern provinces. He had been ele-
vated in rank, and treated with great consideration by Go-Daigo, even
granted exceptional favours.[6] Chikafusa did not like Takauji, whom he

---

[5] The rinji was a document conveying an imperial command. It came into use
to simplify procedure in the late Heian period. It was issued in the name of the sovereign, but did not bear his seal, being signed by an official after the words "by
imperial order."

[6] Takauji was allowed to use in writing his name the character for "Taka" which
the Emperor had used in his own name as Prince Takaharu. The grant of this un-
precedented honour shocked the Court nobility.

regarded as a greedy soldier of no great merit and not of a really good family, since the Ashikaga belonged to the Seiwa Genji, while Chikafusa's family was of the Murakami branch, senior in descent and much more distinguished.[7]

Ciphers of the Emperor Go-Daigo (LEFT) *and Ashikaga Takauji*

Chikafusa was an aristocrat, and his hatred of the warriors was not based entirely upon political grounds. All the nobility continued in their hearts to despise the upstart soldiers who had deprived them of their rights for more than a century. Now the young noblemen and even the commoners in the capital made fun of the soldiers, who did not know how to behave at Court, wore the wrong clothes, and spoke with the wrong accent. They laughed at the petitioner from the country, carrying his documents in a basket as he trudged to the Office of Awards.

But the Court nobles could not treat the descendants of the great Minamoto leaders with the disdain which they felt for a rustic gentry. The aristocrats of the capital may have hoped for a return of the days when both Taira and Minamoto men-at-arms were mere servants and policemen, but Takauji and his men had other ideas, and the power to carry them out. They knew that it was their arms that had restored the Emperor, and what they had raised up they could if they wished strike down. Such was the weight of tradition that some of the high-born eastern families regarded the destruction of the Hōjō clan not as a blow to the warrior caste in general, but only as the end of the Taira and the prelude to a great Minamoto revival. Only a strong and bold leader was required, was indeed probably awaited, for by the end of 1335 (the second year of Kemmu) the warrior class as a whole appear to have lost what faith they may have had in the so-called revival or reform. The wiser heads of the reform government had done their best to preserve harmony between the civil and military elements in the state, but this attempt failed, as it had done in the past and was to do in the future—

[7] In his *Jinnō Shōtōki* Chikafusa refers rather contemptuously to the Ashikaga family, saying that when Sanetomo was Shōgun they were ordinary vassals, who formed part of Sanetomo's escort *on foot.*

even as late as the mid-nineteenth century.[8] In the pattern of national life there was woven a strong contrast between the courtier and the soldier.

One of the chronicles described the position at the end of 1333 by saying that the warriors and the Court nobles were as fire and water—incompatible.

2. Provincial Affairs

While the Emperor and his advisers naturally devoted most of their attention to affairs in the capital, they could not neglect the more distant parts of the country, notably the eastern and northern provinces, which hitherto had been under the direct control of the Bakufu. To appoint a Shōgun to reside at Kamakura would be a step in a return to military rule, and therefore some compromise had to be sought. Consequently a new appointment was made, limited in its scope. In late 1333 Kitabatake Akiiye, the son of Chikafusa, was ordered to escort the eighth son of Go-Daigo, Prince Norinaga (then in his sixth year), to the province of Mutsu. There the Prince was installed as Governor-General of the whole northern region, comprising both Mutsu and Dewa. He was accompanied by Chikafusa and a suite of warriors and civil officials. They resided in the stronghold of Taga, which had been a frontier post in the ninth century, when settlers were trying to push the aborigines to the north.[9]

No doubt as a countermove to this appointment, early in 1334 Takauji's brother Ashikaga Tadayoshi (apparently without imperial warrant) escorted Prince Naringa, another of Go-Daigo's many sons, then in his eleventh year, to the East, where he was installed in Kamakura as Governor of the province of Kōtsuke with Tadayoshi as his deputy.[10] This did not betoken a revival of the Shōgun's government in Kamakura, but the appointment of Tadayoshi to a key position was a sign that the leading warriors, of whom Takauji was the most powerful, were not prepared to leave all political decisions to civilian ministers in the capital. Soon after Go-Daigo's return to Kyoto in 1333 a new office had been set up for the control of warriors in the city, who were already violent and disorderly. It was in name the same as a previous body, the Mushadokoro, which was intended to keep order among warriors stationed in

[8] When there was an unsuccessful call for *kōbu gattai*—the unity of civil and military. For details see *The Western World and Japan*, pp. 272, 311, 317.

[9] Chikafusa left soon and thereafter travelled widely; he is said to have visited Go-Daigo secretly at intervals. He and Norinaga returned to the south in 1336. Norinaga was later named Crown Prince, and succeeded Go-Daigo as the Emperor Go-Murakami in 1339.

[10] It should be noted here that Go-Daigo and his advisers showed considerable foresight in sending young princes with capable guardians to establish themselves at key points in distant provinces as representatives of the Crown. Even as late as 1375 Prince Kanenaga, who had gone to the West as a child, was a power in Kyūshū.

Kyoto for the protection of the restored sovereign and his palace. The new Musha-dokoro was placed under the command of the Nitta family, with a staff of sixty-four officers, including Kusunoki and Nawa. The composition of this body suggests that it was opposed to Takauji; and no doubt Takauji had contrived to bring the Nitta men away from the East, where they might brew mischief, to Kyoto, where they could be under observation. They were probably in touch with Prince Morinaga, who had divested himself of his holy office as Tendai Abbot and was feeling his way in public life—under the careful surveillance of Ashikaga agents.

Morinaga had been named for appointment as Sei-i Tai-Shōgun by Go-Daigo, and thus had incurred the hostility of Takauji, who coveted that post. In point of fact Morinaga was never formally invested with the rank of Shōgun, but Takauji continued to consider him an obstacle to his own advancement. As we have seen, Takauji did not believe that the defeat of the Hōjō and the destruction of the Kamakura Bakufu heralded the decline of the military class as a power in government. He saw himself replacing the late leaders of the Kamakura Bakufu, not as a usurper but as restoring and continuing the true Minamoto tradition, for he himself was in a direct line of descent from great Genji forebears, and was fully qualified by birth and talent to succeed to the leadership of the military class.

When the Rokuhara garrison was destroyed in 1333, Takauji at once stepped in and set up a Control Office (Bugyōsho) in Kyoto. Its purpose was to keep order in the city, then swarming with military, and it took over not only the premises but also the functions of the former Rokuhara headquarters. This was a clear sign that Takauji intended to preserve a continuity of military power in the state, for not content with applying disciplinary measures to unruly soldiers and others misbehaving in the city, he extended the functions of this office to the surrounding country, controlling travel along the highroads, issuing passports, and generally exercising powers which had formerly belonged to the deputies (Tandai) of the Bakufu.

From that time onwards, though he continued to enjoy the favour of Go-Daigo, Takauji did nothing to identify himself with the civil power. He stood aside when the Office of Awards and other tribunals were formed to investigate claims; and disappointed claimants naturally turned towards him. His military strength was at that time greater, potentially if not actually, than that of any other feudal commander. Nitta Yoshisada came nearest, but not near enough to challenge him; and in a feudal society where ancestry counted for much, Nitta was outranked by Ashikaga. Only Prince Morinaga was of sufficient stature to hinder Takauji's plans. The Prince was devoted to the imperial cause and by temperament he was in favour of a purely civil government, in which there would be no place for an ambitious generalissimo or for a military establishment like the defunct Bakufu. There was bound to be a clash between these two strong-minded men, and it was not long in coming.

It makes an unsavoury story. In March 1333 Morinaga had remained in seclusion in Yoshino, and had deliberately kept away from Kyoto, watching events from a distance until later in the year. Then he went to the capital, where he was highly esteemed by the Court party, who looked on him as the chief architect of the restoration of imperial rule. Takauji meanwhile saw himself as the destined head of the feudal order. Presently, when the new government made its inevitable mistakes, in the minds of the discontented warriors he grew in stature as the man who could save them by bringing back the firm and just government of the Bakufu in its prime. Although the latter-day heads of the Hōjō family had been of poor quality, the people in general still felt that the Kamakura government had for a century or more stood for efficient rule and impartial justice. Thus the Ashikaga had a considerable following, which grew as hope of good civil government diminished.

Morinaga, on the other hand, could count upon the sympathy and in due course the active help of men like Nitta Yoshisada and Nawa Nagatoshi, whom Takauji had offended. As Takauji's designs became clear, the Emperor and his advisers were tempted to resort to force, but they were not yet strong enough and therefore tried to avoid the appearance of discontent. But in July 1334 a rumour reached Takauji that Morinaga was about to attack him, and he suspected Yoshisada and Nagatoshi also. (The Emperor's favourite consort, the lady Renshi, hated her stepson Morinaga, and it is probable that she inflamed Takauji against him.) Takauji put his Kyoto mansion in a posture of defence and filled the nearby streets with armed men. The day of the expected attack passed without incident, and for the moment Takauji took no further step.

Go-Daigo knew of all these things, but when Takauji complained, he protested his own innocence and put the blame upon Morinaga. After biding his time for several months, Takauji had Morinaga seized by imperial warrant and confined in the headquarters of the Mushadokoro. Some weeks later Morinaga was taken to Kamakura with certain of his followers who had also been arrested. There he was kept in close custody until late in August 1335, when he was killed by the order of Takauji's brother Tadayoshi.[11]

In this melancholy story the Emperor Go-Daigo plays a sorry part. In conventional Japanese historical works he is usually a romantic figure, the victim of evil forces against which he struggled in vain. But it is

[11] Thus, according to Chikafusa, carrying out a long-cherished design. Probably the most reliable account of the differences between Morinaga and Takauji, and their respective ambitions, is to be found in Imagawa Sadayo's *Nan-Taiheiki*, a critique of the *Taiheiki*.

hard to admire or even to excuse a man who time after time denied his friends and adherents. It was Go-Daigo who swore that he had no knowledge of plots which the Bakufu uncovered, who without even a mild protest allowed his most loyal supporters to be arrested and tortured, and who did not move a finger to save his son. If the records of his reign are truthful, his was not a character to compel admiration. Had it been, the history of Japan might well have followed a less sanguinary course during the next half-century.

Go-Daigo did not want for brave and loyal advisers, men of talents in peace and war, but he seems not to have made the best use of them. Among them was Madenokōji Fujifusa, a son of that Nobufusa who had been an ardent supporter of the junior line. He was appointed judge in the Office of Awards, but he had no faith in Go-Daigo's policy, resigned from all offices, and disappeared. The great Japanese historian and scholar Arai Hakuseki (1657–1725) gives an unflattering estimate of Go-Daigo's capacity as a ruler, summing up with the words: "No wonder the country was in a state of confusion." A similar opinion is expressed in the *Nihon Gaishi*.

There is further support for an unfavourable view of Go-Daigo in a sermon preached by Musō Kokushi in 1351. Regarding Morinaga's feelings, there is a passage in the *Baishō-ron* which says that he hated his father for his treachery more than he disliked the warriors for their enmity. It might be argued in defence of Go-Daigo's behaviour that in a disturbed society where cruelty was common, those in power incurred little blame by resorting to barbarous methods; but after all courage and compassion are virtues in any civilized society in any age.

All things considered, there is not much to be said in favour of the official class in the capital. After two centuries or more of delegated rule they were without experience in the applied arts of administration. When the time came for them to exercise authority, they had lost the habit of command and did not know how to persuade. Thus while older men were conniving at bad government, the young courtiers were ardently discussing the new Confucianism and endeavouring to apply its principles to the conduct of state affairs. At best they were as effective as earnest young students of political science might be today in tackling the harsh quotidian realities of government in a period of stress.

The plain truth was that the warrior class throughout the country was in a ferment which words could not reduce. For every successful claimant there was at least one, and usually there were several, who felt injured; so that even had the judges and assessors in Kyoto been prompt and just in their verdicts, still the provincial gentry would have been angry and mutinous. It was not only dissatisfied claimants who created ill-feeling in the provinces. The distribution of offices in provincial governments also caused great tension between civil authorities and the leading feudal notables in the country.

Go-Daigo had hoped to arrange some kind of collaboration between the civil and military parties in the central government, and he took steps to that end, as for example in appointments to judicial bodies. But he must have been acutely aware that the real test of his power would take place at a distance from the capital. It was impossible—such were the vested interests in land—to revert to the old system of provincial governors appointed by the Crown and carrying out the instructions of departments in Kyoto. The appointment of Stewards and Constables by Yoritomo had destroyed the former fabric of local administration, and their successors were too well entrenched to be displaced by the civil officers of the Crown.

The whole situation was anomalous, for in the first distribution of awards in 1333 the Emperor made appointments of both Governors and Constables, although the office of Constable had been invented by Yoritomo to keep representatives of the feudal order in key positions in those provinces which were of strategic or economic importance to him. The Constable (*Shugo*) was in effect the military governor, and was usually in a position to override orders given by the civil governor. The first appointment of a Constable by the Crown seems to have been that of one Iwamatsu Tsuneiye, who was named Constable of Hida province in August 1333. Iwamatsu had been with Nitta in the attack upon Kamakura, and the need to recompense such military leaders for their services was one reason why civil and military candidates could not be treated on an equal footing.

Perhaps an extreme example of the excessive rewards given to warriors by the Emperor in the first distribution of prizes and honours is the case of Chigusa Tadaaki, who had accompanied him in his banishment and later had led an advanced column in the attack on the Rokuhara garrison. Chigusa was awarded three provinces and a number of confiscated estates. This lavish recompense proved too much for him, and his name became a byword for extravagance and dissipation. He was a picturesque character, but his entertaining follies scarcely can be said to have warranted such magnificent compensation, especially in view of the Emperor's shabby treatment of such a deserving warrior as Akamatsu Norimura. That bold fighter had harried and defeated Hōjō forces by raids from his province of Harima, thus hastening the fall of Rokuhara. He was rewarded by the gift of one single manor, and at the same time he was relieved of his post of Constable.

In the instructions given to Kitabatake Akiiye on his appointment to Mutsu, the Emperor enjoined him to employ civil and military persons in equal proportions. But in Kamakura the organization of Tadayoshi's new headquarters was like that of the former Bakufu in kind, though of course narrower in scope. Kamakura was a base for such military operations as Takauji might find necessary in the future. Elsewhere throughout the country, whatever new appointments the Crown might choose to make, the great provincial officers, whether Governors or Constables, tended to become territorial lords enjoying an increasing degree of autonomy and controlling sometimes two or even three wide provinces. To put the matter briefly, events in Kyoto—the appointments made, the honours granted, the orders issued—were of little importance alongside the growth throughout the country of centres of military power which for the next few decades were to coalesce and disperse in unpredictable patterns. The revival or restoration movements headed by the loyalists had so far done little more than touch the surface of national life.

3. *The Failure of the Revival Movement*

The first serious clash between the civil government and the military leaders took place when Ashikaga Takauji disobeyed an imperial command. He had left Kyoto for Kamakura without permission and later refused to return to the capital, although told to do so in an order from the Throne. His action is best explained by describing the train of events which led to his departure from Kyoto and—to anticipate—his return in February 1336 as a triumphant warlord from whom the Emperor had to escape by hurried flight.

Early in March of 1335 two chieftains from Sagami had started a revolt and attacked the city of Kamakura. They were defeated by one of Takauji's adherents in a desperate fight near the Gokurakuji, but news of their rising caused alarm in the capital, where it was interpreted as evidence of a major effort to return to power on the part of the Hōjō family. Takauji, for his part, suspecting a coup de main on behalf of the imprisoned Morinaga, ordered a strong force to fill the main streets of the capital. Morinaga's faction was afraid to move, not knowing what force Takauji could count upon.

There was some ground for suspecting an attempt by Hōjō supporters, for (as it turned out) a member of the Saionji family, who had spent much of his life in military circles in Kamakura, was in touch with remnants of the Hōjō clan, and had hoped by its revival to bring about the succession, through Kōgon, of the senior line of emperors. By the late summer of 1335 most of the sporadic revolts of the remaining members of the Hōjō family had been put down, but in August Tokiyuki, a son of the late Regent Takatoki, was still at large and in command of a moderately strong force. He attacked Kamakura and succeeded in driving out the young Prince Narinaga and his regent, Tadayoshi, who before leaving gave orders for the murder of Prince Morinaga.

Tokiyuki's vigorous pursuit drove Tadayoshi far along the coast road into the province of Suruga. On hearing of his brother's predicament, Takauji asked the Emperor for a commission as Commander-in-Chief and Constable-General (Sei-i Tai-Shōgun and Sōtsuibushi), in order to suppress the rebels. When his request was not granted, he pleaded family duty and set forth with his troops on August 21, 1335, upon his own responsibility.[12]

He met Tadayoshi at the Yahagi River in Mikawa province, and they prepared to move together along the coast road in the direction of Kamakura. Tokiyuki had put up very strong defence works in Tōtōmi near the mouth of the Ōigawa, a broad but shallow stream not difficult to cross. The leader of Takauji's vanguard crossed at a ford by a bold movement and turned Tokiyuki's flank. Takauji now pursued the retreating forces of Tokiyuki and defeated them in one engagement after another in Tōtōmi and Suruga, and finally in front of Kamakura. He gave them no respite and stormed into the city on September 8, 1335, killing Tokiyuki and scattering the survivors of his army. Thus after only a little more than twenty days in the field Tokiyuki returned to the home of his Hōjō ancestors to meet his death. He was only a youth and he had no wise counsellors. His generals and their families, Osaragi, Gokurakuji, and kinsmen of Nagoshi, once the leaders of feudal society, escaped with their lives and became menials in Zen monasteries in the vicinity.

Takauji installed himself in the Nikaidō apartments of the Eifukuji monastery at Kamakura, where he received the submission of a number of former supporters of the Hōjō. From Kyoto there arrived messengers to congratulate him on the defeat of the "eastern barbarians" and to bring messages of praise and encouragement. He was pressed to return to the capital, where festivities and ceremonies of thanksgiving and reward would be held. Tadayoshi, replying in the name of his brother (who made a point of keeping modestly in the background), informed the Emperor that whereas in Kyoto Takauji had been in constant danger of attack by conspirators among the Court nobility and by Nitta Yoshisada, he felt safe in Kamakura and proposed to stay there. So Takauji began to build a palace on the site of the residence of the former Shōguns. Feudal chieftains like Moronao built their mansions nearby and soon the city was rich in handsome edifices.

News of Takauji's activities began to reach Kyoto, and it became evident that he had assumed powers which had not been granted to him by the Throne. He was conferring rewards upon warriors for their exploits and had even granted certain manors in Shinano and Hitachi to followers who had served him well. This was to usurp the imperial prerogative, and the possibility of commissioning Nitta Yoshisada to command a punitive force was discussed in Kyoto, especially after Takauji was reported to have appointed a member of the Uyesugi family

[12] There are other versions of the request of Takauji and the response of the Emperor; but it is clear that he was refused the full rank and title of Sei-i Tai-Shōgun. Not long afterward he was given a similar rebuff. According to one account, on the day after Takauji asked to be authorized to destroy Nitta Yoshisada, Prince Takanaga and Nitta were granted swords as signs of their commission to proceed against the rebels. This was at the end of 1335.

to the post of Constable of Kōtsuke, which was Nitta's own native province. Now the members of the Court party began to hurry from the East back to the capital, and those whose loyalty lay in the East hastened to escape to Kamakura, so that the highroad was crowded with traffic in both directions—like a shuttle, the chronicler says.

In the late fall of 1335 the country was in a state of bewilderment, heightened by news that an imperial army of tens of thousands was about to move against Kamakura, while to resist it a great force was to move westward from Kamakura, under the command of Kō no Moroyasu.[13] The orders given to Moroyasu said that he must pass through the province of Mikawa, "anchor himself" to a base on the left bank of the Yahagi River, and there await the arrival of reinforcements from Takauji's own province. He was on no account to cross the river, since that would take him to Mino, out of Takauji's sphere of influence. On November 17, 1335, Tadayoshi issued a call (in the name of Takauji) to all warriors throughout the country, saying: "Nitta Yoshisada must be destroyed. You are to assemble your clansmen and hasten to join me."

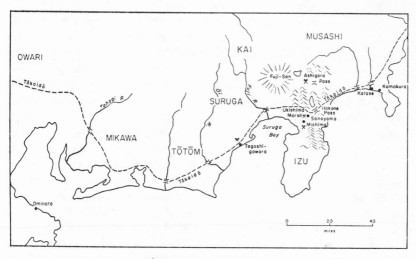

The campaigns of 1335–36

The Court meanwhile, displeased by Takauji's independent actions, issued a proclamation to all provinces commanding the warriors to proceed to Kamakura in order to suppress Takauji and Tadayoshi, who were fomenting rebellion. The Emperor's second son, Takanaga, was appointed Seitō Shōgun, or Commander-in-Chief for the chastisement of the eastern rebels, and under him as general came Nitta Yoshisada with a commission to destroy the two brothers, dated at the end of November 1335.

---

[13] The Kō brothers Moronao and Moroyasu were Takauji's leading generals. The Kō family were hereditary vassals of the Ashikaga.

By that time, however, a majority of the warriors throughout the country were disappointed by what they regarded as the failure of the imperial government, and were ready to answer the call of a leader fitted by birth and talent to command. In the minds of most of them Takauji fulfilled all these requirements, especially since he could claim to be restoring the supremacy of the great house of Minamoto. As to the ordinary man, he had but little to say; but most cultivators of the soil had come round to the view that, after all, they had been better off under stewards disciplined by Kamakura than under the direct control of land-lords owing their estates to the Crown.

Nitta's army arrived at the right bank of the Yahagi River on about December 10. The two armies faced one another for some days without any movement beyond a few skirmishes. Then Moroyasu divided his army into three parts, of which the north and south forces were to cross the river and engage the forces opposite to them; the centre, which was opposite Nitta's position, made no move. The two armies did not join battle until a warrior named Horiguchi rode out from Nitta's side and laid about him. Nitta's whole force followed him across the river, and pressed Moroyasu so hard that he had to retreat in the direction of Suruga, where he made a stand. But his position was insecure, and on December 20 he was thoroughly defeated in a general engagement at Tegoshi-gawara,[14] even though he had been reinforced by the arrival of several thousand men under Tadayoshi. A great number of warriors surrendered to Nitta, but their names were suppressed by the chroniclers "to save them from shame."

After this defeat Tadayoshi withdrew into the Hakone mountain region, where he entrenched himself in a strong position and prepared to make a desperate stand with the redoubtable Kō brothers and other commanders. So far the outlook for the loyalist armies was promising. But Takauji, who had come to the help of his brother, by a clever ruse caught Nitta's men unawares on the western side of the Ashigara pass, and inflicted great damage upon them, pressing them back for several miles to a point where they were obliged to halt and make a stand.

Takauji saw that this was a crucial moment in the campaign, and to encourage his supporters he awarded them certain manors which he regarded as being at his disposal. Here he was assuming the kind of powers which Yoritomo had exercised. He had in fact gone further than Yoritomo, since he made these awards on the battlefield. This new device for stimulating warriors succeeded because, as one ingenuous chronicler remarks, "the fish rises to a savoury bait."

On December 27 the imperial troops withdrew into Suruga and took up a position at Sanoyama. Here they were fiercely attacked, hav-ing lost the support of a Kyūshū warrior chieftain of the Ōtomo family,

[14] A point on the eastern coastal highway on the site of the present city of Shizuoka.

who suddenly offered his following of several hundred good fighting
men to Takauji. Owing to this defection (which was of a kind by no
means rare at that time) the loyalists were broken and routed. They
fell back southward towards the township of Mishima. Rain fell through
the night, and in the morning the Kamakura army, much enlarged by
reinforcements which now flocked to its successful banner, looked down
upon Mishima from its encampment on the heights. Not waiting for the
weather to clear, they stormed the town and forced Nitta to abandon his
position and to retreat through the night in the direction of the coast.
He was overtaken by Takauji just as he reached the highroad along the
shore of Suruga Bay soon after daylight. A desperate battle was fought
there, in which "the tramp of armed men sounded like a thousand convulsions of the earth," if we may believe one narrator. Nitta's remnant
with difficulty reached the Fujikawa and crossed the rushing river by
a hanging bridge.

Now Takauji and Tadayoshi joined forces and hastened on to Uki-
shima, where they halted and encamped on flat ground near the highroad. Here they held a council of war to decide whether one of them,
or perhaps both, should return to ensure the safety of Kamakura. It was
agreed that both should press on together to Kyoto. This was in mid-
winter, and snow lay so thick over the land that it was not possible to
tell the hills from the plains. It had always been a common saying that
the eastern warrior faced the west. This had been true of Noriyori and
Yoshitsune, of Yasutoki and Tokifusa, and now of Takauji and Tadayoshi. They pressed on to Kyoto.

As Takauji followed the retreating imperial forces, he was joined by
warriors from all the eight eastern provinces and the coastal regions,
and by the time of his arrival in Mino his troops were so numerous that
they overflowed in the mountain villages. At this juncture an attempt
was made by some monks of a mountain fraternity who favoured the
loyalists to deliver a surprise attack upon the rear of Takauji's army, but
their plot was discovered and they were put to flight. The edge of Lake
Biwa was quite near, and many of the fugitives escaped in boats from
the battlefield.

From this point the Kamakura army was divided into three separate
forces, which were to attack the city by the traditional approaches—
across the bridges at Seta and Uji and along the road from Yodo. Battle
was joined on the third day of the new year, corresponding to February 16, 1336. Nitta had erected a tower in the middle of the Uji bridge.
On the night of February 21 Takauji's men launched a desperate attack
on the bridge, but Nitta maintained a strong defence, buoyed up by the
hope that Kitabatake Akiiye would reach him from Mutsu with a considerable force. Away from the river fighting went on day and night.
Meanwhile Takauji was being joined by more and more warriors, men
who had come from Kawachi, Settsu, and farther west, even from Shi-

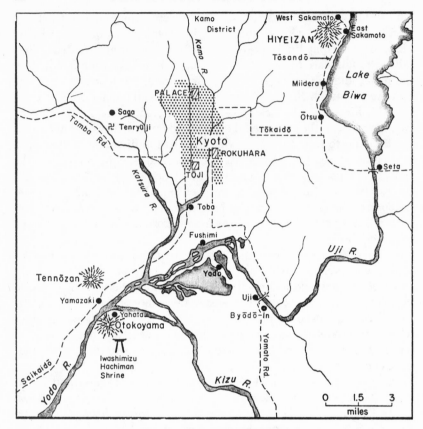

Kyoto in the fourteenth century

koku and Kyūshū. Among them was Akamatsu from Harima, the bold leader whom Go-Daigo had neglected to reward.

On February 22 these new allies proposed to attack the imperial forces in the Yamazaki area early the next morning, sending up a smoke signal at a suitable moment so that a general attack on all fronts might then be delivered. Waiting for the dawn impatiently, Akamatsu moved forward, forced his way through the gate, and took Yamazaki by storm before noon. Thence the attackers rushed on to Kuga and Toba in a furious drive which sent the imperial troops fleeing through the streets. By the night of February 23 the battle was won. The fighting in Kyoto and its suburbs had continued day and night from the first exchange of arrows. With Takauji's victory a new era had begun; Go-Daigo's plan to restore the powers of the Throne had failed, and he was once more a fugitive.

CHAPTER III

THE RISE OF ASHIKAGA TAKAUJI

1. *Takauji in Kyoto, 1336*

ON FEBRUARY 23, Takauji's vanguard, led by Hosokawa Jōzen, entered the capital after a forced march. The Emperor, apprised of his approach, had escaped by night and taken refuge in East Sakamoto under the protection of the Enryakuji. That day and the next Hosokawa's men passed through the streets leaving flames behind them as they destroyed the Palace and the mansions of Court nobles and generals, notably those of their enemies Kusunoki, Nawa, and Yūki.

On the following day, February 25, 1336, Takauji arrived in Kyoto and took up residence in the mansion of the Minister of the Right, Tōin Kinkata. But he was not to remain undisturbed, for very soon strong forces led by Kitabatake Akiiye and Yūki Munehiro (though under the nominal command of Prince Norinaga, then nine years old) reached Hiyeizan from the north, while Prince Takanaga's contingent advanced towards Kyoto from the east by the mountain road (Tōsandō). Akiiye had made a tremendous effort to pursue and overtake Takauji, causing his troops to bear great hardships on the long march.

These attacking columns reached Sakamoto on February 27, after crossing Lake Biwa, and were enthusiastically welcomed by the monks of the mountain sects, among whom the Emperor had sought sanctuary. Since the monks of the Onjōji (commonly called Miidera) were hostile to the Enryakuji, it was natural that Hosokawa should establish himself at Miidera, and that Akiiye should attack him there. Takauji's commander was routed in this action, and Miidera was completely destroyed by fire. Takauji fell back and took up other positions, but could not hold them against the fierce assaults of the loyalists, and after three days of heavy fighting the city was lost and Takauji was driven to retreat into Tamba province.

Takauji saw that there was no prospect of quick recovery, and to avoid further encounters he took a roundabout route to Settsu, guided by his captains through Tamba and Harima. He reached the coast at Hyōgo in the middle of March, but the loyalists found him out and pressed him hard for ten days, until he had to accept defeat and escape by sea to Kyūshū.[1] Many Ashikaga adherents at this time surrendered

---

[1] According to one version, at this juncture, after a serious reverse in the neighbourhood of Hyōgo, Takauji was in despair and decided to commit suicide with Tadayoshi, but was persuaded by Hosokawa Jōzen to leave for Kyūshū. This sounds improbable; but certainly there was hesitation as to the next step, and Tadayoshi seems to have favoured a desperate attack on Kyoto. There was much argument

to Nitta and Kusunoki, who returned to the capital in triumph. On March 16 the Emperor came down from Hiyeizan.

2. Retreat to the West

Takauji's troops had been routed in one engagement after another. Following their last stand at Hyōgo, Takauji saw that he had no recourse but to secure allies and reinforcements in the western provinces and in Kyūshū. This was not a new design, for Takauji had already taken care to win favour among some of the chieftains in the western provinces. He was carried west in one of a group of war vessels which had brought him five hundred picked horsemen from Suō and Nagato, provinces whose Constables were already his partisans. Those of his captains who were familiar with local conditions in the Home Provinces, in particular Akamatsu Norimura of Harima, had told him that even if he should defeat Kusunoki and return to the capital he would not be able to hold it: he must transfer his headquarters westward, give his men and their animals a long rest, and prepare his army for victory by raising the spirits of the soldiers. In this last respect he was already well aware of the weakness of his position. He knew that men want a flag to fight under, and that as things stood, the loyalists were inspired with ardour for the Brocade Banner, whereas the Ashikaga leader appeared as an enemy of the Throne (chōteki).

The remedy was simple. All that was needed was an order from the true heir to the throne, that is to say the representative of the senior line. This was arranged with the help of the influential chamberlain Hino Sukena, and after some going and coming of confidential messengers a commission was granted by the cloistered Emperor of the senior line, Kōgon-In. The document (called an Inzen) commissioned Takauji to act in the name of Kōgon-In, and it was followed by a supplementary Letter of Instruction (Mikyōjo) ordering him to destroy Nitta Yoshisada and other rebels.

There is some doubt as to the time and place of delivery of the Inzen, but it appears that Takauji had word of its issue and therefore anticipated its arrival by announcing when he reached the port of Tomo in Bingo province that he was commissioned by the cloistered Emperor. He began to summon warriors in all provinces to follow him in chastising "the rebel Nitta Yoshisada."

In the next few months Takauji spent much time and effort gathering support in the western provinces of the main island and in Kyūshū.

---

through the night of March 25, and finally Takauji agreed to embark from Hyōgo. He reached there early in the morning of March 26, embarkation was begun in the late afternoon, and the vessels left after dark. Tadayoshi had at first turned back and camped at the foot of Maya-san, eager to risk his life in an attack upon Kyoto. But he was overruled, and boarded the flagship late that night.

Even during the short stay of his ship at Muro in late March, he was active in approaching influential persons in those regions and allotting them spheres of influence and military commands in specified areas. Thus the whole island of Shikoku was allotted to the Hosokawa clan, Akamatsu was confirmed as territorial lord of Harima, and great families like Imagawa in Bitchū, Ōuchi in Suō, and Momonoi in Aki were given authority over wide areas. These arrangements were not easy to make, since the Ashikaga clan had but little connexion with the western feudal barons, and no real control over them. Indeed these western magnates could, if they chose to combine, determine the fate of Takauji. Moreover, it was clear to them from his failures in the vicinity of Kyoto that he could not hope to restore his prestige without their help.

Of these things Takauji also was well aware. Even during the revolt against Kamakura in 1331 he had made a point of conciliating the powerful Ōtomo, Shōni, and Shimazu chieftains of Kyūshū and seeing that they were appointed to high posts. He had kept in touch with them thereafter and had gained their good will; it was the timely (and treacherous) support of an Ōtomo detachment that had enabled him to turn the loyalist flank and win the battle at Sanoyama in Suruga. Now, in addition to Ōtomo, Shōni and others were disposed to follow Takauji with considerable numbers of fighting men; and by the time of his arrival in Nagato at the end of March 1336 he was in a fair way to obtaining a favourable reception in Kyūshū. Reaching Shimonoseki early in April, he crossed at once into Chikuzen, where he was welcomed by a number of Kyūshū notables, and was presently visited by members of the Shōni family, who brought a troop of five hundred warriors with gifts and greetings from their chieftain Sadatsune.

Not all the great Kyūshū families were on Takauji's side. Certain powerful chieftains, notably Kikuchi Taketoshi, were opposed to him. Taketoshi had already gone to the assistance of Nitta in the East, but his younger brother, together with other Kyūshū leaders, remained on the alert in Higo, where the Kikuchi family had its stronghold. Thus Takauji had to reckon with an influential group, including such prominent men as Aso, Mihara, and Kuroki, who were at one in desiring to check his progress in Kyūshū. They had entered Higo for that purpose a few days before Takauji crossed the Straits.

Early in April Kikuchi attacked the Shōni stronghold at Dazaifu in Chikuzen. He succeeded in reducing the fort and driving out Shōni Sadatsune,[2] who then made a stand in the neighbouring hills but was thoroughly defeated and committed suicide with several of his kinsmen.

[2] Sadatsune had retired from leadership of the clan and entered religion, taking the name Myōye. But he felt obliged to go into battle for Takauji because his family were traditionally liegemen of the Shōgun. His son Yorihisa later went into action against Kikuchi wearing a suit of armour that had been given to one of his ancestors by Yoritomo.

The Inland Sea

Meanwhile Takauji had set out from Ashiyaura by road, led by another Shōni, Yorihisa, the eldest son; but before they reached the house of the warden of the shrine at Munakata (a place where heavy fighting took place during the Mongol invasion) they learned the bad news of Sadatsune's defeat and death. Takauji, after assessing the situation, managed to enlist a force of warriors in the vicinity of Munakata. Kikuchi responded by moving against Takauji with the troops that had stormed Dazaifu and others collected at Hakata. Takauji left Munakata on April 15 and marched southwest about fifteen miles to a place called Tadara-no-hama, on Hakata Bay. Here, says the account in *Baishō-ron*, "there is a stretch of over three miles of dry foreshore, crossed at the south end by a small stream. The precincts of the Hakozaki Hachiman Shrine consist of some five square miles of pine forest. To the south lies the city of Hakata, on the east five or six miles distant is hilly country, and to the west is the open sea stretching as far as China."

On this battlefield of white sand and green pine the two armies clashed, and after bitter fighting the Kikuchi force had to surrender. The victory was due largely to the efforts of Ashikaga Tadayoshi, who drove the enemy before him all the way to Dazaifu. Kikuchi took to the hills and then withdrew into the province of Chikugo, while other chieftains who had resisted Takauji either surrendered or, like Aso and Akizuki, killed themselves.

Much gratified by this result, Takauji rewarded the successful commanders. Speaking as a representative of the Throne in putting down rebellion, he confirmed them in their holdings. But he also abstained from punishing those who had resisted him, and his clemency won over to his side many of the men whom Kikuchi had recruited. Thus at one stroke the Ashikaga leader became virtually master of Kyūshū. After discussions with Shōni Yorihisa he invited all the most influential chiefs in the northern half of Kyūshū to join him. Most of the men invited, including such important leaders as Nabeshima and Gotō, quickly assembled at Dazaifu, and thus there was formed an amalgamation strong enough to suppress all opposition in the important Chinzei (Western Defence) region.

3. Return from Kyūshū

After this meeting Takauji assigned the task of subduing further opposition to certain chosen leaders, who severally succeeded in defeating his remaining adversaries and capturing their strongholds. Thus with the help of these supporters, in particular Shōni and Shimazu, he had gained an assured position in Kyūshū in the space of a few weeks. Kikuchi and Aso had been strong—in fact, they had outnumbered the Ashikaga force at Tatara—but the victory of Takauji and Tadayoshi was complete. It was a great stride towards mastery of the whole country.

Takauji now felt safe in leaving Nikki, Isshiki, the Matsuura lea-guers,[3] and other trusted officers at Hakata in command of all the Ashi-kaga forces remaining in Kyūshū, while he and his brother set out from Dazaifu on May 15 with picked troops of Shōni, Ōtomo, and other re-liable adherents. This army was embarked at Hakata for Shimonoseki, while Takauji and Tadayoshi proceeded northward by land, crossed the Straits, and set up their headquarters at Fuchū, the seat of government in Nagato. From that point Takauji began his eastward movement.

The Court party seemed helpless, for the Ashikaga forces met with no serious challenge as they marched along the coastal road. The inert-ness of the loyalists throughout April was in strong contrast to the activity of Takauji. Even when he had been in virtual flight to the West, he had taken care to leave detachments at key points in Shikoku and the central provinces, together with stores of food and weapons in prep-aration for his return. To be sure, shortly after the loyalist defeat at Tatara Go-Daigo appointed Yūki Munehiro Constable of Shimotsuke and Aso Constable of Satsuma, but these were acts of no practical impor-tance, since Shimotsuke was Ashikaga country and Satsuma had for centuries been the domain of Kyūshū families, notably of the Shimazu clan.

The loyalists did, however, take some practical steps against Takauji in the East and in the North. By early April Prince Norinaga, who in 1333 had been appointed Governor-General of Mutsu and Dewa, was back at his post with Kitabatake Akiiye as his adviser. At this time Akiiye was appointed Chinjufu Shōgun—the old office of Commander-in-Chief of the Defence of the North which had been held by Minamoto Yoshiiye two hundred years before. A number of chieftains in the northern provinces (Ōu) formed a league under Akiiye's direction, among them being such strong families as Yūki, Nambu, Date, Soma, and Tamura. Further, certain clansmen of Kusunoki joined warriors in Hitachi and the surrounding country to form a useful concentration. These two groups provided stalwart support for the loyalist cause in eastern Japan (the Kantō), where the Ashikaga family, despite its prominence, was relatively weak in a purely military sense—so weak in fact that of the three strategic areas in Japan, the Home Provinces, Kyūshū, and the Kantō, it was now the Kantō in which it was easiest for the loyalists to attack the Ashikaga. Takauji was aware of this, and he managed to get Soma and some other chieftains to change sides and resist Akiiye in Ōu while, in his capacity as Commander-in-Chief in the East,[4] he ordered Satake and others to harass loyalist forces in Hitachi. At the same time Nitta was ordered by the Court to proceed against Takauji in the West.

All these loyalist steps against the Ashikaga were rather belated, for they were not taken until about a month after Takauji left Kyoto. As part of his strategy, Nitta first attacked Akamatsu at Ikaruga in Harima province, on April 26. Akamatsu was forced to retire to his stronghold of Shirohata in the western part of that province, and there he held out stubbornly, knowing that the loss of his positions in Harima would close Takauji's path to the East. Nitta's object was to capture the place before Takauji could send relief. He surrounded it early in May and hoped to starve it out, at the same time sending separate forces to invest strongholds in Bizen, Bingo, and Mimasaka. Most of these fell, but Shirohata and Mitsuishi (in Bizen) held out.

News from Akamatsu had decided Takauji to move eastward rather sooner than he had planned, since it appeared that the defenders of Shirohata and Mitsuishi could not hold out much longer, being short of food. But he had long intended to return to attack Kyoto sometime in the late spring or early summer of 1336, and his preparations were already made when he received the message from Akamatsu. Having left Dazaifu about May 15, as we have seen, Takauji stayed for three weeks in Fuchū, no doubt while there overseeing preparations for the great expedition to Kyoto and also surveying the political situation and keeping an eye upon his allies and adherents. He moved on to Kasado in Suō and thence to Itsukushima on June 10. He worshipped at the shrine and left handsome gifts for its maintenance. On June 13 he reached Onomichi, and there he visited the Jōdoji, an ancient Shingon chapel, where he gave a poetry party and himself recited thirty-three stanzas, which he copied out in his own hand and presented to the monks.

This leisurely progress may have been meant to induce the loyalist commanders to relax their precautions, for Takauji showed no signs of haste. But he moved steadily forward. When all his forces had reached the environs of Tomo, he held a council of war,[5] at which it was decided to advance in two bodies, one by sea under Takauji, the other by land under Tadayoshi. Accordingly on June 19 both armies left Tomo. The land army was preceded by a vanguard of 2,000 horse under Shōni Yorihisa. It is significant that this post of honour was entrusted to a Kyūshū warrior, a man who owed no traditional allegiance to the Ashikaga family. As the land force marched forward they could see Takauji's vessels under way. When the fleet had made three or four miles eastward, the lookouts saw approaching a large number of vessels, one of which displayed Takauji's emblem. For a time this was thought to be a ruse of Kusunoki, but it soon became evident that it was a large reinforcement from Shikoku, led by Hosokawa.

According to the *Baishō-ron* Hosokawa's vessels, five hundred in

---

[5] The council of war was held on June 14; two days before at Itsukushima Takauji had received news of the death of Go-Fushimi.

number, carried over 5,000 men. Nothing is said about the sizes of these craft, but they no doubt included war junks and fairly capacious ships for transporting men and supplies. The force included several thousand mounted men, and therefore (if the number is correct) the transports had to carry an average of about ten warriors, their horses, and some grooms as well as a crew. Takauji with his fleet reached Kojima in Bizen on June 24, while Tadayoshi, after overcoming some opposition at Fukuyama, kept pace with him by land. Several days later, pressure from Tadayoshi's large army obliged the loyalist forces to abandon their assaults upon Shirohata and Mitsuishi and withdraw to Hyōgo.

On about July 2 Takauji's flotilla left Muro on the ebb at moonlight and with a fair wind sailed until the evening of July 4, when they dropped anchor off Akashi Ōkuradani.[6] The van of this seaborne division was under the command of Hosokawa Jōzen. At the same time the land army led by Tadayoshi had reached Suma and Ichinotani (the scene of Yoshitsune's great feat of arms in 1184), and camped at Shioya and Ōkuradani. The troops on shore lit signal fires, and the ships responded by showing flares through the night. This was the dramatic prelude to a conflict that was to take place next day—one of the decisive battles in Japanese history, the battle of the Minato River or Minatogawa.

4. Minatogawa

Immediately after withdrawing from Shirohata, the loyalist commander-in-chief Nitta Yoshisada had hastened to inform Kyoto of the military situation. Alarmed, but not panic-stricken, the Emperor sent for Kusunoki and ordered him to proceed forthwith to Hyōgo to assist Nitta. According to the Taiheiki, Kusunoki did not agree with Nitta's plans and recommended that a pitched battle should be avoided for a time. The Emperor should take refuge at Hiyeizan, and Kusunoki himself would temporarily withdraw into Kawachi province, so enticing Takauji to enter the capital. Then Takauji would be attacked from Hiyeizan and from Kawachi, while Nitta would cut his line of supply. Finding that the Emperor's advisers would not agree to this proposal, Kusunoki loyally made up his mind to die in battle and marched down towards Hyōgo.

This version of the events leading to the battle of Minatogawa is

---

[6] The fleet was delayed some days at Muro, waiting for good weather. There was much argument before it was decided to risk departure, since the clumsy and heavily laden craft could make no progress against a head wind either by sail or by oars, and in a storm were likely to collide or drift ashore. The Baishō-ron gives an interesting account of precautions taken by the superstitious warriors. Dreams were read, oracles were consulted, and a priestess of the Sumiyoshi shrine (guardian of ships and sailors) declared that Takauji's enterprise would succeed. Best of all, a weather-wise boatman disagreed with his mates and predicted that the fleet would ride smoothly forward on a steady breeze.

not improbable.[7] Kusunoki was a gifted strategist, and his plan of campaign might well have succeeded. But the Court always vacillated in times of danger, and its tardy decision played into Takauji's hand. The preliminary clash between the two armies took place early on July 5. The course of the fighting is described in abundant detail in the chronicles of the period and in the archives of many of the families involved in the conflict. Here it will be enough to recite the main features of the battle.

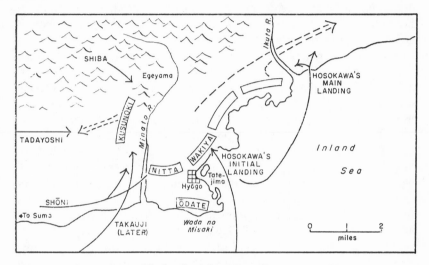

The battle of the Minato River

The loyalist army took up a defensive position in a line from Wada no Misaki to the Ikuta River. Nitta (who had received some reinforcements from the adjacent provinces of Mimasaka and Bizen) was in command of all troops. He placed his main body on the rising ground of Wada no Misaki facing the sea, while his wings occupied the shore line. Kusunoki, standing with his back to the Minato River, held the zone from Egeyama to the village of Nagata, thus facing the land force of Tadayoshi.[8] The loyalists also detached a fairly large body to hold the Suma entry on the Harima road.

[7] The *Baishō-ron* has a very different version, as follows. Shortly after Takauji's defeat near Kyoto and his flight to Hyōgo, Kusunoki advised the Emperor to have Nitta put to death and to call Takauji back to the capital, there to work in harmony with His Majesty. He undertook to carry the message to Takauji himself. When the courtiers ridiculed his plan, he retorted that in truth Takauji was more loyal than Nitta. He predicted Takauji's victorious return, and said that for his own part he would die in battle against him. Whether this is a true story it is hard to say; but it is probable that Kusunoki disliked and mistrusted Nitta.

[8] The Minato estuary has frequently changed. In 1180, to protect his new city of Fukuwara (Hyōgo), Kiyomori diverted the river to its present course. In Ashikaga times the river bed was dry except after heavy rains, and it was on stony ground that Kusunoki fought.

On the Ashikaga side, Tadayoshi's army took up positions in three sectors, opposite those of Nitta. Tadayoshi took the centre position, meaning to attack Kusunoki's centre, while Shiba's corps took a position on high ground with the intention of falling upon Kusunoki's rear. A third corps, under Shōni Yorihisa, was drawn up on the shore line and moved gradually eastward, so as to keep touch with Takauji's seaborne army. The fleet of war junks great and small was led by Hosokawa's vessels. It moved along parallel to the shore, leaving the Minato River and Hyōgo on its port side and then bearing in towards the mouth of the Ikuta River in order to land Takauji's army east of Hyōgo, where it could cut off the loyalists' retreat.

The action began with Hosokawa's attempt to force a landing, which failed and resulted in heavy losses. He was obliged to move further east and land near the mouth of the Ikuta River. Meanwhile Nitta's division was attacked and badly punished by Shōni's picked men. Nitta withdrew in haste as soon as it was clear that his rear was endangered by Hosokawa. This retreat of Nitta proved to be a fateful blunder. It left Kusunoki in the air, and resulted in the defeat of the whole loyalist army, for Tadayoshi quickly took advantage of Nitta's retreat to fall vigorously upon Kusunoki. Kusunoki fought back desperately, and for a time Tadayoshi was in difficulties. But Kusunoki could not sustain the counterattack without support, and presently he had to face not only reinforcements sent to Tadayoshi by Takauji but also pressure from Hosokawa's men, who had driven Nitta from the field and now appeared in Kusunoki's rear. Thus attacked on all sides, and having lost his one road of retreat upon Tamba, Kusunoki fought on against overwhelming odds until he and all his clansmen (including his brother) were killed or died by their own hands. The number of their dead, according to the Ashikaga record, was more than seven hundred. They had fought continuously for six hours in the great heat of the afternoon of July 5, 1336.

In the chronicles of Japan Kusunoki Masashige appears as a paragon of martial valour and of loyalty to the Throne. He was evidently a man of high character and his reputation was well deserved. But he was an almost solitary figure, for the occupant of the throne could count upon very little disinterested support from members of the military class. In attempting to restore the power of the Imperial House, both Go-Toba in 1221 and Go-Daigo a century later had sadly overestimated the strength of their adherents. They depended principally upon the sympathy of some of the great monasteries, and such military aid as might be furnished by provincial gentry who disliked the rule of Kamakura or were lessees of Crown lands and therefore inclined to side with the Court.

Of all Go-Daigo's supporters, Kusunoki was the one who made the greatest sacrifices for the Throne. He was a well-to-do member of the rural gentry in the province of Kawachi. Though of only middling estates, he could claim descent from Tachibana Moroye, a great nobleman of the eighth century. He was a scholar and a devout Buddhist, familiar with the mystic Shingon teaching and intimate with some of the leading clerics of the day. It is not certain whether he held his lands in fief from Kamakura or as a Crown lessee; in any event, it seems that his espousal of the loyalist cause arose from his connexion with the superiors of such monasteries as the Izumi Kumeta-dera and the Kanshinji, upon which (it will be remembered) Prince Morinaga had called for help while Go-Daigo was in exile.

No doubt some of the accomplishments ascribed to Kusunoki are only legendary, but he stands in the history of his country as the ideal figure of a warrior, compact of civil and military virtues in a high degree. The loyalist cause suffered a great loss by his death, for unlike him many of the supporters of the junior line were moved less by their duty to the sovereign than by their antagonism to the Ashikaga. This was particularly true of Nitta Yoshisada, whose first motive for fighting was a desire to prevent Takauji from dominating the country and dictating to the Nitta clan. But it must be admitted that even after the defeat at Minatogawa the indefatigable Nitta continued to lead the resistance against Takauji with surprising success.

Kusunoki's loyalty was exceptional in that it was entirely unselfish. The war which developed from Go-Daigo's determination to retain the crown was not in reality a dynastic struggle, though it took that form. It was essentially a struggle for land, and most of the members of feudal houses took sides not to put this or that claimant on the throne but to promote the fortunes of their own families. Often there was a deliberate division of allegiance within a clan, so that whatever the outcome of a civil war one part of the family would be on the winning side. This not uncommon feature of the feudal wars is best seen in the example of the powerful Shimazu family. The head of the whole clan was Sadahisa, and his fiefs included great domains in Satsuma and Ōsumi. When the civil war spread in Kyūshū in 1360, Sadahisa took the Satsuma estates and declared his loyalty to the Bakufu, while his younger brother took the Ōsumi lands and declared himself for the Court party. Sometimes such family breaches were genuine conflicts of principle, but as a rule there seems to have been an understanding between the two branches, and the division between them was superficial.

5. *Takauji's Success*

Minatogawa has been described as a decisive battle, but its effect was not immediate. Takauji was not able to take the sting out of Nitta until early October 1336.

Nitta extricated his army from Minatogawa by a series of bitterly fought delaying actions as he fell back on Kyoto. He entered the city on July 6, and the next day it was decided that Go-Daigo should take refuge on Hiyeizan. The Emperor at once returned to East Sakamoto, carrying the sacred Regalia. It was a melancholy procession, but it was escorted by a band of seasoned warriors, Yoshisada at their head. With him were other members of the Nitta family and such well-known warrior chieftains as Utsunomiya, Chiba, Kikuchi, Doi, and Nawa Nagatoshi. The Emperor was well received by the mountain monks. The procession had included the ex-Emperor of the senior line, Kōgon-In, but he had pleaded illness and turned back to the capital. Soon after this Takauji established his headquarters at the Otokoyama Hachiman Shrine, and there he received Kōgon-In and the Prince Yutahito (later the Emperor Kōmyō).

The position of the Ashikaga forces at this time was very favourable. Nikki and Imagawa had entered the city from the Tamba road, Tadayoshi had followed with his army and established himself in Kyoto two or three days later, while considerable forces brought by Ashikaga adherents from Mino, Owari, Iga, and adjoining territory had poured into Ōmi province and were allotted positions north of the city, with headquarters at the Shūgaku-In villa.

Tadayoshi took command of all troops and prepared to assault Hiyeizan. The attack began on July 13, but after two weeks' fighting little progress had been made. Takauji, who evidently had not foreseen such poor results, decided to enter Kyoto where he installed Kōgon-In in the Tōji monastery with the idea of stimulating his supporters. Meanwhile, loyalist flying columns were active in Settsu and south of the capital. The loyalists thus threatened to squeeze Tadayoshi between north and south, and before long the Ashikaga force in West Sakamoto was in such danger that Tadayoshi was forced to evacuate his headquarters there and retreat to Kyoto.

On August 7 the loyalists attacked Kyoto in great force at dawn, setting fire to buildings in most quarters of the city. A rapid drive towards the Tōji by Nawa Nagatoshi threatened Takauji himself. At this juncture Takauji took charge, and with the help of his allies managed to turn an imminent defeat into a victory. Nawa was killed.

The loyalist forces thereupon fell back on Hiyeizan, the Ashikaga army remained inactive, and a period of stalemate ensued. Occasional raids and sallies by loyalist flying columns continued to endanger the Ashikaga positions, however, and ultimately forced Takauji to decide upon a vigorous reprisal. Early in October a determined assault was made on the loyalists in the vicinity of Yodo and they were forced to retreat. The indefatigable Nitta counterattacked, but without success. This was on October 5, and from that day the fortunes of war went against the loyalists. They continued a scattered resistance at Uji and elsewhere, but gradually the position at Hiyeizan was isolated and rendered untenable.

At this point Takauji decided not to prolong the fighting. He offered terms to "the Mountain," that is to say to the monastery sheltering Go-Daigo. He said that although he had so far appeared as a rebel, he had fought only in order to destroy Nitta and his clan. Now that Nitta was reduced to impotence, he, Takauji, begged His Majesty to return to Kyoto and govern the country. According to this version (in the *Taiheiki*), the Emperor agreed and ostensibly for the purpose of consultation went down from Sakamoto to the Kazan-In palace on November 13, 1336.

This was merely a tactical move on the part of Takauji, timed when the condition of the loyalist forces was unfavourable and Go-Daigo was helpless. His Majesty no doubt thought it prudent to agree, while not ceasing to hope for a full restoration of his power. This at least was the attitude of Chikafusa, who observes in his *Jinnō Shōtōki* that important forces in the northern provinces were still available to the Princes Tsunenaga and Takanaga, who were ready to establish a base at Tsuruga and were in close touch with Nitta.

According to a story quoted by Arai Hakuseki in *Dokushi Yoron*, before Go-Daigo went down he received a visit from a member of the Nitta clan who protested that in fighting for His Majesty Nitta Yoshisada had lost 163 members of his own family and 7,000 soldiers. If His Majesty meant to go to Kyoto at Takauji's request, he should first cut off the heads of the fifty surviving members of the family. It may have been in response to this protest that Go-Daigo entrusted Princes Takanaga and Tsunenaga to the Nitta leaders to be escorted to Echizen.

As soon as Go-Daigo reached the Kazan-In palace, he was placed in confinement and obliged to surrender the Regalia to Kōmyō-In, after which he was himself given the style of Dajō Tennō or Grand Sovereign. Kōmyō-In was the younger brother of Kōgon, who with the approval of Kamakura had assumed the title of Emperor while Go-Daigo was in exile, but had not been recognized in 1333 upon the return of Go-Daigo. According to the statements of a prominent courtier of the time, the Regalia which Kōmyō-In received were counterfeit. Kōmyō's accession was declared on September 20, 1336, and thus began an age of conflict between the two Courts.[9]

According to the *Taiheiki*, on the day before Go-Daigo surrendered to Takauji he secretly relinquished the throne to his heir-apparent, Prince Tsunenaga. There is nothing to confirm this in other chronicles, but it is a fact that Tsunenaga left with Takanaga for northern Japan that

[9] Kōmyō, who was Prince Yutahito, the second son of Go-Fushimi, was made emperor after Kōgon had nominally returned to the throne in June 1336, in order to establish the legitimacy of the senior line. Kōmyō's enthronement ceremony was not performed until the end of 1337, though his accession was in September 1336.

day. Further, he is known to have issued a formal imperial decree on at least one occasion from his headquarters in the North.

On November 17, 1336, Go-Daigo's son Narinaga was named Crown Prince. It seems that Takauji still regarded Go-Daigo as the legitimate sovereign now retired, and therefore thought it would be proper to name a member of the junior line to follow Kōmyō; but Chikafusa says that Takauji wished to please Go-Daigo and had hope of reconciling the two lines. However that may be, Go-Daigo was a stubborn man and did not intend to submit or to abandon his dynastic claims so long as he could see a possibility of escape.

Takauji took other steps to encourage a favourable opinion of his actions. He confirmed the title to land of most of the shrines and monasteries in the Home Provinces, and he ordered that the estates confiscated since the end of 1333 be returned to their former owners. At the same time he cut down the functions and privileges of Court nobles and officials, and in general moved towards the establishment of a new Bakufu.

In late 1336 he was promoted to the rank of Gon-Dainagon (Acting Grand Counsellor) and become popularly known as the Kamakura Dainagon, an indication that he represented the ideas of which Kamakura was a symbol—the rule of a warrior class. He would probably have moved to Kamakura had not the strain between civil and military been so severe that he could not be absent from the capital. He decided to establish his headquarters, his Bakufu, in Kyoto.

Once established there, he summoned important officials and scholars versed in the laws and discussed with them the main principles of government. He wished in principle to conduct his administration in accordance with the provisions of the Jōei Formulary (Jōei Shikimoku) which the Minamoto leaders had laid down in 1232, but it was thought desirable by his consultants to supplement this by a further statement of principles. This statement, known as the Kemmu Shikimoku, was issued before the end of the year. It deserves notice for the light it throws on contemporary ideas, but it must be read as the work of lawyers and officials, and not necessarily as a statement of Takauji's intentions.[10] For wherever the Bakufu was to be situated and whatever law it was to administer, Takauji was determined to settle the dynastic issue without diminishing his own powers. He would not be bound by any rule or precedent. If Go-Daigo proved stubborn, he would favour the senior line and see to it that only youthful and subservient monarchs came to the throne.

[10] In the preamble to this document the authors discussed where the new Bakufu should be situated. It was argued by Nikaidō (an aged member of the highly respected Nikaidō family of hereditary civil servants) that despite Kamakura's strong historical and traditional claims, whether a new Bakufu should be situated there or elsewhere was a matter to be decided not by precedent but by majority feeling. It was decided, as we have seen, by Takauji.

6. *The Kemmu Shikimoku*

The Kemmu Shikimoku consists of seventeen articles, seventeen being a magic number for such documents since the date of the Constitution of Seventeen Articles attributed to the Crown Prince Shōtoku (A.D. 604). It does not deal with theory, being rather a set of rules ad hoc, designed to furnish guidance in dealing with current problems. A summary of its contents is as follows:

1. Enjoins economy.
2. Condemns drinking and gambling.
3. Declares that order must be kept and crimes of violence prevented.
4 and 5. Deal with reconstruction after the great damage caused by the civil wars: Property is not to be confiscated without careful enquiry. Rewards and punishments are to be decided on the merits of individual cases, and there is to be no indiscriminate punishment of former enemies.
6. In rebuilding, fireproof construction is to be the rule.
7. For the office of Constable men of special integrity and ability are to be chosen; the function of the Constable since early times has been to keep the peace. Deserving warriors will be rewarded by the grant of estates.
8. The administration must put an end to the interference of courtiers, palace women, and monks in the granting of rewards or promotions.
9. Discipline among public servants is the rule and it must be enforced.
10. There is to be no bribery.
11. Presents offered to palace functionaries and government officials must be sent back.
12. Personal attendants of the Emperor and the Shōgun must be selected for merit.
13. Ceremonial must be correctly performed and distinctions of rank scrupulously observed.
14. Good service must be specially rewarded.
15. Those in authority must listen to the complaints of the poor and lowly.
16. The claims and petitions of shrines and monasteries must be carefully scrutinized, since the professed motives are not always the true ones.
17. Justice must be firm and prompt. There are to be no needless delays, no ambiguous judgments.

The Kemmu Shikimoku is little more than a restatement, in the light of recent events, of the main features of the Jōei Shikimoku of a century before. It has a more decided political flavour, no doubt because it was issued at a critical juncture. From its text the nature of current problems can be easily inferred. It represents the views of a group of experienced officials, concerned with practical questions of government rather than theory. It reads almost like a rebuke to Go-Daigo for the failure of his administration to remedy even the most obvious abuses. It is not a judicial document but a statement of guiding principles for the feudal leaders.

Ashikaga Takauji, having assumed the title and office of Shōgun, established his headquarters in the capital city in a mansion at Nijō-Takakura.[11] He appointed as his Deputy (Shitsuji) the successful general Kō no Moronao, and a member of the Ōta family was put at the head of the Monchūjo, the chief judicial organ.[12] In general Takauji followed the pattern of the Kamakura Bakufu, though his staff had no comparable physical facilities. Owing to the destruction caused by constant street fighting (in which setting fire to houses was a usual practice), there was no special building to accommodate the officials of the new Bakufu until 1378, when a palatial structure for this purpose was completed in the quarter called Muromachi.[13]

Takauji and his colleagues did not neglect civil administration, but most of their effort during the next few decades was devoted to the conduct of a civil war against the supporters of Go-Daigo and the junior line.

[11] The city of Kyoto being a rectangle with parallel streets running north-south and east-west, it was the practice to describe the position of a building by naming the intersection at or near which it stood. Thus a palace near the intersection of Nijō Avenue and Takakura Street was called the Nijō-Takakura Palace. See the map of Kyoto in A History of Japan to 1334, p. 472.

[12] The post was hereditary in the families of Ōta and Machino, descendants of Miyoshi Yasunobu, its first occupant in 1191.

[13] The district called Muromachi lay north and west of the intersection of Shichijō and Higashi-Tōin, and the street called Muromachi formed its western boundary. Takauji established his residence and military government offices in this area in 1338. The Ashikaga Bakufu thus founded was commonly styled the Muromachi Bakufu from that date until its collapse in 1573, and the period of the Ashikaga Shōgunate is often referred to as the Muromachi era. The district was close to the Imperial Palace, whereas the Hōjō deputy in Kyoto had had his headquarters at Rokuhara, outside the city.

CHAPTER IV

THE SOUTHERN COURT

1. Go-Daigo's Resistance

ONCE Takauji felt free to act without interruption by the loyalist forces he kept the Emperor in close confinement under military guard— a fact so well known to the Kyoto gossips that they used to ask in jest: "To which island will His Majesty next pay a visit?" But Go-Daigo was a stubborn man and had by no means abandoned his life's purpose of restoring imperial rule. He had friends and supporters and he somehow contrived to escape from custody and take refuge in the remote parts of Yoshino.[1] This was in January 1337.

When Takauji and his officers learned of Go-Daigo's flight they professed to take the matter lightly, but in fact they were crestfallen and made a great to-do to trace the movements of the fugitive monarch. But they could not find him. At that time one of the Emperor's loyal supporters (Shijō Takakuni) had collected a force in the district of Kawachi where Kusunoki had had his estate, and it was probably he that escorted Go-Daigo over the mountain road to Yoshino a day or so after his escape. Shortly after reaching Yoshino, Go-Daigo sent a prayer to the great Shingon monastery of Kōyasan, in which he asked for support and vowed to enter the sect, to endow it with lands, and in general to promote the Buddhist faith when peaceful times should come again. This document he signed "Tenshi Takaharu" to show that he (Takaharu) was the "son of Heaven" and had not surrendered his throne to Kōmyō.

He established his Court in Yoshino, and decreed a new era, named Engen, of which the first year coincides with 1336.[2] This begins the period known as Nambokuchō, or the age of the Northern and Southern

[1] Yoshino is the name of a large tract of mountainous country, wild and sparsely populated, in the southern part of Yamato province. The hills rise steeply and the valleys are narrow. The highest peaks reach to over 5,000 feet and the slopes are thickly covered with forest. This was a most suitable place of refuge for the Court, remote from towns and highways, in a terrain where large bodies of troops could not be deployed. To the east of Yoshino and Kōyasan lies high moorland country, rising to an eminence called Odaigahara from which there is a distant view of Ise Bay.

[2] From this date the era names for the Northern and Southern Courts differ. The era names for the years 1334–40 are given below.

	1334	1335	1336	1337	1338	1339	1340
Northern Court	Kemmu 1	Kemmu 2	Kemmu 3	Kemmu 4	Ryakuō 1	Ryakuō 2	Ryakuō 3
Southern Court	Kemmu 1	Kemmu 2	Engen 1	Engen 2	Engen 3	Engen 4	Kōkoku 1

Courts, respectively the "senior" line of Kōmyō established in Kyoto and the "junior" line of Go-Daigo established in Yoshino.

Go-Daigo was joined in Yoshino by a number of ministers and Court officials of high rank, but his military strength was uncertain. After the death of Kusunoki and the defeat of Nitta Yoshisada, it would seem as if an effort to resume the struggle against Takauji's superior numbers could be nothing but a forlorn hope. Yet Go-Daigo could still count upon a surprising amount of political sympathy and a degree of military strength which, if skilfully used, was by no means negligible. He also had certain topographical advantages, in that the mountainous terrain of Ise, Kii, and Yamato, where he had active partisans, was ideally suited to his military needs, being at once hard to attack and convenient as a base for guerrilla raids on other provinces. It was thanks to these circumstances that Go-Daigo's hastily established Southern Court was to hold out for half a century.[3]

Fortunately for his cause Go-Daigo had supporters in many other provinces as well—in twenty-five out of the sixty-six, according to some accounts. Even though the direct military effort which these forces could contribute was small, it was often sufficient to create useful diversions or to immobilize enemy forces at a long distance from the main field of operations. Of particular value was the strength of the loyalists in the North, which kept Ashikaga troops on the watch to prevent sudden descents upon important centres in the eastern provinces. During Takauji's absence in Kyūshū, Kitabatake Akiiye had collected a large following in Mutsu and Hitachi, and other adherents of Go-Daigo encouraged resistance movements among the rural gentry in the North, many of whom feared that their interests would suffer at the hands of ruthless feudal overlords like the Ashikaga.

Accounts of battles long ago are tedious, but since these battles are the substance of a national legend and elements in the formation of a national ethos, it will not do to pass over them in silence. In the warfare that followed Go-Daigo's escape to Yoshino, the winds of fortune blew to and fro, the tides of conflict ebbed and flowed. Each side had its defeats and victories, and for a long time no definite result was reached. Perhaps the most striking feature of this prolonged struggle was the persistence with which the loyalists returned to the attack after what seemed like crushing reverses.

After the failure at Minatogawa, Nitta had evaded pursuit and now, accompanying the Crown Prince Tsunenaga and his brother Prince Takanaga, he hastened to Tsuruga in Echizen. The Prince-Abbot Sonchō (Munenaga) made his way from Hiyeizan to Ise, where he joined Chikafusa. Other loyalist leaders had gone into hiding in Kawachi or

---

[3] Go-Daigo left Yoshino sometime in 1337; his movements thereafter are not exactly known, but he appears to have gone from place to place during 1337. Later (1349) the Court was situated south of Yoshino in a remote locality called Anau (pronounced Anō).

Kii to prepare for a new rising. The wild country of Yoshino was like a natural fortress, well suited to serve as headquarters of a volunteer army to be raised in those adjoining provinces.

At the end of the third year of the Kemmu era, on a date corresponding to January 27, 1337, a few days after settling in Yoshino, Go-Daigo sent word to Akiiye in Mutsu, ordering him to come to the aid of the Southern army, that is, the troops in the country south of Kyoto. Akiiye replied that he had been forced to yield the stronghold of Taga to the powerful enemy forces operating in that region, and had withdrawn with Prince Norinaga to a fortress called Ryōzenji (in Date's country). Later in the year a loyalist force under Date and Yūki that had been operating in the neighbourhood of Utsunomiya made a sally to Ryōzenji, and gave some help and encouragement to Akiiye, who was thus enabled to reach Utsunomiya, escorting Norinaga and picking up adherents on the way.

Akiiye's men were in such good heart that from Utsunomiya they began to attack enemy forces in the vicinity, and towards the end of 1337 they set out on a westward drive. They were opposed by Takauji's son, Yoshiakira, based upon Kamakura, who had raised a force for service in the eastern provinces, but he was defeated at the Tonegawa (December 24, 1337) and fled to Miura, while the loyalists passed unhindered through Musashi to Fuchū, and thence proceeded to occupy Kamakura.

At this point the outlook for the loyalists in the eastern part of Japan was not unfavourable, but it was not to remain so for long. In the early spring of the following year (February 1338) Akiiye marched westward along the Tōkaidō, being met in Tōtōmi province by local reinforcements. He next entered Mino province, but here he was checked by Tadayoshi and Kō no Morofuyu (a younger cousin of Moronao) with a strong array, at the same time being pressed from the rear by another Ashikaga force. The two armies met in battle on March 22, at a point of strategical importance which was to figure nearly three centuries later under the name of Sekigahara as the site of perhaps the most decisive battle in the history of civil wars in Japan.

Here Akiiye was halted and obliged to fight his way through Iga, reaching Nara a week later. After resting and reorganizing his forces, he was planning to attack Kyoto when he was fallen upon by a great Ashikaga Bakufu army under Kō no Moronao and barely escaped into Kawachi, while Prince Norinaga made his way into Yoshino. In Kawachi Akiiye was able to re-form his defeated force, and at the end of April he drove through enemy resistance to Tennōji (some ten miles southwest of Kyoto and the site of one of the first Buddhist monasteries in Japan), whence he pursued the enemy commander (Hosokawa Akiuji) towards the capital. Alarmed by the loyalists' progress, Tadayoshi went to the Tōji monastery to organize the defence of the city, and took the Emperor Kōmyō into protective custody. He sent all available

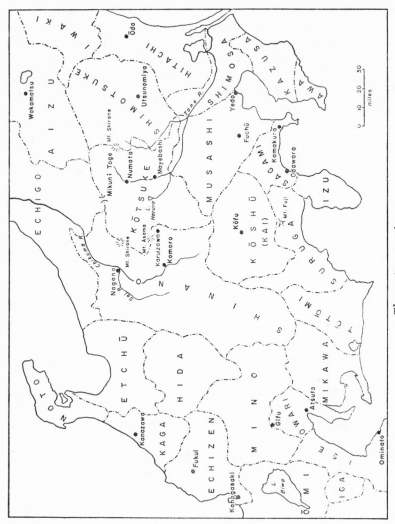

The eastern provinces

troops against the loyalist forces at Tennōji and Otokoyama, the hill on which stood the celebrated Iwashimizu Hachiman Shrine. At Tennōji, after desperate fighting, the loyalist force had to give way, and Akiiye led his tired troops to Izumi, where he was again attacked by a rein-forced Bakufu army. He was at length utterly broken, and died fighting at a place called Ishizu in Izumi, early in June 1338. He was only twenty years of age. There is a tearful description of his death in his father's *Jinnō Shōtōki*, and the *Taiheiki* contains a passage of mournful praise, calling him an incomparable leader.

Akinobu, his younger brother, had held out against heavy assaults upon Otokoyama, but he was forced to withdraw for lack of provisions and escaped into Kawachi. In August Moronao and his colleagues wan-tonly set fire to the shrine, which was entirely destroyed. Thus loyalist resistance to the Ashikaga in the neighbourhood of the capital city was overcome, and in other parts of Japan the outlook was not encouraging for Go-Daigo. The defeat of Akiiye was regarded as so important that Takauji was rewarded by the Emperor Kōmyō and appointed Sei-i Tai-Shōgun—the rank which Go-Daigo had been unwilling to grant him.

Another loyalist force in the North was that of Nitta Yoshisada in Echizen. As we have seen, Nitta had set out for Tsuruga in November 1336, after being entrusted by Go-Daigo with the care of the Crown Prince Tsunenaga just before the Emperor's descent from Hiyeizan. Nitta's northward advance was checked by the Constable of Echizen, Shiba Takatsune. The weather was intensely cold, and Nitta's men struggled against wind and snow until they reached the stronghold of Kanagasaki[4] in a state of exhaustion late in November.

An Ashikaga force was immediately sent from Shinano to hold Nitta, followed at the close of the year by a large-scale expedition under the joint command of Moronao and Moroyasu. Nitta, who seems never to have been alarmed by the predicaments in which he involved himself, raised some local levies and sent his brother Wakiya Yoshisuke[5] to make contact with the prominent Echizen loyalist Uryū Tamotsu, in his for-tress at Somayama. With this addition to his strength and with the pros-pect of further help from Yūki Chikatomo in Ōshū, to whom he sent a summons in the name of the Crown Prince, Nitta felt ready for action on a grand scale. At this juncture his forces repelled a series of fierce attacks upon Kanagasaki. Meanwhile Uryū took the offensive from Somayama and captured the stronghold of Shiba, the Constable of Echizen.

If the liaison between Nitta and Uryū had been perfected, the two together might have made an impressive force, but they allowed the enemy to nibble at their strength and finally Uryū had to fall back on

---

[4] Kanagasaki is on the seaward side of Tsuruga, overlooking the harbour.

[5] Yoshisuke had upon marriage formed a new branch of the Nitta clan named Wakiya.

Somayama in the middle of March 1337. Kanagasaki, after a three-month siege, was now isolated and short of food. The indomitable Nitta secretly left the besieged castle and with Yoshisuke and others entered Somayama in the hope of devising a plan to save Kanagasaki. But Kanagasaki's defenders were exhausted and starving, reduced to eating horseflesh.[6] They held out for another twenty days against attacks by day and night, until on April 7 at dawn Moroyasu broke down the main gates and stormed in, Shimazu's contingent leading the way. The Prince Takanaga and Nitta's son Yoshiaki took their own lives. Tsunenaga was able to escape in the confusion, but was captured on his way to seek shelter in Somayama. He was taken to Kyoto, where he was given poison by Takauji—a fate also met by his brother Narinaga, who was captured a few days later.[7]

Upon the fall of Kanagasaki Takauji announced the victory to the western provinces, saying that Nitta and all his followers had been put to the sword and the castle destroyed by fire. This report was premature, for although Nitta's plans for victory in the North had failed, he himself was still active, and with his younger brother was in Somayama working out schemes for raising troops and continuing the struggle against Takauji. He rallied the many members of the Nitta clan settled in Echigo, and he found other adherents, including the armed monks of the Heisenji monastery. In the course of time he was able once again to get a considerable force together. In response to calls from the Court in Yoshino in April 1338 he sent Yoshisuke to help in the attack on Otokoyama, but he retained the main body of his new army for his own project. It must have been of important dimensions, for Takauji was so alarmed that he gave strict orders to the Constable Shiba Takatsune to attack Somayama. Shiba's attack proved unsuccessful, and he had to withdraw to a district now comprising the town of Fukui and its environs, where he built defences across the plain to stop Nitta's advance.

At this point fate took a hand. Takauji sent reinforcements under the command of Hosokawa Akiuji to assist in the defence of Shiba's stronghold of Kuromaru (the Black Fort), and a contingent of Hosokawa's troops came across a small group of about fifty horse, led by Nitta himself. In the melee that ensued Nitta was mortally wounded by an arrow. This was in August 1338, when he was not yet thirty-eight years old. It seems that the unfortunate encounter was due to a change of front by the Heisenji monks, who had been bribed by Shiba. Nitta had hurried to the gap in his line created by their defection, and had run into Hosokawa's force by sheer accident.

---

[6] For a Buddhist to eat horseflesh was held to break his karma and return him to an animal stage of existence.

[7] Among others who lost their lives here was Ichijō Yukifusa, a celebrated calligrapher who had long been a loyal supporter of Go-Daigo. He was killed alongside the Prince Tsunenaga, whom he was escorting.

There is little detailed information about the reputation of Nitta Yoshisada at the time of his death; but contemporary references to him suggest that he was not highly esteemed as a general by his own side. The *Taiheiki*, although relating events before and after his death, has only one brief reference to his character. Chikafusa in the *Jinnō Shōtōki* says of Nitta that he was frequently summoned by the Emperor but was never available, and that he died in battle without having achieved anything of importance ("sa seru koto naku shite"). This passage follows upon a mention of the death of Chikafusa's son Akiiye, a bitter loss which might have been prevented (he doubtless felt) had Nitta not stayed fighting in the North.

The story recounted in the *Taiheiki* of Nitta's marriage shows him as an elegant young man rather than as a budding commander. His wife (known as Kōtō no Naishi) was a daughter of Ichijō Tsunetada, a Court noble of distinction. At the age of fifteen, according to a lyrical description in the *Taiheiki*, she was "of a delicate beauty like the petal of a flower. She wore no rouge or powder but her face looked as if it had been lightly brushed by a roving cloud and her complexion was as clear as autumn moonlight." She entered the Palace as a maid-of-honour (Naishi) and Yoshisada, a young officer on guard duty, fell in love with her at first sight. News of this came to His Majesty's ear and he encouraged the young pair to marry. Yoshisada was so happy and lovesick that (it is said) he dragged his feet when he went to the wars, forgetting that he was a warrior by descent and calling. While campaigning in the North he sent for her, but before she could reach him he had been killed in battle. She spent the rest of her life praying for his salvation. In later years there grew up a legend that the unhappy girl had drowned herself in Lake Biwa to follow her husband to the shades; and until very recent times the village near her burial place staged every year a simple play to soothe her departed spirit.

There is no doubt that Nitta Yoshisada was a great fighting man, but after his victory over the Hōjō he had no real success as commander-in-chief of the loyalist armies. His strategy was bold, but never thoroughly carried out, perhaps because he had more confidence than prudence. He had failed his comrades at Minatogawa, and his decision to remain in the North instead of joining Akiiye's forces operating in the East and South was probably a blunder if, as his critics thought, the best hope for the loyalist cause was to concentrate the greatest possible numbers on the recapture of Kyoto, the seat of the dynasty.

Like many other warrior chieftains, however, Nitta had private reasons for his public actions. He was born in a family long settled in the northern provinces, and it may be that he chose to fight there because at the back of his mind he also had a prospect of restoring the fortunes of the Nitta clan. He was driven also by animosity against Takauji, who had asked the sovereign for a commission to destroy Nitta and had even dared reward Ashikaga adherents with lands which had for generations been the territory of the Nitta clan.

The position of the Southern Court in the fall of 1338 was discouraging. It had lost all but a few of its most valuable supporters. Kusunoki, Nitta, and Akiiye were dead, together with many other brave and skilful captains, and after all the heavy losses sustained since the battle of Minatogawa, the military situation was desperate. But still the Emperor and his Court did not despair. Realizing that there was no immediate hope of regaining Kyoto, they began to think of forming a nucleus of power in the East and the North, with special reference to the provinces in Mutsu, from which, it was hoped, they might in time extend their influence southward.

To this end, even while Nitta Yoshisada was fighting his last battles, a party consisting of Prince Norinaga and other members of the Emperor Go-Daigo's family made its way into the province of Ise, escorted by Chikafusa and his son Akinobu, who was in command of a small force which he increased by enlistments on the way. The purpose of this journey (in August 1338) was to establish a centre of resistance which, while not too difficult of access from Yoshino, would be strategically placed as a base from which raids could be made on other provinces and communications with the northern provinces could be maintained by sea.

In October 1338 Norinaga, according to plan, embarked at Ōminato in vessels carrying men and supplies destined for Mutsu, where he was once again to take up his post as Governor-General. Akinobu was at the same time appointed Vice-Governor and Commander-in-Chief of the Northern Defences (Chinjufu Shōgun), the post formerly held by his brother Akiiye. It was at this time determined that Norinaga should be heir to the Throne and he was named Kōtaishi (Crown Prince).

The date of the departure from Ōminato is not exactly known, but it may have been as early as October 15. Soon after sailing they ran into a storm and the ships were separated. Norinaga's vessel, carrying Akinobu and Yūki Munehiro, was driven back to Shinoshima in Ise, while by good fortune or skilful handling Chikafusa's reached a harbour in Hitachi. Chikafusa at once sent a message to Yūki Chikatomo (Munehiro's son) in his stronghold at Shirakawa, at the entry to Mutsu, explaining the situation and asking him to search for the other ship, since it had no doubt been driven ashore not far away. Chikafusa now devoted his energy to establishing connexions with friendly chieftains in the neighbourhood and confirming the support of warriors in nearby strongholds, including members of the Date family. He established his headquarters in the main stronghold and residence of Oda, at the foot of Mount Tsukuba.

The news that Norinaga's ship had been driven back to Ise soon reached Chikafusa in Hitachi. He felt that it would be useful to visit Mutsu as soon as possible, but found the way barred by Ashikaga adherents. Norinaga and Akinobu meanwhile made their way back to Yoshino. Thus the year 1338 drew to a close, and when 1339 opened there was still no sign of the arrival from Ise of Akinobu with the reinforcements without which it would clearly not be possible to proceed to Mutsu. An attempt was made in March by local forces to reduce strongholds which stood in the path to the north; but this was not successful. Chikafusa then appealed to Yūki Chikatomo to open a way north, and when this appeal met with no success he settled down to await further news from the Southern Court.

2. Go-Murakami

In the late summer of 1339 Go-Daigo's health failed. He died after a short illness at the age of fifty-two on September 19. He had already named as his successor the Prince Norinaga, his son by the favourite consort of his later years, the Lady Renshi. A simple enthronement ceremony took place in Yoshino a few weeks later, when Norinaga took the name of Go-Murakami.

The Emperor Go-Daigo, whatever his faults, was a man of strong convictions. He remained firm in his determination not to come to terms with the Bakufu, and he submitted to exile and hardship rather than give way on a matter of principle. No doubt his resolution was fortified by Chikafusa, a man of unconquerable spirit; but Go-Daigo's own will was very strong. On his deathbed he issued an order (rinji) to his supporters in every province, urging them to continue the struggle with unabated loyalty.

The young sovereign—he was under twelve years of age—had no important advisers with him. However, Chikafusa was able to keep in touch by messengers, and he sent Norinaga his two celebrated works, the Jinnō Shōtōki and the Shokugen-shō, the former prepared for the guidance of the young monarch, the latter for the instruction of his advisers.

Chikafusa's Jinnō Shōtōki relates the history of Japan in terms of the reigns of its sovereigns, tracing the dynasty from the age of the gods to the Emperor Go-Daigo and his successor the Emperor Go-Murakami. Its main purpose was to support the Southern Court. Chikafusa, in a preface to a later copy, said of his work: "This record was completed in the fourth year of Engen [1339]. An old man's pen raced to instruct the young. While on my travels I had not a single volume to refer to, and it was with difficulty that at last I found a most abbreviated list of the reigns, and on this I had to depend. I did not see what I had written for five years, when I heard that it was being copied and passed from hand to hand. Alarmed by this, I examined it and found it full of errors. I made some corrections in the fourth year of Kōkoku [1343], and this is the book. At least, I hope, it will not be ridiculed by those who read it before."

The finished work was sent to Yoshino late in 1339 from the province of Hitachi, where Chikafusa was besieged in his stronghold. It is an interesting chronicle, written in a clear if ornate style, with some exaggerations;[8] but for the last few reigns it is a valuable historical source, since Chikafusa served five emperors (Go-Fushimi, Go-Nijō, Hanazono, Go-Daigo, and Go-Murakami) and knew all that was going on in politics and war. He was an accomplished scholar and a fine soldier.

The Shokugen-shō was also a tour de force: it was compiled in 1339 entirely from memory. It is an account of the origin and nature of the offices of the central and provincial governments and an essay on the selection and promotion of officials.

As may be imagined, however, there was little time for such niceties at the anxious Court in Yoshino. As soon as Go-Murakami was enthroned, Yoshisuke was ordered to attack Shiba Takatsune's fortress of Kuromaru in Echizen, in front of which his brother had been killed. The attempt succeeded, and Shiba was obliged to surrender. Then in 1340 the loyalists had some local successes in the northern provinces and also in Mino, where the Bakufu were not in great force. But the outlook for the loyalists was anything but bright. While their strength was limited, the fortunes of Ashikaga Takauji were clearly rising, and as Sei-i Tai-Shōgun he could look forward to new supporters and to further successes.

3. Loyalist Efforts in the Northern Region

With the death of Go-Daigo much weight fell upon the shoulders of Chikafusa in his Hitachi stronghold of Oda. As we have seen, Chikafusa's efforts to clear a path northward from Hitachi were checked by the opposition of the influential warrior Yūki Chikatomo, who held the key position of Shirakawa and remained stubbornly neutral.[9] At about the same time the fortress at Taga, which was the seat of government in Mutsu, had been captured and held by a member of the Shiba clan, Ishidō, who resisted all attacks by the loyalists. To add to Chikafusa's difficulties, Kō no Morofuyu left Kamakura with a large force and

---

[8] Like many Japanese chroniclers, Chikafusa was weak on figures. In his account of the Mongol invasion he says that in the great storm the enemy lost "several hundred thousand" ships.

[9] Chikatomo's stronghold was at or near the old barrier (seki) and military post controlling entry into Mutsu. It was on high ground overlooking the upper waters of the Abukuma River, at a place that commanded access from Kōtsuke and Hitachi to Taga in the north and to Aizu in the west. This was a key position, and Shirakawa was still an important castle town in 1868.

attacked loyalist groups in Hitachi at the end of 1339 and in the spring of 1340. That summer, Akinobu at long last left Yoshino to take up his appointment as Commander-in-Chief in Mutsu. After stopping at Oda to help Chikafusa, he proceeded to Taga, where he was checked by Ishidō.

In the following year neither Akinobu nor Chikafusa could make any headway. One after another the strongholds of the loyalists fell to the onslaught of much superior numbers brought against them by Morofuyu in July 1341. Chikafusa appealed time after time to Chikatomo, invoking the name of Yūki Munehiro, Chikatomo's father, who had been a fervent loyalist and had died in 1338 after marching with Chikafusa.

But Chikatomo was obdurate and at the coming of spring in 1342 all the loyalist strongholds were surrounded and isolated, including Seki, which Chikafusa stubbornly held. He made a last desperate appeal to Chikatomo in June 1342, but without result. Meanwhile Takauji, well aware that the Yūki fortress at Shirakawa was the key to success for the loyalists if they could win it or keep it neutral, was bringing strong pressure to bear upon Chikatomo, and at length in July Chikafusa learned that Chikatomo had gone over to the side of the Bakufu. He could do nothing but write Chikatomo a bitter reproach.[10] For the loyalists in Hitachi the end was near. In September Morofuyu surrounded and attacked the two loyalist forts that still held out—Taihō and Seki.[11] This was the third year of siege, and at last their garrisons, exhausted and starving, were overcome.

Chikafusa managed to escape and probably reached Ise by sea, thence going on to Yoshino. He had carried on the struggle for four years from these Hitachi strongholds; but now his plans for the East and the North had failed. The bad news reached Akinobu in Mutsu but he decided to stay there, and retained some measure of influence in the region.

In another part of the North (that is, of the Hokurikudō[12]) the loyalist cause had suffered from the defeat of Nitta but the loyalist forces had not been destroyed. Not long after Nitta's death they regained possession of Kanagasaki and gradually extended their influence to Tsuruga, under the command of Yoshisuke. But his success was of short duration; by October 1339 he had been driven out of Echizen and his loyalist army had faded away. With its scanty remnants Yoshisuke made his way to Ise and then to Yoshino.

[10] Some of Chikafusa's letters from the besieged place to Chikatomo have been preserved. They are touching documents.

[11] Seki was on the northwest shore of the Taihō lagoon, which was about eight miles to the west of Mount Tsukuba. The Taihō stronghold was across the lagoon, on the southeast shore.

[12] The Hokurikudō or Northern Land Circuit is usually understood to comprise the great provinces of Mutsu and Dewa, north of the eight provinces of the Kantō.

可以安諸三國海田庄地頭職俣神高野山
蓮花乗院勸學料所事

右為代、祖考及已息贈從一位右大臣等可
於當山建立一院始置近善勤行由年來至
素意心中之所念也而如聞者當院學業
殆為一山傳法之惠余料所錯乱之後
學頭學衆之依怙一向如無令思此事
不勝嗟息然乃聊聞彼發願欲便補
件闕分仍以當庄地頭職一所充料所々備
衆物理於新造寺院始置勤行不如継欲
絶之錢興欲廢之學　高祖照見此志
可感者已視得達其理不疑欲但料所復
本學衆安緒者且應衆望且迴思慮近可
計沙汰者襲勒書状啓白如件
正平七年四月一日進三宮一品沙門〔花押〕

A letter (holograph) from Chikafusa, presenting the Steward's rights of a manor in Aki province, as income for the support of a seminary at Kōyasan. Photograph by favour of Tokiwayama Bunko.

At the time of Chikafusa's return to Yoshino the prospects for the Southern Court had never been darker. The loyalist forces, despite heroic efforts, were at a disadvantage on almost every front, outnumbered and short of supplies. Yet their leaders did not give up hope.

There were certain good reasons for optimism. One of these was perhaps inherent in the nature of mediaeval warfare in Japan. It will have been noticed that even after what seem to have been crushing blows, the defeated side was usually able within a short space of time to recuperate and often to resume the offensive with success. In most battles armies were not destroyed or so weakened by slaughter that they could not revive. It would appear that although the weapons used were deadly in hand-to-hand fighting, the tactics were not such as to inflict really crippling losses. Mass movements of troops sufficient to overwhelm a large enemy force were uncommon, for the Japanese warrior preferred single combat, and even engagements which began with large-scale attacks in close order often developed into encounters between individual combatants or small groups, especially among mounted men who after an exchange of arrows would clash in sword fights.

Further, seeing that the contending armies had no heavy gear to transport, it was not difficult (if there was room to manoeuvre) for a hard-pressed force to extricate itself by rapid retreat when, in another kind of warfare, it might have been cut to pieces, as for instance where a cavalry charge could scatter and decimate a body of infantry in flight.[13] Thus Nitta Yoshisada after his first victory over the Hōjō was defeated in action time after time and yet managed to keep a considerable force intact for long periods. Chikafusa also knew how to keep the field for weeks on end despite inferior numbers. His resistance in Hitachi, his ability to preserve his force under fierce assault, was due in part to his exceptional skill and tenacity. Indeed it is possible that had he been able to persuade Chikatomo to remain neutral he could have gained the upper hand in Hitachi and thus broken the Ashikaga hold upon the North.

The forces of the Southern Court had a further advantage in that their adversaries were not united. There were constant dissensions in Kyoto among the great warlords, and clashes of pride or interest between Tadayoshi and the leaders of the Kō family. The unanimity of the loyalists was one of their strongest weapons.

4. Kanenaga's Mission in Kyūshū

The reverses which the loyalists met in the East and the North were to some degree counterbalanced by successes in western Japan and in Kyūshū. It will be remembered that when Ashikaga Takauji left Kyūshū in 1336, he had put his interests in the charge of such powerful families as the Shimazu, the Ōtomo, and the Shōni. The Southern Court had for its support the Kikuchi and Aso families; but its general situation was unsatisfactory, for it had no unified force, its supporters wasting their strength in small and probably personal conflicts. For that reason Go-Daigo, while still at Hiyeizan in late 1336, had sent the seven-year-old Prince Kanenaga as Chinzei Shōgun (Commander-in-Chief of the Western Defence Area) to look after loyalist interests throughout Kyūshū.

At that time it was impossible for the Prince to reach Kyūshū by the land route to Nagato. He arrived at Sanuki by ship at the end of 1336, having presumably made contact with the Kumano pirates and obtained a passage from them. Proceeding along the coast, he came first to Iyo

---

[13] The Japanese horses were sturdy but small, and had little or no protection. They were therefore not well suited for mass charges, nor were there as a rule any large bodies of infantry, any "serried ranks," for them to ride down. It was not until later in the Muromachi period that a large class of foot soldiers was developed and gave rise to the use of infantry tactics in certain kinds of engagements. Foot soldiers first proved their usefulness in street fighting, where mounted men were at a disadvantage.

The best early Japanese example of the almost complete destruction of an army was the battle of Dannoura in 1185, which was a sea fight in which most of the vanquished army were drowned. Pitched battles on land were exceptional; or perhaps it would be better to say that they were not as a rule fought to a finish, unless the terrain was such as to make flight or rapid retreat difficult.

and then to the Seven Islands (Kotsuna Shichitō) in the Iyo Channel, the base of the powerful Kotsuna clan.[14]

The Kotsuna family had been a powerful force in this area for a long time. As both warriors and freebooters they controlled the traffic through the Inland Sea, thanks to their enterprise and the commanding position of their islands, which stretched across the Iyo Channel for two sea miles east and west. They were, moreover, the leaders of pirates who made their living in the Inland Sea, without whose good will the loyalists would have found it difficult to maintain bases in the West or in Kyūshū. Fortunately for the loyalist cause, the Kotsuna were good loyalists; in 1333 their chieftain had responded to a summons issued by Prince Morinaga, and had rendered great service to the loyalist forces fighting against the Hōjō. Subsequently the family had taken the loyalist side in other provinces (Yamato, Kii, Suō, Aki, Izumi). There is an impressive list of their services—men and supplies—in the family archives.

Kanenaga, together with his guardian Isshiki Noriuji, arrived at the Seven Islands in 1337, and was warmly received by the Kotsuna. He stayed with them for three years, during which time conditions in Kyūshū were not favourable to the exercise of his powers. At length the wind shifted. Early in 1339 he established liaison with Kikuchi and Aso, and in late summer of that year, after acquiring further adherents, he prepared to leave the Islands.

In the autumn of 1339 news of Go-Daigo's death reached the Prince and his advisers, and they learned that Norinaga had been designated as his successor. The news caused them to delay their departure, but in 1340 they at last set forth, reaching the coast of Bungo-Hyūga in late April or early May. The direction of affairs in Kyūshū at this time was left to the Prince and his adviser Gojō Yorimoto, who was frequently sent news and advice from Yoshino by Shijō Takasuke, a comrade of Chikafusa.

Kanenaga could rely on some support from loyalists in Kyūshū, but he had no troops and was without any great military leader. It is for this reason that Wakiya (Nitta) Yoshisuke was appointed to command the Western Defences in 1341. The movements of Yoshisuke at this time are not exactly known, but it appears that he left Yoshino in 1341 and started for the West, recruiting support on the way to replace the men lost in and after his campaign in Echizen in 1339–40.

He called to worship at Kōyasan, and then went down to the Kishū coast, where he prepared sea transport. He contrived to get hold of no fewer than three hundred pirate vessels in Kumano, and received encouraging messages from landowners in central Japan and Shikoku, with offers of men. Relatives of two important warriors, Doi Michimasu and

14 Also called Kutsuna. They held appointments as Steward (*Jitō*) and Chief Constable (*Sōtsuibushi*) from the Kamakura government in the twelfth century.

Tokunō Michitsuna,[15] sent large reinforcements, and Yoshisuke arrived with a new army in Iyo some three weeks after leaving Yoshino. He was well received in Iyo, for the Constable there was Ōdate, a member of the Nitta clan, and the Governor was a son of Shijō Takasuke.

His prospects at that time were encouraging, and in fact were beginning to cause some misgivings to Takauji. But he was suddenly taken ill in Iyo, and died there a month after landing. His army was at once attacked by a member of the Hosokawa family, the leading warrior of the region (Awa, Sanuki, and Tosa); and within a short time the loyalist support in Iyo was destroyed.

We may presume that the death of Yoshisuke was a serious blow to loyalist hopes in Kyūshū, where altogether the Bakufu held the upper hand. The Shōni in Dazaifu and the Isshiki in Hakata were very strong, giving the Bakufu control over the north, and in the south, in Satsuma, was the powerful Shimazu clan. Loyalist support, drawn mainly from the Aso and Kikuchi clans, was concentrated in northern Satsuma and in Higo, and had there been a successful military leader to unite these forces they might have been able to make important gains.

There is scant information about Kanenaga's activity for two years after his arrival on the coast of Hyūga in 1340. We learn only that in 1341 he wrote to possible supporters in Higo and Hyūga, and that in early June of 1342 he seems to have arrived at a harbour at Satsuma and called upon the Aso family for help. Apparently receiving no encouragement from the Aso, the Prince took up residence in the castle of a warrior named Taniyama, and stayed there while getting in touch with local loyalist gentry. His plan was to improve or consolidate his position in Satsuma province and then to advance into Higo.

To a point the loyalists in Higo were able to hold their own against Ōtomo and Isshiki forces, who had been ordered to attack the loyalists in 1342. But when the Prince sent an envoy north to stir up resistance by the Kikuchi family in 1343, Isshiki and others attacked and defeated Kikuchi, leaving the Prince's forces in Satsuma almost entirely cut off.

The southern part of Satsuma was controlled by the Shimazu clan, which particularly since the beginning of the century had developed a military strength unmatched in Kyūshū. Upon learning of the Prince's intentions, the chieftain Shimazu Sadahisa attacked Taniyama's castle, but the castle was stoutly defended and the attackers were driven off. This made an impression upon neighbouring chiefs, a number of whom came to join the loyalist cause. Such valuable accessions brightened the prospects of the loyalists, whose support in Kyūshū had hitherto

---

[15] Tokunō and Doi had fought alongside Nitta in the North, and Tokunō was with Nitta at the fall of the Kanagasaki fort. His family were powerful in Iyo and were on good terms with the Kotsuna. In fact, this Tokunō seems to have been related to them.

been drawn from a number of small groups with no cohesion. In time the Prince and his advisers felt able to plan an offensive against Sadahisa (who had entered central Satsuma), and eventually to gain some measure of control in northern Satsuma. They began to discuss the proper strategy for this purpose by renewing correspondence with members of the Aso family.

But while these exchanges were taking place, Sadahisa's forces descended upon the loyalists in front of Taniyama and at other points and routed them, and by July 1344 Sadahisa occupied the whole of central Satsuma. Thereafter the two armies were at a standstill, and the Prince was obliged to remain inactive in the castle. He had not abandoned his plan of entering Higo, but his hope of success depended upon the two Aso chieftains, Koretoki and Korezumi, and by mid-1344 these hopes had been disappointed.

The actions of Koretoki and Korezumi suggest that this was one of the cases where members of the same clan deliberately took opposite sides. Korezumi remained loyal to the Prince, but his force was in a difficult position, almost surrounded by Isshiki and Ōtomo troops. At the Prince's order a letter was sent to Korezumi, saying that Korezumi's life was of more value than his own, since the Prince depended upon him; and this letter was followed by further commendations and rewards. Koretoki, however, while remaining on good terms with the loyalists, was not so quick to choose sides. In August 1342 Chikafusa called upon Koretoki to be loyal to the Southern Court, presumably having some reason to suspect his good faith. But Koretoki remained neutral, and when Takauji, who also knew of the situation in Kyūshū, offered him great rewards in 1343, he finally decided to take the Ashikaga side. He no longer concealed his alliance with the Shōni, and urged Takauji to reward him further. His greed was insatiable, and he was evidently trusted by neither side. His defection made it impossible for the loyalist forces to enter Higo (just as Chikatomo's had prevented Chikafusa from entering Mutsu), and a stalemate ensued. The Shōni provided a further obstacle to the Prince's entry into Higo.

Thus for a time the Prince's forces were almost completely cut off. When this state of affairs became known to Chikafusa, he and his colleagues decided to call upon the maritime strength of allies in Kii and Ise and along the Inland Sea. They addressed themselves especially to the pirates, whom they now invited to threaten the coast of Kyūshū at points useful to the loyalist army. By 1345 the assistance of these pirates had made it possible for the loyalists to consolidate their postions in southern Kyūshū and to advance up the coast to Yatsushiro in Higo; by then, moreover, the Court in Yoshino had begun to see a new prospect of regaining the capital. In June 1347 a fleet of pirate vessels attacked the coast of Chikuzen. A few days later some thirty vessels from Shikoku and the opposite shore of the main island appeared off Hyūga and Osumi, and then landed at Kagoshima.

1

2

The situation had now become favourable to the Prince. A report from one of the Ashikaga warriors engaged in the defence of Satsuma said that "several thousand" pirates from Kumano had attacked from land and sea, overwhelming the defenders, who could do nothing but throw away their lives.

Early in 1348, a message from the Court at Yoshino acknowledged with pleasure the news that the Prince and his company had left Taniyama by sea, under pirate escort, and sailed northward to new headquarters in Higo. The same message struck an optimistic note about developments in the Home Provinces.

5. Prospects in the Home Provinces

In the Home Provinces the loyalists' position had been unfavourable after the death of Akiiye in battle in 1338, and they had been almost without resources from 1340 until 1343, when Chikafusa returned to Yoshino and began to plan a concerted strategy. It was important to keep the offensive going, and not to think too much in terms of the protection of Yoshino, since in an emergency the Court could be moved. A gifted military leader was at last found in Kusunoki Masatsura, who, following in his father's footsteps, had been bold and active since 1340. In 1347 he led a force into Kii and there attacked Bakufu sympathizers with such success that he found his army growing and even attracting adherents from Kii and Kumano, as well as Izumi and Settsu.

Thus a condition was created which caused some alarm in Kyoto; and Hosokawa Akiuji was sent down to Sakainoura in Izumi. But he was met by Masatsura with a much superior force and broke off his attack, reporting to Kyoto that he would not be able to withstand an offensive. This news caused consternation in the capital—among the warriors because it was shameful, among the populace because the danger was so near. According to the diary of Tōin Kinkata[16] a real fear of disaster swept through the Bakufu, and he observed: "Just when the Bakufu is governing in a suitable manner this devilish thing happens. . . . Inscru-

---

[16] This is the diary known as *Entairyaku,* the most valuable single contemporary document describing events between 1311 and 1359. Tōin Kinkata kept his diary with scrupulous care and regularity during the whole of this period, and since he held high office during most of his career and was Chancellor of the Realm (Dajō-daijin) when he resigned in 1350, he had an intimate knowledge of Court life and of politics behind the scenes. He was consulted frequently after his retirement and had more influence than the Kampaku Yoshimoto.

It is unfortunate that the extant portions of the diary do not include the entries for the years from 1311 to 1342, since this interval covers the period during which Go-Daigo was on the throne and Kinkata was one of his ministers. The first extant entries concerning the Bakufu are under dates in 1347, and subsequent entries give interesting accounts of the complex relations between Takauji, Tadayoshi, and Yoshiakira, and of the course of events in the struggle between the rival Courts. Kinkata entered religion in 1359, and died in the following year at the age of seventy, on all sides greatly regretted.

table are the ways of Heaven." That night (September 26) the holy places in the capital were filled with the sound of prayers.

Now Masatsura turned back into Kawachi and there clashed with the enemy on September 29 and again on October 13 and October 21 in hot engagements, defeating Hosokawa and in a night attack crushing the Bakufu army with (said Tōin) innumerable casualties. Just as this news reached Kyoto, couriers arrived from the Kantō, reporting successes by the loyalist forces there. It became clear to the Bakufu that these were not isolated incidents but part of a far-reaching strategy, planned and stimulated by Chikafusa and others at the Yoshino Court.

Hosokawa fell back on Tennōji after his defeat, and the Bakufu sent Yamana Tokiuji to his aid; but the two forces remained inactive for a whole month. Observing their inaction, Masatsura attacked (with Wada as vanguard) on December 28, 1347. Hosokawa had not the spirit to resist, and although Yamana did his best, the odds were against him. His brothers were killed, and he and his sons were wounded but managed to escape. The shock to Kyoto was great. The generals were depressed; the civilian ministers and Court nobles were panic-stricken.

The news of Kanenaga's successes in Kyūshū had been discouraging to Takauji and his generals, but the growth of the loyalists' strength in the Home Provinces presented a threat under their noses which they could not disregard. A great army led by Moronao and Moroyasu was sent to attack Masatsura's base in Kawachi in February 1348. Chikafusa, who was there with his own troops, endeavoured to divert part of the attack by moving into Izumi while Masatsura opposed the advance of Moronao's force. In this attempt Masatsura was killed, with some forty of his kinsmen. This was a tragic loss to the Kusunoki family, and a blow to the loyalist cause.[17]

Moronao was now free to advance into Yoshino, in the hope of securing the person of the Emperor Go-Murakami. He reached the place where the Southern Court had been residing, but the Court had moved away, leaving nothing but some deserted buildings, which Moronao burned.[18] Upon turning to pursue the fugitives, however, he was unexpectedly trapped and defeated with heavy losses by Kusunoki Masanori, a younger brother of Masatsura. At the same time Moroyasu was severely handled by loyalists in Kawachi, and altogether it might be

[17] The battle is known as the battle of Shijō-Nawate, from the locality where it was fought in Kawachi. Masatsura had defeated the Bakufu armies in at least four engagements by the end of 1347, and the Bakufu commanders had felt obliged to make a great effort, raising levies in more than twenty provinces. In the battle Masatsura had been on the point of taking Moroyasu's head in single combat when he was severely wounded by an arrow and took his own life. His age was twenty-two. He is a touching figure in Japanese legend, which says that, knowing he must face fearful odds and prepared for death, he had gone to Go-Daigo's tomb before the battle and written a verse on the door of the shrine together with the names of his kinsmen who were to be with him.

[18] Tōin describes the behaviour of his troops as "unspeakable."

said that the flag of the Bakufu was drooping, or, in the Japanese phrase, its colour was bad ("hatairo ga warui"). It was now autumn in the year 1349.

There was at last good reason for the Southern Court to rejoice, after nearly thirteen years of struggle. The Bakufu was still pre-eminent in the land, but its pre-eminence, like its hold on Kyoto, had never been so shaky. On the face of things, the two Courts were now essentially equal. For the first time in years men on both sides began to speak of bringing the conflict to an end by uniting the two dynasties, the senior and junior lines.

CHAPTER V

DISSENSION IN THE BAKUFU

1. *Opposition to Takauji's Policy*

I N T H E struggle between claimants to the throne, the Southern Court no doubt hoped to profit by any internal weakness that might develop in the Bakufu; and it is true that serious disagreements among Takauji and his colleagues gave renewed hope to the loyalists in 1349, only a year after their serious reverse at Shijō-Nawate.

But the disagreements, although complicated by those jealousies which usually afflict military commanders, were not of vital military importance. They may have prolonged the civil war, but their real significance was political. Takauji, Tadayoshi, and the Bakufu generals were all strong-willed men, and the Kō brothers, Moronao and Moroyasu, were especially vain, violent, and quarrelsome. But beneath their personal grievances there was a serious difference of opinion, not only regarding military affairs but including all aspects of Takauji's policy in matters of civilian government.

When Takauji had destroyed the Kamakura Bakufu and restored Go-Daigo, he was almost master of the whole country, and he had to decide what course he should next follow. Should he completely destroy the power and influence of the Throne, set up his own central government, and incorporate rural society in a new system which he would construct? Such a policy would involve the abolition of the manorial system and the development of a new feudalism. It would require revolutionary methods and would produce friction and antagonism throughout the country among those whose interests were endangered.

Alternatively, he could compromise as much as possible with the monarchy and gradually destroy it by assuming arbitrary powers.

As we have seen, it was this course which he chose to follow when, after an early military setback in 1335, he drove the Emperor Go-Daigo out of the capital and raised up Kōmyō as his puppet. While engaged in this reduction of the power of the Throne and the consequent increase of his own authority, he thought it prudent to placate the great monastic bodies and some of the leading Court nobles by threatening to punish any warriors guilty of forcible entry into their estates.

It was on this point that Takauji's policy aroused antagonism among his colleagues in the capital. The alignment of the parties in this dispute is not quite clear, but it is certain that the Kō brothers, Moronao and Moroyasu, were against making any concessions and in favour of drastic measures. They had no respect for the Throne and believed only in force. They thought that Takauji's policy had been mistaken from the beginning, and they were bitter because they had not been fully rewarded for their victories. They particularly hated Tadayoshi, whose advice on political matters was usually followed by Takauji.

The quarrels and warfare of the following two decades were the reflection of personal hatreds, but in historical retrospect they are revealed as a clash between conservative and revolutionary factions in Takauji's government. There is another aspect to this clash which is not at first sight obvious, and that is the effect of Takauji's policy upon opinion in the country at large.

Most minor landowners of the warrior class had counted upon the destruction of the Hōjō regime to release them from tax and other obligations. As we have seen, Go-Daigo's regime did nothing to remove their grievances, and Takauji introduced no measures of land reform. Accordingly, when Takauji forbade the warriors to take matters into their own hands, to break into manors and confiscate the property of others, their disappointment was great. In the long run it was the opposition of rural gentry and emancipated peasants rather than the disagreements of metropolitan grandees that was to contribute most to the collapse of the Ashikaga Bakufu. These land-hungry countrymen did not want to preserve the old order. They even preferred anarchy because it would give them a chance to gather spoils.

2. Moronao and Moroyasu

The Kō brothers, whatever their prowess in the art of war, were violent, arrogant men who did not understand milder forms of persuasion. The news of their victory at Shijō-Nawate in 1348 caused great rejoicing in the capital, and a kind of national holiday was proclaimed in the expectation of peaceful days to come. But Moronao and Moroyasu, not content with their successes, began to ride high, and their intemperate conduct soon caused ill-feeling.

Moronao, as we have seen, indulged in wanton destruction of the deserted buildings of the temporary Court in Yoshino, having on his way there plundered and set fire to houses of the country people. He then went on toward Anau, where the Court had taken refuge, but before he could get there he was beaten by a loyalist force with the assistance of a large number of monks of the fraternities of Hasedera and Tōnomine. On his way back towards the capital he set fire to more monastic buildings before withdrawing to Nara, where he boasted that he had pacified the province of Yamato and forced hundreds of loyalists into submission. Moronao's action, far from serving the Bakufu, caused trouble and ill-will.

His brother Moroyasu was no better behaved and had no better fortune. On his way to attack the loyalist force under Masanori at Tōjō in Kawachi, he burned and smashed houses and shrines. He was roughly handled by Masanori, and had to fall back. The two armies sat facing one another until September 1349, when Moroyasu was called back to Kyoto by Moronao, which means that the loyalists had held out for a year and a half from the battle of Shijō-Nawate. Though not a victory, this was at least a promising situation for the loyalist arms, and the news of Moroyasu's departure was quickly sent out to comrades in other regions, even as far as Kyūshū, for their encouragement.

When Moronao returned to Kyoto from his none too glorious feats in Yamato, he found the atmosphere unpleasant. For some time relations between the Kō brothers and Tadayoshi had been near the breaking point, and by July 1349 there was talk of open warfare between them and Tadayoshi. At Moronao's request Moroyasu returned, and the citizens trembled, expecting a violent outbreak at any moment.

The breach was of some seven or eight years' standing, and was by no means a merely personal quarrel. The Kō family, it will be remembered, were relatives and vassals of the Ashikaga, whereas Tadayoshi was Takauji's own brother and had served him well. Takauji, when he disobeyed the Emperor Go-Daigo in 1335 by going to Kamakura, had remained in the background, living apart in a monastery and leaving the conduct of affairs to Tadayoshi, hoping thus to avoid charges of rebellion and treason. After defeating Nitta near Hakone at the end of 1335, he decided to return to Kyoto where he assumed nominal charge of all affairs, both civil and military. At that time he worked in close harmony with Tadayoshi, who devoted his attention mainly to administrative matters, a field in which he proved himself perhaps more capable than Takauji. But with the lapse of years, and as difficult problems arose, this harmony was strained until it seemed to observers in Kyoto that an open breach could not be avoided. The immediate cause of disagreement was a quarrel between Tadayoshi and the Kō brothers. Moronao had proved a successful leader in several campaigns, and he had done good work in organizing the Bakufu in its earlier stages. For this and similar reasons he and Moroyasu began to gain Takauji's confidence until their influence rivalled that of Tadayoshi.

Even as early as 1342 there were signs of this state of affairs in the capital, and news of the quarrel had reached Chikafusa, then under siege in his stronghold of Seki in Hitachi. By 1349 it was a commonplace of gossip everywhere, and no doubt this internal strain in the Bakufu was encouraging to the loyalists. Tōin Kinkata's diary at this time records that there was much trouble in the neighbourhood of Tadayoshi's headquarters. Small buildings and other obstacles, he says, have been cleared away as a precaution against sudden attack and "it is rumoured that an armed clash between Tadayoshi and Moronao is imminent. Men and women in the capital are rushing wildly from west to east and from east to west. This is the work of devils!"

It seems that some Zen monks were involved in this affair, and it was rumoured that Tadayoshi's counsellor Myōkichi and perhaps Musō Kokushi had inflamed Tadayoshi against the Kō brothers, whom they thought of as evil men. Tadayoshi visited the Jimyō-In, the home of the senior line, to complain, and shortly after this Moronao was relieved of his post as Deputy (Shitsuji) of the Shōgun; it was at this point that he called Moroyasu back from Kawachi. The two brothers put a strong guard of troops around their own house, and Tadayoshi took similar steps to protect himself in Takauji's new mansion at Sanjō-Takakura, in which he had taken temporary residence. Thereupon (September 26) Moronao and Moroyasu surrounded the mansion and ordered Takauji to hand over Tadayoshi's two deputies, whom they blamed for the present quarrel.[1] Takauji would not agree to this but promised to banish both men together with Myōkichi, and also to replace Tadayoshi by his own son, Ashikaga Yoshiakira.

Takauji was in a difficult position, because the force then at his disposal was less than half that of the Kō brothers. It was said at the time that he wished to come to terms with Moronao, but thanks to the intercession of Musō Kokushi, Tadayoshi was restored to his former position as the Shōgun's Deputy. In October the usual conferences were resumed at his official residence and attended by Moronao and his associates. However, Moronao's anger did not subside, and he showed his temper by despatching an expedition as far as Tomo in Bingo province to attack Ashikaga Tadafuyu (a natural son of Takauji adopted by Tadayoshi), whom Tadayoshi had had appointed to govern the eight western provinces as Tandai of Nagato in May 1349. The professed purpose of this appointment was to subdue loyalist risings in the West, but it was in reality intended by Tadayoshi to restrain the partisans of Moronao there.

As we have seen, Takauji and Moronao had agreed that Takauji's son and heir Yoshiakira, who was then governing the Kantō, should leave Kamakura for the capital to take over the functions of Tadayoshi. Accordingly Yoshiakira arrived in Kyoto at the beginning of December and took up residence in Tadayoshi's mansion. Tadayoshi moved to the Nishikikōji house of his old comrade-in-arms Hosokawa Akiuji. To replace Yoshiakira a younger son of Takauji was sent to Kamakura with Kō no Morofuyu and Uyesugi Noriaki as his deputies. Tadayoshi was gradually edged out of his other functions by pressure from Moronao, until early in 1350 he shaved his head and entered the religious life, shunning all intercourse with the outside world. Moronao embellished his triumph by despatching assassins to Echizen to do away with Tadayoshi's two deputies, who had been sent there in exile. He had already

---

[1] These deputies were Uyesugi Shigeyoshi and Hatakeyama Naomune, men of high standing who despised the Kō brothers and through the monk Myōkichi had urged Tadayoshi to get rid of them. Myōkichi had great influence upon Tadayoshi.

begun to persecute Tadafuyu, driving him to escape from western Japan into Kyūshū.

Tadafuyu, however, was not ruined by this action. He had made valuable friends in the West, and in Kyūshū he found supporters who were against the Bakufu. There was a confusion of loyalties everywhere, mainly because dissensions within the Bakufu were reflected in provincial politics. Much more was involved than the issue of loyalty to the Throne, for what was now taking place was a redistribution of feudal power in the western provinces. The former feudatories were beginning to act as independent territorial lords, and in Kyūshū in particular there were such convulsions that not long after Tadafuyu's arrival, Takauji decided upon a great expedition to suppress disorder there. He left Kyoto at the end of November 1350, accompanied by Moronao. He reached Mitsuishi in Bizen about January 18, 1351; and now Tadayoshi, who had seemingly abandoned all worldly ambition, began to show his true colour.

Most of the incidents just related are recorded in the diary (known as the *Entairyaku*) of Tōin Kinkata, at that time Chancellor of the Realm. He refers frequently and with unconcealed distaste to the turbulence of the warriors. His description of life in the capital gives an impression of alarming disorder, yet among his daily entries are careful accounts of regular Court ceremonies, discussion of fine points of etiquette, and (in a separate volume) a full account of the enthronement ceremonies of the Emperor Sukō in January 1351, which had been postponed for more than a year by the uncertain conditions prevailing in 1349 and 1350.

During all those days of violence, when the scene was dominated by angry warlords, the Northern Emperor and his ministers continued to perform their usual ceremonial duties, and the Shōgun treated the titular and the abdicated sovereigns with outward forms of deference. In the midst of the uproar caused by the Kō brothers, Takauji planned an entertainment to celebrate his move to a newly built mansion; and Kinkata gives the text of a simple letter from the Shōgun's household to a Court lady, asking what are the correct sweetmeats to serve on such an occasion. Her reply is courteous, and gives the names of five confections, which must be served on a silver tray with silver chopsticks.

3. *Tadayoshi and the Southern Court*

In November 1350, a few days before Takauji set out for Kyūshū, Tadayoshi suddenly left the capital by night and made his way into Yamato wearing his monastic robe. The Bakufu soon learned of his movements, but Takauji, though urged by Moronao to dispose of Tadayoshi once and for all, gave no order to pursue him. Tadayoshi meanwhile professed to be acting for the Southern Court, and about January 12, 1351, he sent out imperial orders (Mikyōjo) calling upon certain warriors to join in punishing Moronao and Moroyasu.[2] One of these documents has been preserved. It simply says: "Moronao and Moroyasu are to be destroyed. You are to attack them at once." Tadayoshi had submitted, that is to say declared allegiance, to the Southern Court some ten days before, and had not yet received a reply. But he knew that the Kō brothers were hated, and felt sure of support. He went into Kawachi, and from there sent a message to Takauji, then in Bizen, explaining that he was not disloyal, only angered by the behaviour of the Kō brothers. He urged Takauji to rid himself of these men. But the messenger was seized by Moronao, and sent back to the capital in bonds.

Tadayoshi urged the recapture of Kyoto before Bakufu armies could return there, but he found that he could not count much on the support of loyalist forces in the vicinity. He hurriedly took up a position at Yahata, and soon began to receive reinforcements brought by friends from the northwest, notably Momonoi, who came to his aid through snow and ice. During February 1351 there was bitter fighting. Yoshiakira, then in charge of Kyoto, felt that he could not cope with this assault, and left the city to join Takauji. Takauji had by then turned back to help Yoshiakira and sent Moronao ahead; but their combined force failed to recover the ground they had abandoned.

Takauji now retreated along the road to Hyōgo—not a new experience for him—and in March 1351 he was defeated in a battle at Uchidehama in Settsu. Both the Kō brothers were wounded. A truce was arranged through the intervention of Musō Kokushi, and Takauji was forced to tell the Kō brothers that they would be spared only if they became monks. A week later Takauji left Hyōgo for the capital, escorting the two men, Moronao in a Zen monk's habit and Moroyasu robed as a member of the Nembutsu fraternity. But they were not to complete the journey, for on their arrival at the Muko River they were halted by a body of armed men under the command of Akiyoshi, a son of that Uyesugi Shigeyoshi whom the Kō brothers had ordered to be killed. Akiyoshi now claimed the brothers as his prisoners, and shortly afterward, in revenge for the murder of his father, killed them, together with several score of their clansmen.

Moronao and Moroyasu had rendered great service to Takauji, and in their rise to power they had invited much hostility. The *Taiheiki* view of their characters is perhaps prejudiced, but its charges of arrogance and criminal behaviour are surely well founded.

4. Rivalry between Takauji and Tadayoshi

Having delivered the two victims to Akiyoshi, Takauji returned to Kyoto, where Tadayoshi was now in power. Takauji appeared to be

[2] Mikyōjo is an order issued by officers of prescribed high rank, with the force of an imperial edict.

in a dejected mood, whereas Tadayoshi was elated and confident. The two seemed to be reconciled, and Tadayoshi resumed his functions as administrator, with Yoshiakira as his superior. In the flowery month of April the three made an excursion to the garden of the Saihōji, a monastery in the western suburbs. They enjoyed looking at the blossoms and listening to the improving conversation of the great Kokushi.

But under this surface of elegance and urbanity passions were seething. For one thing, Takauji was angry with Tadayoshi for his lenient treatment of Uyesugi Akiyoshi, who had stabbed Moronao. Takauji wished to punish Akiyoshi by death; Tadayoshi reduced the punishment to exile. But there were more serious differences than this. The recent fighting, which had involved great warrior families throughout the country, had created antagonisms among them which were beyond hope of reconciliation. Hatreds arose first from conflicts on the battlefield and later from a clash of interests when the time came to settle rewards for good service. All these difficulties stood in the way of a real peace between the two brothers. Moreover a matter of paternal pride was involved, for Takauji wished to make sure that upon his death he would be succeeded by his sons Yoshiakira and the younger Motouji (as a child called Mitsu-ō) in various offices, and not by Tadayoshi or his offspring. But because Takauji doubted whether Yoshiakira was capable of holding an office that called for good judgment and steady character, he decided that Motouji should be in charge at Kamakura as Kantō Kanrei, the Shōgun's Deputy in the East, a truly important post because its holder had to control and direct the eastern warriors.[3] The office of Shōgun would naturally fall to Yoshiakira, the eldest son, who would have the benefit of experienced advisers.

Tadayoshi, it will be remembered, had tried (after a fashion) to make peace between the Northern and Southern Courts at the end of 1350, and in April 1351 he tried again. He proposed a discussion between the two lines, for which Go-Murakami was to go to Kyoto. Go-Murakami had already shown a willingness to negotiate in a message carried to Tadayoshi by Kusunoki Masanori, who was acting as go-between. But when definite conditions were proposed in writing to the Southern Court, a reply came back in June to say that Chikafusa strongly opposed a reconciliation between the two lines. The failure of these pourparlers annoyed Masanori, who had hoped to negotiate a practical solution. It also put Tadayoshi in an awkward position, and it caused anxiety in Kyoto because it seemed to presage a renewed antag-

---

[3] When the Bakufu was in Kamakura, the Shōgun's Deputy resided in Kyoto. The first regular appointment was that of the Rokuhara Tandai in 1219, and after that the post was held by members of the Hōjō family until 1333. When Ashikaga Takauji came into power he created the post of Kantō Kanrei. It was first held by Yoshiakira and successive members of the Ashikaga family, from 1337 to 1455, and then by members of the Uyesugi family. In Kyoto the Ashikaga Shōguns appointed a general as Deputy, with the style of Kanrei, and this practice continued from 1379 to 1552.

onism between the two brothers. Their respective supporters wished to avoid entanglement in such a quarrel, and most of them left the capital in July and August, returning to their own fiefs, with their own forces. It was a sign of the times that several former Bakufu supporters were now ready to submit to the Southern Court; but Takauji was against coming to terms.

Tadayoshi, beginning to suspect Takauji's and Yoshiakira's intentions towards him, now left Kyoto and made his way into Etchū province, followed by some of his allies. These movements excited misgivings in the country. The *Taiheiki* says of this time: "The people were ill at ease. The whole country was divided into three parts and it seemed that they would go on fighting forever." The situation was indeed fantastic, and the outlook grim. Takauji moved against Sasaki Dōyo; Yoshiakira planned to attack Akamatsu Norisuke, a faithful supporter of the Southern Court; loyalist forces were active in Kawachi, where they were sure to engender conflicts; and Tadayoshi was in the field with Momonoi and other allies from the North.

After some fighting and some negotiations, hostilities were broken off just when Tadayoshi had moved with fresh levies into Ōmi province and was there joined by a friendly chieftain with reinforcements. But he seems to have lost confidence, for he met Takauji about October 15 and the brothers came to terms. Their harmony, however, did not extend to their supporters. The divisions and feuds between members of the rival parties were even intensified, for throughout the land fighting had become a chronic disease, and could not be stopped by agreement between the two leaders. Tadayoshi returned to Kamakura, where he busied himself with the affairs of the Kantō.

These internal troubles of the Ashikaga Bakufu gave the armies of the Southern Court numerous opportunities for action, and some loyalist leaders were now inclined to move on Kyoto. This proposal was premature, but it shows that the Court was moving from the defensive to the offensive and was watching for the next moment of confusion within the Bakufu.

Takauji must have sensed this, for he now proposed to submit to the Southern Court and expressed himself in favour of an agreement between the two Courts. He felt that he must not miss a chance which might prove favourable to him in the long run. He thought it wise to make a show of support for his proposals; and he persuaded Akamatsu Norisuke to urge the Southern Court to accept his submission and his proposal for the amalgamation of the two dynastic lines.

After a short delay the Court consented in November 1351 to accept the submission of Takauji and Yoshiakira. They sent a monk to Kyoto to deliver this message and to state that there must be a return to the conditions of "the early days of Genkō" (1331–33), when the empire was united under the Crown.

At the same time Takauji was commissioned to chastise Tadayoshi.

Takauji ordered the cessation of hostilities throughout the country and declared that he surrendered to the judgment of the Emperor. He said he would obey every word of the imperial command. This was on November 22, 1351. A few days later the Emperor Sukō and his Crown Prince, Tadahito, were "retired," and the era name of the Northern Court was cancelled, both sides now using "Shōhei." At the end of the year the Regalia were handed over by the senior line to the junior line, which accepted them, though saying that they were counterfeit.

It is scarcely necessary to say that Takauji's humble submission was a mere tactical move, designed to gain time. Possibly his only true motive was to obtain a commission to attack Tadayoshi. Similarly the Court must have been well aware of Takauji's duplicity—it was something which Chikafusa would at once detect—but it would have been a mistake to miss an opportunity to return to the capital; and even a simulated agreement between the two Courts might lead the way to a genuine union of both against the Bakufu.

Takauji announced his commission to all the provinces. He left Kyoto in December and entered Suruga early in January 1352, establishing a base near Tegoshi-gawara.[4] He invited Utsunomiya and Yūki Chikatomo to join him, hoping thus to "scissor" Tadayoshi, who had established himself in Izu province. The two armies met when Tadayoshi advanced to Sattayama, east of Okitsu, in Suruga. He was roughly handled by Utsunomiya's force, and withdrew to Hōjō and then into the hills of Izu. He seems to have been mentally disturbed. He could find no place of safety and was on the point of suicide when peace proposals were made. He surrendered and was taken to Kamakura and kept in confinement within the precincts of the Jōmyōji monastery, where he died—beyond doubt poisoned—during the month of March, at the age of forty-six.

Opinions vary as to the character of Tadayoshi. The *Taiheiki*, which is not generally favourable to him, says, after recording his death, that he was "much interested in government and aware of the claims of humanity and justice." It is hard to believe this obituary praise. Tadayoshi was disliked in his time for his evil deeds, especially the murder of Prince Morinaga and the poisoning of the young Prince Tsunenaga, which were regarded as unforgivable offences. When Tōin Kinkata heard of his death he observed that this might be a good occasion for bringing an end to the everlasting warfare. He no doubt felt that all this bloodshed was the work of guilty men.

The *Nan-Taiheiki* says that Takauji never forgot the debt of gratitude which he owed to Tadayoshi for his services in their early days. He did not even blame him for instigating Moronao and Moroyasu to evil courses. He was ready to work with Tadayoshi, but he was deter-

---

[4] Tegoshi-gawara was a dry river-bed near Shizuoka, and was the scene of a loyalist victory under Nitta Yoshisada in December 1335.

mined that Kamakura should go to his own descendants, and his infatuation for Yoshiakira was probably the real cause of his breach with Tadayoshi. The private lives of both Takauji and Tadayoshi are said to have been blameless.

In discussing the relations between Takauji and Tadayoshi, Arai Hakuseki says that Takauji was inferior to Tadayoshi in intellect and in political skill, but far superior in the art of war.[5]

5. *The Struggle for Kyoto, 1352–55*

After Tadayoshi's defeat, the Southern Court had only one great enemy to reckon with, and felt that the moment had come for a desperate effort to break the power of the military society, which was now divided in its loyalties. A plan was formed to attack Takauji in the East and Yoshiakira in Kyoto.

Accordingly, in the Kantō the Nitta clan, joined by the majority of Tadayoshi's adherents, went into Musashi, while other former Tadayoshi men combined with Nitta partisans to attack Kamakura, which Takauji had hurried to defend. They drove Takauji out of the city in April 1352. Further to the north the loyalist governors became active. All these movements were coordinated by a previous plan devised under Chikafusa's direction at the Court in Anau.

Although the successes of these loyalist armies were striking, they were by no means complete. Nitta Yoshimune (the third son of Yoshisada), with a strong force from Echigo, attacked Takauji and defeated him in several short engagements, but he was at last driven back in a fight at a place called Kotesashi-hara, and withdrew to a position on Fluteplayer's Pass (Fuefuki-tōge, now known as Usui-tōge and familiar to travellers from Karuizawa). He was presently dislodged from this position by Takauji, and fled to Echigo. Similarly, the drive of the other Nitta brothers was checked. Takauji was able to recapture Kamakura, and although the loyalists held a stronghold in Sagami against repeated attacks until the spring of 1353, their resistance then collapsed and they scattered in the hills. But their efforts had kept a large Bakufu force engaged, and thus had taken pressure off the loyalist operations in the neighbourhood of Kyoto.

The Bakufu's position in the Kyoto area was in serious danger. After the agreement between the two Courts, Yoshiakira learned that Go-Murakami intended to move on the capital and had already reached Tōjō in Kawachi on the way to a temporary residence at Sumiyoshi in Settsu. He entered Sumiyoshi on March 14, 1352. After a short period

[5] It may be useful for students of this period to know that the chronicles rarely refer to the Ashikaga leaders by name, but by one of their titles, as follows: Takauji is called Ō-Gosho or Dainagon; Tadayoshi is called Gosho or Daikyūji-dono; Yoshiakira is called Bōmon or Hōkyō-In.

of preparation he moved to Tennōji early in April. Yoshiakira was obliged to act, for he saw that the purpose of the Southern Court was not a mere union, but a full-scale attack upon Kyoto. He was taken by surprise. He knew he could not depend upon Takauji, then engaged in the Kantō, and he did not feel strong enough to make a stand alone. He therefore decided to prepare a way for retreat, and to convey to the Emperor certain proposals for a settlement. To meet the first need he had the long bridge at Seta put in order and strengthened so that it could carry a large force moving rapidly to the east. For his next step he seems to have made offers which included the transfer of valuable estates to members of the Court nobility.

The Emperor gave no definite reply, but told Yoshiakira's emissary, the monk Eichin, that he would answer after arriving at Yahata. He reached the Hachiman Shrine on April 4 and took up residence in the house of the Grand Warden, but he gave no reply to Eichin's repeated enquiries. According to Tōin's diary, that night the Bakufu troops were busy preparing to leave, and the citizens of Kyoto "were pale with fright." On the following day, April 5, the loyalist army, which had assembled at Yahata, poured into the capital in columns led by Kitabatake Akiyoshi, coming from Toba; Kusunoki Masanori, coming from the Katsura River; and Chigusa Akitsune, coming from Tamba. Yoshiakira met this attack but was routed by Akiyoshi and fled across the Seta bridge into Ōmi province.

On the next day (April 6) the three abdicated Emperors of the senior line (Kōgon, Kōmyō, and Sukō) with the Crown Prince Tadahito were taken by officers of the Southern Court to the Rokujō palace, where they were detained for a short time. They were then removed first to Yahata, next to Tōjō in Kawachi, and finally to Anau, thus reversing the road taken by Go-Murakami himself. There was confusion in the city, and Kitabatake Akiyoshi tried to establish order, with the help of his father Chikafusa, who as always stayed close to his sovereign.

The capture of Kyoto was a brilliant victory, the result of sound strategy and hard fighting against seasoned warriors. But like many battles in the warfare of this period, it resulted in the defeat but not the destruction of the enemy's army. Yoshiakira had performed what in modern parlance is styled a strategic withdrawal. This may not have been his purpose, but after reaching a suitable point in Ōmi, he did in fact halt to reassemble his scattered forces and to obtain additional strength from neighbouring leaders. Thus refreshed he confidently launched an attack upon Kyoto on April 25, some twenty days after his retreat. The defence was weak, for Akiyoshi had not enough men to keep order in the city while holding all the approaches to Kyoto. Within forty-eight hours the Ashikaga forces had re-entered the capital and had established themselves in strong positions on the high ground in the Higashiyama district, which commands the city. Soon after that

Yoshiakira moved his headquarters to the Tōji monastery, and thence on June 7 he opened an attack upon Otokoyama. At about this time he received reinforcements from Hosokawa Akiuji and also from Akamatsu Norisuke. The Akamatsu family, once great fighters for the Southern Court, had contracted the increasingly common habit of changing sides.

With such assistance Yoshiakira had not much difficulty in forcing the loyalists back on Yahata. Early in May Hosokawa and some other commanders took a circuitous route by Uji, crossed the Kizu River, and came out over the pass onto the rear of Masanori. He also was obliged to fall back on Otokoyama, so that now the whole of the loyalist army was concentrated there, to make a last stand. A few days later—it was in the middle of May—Yoshiakira received further additions to his strength from Yamana, who came from the Sanindō; from Shimazu, who came out of Satsuma; and from Kōno, who had crossed from Iyo. Thus the total array of Yoshiakira was very imposing, and in the early part of June he was able to deliver a most powerful attack upon Masanori and Akiyoshi. Their defence was stubborn and their losses great. They fought back, encouraged by the Emperor, who showed himself to the troops. In a night counterattack they even succeeded in breaking into Hosokawa's formation and obliging him to retreat with speed so as to recover his balance.

After some days of fierce and almost incessant fighting, the defenders settled down to withstand a close siege. They were at length exhausted. There were some desertions, and provisions were running short. They felt that they could no longer protect the Emperor, and they decided to withdraw. They left stealthily during the night of June 23, pursued by some hundred enemy horsemen as they took the road into Yamato. In the rear guard was the faithful Shijō Takasuke, a nobleman who had served the Southern Court for twenty years and more. He died in defence of the Emperor on the way back to Anau. On that journey (according to the *Entairyaku*) the Emperor was inconspicuous as he rode in armour with a troop of horsemen. He was struck once or twice by arrows from the pursuing force, but they did not pierce his coat sleeves. He carried the Seal in a basket attached to the front of his saddle.

This was not the end of the struggle for the capital, but perhaps the best opportunity for success had been lost. According to the *Taiheiki*, if the defenders could have held out for a few more days, they could have inflicted upon Yoshiakira a defeat from which it would have been hard to recover. This of course is only a conjecture; but it is of interest to note the report that Nitta Yoshimune left Echigo with 7,000 men, and was joined by Momonoi with 3,000. Kira and Ishidō left Suruga and reached Tarui in Mino with a considerable force, and Doi and Tokunō were ready to march from the seashore, where they had landed men in 700 transport craft.

These figures are significant, showing that between 10,000 and 20,000 men might have come to the aid of the defenders at Yahata. The numbers are perhaps exaggerated, but they seem more credible than the usual imaginative or careless estimates of the chroniclers. At least they indicate that the loyalist cause had attracted more and more adherents as its leaders showed their determination and the Bakufu showed signs of weakness. The near success of the loyalist army showed that the military strength of the Southern Court was greater than it had ever been.

After Tadayoshi had been poisoned in Kamakura, the internal condition of the Ashikaga Bakufu had deteriorated, a number of clansmen turning against Takauji and, if not actually opposing him, at least withholding their support. Thus the antagonism between the two brothers was perpetuated after Tadayoshi's death, and it tended to spread from the leaders of feudal society in the metropolitan area to warrior chieftains in the distant provinces. Those members of the rural gentry who joined the party of Tadayoshi were not necessarily moved by disapproval of Takauji's offences. They saw a great conflict growing and felt that they must take sides, because it was only in such clashes between great chieftains that they could hope to earn rewards in the shape of lands or lucrative offices. Moreover, if they did not take sides, they might find themselves punished for their neutrality.

The main opposition to Takauji was continued in the form of support to Ashikaga Tadafuyu, who was a nephew of Tadayoshi and a natural son of Takauji, neglected and for long unrecognized by his father. Tadayoshi had treated the young man kindly and had secured for him the important post of Tandai in Nagato, with authority over the eight western provinces of the main island. This was in 1349, and thereafter, when the breach between Takauji and Tadayoshi led to bitter conflict, he took the side of his uncle. The death of Tadayoshi was a great blow to him for, quite apart from family affection, it left him without support in high places. By 1351 he dominated northern Kyūshū as well as Nagato, and had resided at Dazaifu for some time. At the end of that year he was attacked in his residency there by Isshiki Noriuji,[6] together with loyalist forces which had maintained a strong position in central and southern Kyūshū under Prince Kanenaga. Tadafuyu was forced to escape from Kyūshū and take refuge in Nagato.

He could not return to Kyoto, since Takauji and Yoshiakira were now his enemies. Not knowing where to turn, he appealed for help to some of the leading families in his jurisdiction. Among those who responded were first the powerful Mōri clan in the province of Aki, and then other influential parties in Iwami and Izumo. With their aid he was able to improve his own position to such a degree that he became virtually master in the West, but he was not yet strong enough to ven-

---

[6] The Isshiki family had long been supporters of the Ashikaga; Noriuji, whom Go-Daigo had appointed as Kanenaga's adviser, was an exception. Sometime in 1352, however, he went over to the side of the Ashikaga.

ture upon an expedition against Isshiki in Kyūshū. His future was therefore uncertain unless he could find a powerful ally. He soon bethought himself of the device to which his father and his uncle had already resorted, namely an offer to submit to the Southern Court and thus to gain the collaboration of the loyalist army in resisting his own enemies. He made his request and it was granted.

With this advantage he approached Shōni Yorihisa and other leaders, planning to attack Isshiki, who himself had fought as a loyalist against Yorihisa not long before. The situation was confused, but that was not unusual, for at this time, as we have seen, shifts of allegiance were common. Here in Kyūshū, Shōni Yorihisa, who had once been a loyal supporter of Takauji, was now ready to join the supporters of the Southern Court. Yet according to the *Baishō-ron* the loyalty of Yorihisa was deep and enduring. His father had committed suicide because he felt that he had failed Takauji in battle, his brothers had thrown away their lives for Takauji, and he himself had followed Takauji in campaigns on the main island, where he had earned great praise and broad estates.

In Ashikaga times the turncoat is a common figure. His feats are startling but they may be explained if not justified by the inconstancy of the great leaders, whose conduct was rarely guided by thoughts of rectitude. Their subordinates, the general run of warriors, were for the most part concerned with the private interests of their own families and not with matters of principle. They wanted rewards, and civil wars offered the best opportunity for gain, since the victors could take the land of the vanquished. Yorihisa's own history is a case in point.

So the loyalist cause found supporters in unexpected quarters and the loyalist leaders welcomed new volunteers without too close enquiry into their motives. A story in the *Taiheiki*, though perhaps not entirely truthful, illustrates well enough the common practice of the warrior families in the era with which we are concerned. It describes the conduct of a member of a leading warrior house in western Japan, the Yamana family of the province of Hōki. This man had fought well in the attack on Otokoyama in June 1352 and as a reward asked for a certain manor in Wakasa. The grant was made, but Yamana was told that it was subject to the claims of the domanial lord at that time, probably a powerful landowner whom the Ashikaga leaders were anxious not to offend. Consequently Yamana was unable to collect any revenue from the Wakasa estate. He appealed to Takauji's lieutenant, Sasaki Dōyo, who refused to see him. It was this neglect that made him change sides.

When a warrior had a grievance of this kind, the conflict between the two Courts offered an opportunity for revenge and even a hope of recompense. This was one of the most important and common causes of the support given to the Southern Court by men who had so far fought for the Ashikaga and the Northern Court. To join a new leader offered no certainty of success, for the balance of forces was altered from day to day, but there was some prospect of permanent advantage for those loyal to the Southern Court. Moreover, not a few leading warriors disliked the prospect of subordination to Takauji as Shōgun. He did not command the traditional allegiance which the Minamoto vassals had given to Yoritomo in 1180.

The Yamana case is a good example. The family was of Seiwa Minamoto origin, with estates in Kōtsuke near those of the Nitta family. Its chieftains were favoured vassals (*go-kenin*) of Yoritomo. Under the Muromachi Bakufu they rendered valuable services to Takauji, and were awarded large domains in the province of Hōki. It was from there that after their disappointment they drove Sasaki Dōyo out of Izumo, got into touch with Tadafuyu, and declared themselves against Takauji. Their stand persuaded a large number, perhaps a majority, of the warrior families in the Sanin region to join the resistance to Takauji, and within a short time the western provinces in general were giving aid to Tadafuyu and thus to the Southern Court.

After Go-Murakami had been driven back to Yoshino in 1342, the body of the loyalist army, still based upon Tōjō in Kawachi, continued its activity under Kusunoki Masanori, while former adherents of Tadayoshi, including Kira and Ishidō, gave valuable support. The capital was threatened more than once, and Tadafuyu's success in the West was gratifying. By early 1353 Yoshiakira was obliged to order an attack upon Tōjō, but to no effect; and in the summer the converted Yamana Tokiuji set out from Hōki to strengthen the loyalist army. His vanguard reached the outskirts of Kyoto (Saga) from Tamba in July. To cooperate, Masanori had marched to Tennōji and captured Yahata, while reinforcements were moving north from Kii under Shijō Takatoshi, son of the faithful Takasuke. The change of front by Tadafuyu had raised the spirits of the loyalists, and encouraged them to make a great effort. From the beginning of the new year the return of the Southern Court had been expected in the capital, with mixed feelings, to be sure, because it was bound to make trouble for many. Excitement grew as word reached Kyoto of new alliances. Already in the middle of May there were rumours that Yoshiakira would be attacked by loyalist factions in the city, and the Bakufu arrested certain suspects, of whom some were executed. This did not prevent popular talk about Tadafuyu's successes and Yamana's intentions.

In July the loyalists delivered a strong attack; Masanori moving north from Yahata and Yamana advancing from the direction of Nishiyama joined with other attacking parties, setting fire to buildings as they moved into the city. Yoshiakira managed to escape, falling back on Kaguraoka, north of the city, and then retreating to East Sakamoto.

Very soon Kyoto was in the hands of the loyalists, and Yamana hastened to send congratulations to Go-Murakami in Yoshino, while confiscating the property of those nobles who had sided with the Northern Court during the recent occupation of the capital by Ashikaga forces.

In Tōin's diary for August 1, 1353, he describes the situation as it was known to persons in his position: "The Emperor Kōgon-In with Yoshiakira is said to be withdrawing to the Kantō owing to the superior strength of the attackers. They are already on the way. There will no doubt be changes. All kinds of rumours are current. Some say that Yoshiakira is in great difficulties, short of weapons and provisions. To know the truth is impossible. Some say black and some say white. What is true and what is false there is no way of telling. The only thing to do is to trust to one's own good fortune." The entry shows what little knowledge the highest civil officials had of the actual situation. Tōin seems to have supposed that the retired Kōgon was in Kyoto, whereas he was with the other two retired Emperors in the custody of the Southern Court at Anau.

After the loyalist victories of April 1352 the position of Takauji and Yoshiakira in regard to the succession to the throne had been difficult. The three retired Emperors of the Northern Court together with the Crown Prince Tadahito were confined in Anau under careful watch, and the Regalia were in the hands of Go-Murakami. After long discussion it was decided to name as the successor of Sukō a younger brother of Tadahito, named Iyahito. He was enthroned as the Emperor Go-Kōgon on September 25, 1352. There was no true precedent for an enthronement without the Regalia, and the ceremony was therefore invalid.[7] Yoshiakira himself seems to have had some misgivings about this irregularity, and since Go-Kōgon was only fourteen years of age he suggested a kind of provisional "curtain" government by Go-Kōgon's mother, the Lady Kōgimon-In (formerly Fujiwara Yasuko). She was a clever woman, and she sensibly refused the offer, knowing that there were strong objections to government by a female, and cloister government at that.

Now in 1353, when the loyalists were once more in the capital, Yoshiakira could not afford to endanger the young sovereign, and he thought it prudent to remove the Court to a safer place than the Enryakuji, where Go-Kōgon had taken refuge. He escorted Go-Kōgon and his attendants into the province of Mino, fighting off pursuers as he left. The party halted at a place called Tarui in Mino, where Yoshiakira established the new Northern Court.

His reverses had caused a strong reaction among Ashikaga adherents throughout the country, stimulating them to greater efforts to recover

---

[7] It was said in jest on one occasion, when the difficulty of enthroning a sovereign without the Regalia was being discussed, that the Kampaku Nijō Yoshimoto might act as the Seal and Takauji as the Sword.

the ground they had lost. Takauji, having put down the last loyalist resistance in the neighbourhood of Kamakura, also decided that he must go to Yoshiakira's assistance, and Yoshiakira left Tarui to set about gaining support in the surrounding provinces with the intention of delivering a most powerful assault upon the capital. Support was beginning to arrive from the West. At the summons of the Bakufu Akamatsu brought troops from Harima and Bizen, reaching Hyōgo on August 11. Shiba entered Settsu with troops from Shikoku. Loyalist attacks on these newcomers delivered by Masanori and Yamana were unsuccessful, and together with Ishidō and Kira they were forced to retreat. On the following day Yoshiakira entered Ōmi with his contingent. With this addition the Ashikaga force simply swept the loyalists aside as it advanced on Kyoto. On August 24, 1353, the capital was once more in the hands of the Ashikaga, and the loyalists scattered in all directions.

Takauji did not leave Kamakura until early September. He reached Ōmi in about ten days and arrived at Tarui on October 11. There he was awaited by the anxious Go-Kōgon. The scene is described by a contemporary diarist in enthusiastic language: "It was a happy and lively occasion. For two or three days troops had been arriving incessantly. The roads were crammed with their baggage, and they were in a cheerful mood after their long march. They came in continuously, like a long ribbon or a bale of cloth being unrolled. The Dainagon [Takauji] wore a brocaded mantle over a light coat of mail, and rode a chestnut horse. He was escorted by Yūki, Oda, Satake, and other warriors. Armour flashed in the afternoon sunlight, making a gay and lively scene. The rear guard was led by Niki and other captains, and included innumerable warriors from the eastern provinces."

There follows a eulogy of the horses ridden by Takauji and his commanders, and then a description of the approach of the procession to the house of the headman of Tarui, which was now the residence of the Emperor. The Shōgun halted the column and went forward alone to the gateway, where he was met by a Court chamberlain and led into the presence. He stayed for a short audience and came out after paying homage.[8] A few days later Yoshiakira arrived from Kyoto to pay his respects to Go-Kōgon. Takauji and Yoshiakira, father and son, escorted the Emperor and his court to Kyoto. They arrived on October 18, 1353, and from that time until the middle of the year 1354 the capital enjoyed an unaccustomed peace.

Takauji was not content with occupying the city. He had earlier sent a punitive force against Yamana, whom he understandably con-

---

[8] The diarist was the Kampaku Nijō Yoshimoto, who had accompanied the Northern Court on its journey, in attendance upon the Emperor. The diary, known as *Kuchi-ura*, gives considerable detail. Most descriptions of military occasions in this period pay great attention to the pictorial aspects of the warrior's life, and the heroes took delight in the appearance as well as the efficacy of their armour and weapons.

sidered a traitor. Yamana had appealed to Tadafuyu for help and through Tadafuyu had received from the Southern Court a commission to punish Takauji. In March 1354 Takauji ordered Shimazu of Satsuma to attack Tadafuyu, and in the summer Yoshiakira himself proceeded to "subdue" the central provinces. But he met with powerful opposition and could make no headway against the combined forces of Tadafuyu and Yamana. Indeed, the tide was turning once again, and Yoshiakira was soon in retreat. In late 1354 Takauji, judging the situation to be desperate, fled with Go-Kōgon into Ōmi province, where he took refuge in a monastery called Musadera. Shortly afterwards, in the first month of 1355, the army of the South, under Momonoi, and other supporters of Go-Murakami, recaptured the capital, and were joined there by Tadafuyu, Yamana, Ishidō, and other warriors from the central provinces, all of whom had a grievance against the Bakufu.

CHAPTER VI

THE FAILURE OF THE SOUTHERN COURT

1. *Takauji Recaptures Kyoto*

IN FEBRUARY 1355, with the arrival in Kyoto of Tadafuyu's powerful army and the victorious forces of Yamana and other commanders, the outlook for the Southern Court was promising. But Takauji had no intention of abandoning the conflict, and at once began preparations to regain the capital. He had been at work on strengthening the Seta bridge with pontoons and timber baulks even before Tadafuyu entered the city. When his preparations were complete he ordered prayers for victory to be said at monasteries and shrines, and early in March he announced to the Emperor Go-Kōgon that he intended to advance upon Kyoto without delay.

He set out the next day, and on March 5 had crossed the Seta bridge and was on his way to East Sakamoto, where he made camp soon afterwards. He then moved headquarters to West Sakamoto, after learning that Yoshiakira had rallied his forces and with Akamatsu Norisuke and Hosokawa Yoriyuki had moved into Settsu to take up positions to the west of Yamazaki.

Hearing of Takauji's movements, the loyalist leaders made frantic preparations to resist. Tadafuyu and Masanori took up their positions at the Tōji and at Otokoyama, while Yamana Tokiuji prepared to meet the advance of Niki Yoriaki, who was coming in from Tamba.

On March 20 Yamana joined Masanori in a stand against Yoshiakira at a place called Kaminami, to the west of Yamazaki. The fighting was desperate here, and the losses on both sides were heavy. Yamana was obliged to retreat towards Yodo, and Yoshiakira established his force at Yamazaki.

On March 22 Takauji came down along the Kamo River from Sakamoto and engaged the Southern army in the city, fighting in Nishikinokōji, at Inokuma, and in the vicinity of Ōmiya. The struggle was desperate but indecisive. On the next day Takauji moved his base from Sakamoto to Higashiyama and thence to the Kiyomizu hill. A few days later there was more fierce fighting in the city, again without decisive result. The conflict continued into the following month. On April 20 Takauji moved to Hosokawa's headquarters while two of Hosokawa's generals took up positions in palaces at Shichijō-Higashi Tōin and Nishi Shichijō respectively, and then challenged the defenders. After a struggle they drove Momonoi out of his position in the Kaikōji.

Meanwhile Takauji and Yoshiakira had been busy blocking the highroads from the west into the city, and three or four days later they advanced in force against Tadafuyu, who fought stubbornly and in-flicted heavy losses upon the attackers, wounding Hosokawa Yoriyuki himself and killing several of his captains. But this was no more than a local success, and before long the Southern army was obliged to begin a general withdrawal, being unable to hold any ground but Yahata and in general being short of supplies. By April 25 Takauji was able to enter the Tōji and Yoshiakira the Hōshōji, and the capital was once again in the hands of the Ashikaga.

Kyoto was again at peace, and though the blow to the loyalist forces would seem to have been no more severe than many from which they had recovered in the past, they could no longer mount a threat to the capital. The Emperor Go-Kōgon, who had taken refuge in Ōmi prov-ince, was now escorted back to the city. Over the next two years the former Emperors (Kōmyō, Kōgon, and Sukō) found it easy to escape from custody and return to Kyoto.

At the end of hostilities in 1355 the capital was sadly damaged by year after year of fighting. A passage in the *Taiheiki*, which there is no reason to disbelieve, says that nearly all the royal palaces, the mansions of the nobility, and the offices of the ministers of state were destroyed by fire, only two or three buildings in ten having escaped. In some parts of the city there were wide areas in which no houses were left standing, only the barracks of the soldiery. On the outskirts of the city grass had grown over the ruins and all that could be seen was the bleached bones of the victims. Many had starved and many had drowned themselves in despair. It was the cities and towns that suffered most in the civil wars, for the great enemy was fire. The rural areas were usually spared by the armies, who needed their crops.

Thus ended a civil war in which the protagonists were father and son—Takauji and Tadafuyu. In April 1355, with the entry of Takauji into the capital, the effective opposition of the Southern Court had temporarily come to an end, although loyalist forces fought on in Kyūshū under Prince Kanenaga, in Shinano under Prince Munenaga, and elsewhere. Tadafuyu at this point disappears from the scene, re-tiring to the western provinces and sinking into obscurity.

Takauji settled in Kyoto and spent the next three years consolidating the administrative position of the Bakufu. In March 1358 he was dis-turbed by reports of successful anti-Bakufu activities in the Western Defence Area, and was on the point of leading an army to Kyūshū when he fell ill with a malignant tumour. After a short sickness, he died in Kyoto on June 8, 1358, being then in his fifty-fourth year. His son Yo-shiakira was appointed to succeed him as Shōgun at the end of the year.

Takauji's most gifted and resourceful opponent, Kitabatake Chika-fusa, had died at Anau four years earlier, having lived to see the for-tunes of the Southern Court rise and fall and rise again time after time.

He had never lost hope of final victory. He and Takauji were the two great men of their generation, and their characters deserve some special notice here.

2. Takauji

The period of civil wars under the Ashikaga Shōguns has been described as an age of turncoats, and a study of Takauji's career gives point to that title. He began by turning against the Hōjō Regent who was his overlord and the head of the great Hōjō clan, to which the Ashikaga family was closely related by marriage. He was the chief agent of the destruction of the Hōjō Regency and after that achievement he supported, or at least did not oppose, the Emperor Go-Daigo's attempt to restore the power of the Throne; but not for long, since when it suited him he turned upon Go-Daigo and forced him to take refuge in a remote hamlet in the hills of Yoshino.

There is no doubt that Takauji was guided only by ambition and deterred by no moral scruples. This is the view of Arai Hakuseki, one of the great historians of Japan, who wrote: "Though he received rewards far in excess of the value of his services to the Crown, his purpose had always been to promote his own interests." Hakuseki thought, however, that certain acts of treachery and cruelty of which Takauji was accused were really the work of his brother Tadayoshi, for on the whole Takauji's actions show him to have been of an open, easy-going temperament. The murder of Prince Morinaga and the poisoning of the two younger princes, Tsunenaga and Narinaga, were planned by Tadayoshi without his brother's knowledge. It is also probable that it was Tadayoshi who in 1335 prevailed upon Takauji not to obey the Emperor's order to return from Kamakura to the capital. From that time until their falling-out Takauji left to Tadayoshi all decisions upon purely political matters, and took no part in them.

Indeed, Takauji had little time for anything but military matters, for from the day when he first raised an army to the day of his death, a space of twenty-six years, the clash of arms never ceased. Such a state of affairs, says Hakuseki, was without parallel in ancient and modern times, and it was due to the character of Takauji. He was not an upright man, and therefore he could not make others upright. He rose to the summit of the warrior society because the warriors were manifestly more capable than the nobility of governing the country. Of this the people were well aware, and they were prepared to accept any leader who could bring back the rule of the military chieftains. Hakuseki was a severe Confucian moralist, and he allowed few merits to Takauji; but as a servant of the Tokugawa Bakufu he was a believer in firm government and he did not condemn Takauji as an enemy of the Throne. He said that if Takauji had firmly established the Emperor Kōmyō on the

throne, he would have left a good name to posterity. It was Nitta Yoshisada who was to blame for the break between the Northern and
Southern Courts, for while professing to fight for the Southern Court
he was in fact striving to destroy the enemy of his own clan, and Takauji had no choice but to resist.

Some modern Japanese historians take a rather more favourable
view of Takauji. They excuse him for his betrayal of the Hōjō and his
disloyalty to Go-Daigo on the ground that as leader of the Minamoto
clan he was bound to put his duty to the warriors above his allegiance
to the Emperor. This is not a very convincing argument, especially as
Takauji was generously treated by Go-Daigo and given rewards which
others thought excessive. Takauji was aware of this weakness in his
position and tried to cover it up by placing responsibility for acts of
treason upon his brother Tadayoshi; but it is clear that his purpose was
to revive and strengthen the Bakufu, with himself as its leader, the
successor of Yoritomo. Thus his ambition easily overcame such loyalty
to the Throne as he may have felt. He knew that his conduct was reprehensible, for in 1336, shortly after he had seen the Emperor Kōmyō enthroned, he prayed for the mercy of Kannon, asking that he should not
be forced to suffer in the next world for his offences in this. Life on
earth, he said, was a dream, and it was in the future life that he saw
reality. But for Tadayoshi, his brother, he desired worldly success.

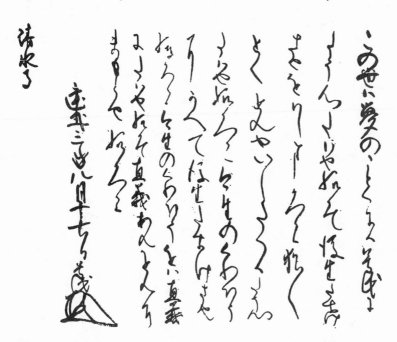

Takauji's vow to the Kiyomizu Kannon (holograph), dated Kemmu III, viii, 17

These professions of repentance, these bargains with the divine powers, make a disagreeable impression that is not removed by the frequent and indeed excessive works of piety by which he hoped to atone for his sins. He had a special feeling for Kannon, who he said had appeared to him in a vision on his flagship at Tomo (1336). He also asserted that the Bodhisattva Jizō came to him in a dream when he was on the point of defeat and death. It is even said that he ordered many thousands of small images of Jizō to be cast, intending that each one should express his compassion for the soul of one man whose death in battle he had caused. One gruesome calculation says that in all the slain numbered six hundred thousand, though this no doubt was bad arithmetic; but sixty thousand might not be far out as an estimate of the numbers killed in battle during his campaigns. He also had prayers said for the Hōjō family, which he had destroyed, and he repeatedly expressed deep sorrow for the suffering he had inflicted upon Go-Daigo and his supporters.

Yet he took no steps to relieve the distress or repair the damage he had caused. Although he shed tears freely for the dead, he never ceased to make war, and he was on the point of leading an army to Kyūshū when he was stricken and died. It is hard to believe that his religious sentiments were genuine, for it is clear that he was of a highly emotional and even unstable character. He was a man of action, without great learning; but he was also something of a dilettante, fond of poetry and sensitive to the beauties of nature. The learned Musō Kokushi, who at times gave him spiritual advice, praised his taste, spoke well of his verses, and often sat with him at poetical gatherings far into the night. Other accounts agree with Musō's judgment that Takauji was utterly fearless in battle, without malice, open-handed; at times gay, laughing, and high-spirited, at times deep in melancholy.

Today a butcher, tomorrow a penitent, he presents contradictions which cannot be resolved, since frank contemporary statements about him are scarce. That he was a great figure in his country's history cannot be denied, but it is doubtful that he did his country good service by plunging it into decades of incessant and needless war.

A modern scholar, Nakamura Naokatsu, has written a study of Takauji portraying him as a conservative anxious to preserve the warrior society ("buke shakai"), and this seems a reasonable view. Certainly Takauji had no such extreme views as those held by Kō no Moronao, who was completely iconoclastic and revolutionary; and it can be plausibly argued that Takauji, if skilfully handled, might have been persuaded to collaborate with Go-Daigo rather than to banish him.

In the early years of his power, Takauji introduced no very drastic changes in the Kamakura system. If he intended to make such changes, he was careful to proceed slowly and to avoid attacking the economic privileges of the leading nobles and the great ecclesiastical bodies. He preserved most of the machinery of the Kamakura Bakufu and at first gave to his provincial representatives, the Constables, no greater powers than those held by their predecessors.

Musō Soseki was in close touch with Takauji, and apart from that direct relationship his career bears witness to the attitude of the Ashikaga brothers towards religious matters. It therefore deserves some attention here.

If Musō is correctly reported, his statements tell us more about his own character than Takauji's. In the *Baishō-ron* he is quoted as saying that Takauji was a greater man than Yoritomo because he combined virtue with benevolence, serving the Throne by suppressing rebellion and keeping the peace; the country ought to be grateful for such a Shōgun. Musō does not say which sovereign Takauji served, but he could scarcely argue that Go-Daigo, whom Takauji served very roughly, was not the legitimate sovereign.

The truth is that Musō had a weakness for the company of the great and powerful. He was, moreover, indebted to Takauji for munificent contributions to the founding of Zen monasteries, especially the Tenryūji (which later played a great part in promoting commerce with China by subsidizing the voyages of merchant ships). Another instance of the Ashikaga's regard for Buddhism was the plan of Takauji and Tadayoshi, announced in 1338, to set up in each of the sixty-six provinces a memorial stupa and a chapel or monastic building named Ankokuji[1] in which prayers could be recited for the souls of the victims of the wars. This plan was suggested by the provincial chapels, called *kokubunji*, founded by edict in the Nara period.

In the circumstances it is not surprising that Musō Soseki figures prominently in the chronicles of the fourteenth century. Like other distinguished Zen monks he was used by the military leaders as an adviser and as a go-between in negotiations, and he was at home among the warriors as well as at Court. He had a high reputation for discretion and was regarded as a great scholar, but his character and his achievements seem to have been somewhat overestimated both during his lifetime and in retrospect.

He was an ambitious, clever young man, and received favours from Go-Daigo and also from the Hōjō Regents, in particular Takatoki, who like most of his family enjoyed the company of learned Zen monks. He prided himself on his ability as a negotiator and he undoubtedly had a gift of persuasion, aided by his prestige as a scholar. Midway in his career he was rewarded by the Throne with the title of Kokushi or National Teacher. But Soseki liked to be on the winning side, and when

[1] Ankoku means "a country at peace."

Go-Daigo went into the wilderness he transferred his loyalty to the Ashikaga brothers and the Northern Court. He served them well; and with their patronage he became head of the Rinzai sect and the leading Zen prelate of his day. He was born in 1275 and died in 1351.

Some light is thrown on his career by a passage in the diary of the retired Emperor Hanazono, written in November 1325, when Go-Daigo was on the throne. Its gist, in translation, is as follows:

*

Today I saw His Reverence Sōhō [Daitō Kokushi] and the Superior of the Zenrinji [Musō Kokushi]. The Superior said that they had been received at the Palace by the Emperor Go-Daigo for the purpose of religious instruction, which he described.

The Superior has of late gained a great reputation for learning, and that is why he was summoned. But from his account of the discussion it seems to have been nothing more than a commonplace talk on elementary points. Dear me! It is sad to think that the sect of Dharma is fading away.

It appears that the interview is to be kept confidential. The Superior is trusted by the leaders of the Bakufu, and the Emperor does not wish news of his conversations to reach them. This was confirmed by His Reverence Sōhō. But I cannot understand why the Emperor is afraid that particulars might leak out. It seems absurd! We are told that His Majesty earnestly desires the Law of the Buddha to flourish, and yet he is afraid that this or that should be known about his association with a great churchman. Why then is this man [Musō] made the Patriarch of the Zen sect? Is this not the destruction of the great line of succession since Dharma? One cannot but grieve.

*

Since Hanazono had been obliged to abdicate in favour of Go-Daigo, it might be supposed that he was unfair to his successor. But throughout his diary, although he is often cynical and usually pessimistic, he is remarkably free from prejudice. His estimate of Musō Kokushi is probably not far from the truth. Hanazono was not himself a convert to Zen, and perhaps he derived some satisfaction from finding fault with its dignitaries; but he was not malicious, and he genuinely thought that the appointment of politically-minded clerics to high offices in the Church was likely to confuse believers and so to undermine the faith.

3. Chikafusa

Chikafusa's family was of Murakami Genji stock, and his ancestors, whose home was in Ise, had held appointments under the Crown for several generations. He was an aristocrat, a member of the Court nobility with no liking for the new military leaders, who were to his mind ignorant upstarts. He was beyond doubt the most impressive figure of his age, a versatile genius who combined much learning with a gift for long-range planning, and great courage with a keen strategical insight. He certainly is one of the most praiseworthy characters in the history of his country.

His association with the Court was intimate, and in 1323 he was entrusted with the post of tutor to the third son of Go-Daigo, Prince Tokinaga. The boy died in 1330 and Chikafusa entered the religious life; but he resumed his secular pursuits when Go-Daigo returned from exile in 1333, entering Court circles again and placing himself at the Emperor's disposal. When Go-Daigo took refuge on Hiyeizan in 1336 in order to escape from Takauji, Chikafusa remained in Kyoto, but when at Takauji's instance Go-Daigo returned to the capital, Chikafusa, who disliked and mistrusted Takauji, made his way to Ise province and there began to plan for the future of the dynasty. He was a far-sighted man, and he saw that he would have to fight hard and long for the restoration of Go-Daigo, whom he ardently supported as the legitimate sovereign. To that cause he dedicated the whole of his adult life.

When Go-Daigo escaped to Yoshino in January 1337, the issue was clear. The Southern Court must establish itself in a place easy to defend and must devote all its efforts to building up a military and political force sufficient to defeat Takauji. This called for bold and careful planning, and it was here that Chikafusa's remarkable talent was displayed. His strategy, his resolution, and his personal courage were such that within a few years the hunted monarch of 1337 commanded the loyalty of supporters in all parts of the country, whose combined military effort enabled them to carry on a campaign of resistance that lasted for fifty years and more than once successfully challenged the might of the Ashikaga leaders.

Behind every important move made by the loyalists there can be discerned the forethought and the imagination of Chikafusa. He believed with a fanatical devotion in the cause of Go-Daigo, and he planned for the defeat of Takauji with scrupulous care for detail yet on a grand scale. It was he who thought of using the many sons of the Emperor to serve in different parts of the country, each as a focus of loyalty to the Throne—Norinaga in the northern provinces; Munenaga in Shinano; Takanaga and Tsunenaga with Nitta in Echizen (both to lose their lives in the cause); and Kanenaga in Kyūshū.

Chikafusa also established a network of intelligence posts, with which he kept in touch by messengers carrying advice and encouragement. He knew what was going on everywhere. Aware that the loyalist forces could not match the armies of Takauji in numbers, he devised a strategy designed above all to promote operations at different times and in different places, so that the enemy did not know where he would strike next. These guerrilla tactics obliged his adversaries to divide their forces and thus to weaken their total effort. Meanwhile the number of adherents to the loyalist cause increased, thanks to Chikafusa's persuasion and to growing dissension within the Bakufu.

He never spared himself. He travelled widely, visiting the distant fronts, and concerned himself especially with encouraging resistance in Mutsu and Kyūshū, with a view to keeping the enemy forces engaged at a distance and thus diminishing the pressure in the Home Provinces.

After the loyalist defeat of June 1338 in which his son Akiiye was killed, he decided that a new effort must be made in the North and West, and because the land route was unsafe he organized a base of supplies in Ise, at the port of Ōminato, whence he could reach Hitachi by ship. Upon arriving in Hitachi, he took command of all loyalist forces in that region and established himself in strongholds where he was able to resist repeated attacks by Ashikaga forces. It was at this time that in the intervals of fighting he wrote the *Jinnō Shōtōki* and the *Shokugen-shō*, and sent them to Yoshino in circumstances that have already been described.

He struggled against mounting difficulties in Hitachi year after year, still keeping in touch with other fronts, but after the death of Go-Daigo he was at last compelled to abandon his effort and return to Yoshino, where he continued to direct the policy of the Southern Court until his death in 1354. To the end he remained firm in his principles and resisted all proposals by the Bakufu based on an agreement between the two lines of succession.

Quite apart from his skill and courage as a military leader, he was a gifted scholar. His *Jinnō Shōtōki* is a remarkable work, which (if one accepts his premise) argues the legitimacy of the Southern Court in a well-reasoned and convincing manner. It is a fine piece of historical special pleading, and at the same time a call for political reform. He starts from the belief that Japan is the country of the gods, and that the line of divine emperors (Jinnō shōtō) must be preserved. He points out a few instances of departure from the true line of succession in the past, but says that these have been rectified by subsequent returns to the proper sequence. He is careful to point out that a sovereign can do wrong, citing in particular the case of Go-Toba, whose mistakes were punished in 1221 by his own banishment and that of two other abdicated emperors. The sovereign, he says, may use force against wrongdoers, but not against persons who have committed no offence. Go-Toba erred when he resorted to force against the Hōjō family, who had done no wrong and had not lost the confidence of the people. So imbued was Chikafusa with the concept of a true line of descent that he praised the Fujiwara family, who had been hereditary Regents for over three hundred years.

Chikafusa was well versed in Buddhism and believed in the doctrine of karma, which suited his ideal of continuity, of inheritance from a remote past; but his general line of religious thought was closer to Shintō doctrine, as might be expected from the nature of his views on the descent of the imperial house. He was influenced by a line of thought which gave rise to the cult called Ise Shintō, according to which buddhas and boddhisattvas are the manifestations on earth of the primordial gods of Japan, rather than the national deities' being the avatars of the Buddha.[2] He was firm in his convictions, but he had a wide-ranging curiosity and a fresh mind. Like many of his contemporaries he was attracted by the new Confucianism of Chu Hsi. Some writers suggest that he had studied the abridgment by Chu Hsi of the *Tzu-chih t'ung-chien* of Ssu-ma Kuang, especially the portions discussing the rival Courts in China.

In addition to the works for which he is well known, some of his letters have been preserved. In all his writings he displays clear judgment and a vigorous, lucid style expressive of his own decided and somewhat self-righteous character. He was a man of remarkable distinction.

The student interested in the growth of political ideas naturally turns to Chikafusa's works hoping to discover how political theory developed in Japan. But he is bound to be disappointed, for Chikafusa deals almost exclusively with the myth or mystique of a succession of sovereigns of divine origin. He wishes to describe and preserve the purity of early doctrine, not to show a continuous stream of thought flowing through centuries from a simple legendary source. He has little to say about the functions of the monarch, and ascribes no duties to the people beyond absolute loyalty and obedience. The subject has no rights and the sovereign is bound by no conditions, though he is expected to be just and compassionate.

It is clear that from the point of view of the leaders of the warrior class, little respect was due to Chikafusa's views. Indeed his writings were scarcely known in his day, and they had no effect except to encourage a few ardent loyalists already devoted to the Throne. Only at a much later date were they to gain great consideration; new editions printed in the seventeenth century and thereafter were to be found extremely useful by persons who wished to destroy the Tokugawa Bakufu and restore the power of the legitimate sovereign. In that sense it may be argued that Chikafusa influenced political thought in Japan, although it would be nearer the truth to say that his arguments were found useful by persons who wished to overthrow the current regime but had not yet formed a coherent political doctrine in their own minds. It was in action that they later developed their principles of government.

There is little evidence to suggest that Japanese thinkers after the succession war were concerned with working out a rational theory of the state from their country's own past. Such fundamental notions of

---

[2] A later development of this idea turned upside down the doctrine of "honji suijaku" familiar to students of Japanese religion.

power and duty as are cited in mediaeval Japanese writings seem to be derived from Confucian teaching or Buddhist ideas, and are used empirically rather than systematically.

The period following the struggle between the rival Courts was one of internecine warfare, with few and brief intervals of peace. Its leading figures had no thought of following an old political tradition or founding a new one. Their chief aim was to destroy the existing order, and if they had a political principle, it was a belief in naked power. Thus in the days of Ashikaga Takauji, his general Kō no Moronao had openly said: "What is the use of a King? Why should he live in a Palace? And why should we bow to him? If for some reason a King is needed, let us have one made of wood or metal, and let all the live Kings be banished."

Such views were not uncommon after the collapse of the Hōjō Regency, and iconoclasm grew more violent as the Ashikaga family gained power. After Takauji's death the very possibility of constructive political thought ceased to exist. Indeed no kind of thinking could have rationalized the political chaos for which the Ashikaga were to blame, and which can best be suggested by the words of Milton that introduce this volume.

Only of the early days of the Kamakura Bakufu can it be said that government followed a clear political principle. Its leaders formulated a simple theory, which is clear from the direct language of the Jōei code and the nature of their actions. They held that good government is firm government, and they believed in justice. Their social theory, if they had had one, would have postulated a rigid division of functions and a fixed pattern of classes.

4. The Last Phase of Loyalist Resistance

After the death of Chikafusa the Southern Court moved from Anau to Amano in the province of Kawachi, making the Kongōji its headquarters. It was from this base that the campaigns of 1354 and 1355 were directed. Following the loss of Kyoto in April 1355, the Court saw the futility of further military operations and for a time ceased active opposition. When Yoshiakira became Shōgun at the end of 1358, he thus faced no immediate threat from the loyalists, although there remained centres of resistance in Shinano and in Kyūshū, where Kanenaga continued to gain ground.

Rather than carry out Takauji's design to invade Kyūshū, Yoshiakira elected to take advantage of the weakness of the Southern Court and attack Amano. He ordered his younger brother Motouji (his Deputy in the Kantō) to collect a force in the eastern provinces, where he had dependable adherents. Early in 1359 this was put in hand; but it was not until nine months later that an army, under the general Hatakeyama, reached Kyoto. Yoshiakira and Hatakeyama agreed upon a plan of campaign, and Yoshiakira led a large force southward, reaching Amagasaki in January 1360, while Hatakeyama led his force into Settsu, where he clashed with the loyalist army at Shijō-Nawate. The news of the great enemy host reached Amano, and the Court hurriedly moved from the Kongōji to the remoter Kanshinji.

Shortly after reaching Settsu Hatakeyama moved into Kawachi, and Yoshiakira's vanguard camped near Mount Kongō. The prospect for the Southern Court was so dark that certain loyalists went over to the enemy. The opposing forces were now in the country over which the Hōjō generals had fought against Prince Morinaga and his friends in 1332 (see pp. 10–12). Kusunoki Masanori was based upon the fort at Akasaka, in liaison with other strong-points in the vicinity, and here he formed a line of defence. Shijō Takatoshi at first held Yoshiakira in check. But one after another the strongholds fell under the attack of superior numbers until only Akasaka was left. What happened next is not clear. Masanori withdrew in June; but he was not pursued by the enemy, nor did Yoshiakira attempt to interfere with the temporary court at Kanshinji. He and his generals returned to the capital in triumph.

It is said that before leaving the field Yoshiakira proposed an agreement to the Southern Court. Whether or not this is true, the time was ripe for such a proposal, since the nobles supporting the Southern Court were losing hope and courage. Some of them offered to help the other side—even, according to one account, the young prince Okinaga, who proposed himself as deputy for the Shōgun in Yoshino. Never before in the protracted civil war had the outlook for the loyalists been so dark.

The Bakufu, however, had its own troubles. The observant Tōin Kinkata, writing in the spring of 1355, describes conditions in the capital as frightful: "The bitter quarrels and jealousies among the generals are such that we might be living in the infernal regions." After Takauji's death the situation was even worse. Men of high rank were so involved in feuds that they paid little attention to the campaign against the Southern Court. After Yoshiakira's return to Kyoto, the Bakufu general Nikki Yoshinaga moved into Ise and took sides with the loyalists fighting there, while Hatakeyama, annoyed by Yoshiakira's conduct, returned in anger to Kamakura with his army. Yoshiakira's position became increasingly difficult. Later in the year he tried to punish one of his insubordinate barons, Hosokawa Kiyouji, but Hosokawa escaped and went over to the Southern Court in 1361.[8]

By these defections and dissensions in the Bakufu, the military position of the Southern Court was much improved, and its leaders once again took the offensive, encouraged by Kiyouji, who suggested an at-

---

[8] After fighting for the Southern Court Kiyouji left Kawachi in 1362, and went home to Shikoku, where for a time he was supreme. But Yoshiakira ordered his death, and he was killed by Hosokawa Yoriyuki, his cousin, a man who figures prominently in the early history of the Ashikaga Bakufu. This was a ruthless age.

tack upon Kyoto. Early in 1362 a considerable force advanced from Sumiyoshi in Settsu (where Go-Murakami had established his head-quarters), and Yoshiakira thought it prudent to withdraw. He escorted Go-Kōgon to Hiyeizan and then to Ōmi. Masanori and his comrades entered Kyoto without fighting. This was the fourth time that a South-ern army had entered the capital; but once more they had to with-draw. Within a short time Yoshiakira had assembled a strong force, and at its approach Masanori and his allies withdrew southward in the di-rection of Uji. They had been less than twenty days in occupation of Kyoto. Now Go-Kōgon was brought back and installed in the Kitayama palace (which had been the home of the noble Saionji family).

Though Masanori and his friends were still unsubdued, they were not effective. They were safe in their mountain stronghold, but were not strong enough to take the offensive. In 1369 even Masanori gave up the struggle, leaving Kyūshū the last stronghold of the loyalists.

A review of the loyalist resistance after 1355 leads to the conclusion that it was doomed to failure. Except in Kyūshū the loyalist forces were outnumbered, indifferently led, and demoralized. There was only one hope: the manifest discord within the Bakufu. It was this that encour-aged the Southern Court to keep up the struggle after the death of Chi-kafusa, when by any unprejudiced judgment it had no prospect of en-during success.

In 1368 Go-Murakami died at Sumiyoshi in Settsu. He had been a good fighter in his day and had cheerfully undergone danger and hard-ship as he moved from one refuge to another. One of his brothers might have succeeded him, but the survivors were in distant places, and one of his sons stepped into his place as the Emperor Chōkei—an empty dignity, since he had no support. The mainstay of the resistance was Kusunoki Masanori, and he went over to the Northern Court in 1369. He had not the reckless idealism of his father Masashige, but he had practical wisdom. He had played his part loyally in the long struggle, but when the loyalist army failed to hold Kyoto in 1362 he began to lose hope of military success and turned his mind to a political solution of the dynastic problem. He had already opened discussions with Sasaki Dōyo in secret (1367), but they came to nothing, mainly because the Southern Court behaved as if the Bakufu were suing for peace, and made such impossible conditions that Yoshiakira angrily broke off the talks. Masanori tried again, but discussions were not resumed after the death of Go-Murakami.

Masanori was regarded as a traitor by some of the nobles at the Southern Court and even by his own family, but criticism did not come well from men who had not risked their lives in battle year after year. There were sound reasons for seeking an agreement.

Yoshiakira died in January 1368 and was succeeded by his son Yo-shimitsu, who was a minor. For a time the affairs of the Bakufu were conducted by Hosokawa Yoriyuki, who had been marked down by Ashikaga leaders as one of the most capable men of the day.

5. *The Kyūshū Campaign*

It was clearly essential for the Bakufu to reassert its authority in Kyūshū, where Prince Kanenaga had gained the upper hand. A Kyūshū campaign was desirable not only to complete the task of suppressing the loyalists, but also to restore the prestige of the Ashikaga Shōgun, which had continued to decline after Takauji's death despite repeated efforts to restore it.

By 1365 the whole of Kyūshū was under Kanenaga's control. The great families of Shōni, Ōtomo, and Shimazu had lost their primacy, and the deputies of the Bakufu, the Kyūshū Tandai Isshiki and Shiba, had been defeated in battle and shorn of their power. Kanenaga at this point was so confident of his strength that he began to think of leading an army against Kyoto. Yoshiakira's position, already weakened by the unruly behaviour of the barons in central and eastern Japan, was still further endangered by the situation in Kyūshū. Shortly before his death he sent an expedition to Kyūshū, but it failed to cross the straits, and its general, Shibukawa, turned back to report that Kanenaga was contemplating a journey to the Southern Court in order to plan further resistance. In the confusion following upon Yoshiakira's death this appeared possible; but Hosokawa Yoriyuki and other leaders saw the danger, and prepared a great force to meet Kanenaga should he attempt to cross over to the mainland.

The creation of this force ended the last opportunity for Kanenaga and for the loyalist cause. His military advantage in Kyūshū began to diminish as his enemies recovered from their defeats and built up new strength, and the Bakufu soon returned to the offensive. In 1370, on the advice of Yoriyuki, who was summoned to Kyoto for consultation, the Ashikaga leaders decided to send to Kyūshū as Tandai the most capable man in their service. This was Imagawa Sadayo, a distinguished soldier and a man of letters well known in poetical circles. Born in 1325, he had spent most of his early life campaigning for Takauji. When the Bakufu's call came he had entered religion and was living a quiet life in Kyoto under the name of Ryōshun.

He left for his new post late in October 1370. Warned by the failure of his predecessor, who had never so much as crossed the straits into Kyūshū, he planned carefully. So as not to leave enemies in his rear he came to an understanding with Ōuchi, the Constable of Suō, and he took similar steps in Shikoku, where he charged the Hosokawa family with the duty of keeping order. As his spearhead and for a reconnaissance in force, he sent a contingent under his son Yoshinori from Onomichi to Kyūshū by sea. Yoshinori landed in the Ōita district and occupied the

stronghold of Takasaki during August 1371. After attacking loyalist
forces in the neighbourhood, he was attacked by Kikuchi Takemitsu,
whose family was the strongest and most dependable ally of Prince Kanenaga in his struggle against the Bakufu. But Yoshinori held out and
Takasaki was never recaptured. At this time Imagawa, who was still
on the mainland, ordered his younger brother Tadaaki to drive into
Hizen and attack Dazaifu from the rear. Tadaaki met with obstacles,
and could not make his way into Kyūshū and across country to Hizen
until the end of the year, when he reached Matsuura and was helped by
local warriors.

Imagawa meanwhile was riding along the western coast road, enjoying the scenery and humming his favourite poems. He made a leisurely progress, and when he saw that his strategy was beginning to
work out as he had planned, he left Aki and proceeded towards Buzen
in Kyūshū, crossing to Kokura, which is about five miles over the water
from Shimonoseki. He then moved westward along the coast to Munakata and pressed on to Dazaifu. He was thus between Yoshinori, making a stand at Takasaki, and Tadaaki, placed at a point in western Hizen.
This triple threat obliged Kikuchi to raise the siege of Takasaki and
address himself to the defence of Dazaifu. Imagawa himself, joined
by Ashikaga partisans, had fought his way from Kokura and occupied
a point which was the key position in the defence of Dazaifu. The three
Ashikaga armies now enveloped Dazaifu, which fell into their hands
before the end of September 1372. Kikuchi was obliged to retreat and
escaped into Chikugo province, escorting Prince Kanenaga.

Thanks to Imagawa's plans and their well-timed execution, the
greater part of northern Kyūshū had been subdued. The commanding
position which Kanenaga had achieved by arduous work since 1361 had
been lost in a few days—twelve years of effort gone! The loyalist cause
was not lost, but great strength and good fortune were needed if Imagawa was to be checked. Kanenaga now took up a position—as a refuge
and at the same time a defensive base—on a plain in the basin of the
Chikugo River. Imagawa was careful not to move unless he could see
a real advantage. He intended to choose his own time and place, and
he addressed himself to gaining the support of the leading families in
the southern part of Kyūshū, inviting them to join in an attack by whose
success they could profit.

Kikuchi divined Imagawa's intention, and decided that he must take
the offensive quickly, before Imagawa's plans were ripe. In March 1373
Kikuchi launched a night attack in force that came near to breaking
Imagawa's defences, but in the end the loyalists were beaten off and
forced to withdraw. A deadlock ensued, and for some time Imagawa's
position was not comfortable. Later in the year, however, Kikuchi died,
leaving the loyalist defence without a really tested leader, and Kikuchi's
heir Takemasa, a promising soldier, died in 1374.

At that time Imagawa had already decided to bring his full strength to bear upon Kanenaga's force, which was sitting at Kōra-san. He succeeded in driving the Prince into Higo province. At this point he was circumspect, and resisted the temptation to follow the enemy into Higo and seek a decision there. He found other means of attacking the Kikuchi clan, and before long he was virtually master of the whole of Chikugo province. In 1375 Imagawa moved his base forward to a point about two and a half miles west of the Kikuchi stronghold, in the neck of the Mizushima plain, and planned to deliver a frontal attack with his entire force upon the main Kikuchi defences.

At this time he appealed to Shimazu, Ōtomo, and Shōni for help. Shōni Fuyutsugu resented the appointment of a new Tandai and at first refused to come. However, when pressed by Shimazu Ujihisa he grudgingly assented and arrived in due course at Mizushima. Imagawa seems to have suspected Shōni of treachery, and (it is said) ordered his brother to stab him at a drinking party. Shimazu, who had persuaded Shōni to join him, was disgusted and returned to Satsuma, where he arrayed his forces in open challenge to Imagawa.

It is astonishing that men who are in most respects capable and wise enough to rise to heights of power sometimes perform such idiotic acts. Imagawa, a supposedly brilliant and sensitive man, by this blunder lost two valuable allies—Shimazu, the most powerful single chieftain in the country, and Shōni, who was a hereditary vassal of the Shōgun.

From the point of view of the struggling loyalists Imagawa's error was a blessing. This wanton murder of one of their kind induced many wavering families in Chikugo to enter the struggle against Imagawa. With their help the new Kikuchi was able to attack him in October 1375 and drive him to retreat into Hizen with loyalist troops at his heels. Imagawa's triumphant advance was now checked, and he found himself on the defensive. In the words of a modern Japanese historian, "His spear was blunted."

Imagawa reported his position to the Bakufu in Kyoto and asked for help. The Bakufu sent an emissary to Suō and ordered Ōuchi to assist Imagawa. This was a risky or at least not very promising move; and Imagawa felt that his position in Kyūshū was deteriorating so rapidly that he could not wait for help. He strove urgently to get certain Kyūshū warriors to join him in an attack upon the Kikuchi combination, and he implored warrior families in southern Kyūshū to raise levies for his support. He saw that the relationship between the loyalists and the Shimazu chieftain Ujihisa must somehow be broken. Ujihisa resisted, although a number of warriors in the three southern provinces (Satsuma, Hyūga, and Ōsumi) joined the Imagawa leaders.

In September 1376 the Bakufu deprived the Shimazu leaders of their offices as Constable in Satsuma and Ōsumi, Imagawa being appointed to replace them. Presently the tide turned in favour of Imagawa, and the Shimazu forces were gradually isolated. The Shimazu leaders saw that the loyalist army under Prince Kanenaga's command was gradually losing strength, but they were too proud, too conscious of their position as the leading magnates in Kyūshū, to go over to the Bakufu. They hesitated and did not make a definite stand, did not show their colour. The death of Shimazu Ujihisa in 1385 marked the end of this phase. His successor declared himself an ally of the Ashikaga leaders, so that the three provinces then fell into the Bakufu's sphere. Even then, however, nothing was conceded to Imagawa. When he was recalled to Kyoto for duty, Shimazu willingly obeyed orders from the Bakufu; but he and his kinsmen were loth to serve under a man who had put them to shame at Mizushima by ordering the murder of Shōni, their companion in arms.

To the north, the war was over by this time. In 1377 Imagawa's forces inflicted severe punishment upon the Kikuchi family in Hizen and forced them to retreat into Higo. Imagawa pressed hard, pursued them across the Chikugo River, entered Higo, and captured Kumamoto. Ōuchi entered Chikugo province and continued the offensive against Kikuchi. The next year, 1378, there was a pause while both sides repaired the damage they had suffered. Then in October Imagawa delivered a joint attack upon the Kikuchi stronghold with Ōuchi, the new Shōni, and Ōtomo. The main engagement was a battle at Takuma-hara, near Kumamoto. It was bitterly fought. The loyalists, in high spirits despite the great numbers against them, fought desperately, and many members of the Kikuchi family were killed; but in the end Imagawa was driven off and had to retreat into Chikugo. He reorganized his forces and attacked again. Kikuchi avoided a pitched battle, and 1380 went by without any decisive action. In the spring of the following year, however, the Bakufu army gradually wore down Kikuchi's resistance, and his chief stronghold, Kumabe, fell in July 1381, to be followed by the capture of all his remaining defences.

Thus the loyalist resistance in Kyūshū gradually collapsed, and with the death of Kanenaga in 1383 all hope of recovery seemed lost. Thanks largely to the stubborn fighting of Kikuchi and the adroit leadership of Kanenaga, the loyalist forces had held out against a strong army under a good general for twelve years from the time of Imagawa's appointment as Tandai in 1370.

There is no doubt that Kanenaga was an exceptionally capable man. Quarrels between great clans in Kyūshū gave him a certain advantage in the choice of willing allies, but he must have used great skill in negotiation. He was in a strong position at Dazaifu, where he received envoys from Ming China, and indeed he sent his own envoys to the Ming Court in 1371. His relations with Japanese pirates were useful to him, since it was in the hope of stopping Japanese piracy that the Ming Emperor sent his first envoy in 1369. Kanenaga maltreated members of this mission, but soon saw that it would be to the advantage of the Southern Court to be on good terms with China, and (according to Ming records) he went so far as to call himself a tributary of the Ming. By 1372, however, Imagawa had established himself as Tandai and driven Kanenaga out of the Dazaifu region. The next Chinese mission arrived after this, and its traffic was with the Northern Court.

Speculating upon the reasons for Imagawa's success, one is tempted to think that the war between the Southern Court and the Bakufu produced a new kind of army commander in such men as Kusunoki Masashige, Kitabatake Chikafusa, and Imagawa Sadayo, and led to some advances in the art of war. The Gempei War of the twelfth century had been fought by generals who had no experience of handling very large numbers. At times they showed tactical skill, but they do not seem to have looked ahead and planned their battles. Most of the generals of the fourteenth century were no better. Nitta Yoshisada was not a wise strategist, and Takauji's generals, especially Moronao, relied upon brute force and not upon judgment. When things went against them they made a poor showing. Takauji had confidence and a good eye for terrain. He knew when to seize an opening, but he was not a first-class military leader, able to see a long way ahead and make his dispositions accordingly.

By comparison, Kusunoki, Kitabatake, and Imagawa were careful and successful planners, and it is not a mere coincidence that all three were men of good breeding, of intellectual and aesthetic interests, and of a thoughtful nature. The characters of Kusunoki and Kitabatake have already been described. It is appropriate to say something here about Imagawa, who like them was distinguished for his strategic skill.

6. Imagawa Sadayo

The Imagawa family was an offshoot of the Ashikaga, and held a manor at Imagawa in the province of Mikawa. Sadayo's father was a follower of Takauji, in whose campaigns he rendered valuable service. He was rewarded with the appointment of Constable of Suruga, and after that the family was prominent among the gentry of the eastern coastal provinces and formed connexions by marriage with families of the Court nobility. Such matches were unusual in feudal society under the Kamakura Bakufu; the relationship between military leaders and the Court in that period was friendly but not intimate. In principle at least, the Ashikaga Bakufu, like its predecessor, had discouraged close intercourse between the civilian and the military. But when the Ashikaga Shōguns established themselves in the capital, occasions for social intercourse were naturally more frequent, especially since many of the problems with which Takauji and his successors had to deal concerned the treatment of members of the imperial family and their circle. The very disagreement of the rival Courts multiplied the occasions for contact.

No details of Sadayo's early life are known. He was born in 1325 and entered the service of Yoshiakira as a young man. He must have spent some time in the capital in the intervals of his military duties, and it is known that he studied the art of composing linked verses (*renga*) with Nijō Yoshimoto, a man of about his own age, who later not only rose to the high offices of Chancellor and Regent but became an arbiter of taste and patron of the school of poetry known as the Nijō School. It is clear that the ruling passion in Imagawa Sadayo's life was the study and practice of the poetic arts. We have seen how on his way to Kyūshū at the head of his army he rode along composing and chanting stanzas in a happy mood. Few of his poems have survived, but among them (in his travel diary called *Michiyukiburi*) are some of the poems inspired by the scenes through which he passed on his way to the wars.

He took a very strong line in the great poetical dispute which split the fourteenth-century literary world into two bitter factions and even had political sequels. The opposing schools were those of Reizei Tamehide and Nijō Tameyo—two lines of descent from the famous Teika, the greatest star in the poetical firmament of the thirteenth century. It is a fascinating quarrel which we must not stop to explore and relish; but there is a certain historical interest in the conflict, for it involved persons who were not poets, and it was one of the consequences of a revolution that was taking place in most aspects of the national life. In simple terms, the issue between the two schools was between old tradition and new freedom—new license even—and thus it reflected social trends of the day, a mingling of classes and an impatience of precedent.

Imagawa was on the side of freedom and argued vigorously that the strict canon of the Nijō School was stifling, while the Reizei School inspired and encouraged spontaneous expression. He enjoyed teaching both the conventional *uta* and the *renga*. His own poems were not much esteemed by connoisseurs, but he fought hard in the literary arena as he did on the battlefield. He wrote essays on poetical matters, and one of his last works was a protest addressed to the Bureau of Poetry against attacks upon his own, the Reizei School. But he did not hesitate to attack the Nijō School himself, or to oppose Yoshimoto, despite their amiable intercourse at an earlier time.

He remained in Kyūshū as Tandai until 1395, when he was recalled to answer charges brought against him by Ōuchi and Ōtomo, his former allies in Kyūshū, who said that he was guilty of conspiracy against the Shōgun Yoshimitsu. Their accusation was almost certainly false, and their proposal that Imagawa be replaced as Kyūshū Tandai by Shibukawa Mitsuyori was obviously inspired by a desire to rehabilitate the Shibukawa family, since it was the craven conduct of Mitsuyori's father in 1368 that had led to the appointment of Imagawa.

A few years later there seem to have been better grounds for questioning Imagawa's loyalty to the Shōgun, one of them being the fact that Imagawa's province of Tōtōmi did not respond to a levy made by or on behalf of the Bakufu in 1400. Presumably for this reason Yoshimitsu sent word to Kamakura ordering Imagawa's offices as Constable in Suruga and Tōtōmi to be forfeited. It was seemingly at this point that Ryōshun (as he was then styled), feeling that he could not sit back and await assassination, endeavoured to raise opposition to the Ashikaga.[4] He was not successful, and appears to have retired to the country for his last years. He wrote his *Nan-Taiheiki*[5] in 1402 and nothing is known of him after that, except that he stayed quietly in the country, with occasional visits to Kyoto presumably on poetical business only.

He died in 1420. It was remarkable that a member of the warrior class should have become a prominent figure in the literary society which had its centre at the Court. The very fact that he was accepted on terms of equality in such an exclusive group shows that a spirit of change was in the air, and a new model of warrior was coming into fashion.

[4] There is evidence that Yoshimitsu tried to get Sadayo assassinated. He wrote to Sadayo's kinsman Yasunori hinting that Sadayo was planning treason and should be put away. "If you could arrange some device, I should rejoice," he says in a letter preserved in the Uyesugi archives.

[5] One literary work of Imagawa which is of particular interest to historians is this criticism of the *Taiheiki*, in which he points out certain errors in that chronicle, especially such errors of omission as a neglect to give due credit to the exploits of members of his own family. One must read between the lines of the *Nan-Taiheiki*, since when he wrote it he was in a dangerous position.

CHAPTER VII

THE END OF THE CIVIL WAR

1. *Agreement between the Northern and Southern Courts*

W H E N Yoshiakira was succeeded as Shōgun by his son Yoshimitsu in 1368, the Ashikaga house was well established. Yoshimitsu, then a child of nine years, was fortunate in inheriting the services of capable and loyal men as his advisers and deputies. Imagawa Sadayo was a gifted leader, and Hosokawa Yoriyuki was perhaps the ablest administrator of the day.

Yoriyuki had been chosen by Yoshiakira to act as his Deputy (Kanrei) and he carried out his duties faithfully, with an unyielding insistence upon high standards of conduct in his subordinates. His stern attitude towards loose behaviour aroused ill-feeling, especially among certain Zen monks and some of the leading warriors whose conduct he found cause to condemn. He was at one time impeached by his enemies, and his pride led him to resign and return to his country estate. The question at issue on this occasion was the treatment of the Southern Court.

One of the reasons which persuaded Kusunoki Masanori to go over to the Northern Court was his association with Yoriyuki, by whose character and ability he was much impressed. It was in fact Yoriyuki's arbitrary policy (which included military assistance to Masanori) that offended Yoshimitsu and caused some of the warlords to turn against him. Angered by their opposition, he wished to resign but was more than once persuaded by the young Shōgun to remain in office, especially during the year 1372. In 1379 Shiba and other barons pressed for his dismissal. Yoshimitsu tried to placate them, but failed; and it was then that Yoriyuki resigned, having first shaved his head and taken vows. Later Yoriyuki felt some regret for his action and tried to make amends. In 1391 he was recalled to Kyoto, where he was given his former post as Deputy and once again advised the Shōgun on matters of high policy. But he died a year later, in 1392.

At the time of Yoriyuki's impeachment in 1379 the Bakufu armies in Kyūshū under Imagawa's leadership were gaining the upper hand, and even where it had been strongest the military position of the Southern Court was gradually crumbling. For years the time had been ripe for reconciliation between the two lines, for since the death of Yoshiakira in 1367 all the leading figures in the struggle had vanished from the scene, and their places had been taken by men who had no strong feelings about the succession. But still the unequal struggle dragged on. In 1373 Go-Kameyama succeeded as Emperor at the Southern Court, and in 1383 Go-Komatsu was installed in Kyoto. It was now nearly fifty years since Go-Daigo's line had gone into exile. Enthusiasm for the Southern Court had almost evaporated. Losses in the field had made a loyalist revival all but impossible; and indeed the very safety of Go-Kameyama and his courtiers at Amano was endangered by attacks from adjacent provinces led by Ashikaga generals.

The Bakufu might have tackled the succession problem soon after Yoshiakira's death, but Yoshimitsu and his advisers had more urgent problems to deal with. The long campaign in Kyūshū did not end until 1383, and apart from that large undertaking Yoshimitsu had to deal with certain recalcitrant warlords, notably the arrogant Yamana family, who had made themselves the masters of eleven provinces in western Japan—one-sixth of the provinces in the whole country. They challenged the authority of the Ashikaga Shōgun, and had to be put down. It was not until late in 1392 that, having at last disposed of the Yamana, he could turn to discussions with the Southern Court.

Details are scanty, but it appears that the Bakufu opened the negotiations by proposing a union (*gattai*) between the two lines.[1] The Southern Emperor, Go-Kameyama, at length gave his consent. He undertook to return the Regalia to their proper seat and to transfer them to the Northern Emperor. This was agreed by all parties, and it was understood that in future the succession was to alternate between the senior and junior lines—Jimyō-In and Daikakuji. An important condition was that Crown estates in the provinces should belong to the junior line, and the rich Chōkōdō estate to the senior line. The agreement was concluded in December 1392.

On the face of it this was a fair agreement, and it was faithfully carried out by the Southern Court. Go-Kameyama left Yoshino in December and proceeded to the Daikakuji monastery (which gave the junior line its name and was at Saga, on the western outskirt of the city), arriving there on December 16. His intention was to perform a solemn act of abdication in which the transfer of the Regalia was an integral part. Abdication was a customary practice in Japan, and this was the traditional procedure by which it was accomplished. Only by following precedent could Go-Kameyama establish the legitimacy of his own reign, and even to have dealings with the senior line was a denial of the firm stand taken by Go-Daigo, who had spurned all claims of the Northern Court. To give way on this point must have been a

---

[1] The terms of an agreement are set forth in a letter from Yoshimitsu to the Southern Court, dated October 29, 1392, of which a copy has been preserved in the Konoye family archives. It accepts the Southern Court's stipulation that an act of abdication should not take place until after the transfer of the Regalia, and that thereafter the succession should alternate between the two lines.

bitter end to so many years in exile. Yet as if the Ashikaga Bakufu were doomed to continue the treachery out of which it arose, the Shōgun was false to his pledge. Yoshimitsu ordered the Regalia to be surrendered, and on December 19 a small escort of courtiers carried them through rain and by a muddy road from Saga to the Tsuchimikado palace, where the Northern Emperor Go-Komatsu was residing.

There was no ceremonial transfer of the Regalia and there was no meeting between Go-Kameyama and Go-Komatsu, still less the ritual act of "surrendering the state" (Jōkoku) which convention required. Nor were other conditions of the agreement kept by Yoshimitsu. In 1412 Go-Komatsu abdicated in favour of his own son, and there was no objection from the Shōgun, despite his promise of alternate succession between the two lines. Further, the estates allotted to the Daikakuji were not available, or more accurately their revenues were difficult if not impossible to collect.

There is no doubt that the Bakufu were not convinced of the claims of the Northern Court, but they wanted to keep clear of the niceties of succession, for their only concern was to install an obedient sovereign, and as practical men they considered that possession of the Regalia was the best certificate of legitimacy. Altogether the Northern Court and the Bakufu made a discreditable showing in this matter of reconciliation. The Southern Court lost everything but its dignity.

After his abdication Go-Kameyama was treated coldly, even contemptuously, by the Northern Court, who said that he had no right to the title of Dajō Tennō (Supreme Retired Emperor) since he had never been enthroned; and it was only after nearly two years' delay that Yoshimitsu took the trouble to secure it for him. Offended by the neglect and deceit of the Bakufu and its puppets, Go-Kameyama withdrew to Saga, where he lived a solitary life. He seems to have offended the fourth Ashikaga Shōgun, Yoshimochi, for not long after visiting the Muromachi palace he suddenly left Saga, and was reported to be wandering in a distressed condition among the hills of Yoshino. But he returned to Saga and was buried nearby in 1424.

Viewed in the light of subsequent events, the struggle between the two Courts failed to decide the issue of legitimacy. It has never been settled. Arguments based on the possession of the Regalia are not decisive, nor is it possible to substantiate charges that the Regalia held by the Southern Court were counterfeit. Some modern scholars have argued that Chikafusa's evidence is incorrect in certain particulars, and have challenged the claims of the Southern Court. This view was current in the early years of the present century, even in official circles. But it was rejected by the Household Minister in 1911 in an official statement.

It might therefore be said that the civil war was fought in vain, and this would be true if its real purpose was to settle the issue of legitimacy. But seen in its historical setting the war was a struggle for supremacy not between two Courts but between two military factions, each seeking its own material advantage and very little else. It was revolutionary in its effect, because it destroyed the feudal hierarchy as it had been developed by the Kamakura Regents, and put in its place a new kind of military society, consisting of great barons enjoying almost full autonomy and giving only a qualified submission to the Ashikaga Shōguns.

The half-century of strife destroyed or damaged many institutions, and it was naturally followed by an era of change, sometimes violent and always lively. It is therefore best to regard the years between the flight to Yoshino in 1337 and the agreement between the Courts in 1392 as a period of transition not only in the political life of the country but also, and notably, in its economic life. Like most wars, the war between the Courts was fought about one thing and settled something else; and while the fighting was going on, unperceived changes were taking place in the life of the people whose occupation was peaceful.

In the foregoing chapters little has been said about the condition and behaviour of the workers on the land. There is not much direct evidence on these points, since the chronicles rarely stop to notice the peasants. But it is clear that although most farm labourers were still in a state of qualified serfdom, they were being gradually emancipated. This change was not due to any reforming spirit among the landowners, but to the practical sense of the masters, who had to go off to the wars and as a rule left their most capable workers in charge of their estates. Thus they created a new class of peasant enjoying a degree of independence hitherto unknown. The culmination of this process is described in later chapters dealing with the breakdown of the manorial system and the frequent agrarian risings that are characteristic of the age of the Ashikaga Shōguns.

2. A Note on Mediaeval Warfare

One thing which strikes the student of the period of almost continuous war (say from 1300 to 1400) is the monotony of its military history. There are clashes of arms, pitched battles and skirmishes, victories and defeats, death and disaster, all the ingredients of a military classic; yet one encounter is very like another, and in no campaign is any great strategic talent displayed. There is no commander of genius, nothing— it would seem—to correspond with the inventive planning and the brilliant execution which in Western literature are attributed to leaders like Alexander the Great and Julius Caesar, and to later and lesser figures as well.

It may be that the chronicles give this impression because Japan failed to produce literary generals like Xenophon and Caesar. Whereas since antiquity commanders in Western countries have had a habit of writing despatches or memoirs describing their own campaigns, the mediaeval accounts of battles upon which Japanese historians depend are for the most part written by monks or by scribes in the employment of great feudal houses, men without understanding of the art and science of war. They even have very little idea of the numbers of men engaged in the battles which they describe.

The chronicles of the Gempei War of 1180–85 give absurdly exaggerated accounts of the size of the armies engaged. The *Heike Monogatari* is a romance in which accuracy was not the writers' aim, but the *Azuma Kagami* has some claim to be treated as a historical document, since it was based in part upon official records. Yet, to take a simple instance, both works give impossible numbers for the armies commanded by the Minamoto generals Yoshitsune and Noriyori when they were commissioned to destroy Yoshinaka at the end of 1183. The figures in both works are of the order of 50,000 for Noriyori and 20,000 for Yoshitsune. To supply, bivouac, and move such numbers would have been a colossal task in twelfth-century Japan, even in favourable conditions of topography and climate, the more so because at that time most of the fighting men were mounted. In modern times a force of 1,000 mounted men is about half a cavalry brigade, which in quarter column would extend half a mile. It is obvious that a force of ten or twenty thousand mounted men could not perform the feats attributed to Yoshitsune's force, such as riding fast over thirty miles or so of rough, hilly country and fighting a stiff action at the end of the day. There is no doubt that the strength of a force reported as 10,000 was frequently not more than 1,000 or 1,500.[2]

It is true that in the fourteenth century conditions of transport and supply had much improved, and it was easier to move large bodies of men. But the numbers in the *Taiheiki* are no less exaggerated than those of the earlier chronicles. It is unfortunate for the study of Japanese military history that this fundamental weakness persists throughout the fourteenth century and into the fifteenth.

Chapter VI of the *Taiheiki* describes the preparation by the Kamakura Bakufu of a great host to put down rebellion in the Home Provinces. It says that more than 307,000 horsemen left the eastern provinces

---

[2] There is an interesting confirmation of this ratio in *Gyokuyō*, the diary of Kanezane, the Fujiwara Regent during part of the Gempei War. He notes that one of his servants counted a Taira force as it passed through the city, and found that it numbered just over 1,000 men, although it had been publicly stated to number from 7,000 to 10,000. It was proceeding to assist Yoshinaka. This passage in *Gyokuyō* is pointed out by Major Hayashibe, co-author of a work on military history discussed below. He thinks that 3,000 would be a likely figure for the combined force of Yoshitsune and Noriyori.

in October 1332, and the vanguard reached Kyoto in about twenty days, while the rear guard was still near Hakone. At the same time many thousands of men marched towards the capital from the west, bringing the total to 800,000, or according to one version, one million. These are fantastic figures; yet the *Taiheiki* is a work upon which modern historians must depend for a description of the campaigns during and after the revolt against the Hōjō in 1332. There are numerous texts of this chronicle, nine of which are collated in an excellent work entitled *Sankō Taiheiki*. A study of the numbers of men engaged in the important battles reveals most surprising discrepancies. In the usually accepted text (*rufubon*), the number engaged in the Hōjō army's attack on Kusunoki's stronghold at Akasaka in 1333 is given at 300,000, whereas other texts have 200,000 and 20,000. The first two figures are absurd, the third may be correct. For later fighting in this vicinity the numbers given vary from 100,000 to 10,000.

The size of Takauji's army leaving Shinomura is given as 20,000 in the standard text, and its strength on reaching Kyoto is given as 50,000, with 5,000 and 20,000 as variants.

It is obvious from examples of this kind that the chroniclers had very little idea of the size of armies, and that they did not distinguish between *sen* for 1,000 and *man* for 10,000. Thus, of the important battle of Kotesashi-Sekido (1333) one text says that the fighting opened with a volley of 3,000 arrows, another says 300. The lower figure is most probable, since it was a custom to begin actions with a challenge by a flight of whistling arrows. The total Hōjō force in this battle is given as 200,000 or 300,000, both unlikely, indeed impossible, figures. As the Hōjō army made repeated attacks on the enemy (Nitta Yoshisada), he was pressed back and stood on the defensive until he received an unexpected reinforcement from Miura, bringing his total strength to 40,000 according to one text, 100,000 according to another.

A total somewhere between 50,000 and 100,000 for Nitta and his allies is not improbable, and the opposing army may have been rather larger. Another chapter of the *Taiheiki*, describing Nitta's attack on Kamakura in 1333, says that he collected three divisions after crossing the Tamagawa, one of which entered the city by the "back door" (*karamete*); but the total strength of a division is not stated. In another passage his force with that of his allies is given as 507,000, obviously an error for 57,000.[3]

If little is known of the numbers engaged in feudal battles, it is not

---

[3] The total force available to Nitta for attacks upon the Hōjō may well have been greater than the force actually engaged in the capture of Kamakura. In different parts of northern and eastern Japan he could probably count upon help from many strong families, so that the number on his side, though not necessarily under his command or even available to him, may conceivably have been as high as 200,000; but even this figure is not at all likely.

surprising that there is only scanty reliable information of other kinds
to help historians in forming an opinion of the skill with which commanders planned and fought their campaigns. On such evidence as is
available, Minatogawa may be looked upon as a well-planned battle,
having regard to the terrain; but it may be that Takauji's success was
due less to his strategy than to Nitta's hasty retreat. We know that
some of Go-Daigo's advisers were against Nitta's plan of defence, and
wished to avoid decisive action; and we know also that more than once
both Nitta and Akiiye neglected Kusunoki's advice with unfortunate
results. On the other hand, Takauji's amphibious progress eastward to
Minatogawa was certainly better organized than any of Nitta's marches.

Imagawa Sadayo was a seasoned warrior, thoughtful and cautious,
a good organizer. Perhaps he may be regarded as the best general
of his day, and it is interesting to note that he comes nearest to those
Western commanders who like to write about their campaigns. But
neither he nor any of his contemporaries appears to have devised important changes in methods of warfare—nothing like the phalanx or
the open square in infantry tactics, or a new use of cavalry. The one
really important change in the armies of this period was social rather
than military, the growth of a class of foot soldier, the *ashigaru*, used
for street fighting.

We do not know what strategies and tactics occupied the minds of
the warrior chieftains who presided over the great engagements. But
the truth is that once the opposing generals had taken up their respective positions, they had little control over the subsequent fighting.
No doubt they had their battle plans, but there appears to have been
no fixed line of command during actions, which soon developed into
unregulated single combats between knights or clashes between small
bands of retainers, with little or no reference to the tactical needs of
the situation. Consequently, the highly coloured accounts of battles
given in such works as the *Taiheiki*, though they make excellent blood-
and-thunder reading and tell stirring tales of heroism and panache,
leave the reader in a state of confusion which perhaps reflects the nature
of the conflict better than a strict analysis.

For a country with so great a warlike tradition there is surprisingly
little evidence of the nature of campaigns and the course of separate
actions after the days of Hachiman Tarō (1041–1108), whose exploits
seem to be truthfully reported in the *Mutsu Waki*. There is an interesting modern work on Japanese military history by Major General Y. Hayashi and Major Hayashibe.[4] It is a careful study, but it gives little
detailed information about the strategy of the mediaeval wars, doubtless for lack of trustworthy material. The authors think that the five
greatest generals in Japanese history are Yoshitsune, Kusunoki, Nobu-

[4] *Nihon Senshi no Kenkyū* (Tokyo: Kaikō-sha, 1940).

naga, Hideyoshi, and Ieyasu. Of these only the first two belong to the middle ages, and Yoshitsune was perhaps a shrewd and bold tactician rather than a far-sighted strategist. But about Kusunoki Masashige there can be no doubt. He was a great commander. His genius is apparent even in the scanty accounts of the defensive campaign which he waged in the hills of Kawachi and Yamato, holding off great armies with a handful of men.

There is a special interest in his successes, because they bring out the weakness of the conventional methods of the Bakufu commanders.

He was summoned to Kasagi in October 1331 by Go-Daigo, for consultation about raising troops against the Hōjō commanders. He got together a small force, consisting of his own kinsmen, their retainers, and some volunteers from the neighbouring gentry, and assembled them behind defence works at a place called Akasaka on Mount Kongō; but being untrained they were easily overcome. Kusunoki escaped, to plan in secret, biding his time. He saw that he must develop a much stronger system of defence. In the winter of 1332 he decided to make a stand behind a fortress called Kami (Upper) Akasaka, on higher ground than the place (Shimo Akasaka) which had been taken by the enemy a year before. This was to be the forward point of a defence system which he devised. It is described as "the front gate," in a work called *Kusunoki Kassen Chūmon*, which gives the order of battle and some interesting details of the fighting during repeated assaults upon Kusunoki's defences.

Kami Akasaka was sturdily defended but was captured by cutting off its water supply. Now the brunt of the attack had to be borne by the defence works at Chihaya, which had been devised by Kusunoki for that purpose. With a very small garrison he repulsed assaults over a period of some ten weeks, even at times vigorously counterattacking. Thus a great Hōjō army was practically immobilized, and when news came of the defeat of the Rokuhara garrison the commanders Aso, Osaragi, and Nikaidō withdrew, in a state of alarm and distress.

It is worth while to describe briefly the strategy used by Kusunoki, since his success, quite apart from its immediate military value, encouraged the loyalist forces and showed Go-Daigo's supporters that they had good prospects of keeping the field and inflicting punishment upon the enemy despite inferior numbers.

The force which captured Kami Akasaka after six days' hard fighting in April 1333 had been led by Aso along the Kawachi road. At about the same time a powerful attack was delivered on Chihaya by Osaragi, approaching by the Yamato road. It is clear that Kusunoki expected this and had planned accordingly. He had not intended to hold out for long at Akasaka, which was a strong-point meant to delay Aso's contingent. He could have built more strong-points in front of Chihaya, but he had only a small force, probably not more than 2,000

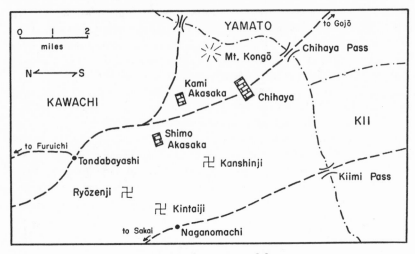

Kusunoki's defences at Chihaya

men, and he decided to depend upon the difficult terrain. His men could sally from the well-protected stronghold of Chihaya, which he had carefully fortified with rocks and felled trees. He had taken care to have a good reserve water supply, and great boulders were placed so that they could be dropped or rolled down upon attackers. Brushwood screens were erected as a defence against arrows. His object was to induce the attackers to fight where their numbers were not of much advantage, near the summit of Mount Kongō, where ridges and ravines and other features were known to him but not to the enemy. This strategy was so successful that although Aso and Nagoshi and Nikaidō sent help to Osaragi, the Chihaya defences were still not penetrated after weeks of bitter fighting.

If Chihaya had surrendered, it is probable that the loyalist resistance would have collapsed, and therefore Kusunoki's strategy may be regarded as one of the finest achievements in the military history of Japan.

3. *The Ashigaru*

With the growing frequency of street fighting during the war between the Northern and Southern Courts, when both sides attacked Kyoto repeatedly, there came certain changes in the method of warfare. The conventional battle, usually fought in open country, consisted of a large number of small encounters, often largely of single combats of mounted men (known as *ikki-uchi*, or one-horseman fights), and what may have started as a battle of manoeuvre often ended as an uncoordinated group of minor engagements. During the civil war this kind of fighting tended to give way to the movement of troops in formation, but usually, it would appear, not in very large numbers.

Street fighting, however, called for special methods, since large bodies of men, especially of mounted warriors, could not safely be deployed in narrow lanes and passages. There thus developed a special kind of fighter known as *ashigaru*, or light foot soldier. The *Taiheiki* mentions such men as being engaged in a surprise night attack on a stronghold in Yoshino, but the ashigaru do not seem to have been generally used until the Ōnin War (1467), when they played a murderous part. According to contemporary records, both Yamana and Hosokawa made use of "picked troops called *ashigaru*," who carried only one weapon—a sword, a spear, or a halberd. They would stealthily enter an enemy camp and take prisoners, or under cover of darkness they would set fire to watchtowers or other structures. They also engaged with enthusiasm in sheer looting, and fire was their favourite weapon.

The great scholar and statesman Ichijō Kanera, who fled from Kyoto to Nara during the Ōnin War, later wrote a memorial on the principles of government in which he recommended the abolition of such fighting men as the ashigaru. "These men, who have recently been used by the armies, are excessively dangerous rascals. They tear down or set fire to any place in or out of the city where they know they will not be caught by their enemies. They do not spare either private dwellings or monastic buildings. They search only for loot, and they are nothing but daylight robbers. They are a new evil and should be done away with. They are a disgrace to our country."

What kind of men became ashigaru is not exactly known, but some of them were probably absconding peasants, others men who took service under the samurai of their own district, looking for adventure and freedom.

The records of the Muromachi era are full of details about absconders. Thus in the Abbot Jinson's journal a report from one of the great Kōfukuji manors in Echizen shows that in the year 1460, owing to poor harvests and epidemics, 9,268 persons had died of starvation and 757 had absconded.

4. *Wives and Children*

The chronicles of the dynastic war tell little about the family life of the warriors, although it is known that the position of women was better in the Muromachi than in subsequent periods. When wives or children are mentioned, it is usually to praise their virtue or their piety. One of the most disagreeable examples of literature of this genre is to be found in the *Taiheiki*. It concerns the head of Kusunoki Masashige, who died on the field of battle at Minatogawa, and it runs as follows:

*

The head of Kusunoki was exposed in the river bed at Rokujō, and since the head of some other man had been labelled as Masashige's in the spring, many people said that this head too was probably a fraud. . . . But later Takauji sent for the head, and despatched it to Masashige's home, with a message saying: "I cannot help feeling sad when I think of how long we were associates, both in public and in private. No doubt his widow and child would like to see him again, even in death." His lordship's generosity was admirable indeed!

At the time of his departure for Hyōgo, Masashige not only had left all kinds of instructions, but had told [his son] Masatsura to stay behind, saying, "I shall certainly fall in the battle that lies ahead." Accordingly, his wife and son had thought from the beginning that he would never return. Still, when they beheld the head, which, though unmistakably Masashige's, was completely altered, with closed eyes and changed colour, sorrow filled their hearts and they wept uncontrollably.

Masatsura was ten years old that year. After gazing at his father's lifeless head and marking his mother's inconsolable grief, he started toward the Buddha Hall, with his sleeve pressed to his streaming eyes. His mother, alarmed by his sudden departure, went to the Buddha Hall through a side door and saw that he was preparing to kill himself. His skirt strings were loosened to expose his belly, and in his right hand there was a drawn sword bearing the family crest; the very sword which his father had given him as a keepsake at the time of his departure for Hyōgo.

Masatsura's mother ran up to him, caught hold of his arm, and spoke tearfully.

"They say that Sandalwood is fragrant even in seed leaf. You are still very young, but if you are your father's son, you ought not to be so ignorant of what is right. Even though your mind is that of a child, consider the matter well. When the late Hōgan left for Hyōgo, he sent you home from the Sakurai stage. His purpose was by no means to make sure that there would be someone to mourn for him, nor did he leave you behind so that you might kill yourself. 'Even if my luck becomes exhausted and I lose my life on the battlefield,' he said, 'if you hear of His Majesty's whereabouts, you must give pay to my surviving kinsmen and retainers, raise an army, destroy the enemies of the Crown, and restore His Majesty to the throne.' You have been quick to forget these last words from your father, which you once repeated to me faithfully. If you kill yourself, you will dishonour your father's name and fail His Majesty the Emperor."

So she admonished him, weeping, and took away the drawn sword.

Masatsura was quite unable to commit suicide. He fell down in tears from the altar and joined his laments to those of his mother.

CHAPTER VIII

THE LIFE OF THE COURT

In a strictly political sense, the ruling dynasty of Japan entered
upon a slow decline in the age of the Fujiwara Regents, lost its claim
to sovereignty in 1221, when the Kamakura Bakufu banished the Emperor Go-Toba, and thereafter retained only a shadow of authority and
a bare vestige of public esteem. Go-Daigo's attempt to exert sovereign
powers, and the subsequent division into rival Courts, left the fortunes
of the imperial line at their lowest ebb.

It is true that the emperors of both Courts continued to perform
their ancestral duties as representatives of the people in the worship of
their national gods. In this capacity an emperor was still the object of
reverence and to a diminished degree a focus of national loyalty. There
remained, however, one respect in which the influence of the Throne
was of great importance. In an age of upheaval and disorder, when
power was in the hands, often the blood-stained hands, of unlettered
warriors, it was the sovereign and his nobles who kept the flame of
learning alive.

Readers of the *Tale of Genji* are apt to form the opinion that life
at Court was devoted to frivolous pleasures and Palace intrigue. No
doubt there were voluptuary young noblemen and scheming ministers
at the Court of Go-Daigo, who lived under the shadow of the military
headquarters in the capital. But the royal Court, steeped in tradition,
always had its serious, even solemn, side, and usually frowned upon
the empty-headed and the dissolute members of the aristocracy.[1] It
happens that the diaries of several mediaeval sovereigns and princes
have been preserved. These precious documents reveal to careful study
aspects of Court life which come as a surprise to the student who has
expected only a dry chronicle of ceremonies, spiced with a little Palace
gossip.

Most interesting of these works is the diary of the Emperor Hanazono, and some account of its content will serve as a picture of Court
life, while displaying the character of a remarkable man. This emperor
was born in 1297, the second son of the Emperor Fushimi. He was thus
in the senior line, and succeeded Go-Nijō of the junior line in 1308.
He reigned until 1318, when he abdicated in favour of Go-Daigo. His
diary covers the years from 1310 to 1332, thus including most of his own
reign and fourteen years during which he was the junior retired Em-

---

[1] The Admonitions of Kujō-dono, written in the tenth century, are an expression of rigid moral principles by a celebrated statesman (Fujiwara Morosuke), and
such documents were not uncommon in later times.

peror. He died in 1348 in his fifty-second year. Many of his daily entries include interesting information on political events, some of it first-hand, some of it from reports that were not always reliable. But still more interesting and perhaps more valuable as historical material are the passages in which he describes his own daily life, examines his own character, comments upon passing events and prominent figures, and generally presents a picture of himself as an exceptional man—a scholar, a poet, an artist, a devout Buddhist, and something of a philosopher.

The first entries in his diary belong to the winter of 1310, when he was in his fourteenth year. The following slightly abridged translation will show their nature:

*

Tenth month (December 1310)

x.1. Summer clothes of Palace officers changed to winter clothes as usual. Genkimon-In [widow of Go-Fukakusa] ill.

x.2. Clear sky. Linked verse. Tonight meeting to decide promotion of monks. Presiding official, Kinkata.

x.3. Tonight my new reader came for the first time. He came to the edge of the gallery. I reclined on cross-bench and read Kobun Hongi. Genkimon-In no better.

x.4. Private meeting for linked verse. Archery practice.

x.5. Clear weather. Linked verse. Practice with small-bow. Genkimon-In now up. Good news.

x.6. Clear. Linked verse. Small-bow practice.

x.7. Rain. Private gathering for composition of poems in Chinese and for linked verse. Theme for poems: "Winter comes to the moorland."

x.9. Clear. This morning I heard of the death last night of Saku-heimon-In. She was my sister. As a sign of mourning the Five Annual Festivals [Go-Sechiye] are suspended.

x.10. Clear. Today I take the first of seven daily doses of medicinal herbs.

x.13. No court today. Sukena excused, and Tōin Chūnagon [Kinkata] in attendance.

x.19. Today Festival of the star of the year. Service conducted by the Monk Eisan.

x.23. Date of Gembuku ceremony fixed. It is to take place in the In's palace.

x.25. Owing to pollution [of sacred precincts] by death of a dog, daily worship suspended.

x.28. Monk-Prince Kakunyo completes religious vows in special service.

x.30. Abbot Shinjū completes service of administering vows. [Names of participants follow.]

It will be noticed that ceremonial duties were not heavy, and that Hanazono frequently held poetry meetings in his own apartments. In the following month, however, there are several observances over which the sovereign himself must preside. For although he did not take an active part in all ceremonies, often sending deputies or messengers to act for him, there were certain great national ceremonies in which he was the intermediary between the people and the gods. Among these special occasions were the Prayer for Harvest (Toshigoi), the Festival of the First Fruits (Niiname), and the Festival of the Kamo shrine, which was by tradition closely connected with the Imperial House.

*

Eleventh Month

xi.1 The calendar submitted. Presiding official Fujiwara Ason Gon-Chūnagon. From today gifts and offerings as usual. Owing to illness of Naishi [attendant in Naishi-dokoro, the inner sanctum where the Emperor worships and the Regalia are enshrined], her place was taken by a young Court lady. Imibi [Pure Fire] as usual.

xi.2. Special service fixed for the Night Duty Room. Today Thanksgiving for freedom from natural calamities.

xi.7. First snow, about two inches.

xi.10. Today messengers to leave for the Festival of Kasuga Shrine. They came late, and did not leave the Seiryōden until after midnight. Lustration as usual. Tonight to separate apartment.

xi.12. This morning Festival of Hirano Shrine. Lustration as usual.

xi.13. Festivals of Matsuo and Umenomiya Shrines. Kamo special festival arranged.

xi.14. Sacred dance and music (Kagura) in Naishi-dokoro. I listen from Naden.

xi.15. Kantō sent usual gifts of gold dust and other articles.

xi.16. Festivals of Sonokara-kami [worship of Korean and other foreign deities].

xi.17. Chinkonsai Festival [for pacification of spirits].

xi.18. Niinamesai [Festival of the First Fruits].

xi.19. No regular festival. Ordinary court. This because of mourning for Sakuheimon-In.

xi.21. Minor promotions.

xi.22. Special festival. Inspection of Imperial Stables.

xi.23. Festival of Yoshida Shrine.

xi.24. Special Festival of Kamo Shrine. Usual procedure. Messenger sent was Arinaka.

xi.28. The Regent brought the order of procedure for the Gembuku ceremony [of son of Go-Fushimi].

xi.29. The messengers carrying offerings to the Usa Shrine came to report date and time.

xi.30. Tonight six sacred cars [*mikoshi*] are to be returned to their seat in the Hie Shrine.

❉

The entries for the following month are similar. The last two months of the year and the first month of the new year were especially busy with public ceremonies, but throughout the year the Emperor had almost daily duties to perform within the Palace, notably his prayers in the Naishi-dokoro, where the Regalia were kept in the charge of vestals. There were also certain symbolic governmental tasks, such as receiving reports from ministers of state and watching over the numerous Palace offices, notably the Kurōdo-dokoro (Kurando-dokoro). Another obligation, sometimes onerous, was a ceremonial visit to the three retired sovereigns, to whom he owed some family duty and, though himself the reigning Emperor, an obeisance.

The sovereign led a dull and confined life. Most of his functions were of a formal nature, and he had almost nothing to do with practical questions of government. These were dealt with by the Bakufu, and often did not come to his knowledge until after action had been taken. It is not surprising that most emperors in those times, after ten years or so of ceremonial duties, were glad to abdicate and live in honoured leisure.

Hanazono was a young man of active and sensitive mind, who naturally took refuge in serious studies, relieved from time to time by poetical gatherings and small drinking parties. In 1312 he records a private poetry meeting when the theme was "Peach blossoms mirrored in a stream"; a discussion of plans for rebuilding the Palace; a decision to change the era name; and details of the procedure at a Court function. There is an eclipse of the sun, which involves much consultation with astrologers and diviners; and there are frequent gatherings, private and informal, in the Emperor's own apartments, which often last until long after midnight.

Sometimes there were troublesome issues, as when in September 1312 the city was alarmed by a demonstration of priests from a Nara shrine, who brought their sacred emblem as a threat and a safeguard against arrest. Such occasions were frequent, and always caused the greatest anxiety in the Palace, since if the sovereign were to show any partiality, he would offend one of the great foundations, whether the Buddhist Tōdaiji or the Shintō shrine of Kasuga, which belonged to the Kōfukuji. During the time a Shintō party was making a disturbance, the Emperor always took care to avoid any Buddhist observance, even to the point of breaking a fast which he had begun or cancelling some Buddhist ritual within the Palace.

In this dispute of 1312 a riot was feared. Fully armed guards were placed at all gates, and mounted patrols rode around the Palace area. The sacred emblem was escorted to the Hōjōji, and as a sign of reverence during its presence the Emperor sat in hieratic style on a ceremonial mat in the Palace courtyard, attended by a Court officer carrying the Sword of the Regalia. This awkward dispute was resolved peacefully, and the Nara priests departed.

When calm returned, an easy-going life could be resumed. In October, we learn, the Lady Genkimon-In paid a private visit to Hanazono with her ladies-in-waiting. She used the private carriage of the Grand Counsellor Tamekane. This was an important occasion, for Tamekane was not only a clever statesman but also a great figure in the poetical world. The light of the moon was clear and all went well. Care was taken that the gathering should be kept strictly private, for this was on the eve of a religious festival. Hanazono was intensely interested in all forms of expression, painting as well as poetry, and he was now going through an exacting curriculum in classical literature, of which his diary shows signs. But poetry was his chief delight and means of relaxation, and thus the company of a man like Tamekane gave him much pleasure.

In 1312 Tamekane completed an anthology called *Gyokuyōshū*, in which he included a poem by Hanazono, still a youth but older than his years. It is explained as a Buddhist allegory, but it has a beauty of expression in its own right:

Tsubame naku	The light of evening sun
Nokiba no yūhi	fades from the eaves
Kage kiete	where swallows chatter
Yanagi ni aoki	and in the garden the Spring breeze
Niwa no harukaze.	blows green through the willows.

Hanazono's father, the Emperor Fushimi, was also a good poet, and many of his poems are included in the same anthology. Poetry was one of Hanazono's passions, and he was able to gather round him a number of eager associates. The gatherings for linked verse were in the nature of a game, in which two teams competed; but the Chinese poems and the native stanzas (*waka*) were serious literary efforts and called for skill and feeling.

In the spring of 1317 a monk just returned from the Kantō reports that bad news is to be expected from Kamakura. The choice of a successor to the throne has been made, and a messenger will shortly arrive. It appears that opinion in the East favours Prince Takaharu (later to reign as Go-Daigo) of the junior line, who is learned and wise, older than Hanazono, and generally well suited to rule. Hanazono's first comment on this news is that despite his lack of virtue he has already been on the throne for nine years, longer than either of his two predecessors. He is quite ready to retire at once, his only regret being that he cannot move to the new palace just completed. He adds: "I rejoice at the will of Heaven. I feel no anger or envy."

Several months passed before the Bakufu made a definite decision. In the meantime we see Hanazono working hard at his studies as usual. Tutors visit him regularly and he reads both Chinese classics and Buddhist writings. A learned abbot comes to expound the *Jōyuishiki-ron*, a Chinese version of a formidable Indian work on an idealist philosophy; he works at this for several days. When he feels that he has grasped its meaning, he turns to poetical exercises with his friends, staying up all night.

A few days later he learns through a secret channel that a messenger from the Kantō has brought a letter for his brother the In (Go-Fushimi) saying that it is proposed to name as heir apparent the first son of Go-Nijō, to be followed by another prince of the junior line. This contradiction of previous news infuriates Hanazono, who writes "I cannot understand this. . . . That the destiny of the nation should be decided by commonplace minds is most alarming. To announce a decision on a grave matter of state in this casual way is truly reprehensible. It must be the work of ignorant rustics. Of late the manners of the Easterners have sadly deteriorated. It looks as if they had no men of consequence there." Hanazono's chief objection to the alleged proposals of the Bakufu was that they amounted to a public announcement that two members of the junior line would rule in succession, thus running counter to the understanding that the two lines should alternate.[2]

The exact date of Hanazono's abdication is not recorded. He moved to the new palace, after all, in the spring of 1317. It was at Nijō-Tomino-kōji, built on the same lines as the Kanin palace, but with fewer rooms. There is a gap from the middle of 1317 until the first month of 1318, when there is a long passage on one of the New Year ceremonies, and then nothing until the first month of 1319. Presumably Hanazono abdicated in the first month of 1318, since Go-Daigo's accession was announced in the second month and his enthronement took place a few days later.

Beginning with the year 1319, in which Hanazono reached the age of twenty-two, the diary displays a rapidly maturing mind. He takes his responsibilities seriously and blames himself for faults in his own conduct, going so far as to say of various disasters afflicting the country that they are due to his lack of virtue. His health at this time is poor; he is of a valetudinarian habit and suffers from fits of melancholy. In the first month of 1319 he describes certain New Year observances in detail, including card games and poetry contests between two teams of Court nobles and ladies, one led by the In's consort and the other by

[2] The understanding between the Bakufu and the Court was reached in the compromise of 1317, which is discussed at length in *A History of Japan to 1334*, Appendix IV.

Hanazono himself. But he seems to have suffered from these festivities, for on the following day he writes:

"The rain has ceased but the clouds have not dispersed. Since last night I have had a severe bout of kakke [beri-beri], and today it seems to be worse. Especially since last summer this complaint has grown worse, and the continuous treatment of the past two or three years has done me no good. The truth is that I am a sickly man, by nature of a retiring habit of mind. From early childhood I have been a solitary. Yet I have not been able to find peace, and I cannot express my sense of disappointment. My spirits are weak, and there is no doubt that my life will be short. In my heart I am devoted to learning and to the teachings of the Buddha, yet my efforts fall short of my desires."

He goes on to develop this melancholy theme, complaining that he has not the strength of mind to cut himself off from the world and enter into monastic seclusion. And so he is condemned, he says, to day after day of idle and useless life. The most he can do is to express the feelings that fill his bosom. Yet this melancholy temperament does not prevent him from the exercise of an alert mind.

He is now himself a cloistered emperor, and this brings him to a new phase of life, causing an emotional strain which is perhaps somewhat relieved by confession in his diary. But as the passage already quoted from his diary shows, he does not regret the abdication forced upon him in 1318 to make room for Go-Daigo, because he has no real interest in most of his imperial functions.

The entries for the third month of 1319 describe another of those outbreaks of violence by disorderly monks that so often alarmed the Court and harassed the Bakufu deputies in Kyoto, whose duty it was to keep the peace and to prevent the spread of insubordination of any kind. This time it was a quarrel between Miidera and Hiyeizan, on a question of rights of ordination, which were jealously preserved by certain foundations. The matter was a serious one, for it aroused not only sectarian passion but also a violent greed for material advantage. The dispute ended in a tragic way, with the Hiyeizan rabble setting fire to the Miidera buildings, most of which burned to the ground. Clashes of this sort were horrifying to the devout Hanazono, who saw in them "the end of the Holy Law."

At about this time he records visits to Go-Fushimi and gives some account of his own studies, his regular discussions with learned monks and lay scholars, the books that he reads, and the pious tasks that he imposes upon himself. It is a serious life, and though he is no longer on the throne, he does not escape ceremonial duties. Family obligations also are at times exacting. In July he has to attend at the bedside of his sister-in-law, the Lady Kōgimon-In, when she is giving birth. He recites charms and whispers prayers into the left ear of the infant, saying three times: "Heaven your Father, Earth your Mother. Take these ninety-nine pieces [coins] as signs of a long life." As usual on such occasions the ritual is elaborate and exhausting. There are clusters of monks, diviners, and exorcists for processions, spells, petitions, and prayers. No precaution is omitted.

In the following month there is a long and elaborate state visit to the Chōkōdō[3] to visit the two retired Emperors, Go-Uda and Go-Fushimi. There are religious rites such as the *kuge,* an offering of flowers before an image of the Buddha, as part of a mass for the dead. For several days after this there are more elaborate ceremonies to be performed. Then Hanazono resumes his ordinary life, which includes frequent discussions with learned monks, catechisms, and arguments on points of Buddhist doctrine. Thus the question is put: "The continuous worship of Kannon removes the Three Poisons. Is this due to an act of faith or to continued devotion?" The answer is: "To an act of faith. But devotion can produce results."

There are occasional distractions from these solemn tasks. It is August, and the heat is great. Hanazono and Go-Fushimi go on a private excursion in search of cooling airs. Their party includes a number of Court ladies. They visit the country villa of a retired Regent, a beautiful place, elegantly furnished and containing precious paintings and other artistic treasures. The guests first rest in a pavilion, to which their host comes to pay his respects. He then withdraws, but he is called back, and later, after an exhibition of archery, is invited to partake of some refreshments. He drinks several cups, and so do others, and soon there is a tipsy party. The Regent presents his favourite dancing girl, who performs several pieces. The Regent becomes drunk, and falls down, but he is at once picked up and led away.

In the early fall we find Hanazono in an argument with the cloistered Go-Uda about an estate in Ise which should have been inherited by Hanazono from his father (Fushimi) but has been taken away by Go-Uda. Hanazono is not covetous, but he has a sense of justice. He speaks to the Minister of the Left and receives an evasive reply. He does not lose his temper, but he notes in his diary that he cannot understand how Go-Uda could act in such a remarkable manner, "seeing that he is a man of great learning, familiar with the classical literature of China and Japan." Hanazono is interested in human behaviour. He wants to find out the reason for Go-Uda's error, not to blame him; and he characteristically quotes Mencius on moderation.

Hanazono at this time begins to find Court life burdensome, and although he has his gay moments, he is always thinking of holy orders. He is restrained by his brother, and finally he decides that he "cannot turn his back on a layman's life." But he is always ready to discuss religion. He talks with a cleric about the Ikkō (Single-Minded) sect

---

[3] A religious establishment owning great estates which were the chief source of income for the Imperial House.

of Nembutsu, or Buddha-calling. This is a branch of the worship of Amida developed from the teaching of Shinran into an aggressive doctrine of salvation by faith. Hanazono approves of the idea of salvation by faith and regards Amida-worship as a "deep" teaching, but he feels that Ikkō believers are tragically wrong when they say that the Hinayana and the Mahayana, all the open and the mystic teachings, should be abolished. He would rather suppress the worship of Amida than see it pursued to the exclusion of all else. For his part, he wishes to promote both the Tendai and the Shingon doctrines.

His thoughts constantly revert to the misery of this life and the bliss of Paradise. One day (February 8, 1319) he writes: "This morning I dreamed that I should soon be reborn. This is my heart's desire, and it is the third time I have had this premonition. I must now devote myself to thoughts of the after-life. I shall not tell anybody of this dream, because of the great joy it gives me." The next day he makes a New Year's resolution to study the Ōjōyōshū, Eshin's work on the Essentials of Salvation, the gospel of the Buddha-calling sects. He must study the sutras earnestly. But the New Year festivities cannot be avoided, and for a few days he is attending evening parties, some convivial, others devoted to music, games of chance for forfeits, or poetical contests.

There is much about his studies in the diary for the years following directly upon his abdication. He sits up with his friends talking of books until far into the night. He notes that whereas classical literature and the Holy Law may not prepare the mind for the task of government, they are moral exercises which form the character. He is scrupulous in attending Buddhist services; he works hard at the scriptures, and even at codes of law. "Except for mealtimes," he writes, "I have a book in my hand all day long. I am not quick of understanding, but I have great powers of application. I hope to arrive gradually at a knowledge of the Truth. I have not yet attained wisdom, and this is the regret of my life."

There is no doubt that he set himself very rigid standards. He is distressed by contemporary behaviour. Men in high places are "sunk in greed for pleasure." The education of young persons is so poor that they learn only words and phrases that may be useful in making rhymes or linking verses. They learn nothing of what is needed for an understanding of the scriptures, and classical learning has given way to belles-lettres.[4] Despite his own devotion to poetry, he holds that classical learning must come first. It is clear that he is well drilled in the classics, for recondite allusions abound in his diary.

In the flowering springtime of 1320 he joined the In, his brother, on an excursion to his Kitayama villa. They strolled round the garden

---

[4] The word he uses is fūgetsu ("wind and moon"), which means elegant prose and poetry, mainly about the beauties of nature.

and examined the buildings; only a few courtiers were in attendance. The Prime Minister came to pay his respects. There was pleasant conversation and then a little wine. Towards sunset they boarded boats that awaited them at the bank of the Kamo River, and rode downstream on the current. There were certain important Court ladies in the first boat, others in the second, and men in the third. His Majesty the In did not embark until after dark. Then in one boat the Ōmiya Dainagon played the flute accompanied by the Chamberlain of the Empress plucking at his lute, while the In himself struck a chord from time to time. "Now the moon shone bright, the music matched the song, the sound of waterfalls filled the ear. As the boats floated down we heard the dawn bell."

In the following month there was a great Buddhist mass at the In's palace. The Lady Eifukumon-In, widow of the deceased Fushimi, came in from the Kitayama villa. The mass was the culmination of one thousand daily recitals of the invocation to Amida, and on the altar as objects of worship were a painting of Amida, three Pure Land scrolls, one thousand miniature figures of Amida, and sutras copied by the In and by various princes and princesses. The picture is not identified, but throughout the diary there are many references to paintings which show that Hanazono had a strong liking for the graphic arts. He had a fine taste, and to judge from sketches in the diary he was an artist of talent himself. The celebrated picture scroll known as the *Tōhoku-In Utaawase*, which contains vivid sketches of participants in a poetry contest, was among the papers kept in the Hagiwara-dono, where Hanazono lived in retirement after 1337. It bears an inscription by Sukō-In, suggesting that it was the work of Hanazono himself. He was well acquainted with the work of the leading Court painters. His own portrait, showing him at the age of forty-two in his monastic robes and holding a rosary, was painted by Gōshin, a descendant of Takanobu, and is described by a contemporary (Tōin Kinkata) as an excellent likeness. Drawn with few but certain strokes, it presents the lineaments and the posture that a study of his diary leads one to expect. The thoughtful face is sensitive; a lively mind looks out from bright eyes.

The years from 1320 to 1324 show an increasing interest in religion. At the end of 1324 Hanazono sets out an imposing plan of studies, including sutras and exegeses, history, and Chinese classical works and commentaries, among which the writings of Chu Hsi are mentioned. In those years the political situation in the capital was growing more and more difficult. Hanazono lived a secluded life and took no active part in politics, but he had informants who gave him news from time to time.

In the first entries for 1325 the New Year Poetical Gathering is described. The themes chosen by the Emperor were "Moonlight on Kasuga" and "Mist on the fields." The reader was Sukeaki, a courtier close to Hanazono and the frequent companion of his leisure. A day or two later there came a message from Kamakura to say that two of Go-Daigo's supporters, Hino Suketomo and Hino Toshimoto, had been held and examined on a charge of conspiracy; and shortly there followed the news of Suketomo's sentence of banishment and Toshimoto's release. At this time the Bakufu were trying to force the abdication of Go-Daigo. The course of events was watched carefully by Hanazono, since the fortunes of the senior line were at issue. Despite his growing preoccupation with religion he kept his eyes and ears open, and made sage observations from time to time. There is a great fuss about the presentation of a sword to the infant son of the Hōjō Regent Takatoki, and Hanazono objects to the humble language used in the In's letter to Kamakura; but he fears that "this is how things are done nowadays." Here and there the diary affords a glimpse of his practical wisdom, as when he advises his sister-in-law about her property or makes sardonic observations on the haste of claimants in lawsuits about property or succession to rush to and fro between the capital and Kamakura to plead their cases.

Throughout 1325 he writes about his poor health, colds, fevers, headaches, sweats, and fits of depression. Both physicians and exorcists are summoned, but their prescriptions do no good, and he continues to complain that he has no energy for study.

The Court in Kyoto is ill at ease, wondering what the next move of the Bakufu will be, but in the sequestered society of the retired emperors life continues with little change. Monks and scholars seem free to enter and leave their palaces at will, to conduct services or to discuss religious problems. Hanazono has long talks with leaders of all sects and seems to listen to them impartially, though certain aspects of Zen do not attract him and he does not think highly of all its exponents. He favours Tendai and Shingon, as he says himself, and he is deeply interested in subtleties of doctrine. He enjoys reading Mencius without accepting all his arguments, and he is critical of the "new" Sung philosophy. At times, however, he turns aside from his studies to take up some question of revenue from provincial manors, for even the royal family are bound to keep a sharp eye upon their landed estates in these days when Land Stewards are voracious and undisciplined.

In the last entry for 1325 he laments his failure to carry out the plan of studies which he drew up at the beginning of the year. He gives a short list of books to be read, and says that although he could plead frequent illness as an excuse, he is ashamed of his indolence.

In the extant portions of the diary there is a gap from the end of 1325 to the autumn of 1331, the time of Go-Daigo's flight from the Palace to the stronghold of Kasagi. Hanazono's entry for November 1, 1331, repeats an account of Go-Daigo's capture. In sympathetic language it records that when the fugitive monarch was seized by the soldiery of

Kamakura he was thinly dressed, his hair dishevelled. A day or two later he was taken in custody to the Rokuhara headquarters, and there ordered to surrender the Regalia. Hanazono refers to Go-Daigo as the "former Emperor," because Go-Fushimi's son has recently been enthroned as the Emperor Kōgon with Bakufu support and connivance. He quotes reports that Go-Daigo has agreed under pressure to hand over the Regalia for transmission to the young Emperor.[5]

While in custody at the Rokuhara headquarters Go-Daigo was allowed to receive some visitors, and they reported to the Court that what the Bakufu had done was "the work of demons." Hanazono describes the behaviour of the Bakufu as abominable and shows pity for Go-Daigo's plight, in which he seems to have seen a threat to the Imperial House that transcended the quarrel between its junior and senior lines. Yet he continues to note down the trivial incidents of daily life, the minutiae of ceremonial, the calls paid by Court officials and holy men, and such family matters as repairs to a palace, visits to relatives, who rode in which carriage, and where they went.

At the beginning of 1332 there is an elaborate account of the New Year ceremonies and of a grand state procession by the Emperor Go-Fushimi, now the active retired Emperor, since his son, though not yet enthroned, has gone through the accession ceremony. Early in April Hanazono notes briefly that Go-Daigo has left on his long journey into exile; he will reach Izumo province in about seven days, and then embark for Oki. Towards the end of this month Hanazono records the death of the "Dainagon Nyūdō" (Grand Counsellor in Holy Orders), that is to say, the poet Kyōgoku Tamekane.

The biography of Tamekane is of special interest, for it shows the link between poetry and politics which is a traditional feature of Court life in Japan. It is always the Court that leads the way in the encouragement of poets, in the compilation of anthologies, and in the establishment of a canon of verse; and because poetry is of such importance, it is almost inevitable that quarrels between schools of poetry should be reflected in political strife.

Tamekane (1254–1332) led the innovating Kyōgoku-Reizei School, and was opposed by Nijō Tameuji, leader of the conservative Nijō School. Both were descendants of the famous poet Teika. Their disagreement was principally a matter of sentiment, since Tameuji did not like the "new" poetry (which grew under the influence of Zen monks steeped in Sung philosophy).

[5] On November 4 Hanazono writes: "At dawn today the former Emperor entered the quarters of Hōjō Tokimasu [the southern Kyoto Tandai]. He was in a procession, accompanied by some Court nobles. He was carried in a palanquin heavily guarded and escorted by several thousand mounted warriors. They had travelled by night, and the flames of the torches lit up the scene as if it were midday. Today His Majesty is to hand over the Regalia."

3

4

5

CARPENTER

GAMBLER

6

MOULDER OF POTS AND PANS

SORCERESS

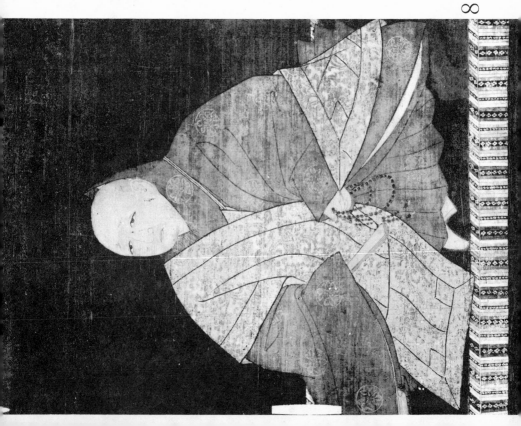

As a boy Hanazono much admired Tamekane, and both he and his brother Go-Fushimi were impressed by the poet's great gifts and wide learning. But as he grew older, Hanazono noted the flaws in Tamekane's character that inclined him to a dangerous course of intrigue. During the reign of the Emperor Fushimi, Tamekane had begun to dabble in politics and had been denounced to the Bakufu, who obliged him to retire and live in seclusion. But he was again denounced and was banished to Sado. After some years of exile he returned to the capital, where he was again involved in conspiracy. In 1312 he completed his well-known anthology, *Gyokuyōshū*, and in 1313 he was banished once more, this time to the province of Tosa. In the years after Go-Daigo came to the throne he continued to intrigue on behalf of the senior line, and thereby incurred the resentment of Saionji Sanekane, his onetime friend and patron, a most powerful nobleman who was in close touch with Kamakura and pressed the claims of the junior line. Tamekane's later exile appears, from a note in Hanazono's diary, to have followed upon his denunciation by Saionji.

It is clear that Tamekane, though a sensitive and gifted poet and a good scholar, had a disagreeable side to his character and gave offence to many of his associates. He is described as jealous and intolerant; and it must be said that from very early times in the disputes between schools of poetry acrimony was the rule and sharp practice not the exception.

Tamekane, being much admired by the Emperor Fushimi—himself a poet of talent—was trusted by the senior line, and when Fushimi retired (1298) his position as political adviser was very strong. There can be hardly any doubt that he was deeply involved in anti-Bakufu movements. Yet on the whole he was leniently treated by the Regents at Kamakura. The junior line regarded him as a dangerous adversary and warmly supported the opposing school of poetry, the Nijō School.

The long-drawn-out conflict between the two schools of poetry was as bitter as the dynastic quarrel. That the two were so closely related testifies to the importance of the Court in the intellectual life of the nation, as patron and protector of literature and the arts. Some of Hanazono's observations in his diary suggest that he felt poetry and religion to be of the same essence.

Not much is known of Hanazono's life in the years after the last extant entries in his diary. In the spring of 1333 he and Go-Fushimi were taken for safety to Rokuhara by the Hōjō Tandai, who was then under attack from Go-Daigo's party. They then moved to a remote monastery in Mino province (Ibukiyama) and returned to Kyoto when conditions were less unsettled. Hanazono took the tonsure in 1337 and lived in seclusion at his country house (Hagiwara-dono) until his death in 1348.

Hanazono took his royal duties very seriously and set a high standard of conduct for the sovereign and his Court. He wrote a Paper of Advice

to the Crown Prince (Go-Daigo's heir), warning him against a superficial belief in fashionable philosophies, which might lead to neglect of
the classical ideals of probity and piety.[6] He was not antagonistic to the
"new" Sung Confucianism, but deplored its indiscriminate acceptance.
He was not opposed to Go-Daigo's views, thinking them based on true
learning, but he feared for the morals of the Court if loose thinking were
to become the rule.

During the war between the Courts life in the capital was often
disturbed, and there were times when the Northern Emperor had to
leave the city. But there is ample evidence that despite such interrup-
tions members of the royal family and the leading Court nobles continued to apply themselves to learned or artistic pursuits. Some of them
lived quietly in country retreats, where they had abundant leisure for
classical studies or poetry or painting. Two important anthologies of
verse were prepared in the second half of the century, one by the Regent
Nijō Yoshimoto in 1356 and one by Go-Daigo's son Prince Munenaga in
1381. The diary of Prince Sadashige (later Go-Sukō-In), which covers
events of the fifteenth century, shows clearly that the writer was a man
of taste who had the advantage of being brought up in a society devoted
to literature and the arts.

Surveying the history of the fourteenth century, one cannot but con-
clude that, in an age of incessant warfare, the fine spirit of Japanese
culture was in danger. It was saved from destruction principally because the high tradition of art and letters was preserved by the aristo-
cratic society, and so provided a foundation upon which the culture of
the Muromachi era could be built.

There was one other stronghold of learning and civil virtue, the
Buddhist Church, but there can be no doubt that the literary and artistic
accomplishments of the Buddhist clergy depended in great part on material and moral support from the Throne. By the end of the fourteenth
century the Imperial House had lost most of its mystic or magical
authority, and its actual political power had almost vanished. But
authority takes many forms, and in a society in which refinement of
manners and morals commanded widespread respect as an ideal if not
a rule, the sovereign and his Court may be said to have retained a very
important measure of supremacy.

[6] This document is called the *Kai-Taishi sho.*

CHAPTER IX

ASHIKAGA SUPREMACY

1. *The Throne Humiliated*

WITH THE UNION of the two imperial lines Japanese political history enters upon a new epoch.

The prestige of the Throne, already waning after Go-Daigo's exile, had been maintained for a while by loyalist successes, but it could not withstand the domination of the Ashikaga leaders once the loyalist opposition had collapsed. Go-Daigo's administrative failures had served only to embitter many warriors, and in time their disappointment turned into positive antagonism. Indeed the aim of most of the warriors who owed allegiance to Takauji and his successors was not restoration but the destruction of the existing order. They believed only in naked power, and their attitude was well if crudely expressed by the words of Kō no Moronao: "What is the use of a King? . . . And why should we bow to him? If for some reason a King is needed, let us have one made of wood or metal, and let all the live Kings be banished." This was an extreme expression of a common feeling, as can be seen from the frequent accounts in the *Taiheiki* of brawls and clashes between warriors flushed with success and Court officers trying to keep order.

Best known of these is the story of a warrior named Doki. He behaved disrespectfully towards the In, the cloistered Emperor, whom he encountered passing with his retinue along a city street. Upon being rebuked for his insolence by a Court attendant, he shouted in drunken folly: "What is this In you talk about? If it is an Inu [a dog] I'll shoot it!" He and his men then charged up to the In's carriage and shot arrows at it. In the ensuing fracas the harness was cut and the oxen ran away. The grooms were helpless, and the In stood there as if in a dream, unable to repress his tears when a courtier asked whether he was hurt. Doki's conduct was condemned by Takauji and Tadayoshi, but as a breach of discipline rather than an offence against the person of the cloistered sovereign. He was arrested and in due course executed, because the Shōgun could not afford to tolerate the excesses of unruly vassals.

By 1368 the Bakufu no longer pretended to govern in the name of the sovereign. Takauji had made a cynical pretence of loyalty, but Yoshimitsu, as soon as he felt firmly established, worked steadily to reduce the Throne to impotence. In the view of some historians he even planned to found a new imperial dynasty of his own. The evidence for this reading of Yoshimitsu's conduct is strong, though not entirely con-

1368   Ashikaga Yoshimitsu succeeds as Shōgun. Ming dynasty founded in China

1369   First mission from Ming China arrives in Kyūshū

1378   Yoshimitsu builds the Hana no Gosho in Muromachi

1392   Union of the Northern and Southern Courts

1394   Yoshimitsu becomes Chancellor. Ashikaga Yoshimochi named Shōgun

1397   Yoshimitsu builds Kinkaku in Kitayama

1399   Ōuchi Yoshihiro rebels against Yoshimitsu

1401   Yoshimitsu proposes renewal of relations with China

1402   Yoshimitsu suppresses piracy at request of Chinese government

1405   Licensed trade with Ming China begins

1408   Yoshimitsu dies. Yoshimochi assumes power

1409   Ashikaga Mochiuji becomes Kantō Kubō

1411   Yoshimochi breaks off relations with China

1417   Mochiuji puts down rebellion of Uyesugi Zenshū

1419   Korean attack on Tsushima

1420   Serious famine with great loss of life

1422   Ashikaga Yoshikazu succeeds as Shōgun

1425   Yoshimochi resumes office upon Yoshikazu's death. A great famine and plague

1428   First large-scale peasant uprisings in Home Provinces. Yoshimochi dies

1429   Ashikaga Yoshinori succeeds as Shōgun. Risings in Harima and Tamba

1432   Yoshinori resumes licensed trade with China

1438   Mochiuji revolts

1439   Mochiuji commits suicide. Collapse of the power of the Kantō Kubō

1441   Yoshinori murdered by Akamatsu, who in turn is defeated and killed by Yamana. Ashikaga Yoshikatsu becomes Shōgun

1443   Yoshikatsu dies. Ashikaga Yoshinari (later known as Yoshimasa) succeeds. Violent agrarian riots in Yamashiro. Kyoto attacked by rioters

1449   Bakufu resumes licensed voyages to China

1467   Ōnin War begins

vincing. He did his best to break the power of the Court nobles by heaping indignities upon them. He would order them to perform almost menial functions, and at times he obliged the highest officers of state to take part in his ceremonies and processions as if they belonged to his own retinue. By threats or by bribes he kept them in the palm of his hand, and when he went on a pilgrimage his train included so many nobles of high ancestry that it looked like an imperial progress. He was on friendly terms with the Emperor Go-Kōgon, whom he treated with familiarity.

2. The Structure of Government under Yoshimitsu

The structure of the government over which Yoshimitsu presided had been developed by the loyal and capable Hosokawa Yoriyuki during the minority of Yoshimitsu in the years from 1368 to 1374. Thanks to Yoriyuki's experience and integrity, government under his guidance was stern and just, and unruly vassals were subjected to a discipline not unlike that of the Hōjō Regency in its prime.

This was the first time since the fall of the Hōjō that law was enforced and order maintained, although many barons chafed under its restraints. It may well be asked why necessary reforms had been so long delayed, since Takauji had become Shōgun some thirty years before and had exercised almost absolute power. The truth is that Takauji and his successor, Yoshiakira, were warriors, not statesmen. Both spent their lives campaigning and were often absent from the capital; indeed, they were more than once ejected from Kyoto by the forces of the Southern Court. Further, it is clear that Takauji had no interest in constructing a new system of feudal government, but was content to leave political problems to be solved by his brother Tadayoshi or other subordinates, who turned out to be unreliable. Thus the early Ashikaga system, unlike the Hōjō system, lacked a strong central administration able to devise and direct policy at the highest level. There was no person or organ fitted to control the great barons as the leaders of the Kamakura Bakufu had done in the previous century.

Towards the end of 1336 Takauji established his Bakufu in Kyoto and issued the Kemmu Shikimoku. The Kemmu Shikimoku was supposed to be a kind of political charter of the Ashikaga Bakufu, but it was in fact little more than a collection of moral platitudes drawn up by civil servants of the old Kamakura regime. It made no change in the laws enacted by the Hōjō Regents, and the Jōei Shikimoku (1232) with its supplements continued, if only in theory, to guide the administrative and legislative acts of the Ashikaga Shōguns until the accession of Yoshimitsu. The Ashikaga Bakufu took over, with little change, the offices and councils of the Kamakura government, the Monchūjo, the Mandokoro, the Samurai-dokoro, the Hyōjōshū, and the Hikitsukeshū, and the working of this apparatus remained in the hands of the subordinates who had controlled it under the Hōjō regime.[1] But although these organs continued under the Ashikaga Bakufu, they were less important than in Kamakura times, because the Shōgun and his high officers were inclined to make summary decisions. The Monchūjo, for instance, lost its judicial powers to the Samurai-dokoro, which was also charged with protecting the Bakufu, keeping order in the city, and administering the province of Yamashiro. The head of the Samurai-dokoro in Kyoto was an important functionary, responsible for public safety.

After Hosokawa Yoriyuki became responsible for the Shōgun's government, he was guided by the spirit of the Kemmu Shikimoku. It was a rather puritanical document, inveighing against what in current parlance was called *basara*, meaning addiction to what was smart and up-to-date. A hint of Yoriyuki's character can be caught in an edict issued in 1368, the year of Yoshimitsu's accession. It forbids, among other things, the exchange of New Year's gifts, the wearing of certain kinds of dress and ornaments, and the use of expensive sword hilts by warriors. It was mainly on such points as these that the adult Yoshimitsu, who did not care for frugality, was to take issue with Yoriyuki.

Yoriyuki's purpose was to strengthen the Shōgun's government, and his chief concern was to prevent both rivalry and combination among the great warlords, since either was likely to endanger the Bakufu. In 1368 the most powerful of these warlords were three generals who had won victories for Takauji and Yoshiakira—Shiba, Hatakeyama, and Yoriyuki himself.

Yoriyuki had been chosen in 1367 by a council of his peers to act as Deputy[2] for the ailing Shōgun Yoshiakira, who on his deathbed entrusted Yoshimitsu to his care. Yoriyuki took steps to secure the loyalty of his two ambitious colleagues by proposing that the post of Deputy for the Shōgun should be held in turn by members of their families. They were to bear the title of Kanrei (which took the place of Shitsuji) and were known as the Three Kanrei (San Kan), though it must be understood that only one at a time could hold the office. Yoriyuki held it first, for eleven years (1368–79), and was succeeded by Shiba Yoshimasa, who was followed by Hatakeyama Motokuni in 1398. The order

---

[1] In the Kamakura system the Mandokoro was the highest administrative organ, and the Monchūjo, the Shōgun's Court, was the highest judicial authority. The Hyōjōshū were the members of the deliberative assembly, and the Hikitsukeshū were coadjutors to the Hyōjōshū. The Samurai-dokoro, first charged with the discipline of the military class, assumed new functions under the Ashikaga Bakufu, including the protection of the capital. For details of the origin of these bodies, see *A History of Japan to 1334*, chap. xvi, "The Feudal State."

[2] An office which was founded in 1336 when Takauji appointed Kō no Moronao as his representative in Kyoto, with the title Shitsuji (Steward or Deputy).

of alternation among the three families was thereafter not strictly followed, but it continued in principle for a century.

Yoriyuki's position was much strengthened by this arrangement. He followed his first sumptuary edict by a program of legislation designed to assert the authority of the central government and to bring under control the warriors who were disturbing the country by their depredations. The laws which he promulgated were designed to protect the legitimate property rights of the Throne, of religious establishments, and of hereditary landowners. These measures were needed not only to protect the landowners (who were subject to illicit or excessive taxation imposed by the Constables as well as to the actual loss of land and revenues) but also to strengthen the authority of the Bakufu, which was being challenged by provincial warriors who assumed and forcibly exercised rights in property and powers of jurisdiction to which they had no valid claim.

Before Yoriyuki took office, Kō no Moronao and men of his stamp had been arbitrarily settling claims and issuing orders in the name of the Shōgun, and had thereby given rise to a series of disputes about land amounting in some provinces to complete revolt. Yoriyuki endeavoured to see that the claims presented before the court of claims were given cognizance, and he cancelled most of Moronao's orders. At the same time he relieved the Constables of certain onerous obligations imposed upon them by Takauji and Tadayoshi, reducing the annual levy of the Bakufu from five per cent to one per cent of their revenues. He also tried to improve the behaviour of certain monks of the Zen sect who, under the protection of Takauji and Tadayoshi, had become lax and unseemly.

In the execution of his policies Yoriyuki was at pains to consult and use the organs which had survived from the Hōjō administration. The hand-to-mouth administration of Takauji and Yoshiakira, which they regarded as a family affair, gave place under Yoriyuki's guidance to a well-organized and effective central government.

But despite his earnest efforts to improve and strengthen the Shōgun's government, Yoriyuki was not able to complete his work of reform, for his successes aroused the antagonism of powerful warriors, who resented his assumption of power and his strict judgments. The warriors pressed for his dismissal, and in 1379 Yoshimitsu, who feared that these great barons would revolt, forced Yoriyuki to resign. Thus Yoriyuki may be said to have failed; but the central organization which he had created continued to function to the advantage of the Bakufu.

(a) The Kantō Kanrei

The habit of appointing deputies (daikan) seems to have grown under the Ashikaga Shōgunate. The Kyoto Kanrei were within certain

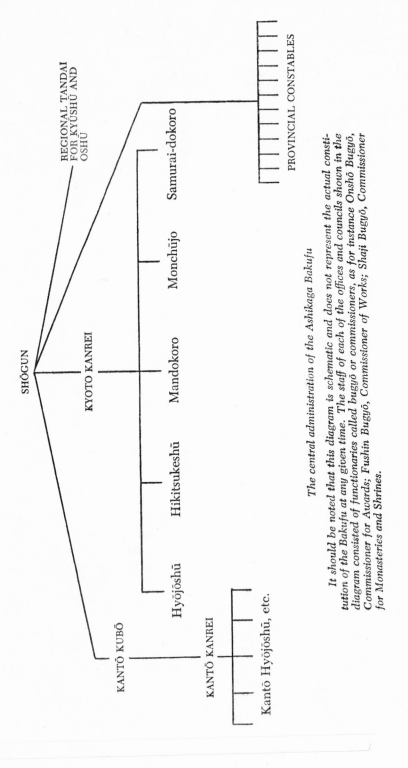

The central administration of the Ashikaga Bakufu

It should be noted that this diagram is schematic and does not represent the actual constitution of the Bakufu at any given time. The staff of each of the offices and councils shown in the diagram consisted of functionaries called bugyō or commissioners, as for instance Onshō Bugyō, Commissioner for Awards; Fushin Bugyō, Commissioner of Works; Shaji Bugyō, Commissioner for Monasteries and Shrines.

limits deputies of the Shōgun, and most offices had regular deputies. A Shugo-dai, for example, was a Deputy Constable, and the head of the Samurai-dokoro himself had deputies styled Shoshi-dai, a title which continued in succeeding centuries and was borne by the Tokugawa Shōgun's representative in Kyoto when the Bakufu was again established in the East. In some offices there were two or more deputies; there were normally four Shoshi-dai. In the Muromachi era the deputy tended everywhere to displace the principal, and this in turn brought about far-reaching changes in the constitution of feudal society.

After Yoriyuki's dismissal the Kyoto Kanrei held an advisory and executive position, and no longer acted as the Shōgun's Deputy. He did not make policy, but only carried out the Shōgun's orders, with the collaboration of the various organs and councils that formed the central government. In contrast to this limitation of powers, the Deputy appointed by the Shōgun to reside in Kamakura and govern the eastern provinces was a quasi-independent ruler, with authority similar to that of the governor of a British dependency.

The development of this office throws an interesting light on conditions in eastern Japan during the fourteenth century and after. In 1335, soon after the destruction of the Hōjō, Takauji had thought of establishing himself as Shōgun in Kamakura. But events forced him to return to the Home Provinces early in 1336, and he established his Bakufu in Kyoto at the end of the year. On leaving Kamakura he appointed his eight-year-old son, Yoshiakira, to represent him (under a guardian) as his Deputy. Yoshiakira was succeeded by Shiba Yoshimasa, and then by Yoshiakira's younger brother Motouji, who as Kantō Kanrei held the eastern provinces for the Shōgun from 1349 to 1367. Since Motouji was a child in 1349, the head of the Uyesugi family, then the most powerful baron in the East, was chosen to assist him as Deputy (Shitsuji).

Motouji was followed in hereditary succession by Ujimitsu (1367–98), Mitsukane (1398–1409), and Mochiuji (1409–39). The office which these men held was of great importance, since it was especially in the eastern provinces that discipline must be preserved in order to curb the strong aggressive spirit of the Kantō warriors. The Shōgun's representative in the East had powers so extensive that his office was known as Kamakura-Fu or Kantō-Fu, terms equivalent to Kamakura Government; and his authority reached over a wide area comprising not only the eight Kantō provinces but also Kai and Izu, to which the northern regions of Mutsu and Dewa were added in 1392.

Late in the fourteenth century the titular head of this government was given or assumed the style of Kantō Kubō. This in itself was an assertion of equality to the Shōgun, for Kubō (a term of Chinese origin used to denote the ruler) was a piece of Court language adopted by Takauji as an honorific title for himself and his successors. The Kantō

Kubō was at times called the Kantō Shōgun, and like the Shōgun in Kyoto he needed the assistance of a Deputy. This post was held by successive members of the Uyesugi family, who bore the title Kantō Kanrei. As the Deputy of the Kantō Kubō, the Kanrei carried out the government's policy in detail by means of an official organization almost identical with that of the central government. It included deliberative bodies such as the Hikitsukeshū and executive bodies such as the Samurai-dokoro.

The Kantō government caused trouble and anxiety to the Bakufu in Kyoto, because its successive leaders showed an attitude of independence so aggressive that it amounted to a constant threat of disloyalty. In 1399 Mitsukane was on the point of taking sides with Ōuchi Yoshihiro against Yoshimitsu, and some thirty years later the Bakufu had to send an expedition to Kamakura to punish Mochiuji for insubordination. Power in the Kantō was then seized by Uyesugi Norizane, and the office of Kantō Kubō came to an end in 1439 except as an empty title. But soon the Uyesugi family split into two factions contending for the post of Kanrei, and this also became an empty office, leaving the reality of power in the Kantō to be seized by a strong claimant from outside its borders.

(b) The Western Provinces

In western Japan there were the Kyūshū Tandai, provincial officers with limited powers, first appointed by Takauji in 1336. After Imagawa Sadayo's long term of service the post dwindled in importance, and by 1400 it was little more than a name. It is important to understand that neither in Kyūshū nor in the western provinces of the main island was there any true loyalty to the Ashikaga Shōguns. No Constables were appointed to those two regions without prior consultation with local magnates. In Kyūshū the great barons (Shimazu in particular), though not positively hostile, held aloof; and even after Imagawa's successful campaign of the 1370's the Bakufu seems to have chosen to regard Kyūshū as outside the range of its effective dominance.

3. The Enemies of the Bakufu

There were sporadic risings against Yoshimitsu after 1368, but he was able to defeat his two most powerful enemies, and his later years (1400–1408) were peaceful enough. Once the Yamana family had been dealt with, his only dangerous rival was Ōuchi Yoshihiro (1356–1400), Constable of several provinces in western Japan. There is a special interest in Yoshimitsu's campaign against the Ōuchi leader, political interest rather than military, for Yoshihiro's strength depended partly upon his influence over other western warlords and partly upon his close links with pirate chieftains in the Inland Sea, some of whom were engaged in freebooting in Korean and Chinese waters on his account.

The immediate cause of Yoshihiro's revolt was his anger at being ordered to contribute to the cost of building the Shōgun's Kitayama villa; but he had always been intractable. He had been preparing to attack Yoshimitsu for some years past, and his plan was carefully laid. Before making a direct assault on the capital, he intended to defeat Yoshimitsu in the field. He had the good will of Ōtomo, and before moving eastward in 1399 he saw to it that the Constables of Aki, Bizen, Nagato, and Suō (the most westerly provinces) were alert to protect his rear. As he was not confident that he could match Yoshimitsu in numbers, he sought and obtained further reinforcements from certain discontented warriors in the Home Provinces. He even contrived to get a promise of support from Ashikaga Mitsukane, the Kanrei at Kamakura. Having completed these precautions, he withdrew to the town of Sakai, which he proposed to make his base pending an attack upon the capital.

Thanks to the rapid growth of trade in the fourteenth century, Sakai had become a thriving commercial centre and a port rivalling Hyōgo in its traffic with Ming China and with other ports in Japan. It was an almost independent city. Early in November 1399 Yoshihiro installed himself there, building a number of turrets (*yagura*) as defences against attack across the Izumi plain and sinking wells to provide against siege. On the seaward side he depended upon a force of pirates, with whose help he expected to keep contact with supporters in Shikoku and Kii.

Yoshimitsu heard of all these preparations and decided not to risk an immediate attack on Yoshihiro. He sent his favourite Zen adviser, Zekkai, to persuade Yoshihiro to come to terms, but Yoshihiro was obdurate. Instead of giving way he took a firmer line than ever and produced a long list of his grievances. Zekkai therefore was obliged to return empty-handed, and Yoshimitsu saw that he must attack at once. He took command of the three divisions under the three Kyoto Kanrei (Hosokawa, Shiba, and Hatakeyama). From his base at the Tōji, he launched frontal pushes against the three landward quarters of Sakai, while on the seaward side pirates from Shikoku in the pay of the Bakufu sought to cut the line of communication from the western provinces. A general advance was ordered but was checked by the strong defence works that Yoshihiro had put up. For some weeks the fighting was indecisive, but in the middle of January (1400) the Bakufu troops, taking advantage of a north wind, were able to set fire to the town. The flames spread, and most of the warehouses and the merchants' quarters were destroyed. Yoshihiro's central strong-point presently caught fire, and soon after that assaults from every side broke down the defences and crushed the rebel army. Yoshihiro killed himself on the field of battle.

Yoshihiro received no help from Mitsukane, who had not moved far from Kamakura and was able to assume an air of innocence which did not deceive Yoshimitsu, but at least spared him from a clash with the Bakufu. This battle is important in political history because it was the prelude to a decade or more of peace and for a time established the position of the Ashikaga Shōguns. It is also of some military interest, since it marked the first complete investment of a large town which was not a military post,[3] and because pirates were used in the seaward approaches.

Early in 1400 Mitsukane swore fidelity to Yoshimitsu, and relations between Kyoto and Kamakura remained friendly until Mitsukane's death in 1409. He was succeeded by a violent and irrational man, Ashikaga Mochiuji, who was on exceedingly bad terms with the Bakufu. In 1415 Mochiuji rebuked his chief adviser, Uyesugi Ujinori, for rash conduct, and goaded him into resignation. Ujinori (who is usually known by his religious name of Zenshū) responded by organizing a revolt against Mochiuji and had some temporary success, thanks to aid which he received from nearly half the chieftains in the eastern and northern provinces. He captured Kamakura, forcing Mochiuji to flee to the hills and appeal for more support.

The Bakufu, though sympathetic to Zenshū, could not tolerate a rebellion against his overlord and were obliged to side with Mochiuji. The fighting continued for some time, but aid sent by the Bakufu to Mochiuji in early 1417 finally turned the tide. Zenshū and his close companions, hard pressed on all sides, made their way through a snowstorm to the Tsurugaoka Hachiman and there committed suicide.

Mochiuji returned to his post and his plots a few days after Zenshū's death. But Zenshū's revolt had put the Bakufu more on the alert than ever. Yoshimochi kept a stern eye on Mochiuji and as much as told him that he was in a state of war. During Yoshimochi's lifetime these uneasy relations continued, though there was no open breach. When Yoshimochi died without a natural heir in 1428, however, Mochiuji aspired to succeed him. He had no friends and no attention was paid to his claim, but he sulked and threatened when Yoshinori was chosen. One of Yoshinori's first acts as Shōgun was to exert strong pressure on Mochiuji, who resisted stubbornly for several years until a huge Bakufu force was sent against him and crushed his army.

It is useful to recall here that Yoshimitsu's defeat of Ōuchi Yoshihiro at Sakai did not put an end to revolts by powerful families against the rule of the Ashikaga. There were sporadic risings against them led by members of families that had fought for the Southern Court—Nitta and Date in the north, Kitabatake in Ise, and others in or near the Home

---

[3] It is true that Kamakura was attacked from all sides in 1333, but there was no prolonged siege. Kyoto was also attacked more than once, but it was never closely invested, since the key positions were at some distance from the city itself, at such points as Yamazaki, Otokoyama, Uji, and Seta.

Provinces. These were either suppressed by force or ended by negotiation during the years from about 1413 to 1415, while Yoshimochi was in power. Trouble with Kamakura was frequent and caused anxiety in Kyoto throughout the Muromachi period.

4. The Extravagance of Yoshimitsu

The ostentation and the lavish expenditure of Yoshimitsu outshone even the display of two illustrious spendthrifts who had preceded him— Michinaga (966–1027) and Kiyomori (1118–1181). The sums he devoted to building were immense. His first great venture was the residence he built for himself in the Muromachi quarter of Kyoto in 1378. This was known as Hana no Gosho, or the Palace of Flowers, from the beauty of its gardens, and strictly speaking the name Muromachi Bakufu dates from that time. After the Palace of Flowers came his splendid monastic villa, the Kitayama Rokuonji. There in 1398 he erected the celebrated Kinkaku or Golden Pavilion, which he used as a retreat after his retirement. The cost of his buildings at Kitayama (including the Kinkaku) was met in part by contributions from Constables and Land Stewards throughout the country. It is said to have exceeded one million *kan*.[4]

Although the Kitayama palace was the most costly of Yoshimitsu's undertakings, there was no end to his building of holy edifices and his contributions to pious undertakings. His very munificence suggests that his motive, when it was not merely an inordinate pride, was a desire to assuage his own feelings of guilt. In this he followed his grandfather Takauji, who in a similar way professed repentance for his sins against the Emperor Go-Daigo by building the Tenryūji. Another costly form of religious exercise in which Yoshimitsu indulged was pilgrimage to holy places, usually accompanied by lavish gifts. One of his earliest pilgrimages was to the Great Shrine of the Sun Goddess at Ise. This was an impressive affair, a procession on a grand scale with great nobles and generals. Its purpose was to conciliate the gentry and the shrine wardens of Yamato and Ise, provinces from which the Southern Court had drawn most of its support and in which Chikafusa was a beloved name.

Yoshimitsu also visited Hiyeizan repeatedly between 1393 and 1396, always in great state and carrying handsome presents. He impressed the Chief Abbot and the leading monks, and his generous expenditure of charm and gold made relations between the Bakufu and the Enryakuji harmonious for the first time in many years. He paid similar visits to the Kōfukuji and the Tōdaiji at Nara, and to important shrines. He

[4] The *kan* was roughly equal in value to one *koku* (five bushels) of rice, the average annual consumption of one person. The usual form of the *kan* in cash was a string of one thousand small copper coins.

was indefatigable in his policy of showing favour to the religious establishments.

Yoshimitsu's attitude towards the Church raises an interesting point
in the history of religion in Japan. The Shintō cult was the state religion
in the limited sense that it included certain traditional observances important in the national life—great rituals such as the Prayer for Harvest
and the Thanksgiving, in which the sovereign addressed the deities in
the name of the people. Buddhism, on the other hand, though not a
state religion, was the professed faith of most members of the ruling
class, and Buddhist rites were performed in the Palace. Moreover, the
state had control over certain institutional features of Buddhism, since
the conduct of monks and nuns was regulated by the Taihō codes of
702 and the Throne could grant or withhold the fundamental right of
ordination.

It would thus seem that the religious leaders of the country could
not directly participate in civil government. This is true, but in practice
the influence of the great religious bodies was an important factor in
political life. From early times the emperor and his great ministers had
been reluctant to risk offending religious leaders, partly out of superstitious fear of the unseen powers and partly because the monks and
shrine wardens could take advantage of their immunities and by a kind
of blackmail prevent the civil government from acting contrary to their
wishes. In short, the religious bodies could not initiate political action,
but they could prevent or delay it by practices corresponding to threats
of excommunication. They could, in other words, bring administration
to a standstill by menaces and even on occasion by acts of violence.
Obviously a determined government could have put an end to this
situation at any time by a display of force, but the sovereign and his
nobles were always averse to bloodshed and anxious to temporize and
negotiate.

It was only to superior armed force that these rebellious churchmen
would submit, and the military leaders were reluctant to use their
strength. Their own interests were not as a rule affected, and at times
they probably enjoyed the embarrassment of the nobles. Thus for several centuries both the Bakufu and the Court had usually abstained
from strong measures against the clergy, and consequently the influence
of the Church was substantial in all but matters of the gravest importance. It was, however, generally negative rather than positive.

The leaders of the warrior society had always been scrupulous in
their worship of Gods and Buddhas. Yoritomo was careful to bestow
favours upon the shrine of his clan deity Hachiman, but he also sought
to gain the friendship of the Nara sects of Buddhism by such pious works
as the restoration of the Tōdaiji. The Hōjō Regents gave handsome rewards to shrines and monasteries after the defeat of the Mongols. They
were strongly influenced by the discipline of Zen Buddhism and were
generous patrons of the sect. But none of them came near to the reck-

less expenditure of Takauji, let alone of Yoshimitsu, who taxed the provinces heavily and levied tolls upon trade so as to furnish the great sums which he squandered. Even this was not enough, and we shall see that he was forced to look abroad for further sources of revenue.

Although most of the numerous sects of Buddhism in Japan were tolerant to the point of indifference in matters of doctrine, they were very jealous of their rights, and would fight hard on a point of privilege. It was therefore not an easy matter for the Ashikaga Bakufu to control them, especially when it was harassed by rebellious vassals and unruly generals. Thus Takauji angered the monks of the Tendai sect in 1345 when he proposed to escort the Emperor Kōmyō to a grand dedication service at the Tenryūji, a Zen monastery, upon its completion. The Tendai monks protested violently and Takauji gave way. He was intimate with the great Zen prelates, but like several of his predecessors he was reluctant to come into open conflict with the militant swarm of the Enryakuji.

Go-Daigo's advisers were not slow to take advantage of this rift in ecclesiastical unity. In their struggle with Takauji they saw an advantage in friendship with the older sects, which were in general hostile to the claims of Zen. Throughout the half-century of the succession war, the Southern Court was careful to seek the aid or at least the good will of Tendai and Shingon monasteries and of the earlier Nara foundations.

Yoshimitsu, although careful to conciliate the older sects, was under the influence of the leading Zen prelates of his time, and it was at their instigation that he built the Shōkokuji, an enterprise begun in 1382 and not completed until 1392. His connexion with the Tōji is well displayed by the prayer (said to be in his own handwriting) which he addressed to that monastery in December 1398, promising to add a valuable estate to its holdings if the rebel (Ōuchi) were quickly destroyed. The Tōji, it will be recalled, had a special relation to the Court; and it had at times served as Takauji's headquarters during attacks upon the capital by the forces of the Southern Court.

Yoshimitsu's expenditures naturally affected the shaping of his domestic policy, and, as we shall see, his foreign policy was governed largely by his financial needs. In considering his domestic policy, it is important to recognize that he was not an upstart provincial magnate. He was by birth and upbringing a Kyoto man, with something of the true Kyoto elegance, at ease in Court circles and learned in points of ceremonial. He was at home in the company of artists and poets. In his maturity he bore the mark of success, for he had subdued his most dangerous enemies and his will was supreme. After the union of the two Courts, he allowed the administration which Yoriyuki had developed to become lax in some respects, and devoted himself to the satisfaction of his private ambition and his very catholic taste. But the administrative machine was well devised, and worked well enough without his close supervision. It should be remembered, too, that the period of his greatest extravagance came rather late in his career, when the country was freed from strife by the union of the Courts. The new society was gay and expansive, and it was not unnatural that its leader should indulge his own lively propensities.

There is another aspect of the Ashikaga dominance which should not be overlooked. The Ashikaga family was proud of its ancestry. Its senior members were of great distinction and commanded respect in the warrior society as heirs to the leadership of the Minamoto clan, which the Hōjō Regents had for a time usurped. This in itself qualified Takauji for the highest military office; but he and his successors could also count upon the powerful support of Ashikaga collaterals of considerable strength and importance. The list is impressive. In the chronicles of civil war, among the names which occur most frequently are: Hatakeyama, Isshiki, Momonoi, Kira, Imagawa, Shiba, Shibukawa, Ishidō, Nikki, Uyeno, and Hosokawa.

All these families were descendants of Ashikaga Yoshikuni, founder of the Ashikaga line. In the Muromachi era they usually, though not invariably, supported the Ashikaga Shōguns, and their leaders commonly held the most important offices in the Bakufu. Another powerful ally was the Uyesugi family, related to the Ashikaga by marriage, who played a prominent part in the eastern provinces.

Most of the important Ashikaga kinsmen were appointed Constable of one or more provinces, for the purpose of spreading the authority of the Ashikaga Bakufu throughout the country. The list is interesting:

Shiba Yoshishige	Echizen, Shinano, Owari
Shiba Yoshitane	Kaga
Hatakeyama family	Yamashiro, Kii, Kawachi, Etchū, Noto
Isshiki Akinori	Wakasa, Mikawa
Isshiki Mitsunori	Tango
Hosokawa Yoriyuki	Settsu, Sanuki, Tosa
Hosokawa Yoshiyuki	Tamba
Hosokawa Mitsumoto	Bitchū
Yamana family⁵ (three branches)	Tajima, Aki, Bingo, Hōki, Iwami

There were a dozen of these appointments as against six of "outside" families, such as Akamatsu, Kyōgoku, and Ōuchi.

In the long run these appointments did not result in the Ashikaga solidarity which Takauji and his successors had hoped for. Ambition was too strong and the Shōguns were, in a military and also a financial sense, too weak.

It will be noticed that the above list does not include the eastern

---

⁵ The Yamana family were not related to the Ashikaga, but they gave allegiance to Takauji and were rewarded with the province of Hōki; at one time they governed eleven provinces, although not with the consent of the Ashikaga.

provinces and Kyūshū. The only Constables in these regions were those originally appointed by the Kamakura Bakufu. As a general rule further appointments at Kamakura could not be made by the Muromachi Bakufu without the consent of the Governor of the eastern provinces. In Kyūshū the Muromachi Bakufu took the line of least resistance and left such families as Shimazu undisturbed as hereditary constables. In 1404 Yoshimitsu confirmed Shimazu as Constable of Hyūga and Ōsumi, and in 1425 Yoshimochi confirmed Shimazu as Constable of Satsuma.

The importance of the Uyesugi family needs some explanation. Its founder was of Fujiwara descent, a nobleman named Kajūji Shigefusa, who accompanied Prince Munetaka to Kamakura on his appointment as Shōgun in 1252. The Kajūji family took the name of Uyesugi on acquiring estates at a place of that name in Tamba, but they settled in the East.

Their (abbreviated) pedigree is as follows:

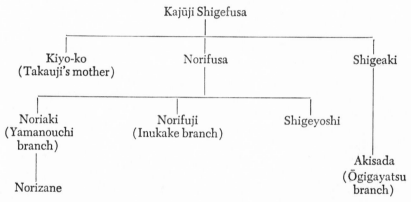

It will be seen that Takauji's mother was a member of the Uyesugi family. Takauji was born in Tamba.

5. Yoshimitsu's Relations with the Throne

If we may believe contemporary diaries and notebooks, Yoshimitsu was not only a King Maker, but took especial pleasure in assuming and exercising kingly powers himself. His term of office lasted from 1368 to his death in 1408, and during that period the reigning Emperors were Go-Kōgon (1352–70), Go-Enyū (1371–82), and Go-Komatsu (1383–1411). When Yoshimitsu became Shōgun there was a split in the Northern Court, and it was the support of Yoshimitsu's tutor Hosokawa Yoriyuki that gave the throne to Go-Enyū. Yoshimitsu could thereafter feel no great respect for the throne, since its occupant was his puppet. But in his private intercourse he was on familiar terms with Go-Enyū, whom he treated almost as a family friend. He used to step into the Palace as if he were at home there, and he would sit drinking with His Majesty

in a most easy-going way. On the surface, relations were close and warm
between them; but from the gossip of the day (as it is purveyed in writing) it seems that there was a quarrel in 1381 and again in 1382 after
Go-Enyū's abdication. Scandalous tales were told of the Shōgun's relations with Palace ladies, including even the favourite of Go-Enyū
himself. In 1383 Go-Komatsu succeeded, a child of six who was growing up as Yoshimitsu approached the summit of his power and his pride.
Yoshimitsu seems to have treated Go-Komatsu with affable kindness,
and he was also on familiar if not friendly terms with Go-Kameyama,
the cloistered Emperor of the Southern Court, who had retired with
dignity when the two lines were joined in one.

The two ciphers of Ashikaga Yoshimitsu

Obviously at this time Yoshimitsu completely dominated the sovereign and his Court. He stood at the head of the warriors, and at the
same time as Chancellor (Dajō Daijin) he was the highest civil officer
in the realm. He even symbolized this dual authority by using two
ciphers, one military, one civil. There were no more peaks for him to
climb, and late in 1394 (when he was approaching his fortieth year,
which in those days was regarded as climacteric), he retired and entered
the religious life,[6] resigning the office of Shōgun in favour of his son
Yoshimochi, then in his ninth year. He retained the office of Chancellor
of the Realm, however, and from his retreat in the Golden Pavilion he
continued to keep an eye on current affairs, to direct high policy, and
to plan the future of his descendants.

He had eight sons and five daughters, for all of whom he made ample
provision. He saw to it that they were appointed to the highest posts,
mostly as Prince-Abbots (Monzeki), or Lady Abbesses in nunneries usually governed by princesses of royal blood. There were two exceptions.
His second son, Yoshimochi, was named to succeed him as Shōgun, and
for Yoshitsugu, his third and favourite son, he seems to have had even
greater ambitions. There is no direct evidence of his intention here,
but it is clear that he secured the services of two most influential noble-

---

[6] After Yoshimitsu had been received into the order of monks, his head being
shaved as he sat before a picture of Musō Kokushi, he obliged a number of eminent
nobles and generals to go through the same ritual, and some of these were shorn
by Yoshimitsu himself.

men to further his designs. These were Nijō Yoshimoto, who had served Takauji and Yoshiakira, and the head of the Konoye family, Michitsugu. The exact nature of their intrigues is not known for certain, but they were without doubt called upon to obtain special treatment for all his children, and they were most handsomely rewarded.

When the Empress Tsūyōmon-In, the widow of Go-Enyū, died in January 1407, Yoshimitsu somehow induced the Court to appoint his own wife to succeed her as Empress Dowager. By this ingenious stroke, suggested no doubt by Yoshimoto, the Shōgun's family was linked with the imperial family. No objection was openly raised to this startling change; Yoshimitsu was now on the level of the Throne.[7]

In 1408, when the Emperor Go-Komatsu paid a state visit to Yoshimitsu in his Kitayama palace, Yoshimitsu's seat was equal and opposite to that of His Majesty, and the young Yoshitsugu, because of his family connexion, was placed higher than the Regent. He was treated as if he were a prince of the blood royal. His coming-of-age ceremony (Gembuku) was performed in the presence of the sovereign in the Seiryōden, the great ceremonial hall of the Palace. Whether in fact Yoshimitsu expected his favourite son to occupy the throne cannot be told, for a day after the ceremony the boy was taken ill, and he died a few days later, on June 1, 1408.

Yoshimitsu's entertainment of the Emperor at his Kitayama villa was a fitting end to his career as a patron of the arts and an illustrious spendthrift.[8] It began at the height of spring and lasted for twenty days. There were banquets, music, and stage plays (including performances of Nō, at that time little known outside a narrow circle). There were poetry contests, games of football, and archery matches. Lavish gifts of paintings, rich brocades and embroideries, and other precious things were offered to His Majesty and the lords and ladies in waiting. Whole nights were passed in drinking and versifying, or in enjoying the company of entertainers of all kinds.

When the festivities ended and the Emperor was escorted back to the Palace, Yoshimitsu set out on a pilgrimage to the Great Shrine at Ise. He died very soon after his return, in the summer of 1408 at the age of fifty, and Yoshimochi slipped into his place. His funeral was attended by several thousand monks.

6. The Influence of Zen Buddhists

In the development of friendly intercourse with China an important part was played by Zen monks, and indeed the influence of Zen teachers

---

[7] Zen monks sometimes referred to him as Rokuon Tennō, and in the Rokuonji there was a memorial tablet (ihai) inscribed with that imperial title. Rokuon means a deer-park, and refers to the deer-park where the Buddha preached his first great sermon.

[8] It is described at length in Kitayama Miyuki as an event of great importance.

on the ruling class in both countries was in some directions very great. Japanese monks who had studied in China were able to give to Yoshimitsu a useful picture of conditions there, especially in the eventful years following closely upon the founding of the Ming dynasty, and some had the ear of the Shōgun on domestic matters as well. But although in general terms it may be correct to say that Yoshimitsu consulted Zen prelates on certain points of policy, it is by no means certain that he was guided by them in decisions of importance. The point is of special interest in the political history of Japan, since any estimate of the influence of Buddhism on Japanese life ought to take into account the degree to which the rulers of the country were guided by its religious leaders.

The respect for religion displayed by many feudal magnates cannot be explained as a mere political device to enlist the support of powerful ecclesiastics. Yoshimitsu and most of the leading warriors of his day wished to be regarded not as upstarts but as well-bred and cultivated gentlemen. Many of them were genuinely interested in the arts, and some, like Yoshimitsu himself, made an effort to understand Zen teaching for its own sake. Historically the military class in Japan had inclined to a belief that there was a science of government which could be mastered if the right teacher could be found. It was this tradition, no doubt, which led men like Yoshimitsu to associate closely with Zen monks, learned men of high character who could not only explain the Buddhist arcana but also discourse upon the latest Confucian doctrine in political philosophy.

The Hōjō Regents had been ardent patrons of Zen teachers in the thirteenth century and had perhaps been influenced by them in their private lives. Hōjō Tokiyori was particularly devout. Later, the renewal of relations with China at a time when Zen Buddhism was prospering in that country had stimulated its growth in Japan. Partly because their monasteries were aloof from the quarrels of the other sects, and partly because they were men of talent and learning, the great Zen clerics gained the respect of the leaders of feudal society, who consulted them on points of literary and artistic taste and at times on questions of domestic policy. Musō Kokushi, as we have seen, was used as a go-between in negotiations with the Southern Court, and may have offered useful advice on matters of procedure. But there is nothing to show that he was asked for advice on major issues. On the contrary, he seems to have been very cautious, and reluctant to take sides.

He was followed by two of his disciples, both highly esteemed as scholars, Zekkai and Gidō. They were poets, men of feeling, steeped in Chinese literature, but they do not appear to have had any particular interest in political questions. They are remembered chiefly as models of piety and ornaments of the school of Gozan Bungaku, or literature of the Five Monasteries (Gozan)[9]—Zekkai for his poetry and Gidō for his learning. The exponents of the wordless doctrine contrived to fill hundreds of volumes with their works in prose and verse on both religious and secular themes. One might say that with but few exceptions, higher learning in the Muromachi era was a monopoly of the Zen monks, especially since they did not fail to combine their bookless meditations with careful study of the Sung Confucians. Some Zen scholars were men of acute perception in worldly matters, and a number of such men found their way into the service of Yoshimitsu, who had literary tastes and was disposed to use a learned cleric rather than an official as an intermediary in some of his negotiations.

Thus Zekkai, after he returned from a sojourn in China in 1376, was installed by Yoshimitsu in the Rokuon-In of the Shōkokuji, where he was close at hand for consultation. He was called upon to draft state papers, and of course he was useful in entertaining Chinese visitors, monks from the Ming Court. It is not likely that these men made policy, even if they helped to carry it out; their functions would best be described as diplomatic. Something of this sort is true also of Gidō, incumbent of the Enkakuji at Kamakura until he was sent for by Yoshimitsu, who gave him important benefices and took pleasure in his company. One useful illustration of the services rendered by Zen monks to the Shōgun is the despatch of Zekkai to Ōuchi Yoshihiro's camp (in 1399) in an attempt to persuade him to come to terms. It did not succeed, but Yoshihiro in his turn used Zekkai as a go-between to state his grievances against the Bakufu. Between quick-tempered fighting men an ecclesiastical dignitary made a useful lightning conductor. The diaries and memoirs of Gidō and Zekkai and their colleagues provide valuable "inside" information on the political history of their times.

These men certainly knew what was going on in Court and camp; and yet if there was a monk upon whose political judgment Yoshimitsu depended, it was not a Zen master but a remarkable cleric known as Manzai Jugō. Born in 1378, the son of a Court official of high rank

---

[9] In point of date the senior Zen monasteries were those founded under Hōjō patronage in Kamakura—Kenchōji, Enkakuji, Jōchiji. Later there was a similar group in Kyoto, where the Nanzenji was, so to speak, the Zen cathedral; in 1345 Takauji added his Tenryūji. Yoshimitsu took a particular interest in these monasteries as well as a number of lesser Zen monasteries in both cities, and rearranged them for hierarchical purposes several times. The order finally reached was:

Nanzenji
(the presiding foundation)

KAMAKURA	KYOTO
1. Kenchōji	1. Tenryūji
2. Enkakuji	2. Shōkokuji
3. Jūfukuji	3. Kenninji
4. Jōchiji	4. Tōfukuji
5. Jōmyōji	5. Manjūji

named Imanokōji, he was made Abbot of Kyoto's ancient Shingon monastery the Daigoji in 1395, and by 1425 he had reached the highest ecclesiastical dignity. He became extremely rich, acquiring estates in twenty
provinces. His advice was constantly sought by Yoshimitsu, who was
his uncle, and in time by Yoshimochi. He has been described as the
Black-robed Prime Minister.

To question the position of Zen monks as political advisers is not to
deny their influence as a class. They undoubtedly did an inestimable
service to their country in tending the light of learning in an age of disorder. There is much to be said against some of the pretensions of Zen
in the history of Japanese thought, but the attempt of Zen scholars in
Japan as in China to harmonize Zen principles with the Confucianism
of Sung thinkers is a sign of vitality in sharp contrast to the sleepy contentment of some of the older sects of Buddhism.

In China after the expulsion of the Mongols there was a revival of
learning under the first Ming Emperors, who claimed to be leading a
restoration of true Chinese culture. As a natural part of that movement,
the works of the Sung philosopher Chu Hsi (1130–1200) were established as the orthodox interpretations of the Confucian classics. With
Confucianism thus in the ascendant it was scarcely possible to grant
any special favours to Buddhism, and indeed Tai-tsu, the first Ming
Emperor, thought it necessary to admonish the clergy and generally to
control them.[10] The third Emperor, Ch'eng Tsu (1403–24, the Yung-lo
era), was friendly to Buddhism, but he set limits to the number of ordi-
nations and on political grounds favoured other sects than Zen. Although
Zen Buddhism flourished in Ming China irrespective of official control
or support, and the Zen doctors proved their worth in many fields of
learning, they never achieved the position of their fellows in Japan, nor
was that to be expected, since they could not hope to rival the leading
Confucian officials or the eunuchs who were near the Throne.

Nearly all Zen monks in China were versed in Confucian philosophy,
and there was among them a strong feeling for uniting the two systems
of thought. The Japanese Zen monks who flocked to China when intercourse between the two countries was resumed in the late fourteenth
century came under the influence of this school, and on their return to
Japan they spread its views widely. Their message was well received,
and it had some effect upon Yoshimitsu himself, for he studied certain

[10] Originally a Buddhist monk, Chu Yüan-chang took the name Ming Tai-tsu
as leader of a rebellion against the Yüan (Mongol) dynasty. He is usually referred
to as the Hung-wu Emperor, or Hung-wu, after the era name given to his reign.
Having been a monk, Hung-wu was familiar with the problems of monastic life.
He employed Buddhists as teachers, but he thought it prudent to establish a registry of monks as a means of supervising their activities and promoting discipline
among them. Yoshimitsu, following the Ming example, set up a Registry of Monks
(Sōroku-shi) under the direction of his favourite, the Zen master Myōchō (Daitō
Kokushi).

Chinese classics under Gidō, thereby (according to Gidō's journal) hoping to learn how to govern a country and keep it at peace. It is not likely that his researches bore much fruit, but he certainly helped to promote learning in his day, and he may be regarded as a patron who inspired some of the literature of the Five Monasteries. It is probable that such benefactions were not all to the taste of Gidō, who frequently said to the monks under his charge: "There is too much learning and too little practice [zazen] in our sect."

An account of Yoshimitsu's patronage of learning and the arts would not be complete without some mention of his interest in theatrical performances. He was reproved by one of his advisers for his addiction to watching the dances called sangaku, sarugaku, or sarugō, a form of entertainment which had been popular for a long time and had been enjoyed by Takauji.[11] There are passages in contemporary diaries alleging that Yoshimitsu's taste for the dances arose from his liking for the young boys who performed them, and this may well be true, for there seems to be a subtle relationship between aesthetics and sexual preferences. But it is certain that his ardent patronage of such spectacles and his association with some of the youthful monks or novices who took part in ritual dances at the great monasteries encouraged the growth from these origins of the Nō theatre.

He liked to hear prayers and sutras recited, and was not in agreement with the usual Zen practice of silent worship. On one occasion he ordered some Zen monks to open their mouths wide and to recite their scriptures in a loud clear voice. Perhaps this taste for the spoken word was one of his reasons for encouraging the Nō plays. It was no doubt thanks to his support that the actor Kwanami (1333–84) and his son Zeami (1363–1444) were able to develop the perfected Nō from its early elements, sangaku and dengaku.

Whatever may be thought of Yoshimitsu's record as a statesman, it must be agreed that by his interest and his bounty he helped to create an aesthetic tradition which was to make a deep impression upon Japanese culture after the middle ages.

7. Gidō and Yoshimitsu

Although it is difficult to point to an instance in which even the most venerated of Zen masters directly influenced the political decisions of the Shōgun and his high officers, there is no doubt that certain distinguished Zen prelates by their piety and learning made a strong impres-

---

[11] The Taiheiki (cap. 27) in a celebrated passage describes a great open-air performance of "Dengaku-Nō" in 1349. It was attended by all the great personages of the day, including Takauji. There were thousands of spectators. It ended in a tragedy when part of the staging collapsed. "Dengaku" is thought to be the archetype of the Nō performances.

sion upon the minds of some of the leading warriors. Musō Kokushi, as we have seen, was a gifted but somewhat worldly churchman, apt to give palatable advice to those in power; but Gidō was a man of a different stamp, for he combined great wisdom with deep religious feeling and true goodness of heart.

His journal is a valuable historical document, for besides providing a detailed account of the daily life of an eminent member of the Zen sect, it shows him in close and frequent intercourse with Yoshimitsu and the principal feudal magnates of his time. His conversations with Yoshimitsu, which are recorded briefly but concisely, help towards an understanding of Yoshimitsu's somewhat enigmatic character. For that reason, and because the journal portrays interesting scenes of life in the Zen monasteries of the late fourteenth century, the following description has been put together from relevant entries.

Gidō was born in 1324, was ordained in 1339, and becoming a disciple of Musō Kokushi, rose rapidly in the Zen hierarchy of Kamakura, where he was on terms of intimacy with the Kanrei Motouji and his successor Ujimitsu. These men respected him for his learning as well as his piety, and in his discourses he always insisted that since knowledge is essential to the man who would govern wisely, they must not let a day go by without study. He was from time to time consulted upon moral questions and always gave firm, straightforward replies. A leading warrior (Uyesugi Tomofusa) fresh from the battlefield said to him one day that it had been necessary "for the sake of the country" to kill a large number of rebels, and asked whose was the guilt. Gidō replied that the men who used soldiers were the guilty ones. The warrior chiefs hoped that religious observances would purge their offences, but Gidō always insisted that right behaviour was more important than prayers and vows and offerings. It seems that at that time a number of warriors felt scruples at least about killing prisoners, if not about slaughter on the battlefield, and perhaps such men were tired of the unending warfare of the era in which they lived; but to a true Buddhist to take life was a grievous sin in any circumstances whatever, and could not be condoned.

Yet, however sharp his rebukes, he was both admired and loved by the people of Kamakura. As incumbent of the Enkakuji he held the highest ecclesiastical place in Kamakura, where the tradition of Zen in Japan had been founded more than a century earlier. But after twenty years in the East he was obliged to quit a situation in which he was altogether content. In March 1380 a monk brought him letters from important persons in Kyoto, announcing that he had been appointed to one of the five Zen monasteries in Kyoto, the Kenninji, as of the beginning of the year. He said nothing of all this, and when asked by high officers in Kamakura whether such an appointment had been made, he said that he had received no order and that he intended to remain where he was. But the next day a courier came from the capital, bearing the paper of appointment. He was pressed to hold firm by his friends in Kamakura, and declared that he would go to Kyoto only to announce his refusal.

When he left he was seen off by a great crowd, which included Uji-mitsu himself. They gave him parting presents, and many of them were in tears. When he reached Kyoto, his protests were overruled by the Chief Registrar of Monks. His installation took place without delay, and it was attended by Yoshimitsu himself, before a congregation which overflowed into the courtyard. Soon after this he was escorted to the Muromachi palace, where Yoshimitsu came forward to meet him and accompanied him to the entrance when he left. From that time for more than eight years Gidō was constantly in close touch with the Shōgun, giving him guidance and instruction and pleasing him with entertaining talk.

When Gidō came to Kyoto from Kamakura, Yoshimitsu was a young man still at an impressionable age, and he was only thirty years old when Gidō died in 1388. In large part the call to Kyoto was due to Yoshimitsu's jealousy; he knew Gidō by reputation and could not bear the thought that his deputy in Kamakura had the privilege of Gidō's presence there.[12] He soon perceived the true worth of his new adviser, however, and saw that the relationship between them was something to be prized.

Gidō, for his part, had a strong sense of duty and a missionary zeal. He first instructed Yoshimitsu on points of Confucian doctrine, and then, by awakening his interest, gradually led him on to familiarity with cardinal points of Buddhist doctrine. Yoshimitsu asked why his Confucian teachers had given him explanations of Mencius that differed one from another, and Gidō showed him that in recent years there had developed two schools, one the old and one the new, the latter being based upon the interpretations of Chu Hsi and his disciples. Gidō added that since Sung times most Confucianists identified themselves with certain aspects of Zen teaching. In general Gidō incessantly urged upon Yoshimitsu the importance of study as a path to knowledge, to understanding, and ultimately to the wisdom which is essential for good government. In his judgment the visible decline in both religious and secular morality during the civil war was due to the decline of pure learning.

Gido's general line was to show that Confucian teaching could not contain Buddhism but Buddhism could contain Confucianism. From about 1382 Gidō seems to have persuaded Yoshimitsu to transfer his belief to Buddhism. The journal after this date contains hardly any reference to Confucianism, while it shows that Yoshimitsu, who was by no means an ignorant man, began to enter into the spirit of Buddhism more deeply than before. He was led gently but firmly into the realm

[12] He also stood in need of a companion in whom he could confide, for he had dismissed Hosokawa Yoriyuki a year or two before sending for Gidō.

of Zen. One day, after a memorial service for Yoshiakira, Gidō sat and conversed with Yoshimitsu in a little pavilion. Yoshimitsu asked questions about the day-to-day life of Motouji, the late Kantō Kanrei. Was it true that Motouji had asked for instruction in Zen? Gidō replied that Motouji was not adept. He could not concentrate his mind and dismiss irrelevant thoughts. He had asked his preceptor for advice and had been further instructed in the stages of comprehension. Yoshimitsu said that he himself was still not clear about zazen, the sessions of concentration which are the essence of Zen discipline, and Gidō endeavoured to explain the true nature of this discipline.

There was much discussion about right and wrong, and Yoshimitsu asked whether to take life was a great sin or not. Gidō replied that the sin was great, that it was a "deep" offence. They who killed would not long survive in this life, and in the next would fall to a lower plane. Yoshimitsu then asked about putting a layman to death for an offence against the law. Gidō said that in his opinion Buddhism did not distinguish between layman and monk in the application of its commands and penalties, but he would have to consult the disciplinary code (*ritsu*). Yoshimitsu again asked about the preparation required for zazen, and Gidō replied that first the mind must be emptied of all notions of good and evil. To think of those matters is to discriminate between this and that, and to discriminate is a source of error (because it conceals the comprehensive truth). Yoshimitsu went on to ask about the Pure Land sect's concentration on the name of the Buddha, and Gidō replied that this was discrimination. There is no division between Pure Land and Not Pure Land, for the Buddha-world is of one essence, he said.

At this point Gidō took leave, and Yoshimitsu sent after him messengers carrying gifts—cushions, paper, a pair of pictures of monkeys by the great Chinese painter Mu-hsi (Mokkei), and various perfumes and incenses.

Gidō liked to encourage Yoshimitsu to talk about religion and literature. He spoke of the great libraries of Chinese classics and the great collections of the sutras, recalled the number of volumes in the Tripitaka, and told how, just after a new edition of the *Genkō Shakusho* had been struck off, the wood blocks were destroyed by fire. Listening to such talk about the scholarly life, Yoshimitsu said one day that he envied the monks, since they lived to a great age. Shiba Yoshimasa, who was present, said that there was once in China a monk known as Chao-shu, who lived until he was a hundred and twelve years old. He was so respected that it was thought too familiar to mention him by name, and that was why he was called Chao-shu, after his native place.

On one occasion Yoshimitsu discussed the government of the country and spoke of the return of power to the Throne. Later, in private in his own apartments, he spoke confidentially to Gidō and another Zen monk whom he trusted. He went so far as to say that if perchance trouble should come—he meant a rebellion—he would take the line which the venerable Dōgen had recommended to Hōjō Tokiyori, namely to quit public life and devote himself to solitary meditation. It is extremely unlikely that he would have abandoned all ambition, but his words show that he had given some thought to the legitimacy of his position. It may be that at that date (1382) he was not confident of overcoming the loyalist armies then in the field against the Northern Court. But it is best not to take his talk at face value. Perhaps that was how he felt in the presence of Gidō, but after Gidō's death Yoshimitsu treated the Throne with very scant respect.

Gidō continued to instruct Yoshimitsu, who was now a firm believer and spent hours in frequent sessions of zazen. But Gidō soon yearned to return to Kamakura, which was his spiritual home and, as he believed, the true centre of his sect. Pleading old age and poor health, he asked Yoshimitsu to release him, but was told that although he might go to a hot spring for a cure and stay there as long as he liked, he must not resign. Gidō then asked the Kanrei Shiba Yoshimasa to plead for him, but Yoshimasa said that the Shōgun, although good-humoured on this point, would not change his mind.

Giving up all thought of Kamakura and seeking only to avoid the arduous routine of a great city monastery, Gidō secretly took refuge in a little hermitage on an island in the Uji River. He was followed by a messenger urging him to return, but he escaped in a woman's palanquin. Again he was followed and pressed to return, but he found his way to another retreat. There he was traced, and a letter in the hand of Yoshimitsu was brought to him. He was ordered to return, and went straight to Yoshimitsu's palace, where he was received in the private apartments. Yoshimitsu treated him with deference, and said that he could go to the Tōjiji, which was an Ashikaga foundation, and stay there without any duties. He then escorted Gidō respectfully to the door. Gidō repeatedly asked to be relieved, but Yoshimitsu was stubborn. He said that he needed Gidō, and that Gidō must not try to leave.

In 1382 Yoshimitsu learned that the Kantō Kubō, Ujimitsu, had selected Gidō to become the Chief Abbot of the Enkakuji, the highest ecclesiastical office in Kamakura. Yoshimitsu was furious, and Gidō, though he felt that he ought to be appointed, felt obliged to placate Yoshimitsu, saying that if he were invited he would go and hide in a forest. But he was growing visibly infirm, and one day when visiting the monastery Yoshimitsu saw this clearly and told Gidō that if he felt he must resign, his resignation would be accepted. But he must first choose a successor. Finally a choice was made, and in the fall of 1384 Gidō left the Tōjiji with the Shōgun's consent. He entered a quiet retreat and sent his thanks to Yoshimitsu in a verse saying that his kindness was like the ocean. Now he was free to enjoy the peace of autumn days and to fall asleep listening to the quiet rain.

Later Yoshimitsu found means of appointing Gidō to the Nanzenji, the highest office of Buddhism in the land. Gidō at first demurred and asked for a delay of one year. The next year, 1385, he was obliged to accept the appointment, but the ritual of induction had to be postponed because Yoshimitsu had a fever. At last in April 1386 Yoshimitsu went to the Nanzenji, accompanied by high officers of state and a great number of distinguished monks. There was a linked-verse party at which both Chinese and Japanese styles were used. The atmosphere was cheerful and the Shōgun was in a good humour, much enjoying Gidō's company. He noticed that Gidō's girdle was old and torn, and insisted on taking it and giving his own in exchange. There was much laughter and applause. When Gidō called to thank the Shōgun the next day, he was asked what girdle he was wearing, and both took pleasure in the jest.

Since the Nanzenji was now recognized throughout the country as standing above all other Zen monasteries wherever situated, Gidō thought that he was too infirm for such great responsibility. He tried to resign, but all the monks and all the lay workers combined to prevent him. They poured into the great hall to stop any ceremony from taking place, and they would not allow the drum to be beaten to summon worshippers. Gidō did at length leave the Nanzenji, only to be raised by the Bakufu to a special rank which placed him above all other Zen clerics in the country.

In March 1388 he went to the hot springs at Arima, ostensibly for a cure but in fact to complete without interruption the revision of an anthology of Zen writings which he had put together many years before. Feeling that his end was near, he made suitable preparations, entrusting his manuscript to Zekkai, telling a physician sent by the Shōgun that he was beyond medical aid, and giving instructions for his own sepulture. He returned to the capital after a month in Arima. Growing weaker day by day, he told his weeping friends that he was ready for death. By the beginning of the fourth month (May) he was sinking fast. On the fourth day (May 10) he asked what the hour was. The monk by his bedside answered that the Zen session of the midnight watch had just ended and the bell was now ringing for the dawn watch. Gidō sat up straight in bed and at that moment expired.

CHAPTER X

FOREIGN RELATIONS UNDER YOSHIMITSU AND YOSHIMOCHI

1. *Trade with China under Yoshimitsu*

DIPLOMATIC intercourse between Japan and China had ceased at the time of the Mongol invasions, but private trading was quickly resumed at the end of hostilities. During the thirteenth century there had been fairly frequent voyages between the two countries. The ships carried as passengers many monks going to China for study and some coming from China to Japan to teach in Japanese monasteries. Early in the fourteenth century private trade was continued by western barons, but the Kamakura government was too absorbed by domestic problems to pay special attention to foreign affairs.

When Takauji was well established as Shōgun, however, he had reason to encourage trade with China. At the instance of Musō Kokushi he had founded the Tenryūji monastery for the repose of the soul of Go-Daigo, but the building was stopped for lack of funds, and it was to earn money abroad that on Takauji's orders a vessel chartered by Hakata merchants carried a valuable cargo to China in 1342 and came back with a great sum in cash. The vessel was known as the Tenryūji-bune, and its voyage opened new trade relations with China of a quasi-official nature.

The early years of Yoshimitsu's rule were the years in which the Hung-wu Emperor, founder of the Ming dynasty, expelled the Mongols and consolidated his power. In order to increase the renown of his dynasty, he worked hard to make adjacent countries declare themselves tributary states. For that purpose he sent three missions to Japan, but they were detained by Prince Kanenaga at the Kyūshū Defence Head-quarters and sent back to China.

Hung-wu's purpose was to induce Japan to enter the Chinese empire as a tributary state so that he might bring under control the Japanese pirates who were ravaging his coasts. But the Japanese, despite their respect for Chinese culture, had a fierce national pride, stiffened by their defeat of the Mongols. They were not likely to submit to Chinese pressure. Moreover, during Hung-wu's reign Japan was split by civil war, and there was no ruler who could speak for the whole country. Even after 1392, when the two Courts were united, not all the great barons had submitted to Ashikaga rule; and before the agreement between the two Courts was reached, the Chinese government was in correspondence with Prince Kanenaga, the loyalist commander-in-chief for western Japan, supposing him to be the King.

The relation between the Ming Court and Kanenaga had an inauspicious beginning, for Kanenaga arrested the leader (Yang Tsai by name) of a Chinese mission which arrived in Kyūshū in 1369.[1] The Ming Emperor, however, kept his temper and sent another mission to Japan in 1370, with a message pointing out the advantages of peaceful intercourse and the perils of offending the Chinese empire by piratical behaviour. This despatch was admonitory rather than threatening in tone, and it was followed some months later by an almost conciliatory message brought by Yang Tsai. This time Kanenaga saw some advantage in friendly relations, and he sent a return mission in 1371. It was composed of Buddhist monks who took with them letters, gifts, and a number of Chinese who had been captured by Japanese pirates near Ningpo. The mission was well received in China, and Hung-wu responded with a mission of Chinese monks, whose leaders were of high ecclesiastical rank. They were given a magnificent send-off in a ceremony conducted by prelates of several sects, whose followers numbered one thousand.

These facts testify to the strength of the Chinese government's desire to reach an agreement with Japan for the suppression of piracy. Chinese pirates were doing perhaps as much harm as the Japanese since they had nests all along the China coast, and there were also many Chinese among the crews of Japanese ships.

Hung-wu's fourth mission reached Kyūshū in 1372, to find that Prince Kanenaga was no longer in power there. He had escaped from Dazaifu, which was invested by Imagawa Sadayo's armies, and had taken refuge farther south. Upon discovering the true state of affairs, the leader of the Chinese mission—he was an abbot named Tsu-shan—saw that he must get into touch with the actual rulers of Japan. This he did, making his way to Kyoto, where he stayed until the summer of 1374.[2]

The Ming Emperor was not convinced by Tsu-shan's reports, and for the next few years the Chinese continued to address their communications to Kanenaga, styling him King of Japan. Among them was a letter of 1376 which contained some threatening language, pointing out that it would be easy to invade Japan from China and that therefore Japan should take care not to give offence.

This language caused anger in Kyūshū and for three years or more no mission left for China. A letter to the Ming Emperor, possibly from Kanenaga or his deputy and despatched probably in 1381, took a very firm and challenging line, almost daring the Chinese to attempt an invasion and suggesting that they might get an unpleasant surprise if they did. But the letter ended on a friendly note, said that a peaceful settle-

[1] If the Japanese at this time had any idea of diplomatic immunity, it was of a rudimentary kind. They had executed several ambassadors from China before the Mongol attacks, and Kanenaga, although only detaining Yang Tsai for some months, executed several members of his staff.

[2] He was presumably not a Zen monk, since he approached the Tendai Zasu, the Chief Abbot of the Tendai monastery on Hiyeizan.

ment was best, and announced the despatch of an envoy. After this several Japanese missions visited the Chinese Court. It is not certain whether they were sent by the Ashikaga Bakufu or were emissaries of powerful warlords in western Japan. Kanenaga's chief supporters, the Kikuchi family, were in touch with China, and so were the Shimazu and Ōuchi families.

But in 1386 the Hung-wu Emperor refused to receive a Japanese envoy, and there was a break in the relations between the two countries. The Ming Emperor was obliged to devise some means of preventing piracy, and he turned to defensive measures. The movement of Chinese ships was restricted, and Chinese subjects were forbidden to go abroad. It was also planned to withdraw persons living on the coast to places a given distance inland, where they would be out of range of sudden raids.

But very soon two forces began working for a resumption of intercourse between China and Japan. The first was the policy of Yoshimitsu, who after subduing Ōuchi Yoshihiro in 1400 was master of the whole country and favoured amicable relations with China and the expansion of trade. The second was the desire of the Buddhist leaders on both sides to revive the free intercourse which they had hitherto enjoyed to the advantage of their faith. An unfruitful approach was made by Yoshimitsu not long after the union of the two Courts in Japan in 1392, but in 1401 an embassy arrived from Japan at the Ming Court carrying presents and a request for the renewal of relations. The letter—it was a memorial rather than a proposal—was couched in a very humble language and evidently gave pleasure in Peking. It was carried by a monk called Sō-a (possibly Sō-ami, an adviser much trusted by Yoshimitsu) and with him was a merchant named Koetomi (Koizumi). It changed the policy of the Chinese government, which seems to have been relenting somewhat after 1392, and certain Chinese monks were ordered to accompany the Japanese mission on its return to Japan. No doubt the accession of the second Ming Emperor in 1399 made a change of policy easier.

Yoshimitsu may have taken steps to suppress piracy before the despatch of the 1401 mission or at least have shown readiness to take action, but his first recorded action was an order (Mikyōjo) of 1402, sent to the Constables of the western provinces, instructing them to inflict drastic punishment upon the raiders.

The envoys of 1401 were well received by the Ming Emperor and a return visit was paid by two Chinese ambassadors. Their ship reached Hyōgo on August 29, 1402, and was met by Yoshimitsu. They were lodged in the Hōjūji and hospitably entertained. Thenceforward intercourse between the two countries continued on an amicable footing and without interruption until 1411.

In 1404, when the Ming envoys returned to China, they were escorted by a monk, Myōshitsu, sent by Yoshimitsu. He went back to Japan with two new Ming envoys, who carried gifts and a letter from their Emperor to Yoshimitsu. This was early in 1405, and the Yung-lo Emperor was on the throne. Several more missions were exchanged and met with a friendly reception. Yoshimitsu having taken action to punish the sea raiders, the Ming Emperor sent him a letter of thanks together with a large quantity of silver and copper coin and precious silks. Yoshimitsu's action against the pirates had been successful, and for some time their raids were suppressed.

In the course of these diplomatic exchanges, the Ming Court sent a special ambassador carrying a seal and a letter addressed to Yoshimitsu. This was the mission which reached Japan in 1405; and according to Chinese records it brought also a crown and robes of state. There can be no doubt that by these acts the Emperor of China appointed Yoshimitsu a tributary sovereign. The letter was addressed to "Minamoto Michiyoshi [sic], King of Japan." The seal was of solid gold, so heavy that it "could scarcely be lifted in two hands." It bore the same inscription.

Chinese sovereigns were in principle always willing to accept tribute from countries which recognized Chinese sovereignty, and it was their custom to make generous presents in return. It was on this basis that a trade agreement was negotiated shortly after the arrival of Yung-lo's letter.

The agreement allowed Japan to send periodical missions to China under a license system which gave a monopoly to the Ashikaga Bakufu and ensured that no other party in Japan could engage in licit trade with China. The missions were to be identified by tallies issued by the Chinese authorities, the whole arrangement being officially regarded as regulating the transport of tribute to China and return gifts to Japan. It provided for only one tribute-bearing voyage every ten years, but no attention was paid to this rule. Similarly there were conditions limiting the number of ships, the crews and passengers carried, and the nature of the cargoes, but it is clear that so long as both parties desired the agreement to continue in force, it worked quite smoothly without strict observance of its terms. The Japanese agreed to suppress piracy, and the Chinese in return not only permitted but even facilitated trade.

Yoshimitsu's measures to deal with the pirates were severe. He ordered them attacked in their bases and in their advance posts on the islands of Iki and Tsushima. Those who were caught were given no mercy. According to a credible account, one of the first missions under the new trade agreement presented a number of captives to the Emperor of China. His Majesty politely returned them to the Japanese leaders, who had them boiled alive.[3] The success of Yoshimitsu's measures was acknowledged by Yung-lo in a rescript at the beginning of 1406.

---

[3] A Chinese account of 1402 reported that the copper cauldron used for this excruciating punishment had been preserved *in situ*.

On the Chinese side, care was taken to treat the members of the Japanese embassies with consideration, and special lodgings were built for them in coastal towns. The terms of trade were very favourable to Japan. Each Japanese mission carried a number of articles described as tribute and accepted as such by the Chinese authorities. These were not treated as merchandise, but the Ming Court sent gifts of equal or greater value in return. The tribute varied little from mission to mission, consisting mostly of horses, swords, armour, ink slabs in ornamental cases, and quantities of sulphur. The return gifts were impressive. They were for the Shōgun and his officers and usually included silver, copper coins, brocades, fine silks, jade ornaments, pearls, incense, scented woods, and fine furniture.

The so-called supplementary articles carried to China by the Japanese were the real substance of the trade. They were sold to Chinese buyers by merchants and also by officials who travelled in the ships. The most important item was sulphur, the remainder consisting of the products of Japanese craftsmanship, such as swords, lacquer chests, bronze vessels, and fans. These were purchased by Chinese merchants and private persons, payment being either in kind or in copper coin. Certain Chinese goods, especially silk fabrics, books, drugs, and porcelain, brought an especially good profit when sold in Japan, as much as two or three hundred per cent.

The expansion of internal trade in Japan had increased the need for currency to a point far above the country's mintage capacity. As a result, Chinese copper coins gradually became an accepted circulating medium, to the point that prices were sometimes expressed in terms of Chinese currency, which was often stipulated in contracts. Thus the importation of Chinese coins was an important feature in the national economy. It throws an interesting light on monetary conditions in both countries. The Chinese had begun to use silver for tax payments in the Yüan era; under the Ming rulers the silver note was the standard currency, and copper coins were only subsidiary. In Japan the government was mistrusted by the rising merchant class, and the mint was technically backward, so that Chinese copper coins were particularly welcome at a time when their use in China had diminished.

In the last years of the official trade, the Japanese need for copper coin seems to have been satisfied, and its place was taken by raw silk and silk textiles of the highest quality.

During Yoshimitsu's lifetime the relations between Japan and China remained harmonious. Yung-lo, a wise ruler, was impressed by the efforts of Yoshimitsu to meet his wishes and was touched by a report that Yoshimitsu had seen his father the Hung-wu Emperor in a dream. He sent a high official and an important eunuch to Japan in 1406, with lavish presents for the Shōgun and a remarkable rescript praising the virtue and wisdom of Yoshimitsu in most flowery language. It prophesied undying fame for him and his descendants.

When this mission arrived in Hyōgo, Yoshimitsu himself went to meet it and escorted the Chinese leader to Kyoto, where he was entertained at a ceremony in which the gifts of Yung-lo were displayed. They were so lavish and magnificent that the Japanese were struck with amazement. A later Chinese rescript (1407) was almost ecstatic in its praise of Yoshimitsu. In response he sent a great tribute-bearing mission to China in 1408. His chosen emissary, the monk Keimi, was a good diplomat, for he asked Yung-lo (in the name of Yoshimitsu) for copies of two books written by Yung-lo's Empress. He received one hundred copies of each.

Whether Yoshimitsu's prime motive in promoting intercourse with Ming China was a desire for the profits of trade or an insatiate ambition is a disputed question. Chinese maritime trade as well as Chinese prestige suffered from the Japanese raids, and Yoshimitsu or his advisers would not be slow to take advantage of this situation to improve their own position. It is also possible to argue that to be saluted as King of Japan by the greater Emperor of China seemed to Yoshimitsu a step towards the throne of his own country. We know that he enjoyed impressive titles and plenty of money, that he liked to wear Chinese dress even at court, and that he professed to see the Emperor of China in his dreams. But there is no real evidence that he wished to succeed to the throne of Japan. It is quite likely that his expansive nature led him on to step after step of grandeur with no specific design in mind other than a general idea of increasing his own stature at the expense of the Throne.

One thing is quite clear. The Bakufu's treasury was almost empty, and both the Bakufu and the Shōgun were in such difficulties that they would sink their pride for a handsome cash revenue from trade. Later in the fifteenth century (ca. 1470–85) the Japanese government three times asked the Chinese government for a gift of money; but Yoshimitsu did not resort to such desperate appeals. The submissive language of his memorials to the Ming Emperor must have pleased the Chinese, but in all likelihood he had learned from monks and traders thirsty for renewed intercourse that the way to get concessions from Chinese dignitaries was to pour out supplications and flattery.

As for wearing Chinese dress and lighting incense before an imperial rescript from China, it was the kind of theatrical performance that Yoshimitsu enjoyed. The lavish use of honorific words and gestures was familiar to anybody who attended the court of Japan, and such a sentence as "In fear and dread, and kneeling again and again, I respectfully state as follows" would not ring false in a Kyoto palace. The letter carried by the Japanese mission of 1401 was accompanied by gifts of gold, horses, fine paper, fans, screens, armour, swords, ink slabs, and a number of

Chinese, doubtless captives of the pirates. Its language was very humble. The Chinese reply addressed to Yoshimitsu was friendly. Its preamble says "Japan has always been called a country of poems and books"—a charming compliment.

Yoshimitsu has been accused of treason because the reply to the Ming rescript was signed by him as King (王) of Japan; but it does not follow from this humble style that he regarded himself as a tributary. He knew his treasury was empty, and he probably thought that a little polite fiction was a fair price to pay for the benefits of peaceful trade. The real historical interest here lies not so much in the rise of Yoshimitsu as in the decline of the Ruling House despite its long tradition of supreme, indeed divine, authority. In all the negotiations between the two countries there is no mention of the Emperor of Japan.

Yoshimitsu died in the summer of 1408, but news of his death did not reach the Chinese Court until the end of the year. The Ming Emperor sent a special envoy to Japan on this occasion, carrying funeral eulogies and a letter of sympathy to Yoshimochi. The eulogies, composed in impressive language, were addressed to the deceased Shōgun, and notified him that special persons would be despatched to Japan to perform rites for the consolation of his spirit in the nether world. Yung-lo appears to have been genuinely grieved, and at the same time doubtful whether Yoshimochi would be as amenable as his father. In a later letter he urged Yoshimochi to follow his father's example and track down the pirates.

2. Relations with China after 1408

The envoy sent by Yung-lo to perform the special obsequies for Yoshimitsu was an important eunuch named Chou Ch'üan, who was also charged with appointing Yoshimochi as the new King of Japan. Yoshimochi, following his father's example, went to Hyōgo to meet the envoy as he came ashore. Chou stayed for four months in Japan, and returned with his suite in Japanese ships. In 1410 another Japanese mission reached the Chinese Court to express thanks for the Ming Emperor's gifts and his confirmation of Yoshimochi as the successor of Yoshimitsu. It seemed that Yoshimochi had accepted Chinese suzerainty; but if he had, he soon found reason to change his mind. In 1411 he refused to receive an envoy from China who (according to Ming records) carried a friendly letter and a gift of money from Yung-lo.

It is not clear why Yoshimochi took this line. His own explanation was that Yoshimitsu, after being attacked by the disease which was to prove fatal, had vowed never again to offend the national deities by receiving envoys from a foreign country. This is the version given in a reliable work called Zenrin Kokuhō-ki, a collection of diplomatic documents exchanged with China from 1118 to 1486. But there may be another and perhaps a deeper reason for Yoshimochi's attitude. Some modern Japanese historians suggest that he felt a deep resentment against his father for neglecting him in childhood, and that in his adult life he tried to banish the memory of Yoshimitsu. There is good support for this view. Yoshimochi would not live in the Kitayama palace, and he had several of the Kitayama buildings removed or destroyed, though he spared the Kinkaku. He opposed a high posthumous rank for his father and—most powerful motive of all—he hated his half-brother Yoshitsugu, the much-beloved child of Yoshimitsu by his favourite, Kasuga no Tsubone. Yoshimochi had Yoshitsugu assassinated in 1418 and was said to have been tortured by Yoshitsugu's vengeful ghost thereafter.

For six years after the refusal of 1411 there was no official intercourse between the two countries. Yung-lo was patient, and in 1417 he sent a message which, though rebuking Yoshimochi, left the way open for a renewal of good relations. But there was no response from the Shōgun, and at the end of 1418 Yung-lo sent another rescript, harsher than the last in tone, but still not closing the door. It is a remarkable document, worth some brief notice as evidence of a lack of mutual understanding between the two peoples. It is long and diffuse, here sublime and there ridiculous. Yung-lo is at pains to warn the Japanese that the Chinese armed forces are not like the Mongol invaders, who had been good at riding and shooting but not at seamanship. There was some truth in this, for the decades between 1400 and 1430 were the times of the great Ming voyages, which reached as far as the coast of Africa. But to point out to the head of a military government that the King of Korea was a sagacious monarch because he obeyed orders from China was not at all a convincing argument.

Yoshimochi's reply was prompt. He brushed aside Yung-lo's complaints and stated firmly that in view of his father's deathbed wish he would not receive any more missions from the Ming Court, and desired the envoys then in Japan to sail away. Accordingly, official intercourse between the two countries again came to an end in 1419, though there is good reason to believe that the Shimazu family in southern Kyūshū continued to trade privately with China.

Yoshimochi's firm attitude caused some anxiety in Kyoto, where it was rumoured that the Chinese were about to attack Japan. A passage in the diary of Manzai, the Shōgun's adviser, under the date of August 26, 1419, reads as follows: "While I was at the Shōgun's palace, in the middle of our talk a courier came with a despatch from the Kyūshū Tandai Shōni. He reports an attack of five hundred Mongol ships on Tsushima. Seven hundred men were hurried to meet the attack, and after severe fighting they destroyed the invading force, taking only a few prisoners alive. These were mostly Korean vessels, but the report warns that 20,000 Chinese ships are shortly to attack the coast of Japan." There was no basis for these rumours, and the story of five hundred

Mongol ships at Tsushima was evidently an exaggerated version of an attack by Koreans upon a Japanese pirate base. Certainly it was a false alarm, as were occasional rumours of Chinese warships approaching the port of Hyōgo. The next Chinese vessel to visit Japan after relations were severed was a peaceful merchantman, for the Chinese government proposed a resumption of trade several years after 1419.

In 1425 the great Ming Emperor Hsüan-te came to the throne. By that time Yoshimochi had entered religion, his son Yoshikazu having taken over his functions in 1423. Yoshikazu was then a youth of about fifteen, but his authority was brief and his policy unknown, since he drank himself to death in two years. In this he was only following his father's example, for the heavy drinking bouts of Yoshimochi with his companions Hatakeyama, Yamana, and Shiba are frequently noted in Manzai's diary.[4]

Yoshikazu's death in 1425 obliged Yoshimochi to resume office, but it is doubtful whether he was then capable of sustained mental effort. He probably paid little attention to the question of relations with China. After a short illness he died in 1428, at the age of forty-two, and was succeeded as Shōgun by a younger brother named Yoshinori.

No response to the Chinese overtures of the 1420's was made by Japan, but the Chinese were persistent. In 1432 the Hsüan-te Emperor sent a rescript through the King of the Luchu Islands, inviting the "King of Japan" to follow the example of Yoshimitsu and send envoys to the Ming Court. He promised generous treatment, using the words "good fortune without end." Yoshinori had no religious or political scruples and responded promptly by sending an embassy headed by a Tenryūji abbot named Dōen. There were three vessels, one from the Bakufu, one from a group of warlords, and one from the Shōkokuji, a Zen monastery founded by Yoshimitsu. The official envoys carried a friendly response to Hsüan-te's proposals and were handsomely treated when they reached China.

In June 1434 a return mission arrived from China. It was on a grand scale, consisting of five ships bearing as ambassadors high officials who had been charged to express Hsüan-te's earnest hope for friendly relations. They brought handsome gifts and made an imposing progress

[4] Indeed, intemperate habits must have been common at this time among the Bakufu leaders and even among officers on duty. The following extracts from Manzai are pertinent. 1419, viii, 22–23: "There was a great display of dancing in the Sentō Palace, before the Emperor and the cloistered Emperor. Muromachi Dono [Yoshimochi] was present. He entered the In's palace to change his costume. When he came out he was very drunk." 1423, i, 7: "On the fifth the younger brother of General Akamatsu died. On the previous day he was riding as an escort to the Kanrei's mansion when, being very drunk, he fell from his horse and was kicked in the head and other vital places."

Yoshimochi seems to have been restless and erratic even when he was not inebriated. He went from one shrine or monastery to another, attending religious services, watching dancers and mimes, then going into retreat.

through the streets of Kyoto to the Muromachi palace of the Shōgun. Yoshinori treated them well, though not with the submissive respect shown by Yoshimitsu. Among questions discussed was the suppression of pirates, who were still ravaging the coasts of China. Some modification of the relations between the two countries was proposed, but its nature is not known, apart from the fact that official trade was resumed. It is clear, however, that the Japanese wanted concessions which the Chinese were not prepared to grant.

We may here anticipate the subsequent course of relations between the two countries by saying that trade continued and the volume of Japanese exports increased until 1453, when it began to decline. The persistent reluctance of Chinese officials to meet the wishes of Japan after 1435 (the year of Hsüan-te's death) may have been due in part to annoyance caused by the behaviour of some members of the Japanese missions. They were forever quarrelling and fighting, and from time to time the Chinese authorities had to complain that Chinese subjects had been wounded or their property damaged. But what most influenced the Chinese government was Japan's insistence upon sending goods for sale to China in increasing quantities. China was not dependent upon foreign trade, whereas it was very important to Japan; moreover, the prevailing Confucianism of the time was hostile to all forms of commerce. The mission of 1435 carried excessive amounts of copper and sulphur, for which the Chinese refused to pay the quoted price. After much haggling the Japanese envoys left Peking under pressure from the Chinese Court, and the ships, having disposed of their cargoes, sailed for home. There were nine vessels in all, four from the Tenryūji and other monasteries, two from the Ise family (favourites of the Shōgun), one from the Kyūshū Tandai, and one each from two western daimyos, Ōtomo and Ōuchi. Thereafter, when the Ming government was faced with trouble on China's northern borders and Japan was afflicted by internal strife, official intercourse between the two countries diminished.

After about 1450 the Bakufu lost interest in the China trade, but ships continued to be sent by certain monasteries and by the four leading daimyos, Shimazu, Ōtomo, Ōuchi, and Hosokawa, the arrangements being put into the hands of merchants at Hakata, Hyōgo, Sakai, and other seaports. After the Ōnin War (1467–77), in which control of the Bakufu was grasped by Hosokawa Katsumoto, there was great rivalry between the Hosokawa and Ōuchi families, which spread from politics into the field of foreign trade. It became so acute that in 1523 a clash took place at Ningpo, where a ship from each party had arrived to unload. Ōuchi's men left after pillaging the neighbouring countryside in revenge for some preference given by the Chinese officials to Hosokawa's vessel. The Ming government thereupon closed Ningpo to Japanese trade. A few years later Ōuchi was permitted to send a ship, but the trade was dying, and it came to an end in 1548.

3. Japanese Pirates

Pirates are mentioned in Japanese records from early times. In the year 934 a celebrated Japanese poet, Ki no Tsurayuki, returned to Kyoto from his post as Governor of the province of Tosa. Describing in his diary his voyage along and across the Inland Sea, he refers to the precautions taken by the shipmaster to avoid pirate craft. Any modern traveller who has taken passage in a coasting vessel in these waters will have noticed the many inlets and channels where pirates could lie concealed in wait for victims.

The Japanese pirates of whom the Chinese complained were principally those freebooters whose land bordered on the Inland Sea or the shores of Kyūshū. There were families like the Kotsuna, who made no fine distinction between piracy and legitimate trade, and most of the western warlords had an interest in seaborne traffic. The Taira clan in general and Kiyomori's branch in particular had received much of their strength from that source, and after their defeat in 1185 the central government never had a firm hold on the warrior families whose property ran down to the shore.

The men who with their small craft had attacked the Mongol invaders or had transported troops along the Inland Sea to Kyūshū found their occupation gone at the end of the war with the Mongols; and since they were stingily treated by the Kamakura Bakufu, they could argue that they were driven to buccaneering. Their numbers increased, and they played an important part during the struggle between the two Courts, when they were organized under a kind of admiral named Murakami Yoshihiro, whose base was in the Iyo channel. As we have seen, they gave valuable assistance to commanders of Go-Daigo's armies, especially to Prince Kanenaga in Kyūshū. Those pirates who were not partisans in the civil war engaged in unlicensed trade, in kidnapping, and in other forms of robbery on the coasts of Korea and the Shantung Peninsula. They were feared in both China and Korea, and were known as the Wakō, the Japanese pirates.

There is no doubt that both China and Korea suffered greatly from the depredations of the Wakō, and that the Hung-wu Emperor spoke truly when he said that pirates were among his greatest troubles. The fault was partly that of the Chinese, for they were opposed to foreign commerce, whereas the Japanese authorities would have been glad to promote legitimate trade. But there were also reasons why the Bakufu was reluctant to go to extremes in suppressing piracy. It was not entirely convinced of the peaceful intentions of China, and looked upon the pirate chiefs probably as Queen Elizabeth looked upon Sir Francis

Drake—as a freebooter or a naval captain according to circumstances. Moreover, action against the pirates depended upon the Bakufu's control over the western warlords, and before 1400 Yoshimitsu was not yet firmly established in power.

With the defeat of Ōuchi, however, Yoshimitsu was able to take positive action, and his order sent to the western Constables in 1402 was couched in very strong terms. They were to take immediate steps not only against pirates caught in the act but against mere suspects as well. The Yung-lo Emperor's letter of gratitude of 1406 was a measure of their success. Yet even these determined measures did not succeed in stopping piracy altogether. It was too interesting and too profitable a profession to be given up by families who had followed it for generations.

4. Trade with Korea

Throughout the Muromachi era the Kyūshū Tandai and the leading western daimyos had kept in communication with Korea by annual or more frequent voyages. During this period Japanese pirates were active along the Korean coast, and in 1375 Yoshimitsu was pressed by the Korean government to deal with them; but he was not at that time strong enough to give orders to the more powerful western chieftains and therefore took no action. The King of Korea (Koryö; in Japanese, Kōrai) pressed him time after time, but to no avail. The damage done by the pirates was so serious that the King had to take defensive measures on a large scale. His efforts had some success, but were not followed up. Internal troubles in his kingdom ended in the fall of his dynasty.

In 1392, when peaceful conditions were restored under a new dynasty, in Korea—now named Chōsen—friendly intercourse with Japan was resumed, and trade relations improved to such a point that a number of Japanese emigrated to southern Korea (through Pusan) and carried on business there. But the Japanese pirates continued to raid Korean ports, sacking towns and emptying granaries, wreaking such havoc that the King made continuous protests. To these Yoshimitsu, through the powerful western baron Ōuchi Yoshihiro, gave an astonishing reply. He said that he would deal with the Japanese pirates, but by way of payment in advance he wished for a copy of the new Korean block-printed Chinese version of the Tripitaka.[5]

Time after time, whenever a mission went from Japan to Korea, the request was repeated; and not only by the Shōgun, for in 1409 the Kanrei Shiba Yoshimasa wrote asking for a gift to celebrate the foundation of a small chapel which he had built. The gift he desired was the complete

---

[5] The Tripitaka (Three Baskets) is the canon of Buddhist literature, completed in 250 B.C. It has three divisions, and its name arose because the palm leaves on which the text was written were kept in baskets.

edition of the Tripitaka in seven thousand volumes. Later Yoshimitsu's successor Yoshimochi was to repeat this request, and at last in 1423 the books arrived, with a prayer for the return of Koreans who had been captured by Japanese corsairs. These unfortunates were traced and sent home. When further requests for the edition were made by Japan, the Koreans said that there were no copies to spare, and for a time intercourse was broken off. But it was resumed under Yoshimochi and presents were exchanged.

It should be added that the Koreans themselves were not innocent of piracy, nor were the Chinese. Indeed it has been said that more than half the crews and many of the vessels of the so-called Wakō were Chinese or Korean.

The island of Tsushima, which had been Japanese territory for centuries, was a favourite base for pirates, being especially convenient for attacks on the Korean coast or on ships in coastal waters. The head of the Sō family was hereditary Constable of Tsushima, and the holders of this office usually tried to keep relations between Japan and Korea on a friendly footing. According to Korean annals, the Constable Sō who had been smoothing out difficulties in trade relations for some time before 1418 died in that year and was succeeded by his son, who was only a child. Thereafter, it appears, the affairs of the island were managed for a time by a pirate chieftain named Wada Saemon Tarō, much to the alarm of the King of Korea. Very soon large pirate craft were seen frequently off the Korean coast, and although most of these were on their way to the Shantung Peninsula, others were stealing supplies of food from Korean granaries. The Korean authorities were on the alert, and the King devised a plan by which in the absence of the Japanese pirates during one of their raids on the China coast, a full-scale attack should be delivered on Tsushima.

He overcame the timid objections of his ministers and issued a declaration of war in the summer of 1419. According to Korean records over 200 ships carrying 17,000 men set sail on July 17 and anchored next day in shallow water off the shore of Tsushima at a point called Ōzaki. They had with them provisions for sixty-five days, and Sō (or his advisers), aware that they meant to land, made careful preparations for defence. The Koreans put ashore a large force on July 19, which Sō cleverly ambushed and defeated. Sō then made a friendly truce with the invaders, who withdrew a few days later.

The story of this affair as it reached Kyoto was incorrect in almost every particular and caused great alarm. The Koreans' demonstrations of anger seem to have had more effect than their military effort, for after this incident Japanese pirates confined their depredations to the coast of China. Relations between Japan and Korea were soon resumed in comparative harmony, and trade flourished.

The chief articles of trade were pottery, cotton thread, and textiles from Korea, and sulphur and copper from Japan. Japan was relatively late among the countries of eastern Asia in cultivating and using cotton, the usual dress material other than silk being coarse or fine linen. The Koreans learned the use of cotton from China and were growing and weaving it before 1400.

One reason why the Bakufu and the western daimyos wished to promote trade with Korea was their desire to obtain copper coins. Both Chinese coins and coins minted in Korea circulated there. Japanese efforts to take them out of the country embarrassed the Korean government, who placed an embargo on their export. But despite this restriction the flow of coins from Korea to Japan seems to have continued throughout the fifteenth century.

5. *Trade with the Luchu Islands*

Among exports from Japan to Korea were certain tropical products brought to Hakata from the Luchu (Ryūkyū) Islands. The trade of the Luchu Islands with Japan is of peculiar interest. In the fourteenth century, Hakata in Kyūshū was an important entrepôt in East Asian trade. It was frequently visited by ships from Ming China and from Korea. According to Chinese records Luchuan ships often called there and also at Bōnotsu, a port in Shimazu territory. From this time the connexion between Satsuma and the Islands was especially close.

Japanese ships frequently entered Luchu ports (principally Naha), where they purchased for sale in Korea and China articles from southern countries—Indonesia and Malaya. The triangular trade began shortly before the fall of Kōrai. The voyages of the Luchuan craft were quite remarkable, for they reached as far as Siam, Burma, Sumatra, and Java. Every year the Luchu traders would collect Chinese porcelain and silk and Japanese swords, fans, and sulphur, and exchange them for tropical products, such as the spices and perfumes of Indonesia. They made use of the monsoons, and in order to find favourable winds the ships went by way of the Fukien coast to Malacca and thence to their several destinations across the seas east and west of Malaya.

The islands were unified under a king in the early years of the fifteenth century. He sent envoys to Ming China and also approached the Bakufu through the Shimazu leader at Bōnotsu.

CHAPTER XI

ECONOMIC GROWTH

1. *Increased Production*

AT THE DEATH of the Shōgun Yoshimochi in 1428, the Ashikaga Bakufu had been in existence for close to a century, and during that time
hardly a year had passed without some episode of violence. The armed
conflict between the two Courts had lasted for fifty years, and when
that issue was resolved, the Ashikaga leaders had to deal with insubordinate warlords from one end of the country to the other.

It might be supposed that the national economy would suffer from
the plague of armies and the depredations of greedy barons. But mediaeval warfare was not in fact especially deadly or destructive. The
damage done by warfare to the true economic foundation of the country,
its rice fields and its forests, was almost negligible. The industrious cultivators were usually unhurt, though from time to time they were incon-
venienced by being conscripted for war service. Even the country's
total loss in manpower was not serious, for death in battle was not so
common as the military romances would have us believe, and few civilians were killed.

Indeed the civil wars in some respects served to stimulate and not
to reduce economic activity. There were campaigns in almost every
province, and armies moved for long distances, thus creating a need for
the services of local entrepreneurs in the procurement, storage, and
transport of supplies and the improvement of communications. There
is no evidence, moreover, that the total product of agriculture and
industry declined during the civil wars. On the contrary, it seems to
have increased; and there is no doubt that the renewal of traffic with
China gave a stimulus to commerce in general, partly because it opened
a new market for Japanese goods, but also because it created a plentiful
supply of copper coins, which facilitated all kinds of transactions in
domestic trade.

There can be no doubt that the economy of Japan at the simple level
of the early days of the Kamakura Bakufu could not have sustained the
almost continuous wars that began with the defeat of the Hōjō in 1333.
There is, it is true, no statistical basis for assuming a great increase in
production during the thirteenth century, but it is only on this assumption that we can account for the nature and scale of the succession wars.
There are doubts about the exact numbers of the contending armies, but
it is certain that very large bodies of men were supplied with food and
arms as they moved often hundreds of miles along and across the
whole country. The wars of succession could not have been fought on

the reckless scale they were had there not been a flourishing economy upon which the generals of the two Courts could depend.

The factors affecting the growth of the economy in the hundred years before 1333 are complex, and need not be discussed in detail here. It is enough to say that the years of peace after the Gempei War (1185) saw a steady increase in the total product of agriculture and an advance in the manufacture and use of farm implements. These trends had their roots in certain social changes that were transforming the rural areas and gradually undermining the foundations of the Kamakura Bakufu. Social developments will be considered in the next chapter, but it is important to notice here the gradual change in the system of inheritance. In the early Kamakura period it was customary for a father to bequeath his whole estate to one of his sons, thus providing the Bakufu with direct vassals and preserving the family in its accustomed position in the complex land-ownership system that was the foundation of mediaeval feudalism in Japan. But gradually the practice of sole inheritance (sōryō)[1] was abandoned, and estates came to be divided more or less equally among the sons of the family, with the result that after a generation or so the area of a single holding fell sharply.[2] It is difficult to express the rate of diminution in averages, but it would not be unusual for a total family holding of 100 chō (250 acres) to fall within a generation to five individual holdings of 20 chō.

The decrease in the size of individual holdings, as one might expect, brought about an increase in the productivity of the land. From midway in the Kamakura period the small landholders devoted their energy to increasing the yield of their farms, and as the new inheritance system gained acceptance they were of necessity emulated by the sons of large landholders. Seeking the maximum yield from every chō, they imposed

[1] The word sōryō, often used loosely to mean "eldest son," strictly speaking means "the whole estate."

[2] This is well illustrated in the history of the Ōno manor in the province of Bungo. This fief was granted to Ōtomo, Constable of Bungo and Buzen, in 1240. Its area was 307 chō, or about 750 acres. When Ōtomo died, his widow inherited the whole estate, which she held for seventeen years. On her death it was divided among her sons, except for a portion which Ōno (the original owner) was allowed to retain for life. In the third generation the whole area had been divided into ten portions held by ten different legatees, their respective areas being 3, 33, 36, 35, 25, 76, 89, 22, 5, and 3 chō. Details will be found in Maki Kenji, Nihon Hōkenseido Seiritsu-shi.

Similar evidence is furnished by analysis of the history of a monastic shō over a longer period. In 1189 it was composed of 90 portions held by different persons, while in 1343 there were 149 holders of portions in the same area. The change in the size of the holdings is indicated by the record that in 1189 there were 7 holdings over 10 chō and 29 holdings under 1/2 chō, while in 1343 there were 96 holdings under 1/2 chō and only one over 10 chō. Full particulars are in Nagahara, Nihon Hōken Shakai Ron.

On the general question of succession and inheritance there is a very clear exposition in Joüon des Longrais, L'Est et l'Ouest (Tokyo: Maison Franco-Japonaise, 1959).

strict discipline upon their workers as they passed from extensive to intensive farming, and even, in some areas, to double-cropping.

As the total product of agriculture and manufacturing increased, there was in many commodities an excess over the producers' needs, which encouraged the development of market places and shops, and ultimately led to an all-round increase in facilities for the exchange of goods. Such an increase in the number of transactions could scarcely have taken place without the aid of a circulating medium to hasten the passage from barter to purchase; and conversely, of course, the availability of cash multiplied the number of transactions. This kind of development, though immediately profitable to individuals, had the effect of raising the standard of living and causing the less efficient cultivators to contract debts, a process accelerated by the rapidly expanding circulation of metallic currency and a consequent rise in prices in terms of coins.

A related factor in the growth of the economy was the improved position of the peasants, who in several areas, particularly in the Home Provinces, had acquired virtually complete freedom. There by the late fourteenth century the peasants constituted an important class of small farmers who found it to their advantage to form associations in their villages, and also to combine with similar bodies in other villages so as to further their interests by joint action. Their freedom gave them an incentive to improve their position, and those who lived near a town or a great city like Kyoto or Nara found it profitable to sell their produce for cash. They had a ready market for their rice and vegetables, and also for articles of handicraft made in their spare time.

This traffic encouraged them to increase production, and the desire for greater and more diversified crops resulted in a steady improvement in agricultural methods. Special attention was naturally paid to intensive cultivation of rice, the staple food crop. Efforts were made to avoid an unbalanced distribution of labour at crucial times, care being taken in the selection of seeds so as to spread the period of growth and ripening. Early, middle, and late crops were cultivated in part because of local conditions of climate, but no doubt also for the purpose of reducing the risk of total loss by storm or other misfortunes. In the collection of seed rice, grades of quality were carefully distinguished.

In the thirteenth century a strain of rice from Indo-China (Champa) was introduced by way of China. It was appreciated by growers because of its early ripening and its resistance to cold and to pests, and by the end of the fourteenth century it was widely grown in the western provinces. According to the records of the Daigoji manors in Sanuki and Harima, about one-third of their tax rice was of this strain. It was a low-grade rice in colour and flavour, but it was consumed in quantity by the poorer classes.

The cultivation of barley was taken up with energy in the thirteenth century, and the total crop increased rapidly. The Kamakura Bakufu encouraged double-cropping, ordering farmers to plant barley in rice fields after the rice harvest. Early in the Muromachi period visitors from Korea were impressed by the rotation of crops (rice–barley–buckwheat) in the fertile area near Amagasaki.

Vegetables were grown in variety, and tea became an important article of commerce. Tea estates were common in the neighbourhood of Uji, where Yoshimitsu ordered the tea bush to be planted. Other crops grown by the farmers where conditions were suitable were hemp, mulberry leaves for silkworms, vegetable dyestuffs (particularly indigo), lacquer, and sesame for lamp oil.

Fresh fruits were not an ordinary article of diet, but the new Muromachi society had a taste for luxuries. This encouraged the supply of melons and persimmons of improved varieties, and also of fresh vegetables grown in market gardens for sale in the city. In general, however, preserved fruits and sweetmeats were most appreciated—pickled plums, dried persimmons, and later flavoured jellies, such as satō-yōkan.

Sugar was scarce. It had been imported in small quantities from China and the Luchu (Ryūkyū) Islands in the twelfth century, and on a larger scale after the opening of trade relations with Ming China, but it was still highly prized as a luxury at the end of the fifteenth century.

2. Money Economy

The use of metallic currency goes back a long way in Japanese history, but the most rapid increase in its circulation took place from the end of the twelfth century. One of the first clear mentions of the growth of monetary transactions is a passage in the *Hyakurenshō* under the date 1179, which says: "There is a strange sickness going round the country nowadays. It is called the money disease." In conservative Court circles the use of coins was thought (not without some reason) to upset the price of commodities, and even so grave a statesman as Kujō Kanezane, writing in the 1180's, said that the decay of government at this time was due entirely to these coins. But no order, whether of the Court or the Bakufu, could be enforced against the use of Chinese copper cash, which were being freely imported and became legal tender in 1226, when certain kinds of barter were prohibited.

Thereafter their use increased rapidly. By 1261, when the Kamakura Bakufu was in its prime, we find the Regent sending gold to China for the purchase of copper coins, and before long they were legal tender for the payment of taxes as well as in ordinary private transactions. By 1300 there was perhaps ten times as much metal currency in circulation as there had been a century earlier.

This increase can be correlated to the growth of market places and market towns, for there can be little doubt that the function of markets became more and more important, and more essential to the total economy, as cash transactions became usual. In addition, the use of metallic currency was of great advantage to producers who had hitherto been obliged to send their goods, whether farm produce or manufactures, for long distances by road as tax or tribute, or as payments to a landlord.

As we have seen, trade with China was severely curtailed during the reign of the Mongol dynasty, with the result that the amount of currency available failed to keep pace with the growth of the economy. These circumstances explain the massive imports of copper coins from China during the years when Yoshimitsu and his successors were in treaty relations with the Ming government and trade between the two countries was flourishing.

An interesting feature of the circulation of copper coins in the fifteenth century is the official recognition of "bad" coins. The relative values of "good," "medium," and "bad" coins were established by regulations on *erizeni* or the classification of coins. The "bad" coins were usually counterfeits made in Japan.

3. The Growth of Towns

The great cities of Japan in the middle ages—Kyoto, Nara, and Kamakura—were originally planned and built as either political or religious centres, although their position was decided principally on economic grounds, such as the proximity of fertile land, the supply of good water, and the ease of communication by road and river. Many of the great cities of present-day Japan grew up in a very different manner, beginning as temporary trading-posts or way stations and growing into markets and then market towns as economic pressures and opportunities increased. Few such towns attained any great size until the fourteenth century.

What population would justify describing a group of dwellings and other buildings as a town must be a matter of arbitrary choice. Perhaps a concentration in one locality of about two hundred houses, with a population on the order of one thousand, might be regarded as a small town in the fourteenth century. The following account should be read in the light of this assumption.

Most large manors in the Kamakura period had within their boundaries or at their gates a market place (often with permanent buildings of a simple kind), and similar settlements commonly grew up outside or just within the gates of monasteries and shrines, many of which owned and managed rich estates. Here buyers and sellers would gather on fixed days of the month, generally at intervals of ten days. Thus the Two-Day Market (*futsuka-ichi*) was not a market lasting for two days, but one held on the 2d, 12th, and 22d days of the month. The fact that more frequent market days were unusual until the mid-fourteenth century is an indication of the still quite limited needs of the time.

So long as the economy remained simple, the great estates were self-supporting in food, implements, and other supplies, except for salt, dried fish, and certain metals. But as the variety as well as the quantity of products increased and the need for markets became greater, these market places grew rapidly in number and size. By about 1350 they were spread in a network over the whole country, with the greatest concentration in the Home Provinces, where the population was dense and the soil fertile. Markets grew up in a great variety of locations, not only near centres of production but also at key points on roads and waterways.

During the fourteenth and fifteenth centuries, as the rural economy developed and the growing use of currency facilitated the sale of produce near the farms, the number of market days rose from three to six each month. Thus traders were encouraged to establish permanent stores in the market place, and to build small houses for themselves in the vicinity. Itinerant vendors also appeared at the market places, bringing merchandise from other provinces—lightweight goods such as cloth carried in bundles on their own backs, heavy goods such as salt or iron tools loaded upon the back of a horse or an ox. These small centres gradually became large villages or modest towns, an evolution revealed by the names of several modern towns, such as Yokkaichi, which began as a market place open on the "four" days of the month (the 4th, 14th, and 24th). By the end of the fifteenth century many of these towns, some of them no longer small, were trafficking in large amounts of goods in great variety.

There is useful information on these mediaeval markets in a somewhat surprising source: the ōrai-mono, or correspondence manuals, which were used as textbooks for the education of young persons either at home or in monasteries. One of the most interesting of these is the Teikin Ōrai, attributed to a Zen monk named Gen-ye who flourished in the middle of the fourteenth century. It is in the form of letters giving useful information about current affairs and institutions. One letter gives a list of the special products from all parts of the country which were on sale at the leading markets. It shows a great variety, including besides agricultural produce a wide range of manufactured goods, such as textiles, plain and dyed; paper; straw mats and reed blinds; pans, pots, and kettles; needles; spades and hoes; cutlery; lacquer goods; and a number of articles made by farm workers in their spare time.

Another letter gives an imposing list of skilled artisans—early evidence of the great tradition of craftsmanship in Japan. It includes workers in silver, copper, and iron; dyers; damask weavers; potters; lacquer makers; artists in lacquer; bowyers and fletchers; painters and sculptors; calligraphers; and makers of rouge, face powder, and other cosmetics, including eyebrow pencils, a specialty of the Ninnaji monastery.

The development of these crafts (no longer the work of half-free servants in a manor) naturally produced a new class of independent artisans, men who welcomed the chance to exercise their calling where

Drawing of a bowyer, after an illustration in "Shichijūichi-ban Uta-awase," a picture scroll portraying a poetry contest of seventy-one matches between competitors of different trades and professions

they could be sure of a supply of materials and tools, and also of a market for their product. Their needs to some extent determined the locations of towns, and conversely they were attracted to towns from the rural areas.

But what chiefly decided the situation of towns, particularly in the earlier period, was the number of buyers who lived in the vicinity or who passed through on some frequented route. Of such positions, those near or within the precincts of an important monastery or shrine and those at relay stations on a well-travelled highroad were the most favourable. The permanent market at the gateway of a powerful religious body could depend upon the protection of that body as well as upon the custom of its members and the crowd of pilgrims and worshippers by whom it was visited.

Consequently the first towns were those known as *monzen-machi* (*machi* meaning a group of houses and *monzen* meaning "before the gates"), which usually consisted of a row of shops and stalls on either side of the approach to a monastery, together with lodging houses for pilgrims. Thus Sakamoto and Ōtsu, places through which travellers must pass on the way to the Enryakuji or Miidera, became important towns from relatively early times;[3] and before reaching the Great Shrine at Ise worshippers usually stopped at Uji-Yamada, where they could find lodgings and make purchases, if only of local products or guides to the sacred places.

Other settlements began as stopping places on lines of communication by land and sea. The highroads leading east and west from the capital came into use soon after the foundation of Kyoto, but apart from officials and couriers, travellers by road were not numerous. The Gempei War brought about more frequent movement along those highroads, but it was not until the Muromachi era that private travel by individuals became common. While the manorial system remained in force, the workers in the manors had no freedom to leave their boundaries; nor had they much reason to leave, since each manor was practically self-sufficient and there was not much transport of goods along the roads, except when tax-goods were carried to a seat of local government.

But as we shall see, the farm workers were gradually emancipated in the Muromachi era, with the result that more and more men were free to travel long distances, whether for purposes of trade or on pilgrimages. Thus a need for lodgings arose, and facilities for travellers on foot or on horseback were provided at intervals along the main highroads, usually at the relay stations where officials and couriers had formerly stopped. These stopping places grew into large villages or small towns as traffic along the roads increased, so that a traveller might count upon lodging at an inn, or hiring a horse, or selling his goods if he was a pedlar. The development of such townships—they were called *shuku-ba-machi*, or post towns—was rather late in the Muromachi era.

Much earlier in developing were the *minato-machi*, or harbour towns, which offered facilities for travel and transport by water. These were places from which goods from inland points could be shipped in bulk. During the Kamakura and Muromachi periods large quantities could only with difficulty be handled by road, since horse-drawn vehicles were very slow to develop and the load that a single horse or ox could carry was small.

Most large inland centres of population had their own port towns. Kyoto had Yodo, Nara had Kizu, the province of Ise had Ōminato, and Hyōgo and Sakai served the Home Provinces in general as ports for ocean-going vessels as well as for vessels plying along the Inland Sea. Most of these port towns were equipped with warehouses and with apparatus for ship repairs and for handling cargo, together with lodgings for seamen. In such ports there were usually wholesale dealers and transport agents doing business on a large scale. According to some documents, Yodo before 1500 had one thousand buildings and therefore

---

[3] Ōtsu was said to have lost 2,800 houses by fire during the Gempei War, a doubtful figure, but one that nonetheless suggests a town of considerable importance.

a population of the order of five thousand. Sakai, the most important of the port towns which became prominent during the Muromachi period, deserves a separate notice.

Sakai is situated at the head of the Inland Sea near the Yamato River and close to the boundary (*sakai*) of the three provinces of Izumi, Kawachi, and Settsu. It is first mentioned about 1320 as part of an imperial manor which produced salt for sale, and it was known to Kyoto nobles for its hot salt-water baths. It was closely connected with the Sumiyoshi shrine, a few miles distant, and it was a base for fishing vessels which supplied the Kasuga shrine near Nara. It was also a stopping place for pilgrims on the way by sea to Kumano, and since from 1400 or thereabouts the peasants were free to travel between planting and harvest, they no doubt contributed to the prosperity of the port.

Owing to its convenient situation, Sakai became a useful base for army supplies during the war between the Courts. When Go-Daigo moved to Yoshino, Sakai was a valuable link in his chain of communication with loyalists in Shikoku and Kyūshū, and also with the Kumano pirates who sided with the Southern Court. The Kusunoki family had a certain indirect control over Sakai, and Kusunoki Masashige obtained information from his agents there about the enemy's movements. Early in the war the town was captured by the Northern army. Loyalist forces attempted to recapture it in 1338, but with no success. After some vicissitudes the town fell into the hands of Ashikaga vassals, among them Yamana; but its closest connexion was with the Ōuchi family, thanks to whose good management it prospered as a seaport and a trading centre. It was almost completely destroyed by fire when Yoshimitsu's army attacked it in 1399; it was then said to have lost 10,000 houses of citizens in addition to warehouses and other buildings. This is certainly an exaggerated figure, but the loss was undoubtedly very great in relation to the total number of buildings. The town was rebuilt soon after 1400, and it prospered; but its height of importance was not reached until after the Ōnin War, when it flourished in both domestic and foreign trade and was granted certain special privileges.

4. *Wholesale Trade*

By a natural transition the establishment of markets led to trade in bulk. Here the use of metallic currency played an important part, for in the absence of a circulating medium great quantities of produce had of necessity to be transported by road or river from the farms to the often far-distant home of the landlord. But when the crop could be sold locally the landlord could receive his revenue in cash, while the estate would sent its produce to nearby markets for sale to merchants dealing, often on a speculative basis, in large quantities which they could sell at places of their choice.

In this way an important wholesale trade developed in certain commodities, principally in grains, of which the most important was rice. By the fifteenth century special wholesale markets had developed, and a small but powerful class of wholesale dealers had obtained a virtual monopoly of the purchase and sale of the major commodities. With the decline of the great manors the volume of agricultural tax-produce transported to the towns, where the landlords usually resided, had fallen so low that it was not sufficient to meet the demands of the townspeople, who were at this time (particularly in the Home Provinces) increasing rapidly in numbers. The amount of grain harvested near Kyoto was very small in relation to the city's needs, and consequently the citizens became dependent for their supplies upon wholesale grain merchants who bought up crops in more distant areas.

The rice dealers were particularly well organized. Their business grew rapidly as the population of Kyoto increased, until it became necessary to form a central rice market. It is not clear when this was founded, but it must have been about 1400. It had a monopoly, and no rice could be stored or sold wholesale elsewhere in the city. It also fixed the price of rice by a kind of auction, and this no doubt affected rice quotations in other parts of the country.

The rice dealers took full advantage of their position to hold the citizens at ransom. A most interesting account of their activities is recorded in the journal of the retired Emperor Go-Sukō-In. In Kyoto in 1431, he relates, certain wholesale dealers withheld rice from the market for a rise in price, thereby causing great distress to the citizens. They were ordered by the Bakufu to supply rice on reasonable terms, but after a display of obedience for one day they refused to make any sale whatever, and even went so far as to hold up cargoes that were on their way to the city. The Bakufu, alarmed by reports of starvation on the outskirts of Kyoto, ordered the ringleaders to be arrested and put to the question by the Samurai-dokoro. They denied the charges against them and were subjected to the ordeal of boiling water; their hands showed scalds or burns, and this was held to prove their guilt. The Deputy Governor (Shoshi-dai) of the Samurai-dokoro was ordered to punish them, but did nothing because he was in league with the culprits.

Encouraged by this example of corruption in high places, the rice dealers behaved more and more outrageously. The Samurai-dokoro still took bribes from them despite severe reprimands, and even the Shōgun Yoshimasa's wife was party to their schemes. This lady, Hino Tomi-ko, even built a fireproof store for pledges in her own money-lending business, and gambled on the rice market.

So lax was the discipline of the Bakufu at this time (especially after the death of Yoshinori in 1441 and under the fainéant rule of Yoshimasa from 1449) that its orders were often derided by men who under a sterner rule would have been put to death for their offences. For example, at one time more than sixty palanquin-bearers took advantage of their immunity as Palace servants to control the distribution of rice by means of their hold on transport and their membership in the guild of rice dealers.[4]

The hold of the rice dealers on Kyoto's food supply was indeed complete, for not only did they exercise a monopoly of sale, but by posting their guards at the main points of entry, such as Sakamoto and Ōtsu, they could completely control the flow of rice into the city. When the rice was admitted, it was carried by transport workers, such as carters (*shashaku*) and teamsters (*bashaku*). For some time there was no clear distinction between dealers and carriers, though specialization came about later. An example of this dual function is recorded in Go-Sukō's journal for the year 1418, where he states that "several thousand" teamsters from Ōtsu have poured into the precincts of the Gion shrine and done great damage, threatening to set fire to the buildings if their complaints are not heard. A strong force of police was sent by the Samurai-dokoro, and arrests were made. Spectators gathered "like clouds and mist" to watch the goings-on, which were very exciting. The cause of the fracas was a dispute about the price of rice, and these teamsters seem to have been at once the purveyors and the carriers of rice from the province of Ōmi.[5]

These details of the Kyoto rice trade suffice to show that the mercantile organization of the capital was well advanced, at least from the point of view of the sellers, in the early years of the fifteenth century. It was at about this time that merchants first began to make a sharp distinction between retail and wholesale trading. This distinction is of social as well as economic interest, since it reveals the development of a new social class—the wholesale merchant, usually a man of low degree but able to stand up against the official class by reason of his control over the supply of necessities.

One of the most interesting examples of the evolution of a mercantile function parallel with a growth in the volume and complexity of domestic trade is to be seen in the history of the *tonya* (*toiya*), a kind of wholesale broker or commission agent. The first mention of such a function seems to be as early as 1175, when a "toi-otoko" is described as providing a boat to take certain Court officials down the Yodo River

[4] The position of these palanquin-bearers (*kago-kaki*) is one of the curiosities of the economic history of these days. They were by trade rice dealers, but along with other traders they also belonged to one of the four companies of palanquin-bearers serving the Palace. This was an honourable position, and its holders were free from arrest because they were servants of the Imperial Household.

[5] Evidently at this time the citizens of Kyoto depended for their rice upon supplies from the fertile plains of Ōmi. Such supplies continued to reach Kyoto with regularity, but in the course of the Ōnin War, which laid both town and country waste between 1467 and 1480, the great daimyos and many citizens left and the streets were deserted. The rice dealers then found themselves in distress, and they were obliged to sell their stocks at "throw-away prices."

from Katsura to the Iwashimizu shrine. Here he appears not as a worker belonging to a manor but as an agent employed by one or more manors near Katsura to act for them in matters outside their boundaries, such as arranging the transport of persons and goods by water. In later documents such agents are mentioned as being able to furnish four or five boats for ferrying passengers or goods or for fishing. From such beginnings there developed the *tonya*, an important intermediary in the wholesale trade, whether as a transport agent, a warehouse-keeper, or a large-scale purveyor of merchandise. In the eighteenth and nineteenth centuries the *tonya* played an extremely important part in Japanese commerce. It is interesting to note that his ancestor was the outside agent of a manor.

In the Muromachi period the most important wholesale merchants apart from rice dealers were the dealers in cattle and horses and the dealers in marine products, notably fish and salt; and in the rapidly developing money economy, an essential function was performed by pawnbrokers or brewers acting as moneylenders, and in some cases as bankers issuing bills of exchange against payment in copper coin.

5. *Trade Guilds*

Trade guilds in mediaeval Japan are thought to derive from an early form of association known as the za. The word za means a seat, and doubtless signified a place reserved at ceremonies or at a market for a group of persons having the same interest. There are early notices of za composed of lay persons performing some voluntary service for a monastery or a shrine or for other manorial lords, and receiving some kind of favour in return. These social groups tended to develop into occupational groups, and soon (in the twelfth century, if not earlier) we learn of za of mimes, dancers, musicians, and other entertainers, usually in some way connected with a religious institution or a powerful patron. The custom has persisted, and to this day a company of actors has a za (e.g., Kabuki-za), and the five schools of Nō players are also called za. Painters, sculptors, and skilled craftsmen of various kinds formed za of a slightly different kind, which might be described as professional societies.

A connexion with some powerful body was important to traders as well as to entertainers and artists because of the protection it afforded, and at the same time a connexion with traders was useful to the protecting party as a source of income. Even where there was no za, there was often another kind of relation between Trade and the Church, for traders found it both convenient and prudent to form themselves into closed groups under the patronage of an institution or of a person of high rank. Thus the yeast-brewers in Kyoto were parishioners of the Kitano shrine, the oil merchants depended upon the great Iwashimizu Hachiman, and the pawnbrokers, a very active and influential body, had as their patron the powerful Tendai monastery on Hiyeizan. This link was very valuable, since when necessary a band of armed monks or priests could descend upon the capital to threaten the Court or the Bakufu on behalf of their clients. Other Kyoto guilds placed themselves under the protection of noble families, the papermakers under the Bōjō, the goldleaf-makers under the Konoye, and perhaps most surprising of all, the fishmongers under the Saionji, at that time the most influential of the noble houses. In return for its services the Saionji family received two-thirds of the income of the Kyoto fish market. This was its largest single source of income after the revenue from its manors began to decrease. It was so important that the Saionji and the Sanjōnishi, two noble houses, quarrelled over the appointment of an overseer in the fish market.

It is evidence of the rapid growth of commercial activity in the Muromachi era that by the fifteenth century the mercantile za were organized primarily by market rather than by commodity; a za was simply a group of traders in a given locality. In the Home Provinces, where economic development was most rapid, there were well-established za, in both town and country, of traders dealing in rice, textiles, iron, bamboo, and many other necessities. In the big cities, by contrast, notably in Kyoto, specialization by commodity was still common practice. Each trade tended to be concentrated in a special quarter; fishmongers, oil merchants, and timber merchants, for instance, all had their own separate za. Some vestiges of this practice survive in modern place names, such as Zaimokuza (timber merchants) in Kamakura, and Ginza (silver merchants) in Tokyo.

In their earlier forms these bodies were not independent, being subordinate to the monastery, shrine, or manor which they served; but before long both workers and traders began to form quasi-independent za not only for protection but actually for the furtherance of their interests. The rigid class structure of the Kamakura period was at this time breaking down, and the members of the za soon found that by joint action they could in some degree influence prices and resist the exactions of landlords and officials.

The rural za were of great importance, since they handled important foodstuffs, primary products such as oil seeds, bamboo, and timber, and raw materials of industry in general. The members of these associations were generally well-to-do peasant farmers who combined to sell their crops in bulk on the market; occasionally outside brokers would be admitted to their za. To be the head of such a za was to occupy a social position of some importance, comparable to that of a small landowner.

Since the main object of a za was to preserve and increase the profits of its members, it was bound to have a monopolistic character, and to strive to maintain its monopoly against the competition of outsiders.

Most of the monopolies applied only to retail sales, but in certain cases a za would make wholesale purchases of raw materials for the benefit of its members, and would prevent competitors from obtaining such materials within a certain area. A good example of this is the za of salt dealers in Yamato province, which was divided into three subsidiary za, of wholesalers, retailers, and pedlars.

Although by the fourteenth century the za were no longer under the orders of a manorial lord, they could not be permanently effective without protection, and arrangements on a simple cash basis (as between the Saionji and the Kyoto fishmongers) were commonly made. By the mid-fifteenth century, however, some of the za had made powerful enemies by abusing their privileges, and others had lost their protectors as a result of political reverses. Ultimately the za as an institution was challenged and forced to give way to other forms of mercantile organization which did not obstruct the free flow of trade.

The za has been compared to the merchant guild of mediaeval Europe, but the resemblance is in the opinion of some specialists only superficial. The za enjoyed certain tax exemptions, and za in different provinces kept in touch with one another, but there was nothing like a Hanseatic League. During the fifteenth century the political tendency in Japan was distinctly separatist, and the great warlords did not favour freedom of communication and trade between different spheres of influence. The za as guilds were not powerful except in making life uncomfortable for consumers and thereby causing trouble for the authorities, and it is doubtful whether in the long run they contributed as much to the growth of the economy as free competition would have done. To the general historian their chief interest lies in their promotion of a new social outlook. Their members were the forerunners of the important and numerous class of townsmen or chōnin (町人), which formed the mass of the population of the cities and towns in the eighteenth century and altered the complexion of feudal life.

CHAPTER XII

YOSHIMOCHI'S SUCCESSORS

1. *Yoshinori*

WHEN Yoshimochi, on the death of Yoshikazu in 1425, was faced with the problem of choosing a successor, he had to decide among four sons of Yoshimitsu, all of whom were in holy orders. He delayed decision, however, saying that whatever choice he might make would be upset by the Constables—an interesting admission of the power of those officers. He recommended drawing lots, and after his death in 1428 the chief men in the Bakufu followed his advice in the hope of preventing succession quarrels. The choice fell upon Yoshinori, the sixth son of Yoshimitsu, a man of thirty-five then Chief Abbot of the Tendai sect (Daisōjō, Tendai Zasu). Fortune here seemed to favour the house of Ashikaga, for Yoshinori proved to be a man of strong character and firm decision, intent upon restoring the authority of the Bakufu.

He revised the procedure for the settlement of lawsuits, issued new regulations concerning Acts of Grace (*tokusei*), and took a firm line with the monks of Hiyeizan and Nara, obliging them to cease their violent bickering. He even went so far as to chasten the impudent priests of the Iwashimizu Hachiman, a shrine which the Ashikaga family held in special reverence.

Unlike his predecessors, who had inclined to conciliatory methods, Yoshinori chose to deal with the insubordination of powerful warlords by a determined policy of repression. This inevitably led to open conflict.

The first to offer resistance to his measures was Yoshimochi's adopted son Mochiuji, the Deputy Shōgun at Kamakura (Kantō Kubō). In part because he himself had hopes of succeeding Yoshimochi as Shōgun, Mochiuji hated the "unfrocked monk" Yoshinori[1] and refused to defer to the Bakufu, against all precedent claiming rights to succession for his own son. In 1430 the powerful Kantō Kanrei, Uyesugi Norizane, rebuked Mochiuji (who had been making himself a nuisance in Kyoto) and advised him to return to his duty in the Kantō. But Mochiuji responded by sending a force to attack Uyesugi, and it became necessary for the Shōgun to take a hand in reducing the power of the Kantō Kubō, for the preservation of the Kyoto Bakufu was at stake. This was in 1432. Yoshinori, having obtained a commission to "punish" the rebel, ordered his generals Shiba and Imagawa, with other military leaders, to proceed with a large army to join forces with the northern provinces (Ōshū)

---

[1] "Unfrocked monk" is a free translation of *genzoku*, meaning a monk's return to lay life.

and to prepare an attack upon Kamakura. In October Yoshinori himself left Kyoto under pretence of an excursion to view the autumnal beauties of the country around Mount Fuji, but in fact for the purpose of inspecting conditions in the eastern provinces and as a demonstration in force. But no hostilities took place at this time.

In the following years Yoshinori was occupied with other matters and an uneasy peace was maintained, but in 1438 Norizane was again attacked by Mochiuji and complained to the Shōgun. Yoshinori sent a numerous host to the east in two portions, one by the coast road and the other by the mountain road. In the autumn of 1439 Kamakura was subdued with ease, and before the end of the year Mochiuji's committed suicide (Norizane had asked the Shōgun to spare Mochiuji's life, but Yoshinori was adamant). Thus the power of the Kantō Kubō was brought to an end, and thereafter the ruling family in the eastern provinces was the Uyesugi clan.

Having thus established the Shōgun's authority in the East, Yoshinori now turned his attention to the most powerful barons in the West. He succeeded in mastering both Ōuchi and Ōtomo, who had shown signs of rebellion, by setting one against the other and so reducing their offensive strength. Similarly he disposed of his opponents in Yamato province, adherents to the cause of the former Southern Court who were headed by Yoshiaki, Yoshinori's younger brother, and included members of the Doki family. He then made a special effort to restore order among the Court nobles and to promote good behaviour. His efforts met with some success, but he earned the enmity of those who stood to lose by his drastic reforms, for he was utterly without tact.

Yoshinori was a man of strong but very disagreeable character. He had something of the heroic stature of his great-grandfather and his father (Takauji and Yoshimitsu), but lacked their open temperament. Although he was a monk when he became Shōgun, he displayed no signs of piety. When interviewing his officials in the first few weeks after his appointment, he would wrap a kerchief round his head to conceal his tonsure. He had a strong feeling for rank and ceremonial and took a lively interest in Court affairs. In this he was no different from his predecessors, for unlike the great Yoritomo, who forbade the vassals to visit the capital or to associate with courtiers, the Ashikaga Shōguns were all on intimate terms with the sovereign and frequent visitors at the royal palaces. Yoshinori seems to have derived much pleasure from pomp and circumstance. An account of his attendance at Court in 1432 shows that he had a retinue of the highest nobility, with a number of lesser officers of state and an escort of Imperial Bodyguards. He liked moving about. He went to Hyōgo to see vessels in the China trade, and thence passed along the coast to visit Suma and Akashi, places famous for their beauty. The ships for China were three in number, one sent by the Bakufu, one by the Shōkokuji monastery, and one by a group of daimyo.

Yoshinori was particularly interested in the internal discipline of the Court and the morals of the nobility. He took a most puritanical line with lords and ladies whose behaviour he deemed improper, punishing their venial offences with unpardonable severity, for he had in his nature a dark strain of cruelty. On one occasion (according to the journal of Go-Sukō-In), he learned that a Court noble had seduced a young lady-in-waiting at the In's palace. Without waiting to make inquiries, he had the pair very severely punished. (The tale proved to be false.) On another occasion, when a lady-in-waiting in his own palace made a mistake in conveying a message, he beat her, made her cut off her hair, and sent her to enter a nunnery.

A long list of such brutalities might be recited. Yoshinori's intentions may have been good, but his temper was erratic and ungovernable and drove him to excesses. According to Go-Sukō-In, "He governed by terror." Some sixty persons in all are said to have been killed by his order, including the highest imperial official in the land, the Kampaku Konoye, as well as Court nobles, monks, and priests. Scores of responsible officials who had in some way displeased him were put under house arrest for indefinite periods, others were banished, and still others were deprived of their estates and condemned to a life of poverty, even of squalor. Ruthless though the age was, his ruthlessness offended almost every rank of society.

It is not surprising that Yoshinori made many enemies, nor that he was ultimately killed by one of them. He had reversed the policy of his predecessors, whose general aim was to be on good terms with the Court and to conciliate the great warrior houses. One of his generals, Akamatsu Mitsusuke, a powerful man in Harima province, had reason to suspect Yoshinori of planning to deprive him of portions of his fief. In 1441 he invited Yoshinori to a banquet in Kyoto, ostensibly to celebrate the pacification of the Kantō in 1439, and murdered him there in circumstances of revolting barbarity.

The Kanrei Hosokawa Mochiyuki felt that this treachery must be punished in a spectacular way. He consulted Hatakeyama and other Bakufu colleagues, who decided that the Yamana family should be charged with the task. In the fall of 1441 the Akamatsu stronghold at Shirohata was captured, and Mitsusuke and most of his kinsmen were killed. The Yamana family, which had been much reduced in strength by Yoshimitsu, was allowed to keep all of the domains of Akamatsu, and now found itself in control of seven provinces.

2. *The Kantō Warriors*

When Takauji's son Motouji was appointed by his father to the new post of Governor of the Kantō (Kantō Kanrei), he said of the warriors of that region: "If once these fellows are allowed to disobey, there will never be a quiet day in the East." The experience of his successors, especially Mochiuji, proved this to be a wise observation. Moreover, in the behaviour of these warriors from about the time of Zenshū's rising (see Chapter IX), there can be detected trends which, beginning as a regional movement, were ultimately to work a revolutionary change in the political and economic life of the whole country.

When Uyesugi Zenshū took his own life in 1417, the rebellion he began was not ended. He had been joined by a great number of warriors less for the sake of his quarrel with Mochiuji than for their own purposes. These warriors were almost exclusively small landowners and tenants, a class whose numbers had over several generations grown as the number of small holdings multiplied. They were all seeking to improve their positions, either by obtaining more land or by reducing their payments of tax; and they were ready to join a movement such as Zenshū's if it offered hope of such benefits.

After Zenshū's defeat, Mochiuji, far from seeking to alleviate the conditions that had given rise to the rebellion, endeavoured to destroy the families which had opposed him. Without consulting the Bakufu he attacked rural gentry in Musashi, the Oda family in Hitachi, the Takeda of Kai, and other long-established houses. The result was fierce antagonism towards the Kantō Governor among the provincial magnates, and grounds for anxiety in the Bakufu, which wanted above all things peace in the Kantō. In 1423 the Bakufu planned an expedition to punish Mochiuji. In 1424 he forestalled this action by swearing obedience, yet he continued to persecute the followers of Zenshū and to bicker incessantly with the Bakufu. It became increasingly clear that the Kantō magnates could depend neither upon the Governor for fair treatment nor upon the Bakufu for firm action, and hostile opinion grew throughout the eastern provinces. The magnates began to develop their own military strength, and although during Yoshimochi's lifetime they kept quiet, they were prepared if need be to disobey the Bakufu. They had in common a desire for independence, and in every village now the local gentry and the small farmers were saving their strength for action.

Much could be written about the activities of these warriors throughout the eastern provinces, but the story would be similar to that of the fertile area west of the Tamagawa in southern Musashi. This area contained a number of rich manors belonging to Kyoto monasteries and other wealthy foundations, to which an annual tax had to be paid by the warriors. As holdings grew smaller, the tax came to seem more and more onerous, and Zenshū's revolt offered a fine opportunity to get rid of this burden.[2]

On the other side, the warriors in the Tamagawa basin who had

[2] The memory of those younger sons who fought to increase their holdings and to gain freedom from tax is preserved in many place names in southern Musashi, such as Rokugō, Shioya, Maruko, Asagaya, Itakura, Umeda, Ishihama, Ushijima, Kanasugi, Kobinata—all in the vicinity of Tokyo.

helped Mochiuji against Zenshū were as a reward excused from paying certain taxes for a period of five years. This remission they interpreted in a very broad sense, and when the five years came to an end they extended it indefinitely. Similar action seems to have been taken in other parts of the Kantō, and most of the Kantō shōen belonging to domanial lords in Kyoto and Nara were in this way dissolved. The careful Manzai noted in his diary at this time: "The wicked behaviour of the Kantō warriors in these days is outrageous. They have been confiscating estates belonging to the Ashikaga family as well as those of Kyoto landlords; and now not one is left."

A student raising his nose from feudal documents and reflecting at large upon Japanese history cannot avoid the conclusion that the eight eastern provinces have had the strongest influence in shaping its course. It was the Kamakura government that broke down the institutions of the Heian age and dictated to the imperial government in Kyoto through a handful of resident officers. It was a feudal house of Kantō origin that ruled the country during the Ashikaga regime, and it was in the Kantō village of Yedo (later Tokyo) that the Tokugawa government established its headquarters in the seventeenth century.

The reasons for the dominant character of the eastern provinces are not entirely clear. The Kantō had a strategic advantage over the Home Provinces as a seat of government, for Kamakura and Yedo were easier to defend than Kyoto, which is open to attack from all sides. Both Kyoto and Yedo were situated in fertile plains, but the Kantō plain is ten times as great in area as the Kinai plain, and could thus support a greater population. The Kantō has a more stimulating climate than the Home Provinces. Moreover, in the middle ages Kamakura was not so strongly influenced by ancient and conservative tradition as Kyoto and Nara, where both the Court and the monasteries of the older Buddhist sects were unfavourable to change.

Whatever the reasons, the facts are that conditions of life in the eastern provinces bred men of vigorous and self-reliant character—hard workers, good soldiers, but not easy to manage. Their stubborn nature was perhaps one of the most important single factors in shaping the new feudal society that was to emerge from the civil wars of the sixteenth century.

This is not to say that men from other parts of Japan were inferior in quality, but to draw attention to the regional differences of character and customs which are an important feature in the national history, just as the differences between, let us say, Yorkshire and Kent are of importance in the political as well as the social history of England.

In mediaeval Japan the western provinces were remote from the centre of government, whereas the eastern provinces, though geographically not much closer, were more intimately connected with the capital by tradition, the Throne having depended since 1185 upon the military strength of the Kamakura Shōguns. Indeed, the Ashikaga Bakufu had no qualms about leaving Kyūshū to itself after Imagawa's long campaign. The Kantō, on the other hand, could be ignored only at the Bakufu's peril, for the road between Kamakura and Kyoto was well trodden, and often by the feet of armed men intent on spoils of war.

A study of the relations between Kyoto and Kamakura in the fifteenth century shows that the Shōgun and his high officers were at pains to conciliate their unruly representatives in the East. A curious sidelight on the attitude of the Bakufu is furnished by the custom of ordering a monastery, usually the important Tōji, to offer prayers for peace in the eastern provinces. The time chosen was usually shortly after the arrival of the annual quota of tax (zatsuzei) from Kamakura. Such prayers are recorded (for example) in the Tōji records for several days in succession during the tenth month of 1437, the year before Yoshinori's punitive expedition against Mochiuji.

A cursory study of the mediaeval history of the Kantō may give the impression that it was peopled solely by fierce warriors, whose only interest was in making war, whereas in truth the eastern provinces had a tradition of respect for learning going back to the early days of Kamakura. The Hōjō Regents encouraged literature and the fine arts, and Kamakura throughout mediaeval times was the home of many learned monks. Most of the great families promoted classical studies. The library called Kanazawa Bunko, founded by Hōjō Sanetoki (1225–76), contained a great number of books (including Sung editions of Chinese works) and many manuscripts. The Ashikaga College was famous in its day, and though it declined it was revived and its library replenished by Uyesugi Norizane, who had a high reputation for wisdom and learning, and was in close touch with literary circles in Kyoto. In general, the rivalries of the great chieftains in the Kantō as elsewhere were not confined to the battlefield; they competed as well for the services of scholars.

3. The Constable-Daimyo

The balance of power which Yoshimitsu had with difficulty achieved and Yoshinori had barely maintained proved dangerously unstable. Takauji's successors (Yoshiakira, Yoshimitsu, and Yoshimochi) had tried to maintain the primacy of the Bakufu over the great vassals by the use of armed strength. But by making war throughout the country for decade after decade they had let loose forces which they could not control, and at the time of Yoshinori's death a period of anarchy was impending. Now a Yamana could swagger and bully in the capital and nobody could check him.

The chief agents of the collapse of the authority of the Ashikaga Shōguns were the Constables (Shugo) whom Takauji and his successors had appointed following the precedent of Kamakura. In most provinces, it will be recalled, trustworthy kinsmen or supporters of the Ashi-kaga family were given appointments as Constable. The distribution of these posts has already been described (see Chapter IX); a more important matter was the powers which were granted to them or which they later arrogated.

The first appointment of Constables by the Kamakura Bakufu had limited their functions to the mobilization of troops, the suppression of revolt, and the control of vassals; but under the Hōjō regime their powers had been extended, and during the dynastic war the Constables appointed by the Ashikaga Shōguns were necessarily called upon to exercise an even wider authority. They began to interfere in lawsuits concerning land, and would evict tenants or install successful plaintiffs according to their own judgment. In the disorder of the time their legitimate and their assumed powers in combination gave them increasing military strength as well as civil authority.

Owing largely to the increasing number of small landowners known as *kokujin* or *ji-samurai*, and to the growing self-confidence of a new class of independent small cultivators, the manorial rights of the great landowners were in constant danger. By about 1400 no great manorial lord could keep order in his estates without the support of the Constable, and the Constables soon began to take advantage of this position to confiscate choice land for themselves. The most striking example of such arbitrary conduct is the fate of the extensive Chōkōdō domains, twenty-three rich manors in different parts of the country, which had long been a source of dispute between the senior and junior imperial lines. A record of the early years of the fifteenth century shows how they had been dealt with during the years of Ashikaga supremacy. Of the twenty-three manors, eleven had been confiscated, and one partially confiscated, by Constables and their subordinates; two had been forcibly taken by local warriors; and four had passed into the hands of other owners, probably under pressure. Only five remained in the ownership of the Imperial House.

Another vivid account of the depredations of Constables and provincial warriors of lower rank is provided in the journal kept by the Chief Abbot of the Daijō-In of the Kōfukuji, the most influential and wealthy of the Nara monasteries. Reduced to its simplest terms, the story is as follows.

In Echizen the Kōfukuji had a number of rich manors, notably the Kawaguchi-shō, the Tsuboye-shō, and the lands adjacent, with a total area of some 1,300 chō (about 3,100 acres). In Kamakura times these lands had been immune from tax and also from the entry of public officials. By about 1300 this great estate, which had been well managed and developed, was extremely valuable to its monastic owners.

It was also very tempting to neighbouring landowners. One of these, soon after Go-Daigo's return from exile, seized part of the Tsuboye-shō, but on complaint to the court of claims, which had recently been set up, an order was issued to eject the intruder. In the following year (1335) certain local officials, declaring themselves to be deputies of the Constable of Echizen, appeared with a body of armed men and forcibly entered the Kawaguchi-shō, where they seized money and other property.

That such conduct was not unusual at this time is clear from many similar reports in the records of several manors, although after about 1340, when the influence of the Southern Court was strong in Echizen, the Nitta commanders gave some protection to the Kōfukuji property. After Nitta Yoshimune's defeat, however, the Bakufu was dominant again in the province, and incursions into the manors were so frequent that an incumbent in Nara complained of a real shortage of supplies "due to the confiscation of our property."

In 1363 Shiba Takatsune, then Constable of Echizen and one of the most important officers of the Ashikaga government, seized the whole of the Kawaguchi-shō and gave it to a vassal. The Kōfukuji, unable to use force, resorted to the device of blackmailing the Court. There was a combined mass meeting of the Nara soldier-monks, who escorted the sacred emblem of Kasuga to Kyoto and left it in front of Takatsune's mansion. As a result of this demonstration, the manor was restored to the monastery. But very soon the warriors grew stronger and bolder, constantly quarrelling over the two manors. They finally adopted the device of *shugo-uke*, a contract by which the Constable undertook to accept in full payment of the tax due the Bakufu an agreed amount of rice, retaining for himself, as a kind of commission, the balance above the amount actually due. This arrangement was at first regarded as a convenience by some manorial lords, but before long the Constable was taking far more than the tax due and converting the difference to his own use. A classic example of the abuse of shugo-uke is the case of Yamana Tsunehisa, Constable of Bingo, who in 1402 received for tax from a monastic shō in his province 18,000 koku of rice and paid out only 10,000.

While the Constables were thus appropriating the revenue of manors on a large scale, the property of landlords was subject to a number of smaller incursions and often to plain theft of land (and sometimes of standing crops) by local small landowners of the myōshu type. The incident of 1335 mentioned above was of this nature, and similar cases grew frequent through the fourteenth century.

Furthermore, with the gradual emancipation of farm workers, the owners of estates were obliged to make concessions to deputations of farmers who would visit them and press for the remission or reduction of taxes. Such deputations were common, especially late in the Muromachi period. Their memorials were generally well argued, as is clear from documents of about 1460, when the *tansen* (a tax on arable land) was proving burdensome. The memorial was usually signed (sometimes

as a round robin) by the Sōbyakushō, that is, by an elected body representing all the farm workers of an estate or a district. The peasants were
obviously well organized and prepared to resist, by force if necessary,
objectionable orders from officers of a manor.

As early as 1414 the journal of the Daijō-In records a visit from the
officers of the Ukesho, the office responsible for collecting the rice due
under the contract of the Constable. These were almost all deputies for
important warriors, two for each of the ten separate farm areas which
made up the Kawaguchi-shō. There was, however, one exception, the
Mizoye farm group, which sent no representative since it had already
been confiscated by a Deputy Constable. It is clear from this record
that the monastery could not count upon supplies from this source.

Nor was the position any more favourable in the remainder of this
great estate. By the end of the Ōnin War (1477) practically all the
lucrative offices of the shō were held by a Deputy or by influential landholders of the neighbourhood, among whom there figures an especially
voracious general named Asakura, a vassal of the Shiba family with a
great capacity for swallowing estates. Among the properties which he
or his family confiscated were those of the retired statesman Ichijō
Kanera. It may well be imagined that by the end of the fifteenth century
very little revenue reached the Kōfukuji from its lands in Echizen.

As a pendent to the foregoing tale of depredations suffered by a
great monastic shō at the hands of warriors it seems pertinent to give
some details of the source from which it is drawn. One of the most
copious fountains of information for students of mediaeval history is
the journal known as *Daijō-In Jisha Zōjiki*, a daily recording of miscellaneous items concerning the complex of ecclesiastical offices forming
the Daijō-In of the celebrated Kōfukuji. This journal was kept by successive incumbents, the most prominent being the Chief Abbot Jinson,
who recorded the events of some forty-five years, from 1458 to about
1503, a year or two before his death.

It is nearly all in his own handwriting and contains detailed entries
for almost every day during that long period, which included the prelude of the Ōnin War, its duration, and its sequels, subjects treated in
the next chapter. Jinson's high rank and his family connexions gave him
a great advantage in obtaining information and learning the gossip of
official quarters. He was a son of the retired Kampaku, Ichijō Kanera,
an aristocrat celebrated as a statesman, a scholar, and a man of considerable wealth. Kanera had made handsome contributions to the
Kōfukuji while he was in office and had no difficulty in securing prefer-
ment for his son, who entered the religious life at the age of twelve.

During the Ōnin War Kanera took refuge in Nara,[3] and so did many

---

[3] Kanera later returned to Kyoto, where he became the Shōgun Yoshimasa's
adviser and at Yoshimasa's request wrote a memorial on the principles of government.

other Court nobles. They kept in close touch with the capital by messengers passing to and fro with news. Consequently Jinson's record of facts is detailed and generally seems accurate. But his running commentary is not so reliable. He was evidently a man of an extremely autocratic and conservative temperament, and his observations on current events are of a kind to be expected from a Church dignitary of noble birth living a comfortable and sheltered life. He shows very little understanding of what is going on in the world outside and is free with such expressions as "dreadful behaviour," to be visited by "divine punishment," and "wicked men" who are nothing but "beasts."

Yet his patient pen has left a fascinating picture of conditions in the metropolitan region during a critical period of disturbance. He was able to move about in the country between Nara and the capital. He had an enquiring mind, and he took a serious interest in the economic affairs of the monastery. He seems to have been a good businessman, and he was without doubt a severe landlord, ruthless in his dealings with the peasants. He was in close touch by messenger with the Kōfukuji manors in Kaga and Echizen. In his latter years his messengers brought him little but bad news, news of the dreadful behaviour of wicked men who were seizing Church lands on a grand scale, wicked men who would be visited by divine punishment, he doubtless thought as he mumbled his prayers.

4. Rural Society

The history of the latter half of the fifteenth century consists of such confused and melancholy details that there is a temptation to dismiss it with a statement of its major disasters. But to do so would be to give a wrong impression of the problems by which the Ashikaga Bakufu was faced. Since the middle of the Kamakura regime great and far-reaching changes had by degrees taken place in the social and economic life of the country. These had not been understood by the Ashikaga leaders, who supposed they could still solve their problems by the traditional methods of a feudal dictatorship, namely the issue of orders and the use of force.

We have seen that in the thirteenth and fourteenth centuries the Japanese economy grew rapidly, and its growth was in part linked with social changes that had slowly begun to undermine the manorial system upon which the power of the Bakufu rested. It is appropriate to examine these changes more closely, for they resulted in the social dislocations of the fourteenth and fifteenth centuries, and ultimately hastened the collapse of the Ashikaga Bakufu.

After the Gempei War, when the Kamakura Bakufu was at its strongest and most efficient, the successful warriors settled down to peaceful life on their estates. They had faith in the justice of the Bakufu. Indeed, for a short time after its foundation the warrior society over which the

Bakufu presided was of a remarkably equalitarian character. The great vassals (*go-kenin*), as stewards of prosperous manors, were in effect all landholders in a favoured situation, enjoying the protection of the state in return for their allegiance.

But this Arcadia was not to last. The Mongol invasions at the end of the thirteenth century placed an increasing strain upon the finances of the Bakufu and involved the most loyal vassals in backbreaking expenditures. The Kamakura Bakufu tried remedies of many kinds, but with poor success; by about 1325 its authority was at such a low ebb that it was on the verge of collapse, and its foundation, the once solid society of direct vassals, was disintegrating.

Under Takauji the place of the go-kenin was taken by the prominent warriors whom he appointed Constables. As we have seen, these men gradually acquired de facto ownership of land once constituting the manors from which the go-kenin had received their revenue. This kind of confiscation was accomplished by various pretences;[4] and its effect in the long run was to destroy the manorial system and to make the Constables into territorial lords who were in practice autonomous, though they might in some circumstances profess allegiance to the Ashikaga Shōgun of the day. The Constables were the forerunners of the great territorial lords who formed the mature feudal society of the seventeenth century; by the fifteenth century there were a score or so of these great lords, who are known as daimyō, a name which reveals their historic connexion with the ownership of land.[5]

The disintegration of the old warrior society and the rise of families loyal to their own interests rather than to the Bakufu was hastened by the war between the Courts, when, as we have seen, a warrior's loyalty to his overlord was weakened to such a degree that the turncoat became a common phenomenon. At the same time the gradual abandonment of the custom by which one son inherited the whole estate was encouraging the growth of a new class of rural landowner engaged in intensive and diversified agriculture on a relatively small area of land. These were men of warrior descent known as ji-samurai or kokujin, terms which

---

[4] The methods by which the shōen system was destroyed are important for the study of feudal land tenure, but the subject is far too complex for treatment here. It can be argued that quite apart from its political destruction, the shōen was bound to disappear as an economic institution when it could no longer be self-sufficient. As the total economy of the country grew in size and variety, the shōen could not supply all its own needs and therefore began to depend upon other organs for its maintenance.

[5] The term myōden (Name-field) was used to describe farm land in the full ownership of an individual as distinct from such qualified possession as the occupation of land in return for rent or services. It was usual to describe the owners of such property by reference to the size of their estates. A small proprietor was called shōmyō, a large proprietor was a daimyō. A generic term for these owners was myōshu (Name-master), but it came to be especially applied to small cultivators, usually emancipated peasants, farming their own land.

might be translated as "local gentry" or "yeoman farmers." They were bound by no loyalty to a great lord, but were men with a strong feeling of independence and of attachment to their native places.

As we shall see, the kokujin played an important role in the agrarian risings of the fourteenth and fifteenth centuries, and they were often joined by farmers of humbler origin. Since the early middle ages there had been at work a gradual process of emancipation, resulting in the formation of a class of farmers who enjoyed some degree of personal independence and rights in land approximating to ownership or at least permanent tenancy. These peasants fall into various categories, differing in the size of their holdings or the amount of the crop which they could retain.

It should be understood, however, that the emancipation of peasants as well as being gradual was also partial, and in the long run only temporary. Throughout Japanese history the peasant has been alternately freed and oppressed; and perhaps the most oppressive phase of all was the phase that followed the emancipation of the fifteenth century.

It may be pertinent here to make some observations on the question of serfdom in Japan. In theory—that is to say, from the strictly legal point of view—the agricultural worker in Japan was never as such in a state of serfdom, never bought or sold or moved about like a chattel. In the Nara and Heian periods there were household slaves, and some of these may have been put to farm work. But the true peasant was not a slave, and the general trend even in these periods was towards emancipation.

In the ninth and tenth centuries the burden of taxation and the general insecurity of life induced many peasants to "commend" themselves and their little plots to a landlord, thus diminishing their freedom; but they did thereby escape tax and paid relatively small dues in kind or in labour to the landlord. In Kamakura times, in the first phase of feudalism in Japan, the peasant was in some ways freer than the warrior-farmer, who could be severely punished by his feudal superiors for slight breaches of law. The Jōei Shikimoku recognizes the right of the humblest peasant to remain on the land which he occupies or to leave it at will. The old slavery had completely vanished by about 1200, except for a few domestic servants, usually females.

By the fifteenth century, with the collapse of the shōen, the liberty of the peasant was diminished to what in practice the warrior allowed him. But in effect this was often considerable, and the emancipated peasant who tilled his own land formed a class that was capable in a crisis of standing up for itself, and if competently led, of challenging the military class with some success. Moreover, the growth of production and trade gave new opportunities to peasants, who could leave the land and set up as traders and artisans.

5. *Agrarian Risings*

The difficulties which harassed the Ashikaga Bakufu are well illustrated by the frequency of agrarian risings beyond the central government's control. These and similar violent expressions of discontent are important features in the economic history of Japan, but they had political overtones as well.

We have seen that among the new classes which had appeared in the course of the thirteenth century, one of the most important was the class of small landowners known as ji-samurai or kokujin. These men resented the interference of representatives of the Ashikaga government, the Constables and other officers appointed to the provinces by the Shōgun. They came from good warrior families, long established in their own districts, and they were determined to protect their interests, both economic and social, against newcomers. Accordingly, they formed leagues (*ikki*) for mutual defence, a natural precaution during a period when disorder was destroying the system of rights and duties to which they belonged.[6] The central government could no longer give them the protection it had afforded to their ancestors. They had to act for themselves.

The word ikki strictly speaking means a league, but was extended to describe the activity of a league, usually by way of revolt. The frequent risings which took place as a protest against the government of the Ashikaga Shōguns, especially after the relatively stable rule of Yoshimitsu, are accordingly described by such terms as Shirahata-Ikki, or "White Flag Uprising," and Mikazuki-Ikki, or "Crescent Uprising."

It was when the Constables and their Deputies tried to impose their control upon a whole province that native-born landowners rose in revolt, and it was because of their wide range that the risings were called Kuni-Ikki (the word kuni here means province). The most important and determined of such risings took place late in the fifteenth century, but there were quite serious revolts of this type in the midst of the war between the Courts. In 1351 the kokujin of Wakasa province ejected a Deputy Constable, and in 1353 they attacked and drove out the warlord Yamana Tokiuji, who had been appointed Constable. The kokujin were extremely stubborn, and according to the records of the time in the course of thirty years there were fifteen changes of Constable in Wakasa because the kokujin made the post untenable.

Similar risings took place in Etchū (1369 and 1377), in Shinano

---

[6] Similarly, supporters of the Southern Court formed leagues to resist the Bakufu. In accounts of the battles fought by Nitta Yoshimune and other leaders of the Nitta clan, the members of the league are identified by their colours. In a battle at Kotesashi in the spring of 1352, for example, the Kodama-Ikki wore an emblem with the design of a fan, the Taira-Ikki were dressed in red from head to foot, and other Ikki had such emblems on their banners or their helmets as a crescent moon, a flower, a spade, and a vermilion (*beni*) lozenge.

(1384–86), and at intervals again in Wakasa (1366–69). Some of these were suppressed by force, others by compromise, or even by appointing one of the rural notables to the post of Deputy Constable. On the whole the Constables in this early period were not strong enough to force the issue, and the Ashikaga Bakufu did not reach its maximum power until the close of the fourteenth century.

There are records of peasants in armour taking part in some of these movements, and even before the war between the Courts true agrarian risings are recorded at intervals; but they were poorly organized and sporadic. However, they do indicate that by the end of the Kamakura regime peasants were already striving to improve their condition by concerted action, and were gaining some success. By the fifteenth century such risings had attained a higher state of organization and the peasants appear to have played a more prominent part. These risings are known as Tsuchi-Ikki. Some were plain revolts against the injustice of landlords, others were attacks upon moneylenders in neighbouring towns; but all were in essence agrarian movements stimulated by the growth of a new class of peasant farmer struggling for independence.

The first example of such a rising is thought to be one which took place in 1428 in the province of Ōmi, led by peasant cultivators in forcible protest against certain financial edicts by which they were injured.[7] In 1441 the farmers rose against the landlords in country districts not far from the capital—Miidera, Toba, Fushimi, Saga, Ninnaji, and Kamo. These were not aimless demonstrations but attacks in force against persons and places. The 1441 rising was joined by farmers from many points in the environs of Kyoto. They seized and occupied houses in the western part of the city (Nishi-Hachijō), and in one instance a force of from two to three thousand men occupied important monasteries at Kitano and Uzumasa. Such risings continued at intervals of two or three years until the end of the fifteenth century, chiefly in Yamashiro province but àlso in the Nara district. Some were put down by force and the leaders executed, but on the whole the feudal leaders failed to stem the movement.

The rising of 1428, which is thought to be the first large-scale appeal to force by a rural population, started as a rising of teamsters (bashaku) in Ōmi province. It soon spread to the capital, and thence to Nara, as well as to Ise, Kawachi, Izumi, and other provinces. The mob broke into the premises of moneylenders, chiefly sake-brewers and pawnbrokers, even into monastery buildings, destroying evidence of debt and seizing pledges. By about 1430 riots against the policy of the Bakufu had become almost endemic in some regions. Aggrieved parties called for

[7] Of this disturbance the journal of the Daijō-In says: "This is the first time since the creation of Japan that the country people have revolted." The statement is not quite correct, since there were some sporadic risings during the war between the Courts; but they were on a small scale.

edicts favourable to themselves, smashed the property of their creditors, seized the articles which they had pledged, and forced creditors to return their written acknowledgments of debt.

Scholars are not all in agreement on certain points, such as the constitution of these ikki and the status of their various members. Subject to this reservation the following account of a series of agrarian risings in Yamashiro may serve as a general description of the Tsuchi-Ikki, or as it is sometimes called, the Do-Ikki.[8]

A few miles to the west of Kyoto, on fertile soil along the banks of the Katsura River, there were a number of prosperous manors belonging to great nobles and religious institutions, as well as smaller properties owned by men of the kokujin class. The peasants by whom all this land was cultivated were united by a common interest, the fair distribution of water from the river for the irrigation of their fields. This work had formerly been carried out by the stewards of the manors, but throughout the fourteenth century there had been in progress a gradual but steady emancipation of farm workers, accompanied by a development of rural organization in the village (mura) and the district (gō), which in the early fifteenth century reached a measure of self-government.

These peasants had thus developed a feeling of confidence, a strong sense of unity, and a habit of cooperation which was naturally expressed in the joint control and management of their water supplies. Because their villages were not far from the capital city, they were also in touch with townspeople whom they would meet when they took their produce to market. They no doubt discussed their grievances and the shortcomings of the Bakufu officials with their customers, and learned from them something about metropolitan life.

Yamashiro was the most advanced province in the country and it is not surprising that its peasants were sophisticated. There were frequent risings by peasants from the Nishioka district, very close to the city, from 1440 until 1466, just before the Ōnin War began. They entered the capital in force time after time, and on at least one occasion they were joined by city workers, including members of the stable-keepers' corporation.

There is excellent evidence for the dates and the general nature of these uprisings, but what is not clear is the usual composition of the ikki. No doubt most of the leaders were middling landowners of the kokujin or ji-samurai type, but it is not certain whether any of the emancipated peasants now cultivating their own small plots of land took part in the planning and direction of the movements at this time. They and the kokujin had the same object, namely to be relieved from the exactions of

---

[8] It is interesting to note that in the documents describing the agrarian risings the word do-ikki is used as an alternative for tsuchi-ikki, and seems to express a contemptuous attitude towards the domin or "soil-people," as if they were thought of as aborigines by men of a superior race.

a corrupt provincial government. The kokujin were determined to resist by force the efforts of Constables and Deputies to confiscate their
land or to break their backs by heavy taxation, and many peasants were
ready to take arms and follow them. One of the difficulties here is the
interpretation of the term myōshu. It means the owner of land in his
own name, but it might apply to an emancipated peasant enjoying the
freehold of an acre or so, or to a great proprietor. Persons styled myōshu
seem to have taken a leading part in some risings (both Kuni-Ikki and
Tsuchi-Ikki), but it is doubtful whether they were free peasants.

6. Yoshimasa

Yoshinori was succeeded by his first son, Yoshikatsu, a sickly boy,
who died in 1443 at the age of ten only a few months after the Court
granted him the office of Shōgun. It was urgent to appoint a new Shōgun, and at a meeting of the leading generals summoned by the Kyoto
Kanrei Hatakeyama, the boy's younger brother Mitora (born 1435) was
chosen. He was subsequently given the name Yoshishige by the Emperor Go-Hanazono, and in 1449 he was formally appointed Sei-i Tai-
Shōgun and renamed Yoshimasa. At the beginning of his term of office
the Bakufu generals collaborated to maintain peace and order. But
Yoshimasa was not interested in affairs of state, and within a few years
the government of the Bakufu had grown so relaxed in strength and
vigilance that it invited rather than resisted the disasters by which it
was to be overwhelmed.

It would be unjust to ascribe the weakness of the Bakufu only to the
misgovernment of Yoshimasa. It was a progressive disease of long standing which even a wise and determined ruler could not have arrested.
Perhaps the most notable error of his advisers was their constant resort
to the Acts of Grace, which were intended to protect the vassals against
economic distress. The early Acts of Grace, belonging to the pre-feudal
period, were called tokusei or jinsei, meaning virtuous or humane government; they were forms of amnesty in times of famine or plague, and
not a part of financial policy, as they later became. The later history of
these edicts, beginning with the Act of Grace issued by the Kamakura
Bakufu in 1297, is a history of economic blunders. By the Act of 1297
personal loans were cancelled, sales of land voided, and the position of
creditors undermined. The result of this measure was an economic
panic, for the suppliers of goods and credit to the military families,
their principal clients, at once refused all further transactions, and stood
firm. The Bakufu was helpless, for it dared not permit a breakdown of
domestic trade, and accordingly withdrew the offensive edict in 1298.

The Muromachi government did not learn a lesson from this example, but under pressure resorted to hopeless conjuring tricks of the
very kind that had failed in Kamakura. Beginning in 1441 a stream of

these tokusei edicts were issued,[9] but with no effect other than to do harm to the national economy, to throw markets into distress, and to bring trade almost to a standstill.

The futility of trying to protect the warriors by such measures was already amply demonstrated by the reception given the moratorium declared in 1441, the first tokusei issued by the Muromachi Bakufu. The country people (as we have seen) at once rose in revolt and their riots extended into adjacent provinces, to points close to Kyoto and Nara, under the nose of the Shōgun. They destroyed evidence of borrowing, seized pledges, and tendered small sums in full payment of their debts. The Bakufu offered a compromise in respect of the rioters' debts, but this was not accepted. The rioters insisted upon a general act applying to all classes of debts and debtors and not to warriors only—a tokusei in reverse. In October 1441 the Bakufu capitulated and issued new edicts in terms acceptable to the rioters. One of their clauses (confirming a long-established custom) provided that land occupied by one tenant for twenty years should become the property of the taxpayer, thus recognizing the ownership of land by small tenant farmers.[10] But violent demonstrations continued.

One of the first of these riots to do serious damage in the capital took place in the summer of 1447. It began in a manor belonging to the great Tōji monastery, but the rioters in their anger streamed into the city, passing down the wide avenues and setting fire to buildings on the way. They forced an entry into the courtyard of the Tōji, where they killed two servants, and then broke into the main hall, where they killed two more persons. They were at length checked by a troop of soldiers hastily summoned to the scene.

Similar riots took place in or near Kyoto and Nara at intervals until 1456, when the Bakufu proclaimed a policy which was favourable to landowners who had pledged their property and to debtors who had borrowed cash, the latter being freed by the payment of one-tenth of the debt. But it did not offer much relief to the aggrieved peasants, some of whom preferred riot and plunder to new rules. In 1457 there was a demonstration in force by farm workers from the environs of Kyoto, who marched through the city beating drums and gongs, and shouting for a new tokusei order. They would not disperse until, at the order of the Bakufu, some of their ringleaders were killed by soldiers. One of the worst riots took place in 1461. The rioters attacked the shops of moneylenders, hoping to destroy evidence of debt, but they also pillaged and burned houses throughout the city. It was some weeks before the generals could subdue them.

Yoshimasa's failures in administration were accompanied by natural

---

[9] Yoshimasa is said to have issued thirteen in all.

[10] The word "occupied" is used here as an equivalent of *chigyō*, which is loosely regarded as meaning the possession of land in fee.

disasters which harmed not only farmers but the country at large. In the year 1457 and during the following decade storms laid waste the rice fields, and the ensuing famine was followed by epidemic sickness. The deaths from starvation and sickness are said to have numbered over 80,000 in two months in the capital, the Kamo River being clogged with stinking corpses. During these calamities the Bakufu does not appear to have taken any measures of relief, beyond arranging the distribution of food at one or two monasteries. Altogether the Bakufu proved incompetent in administration, and Yoshimasa's government was exceptionally bad, being both extravagant and corrupt. No attempt was made to apply the injunctions of the Kemmu Shikimoku, which was the basic law of the Ashikaga government. Monks and Court ladies interfered in matters of policy and they were relied upon by warrior chiefs who wanted to get the Shōgun's ear. It is hard to say what influence was exercised by the monks or the women, but there is no good evidence that they had a say in vital political decisions, and as go-betweens they doubtless exercised influence in personal matters.

Yoshimasa himself was much subject to feminine influence, especially that of his favourite mistresses. His wife Tomi-ko, clever and unscrupulous, was a power at the Shōgun's Court. These women, as well as certain monks, no doubt intrigued in personal questions of title and office, but national policy, in so far as it was subject to planning, was probably determined by the Kanrei in consultation.

Indeed it can hardly be said that there was a national policy once the Bakufu found itself unable to coerce the more powerful warlords. The only question of policy that arose was War or Not War? The answer was usually War, and not of the Shōgun's choosing. Some Japanese historians speak of feminine intrigues as an important cause of the senseless and cruel civil wars of Ōnin and Bummei, but it is doubtful whether cause and effect can be so clearly traced. To follow the history of deterioration in government from the decline of the Hōjō is to gain a strong impression of gradual and inevitable decline, a tragic sequence that had to run its course, because a military society is bound to seek military solutions of its problems. That is its curse.

Apart from his neglect of public duty the behaviour of Yoshimasa offers an interesting and even attractive field of enquiry. His extravagance alone was something to wonder at, and his aesthetic ventures command a certain respect.

Yoshimasa is said to have modelled his behaviour on that of Yoshimitsu, whom he admired. One of his most costly undertakings was the building of a new Muromachi palace in 1458, work which was continued during the famine year of 1461. He was blamed for this expenditure at a time when people were starving, and work was suspended, it is said, because of a satirical poem by the Emperor Go-Hanazono, who was a benevolent sovereign. But it is doubtful whether His Majesty's rebuke was justified, since there is something to be said for expenditure on public works in times of depression. Nothing that the Bakufu could do would increase the supply of food that year, or for that matter improve its distribution, since the Constables and other territorial lords could scarcely have been persuaded to ship grain to neighbouring regions, even if they had a surplus.

Another expensive undertaking was the building of the Takakura mansion for the Shōgun's mother, which vied with the Muromachi palace in the beauty of its gardens. Yoshimasa also spent great sums on monasteries and shrines, for buildings and rich gifts. He made most costly pilgrimages, proceeding with a great retinue to Kasuga, Ise, and other holy places. He also patronized and subsidized performances of sangaku, such as the Tadasu-gawara Nō plays of 1464, which are described in detail in a contemporary record.[11]

It is said that Yoshimasa's lavish expenditures emptied the Bakufu treasury and obliged the Shōgun to borrow from the rich Zen monasteries. It is also suggested that these things combined to produce an inflammable condition, and "it wanted only a spark to produce a great forest fire." But such interpretations are too simple to account for the bitter civil strife of the ensuing years. It is nearer the mark to say that the warrior class was not yet sick of bloodshed. The great chieftains were preparing for conflict by strengthening their own defences and setting up barriers at points of entry into their domains, hoping thus to insulate themselves against spies and sudden attacks. The multiplication of barriers throughout the country, checking the movement of goods and travellers, is vivid evidence of a trend in sharp opposition to the unity which it was the Shōgun's duty to encourage and protect.

The barrier is mentioned in early Japanese history in its use for such purposes as inspection of travellers by police or military guards on the lookout for fugitives. (One of the most celebrated of Japanese legends is the story of Yoshitsune, challenged at a barrier by Yoritomo's officers and saved by the quick wit of his henchman Benkei.) But as the country was settled and unified under the rule of Kamakura many of these barriers were abolished. It was not until the later middle ages that the great landowners—warriors, noblemen, religious foundations—took to erecting barriers on the borders of their territory, and these were used less for protection than for purposes of revenue. Heavy tolls were levied on passengers and goods, a device which proved to be so fruitful that the Muromachi Shōguns forbade private barriers and set up a national

---

[11] *Tadasu-gawara Kanjin-Sangaku Ki.* An earlier occasion is recorded in an account of a great Court performance of Dengaku-Nō in 1445. The performance of 1464 was a state occasion of the highest order. It was directed by the Kanze Tayū Matasaburō and attended by Yoshimasa and his great captains, who were seated in a strict order of precedence. It continued for a week, with several plays on each alternate day.

system under which official barriers were erected in each province and transit taxes were imposed as part of the revenue of the Bakufu.

The injunction against private barriers had no effect, for they were set up in increasing numbers. The tolls exacted were so heavy and so frequent that trade suffered and prices rose. One record states that sometimes a trader would have to pay toll at ten places on a journey of ten miles, and cites the case of a messenger, sent from Nara to a point in Mino province, who had to pay a small toll at each of twenty-nine private barriers. It is no wonder that smashing barriers was one of the ways in which rioters protested against the burdens imposed upon the growing class of small traders; and the fact that the Bakufu could not enforce its own prohibitions is ample evidence of its progressive decline.

Of all the administrative blunders of the Bakufu under Yoshimitsu's successors, and particularly under Yoshimasa, probably the most disastrous was the heavy burden of taxation imposed upon small farmers and tradespeople. The *tansen*, a tax on arable land, began as a special non-recurrent levy in 1371, when all Constables and Stewards were ordered to collect it to provide funds for the accession ceremony of Go-Enyū. It was never abolished, and by Yoshimasa's time it was collected more than once a year.[12] To this were added a great variety of taxes on trade and traders—taxes on buildings, on retail shops, on warehouses, on brewers, rice dealers, and sake dealers—repeated sometimes in the course of a year. The wholesalers could pass the burden to their customers, but the small men were ruined. It is not surprising that many of them left their homes and enlisted in the armies of the warlords, thus swelling the forces which challenged the authority of the Bakufu.

As Murdoch observes in his vigorous chapter on Ashikaga feudalism, the effect of war upon the peasant was not serious, since he had so little to lose. What he most dreaded was the tax-gatherer and the debt-collector, both of whom could be avoided if he took to military service. It was no doubt in part the enlistment of such men that changed the character of warfare in the fifteenth century by increasing the number of foot soldiers.

7. The Finances of the Muromachi Bakufu

Chroniclers writing at the time of the Ōnin War (1467–77) are apt to ascribe the decline of the Muromachi Bakufu to the immoral character of the rulers, especially the corrupt advisers of Yoshimasa. But it would be nearer the truth to say that the hand-to-mouth financing to

---

[12] The ledger of a monastery in Owari shows the payment of tansen for the provision of furnishings to be used at an accession ceremony in 1428. The rate was 50 mon per tan of area. The tan was one-tenth of a chō (about one quarter-acre); thus the amount paid on an area of 40 chō was 20,000 mon—about the price of ten bushels of rice.

which Yoshimasa resorted afforded endless opportunities for bribery and related evils. The real weakness of the Muromachi Bakufu was one which no government, however capable and honest, can long survive, to wit, a lack of fiscal resources.

One of the causes of the collapse of the Kamakura Bakufu was the drain on its finances caused by the Mongol invasions, from which it never fully recovered. But before that disaster it had maintained its fiscal independence for more than a century. The Muromachi government, on the other hand, was not so firmly based. It had been in financial difficulties since its foundation. When Takauji assumed leadership in 1336 he had no revenue to meet military expenditure and was obliged to raise funds by an emergency measure. This was the introduction of a system of collection called *hanzei* (half-payment), which was of the same general character as the *hyōrō-mai* (commissariat levy) collected by Yoritomo's Constables. For reasons of expediency, Takauji authorized the Constables in a few provinces to retain half the revenue due from manorial estates. This was meant to be an emergency measure, but it was never discontinued, and indeed it was soon extended to most provinces. It bore very hard upon the owners of estates. Moreover, it was abused by the Deputy Constables (Shugo-daikan) who would seize and retain property under the pretence of collecting hanzei. By about 1400, if not sooner, the Bakufu was gaining little or no revenue from this source.

In theory the Constables appointed by the Bakufu remitted to Kyoto a proportion of the taxes which they collected from estates in their jurisdiction; but in practice this source of income was irregular. By the middle of the fifteenth century it had almost dried up, and the government was therefore obliged to resort to new forms of direct taxation. It was able to turn to a rising mercantile class for funds, and one of the most fruitful sources was a tax upon rich moneylenders, most of whom resided in the metropolitan area. These levies were made at regular and also irregular intervals, to meet the frequent deficits of the Shōgun's treasury. According to one document, whereas Yoshimitsu levied this *kurayaku*[18] four times a year, Yoshimasa did not stop at eight times a month. Such taxes were naturally resented, especially when they seemed merely to pay for the luxurious tastes of great men.

In short, until about 1400 such special taxes as tansen and a proportion of tax due from Constables appointed by the Shōgun were duly remitted to the capital. But the forces of greed and protest proved stronger than the Bakufu, and by the middle of the fifteenth century the provincial landholders, from the Constables down to the small rural gentry, had forcibly confiscated so many manors from which revenue

[18] *Kurayaku* refers to the *kura* or storehouse in which moneylenders kept their pledges. The tax, however, was not levied upon the storehouse or its contents, but upon the combined wealth of the moneylender.

had hitherto been derived that very little tax reached the Shōgun's treasury. Writing just before the New Year of 1478, at a season when rejoicing is the rule, the Abbot Jinson paints a bleak picture: "There is nothing in the whole Empire to be glad about. . . . The provinces [here follows a list] have paid no taxes since the outbreak of Ōnin, and the provinces which should obey all orders of the Bakufu[14] pay no attention whatever to the commands of the Shōgun. The Constables say that they will obey, but their deputies say that they can do nothing. . . . The whole country is in a state of disobedience."

To round off this account of the fiscal troubles of the Ashikaga government, the even more miserable state of the imperial treasury needs some notice. According to the official soothsayers, 1440 was to be a crucial year, full of difficulty and disorder. At that time the discipline of the Imperial Bodyguards was so lax that robbers entered the innermost private apartments of the Palace, and at another time thieves even found their way into the Naishi-dokoro, the holy of holies where the sacred treasures were kept, and stole the bell and some garments. Bands of robbers roamed the streets by daylight and even boldly ventured into quarters which soldiers were supposed to dominate. The royal Court was so poverty-stricken that it could not find funds for the upkeep of the Great Shrine at Ise, the holiest place in the land. Even the local festivals of such important shrines as Kamo had to be given up for lack of money. Repairs to the Hachiman shrine, important to both the Throne and the Shōgun, could not be undertaken because neither had any money to spare. At last, so the story goes, a fund was raised by selling the Shōgun's armour; but this tale is probably more picturesque than truthful.

Seen in their political aspects many of the economic and social developments of the Muromachi period appear as examples of the failure of the administrative organs of the Bakufu. The abortive Acts of Grace, the agrarian risings, the smashing of toll-barriers, all seem to testify to the political incompetence of the governing class. There is some truth in this reading of events, for it is clear that the Bakufu did not understand the nature of the social and economic changes that were taking place, but even if they had made wiser decisions there was little that they could do. The country was alive with energy in a phase of expansion which could not be checked.

[14] Harima, Bizen, Bingo, Bitchu, Mimasaka, Ise, Iga, and the whole of Shikoku. These provinces were within easy reach of the capital and practically under direct Bakufu control.

CHAPTER XIII

THE ŌNIN WAR

1. *Its Origins*

THE ŌNIN WAR, which lasted for eleven years—from 1467 through 1477—was the most dreadful conflict in the sanguinary history of the middle ages. Its origins are complex, and it is idle to attempt to trace them to specific actions and events. The war arose immediately from a quarrel between angry warlords, but this was only a spark which set fire to a mass of inflammable material. For its true causes we must look to the general condition and temper of society in the Muromachi age.

The century following the collapse of the Kamakura government had shown a great vitality and an expansive spirit of change. The bonds of tradition were loosened; new energies were released, new classes formed, new wealth created. A fierce competition for power and possessions replaced the acceptance of feudal discipline. To the student following these trends, change is visible at every social level. Peasants revolt, trade guilds defy the law, tenants oust their landlords, small shopkeepers make fortunes, and provincial warriors seize the power of the Shōgun's Deputies. Violent succession quarrels break out in warrior families, and the authority of the Bakufu declines until it almost vanishes after the death of Yoshinori in 1441.

No doubt a contributory cause of trouble was the addiction of the Shōgun's great officers to metropolitan life; for while they were competing for influence at the capital, the leading families in the provinces were building up their resources and growing more and more independent of the Bakufu. They formed leagues and alliances designed to resist pressure from the leaders at the centre, particularly the families of Hosokawa, Shiba, and Hatakeyama, and their prospects were the brighter for the incompetence of Yoshimasa, who cared for none of these things.

There was a split in the Hatakeyama family about 1450, and the Shiba family was torn by dissension when a vassal objected to the succession of an adopted son. Such quarrels commonly arose not between members of the family but between third parties, for very often the real antagonism was not between the potential heirs but between their respective vassals or other subordinates. Succession disputes continued down the scale of rank to families of only moderate importance, until nearly every province had its rivalries. It wanted only a clash of arms between two great houses to start a general conflagration. No doubt the faltering government of Yoshimasa contributed to an accumulation of disorders which could be swept away only by a strong revolutionary

Chronology of the Ōnin War and the Age of the Country at War

1443 Ashikaga Yoshimasa becomes Shōgun
1445 Hosokawa Katsumoto becomes Kyoto Kanrei
1449 Ashikaga Shigeuji assumes office in the Kantō
1457 Ōta Dōkan builds Yedo castle. Ashikaga Masamoto sent to govern the Kantō
1458 Yoshimasa builds a new Muromachi palace
1464 Yoshimi assists his brother Yoshimasa in public office
1465 Tomi-ko gives birth to Ashikaga Yoshihisa
1466 Yamana Sōzen and Hosokawa Katsumoto gather troops near Kyoto
1467 Outbreak of the Ōnin War. Yamana is declared a rebel. In November the Shōkokuji is destroyed
1468 Yoshimi goes over to Yamana's side
1469 Yoshimasa names Yoshihisa his heir
1471 Ikkō sect gains strength in the North. Asakura becomes Constable of Echizen
1473 Yamana and Hosokawa die. Yoshimasa retires
1477 Ōuchi leaves Kyoto. End of the Ōnin War
1485 Agrarian risings in Yamashiro
1489 Yoshihisa dies
1490 Yoshimasa dies. Ashikaga Yoshitane becomes Shōgun
1492 Hōjō Sōun becomes master of Izu
1493 Yoshitane abdicates
1494 Hosokawa Masamoto becomes Kyoto Kanrei
1495 Hōjō Sōun captures Odawara
1508 Ōuchi restores Yoshitane
1523 Official trade with China is temporarily suspended
1530 Discovery of silver in Iwami
1542 Arrival of Portuguese castaways at Tanegashima. Introduction of fire-arms. Hōjō Ujiyasu defeats the Uyesugi forces at Kawagoye
1545 Japanese pirates begin large-scale raids on China
1548 Last official trade voyage to Ming China
1549 Francis Xavier lands at Kagoshima
1551 Defeat of Ōuchi by Suye Harukata
1554 Mōri succeeds to Ōuchi lands and power
1555 Uyesugi Kenshin and Takeda Shingen meet at Kawanakajima
1560 Victory of Oda Nobunaga at Okehazama

movement; and it is as such a movement that the Ōnin War, with all its horrors, can be best explained. Its immediate result was only more confusion and more misery, but it was a necessary step towards the restoration of firm and resolute government.

2. *The First Year of Ōnin*

The quarrels between factions within the Kanrei families of Hatakeyama and Shiba spread as the several antagonists came to be supported or opposed by other warlords. Both conflicts were indecisive, however, and none of the claimants proved to be a forceful leader; moreover, since the two houses were of course weakened in a military sense, their influence rapidly declined. By about 1450 the two most powerful warriors in the country were the chieftains of the Hosokawa and Yamana families.

Hosokawa Katsumoto was a gifted man, an exceptionally able administrator who kept his domains in good order and his vassals contented. He remained firm and aloof while his colleagues and his adversaries were creating disorder. He had something of the character of his ancestor Yoriyuki, the statesman upon whom the Shōgun Yoshimitsu had most depended.

Hosokawa's father-in-law, Yamana Sōzen, was a warrior chieftain of a different stamp. His clan had suffered from imprudent leaders in the past, and although its position had improved with the defeat of Akamatsu, Yamana was ambitious and wanted nothing less than to raise his family to the summit. He was a turbulent man, becoming almost apoplectic in his rages. Known by his scarlet complexion, he was called Aka-nyūdō, the Red Monk (for he had entered religion in his later years).

Yamana envied and distrusted Hosokawa, whose family held the position of Kanrei and had long enjoyed the confidence and favour of the Shōguns, and resolved upon his destruction. He could not easily find a legitimate cause of quarrel with Hosokawa, who was a skilful and wary antagonist, and he did not want to precipitate an open showdown until he was sure of his strength. He therefore marked time by intervening in the succession disputes of other families—and not always on the same side, since his purpose was not to bring peace but to seek allies for an attack upon Hosokawa. His advances and withdrawals need not be described in detail, since they were the customary procedures of what we may call feudal power politics.

The political situation was complicated in 1464 by the problem of deciding upon a successor to the Shōgun, who was tired of the cares of office, which interfered with his pleasures. In historical studies of the political events that led to the outbreak of the Ōnin War, part of the blame is usually laid upon Yoshimasa. It is true that he was little interested in the duties of his office and made frequent blunders when called upon for decisions, but it is very doubtful whether even the most heroic efforts on his part could have stemmed the tide of events.

Although Yoshimasa found his official responsibilities irksome, he did not at first neglect them. He did not like Hosokawa Katsumoto, but he recognized his talents and in some matters depended upon his advice. Yet the problems before him were very often unsolvable, and his mind was more naturally drawn to other matters. He was inclined to vacillate after hearing the views of his adviser Ise Sadachika, of his favourite ladies, and most decided of all, of his wife Tomi-ko. Thus by 1464 (after fifteen years in office) he was preparing to resign, though he was only thirty.

The question of succession was naturally of great importance to Hosokawa, who favoured Yoshimi, a younger brother of Yoshimasa and at that time an abbot in a Jōdo monastery. Yoshimi did not wish to leave the religious life, but at the end of 1464 he was persuaded to join his brother and assist him, it being understood that he would in due time succeed to the Shōgun's office. A year later the Shōgun's wife Tomi-ko gave birth to a son, Yoshihisa, which made Yoshimi's position very awkward. However, he remained as Yoshimasa's Deputy and carried out his instructions, relying in general upon advice given to him by Hosokawa.

Tomi-ko was understandably very angry, and sought Yamana's support for the claim of her infant son. The conflict between Yamana and Hosokawa thus assumed a different character. On the one side was the Shōgun, supported by Yoshimi and defended by Hosokawa; on the other side was Tomi-ko with her son, supported by Yamana. The issue was now a succession dispute of a high order, not among vassals but between claimants to the Shōgun's office.

By the end of 1466 Yamana, having increased his support greatly by his political manoeuvres, was feeling strong enough to challenge Hosokawa openly. According to such works as the Ōnin-ki, which are not entirely credible but probably represent the general situation accurately enough, the forces commanded by the two generals were approximately as follows, omitting the speculative figures of possible contributions by uncertain allies:

Hosokawa		Yamana	
Katsumoto	60,000	Sōzen	30,000
Collaterals	20,000	Collaterals	11,000
Allies	5,000	Allies	39,000
	85,000		80,000

The antagonists were closely matched, but the advantage lay with Hosokawa, whose troops were more dependable, as well as more numerous, than Yamana's.

Early in the first year of Ōnin (1467) Yamana, after consulting his kinsmen and allies, approached Yoshimasa and complained that Hosokawa had interfered in a dispute between two candidates from the Hatakeyama family for the office of Kanrei. (The two were Hatakeyama Yoshinari and Hatakeyama Masanaga, each of whom Yamana had favoured as it suited his own purpose.) Yamana asked leave to punish Hosokawa for insubordination, but the Shōgun only reprimanded Hosokawa for his action. That evening Yamana (then living in Yoshimi's mansion) as a move against Hosokawa conducted Yoshimi to the Bakufu headquarters, which he took measures to defend. At this time Hosokawa was already looking around for suitable houses to use as headquarters or defence points should hostilities commence. Both leaders mobilized their forces. It was clear that the capital was to be the battlefield.

Yoshimasa saw that if open war broke out in the capital, the war would spread throughout the provinces, and he ordered the protagonists not to interfere any further in the current dispute within the Hatakeyama family, but to let the Hatakeyama rivals fight it out between themselves. He warned Yamana and Hosokawa that whichever of them was first to fight in the capital would be declared a rebel.

Thus although both generals had brought a large number of troops to the vicinity of the capital, neither side dared to make the first move and their armies stood immobile. Weak as he was, the Shōgun still had a powerful weapon to hand in the formal power to assign the responsibility for rebellion and ask the Emperor for a commission to chastise the rebels. No warlord could afford to be declared a rebel, since the very declaration would alienate his allies and give his rivals just cause for attacking him and confiscating his property.

Tension grew in the capital as time went by. It is interesting to follow the daily events as they are recorded in diaries and other contemporary documents. There are letters from eyewitnesses and journals kept in the great monasteries to which news was constantly sent, and these sources all convey the feeling of strain and fearful anticipation that must have possessed all the citizens.

In the first month of 1467, we learn from these sources, the usual New Year celebrations took place. On the eleventh day there was a national prayer for peace at the Great Shrine of Ise. On the thirteenth day there was the regular poetry gathering at the Shōgun's palace. Then follow reports of the political manoeuvres of Yamana and Hosokawa recounted above. The outlook darkened, but still there was no open breach or clash. In February Hosokawa learned that the great western daimyo Ōuchi, with 20,000 men, was about to move in support of Yamana.

In March Yamana and his generals went to pay their respects to the Shōgun and his brother Yoshimi. The Hosokawa party did not attend, being occupied with warlike preparations. At the end of the month the mansion of a Hosokawa officer was destroyed by fire. The crisis was imminent. In April tax-rice being conveyed to the capital by Yamana soldiers was seized by Hosokawa men in the province of Tamba. There were frequent fires on the outskirts of the city, and in Ōmi, Owari, and Echizen. Those who could leave the city departed, and the guard at the Imperial Palace was doubled. Now Yamana and Hosokawa both began to assemble forces in the city itself, Yamana to the west of Muromachi and Hosokawa to the east. Rumours of coming disasters flew about, and the populace was in a state of great alarm. Writing on the seventeenth day, a Court noble says: "It is reported that there will be desperate happenings tonight. The young princesses are being taken for safety to the outer suburbs, south of the city."

Finally, at the end of May, Hosokawa troops attacked the mansion of Isshiki, one of Yamana's generals. Fighting continued for several days, with many killed or wounded on both sides, and meanwhile a number of buildings—monasteries, shrines, and dwelling houses—were destroyed by fire, some burned by the soldiers, others by marauding robbers in search of loot.

Such was the state of affairs early in the month of June. Yoshimasa sent word in vain to both commanders, ordering them to arrange a truce. By the end of June, if not sooner, thousands of acres had been swept by flames and the fighting was almost incessant. In the first hostilities there had been little room for any but close hand-to-hand fighting at the barricades, but as buildings were destroyed by fire more open tactics became possible in the wide avenues and in spaces cleared of debris. Street fighting of the bitterest kind ensued. Trenches were dug by both sides, notably in the wide avenue Ichijō on the northern edge of the city.

Although Yoshimasa had warned the adversaries that the first to fight in the capital would be declared a rebel, and although Hosokawa's forces were apparently the first to attack, Hosokawa succeeded in inducing the Shōgun to attach the stigma of rebellion to Yamana. Early in July Yoshimasa ordered his brother Yoshimi to chastise the rebel, and appointed Hosokawa as his commanding general. Hosokawa was given a flag symbolizing his position, but the Shōgun refused to procure him the usual commission from the Throne.

This gave a certain moral advantage to Hosokawa, and some of Yamana's supporters deserted; but more effective in the long run was the work of Hosokawa's emissaries in the provinces from which Yamana and Ōuchi and Shiba drew their strength, for they were able to stimulate such disorders that both Yamana and Ōuchi had to send troops back to protect their interests in their own provinces. Yamana, feeling that his position was weakening, sent to Harima province for more troops, which reached Tamba by forced marches early in July, from there fighting their way to the environs of Kyoto. Heavy fighting continued throughout July, together with much incendiarism and looting by undisciplined troops. According to a usually reliable journal, several hundred large buildings were destroyed, and destruction continued day after day. Thousands of small houses also went up in flames, leaving nothing but ashes, so that a once populous area "looked like a lonely moor."

The centre of the fighting in the city was a small space where movement was restricted. Hosokawa's force (called the Eastern Army) held a small area containing the Bakufu buildings, the Jissō-In, the great Zen monastery Shōkokuji, and Hosokawa's own mansion. Yamana's forces (the Western Army) held an area to the south and west of this; their front line of defence ran east from Itsutsuji-Ōmiya, and their main encampment was at the place today known as Nishijin.[1] Hosokawa had little room for manoeuvre; his forces were pressed into a corner at the north of the city, and his communications to the south and east were cut off by Yamana and Shiba. By early September Yamana's reinforcements had arrived, and Hosokawa learned that in addition to these Ōuchi Masahiro with 20,000 men had swept aside all opposition and reached Arima in Settsu. Hosokawa's efforts to stop Ōuchi south of the city failed, and Ōuchi's army passed along the road from Yamazaki and joined Yamana's army at Kitano.

The composition of Ōuchi's army is worth noting. It arrived at Hyōgo in the latter part of August, partly by land and partly by sea. Ōuchi was in the van with 500 boats, and the total number of boats is given as 2,000, carrying troops from Suō, Nagato, and Kyūshū. They were escorted by pirates named Nogami, Kurahashi, Kure, and Kokuya. The land party was composed mainly of contingents brought by their captains from Iwami province. The Ōnin-ki says that when Ōuchi arrived, Yamana felt like a dragon refreshed by water or a tiger sniffing the breeze.

Bolstered by these reinforcements, Yamana decided to cut all Hosokawa's lines of communication, and for that purpose he planned first to attack the Eastern forces in the vicinity of the Imperial Palace. At about this time Hosokawa decided to purge the Shōgun's Court of persons sympathetic to the cause of Tomi-ko and Yamana; but he had to proceed with caution. In September 1467 he surrounded the Muromachi-dono (Hana no Gosho) and demanded the expulsion of twelve offenders known to be in league with Yamana. But since it would have been a breach of loyalty for him to attack the Shōgun's residence, the attempt came to nothing. Hosokawa, however, had heard that Yamana planned to attack the Emperor's Palace and seize the persons of the

---

[1] It means the Western Camp, and has given its name to a well-known weave of silk, Nishijin-ori.

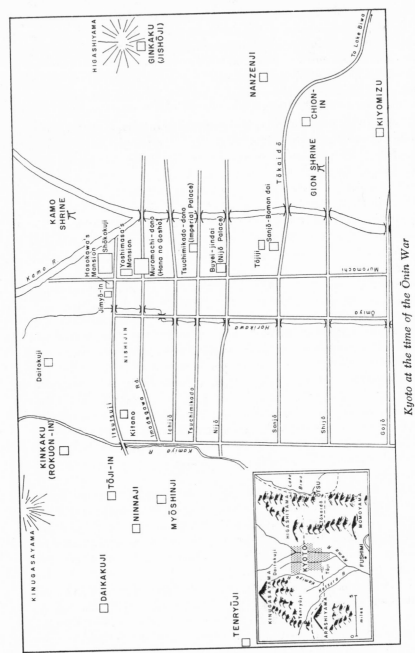

Kyoto at the time of the Ōnin War

The diagram shows the northern part of the city in the mid-fifteenth century, and the principal
monasteries, palaces, and shrines in the eastern and western suburbs.

sovereign and the abdicated Emperor, action which he forestalled by sending a trusted commander to escort them to the Bakufu. Their Majesties were carried as far as the entrance, where they wept to find that they could not enter because the twelve offenders had barred the gate. They were admitted late that night, after the twelve had escaped by a back door.

Late in September Yamana attacked the Sambō-In, a monastic building adjacent to the Imperial Palace, which at that time was situated at Tsuchimikado-Madenokōji, in the northeastern part of the city. The attacking force numbered some 50,000 men. The Sambō-In and several adjacent buildings were destroyed by fire, and other strategic points, including the Imperial Palace, were seized. The outlook for the Eastern Army was poor, and Hosokawa's beleaguered generals sent for reinforcements from their several provinces.

Help came from the Akamatsu family in Settsu and Tamba. The Akamatsu troops were harassed by the Western Army, but made their way to a point in Yamashina and thence to the neighbourhood of the Nanzenji, where they beat off poorly timed attacks by several separate forces sent by Yamana and Ōuchi and routed the attackers. Soon afterwards they arrived at Hosokawa's headquarters in the city.

Yamana's position nonetheless continued to improve. All Hosokawa's outlying defence works had been captured by early October, and all that was left him was a crowded space containing the Shōkokuji, the Bakufu buildings, and his own mansion. He tried to counterattack, but the wide spaces cleared by the earlier fighting gave an attacking force the advantage against a cramped defence. The most vulnerable of Hosokawa's positions was the Shōkokuji, and Yamana's leading generals decided to storm the monastery on November 1. They bribed a monk to start a fire, and as the smoke rose to the sky the attackers leapt forward. The monastery was taken, and the defenders were forced to fall back along Ichijō.

As it turned out, however, the force of the Western Army was spent. Fighting went on from dawn to sunset, until both armies withdrew exhausted, leaving the streets choked with corpses. The chronicles of the time paint a dreadful picture of the carnage. Ōuchi collected eight cartloads of heads, but there were many more, and these he threw into trenches.

The Shōkokuji was adjacent to the Shōgun's palace, and the Shōgun's ladies, fearing fire or rape, asked to be moved to safety. But Yoshimasa, so the story goes, remained calm and began a drinking party with his favourite companions.

After five months of incessant fighting, burning, and looting, the condition of the once beautiful city was appalling. At the end of 1467 it was described by a Bakufu official in the following words: "The flowery capital that we thought would last forever to our surprise is to become the lair of wolves and foxes. In the past there have been rebellions and disasters, but in this first year of Ōnin the laws of gods and kings have been broken and all the sects are perishing." He composed a short poem which may be rendered, though without the elegance of the original: "Now the city that you knew has become an empty moor, from which the evening skylark rises while your tears fall."[2]

3. Later Hostilities

After the destruction of the Shōkokuji in November, one of Hosokawa's generals recaptured the acres of cinders that had once been that imposing monastery. Yamana made no effort to regain the site, and the two spent adversaries faced one another without action for the rest of the year. Both reckoned on a long-drawn-out war of position, in which it seemed that Yamana had the advantage, because Hosokawa commanded only one out of the seven entrances into the city.[3]

Hosokawa ordered an attack on the first day of the New Year, an unconventional move which took Yamana and his roistering troops completely by surprise. After some sharp fighting, however, the attackers withdrew. Following this encounter there was little activity until April, when a raiding party from the Hosokawa forces tried to cut the Western Army's supply line. In the city also there was a sanguinary clash at this time, but thereafter the fighting seems almost to have ceased. Apart from the sallies and excursions of adventurous young officers, the two armies now remained glaring at one another month after month.

They glared at one another over a mass of protective works, for both sides wished to stand on the defensive and accordingly raised barricades and dug trenches. The records say that the central trench between the two parties was ten feet deep and twenty feet wide. The Eastern Army brought in some artificers to construct machines for flinging wood or stone missiles at the enemy. To relieve the tedium many officers on both sides indulged in such elegant and peaceful pastimes as composing poems, dressing in fanciful costumes of bright silk and even taking a hand at Chinese prosody. It was as if the Viscount Wellington's sub-

---

[2] Nare ya shiru/Miyako wa nobe no/Yū-hibari/Agaru wo mite mo/Ochiru namida wa.

[3] These seven entries were as follows:

ENTRY	HIGHWAY
Tōji guchi	Settsu road
Gojō guchi	Tōkaidō (Eastern Highroad)
Shijō-Omiya guchi	Saikaidō (Western Highroad)
Takeda guchi	Kii road (South)
Sanjō-bashi guchi	Eastern road to Ōmi
Ōhara guchi	Northern highroad to Wakasa
Kiyokura guchi	Sanindō (Western mountain road to Tamba)

It was only the last of these that Hosokawa could use.

alterns were to have acted a piece from Shakespeare and done a little Latin verse while waiting at Torres Vedras.

Thus week after week passed, enlivened only by an occasional sortie. There was some heavier fighting in September, chiefly on the eastern borders of the city; but the year drew to a close without any battle on a large scale, though destruction continued as long as the armies were in contact. Among the victims of this phase of desultory warfare were several important monasteries (including the Tenryūji) and the mansion of the Kiyowara family, with all its store of books and documents handed down by previous generations of scholars.

After 1468 there was no significant military activity except in the provinces. In Kyoto the activity of both Hosokawa and Yamana was mainly political. It centered upon the succession dispute, though both parties had to keep a sharp eye on events in other parts of Japan. Yoshimi's claim was sound enough, but he had no real supporters, being little more than a counter in the game between Yamana and Hosokawa.

Yoshimi was in a difficult position, and after various adventures (which need not be described here) soon he found himself one of Yamana's leading generals. This led to an anomalous situation characteristic of an age of broken promises and capricious loyalties. The Shōgun was now able to name the four-year-old Yoshihisa, Tomi-ko's son, as his heir, and this he did early in 1469. Thus the Ōnin War, which had begun as a partisan struggle between Yamana and Hosokawa, now became a war between Yoshimasa and his brother. The Shōgun duly induced the Emperor Go-Tsuchimikado to strip Yoshimi of his Court ranks and declare him a rebel.

On the whole the Imperial House was not seriously involved in the events of the Ōnin War, but in 1471—a remarkable development—there was a revival of the war between the Northern and Southern Courts, or a parody of that war, when Yamana thought to bolster his cause by setting up a Southern Pretender, who, dressed as a woman, arrived in a palanquin at Yamana's camp. This move was not pleasing to Yoshimi, who had not abandoned his allegiance to the reigning Emperor, and nothing came of it. The Pretender soon disappeared and was not heard of again except by rumour.

By the end of 1472 some generals on both sides had left for their own territories to put down insurrections brewed in their absence. Most of those who remained in Kyoto among the ruins were tired of the perpetual clash of arms, and as the months and years dragged on, both Yamana and Hosokawa began to wish for peace. But feeling still ran high among the lesser generals, and a truce was impossible. The weary Hosokawa proposed to enter holy orders and live in retirement, while Yamana, already ordained, said that he would take his own life. These dramatic measures proved unnecessary, however, for in 1473 both men died, Yamana at the age of seventy, Hosokawa at forty-three.

After the death of the two leaders the armies diminished rapidly in strength until Yoshimasa began to fear that if the Eastern Army should grow weaker, he himself might be in danger from Ōuchi and his associates. He sent out an order (Mikyōjo) to all provinces, calling upon them to keep the peace. It was, of course, especially directed against Ōuchi. The two armies now began pourparlers, and although no final agreement was reached, they arrived at a partial understanding upon which a number of generals submitted to Yoshimasa. Ōuchi, however, persisted in the view that he could not surrender until Yoshimasa and Yoshimi had come to terms on the succession. He even rejected a direct order from the Shōgun to lay down his arms, though it was accompanied by a promise of generous treatment. There was still sporadic fighting in and near Kyoto, and also in Yamato, where the peace of the Kasuga shrine was broken by a desperate struggle between Ōuchi and Hatakeyama Masanaga in 1475.

While the war dragged on in this way, increasing numbers of Western Army commanders submitted to the Shōgun, because they wanted to return to their domains. Finally, Ōuchi himself changed his mind, submitted to Yoshimasa, and marched his army home, leaving his base in Kyoto on December 17, 1477. Once he had left, there was nothing for the remaining forces to do but disperse. Yamana's men had already marched out the night before. A diary of the period has this to say of their departure: "Several places in the enemy's position were destroyed by fire. The Nijō palace was burned down. This was the work of the ashigaru." So the last act of the Yamana men was one of wanton destruction.

Even now peace had not come to the ravaged country, for there was still bitter warfare in the Kantō, where Ashikaga warriors fought against Uyesugi rivals for the office of Shōgun's Deputy in the eastern provinces; and at the other end of the empire there were fierce battles among the great families of Kyūshū. Indeed it would have been difficult to find a province where there was no convulsion, unless it were perhaps the Shikoku domains of the Hosokawa family.

The history of this cruel war of Ōnin gives an impression of utter futility. The purposes for which it was fought were never clearly defined, and certainly they were not achieved, except in so far as Hosokawa at the cost of fearful destruction proved superior in statecraft to his clumsy enemy. Looking at the political scene against its background of flames and smoke one seems to see its actors as unfortunate creatures demented by their own ambitions. There are no heroic figures that compel the imagination, for Yamana is a mere bandit and Hosokawa, with greater advantage of upbringing, is disagreeably shrewd and calculating and no less ruthless than his rival. Among the really interesting figures are those blemished characters of a secondary order whose offences seem almost venial in an age of robbery of gigantic dimensions—Tomi-ko, the Shōgun's consort, avaricious and cunning but well-bred and courageous; Ise Sadachika and Hino Katsuakira, his corrupt advisers; and a bevy of mistresses skilled in intrigue, delation, and embezzlement. But most enigmatic of all is the Shōgun himself.

4. Higashiyama

Yoshimasa is often condemned for neglecting his duties and devoting himself to a life of pleasure. There are grounds for this charge, but his behaviour cannot be explained in such simple terms. He inherited a much more difficult task than his predecessors, because social and political disintegration had proceeded fast since the days of Yoshimitsu. Whether he liked it or not, he was obliged by the urgency of the times to make some decisions, to give some orders, and to form some opinions on policy. In his first years of office he seems to have made an effort to govern, but he was very young and he received poor advice from those whose duty it was to guide him.

It is true that he vacillated and made frequent blunders, but it is doubtful whether a wiser man could have done better. The tide of events was flowing too strongly against him. By the time of his succession the subversive movement which already faced the Bakufu had spread to every class, from the arrogant warlord to the poor labouring man. The very fact that even with the power of Hosokawa behind him Yoshimasa was unable to control Yamana is evidence that the warlords were uncontrollable. It was not Yoshimasa but the whole military society that was to blame for the senseless destruction of the Ōnin War, and it is in the light of those circumstances that his conduct seems reprehensible. A clever, many-sided man, Yoshimasa would have made an excellent leader in a peaceful era of renaissance of the arts, but he was not the man to pull together a society rapidly falling to pieces. He saw death and disaster all around and sought distraction. Being of a sensitive character, he naturally preferred feminine society to the company of certain military leaders, whose loud voices and fierce opinions must often have offended his taste. Unfortunately his choice of favourites was far from impeccable, and he allowed them to dabble in affairs of state, which in practice meant to take bribes and accept commissions from petitioners.

There were several of these ladies, but none was so skilled in shady finance as his wife Tomi-ko, who in collaboration with her elder brother Hino Katsuakira made a great fortune by illicit methods. Katsuakira, one of Yoshimasa's advisers, was himself a master of peculation, who said openly that no claimant need approach him without a cash payment in advance.[4] But his sister was even more determined in her pur-

---

[4] The source is the miscellany (Zōjiki) of the Daijō-In branch of the Kōfukuji at Nara; and the issue was a commonplace suit concerning Church property.

suit of gain. Her dealings on the rice market and her moneylending
activities have already been noted. One of her more ingenious practices was to appropriate taxes which she illegally levied at the seven
entrances to the capital, falsely declaring that they were for the repair
of the Imperial Palace. But it is only fair to say of Tomi-ko that Yoshimasa must have been a very difficult husband, and that her unhappy
domestic life explains if it does not excuse her conduct.

Other advisers of Yoshimasa, if less avaricious, were no more trustworthy. Ise Sadachika was in his confidence and had some influence
on his actions, but he was disliked by the warrior chieftains and was
driven out of Kyoto before the war began, only to make his way back
some time later and to resume his service to the Shōgun.

If Yoshimasa's wife and his favourites were remarkable for their
incomes, he was unrivalled in his expenditure. His extravagance was
notorious, and it may perhaps be explained by his despair. He wanted
to escape from his own failures in private and public life. His world
was falling in ruins around him. He thought of entering a monastery,
and he studied under Zen teachers in the hope of finding serenity; but
he ended by devoting all his mind and spirit to aesthetic pursuits,
always seeking freedom from the despondence which had become his
habit. In 1473 he retired from office, naming Yoshihisa as his successor.

Thus the man who failed as the leader of a military society found
some contentment as a patron of the arts and a connoisseur inspiring
new movements in acting, dancing, painting, architecture, and the general practice of aesthetic refinements. He showed that in a strong reaction against barbarity, the arts may flourish in times of war. The dark
ages have their bright side, and to set against the Ōnin War there is
constructive activity displayed in many fields of endeavour during the
Muromachi era. Not least of these in importance is the work of artists
encouraged by Yoshimasa from his retreat at the base of Higashiyama,
a hill on the northeastern fringe of the city.

This is not the place for a discussion of Muromachi aesthetics, but it
is useful to relate here some of the events in the years when Yoshimasa
was indulging his taste for splendid ceremonies, fine buildings, theatrical performances, the plastic arts, and connoisseurship in general.[5]

A new Muromachi palace was built in 1458, and so was the Takakura
palace of his mother; and one of his most elaborate Nō entertainments
was given in 1464, before the Ōnin War. After the war he devoted much
attention to building and restoring, but his most celebrated structure
was the Silver Pavilion (Ginkaku), part of his Higashiyama villa. It is
of peculiar interest because, although it was no doubt influenced by the
Golden Pavilion (Kinkaku) of Yoshimitsu, it expresses the difference

[5] For further details on the arts of this period the reader is referred to Chapter
XVIII of the author's "Short Cultural History" of Japan, revised edition, London,
1952.

Drawing of dengaku (LEFT) and sarugaku (RIGHT) dancers, after an illustration in "Shichijūichi-ban Uta-awase"

between the aesthetic standards of the two periods—one a parade of bright gold, the other a delicate understatement in gray, black, and white. The villa was completed in 1493, three years after Yoshimasa's death. It is doubtful whether any silver foil was applied, though its use had been intended.

It was here in the Ginkaku that Yoshimasa practised the tea ceremony (which he raised to the rank of a fine art) and entertained his favourites, who were no longer the unscrupulous money-grubbers of a former time but artists, poets, playwrights, and men of taste with whom he discussed the Sung paintings and porcelain which he had assembled there at great cost. Today a "Higashiyama piece" is the greatest of treasures. Associated with those years, moreover (the last two or three decades of the fifteenth century), are the names of many celebrated Japanese masters. Zeami, the real founder of the Nō, had died in 1443, but Nōami, Geiami, Sōami, Kanze, and the incomparable painter Sesshū belong to those years.

The aesthetic movement of which Yoshimasa was the leader was not confined to the ruling class. Rich merchants of Kyoto and Sakai contributed to it by their purchases of rare works of art and their general pursuit of refinement in taste. Great barons, who had once fought for provinces, now competed also for small pieces of porcelain.

In some respects Yoshimasa was the most remarkable of mediaeval Japanese rulers, for it was a rare achievement to create and govern an aesthetic society important not only in his own country's history but also in the general history of taste. It may be objected that he did not create this society, but certainly it was he who called it into being by his strong inclinations. In the Japan of his day the artists, playwrights, actors, dancers, and musicians whom he favoured could not so fully have exercised their talents and gained such public esteem without the patronage and the lavish support by which he encouraged them. As a ruler he was a mere puppet, yet in the world of art or letters he was no mere dilettante, but a man of exceptionally firm and penetrating judgment. In this sphere he showed himself able to originate and command. He gave a conscious and positive direction to the aesthetic life of his time.

And despite his political shortcomings Yoshimasa was capable of strong leadership when he chose, and he was not without constructive powers. By his time it was no longer possible for a Shōgun to exercise political authority, since the country was in a turmoil of revolt; but he did what was open to him with great distinction.

It is sometimes said that the masterpieces of Higashiyama were created under the inspiration of Zen Buddhism. This is a dubious statement, which should not be accepted without clear definitions of inspiration and Zen. In so far as Zen inculcates "direct pointing to the soul of man" it must be hostile to what is false, pretentious, confused, obscure, or roundabout. But so is any rational canon of taste in the arts as well as in the life of the individual. We need not turn to metaphysics for an explanation of pure creative instinct at work.

Yoshimasa's own religious beliefs were very catholic. He was interested in the mystic sects, and he also liked the company of Zen monks, who, in his time, were usually more active in literature than in religious thought. But his later life was governed by the Nembutsu teaching, and he was intimate with a powerful monk from Kurodani, one Shinsei, who intoned the Nembutsu at his deathbed.

CHAPTER XIV

THE CAPITAL AND THE PROVINCES
AFTER THE ŌNIN WAR

1. *Hosokawa and the Ashikaga Shōguns*

AMONG the most significant features of the years following the Ōnin War was the complete breakdown of the Ashikaga Bakufu. Yoshimasa died in 1490, and the government of the country, such government as there was, fell into the hands of the Hosokawa family. The Shōguns who followed Yoshimasa were mere puppets, except for Yoshihisa, who (having the courage of his mother Tomi-ko) made a gallant attempt to check the disloyal ambition of some of the leading warriors but died on a battlefield in 1489 before he could carry out his design.

His successor Yoshitane (Yoshimi's son) was made Shōgun in 1490, but he did not remain long in office. In 1493 he fled from Kyoto in fear of the Kanrei Hosokawa Katsumoto, who then set up another nephew of Yoshimasa, named Yoshizumi. Hosokawa Masamoto, Katsumoto's son, became Kanrei in 1494. Yoshitane ventured back to Kyoto in 1499, making the Enryakuji his headquarters; but he was put to flight by Hosokawa, whose troops destroyed many buildings of the monastery. In time Yoshitane made his way to Ōuchi's capital at Yamaguchi. Ōuchi Yoshioki took up his cause, assembled an army, and marched on the capital. In 1507 Masamoto was assassinated in Kyoto; the following year Yoshizumi fled and Yoshitane was restored to office.

From these examples it will be seen that the warlords were using the Shōguns as puppets, much as Shōguns had used the Emperors in the past; for the present war was not a war of succession between claimants to the Shōgun's office, but a scarcely concealed struggle between claimants to the more important office of Kanrei. After Masamoto's death this war was fought chiefly between his adopted sons Takakuni and Sumimoto.

Here the situation became fantastic, if not farcical, since Sumimoto was also a puppet, manipulated by a Hosokawa vassal named Miyoshi. Thus we have a picture of a puppet claimant to an office which manipulates a puppet Shōgun. It is an excellent illustration of the so-called causes of the wars of this period, which were not causes at all but merely pretences or flimsy excuses for making war.

Ōuchi remained in the capital until 1518, protecting the Shōgun Yoshitane against Miyoshi and his fellow conspirators. In this era of reprehensible conduct Ōuchi stands out as a generous figure. He gave financial aid to the Shōgun and to the Emperor, both of whom were in a wretched condition, and there is no doubt that his presence in Kyoto was a contribution to peace and good order. But he had to leave to see to his own affairs in Yamaguchi, and with his departure trouble at once broke out again in and around the capital.

Between 1490 and 1550 Shōguns were appointed or deposed principally at the will of the Hosokawa family. The successive puppets, beginning with the tenth Ashikago Shōgun, were as follows:

Yoshitane ...... appointed 1490, abdicated 1493
Yoshizumi ..... appointed 1493, abdicated 1508
Yoshitane ...... returned   1508, abdicated 1521
Yoshiharu ..... appointed 1521, abdicated 1545
Yoshiteru ...... appointed 1545, murdered 1565
Yoshihide ...... appointed 1565, died   1568
Yoshiaki .... appointed 1568, deposed   1573

The Hosokawa family lost their position to their former vassals in 1558 with the defeat of the last Kanrei, Hosokawa Harumoto, at the hands of Miyoshi and Matsunaga, both of whom owed a debt of loyalty to the Hosokawa clan. These two families were nuisances in Yamashiro and adjacent provinces for a further decade or more, and were then suppressed by supporters of the Shōgun Yoshiaki. The collapse of the Hosokawa family and the later Ashikaga Shōguns is not of great interest in itself, but it serves to illustrate the main features of the political history of the period known as Sengoku Jidai, the Age of the Country at War, which followed closely upon the Ōnin War and lasted for the better part of a century.[1]

In that period only a few of the once prominent feudal houses survived. New men rose to power, new rivalries developed. The pattern is furnished by the case of Miyoshi, mentioned above. Miyoshi was a vassal of Hosokawa, whose authority he usurped; and Miyoshi was in turn ousted by his own retainer Matsunaga. Changes of this kind were taking place all over the country before the close of the fifteenth century, and in the sixteenth century they continued on a grand scale.

Perhaps the most remarkable of these struggles is that in which the Ōuchi family was destroyed by one vassal and avenged by another. Ōuchi, thriving on seaborne trade, kept a kingly state in western Japan (holding in a firm grasp Suō, Nagato, Buzen, Bungo, and Chikuzen). But in 1551, Yoshioki's son Yoshitaka, then the chieftain and a man of high character, was attacked and destroyed by a vassal named Suye Harukata. Another and a senior vassal, Mōri Motonari, was more loyal

[1] "The Age of the Country at War" is a convenient but not exact translation of Sengoku Jidai, which is a term from Chinese history designating the age of the "warring states," which lasted for some two hundred years before China was unified under Ch'in Shih Huang-ti in 221 B.C. The conflict in Japan was not between states or even between provinces, but between individual warlords.

10

11

to his liege lord. He made his preparations and in 1554 began hostilities against Harukata, whom he overcame in one of the most theatrical battles in the history of Japan. It was fought on and around the lovely island of Itsukushima, which according to tradition neither birth nor death was allowed to pollute.

In the season of autumnal gales Harukata, thinking himself safe on the island, was tricked by a surprise attack from the mainland delivered at night in a blinding rainstorm. Pirate vessels on both sides took part in the encounter, and fought in the offing. Harukata fled with the remnants of his force, decimated by Mōri's attack and further reduced by drowning as the fugitives struggled to reach the boats with which the water was littered. Harukata could not escape, and committed suicide with some of his officers. Motonari thus established the power of the Mōri family as successors to Ōuchi, and they continued supreme in the western provinces for three hundred years.

It is difficult to distinguish any single important reason for the outbreak of the civil wars which as they spread engulfed the whole country during the sixteenth century. Some Japanese historians have found a clue in the phrase "gekokujō" (roughly "the low oppress the high"), which was current parlance from the time of the so-called Kemmu Restoration (1334–36), when the streets of the capital were thronged with discontented warriors seeking reward for their services. This is a useful cliché, giving a quick view of a disturbed social order in which things look upside down to a conservative eye; but it does not explain the phenomenon which it describes.

"Gekokujō" has even been interpreted as an expression of democratic ideas, but the changes that took place after the rise of the Ashikaga Shōguns can scarcely be described as a social revolution. What took place was the emergence of new classes, together with the exercise of new powers by certain members of existing classes. The process is clearly discernible at different levels, notably: (a) in the emancipation of a number of agricultural workers, who became independent farmers on a small scale; (b) in the rise of an influential class of traders and moneylenders; (c) in the growing strength of independent local warriors (ji-samurai), who formed associations to resist the depredations of Constables and other rural magnates; and (d) in the seizure of power in both national and provincial government by former vassals or retainers of the leading warrior houses.

These were important and sometimes violent changes, but to describe them as democratic movements is to debase the currency of political terms. It is true that most of the frequent risings of the fifteenth century were expressions of popular discontent in which peasants took part, but they were usually led by small local landowners, and they called for the removal of specific grounds of complaint. They were not inspired by any general political aim, although at times they may have developed a political character.

2. The Yamashiro Rising of 1485

In a previous chapter a series of agrarian risings in Yamashiro province has been described. These were forcible protests by peasants and small landowners against oppressive acts of the Constable or his officers. During the twenty-five years before the Ōnin War they had revolted with some success. After the outbreak of war in 1467 they managed with difficulty to keep their fields in cultivation; and when hostilities in the city came to an end, they looked forward to a real return of peaceful life. They were to be disappointed, however, for the feuds and rivalries of the Ōnin War spilled over into other parts of the country, while the unrepentant Bakufu, or at least its financial officers and the grasping Tomi-ko, resumed their oppressive taxation. In 1479 they imposed a levy on all provinces for the repair of the Imperial Palace; and in 1482 Tomi-ko proposed to restore the barriers and collect octroi, taxes on produce, at the entrances to the city. But when the Yamashiro-Ikki threatened reprisals, the project was withdrawn.

It will be seen that the peasants had by this time developed a strong feeling of unity. We need not attempt to trace its growth in detail, but we should note that along with the improved position of the peasantry there came a certain degree of organization in villages or other rural communities, and also of joint action by such communities. In fifteenth-century documents, such as petitions or protests or agreements, the terms sōson ("all the villages") and sōbyakusho ("all the peasants") occur frequently. Here the prefix sō[2] signifies that the peasants and the villages are united, and that the document speaks for all of them.

After the Ōnin War there developed in southern Yamashiro a continuous strife between warriors who were or who claimed to be partisans of one of the two branches of the great Hatakeyama family, led respectively by Masanaga and Yoshinari, whose feud had been one of the causes, or at least the preludes, of the Ōnin War. The campaign was not on a large scale, the numbers engaged being of the order of ten thousand at most; but the fighting was widespread and conducted with no regard for the life or property of the inhabitants. Dwelling houses and monastic buildings were destroyed by fire, and much damage was done by ashigaru temporarily employed. In some places peasants were dragged off to serve as porters, or were made to pay large sums to escape from forced labour. But at length the peasants formed their own force, under command of capable local warriors, and it looked as if the Hatakeyama partisans on both sides would be obliged to withdraw. Their prospects were so poor that they were drawn together;

---

[2] It occurs in many other terms, such as sōryō, the whole estate, sōkoku, the whole province.

a certain Tsubai, one of the leaders on the Masanaga side, actually applied to the Chief Abbot Jinson in the Kōfukuji for a post in a manor belonging to Yoshinari's side.

The peasants in southern Yamashiro had already done great harm to both groups of partisans by forcibly depriving them of supplies. Now they took the offensive. Towards the end of the year 1485 the peasants and their leaders, the experienced kokujin, met in council and agreed to make the following demands: (1) both Hatakeyama armies were to leave Yamashiro province; (2) all estates theretofore illegally possessed by warriors were to be returned to their owners; (3) all barriers were to be withdrawn. Both Hatakeyama forces began to move away less than a week after this ultimatum. Some of their commanders took refuge in another province, and Tsubai committed suicide.

Early in 1486 thirty-six leaders of the Yamashiro-Ikki met in council at the celebrated Byōdō-In of Uji, the scene of many historic events since its beginning as a Fujiwara villa. There they elected a provisional government of the province, to be administered by officers in monthly rotation. This was a triumphal moment for warriors and peasants, proving the value of their determination to resist oppressive treatment. It should be understood, however, that although the peasants benefited from the new arrangement, the local gentry were still in command. They had chosen to combine with the peasants in revolt, but they had served their own private purposes also, since this new combination protected them against Constables and Deputy Constables.

The provisional government was not a mere temporary arrangement. It lasted for eight years. Its officers met regularly to administer the laws and regulations which the council at the Byōdō-In had approved; but after those years of self-government the Constables and their officers began to resume their old habits, often with the collaboration of kokujin, who accepted appointments as overseers or even as daikan.

3. *The Capital in Ruins*

By the end of the Ōnin War the capital had suffered such destruction of life and property that its inhabitants may well have been sunk in despair, especially since war and rioting continued in the Home Provinces, and Kyoto was now at the centre of a storm affecting the whole country. After the armies withdrew in 1477 the city was for a time in the hands of marauders, and the police functions of the Bakufu were most inadequately performed by the Shoshi-dai, the deputies of the Samurai-dokoro. So weak were they that the rioters, many of them members of the numerous ikki, established themselves in great monasteries or shrines like the Tōji or Gion, and could not be ejected. Once installed, the ikki leaders would ring the warning bells day and night, hoping to terrify the rich citizens. Those who suffered most were not the nobles, but the pawnbrokers and the sake dealers. Private householders who feared attack would try to bribe the rioters by gifts of food and drink; others would put up a fence of bamboo or wood, and fight until they were vanquished. The raids were not furtive affairs but daylight robberies; if they lasted into the night they were lit up by flares. They generally ended in fires. Most of the conflagrations in the city at this time were due to deliberate incendiarism, not only by the ikki rioters but by small bands of hardened criminals who murdered as well as robbed. Soon the tumult and lawlessness of the city spread to the suburbs and along the main roads leading to Ōtsu and Yamazaki.

Yet the citizens rose above these appalling conditions, and even managed to find some recreation. They went on excursions to the countryside, or attended performances of sangaku, or made pilgrimages to Kamo or Gion. They faced the task of repair with courage, and hastened to cover the scorched earth with new buildings, including a new Tsuchimikado palace and new headquarters for the Shōgun. (Evidently the taxes which made this work possible came in from the provinces, though no doubt in much reduced quantities.) Before long the city had resumed its usual busy life. The great avenues (Sanjō and Shijō) were once more lined with shops, and travellers appeared in large numbers.

The truth is that the inhabitants had become used to danger and knew how to enjoy the present without too much thought of the future. Their acceptance of disaster was not a sign of apathy, for they continued to develop the city's municipal administration, which had been in an early stage before the Ōnin War. After the war the Bakufu was ineffective if not helpless, and it was thanks to the organized efforts of the people, led by merchants and shopkeepers, that the city's Upper and Lower Quarters (Kami-kyō and Shimo-kyō) rose again from desolation. A similar form of self-government was growing in other cities and struggling against the destructive forces by which the citizens were so often threatened.

This power of recuperation is displayed throughout Japanese history and testifies to the courage and endurance of the people. It may be added that a society which depends upon wood rather than stone suffers much destruction by fire, but it is a loss that can be repaired in a short time.

The Court nobles at this time suffered great hardship and loss; it is true, for many of the lesser nobles took refuge in the country and were unable to return since their property was destroyed. But the great families somehow managed to continue their usual way of life, with difficulty at times but still without great change. This is the impression given by the diary of Sanjōnishi Sanetaka, which covers the years from 1474 to 1533, four years before his death. Sanetaka saw great changes, but they came slowly at first. Although he had to be content with a reduced and irregular income from his estate, he experienced none of the distress which afflicted the poorer, salaried Court officials. He managed his affairs with skill and found new sources of revenue. The leading nobles, while no doubt secretly despising the warriors, were clever enough to make use of those who had social ambitions. In 1530 we find Sanetaka making a present to a person whom he had contrived (with help from his military friends) to get appointed as manager of one of the Sanjōnishi manors.

He was a man of considerable learning and was much respected for his talents both at Court and in the Shōgun's palace. He was often invited by the Shōgun to discuss literature, and he was asked to copy or read or expound written works in great variety—especially anthologies of verse and such illustrated scrolls as the *Ishiyamadera Engi Emaki.* He was also consulted by the Emperor on the purchase of rare books, and modern Japanese historians owe him a debt of gratitude for saving a complete copy of the *Entairyaku,* which its poverty-stricken owner was on the point of breaking up.

No doubt Sanetaka was more fortunate than most of his peers, but his diary shows that Court society had not collapsed as a sequel of the Ōnin War, and that the Court, while short of funds, was not destitute (as is sometimes suggested). The ceremonial functions of the Emperor were reduced, but he continued traditional observances at shrines and monasteries as well as ordinary ritual within the Palace, including the conferment of ranks and titles. Ceremonies in which all the nobles took part were very rare, and fewer than a hundred were qualified to attend, so that no costly splendours were required except for some special occasion like a coronation, when the Bakufu usually contributed by raising funds from special taxes.

Although shorn of its wealth, the Court was still held in respect by the great daimyos. Ōuchi Masahiro, growing rich on foreign trade, tried to copy Kyoto culture in his domain, and was in close touch with the capital. And when Ōuchi Yoshioki brought the refugee Shōgun back to Kyoto in 1508, he was proud to be rewarded with the fourth rank at Court.

Sanetaka's diary gives evidence of the gradual disintegration of the shōen. It describes in detail the efforts which he was obliged to make in order to obtain revenue from his estates. It is true that he was in a stronger position than other landlords owing to his cordial relations with the Bakufu; but he had to use all his influence to obtain an adequate income, and towards the end of his career—say by about 1530—his total receipts from the manors of the Sanjōnishi family were at such a low point that even small sums are mentioned gleefully in his journal. He was particularly glad to supplement his income by such a perquisite as a royalty on sales of karamushi, a kind of ramie or China grass grown in Yamashiro province.

While receipts were dwindling, claims were increasing. An early example is an order of 1485 from the Bakufu to furnish labour for the building of Yoshimasa's Higashiyama villas. Sanetaka, after consulting the Saionji family (who were joint owners of the manor in question), agreed to send 110 labourers. This was a great drain on the resources of the manor, though still not an intolerable burden. But fifty years later the whole system of shōen was on the point of collapse.

4. *The Provinces after the Ōnin War*

During the Ōnin War, while the western warlords were spending their strength in Kyoto they were losing control of their own domains, partly because of conspiracies by subordinates whom they had left in charge and partly because Hosokawa had sent emissaries to stir up trouble, especially in the territories of Yamana, Ōuchi, and Shiba, his most dangerous rivals. These attempts to foment rebellion show that Hosokawa was well aware of the general trend of feeling in the provinces. He no doubt felt impatient at being obliged to stay under siege in Kyoto while important events were taking place elsewhere.

It is true that the Ōnin War was an exceptionally bloody struggle, but its importance is perhaps overestimated in most historical accounts, probably because it was full of dramatic episodes, was fought in the capital city, and involved the persons of the imperial family and the Shōgun's household. It was otherwise not exceptional, for like all the wars of the fifteenth century it was a conflict between two great warrior houses and no strictly national issue was at stake.

But very soon the aggregate of these so-to-speak private wars became a single war in which the whole country was involved for a century or more. The first signs of this disastrous sequence are visible after Hosokawa's attempt to make trouble in western Japan. The arrival of Ōuchi Masahiro's army in Kyoto in 1468 had been a severe blow to Hosokawa, who felt it urgently necessary to stimulate disloyalty in the West in Ōuchi's absence. This was not an easy matter, but fortunately for Hosokawa some of Ōuchi's subordinates had already taken advantage of their overlord's absence to plot against him with certain Kyūshū chieftains whom he had in the past defeated. The Bakufu, under pressure from Hosokawa of course, ordered Shimazu to combine with other leaders against Ōuchi, promising them his lands should they be successful. These plans did not succeed, but no doubt the dissension within Ōuchi's circle and the generally uneasy situation in the western provinces took some of the strain off the Eastern Army in Kyoto.

This kind of stroke and counterstroke spread over the whole country, involving almost all the leading warrior families. To relate in their complexity the full story of their quarrels and their battles, their shifts of allegiance or alliance, would be to encumber this narrative with confusing detail. Here it is enough to mention only the names of the successful antagonists and the areas of their strife. It should be understood that there was no direct connexion between the Ōnin War and the wars waged in western Japan and the Kantō. Some of these had broken out before Ōnin, others lasted longer, but of course the Ōnin War had an indirect influence upon their timing and their extent.

5. War in the Kantō

It will be recalled that the office of Governor of the Kantō (Kantō Kubō) was brought to an end in 1439 by the defeat and death of Ashikaga Mochiuji. The great Uyesugi family (closely related by marriage to the Ashikaga) took charge of affairs in Kamakura until 1449, when Ashikaga Shigeuji was appointed Kanrei.

This Shigeuji showed signs of disloyalty, and arranged for the murder of the Uyesugi who was his Deputy. The whole Uyesugi family arose in anger at this treachery, and drove Shigeuji out of Kamakura. After some years of fighting they asked Kyoto to send a successor to Shigeuji. This was agreed, and in 1459 the Shōgun Yoshimasa sent his own younger brother Masatomo to Kamakura. But the supporters of Shigeuji would not allow Masatomo to take up his post, and consequently there were now two deputies of the Shōgun in the East.

In this absurd situation, where neither claimant was able to exercise his powers, Shigeuji established himself at a small place called Koga in Shimotsuke, while Masatomo settled with his retinue at Horigoye in Izu. The two men were known respectively as the Koga Kubō and the Horigoye Kubō. They played no part in administration, and they are mentioned here only because in the factional strife which darkened the ensuing years the leaders found it convenient to claim that they were fighting in the cause of a representative of the Ashikaga Shōgun.

The government of the Kantō was now once again in the hands of the Uyesugi family, who were extremely powerful. As they increased they split into three main branches, Inukake, Yamanouchi, and Ōgigayatsu, named after the localities in which they resided. The result of this division was an internecine war which continued for some twenty-five years, and came to a stop, or rather a pause, at the end of the Ōnin War, in 1477.

There is no need to study this conflict in its sanguinary detail, but one episode deserves attention because it reveals the fundamental weakness of these great warrior families as they became swollen with pride and doomed by ambition.

The Uyesugi of the Yamanouchi branch occupied the stronghold of Kawagoye in Musashi, and the Ōgigayatsu branch stood against them in the castle of Shirai in Shimosa. The Ōgigayatsu forces were inferior in numbers, but thanks to the efforts of a vassal, their strength was increased not only in numbers but by the use of a new fortified place. The vassal was Ōta Dōkan, and the fortified place was the castle which he had built at Yedo.

Dōkan was a remarkable man. He was a good general with a quick eye for terrain. He saw that the fortress at Kawagoye was not enough protection along the line of the Tonegawa, and decided that another place should be fortified to complement it. This was done in 1456–57 and was a remarkable achievement. The new castle consisted of triple circular galleries, the whole enclosed within great stone walls, rising to a height of one hundred and fifty feet. It was surrounded by a deep moat. Dōkan's own residence was in the centre, and included apartments furnished in excellent taste, where he held poetry meetings or gave other elegant entertainments, for in addition to his merits as a general he had a fine literary judgment.

It might be supposed that Sadamasa and other Ōgigayatsu leaders would be grateful to this loyal man, but in those days murder was a favourite solution of all problems. Sadamasa killed Dōkan because of a false rumour retailed to him by a rival. This outrage was committed in 1485, after years of valiant service rendered by Dōkan to his lieges.

It would seem as if the incessant strife of those days was the work of barbarous chieftains, bent only on slaughter. Yet the Uyesugi leaders, though belonging to a warlike house, were by no means ignorant men. In their family tradition there was a respect for learning, displayed in particular by Uyesugi Norizane, who was Deputy for the Kantō Kanrei in 1440. He had the proper qualities of a statesman and endeavoured to preserve good feeling between Kyoto and Kamakura; he had scholarly tastes, as we know, and contributed to a revival of the Ashikaga College, furnishing its library with books. His contemporaries spoke of his ability with high respect.

It may be added here that even the brutal Uyesugi Sadamasa had an amiable side to his character. He found that his son Tomonaga had no desire to succeed him but preferred an easy life of pleasure to the anxieties of leadership. Fearing for the future of his family in an age when the chief occupation of men was to make war, Sadamasa drew up a paper of instructions setting forth his idea of the duties of a warrior. It was a serious, thoughtful document, and was deemed so appropriate to the times that its text was later used as a copybook by children learning to write.

In Sadamasa's time, and indeed from soon after the close of the Ōnin War in 1477, few parts of the eastern provinces were at peace. The Uyesugi factions, reduced to two by the death of the Inukake chieftain, resumed hostilities and were fighting hard by 1488, though without decisive results. Large numbers of men were involved, and after a pause the struggle was resumed on a great scale a few years later, at the turn of the century.

By 1500 the Ōgigayatsu branch was declining in strength, but it continued to struggle until 1505. In that year it was at last defeated by the Yamanouchi forces, thanks to help sent from Echigo by an Uyesugi kinsman named Fusayoshi, who was Constable of that province. The Echigo forces were led by a warrior in Fusayoshi's service as Deputy Constable, one Nagao Tamekage, who now found in his hands the future of the Uyesugi house in Kamakura. Tamekage was a soldier of fortune, a *nariagari-mono* or "upstart," as such men were called by their upper-class contemporaries. Upstarts were not uncommon in this era, for almost every great feudal house was plagued by succession quarrels, often instigated and planned by subordinates who sought to improve their own condition. Tamekage's career is of general as well as particular interest, because he is representative of a new type of warrior destined to replace the Constables and other high officers who owed their positions to the Ashikaga family, or even to the Kamakura Shōguns.

Tamekage quarrelled with Fusayoshi and took arms against him in 1507, having by then acquired a large following. Fusayoshi was defeated and killed. He was succeeded as Constable of Echigo by Uyesugi Akisada, and Tamekage's appointment as his Deputy (Shugo-dai) was approved by the Bakufu. Tamekage soon felt strong enough to challenge Akisada, whom he defeated in battle in Echigo in 1510. In this struggle he had the advantage of help from another warrior, one Hōjō Sōun, a newcomer who was already a power in the Kantō and was to become its master within a few years. Fortunately for Tamekage it happened that his interests were parallel with those of Sōun, so that Sōun willingly engaged enemies who might otherwise have turned to attack Tamekage. Before long Tamekage had reduced the Uyesugi in the Kantō to a subjection which led to the ultimate collapse of this powerful house.

Sōun was a man of much greater ability and much wider ambitions than Nagao Tamekage. His origin is so obscure that even his name and birthplace are not known for certain. He is thought to have been born in Ise and to have arrived in Suruga about 1475, when he took service with Imagawa, Constable of that province. He was known then as Ise Shinkurō, presumably a mere cognomen. He gained favour by helping to suppress a rising in Imagawa's territory, and thereafter he made progress as an independent leader, being joined by a number of warriors whom his character and military skill had attracted.

Having far-reaching designs, he kept an eye on the province of Izu; and he carefully watched the sequence of events at Horigoye, where the Kantō Kubō Ashikaga Masatomo had been installed in his empty office. Masatomo died in 1491 and was succeeded by his son, known by his childhood name as Chachamaru. This appointment led to dissension and to armed clashes which provided Sōun with the excuse for intervention that he required. He had a sufficient force ready for action, and he stormed in to capture Horigoye not long after Masatomo's death. The boy Chachamaru was confined in a small room by his stepmother, but he broke out and killed her before committing suicide himself.

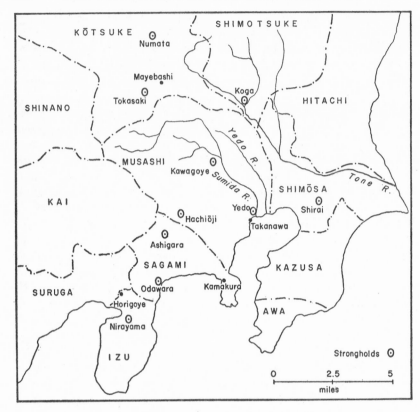

The Hōjō strongholds about 1550

Now Ise Shinkurō was master of the whole province of Izu. At this point he took the surname of Hōjō, thereby associating himself with the Hōjō Regents, who belonged to Izu and were of Taira origin. His purpose was to suggest that he was destined to displace the Ashikaga, as the Hōjō had displaced the Minamoto Shōguns, thus reviving Taira rule. For a given name he adopted the Buddhist appellation of Sōun or Sōzui, and in the history of the early sixteenth century he is known as Hōjō Sōun.

Now well on the way to further success, he built a stronghold at Nirayama in Izu and studied the situation in other provinces. A reference to the above map will show that to protect his position in Izu he needed to hold the strategic position of Odawara, a post town (shukuba-machi) on the high road, giving access from the west by the Hakone Pass and from the east by the coast road passing through or near Kamakura. At that time the castle at Odawara was held by one Ōmori, a youth who had just succeeded his father. Sōun made friends with him, and one day asked for permission to enter the Ōmori domain on a deer hunt. Permission was granted, and Sōun disguised his men as hunters. The hunt turned into a massacre and the castle was captured. By this treachery, of a kind then regarded as a legitimate stratagem, Sōun became master of Izu and of the southern portion of Sagami.

To complete his design he now had to extend his influence eastward in the direction of Yedo Bay and northward into Musashi to points where he could defend himself against invasion from the north. This he accomplished in a series of battles and sieges lasting over twenty years. He occupied Odawara in 1494, and by 1516 he was virtual master of all Sagami. Nagao Tamekage's attacks upon the Uyesugi faction were of assistance to Sōun, enabling him to complete his conquest of Sagami in 1518.

Sōun died at his Nirayama stronghold in 1519, but his son Ujitsuna carried on his work. In 1524 Ujitsuna led a large army into Musashi and attacked the castle at Yedo. At this time the two branches of the Uyesugi, if they had combined, might have checked or stopped his progress. But they were at odds again, and when this news came to Ujitsuna, he hurried into Musashi and defeated one army at Takanawa and another in Yedo castle. He was now in a strong position in Musashi, but in order to secure it he was obliged to hold the line from Yedo along the Sumida River. For this purpose he had to anchor his defence at the stronghold of Kawagoye, which commanded the road from Echigo and at the same time stood in the way of an enemy approaching from the north. Such an attacking force would of necessity be slowed down by crossing the Sumida and Yedo rivers, and would be then in danger of sudden assaults from Kawagoye.

In 1539 Ujitsuna defeated and killed the Koga Kubō (Yoshiaki), and forced the submission of the Satomi clan in Awa province, thus carrying Sōun's design an important stage towards completion. But his success at Kawagoye was not decisive. Time after time the Uyesugi made desperate efforts to regain the fort, and although Ujitsuna pressed them hard, both branches held out stubbornly against his superior forces.

Ujitsuna died in 1541 and was succeeded by Ujiyasu, a man of his grandfather's stamp, who turned his energies to completing Sōun's plan, the domination of the Kantō. At this late hour the two Uyesugi factions saw that they must unite in order to survive. They decided to support the cause of the Koga Kubō and thus to unify Musashi; they failed, though not for want of desperate courage.

They joined in an attack on Kawagoye in 1542, and they were assisted by troops from Koga. Ujiyasu promptly sent a great reinforcement to attack the enemy outside Kawagoye, while the defenders of the fortress sallied out at night to join the battle. The result was a complete defeat of the Uyesugi forces and the Koga contingent. This successful engagement fought in the darkness is celebrated in the military annals of Japan. From that date the Go-Hōjō (Later Hōjō) as they were called, went on to further triumphs, beginning with the destruction of the Uyesugi family. By 1560 most of Ujiyasu's enemies had been crushed or dispersed and he was joined by most of the influential warriors in other eastern provinces.

The Uyesugi branches and the Koga Kubō were destroyed or had vanished. Only Uyesugi Norimasa remained, and he escaped to Echigo, where he put himself under the protection of Nagao Terutora, a son of that Nagao Tamekage whom Sōun had assisted in 1510. Terutora accepted Norimasa's surrender, and had himself adopted as Norimasa's heir, taking the name of Uyesugi Kenshin and (though remaining in Echigo) claiming to be the legitimate Kantō Kanrei. His name is famous in military history, especially for his repeated conflicts with another bellicose figure, Takeda Shingen of the neighbouring province of Kai. These two seem to have enjoyed meeting in battle. They are said to have fought several times at Kawanakajima, a place well suited for tactical experiment, lying in a triangle at the confluence of the Saigawa and the sinuous Chikumagawa in Shinano. Two such encounters (1555 and 1564) are recorded in detail, and there may have been others.

Kenshin also caused trouble to the Hōjō by raids upon territory which they were peacefully occupying. His first attempt was in 1560, when he crossed the Mikuni-Tōge (Three-Province Pass) and after following the course of the Tonegawa, turned off at Umayabashi (the modern Mayebashi) to deliver a sudden attack in the neighbourhood of Odawara. Having no rear guard, he could not follow up these attacks, which did little more than oblige the Hōjō commanders to take special precautions.

He was joined in Kōtsuke by former Uyesugi followers, but to no useful end. While he was occupied by this adventure, Takeda Shingen took advantage of his absence to attack enemies in Kōtsuke and Musashi. News of this activity stimulated Kenshin to make a second attempt, in 1561; but he did not get far beyond Umayabashi and turned back.

These details of Kenshin's raids are of no great interest in themselves, since they were poorly conceived and not well executed; but they throw light on the strategic principles followed by Sōun and his successors. Ujiyasu retaliated by attacking those friends of Kenshin who were near, and making friendly approaches to Kenshin's enemies who were distant. Thus he dealt severe punishment to the Satake family in Hitachi and took special steps to cause trouble in Kenshin's own province of Echigo and in adjacent regions. As part of this policy he proffered help to the Ikkō (Single-minded) sect of Buddhists, who were then firmly established in the province of Kaga, which lies between Echizen and Kenshin's own province of Echigo. Letters addressed to the temple of the sect in Kaga (the Honseiji), written at Ujiyasu's instance in 1561 and 1562 by the then Kubō, have been preserved and show that his policy had been most carefully thought out, and that he had a good understanding of the political influence of the sectarians. He suggested that they should consult their brethren in other districts and devise ways of attacking Kenshin and so extending their own sphere.

The development of the Ikkō sect is one of the most remarkable phenomena in the history of religion in Japan. It derived from the Amidist teaching—the Nembutsu or Buddha-calling—of the great evangelist Shinran (1173–1262), and it had been developed on congregational and anti-monastic if not anti-clerical lines by his apostolic successor in the eighth generation, the extremely gifted Rennyo (1415–99).

Rennyo's unorthodox views, expressed in words and deeds while he was Abbot of the Kyoto Honganji, the cathedral of the sect, had so enraged the monks of the Enryakuji that in 1465 they burned down his house. His life was in danger and he barely escaped into the country, where he travelled and preached for some years with astonishing success. In 1471 he settled at a place called Yoshizaki and built a church which was soon continually thronged by converts, mostly but not all of a simple peasant class. The sect, which was self-governing, grew and flourished to such a point that its influence spread through the northern provinces, particularly in Echizen and the adjoining Kaga. Its believers resented any interference by the civil or military authorities and were quick to resort to force against attempts to control them. In Kaga they rose (about 1486) and drove out the hereditary Constable, one Togashi, thus becoming de facto rulers of the whole province. They were so strong that Togashi implored the Bakufu to suppress them, and appropriate orders were issued. But they defeated a force sent against them by the powerful Asakura of Echizen—a hard nut to crack.

Togashi escaped, but he committed suicide in Etchū. The Ikkō pastors continued to rule Kaga until 1576, when they were ejected by the leaders of a new warrior society.

6. Provincial Autonomies

The foregoing descriptions of almost ceaseless warfare may have given the impression that by the close of the fifteenth century the whole country had lapsed into a chaotic state in which there was no room for progress in the civil arts. But such a dark picture would be far from the truth. To be sure, there was much destruction of property and some loss of life in battle, though perhaps less than is usually supposed, for plagues and famines were much more deadly than mediaeval weapons. But there was much advance as well.

The armies had to be fed, and the landowners great and small, though they may have taken to town life, still belonged to an agrarian society and knew the importance of agriculture. Indeed, in a general way it is fair to say that members of the military class, from the barons holding a province or more down to the owner of a few score acres, began at the time of the greatest disturbance to see that their prospects of taking and holding more territory were far less favourable than their opportunity to increase the yield of their lands by better farming and the promotion of industry. Moreover, the landowners who had freed themselves from the control of the Bakufu soon found that if they wished to keep their independence, they must pay serious attention to organizing their human and material resources. They had to perfect the administration of their domains, to regulate the life of their people, and above all to foster improvement in agricultural and industrial methods. This was done in some places with remarkable success, though not always to the benefit of the peasantry.

As we have seen, a number of new families rose to prominence. Their origins were various, but most of them began as vassals of the great houses, or as small landowners—members of the rural gentry—who had singly or in combination brought others into their orbit. Some reached their position from a similar starting point by being appointed Constable of a province or provinces as a reward or a bribe by the Ashikaga Shōguns of the day.

In effect, the last years of the fifteenth century and the early part of the sixteenth saw a redistribution of power throughout the country. There were now a score or so of warlords of the first rank, independent rulers of territory comprising one or more provinces. There were two or three hundred of less importance, whose land was not of great extent but who were efficient enough to be valuable friends or dangerous enemies in times of trouble. Most of them were in some degree subordinate to the great territorial lords, the daimyos.

It is not possible to give an exact picture of the distribution of power after the Ōnin War, since changes were violent and frequent and it was many years before stability was reached. But for a time after 1500 the position of the prominent warlords was roughly as follows:

Northern provinces: Yūki, Nambu, Date, Ashina
Eastern provinces: Hōjō, Satomi
Eastern seaboard: Imagawa
Northwestern provinces: Uyesugi, Takeda, Asakura, Saitō
Home Provinces: Hosokawa
Shikoku: Chōsokabe
Western provinces: Ōuchi, Mōri, Amako, Yamana, Ukita
Kyūshū: Ryūzōji, Arima, Ōmura, Ōtomo, Shimazu

There were a number of minor warrior families as well, but here the changes were so rapid that it is hardly possible to keep track of them. At a bold guess their number in the year 1500 was less than three hundred. When the position was stabilized in the seventeenth century, there were about one hundred daimyos with a revenue of upwards of 50,000 koku per annum, and the records show that in 1614 there were altogether fewer than two hundred daimyos with a revenue of 10,000 koku or more.[3]

---

[3] This figure is reached by a computation based upon *Daimyō Ichiran*, in *Dokushi Biyō*.

CHAPTER XV

SENGOKU-DAIMYŌ, THE CIVIL WAR BARONS

1. *Asakura Toshikage*

IN THE political history of the age of the Muromachi Shōguns, the most striking feature is the rise of a new governing class composed of warriors of modest origin who by force or threat ejected the high provincial officers appointed by the Bakufu, confiscated public and private property on a large scale, and became independent rulers of wide areas, often a whole province, sometimes more. Their rise is an aspect of the concurrent decline of established civil authority.

To make clear the steps by which this far-reaching change was brought about, an account of the career of one of these successful rebels will serve better than a description of their class in general terms. The most convenient example is that of Asakura Toshikage (1428–81), whose activities in Echizen may be taken as typical, uncomplicated by such extraneous issues as events in the capital and in neighbouring provinces, and amply documented.

Asakura belonged to a family who were hereditary vassals of the important house of Shiba. As a youth he attracted attention by his intelligence and his military skill, and in 1453, when a feud broke into violence between two branches of the Shiba clan in Echizen, he was charged by the Bakufu to settle it, by force if necessary. This required some years of fighting in support of the claim of Shiba Yoshikado.[1] At length, in 1459, Yoshikado was agreed upon as the new Shiba chieftain, and Asakura assumed the function of Deputy Constable.

In this position he gained considerable wealth by eating into the rich manors within his territory, notably those which belonged to the Kōfukuji monastery of Nara. In 1466 he attacked the Echizen property of Ichijō Kanera, the last estate left to that distinguished nobleman, but the peasants on the estate drove out Asakura's men, knowing that they would get better treatment from a nobleman than from a warrior.

The outbreak of the Ōnin War gave Asakura excellent opportunities for adding to his wealth, since both the Eastern and the Western armies wished him to join them and he therefore had little fear of rebuke, still less of punishment. In 1471, when the war was still at its height, he declared that he had cut his ties of loyalty to the Shiba family and henceforth would serve only the Shōgun. Thereupon he joined the Eastern Army and served as Yoshimasa's commander in Echizen. Be-

---

[1] Yoshikado was later (1467) to become the Kyoto Kanrei, but he lost the office about a year after his appointment.

fore this a prominent churchman had observed of such behaviour: "This kind of thing has become the rule among warriors. Everything they do nowadays is something that common sense could not have foreseen."

At the end of 1471 Asakura assumed the office of Constable of Echizen and announced that he meant to confiscate all the manors in that province. He moved to a new castle, wore Court dress, and behaved as if he were a great noble. His behaviour so offended the local warriors that they rose against him. This gave some satisfaction to the former lords of the manors, but had no effect upon Asakura. In 1472 he was attacked by the Kai family (also vassals of Shiba). The struggle between the two armies was bitter and protracted, but towards the end of 1472 Asakura brought his full strength against the Kai forces and routed them. Some of the Kai commanders killed themselves, others fled into Kaga, and Asakura became master of all Echizen. The scale of the campaign was relatively small, the strength of Asakura's main body being recorded as not more than 7,000 men (probably a correct figure, since the province was not thickly populated).

Having disposed of his chief enemy, Asakura was now Constable in fact as well as in name. He need no longer cut slices from the estates of rich monasteries or noblemen; he could swallow them whole. Soon after his victory he ordered manorial lords to pay him half their revenue (under the hanzei system) for the support of his military establishments, and he seized the property of the Kai family for distribution among his followers. Petitions and claims by injured landowners poured into the courts at Kyoto, but the Bakufu was helpless. Asakura pursued his policy of robbery undisturbed. In Echizen the warrior was now the master, and the lord of the manor was at his command. As we have seen in Chapter XII, that was the pattern of land tenure which prevailed in the last decades of the fifteenth century.

In its national setting the history of the Asakura family in Echizen explains the breakdown of the shōen in a most vivid fashion; and it traces the steps by which a new governing class was formed, as the Constables duly appointed by the Bakufu were replaced by self-made men taking advantage of the failure of central authority, the process culminating shortly after the end of the Ōnin War.

It should be recalled that the Shiba family was one of the most important warrior houses in Japan. It was in high favour when Takauji formed the Ashikaga Bakufu. Shiba Takatsune had followed Takauji to war, and his son Shiba Yoshimasa was the first Deputy (Kanrei) appointed in Kyoto. Yoshimasa was also made Constable of half a dozen provinces, and one of his successors was Constable of Owari and Tōtōmi as well; but Echizen was the real headquarters of the Shiba family. The family's domains were so widespread that Shiba vassals were naturally entrusted with important offices in all their provinces, and held the post of Deputy Constable in some. At the outbreak of the Ōnin War the family's leading vassals were Kai and Asakura in Echizen, and Oda in Owari.

Asakura continued his depredations without serious opposition until 1479, when the Shiba family felt obliged to force the issue. A decisive battle took place in the neighbourhood of the Kōfukuji farms, and the Shiba and Kai forces, supplemented by peasants conscripted from the fields, fought back vigorously but were once again defeated. Hostilities continued until 1481, by which time all the Kai men had been driven out of Echizen. During those days of victory Asakura died, and was succeeded by his son.

There followed an astonishing settlement of the rebellion of Asakura. The Shiba chieftain surrendered but formally maintained his position as Asakura's overlord. In 1483 an agreement was reached by which the new Asakura was recognized as Deputy Constable of Echizen, Kai as Deputy Constable of Tōtōmi, and Oda as Deputy Constable of Owari, while Shiba Yoshikado was recognized as overlord of all three Deputies. In fact, however, all but a small portion of the Shiba property was shared by Asakura, Kai, and Oda. The Shiba family lost its prominence, and the three vassals were left to play important parts in the new era.

2. House Laws and Civil Administration

When Asakura's position in Echizen was assured, his thoughts naturally turned to the future, and he laid down rules for his descendants to follow, so as to preserve their inheritance. These have been transmitted to posterity in a document known as the Injunction of Seventeen Articles (*Toshikage Jūshichikajō*), which may have been compiled after his death but undoubtedly followed his wishes.

It is an extremely interesting document, for it not only reveals the sentiments of Asakura but is characteristic of the behaviour of a successful rebel who, having reached a high position by flagrant defiance of the law, announces strict rules of public and private behaviour that his successors are to obey. It should be added that however reprehensible the conduct of Asakura and his kindred may have been, they must be credited with an energy and a determination of which the older families of Constables seemed no longer capable.

The Injunction of Seventeen Articles belongs to a class of literature called Kahō or House Laws, which set forth rules of conduct for members of a family in the administration of its domains. The Articles are worth translating in full as an expression of ideas current among the new warlords. They are as follows:

❖

1. In the Asakura family special appointments will not be given to elders. Advisers shall be chosen for their ability and their loyalty.
2. Even retainers who have served the Asakura family for genera-

tions are not to be given administrative posts unless they are capable.

3. Though the world may be at peace, intelligence agents should be maintained in other provinces, near or distant, to study conditions there.

4. Swords or daggers of famous warriors ought not to be coveted. A sword worth ten thousand pieces can be overcome by one hundred spears worth only one hundred pieces.

5. Actors of the Komparu, Kanze, Hōshō, and Kita schools of Nō must not be frequently brought from Kyoto for performances. The money needed for such a purpose should be spent on the training of clever young dancers of the district for its permanent benefit.

6. Performances are not to be given in the castle at night.

7. Valuable horses and falcons shall not be ordered from the places where they are bred on the pretence that they are needed for the training of officers. This ban does not apply to unsolicited gifts from other provinces, but after three years such gifts should be passed on to some other family. To keep them is to bring sorrow.

8. When wearing ceremonial dress at the New Year, members of the Asakura family should confine themselves to nunoko [? wadded cotton], and this should bear their crest. If they wear costly garments, no samurai in the country will feel that he can attend upon his superiors without dressing up. The result will be that samurai will absent themselves from their duties for long periods on a plea of illness; and in the end they will be of little service to the Asakura house.

9. On the choice of servants. Cleverness is less important than other qualities in a servant. Honesty is important. Even a lazy fellow makes a good servant or messenger if he is of especially good appearance. But do not employ one who has neither good character nor good looks.

10. Do not treat as servants people who are not *your* servants.

11. Do not entrust confidential papers to a samurai from another province, unless it is unavoidable.

12. Do not allow other families to persuade persons with a special talent to leave your service, whether monks or laymen.

13. In preparing for battle, do not waste time selecting an auspicious day or a correct direction.

14. Three times a year you should send honest and capable persons on a tour of inspection throughout the province. They should listen to the views of people of all classes and remedy errors in government. One of you [sons] ought sometimes to take on this duty, wearing a light disguise.

15. No castle or stronghold other than that of the ruler is to be built in the province. All important people must reside in Ichijōgatani [the castle town], and their estates are to be managed by bailiffs or servants.

16. When passing in front of monasteries, shrines, or dwelling houses, rein in your horse. If the place is pretty, praise it. If it is in poor condition, express your sympathy. This will have a good effect.

17. When judging lawsuits be completely impartial. If any wrongful act by an official comes to your notice, punish it severely.

✴

These regulations speak for themselves. They show that the new barons had begun to understand that to develop their territory by good, firm government was more profitable than to expand it at a great cost of life and treasure. Unfortunately for them they usually went to extremes of protection in their desire for self-sufficiency, and thus created tensions which led to further conflicts.

Something of this kind is true of many of the new rulers, the Niwaka Daimyō or Sudden Lords, as they were called by Kyoto cynics. In their efforts to enforce their laws, their treatment of offenders was generally harsh and at times unspeakably cruel. But the public works which they promoted were of benefit to the people at large. Thus in 1537 one of Asakura's successors introduced an irrigation system by which water was carried by channels to groups of ten villages, for further distribution by them. Other important works of this kind were the stone embankments built for flood control of the tributaries of the Fujikawa by Takeda Shingen about 1545, and similar works along the course of the Tonegawa, put in hand by the Hōjō family to regulate its flow through the Musashi plain.

It may be added that Asakura Toshikage himself, for all his coarse brutality, had some literary and artistic leanings, and hoped to establish a centre of culture in his domains. The ruins of his castle at Ichijōgatani indicate that he had handsome apartments, a library, and an elegant garden in correct Muromachi style.

Similarly, the exploits of Hōjō Sōun and his sons were not confined to battle and plunder. Sōun was impressed with the importance of good government. When he took the castle at Nirayama in Izu after his successful occupation of Odawara in 1491 (a few years later than Asakura's successes in Echizen), he at once turned his attention to questions of civil administration.

The *Hōjō Godaiki*, a history of his family, says that he regarded the people as his children. This was a relationship postulated in classical treatises on government, and we need not suppose that Sōun took it seriously. But no doubt he recognized that it would be prudent to treat the people with consideration. He is said to have issued from Nirayama a notice to farmers saying that he would reduce the amount of tax payable by them from five-tenths to four-tenths of the total crop. This ratio was known as "shikō rokumin," or "four to the Prince and six to the People," and was regarded as generous at that time. Sōun also undertook not to impose special levies, such as *tansen* (land tax), *yazeni* ("arrow-money," or war tax), and *kurayaku* (pawnshop tax).

But this relief did not last long. The cost of war was high and the

Hōjō were surrounded by enemies. By the time of Ujitsuna, if not sooner, there were to be many changes. New taxes and surtaxes were imposed, and it seems that many peasants absconded, for in 1550 it was announced that peasants who had left without paying taxes would not be obliged to pay arrears if they came back, but must pay regularly thereafter.

Other measures show that an attempt was made by the Hōjō to improve the treatment of workers, and on the whole the family's administration was lenient by the standard of the time; but life was hard for labouring men, and most of the concessions made benefitted only skilled workers, like stonemasons or shipwrights. However, farmers without special skills who assisted in the opening up of new land in the Musashi plain were encouraged by exemption from taxes and other duties.

The House Laws, as may be inferred from the Asakura articles, are valuable sources of knowledge bearing upon the character of individual rulers and their outlook as a class. Among the best known of these documents are:

Jinkaishū	The code of the Date family
Kōshū Hatto	The laws of the Takeda family
Ōuchi-ke Kabegaki	The "wall-writings" of the Ōuchi family
Sōun no Nijūichikajō	The twenty-one articles of Hōjō Sōun
Yūki-shi Hatto	The laws of the Yūki family
Imagawa Kanamokuroku	The Kana Index of the Imagawa

Of these the Ōuchi wall-writings, which contain some articles dated 1440, are probably the earliest.

The contents of these documents vary from simple rules of personal behaviour to a detailed criminal code. Most of them have two features in common: first, a strict concern for the protection and the survival of the family and its domain, and second, most severe penalties for offences, however slight, which might lead to the advantage of a rival house. The codes are interesting in many respects, in particular because they were attempts by successful men to replace the now obsolete Jōei Formulary and its supplements by rules that were better suited to the new order.

The codes are written in simple language, in contrast to the Jōei Formulary, which could not be understood without some knowledge of legal terms. The Imagawa and Yūki laws are written in kana, and the Yūki laws are in local dialect for easy understanding by the country people. The codes are not statements of principle, concerned with rights as well as duties, but positive disciplinary rules which must be obeyed under penalty. Thus the Kōshū Hatto of the Takeda family contains the rule that both parties to a quarrel leading to violence shall be punished "irrespective of the rights and wrongs" of the case ("zehi ni oyobazu"). The punishment might be death. The purpose of this rule was doubtless to maintain order within the ruler's domain, since constant internal feuds would lead to a loss of military efficiency; but it is doubtful whether it ever prevented high-spirited warriors from drawing their swords in private brawls.

Another feature of these House Laws was the doctrine of joint responsibility (*enza*), according to which the guilt of an offender was shared by his family or by his servants. This was an old principle, applied in the early codes only to such crimes as high treason; but in the late fifteenth century it was extended to more offences and applied to more people. In such cases as failure to pay tax or to apprehend evildoers, a whole village might be punished for the fault of one peasant.

The severity of the law was matched by the cruelty of the punishments which it decreed. Their very descriptions evoke a shudder. Quite apart from the specific barbarities, in general the new laws show a sad decline from the standards of the Kamakura codes, which had their severity tempered by a certain liberal quality.

Despite these oppressive laws, however, self-interest dictated to the new rulers a degree of moderation in their treatment of the most important producers under their control. The benefits accorded to peasants and skilled artisans by the Later Hōjō have already been pointed out, and they were emulated by other daimyos. Sōun and his heirs were men who understood what makes for profitable administration; but in a general way the new territorial lords, even the most backward, soon found that in the competitive society of their day they could not increase the harvest of their farms or the output of manufactured goods unless they gave some thought to the condition of their workers—the mass of peasants and the smaller but no less important body of artisans and craftsmen.

2. Peasant Protection

One of the tasks that occupied the attention of the new class of daimyos was the destruction of the long chain of privileges and claims separating the manorial lord and the producers. When all who profited from the land were satisfied—the landlord, the steward, the officers of the shō, the managers, the tenants, and the unavoidable tax collector—little was left for the man who tilled the soil. It was necessary to sweep away this complex of rights and duties, but that was not easily done, since there is nothing more stubborn than ancient privilege. Even when the shōen was abolished, it was survived by abuses which it had created, and special efforts were needed to protect the peasant. Thus, for instance, in 1587 a daimyo in Wakasa was obliged to issue an order which said: "The headmen and the former shōen officials in the villages are not to employ the ordinary peasants upon private work, even for a short period." Such orders were common, and in some domains, in particular those of the Hōjō family, peasants were allowed to bring petitions or suits against offending parties.

Further measures which gave relief to peasants were the unifying of the rate of tax upon farm products—the usual rate being half the crop—and the abolition of onerous surtaxes. These measures were not dictated by sympathy but by a desire for efficiency. Other measures show that it was thought important to take special steps to keep the peasant on the land; one common measure was an agreement among neighbouring daimyos to surrender fugitive peasants. Peasants absconded then, as always, when they were ill-treated by bailiffs or when they got into debt because of illness, or a poor harvest, or the destruction of their crops by raiders in wartime. War damage was common in those years. For example, in 1479 the whole of the Hosorogi manor in Echizen was destroyed by flames during a battle. In the following year half the ripening crops of the Tsuboye manor were trampled by troops of Kai fighting against Asakura. Two months later one thousand conscripted peasants were forced into the battle area and lost their lives. These were exceptional disasters, but lesser troubles constantly afflicted the peasants.

Among the corvées imposed upon peasants was military service. This was rarely systematic, since at most times they could not be spared from the farms; but they were mobilized as soldiers in emergency. The practice was not at all common until the end of the fifteenth century, by which time the substitution of infantry fighting for the old-fashioned conflicts of mounted warriors was transforming the art of warfare. An early example is the use of armed peasants in the decade 1501–10, during Uyesugi Sadazane's campaigns in Echigo. By about 1570 we find Uyesugi Kenshin telling peasants in his domain to report for military service wearing armour and carrying weapons in company formation, each company with a banner. The form of the summons was a request rather than an order, and a reward was promised to those who complied. But the practice developed, and later in the century peasants were regularly conscripted for military service as combatants or transport workers. As early as 1577 Takeda of Kai issued a mobilization order to all men between fifteen and sixty years of age, of all classes.

An important change took place in rural life as the new barons established themselves in their fortified castles. They grew more and more averse to letting their more important vassals and followers reside on their own estates, where they might plot mischief. Consequently they obliged such important people to reside near the castle, leaving their estates to be managed by stewards. This action resulted in the growth of castle towns (jōka-machi) and the separation of the warrior from the farmer. Hitherto there had been no clear distinction between the two classes, since a warrior might be a farmer living on his own land. But now the professional soldier lived an urban life, and rural society developed on new lines, with an elaborate organization of village life and marked social distinctions between the headman and the plain cultivator.

The affairs of a village or a group of villages were managed by a kind of council in which a strict order of precedence was maintained. The senior members were called *otona,* or elders. They were carefully selected by the council members from among men with certain qualifications of family origin, age, and property. On appointment they went through a ceremony, and usually an honorific affix was added to their names (such as Tayu or Emon or Chōbei). A typical petition, addressed by a village to the landlord of an estate in 1542, is signed by two elders (*otona*), two men of middle age and status (*chū-otona*), and two young men (*waka-shū*), thus representing all classes. It would seem that the elders must have been free peasants of the status of myōshu at least. Village meetings (*yoriai*) were frequent, and those who failed to attend when summoned were fined.

Such well-organized councils were more common in the Home Provinces than in distant parts of the country, and so, of course, were most other evidences of sophistication. But not all places at a distance from the capital were backward. There was little hint of provincialism in the principal towns in the domains of powerful daimyos. Ōtomo's castle town at Funai in Bungo had fine buildings, busy streets, and thriving markets, and is said to have had a population of 8,000 in the late sixteenth century. Similarly the castle town of the Ōuchi family at Yamaguchi in Suō was an important centre of culture, built in imitation of Kyoto, and a favourite place among travelling noblemen, many of whom, being indigent, were happy to be entertained for long periods by rich warlords.

4. *Industrial Growth*

One of the chief concerns of the new barons was the development of industries, and among these the most important was mining. Old mines were developed, improved, and enlarged, and prospecting discovered new ones. The most important at this time were gold and silver mines, since the daimyos could convert their product directly into currency for military and other expenditure. Mining methods were rudimentary until about 1530, when the discovery of silver in Iwami led one of the Hakata merchants—they were noted for their enterprise—to bring skilled men from China and Korea to supervise an improved smelting process. Later (1542) a richer deposit was found at Ikuno in Tajima. Apart from profits in foreign trade, a principal source of the wealth of the Mōri family was the Ōmori silver mine, which fell into their hands during a campaign in Iwami province in 1556.

Gold mining and refining also made good progress, and the daimyo whose territory included gold mines was especially fortunate. The technique of deep mining made rapid advances, and we begin to hear of skilled miners used as sappers during the siege of a castle. In this way, too, as well as by the arming of peasants and the introduction of muskets (see p. 263), the art of war had advanced in the two centuries since

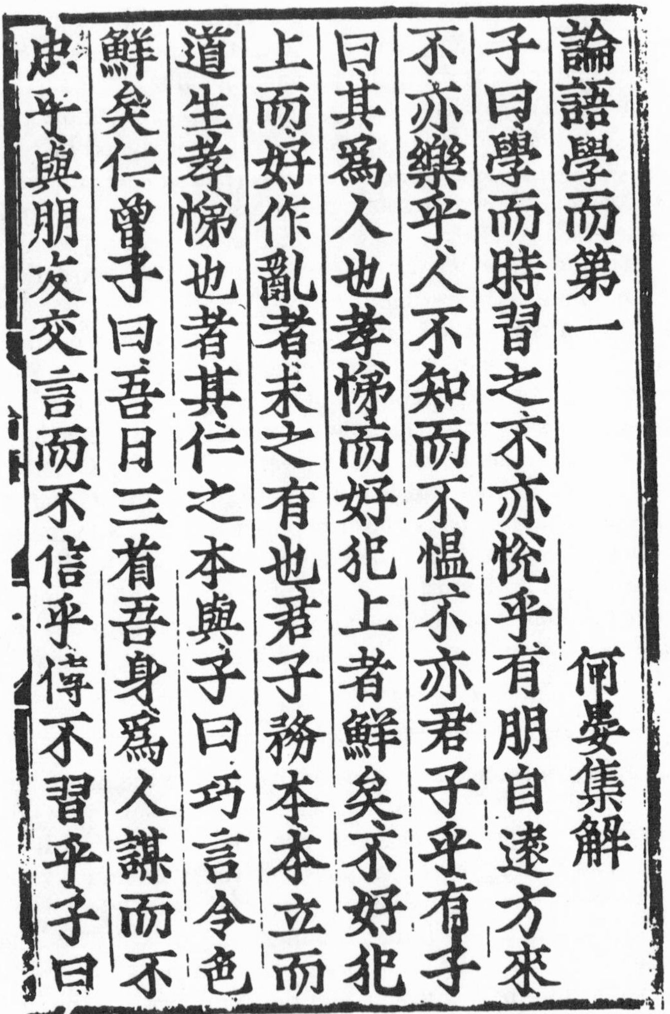

論語學而第一　何晏集解

子曰學而時習之不亦悅乎有朋自遠方來

不亦樂乎人不知而不慍不亦君子乎有子

曰其爲人也孝悌而好犯上者鮮矣不好犯

上而好作亂者未之有也君子務本本立而

道生孝悌也者其仁之本與子曰巧言令色

鮮矣仁曾子曰吾日三省吾身爲人謀而不

忠乎與朋友交言而不信乎傳不習乎子曰

A page from the first extant Japanese book printed from moveable type the struggle between the two Courts. Now there were stone walls a hundred feet high and trained men to undermine them.

Other kinds of mining made little progress during the sixteenth century, no doubt because the leaders of the country were intent upon war and upon production for warlike purposes. Iron ore is scarce in Japan, but there was a sufficient supply of easily worked iron sand, so that there is nothing new to record in the production of iron and steel materials, except perhaps for some advances in the manufacture of cutting tools other than swords.

Weaving, paper-making, block printing, and similar crafts were already well advanced, and made no special progress, apart from some fine editions of books, known as Gozan-ban, produced by Zen monks.[2] It was not until a degree of peace had been achieved that any notable technical advances were made.

The new barons did, it is true, encourage and control the skilled artisans in their domains, especially those who made a direct contribution to military strength. As Sōun treated shipwrights with care, so did most rulers accord favourable treatment to such workers as the iron moulders, who, as well as making pots and kettles, could furnish parts for muskets.

5. Communications, Travel, and Transport

With the development of production in agriculture and industry there naturally arose a need for improved communications within the domains of each daimyo and, granted certain precautions, between one province and another. In eastern and northern Japan, where waterways were scarce, such new barons as Hōjō, Takeda, and Uyesugi paid special attention to the maintenance of roads, and established systems of fast couriers and post stations (shukuba) where travellers were lodged and furnished with horses or other means of transport. By the beginning of the sixteenth century these facilities were well developed. They were devised with wartime requirements in view, but they served the purpose of private travellers, especially merchants in pursuit of their trade.

Travel was unsafe by land or water in many regions, and merchants usually travelled in company. In addition, passage from one domain to another was often difficult, because fear of spies dictated the examination of all travellers at barriers. The post system—the supply of horses

[2] The standard of block printing was generally high, thanks in the first place to the need of the Buddhists for copies of the Chinese translation of the sutras and later, under the Ashikaga regime, to a growing enthusiasm for Chinese classical studies. The Jesuits had a small printing press in Kyūshū in 1590, but the first extant work printed by Japanese from movable type is an edition of the Analects made in 1598 at the command of the Emperor Go-Yōzei. Movable type had been used in Korea from about 1400, and it is probable that the Japanese were impressed by its advantages during the invasions of Korea in 1592–97. Movable type, however, proved unsuitable for popular works in Japan, which needed a running script, and by about 1640 block printing was resumed for all purposes.

and the carriage of goods—was controlled by the daimyo through whose territory the traveller passed, and in many domains horses could not be hired without a voucher issued by the daimyo and presented to officials at each stage.

The tolls levied on passengers and goods were at one time extremely onerous, in frequency rather than in amount. Records state that about 1450 there were over six hundred octroi posts (probably including ferries) along the Yodo River in a distance of twenty-five miles. On the road taken by pilgrims to Ise there were sixty barriers in the ten miles from Kuwana to the shrine. It is true that the toll was very small, like Charon's obol, but the annoyance to travellers was great.

Despite these hardships and restrictions travel by road increased rapidly in the sixteenth century. One of the sights that struck foreign visitors to Japan, beginning with the Jesuit missionaries, was the great flow of traffic on the highroads. It was mostly pedestrian traffic. The main road from Kyoto to the eastern provinces (the Tokaidō) was crowded with people of all classes and callings, officials, merchants, soldiers, couriers, pedlars, countrymen leading strings of pack horses, and (as the peasants gained freedom of movement) pilgrims by the hundred or even the thousand. Some of the pilgrimages took them to distant places, such as Ise or Kumano or provinces farther west; and (rather later) they would climb to the summit of Mount Fuji, wearing white pilgrims' robes and reciting a prayer as they toiled up the steep path.

The express courier service from Kamakura to Kyoto took seven days —or only four in special emergencies—as compared with ten to fourteen days in the twelfth century.

Throughout the middle ages coasting trade flourished, especially in sheltered waters such as the Inland Sea. Most of the Constables took positive steps to encourage this traffic, since few of the central and western provinces were without direct access to the sea. Larger vessels were built with greater carrying capacity; and a "sengoku-bune," a vessel carrying 1,000 koku (5,000 bushels) of rice or other such cargo, was a common sight in busy harbours.

Coasting trade in the Japan Sea was more difficult, owing to the stormy weather and the shortage of safe harbours; but during the fifteenth century this kind of trade increased as harbours were improved at such places as Obama, Mikuni, Sakata, Tsuruga, and Naoyetsu. It was not until after the end of the Muromachi era that the voyage from these ports westward, then south about Chōshū (Nagato) and through the Straits of Shimonoseki into the Inland Sea, was regularly made.

CHAPTER XVI

SEABORNE TRADE

1. *Developments in the Western Provinces*

TRADITIONALLY Kyūshū in particular and the extreme west of the main island in general were regarded as somewhat remote from the main field of political activity, which for obvious historical reasons stretched from the Home Provinces eastward to Kamakura. But during the flourishing period of the Muromachi Bakufu the western daimyos became extremely active and showed a strong spirit of independence. In the course of the fifteenth century, while men like Asakura, Hōjō, Takeda, and Uyesugi were consolidating and extending their baronies in the East, a similar process was going on in the West, with the result that regional differences in political organization between East and West all but disappeared. By about 1500 the most powerful of the western barons—Shimazu, Ōtomo, and Ōuchi—were beginning to play an important part in the national scene. Ōuchi, for instance, gave shelter in Yamaguchi to the fugitive Shōgun in 1500 and later (1508) restored him to office.

Naturally there was a frequent conflict of interest between eastern and western potentates, and one of the puzzles of Japanese political history is the contradiction—or the seeming contradiction—between the fierce rivalries among warlords in the fifteenth century and the search for some kind of national unity which is a peculiar feature of the sixteenth. The warlords of the early period aimed at extending and protecting their domains, but the later military leaders wished to dominate the whole country. Some modern historians are at a loss to explain this anomaly; but apart from a natural desire to restore a central (military) government which had lasted for centuries, there was a social reason which, though perhaps not cogent, is worth taking into account.

With the growth of their military power most of the successful warlords developed an interest in learning, and invited to their castles distinguished scholars, learned clerics, and poets and painters of high repute. These warlike men were anxious to promote the arts of peace, and we need not question their motives. They wanted to keep up with their rivals, but also they felt a respect for learning which is traditional in most Asian countries. This community of taste brought about a certain cultural unity. Thence it was a long way to political unity, but first steps are important though they may falter. It might be said that the craze for linked verses formed a tie between enemies; and this is not astonishing if one bears in mind the part played by poets and poetasters in the national life.

The arts flourished in the West as well as the East, to the extent that Yamaguchi rivalled Sumpu, the capital of Suruga, as a stronghold of poetry. Many successful warriors in western Japan turned their minds to aesthetic matters, and even descended to antiquarian studies. They sought and enjoyed the company of Court nobles, who stood for the traditional culture of Japan. They bought valuable books, and some were such ardent collectors that they might at times be bribed by gifts of incunabula (or the Oriental equivalent) to allow to needy courtiers some revenue from their confiscated estates.

There can have been few castles in the country without some precious manuscripts or pictures, or at least the services of resident scholars and artists. Interest in the fine arts, particularly in painting, had been limited in the past to Court circles and to monastic society, but in the Muromachi age, partly because of Yoshimasa's example, the taste for pictures grew rapidly among the barons, who invited great artists to visit their domains. The Ōuchi family in particular was able to be very lavish, having rich lands and deriving great profit from trade with China.

The best example of the Ōuchi family's interest in painting is the invitation of Ōuchi Masahiro to the great painter Sesshū to come to Yamaguchi, where the celebrated Long Scroll (Chōkan) was painted in 1486. It was one of the beneficial results of the Ōnin War that men of letters and artists took refuge in country places. Kyoto was no longer the predominant cultural metropolis, and the Gozan school of literature had lost its leadership. It is true that when Yoshimasa was Shōgun metropolitan influence was still strong, but it was no longer exclusive.

One of the finest painters of the time was Sesson (ca. 1504–89), a gifted follower of Sesshū. He never even saw the capital, but spent his active life in the province of Hitachi, sometimes visiting other domains, such as those of the Ashina family in remote Aizu. His chief work seems to strike a native note in contrast to the masterpieces of Sesshū, in which a Chinese flavour can be detected—a flavour, the best authorities tell us, not of the Ming paintings which he saw in China but of the earlier Sung paintings which he had studied in Japan. It is an interesting footnote to the history of relations between the two countries that Sesshū did not think highly of the work of his Chinese contemporaries.

So much for the plastic arts. The theatre was in its early stages of development, but the dengaku and other plays were frequently performed in the castles of the warlords, as well as at the courts of Yoshimasa and his successors. Asakura's reference to the various schools of Nō has already been cited, and other barons displayed an interest in this new dramatic form. Ōuchi invited a company of the Kanze school to perform at Yamaguchi, and players of the Komparu school went to the island of Tsushima at the Constable Sō's request in or about the year 1550.

In the light of these facts it may be suggested that the rapid decline of central government from about 1500 served to promote the idea of a national culture shared by all and not belonging exclusively to the capital city. This sentiment did not of course dictate political action, but it did at least counteract in some degree the separatist trends displayed by the new barons. And at the same time it stimulated new local cultures, as when a new school of Confucian studies was developed in Tosa.

The growth of travel by road doubtless served also to moderate the intense localism which has always been a feature of Japanese life. Among the travellers were the *rengashi*, the professors of linked verse, who went from province to province much as the mediaeval troubadours called at one castle after another in France. At times, no doubt, they also acted as spies and gave the warlords news from other territories.

2. *The Arrival of the Portuguese*

While the Hosokawa family were losing their hold in the Home Provinces, and while Hōjō, Asakura, Takeda, and Uyesugi were consolidating their strength in the East, three great warlords whom we have just noticed were developing their resources in the West. These were Shimazu and Ōtomo in Kyūshū and Ōuchi on the mainland. They were rivals, but they were not at war with one another. Ōuchi was to be replaced by a vassal, Mōri Motonari, in 1554, but the balance of power remained unchanged. The three great baronies formed a relatively stable centre of power in western Japan.

The utter collapse of the Bakufu, which may be placed at about mid-century, created a situation calling for some unifying force if the whole country was not to be divided into two or more autonomous regions, or to crumble into anarchy. Such a unifying force was already taking form, but before its full development a new figure, or rather two new figures, intruded upon the national scene—the Portuguese trader and the Portuguese missionary.

The importance of these new elements in Japanese history tends to be exaggerated by Western writers. Naturally the arrival of Europeans in Japan is of peculiar interest to Western readers, and it has many dramatic aspects; but in the long chronicle of Japanese history it is a secondary episode.

The first Europeans to land in Japan were three Portuguese who reached the small island of Tanegashima off the shore of southern Kyūshū in (or about) 1542, when a Chinese junk in which they had taken passage was blown off its course in a typhoon. The muskets which they carried caused excitement among the rescuers, and for a long time after this event the Japanese name for such firearms was Tanegashima. The weapons were soon copied in considerable numbers, but it would be a mistake to suppose that the use of firearms at once brought about a great change in methods of warfare in Japan. For although they were used in the major battles of the sixteenth century, they remained in scarce supply for a century or more, and they did not displace traditional weapons—the sword, the bow, and the spear—until an even later date.[1]

A more important sequel to the landing of these castaways was the arrival of Portuguese merchant ships soon after the castaways returned to China and told their compatriots about their discovery of Japan. The first of these ships entered Kyūshū harbours a year or two later. From the point of view of the great Kyūshū barons its appearance was opportune, for in addition to being intensely curious about the Portuguese and their wares, they saw foreign trade as a source of the wealth they needed to maintain their military strength. The foreign merchants thus arrived in Japan at the right places and at the right time. Soon the barons were competing for the Portuguese trade.

The first ships brought missionaries as well as traders, and when the barons observed that the Portuguese traders treated the missionaries with great respect, they were inclined to accord favourable treatment to them as well. Thus when the Jesuit missionary Francis Xavier landed at Kagoshima in 1549 he was well received by the lord of Satsuma. His further travels—he remained in Japan for more than two years—took him to the port of Hirado, where a Portuguese merchantman had arrived to the great satisfaction of Matsuura, the daimyo. Thence he set out on foot to the Ōuchi castle town of Yamaguchi, which, as we have seen, was a thriving home of art and letters; and ultimately, after a painful journey by land in severe weather, he reached the capital, where he found the city in an unproar, the Shōgun absent, and (he was told) the Emperor living in obscurity. Seeing no prospect of making converts alone in Kyoto, he returned to Yamaguchi. From there he was invited to Funai by the powerful Ōtomo Sōrin of Bungo, whom he described as a King; and when he went back to Goa in 1552 he took with him a mission from Ōtomo to the Portuguese Governor of the Indies. Ōtomo was especially anxious to attract merchant vessels that could bring valuable cargoes and sail the seas without fear of pirates. At that time (1552–53) Portuguese ships were frequently calling at harbours in Kyūshū.

The Jesuit fathers who went to Japan after Xavier's return to Goa numbered only six by 1560 (although a decade later there were some twenty). In the two years following their arrival in Japan (about 1555) they made good progress. Most of their early converts were poor peasants in western Japan, where life was harder than in the more advanced Home Provinces, and the consolations of religion more needed.

----

[1] The introduction of firearms did, however, oblige commanders to change their tactics when attacking a force which included a large number of musketeers; and this state of affairs greatly speeded up the tendency to make less use of mounted men and more use of infantry, so that within a generation or so the use of mounted men had been virtually abandoned.

They had especial success in Bungo, where Ōtomo was well disposed towards them. They were less successful in Yamaguchi. Xavier's reception there had been not unfriendly; Ōuchi had been impressed by his dignity as well as pleased by his gifts. But he had met with some opposition from certain members of the militant Hokke (Lotus) sect, whose manners were bad, and also from some members of the Zen sect, who argued against him but were more polite.

The course of events in the fifteenth and sixteenth centuries thus brought the western clans into a closer relation with the rest of the country than heretofore. Flourishing trade with China, increased maritime activity, closer contact with Kyoto during and after Ōnin, and now the introduction of foreign visitors with new ideas and new weapons, seem to have given to the territories of Shimazu, Ōtomo, Ōuchi, and the lesser western daimyos an initiative which they had not so far enjoyed, and to have launched them on the full stream of national life.

3. *Piracy and Foreign Trade*

Like the practice of piracy, the term Wakō used by the Chinese to denote Japanese sea raiders is of respectable antiquity. Its first recorded use is on a stone monument erected in northern Korea to celebrate the exploits of a king who ruled there for some decades after A.D. 391. It states clearly that "Wakō" ("Japanese robbers") crossed the sea and were defeated by him in the year 404. This raid was probably a legitimate act of war by the standards of the time; but during the middle ages true piracy in Japanese waters and overseas was common. It can often be related to a shortage of food in the pirates' own country, and sometimes it was due to the seclusion policy of Korea or China, whose governments thought that foreign trade was unprofitable and even dangerous. Japan's economy, by contrast, after the Mongol invasions at the end of the thirteenth century, could not develop without foreign trade, and the desire of the Japanese for "free trade," licit or illicit, was therefore strong.

Piratical ventures were abetted by the geography of Japan, which was extremely favourable to them. The Inland Sea and parts of the coast of Kyūshū provided scores of lurking places from which robbers could emerge and take their victims by surprise, and the Straits of Shimonoseki gave fairly quick access to islands within easy reach of the Korean coast. During the war between the Courts many pirate leaders were engaged at home, but some of them, as we have seen, kept up their raids along the coast of China until the Shōgun Yoshimitsu was asked by the Chinese government to suppress them.

So long as the authority of the Bakufu extended to the western provinces, the warrior families whose estates bordered on the sea kept to legitimate trade and at the same time regarded themselves as naval commanders, even adopting the style of Admiral. While the country remained at peace they behaved on the whole correctly, and some were even praised by the Korean Court.

Thanks largely to the enterprise of Japanese merchants, Japanese maritime trade grew rather rapidly in the fourteenth and early fifteenth centuries, and the licensed trade with China brought great profit to the merchants and to the whole country. Authorized trade with the Ming Court continued fairly smoothly from 1405 to 1523, although it fell off in volume after 1453, when both governments found themselves increasingly occupied with internal strife. In 1523 a violent brawl at Ningpo, in which the Ōuchi contingent committed crimes against the persons and property of Chinese officials,[2] caused the Chinese government to declare that the agreement with Japan must be terminated. Under pressure from Japan they relented; but by then the licensed trade was so unprofitable and so hampered by restrictions that the Japanese government had little desire to continue it and the Chinese authorities were eager to bring it to an end. Missions were exchanged sporadically until 1548, when for the last time the Chinese allowed some members of the Japanese trade mission then waiting at Ningpo to go to Peking and pay their respects to the Throne.

Consequently unlicensed trade grew in volume, sometimes with the connivance of Chinese officials, but generally by the piracy of Japanese adventurers, the Wakō. With the downfall of the Ōuchi family in 1551 there was no longer any force to control their activities, and moreover by this time most of the western daimyos were glad to protect the pirates, upon whom they relied for gratifying income. Pirate attacks upon points on the southern coast of China had been renewed as early as 1522, but these were exceptional. Piracy in Chinese waters began in earnest from about 1545, and Chinese chronicles show almost continuous yearly raids from 1545 to 1563. The incidence of these attacks varied according to prevailing winds, but few parts of the littoral escaped. A list of the provinces attacked during that period shows that Chekiang was attacked every year, Chihli and Fukien almost every year, and Kwangtung most years after 1550. Shantung was attacked only rarely; the trend was southward, from Hupeh and Honan to Fukien and Kwangtung. It is interesting to note that the places where the Wakō landed in the Hangchow Bay region were those where Japanese forces landed in 1937—Woosung and Shanghai, for example, though Shanghai in 1550 was a mere village on a creek.

Some expeditions made their way to Nanking, where on one occasion a raid was successfully carried out, even though the city was well defended and its twelve gates firmly shut. There is some question about the numbers and the composition of these pirate forces. Figures from

---

[2] The incident is described in Chapter X.

a few score to a few thousand are mentioned. Some Chinese records refer to the reinforcement of a pirate band by four thousand men, and on one occasion to the capture and execution of two thousand prisoners. There seems to have been no continuing coordination between separate bodies of men. As to the ground they covered going south from Honan, they are known to have been active in Ningpo, Foochow, Amoy, and lastly Bias Bay, which was still a nest of Chinese pirates in the twentieth century.

Throughout the sixteenth century the Ming authorities continued to enforce, though not efficiently, the rule of the first Ming Emperor, who decreed that "not an inch of plank" should go down to the sea. It had been a measure to end piracy, seemingly on the principle that if there were no foreign trade and no flourishing seaport towns there would be nothing for the pirates to attack. The result of this absurd policy was to deprive dwellers on the seacoast of their usual means of livelihood as boatmen or fishermen, and thus to drive them to serve in pirate ships. Consequently at the time when the activity of the so-called Wakō was at its height, say from 1550 to 1560, the crews of the pirate craft were for the most part not Japanese but these distressed Chinese.

Reliable Chinese records indicate that the rank and file of the pirate bands consisted of Chinese and Japanese in the proportion of ten to one, or as some said ten to three. It is probable that the Japanese were the leaders and navigators of the ships, while the crews included fishermen and mariners deprived of employment by the Ming edicts against both coastal trade and foreign voyages. The remainder were no doubt the usual desperadoes of seaport towns. According to some accounts Chinese members of a pirate crew would cut off their pigtails, shave their heads, and pose as Wakō.

The Portuguese had captured Malacca in 1511, and were well established there by 1550, when the Japanese free-traders were making their way southwards from Kwangtung. Enterprising Japanese captains cooperated with Portuguese merchants and persuaded them to visit Canton for the sale and purchase of merchandise, and subsequently the Portuguese invited the Japanese to continue with them in this kind of traffic. Ultimately Chinese merchants also joined in these arrangements, and by about 1560 the former piracy was gradually turning into an almost legitimate trade.

Before long Japanese vessels were making their way to other ports, on commercial voyages that sometimes bordered on piracy, and by the end of the century there were few harbours in southeast Asia, Indonesia, and the Philippine Islands that they had not visited.

The merchants in both Japan and China were anxious for a resumption of normal, private trade relations with China after 1523, although some of the Japanese no doubt profited indirectly from the gains of the Wakō. The Chinese merchants had long been in principle prohibited from engaging directly in foreign trade. However, as the Ming government grew weaker they began to defy the prohibitions and engaged in direct commerce with Japanese merchants not long after 1540. Their ships entered ports in Kyūshū and in other parts of Japan; the usual cargo was silk textiles and raw silk, and the ships carried as passengers Chinese merchants, some of whom settled as residents in Hakata, Hirado, Funai, and ports in Satsuma, where they formed partnerships with Japanese merchants. In Funai and other ports there was a quarter known as Tōjin-machi, or Chinatown.

Chief among these Chinese merchants was one Ōchoku (Wang Chih), whose interesting career might be taken as an epitome of the profits and risks of seaborne trade in his day. In 1544 he was a member of a group of Chinese pirates, and it was as a pirate chief that he was regarded by the Ming authorities. He crossed over to Japan in 1545 and invited merchants there to join him in illicit trade. This was not piracy but smuggling on a large scale, in which Japanese merchants were to exchange goods with Chinese merchants at a rendezvous on certain small islands off the Chinese coast. Trade of this kind gradually took the place of piracy, and through it Wang Chih grew more and more influential. He was established at Hirado before 1555, and from there he directed the activities of his followers. Another version of his activities, brought back from Korea by a Japanese traveller at about this time, said that Wang Chih was still a pirate chief, who from his headquarters in Hirado instructed his two thousand followers to make raids on Chinese territory in his ships, which carried about three hundred men each.

Japanese merchants from Hakata and other ports also braved the Chinese embargo, somehow avoiding the attention of Ming officials and carrying on an illicit trade at hidden bases in Chekiang, Fukien, and Kwangtung. Such simple smuggling could not compete with downright piracy. Yet all was not well with the pirates, for a truly dangerous competitor had now appeared. This was the Portuguese trader, whose ships were armed and could not safely be attacked. In fact these new arrivals could behave as pirates themselves when they chose.

In their first days in southeast Asia, when Albuquerque had conquered Malacca in 1511, the Portuguese behaved with circumspection and were on good terms with the masters of junks lying in the roadstead. These were Chinese, but presently another vessel or vessels arrived, manned by people whom the Portuguese called "Guores." It has not been established who they were. They may have been Japanese or Koreans from Kōrai; but probably they were from the Luchu (Ryūkyū) Islands, since it is known that Luchuan ships frequently visited Malacca, Patani, and other tropical ports in the fifteenth century, if not earlier. The Wakō, it is true, occasionally reached as far south as Patani, but this was later in the century, after their raids had carried them along the China coast to Hainan and beyond, about 1550.

In 1519, while Japan was still carrying on licensed trade with China, a Portuguese commander had behaved so atrociously near Canton that the Ming government put a ban on Portuguese traders which lasted for more than thirty years. They were thus obliged to turn their attention to the illicit trade which was carried on in the hidden bases mentioned above. It is curious that the Portuguese records do not mention any meeting with Japanese, since from time to time they must have been together in harbour; but perhaps at that time the Portuguese did not distinguish between Chinese and Japanese and Luchuan vessels. It is also curious that, although they were so anxious for trade openings, they did not reach Japan until 1542, and then only by accident. Probably they needed a safe base farther north than Malacca, and this they did not obtain until 1550, when they reached an understanding with the Chinese and could make use of Chinese ports. After they had seized Macao in 1557 the Portuguese chose to act as carriers and brokers in the trade between China and Japan. At that time the most profitable trade was the exchange of silver from Japanese mines for Chinese commodities. The export of silver brought advantage to the Japanese merchants engaged in foreign trade, since it attracted both Chinese and Portuguese ships to Japanese ports; and, as we have seen, the possession of a good silver mine was a most valuable asset to any daimyo in Japan.

The depredations of the robber bands were so great that the Ming government was obliged to make a great effort to suppress them. In 1555 a mission was sent to ask the Bakufu to take action and to send home the Chinese merchants then settled in Japan. The envoys met Wang Chih in the Gotō Islands, and he told them that the Bakufu was too weak to take effective steps. The best way to deal with piracy, he said, was to approach the Japanese daimyos under whose protection the pirates carried on their trade. He offered to help if the Ming government would grant him a pardon, and it seems that the envoys agreed; but when he returned to China in 1559 he was executed.

Meanwhile the Wakō were more than ever active. According to Korean records, a fleet of seventy pirate craft attacked Quelpart Island and adjacent parts of the Korean peninsula in 1555. At about the same time it was reported that frequent raids on the coast of Korea were made by ships manned not by Japanese but by Chinese; and a pirate vessel captured in the Yellow Sea in 1559 was said to have carried a crew of over two hundred men, all Chinese.

But by about 1560 the efforts of the Ming government to suppress piracy were showing some signs of success. Wise officials had for long past advised the Chinese government that the true cause of piracy was the prohibition of legitimate trade. Now piracy in Chinese waters began to diminish not because of repressive measures but thanks to a relaxation of the former policy of seclusion. The embargo on foreign trade was withdrawn and Chinese merchant ships put to sea again, on voyages in southern waters to the Philippines, Indonesia, Malaya, and beyond. They carried in addition to their cargoes great numbers of Chinese emigrants, the ancestors of the great overseas Chinese communities of modern times. The prohibition of trade with Japan was not specifically withdrawn, but Sino-Japanese trade flourished, thanks largely to the efforts of the merchants of Sakai and Hakata. Piracy continued in some areas, for pirate ships reached as far as Luzon in the Philippines and points in southern China; but they were smugglers rather than corsairs, and simply to break rules about commerce was not thought of as real piracy.

It may be asked what was the booty sought by the Japanese pirates in China and Korea. Granaries, particularly in Korea, were often attacked, and large quantities of rice and other grains were seized. In China the Wakō sought any kind of property which was easy to transport—silk textiles, for example, and copper cash. In all their successful raids the Wakō took a great number of captives, and these unfortunates were sold as slaves. For despite the gradual emancipation of the Japanese peasant, slavery had not been entirely abolished, and the sale of human beings, though illegal, continued throughout the Muromachi period. Students of Nō plays will recall that the theme of the piece called *Tōsen* or *Karafune* is the tragic life of a Chinese captured at Ningpo and sold in Japan as a slave, and the sale of men, women, and children is the subject of the plays *Sumidagawa* and *Sakuragawa*. Much of the diplomatic correspondence between Japan and Korea at this time deals with the repatriation of captives or fugitives held in either country.

4. Seaport Towns

Among the merchants prominent in foreign trade we have already noticed Koetomi (Koizumi), the Hakata merchant who advised Yoshimitsu that trade with China would solve his financial difficulties. The first phase of the licensed trade with the Ming, lasting from 1405 to 1419, was financed principally by the Bakufu; but in the next phase, from 1432 to 1548, the eleven official voyages from Japan were undertaken mainly by great monasteries and leading daimyos. They were the principals, but the arrangements for chartering, collecting freight, loading, and so forth, were in the hands of experienced merchants from Hakata and other seaports.

Traders also took part in the voyages; sometimes as many as one hundred took passage, each with a prescribed quantity of merchandise for sale. Hyōgo being the usual port of departure, traders from its vicinity were predominant during the early period, but presently traffic shifted to the port of Sakai. After about 1500, Sakai merchants financed and organized most of the voyages originating in the Home Provinces.

Their method of financing voyages was by contract. They paid an agreed sum to shippers, recouping themselves by taking the profit made by sale in China. Thus in 1493 three vessels left Sakai, and on each ship Sakai merchants had put goods worth 10,000 kan, which sold in China for 30,000 kan or more, making the gross profit on the voyage about 60,000 kan. It may well be supposed that Sakai prospered as a seaport, and indeed its history is an epitome of the development of Japan's foreign trade and also of a class of rich and influential merchants.

The growth of Sakai is of interest in the political as well as the economic history of Japan; it shows very clearly the development of a class of well-to-do chōnin, or townspeople, and of merchants of great wealth enjoying an unusual degree of independence. Its early growth has already been touched upon (in Chapter XI), and we may now take up the story at the point where its condition was affected by the Ōnin War.

Early in the days of the Muromachi era Hyōgo had been under direct Bakufu control, and at the time of Yoshimitsu's death it was still a thriving port, looking back to its importance in the time of Kiyomori, who had thought of establishing the capital there in 1180. The reasons for the decline of Hyōgo in the fifteenth century are not entirely clear, but it was no doubt due to causes which favoured the rise of Sakai. Among these was the Ōnin War, when Hyōgo was under the protection of Ōuchi and Hosokawa found it convenient to use Sakai for his connexions with the Home Provinces, in particular Yamato, where the great monasteries of Nara were situated. After the war the powerful Hosokawa family continued to favour Sakai as a port for Kyoto, on the ground that vessels sailing thence for China could go south about Shikoku and Kyūshū and so avoid the attentions of Inland Sea pirates, many of whom were in league with the erratic Ōuchi.

Another advantage enjoyed by Sakai was the presence of refugees who had fled from Kyoto during the worst of the battles. These were for the most part skilled artisans in various trades, and other persons accustomed to town life who could contribute to the prosperity of Sakai. They seem to have succeeded in such a degree that (according to the Chief Abbot Jinson) one summer day in 1481 a group of gaily dressed women claiming to be attendants of the God of Wealth entered Kyoto from Sakai; in response some fifty persons from Kyoto, claiming to be Gods of Poverty, set forth for Sakai wearing comic headdresses in the shape of birds. This may be a piece of fiction, but it surely echoes a feeling that if the citizens of Sakai were doing well, the citizens of Kyoto, though poor, were in good spirits and rebuilding their lives.

Sakai had one other advantage over Hyōgo: its position with relation to Yamato, Kawachi, Settsu, and Yamashiro favoured traffic to many inland points, in particular to Nara. In fact, its progress as a harbour was due in part to its position as a natural point of distribution by land as well as arrival by sea. Rice and other tax goods from places along the Inland Sea destined for the Nara monasteries, or Kōyasan, or even for Kyoto monasteries, could be carried to its destination by an easier route than the approach from Hyōgo by way of Yodo and the Kizu River. Moreover, in Sakai there were ample facilities for converting goods into cash on favourable terms (a commission of 1 per cent), thus saving the merchant the cost of further transport by land. Facilities for the remittance of money by *kawase*, or bills of exchange, were available at Sakai and also at Hyōgo; but Sakai was on the whole more convenient to the traveller, especially at times when the country inland from Hyōgo towards the capital was disturbed by warriors, farmers in revolt, or plain bandits.

One interesting example of the function of the Sakai exchange brokers is their connexion with the Ikkō sectarians established in Kaga. The contributions of the believers to their cathedral in the Home Provinces, the Ishiyama Honganji, were immense, and they were all handled by the Sakai brokers, who were in close touch with the Honganji. The total of such remittances is not known, but we do know from the records of a Sakai broker that one year's contribution from a single small community in Kaga amounted to over 100 kan in 1536. Such commercial facilities improved the position of Sakai as a seaport, and ships arrived in increasing numbers as the country strove, with indifferent success, to return to peaceful life.

The activities of Sakai merchants in overseas trade have already been mentioned in connexion with the licensed voyages to Ming China. They also engaged in coastal traffic along the Inland Sea, despite the risk of capture by pirates; in fact, they appear to have insured themselves against that risk by payments to the pirate chief, whose name was Murakami and who collected such tribute from most vessels in those waters. Evidently Murakami's protection was effective, and he was under Ōuchi's ultimate control.

The use of the southern route for voyages to China brought Sakai merchants into touch with southern Kyūshū at the Satsuma ports of Bōnotsu and Tanegashima, and with southern Tosa at Urado, promoting new activity there. But it was a longer and more dangerous route, so that in the long run the route by way of the Inland Sea and the Straits of Shimonoseki was to be preferred. Towards the last years of the licensed voyages, when the Ōuchi family were prominent in the trade, ships from Sakai commonly sailed to China by the Inland Sea route, and the Sakai merchants at last broke the Ōuchi monopoly. By 1549, a year after the last official voyage, Sakai merchants were organizing voyages to southern China which partook of the nature of smuggling if not of piracy; but as we have seen, piracy on the high seas began to diminish from about 1560, and legitimate traffic took its place.

This is not to say that piracy in home waters came to an end, for in 1581 the Jesuit Valignano, travelling by ship from Bungo to Sakai, was pursued by a pirate ship and barely escaped.

CHAPTER XVII

THE ROAD TO UNIFICATION

1. *Oda Nobunaga*

IN PRECEDING chapters it has been shown that although the two centuries ending about 1540 were marked by almost continuous civil war, the national effort was by no means directed wholly to the support of armies in the field. On the contrary, the needs of the contending parties stimulated rather than hindered economic progress in almost every sphere of peaceful endeavour—in agriculture, in industry, and in trade.

Domestic commerce expanded as merchants travelled freely; and the increased circulation of goods diminished the isolation of small rural communities. Cities, towns, large villages, sprang up to meet new needs, and some of them were strong enough to resist the pressure of powerful barons. The growth of trade and the accumulation of wealth by merchants did not, it is true, reduce the importance of the leading daimyos, but they began to moderate their ideals of self-sufficiency and to understand that they were members of a society composed of inter-dependent parts.

The more enlightened among the daimyos saw the folly of making war merely for expansion of their territory. But the spirit of rivalry was not extinguished, and now that the Bakufu was as good as extinct some unifying overlordship was urgently needed to keep them in order. A process of building up a central authority must soon begin, and its first, possibly its most difficult, phase was undertaken by a small territorial chieftain named Oda Nobunaga. His task was to destroy or reduce the autonomy of the leading warlords, whose number had been reduced to about twenty at the end of the Ōnin War.

It may well be asked how it came about that this burden was carried by a minor chieftain, a mere youth, when in most parts of the country there were powerful barons who could have crushed him with ease. This is an interesting problem which deserves some study in its bearing upon the political tradition of Japan.

Nobunaga of course was not alone in his ambition to bring the country under one rule. Most of the great barons had visions of national hegemony, and the journeys to the Court of warlords like Uyesugi, Hōjō, and Takeda were inspired by a hope of receiving an imperial commission to chastise their rivals. That was the way to gain friends and destroy enemies—the royal road, it might be said—for in spite of all the vicissitudes suffered by the sovereign in those days, authority from the Throne was essential to an aspiring leader.

Chronology of Nobunaga's Rule

1559   Oda Nobunaga becomes master of Owari. Father Vilela arrives in Kyoto

1560   Nobunaga defeats Imagawa at Okehazama

1564   Arrival of Father Frois in Kyoto

1565   Murder of Ashikaga Yoshiteru. The Emperor orders the Jesuits to leave

1567   Nobunaga reduces the stronghold at Inabayama

1568   Nobunaga enters Kyoto. Ashikaga Yoshiaki is named Shōgun. Currency regulations issued

1569   Work begins on the Nijō castle. Nobunaga licenses Frois to preach

1570   Ikkō soldier-monks defeat Nobunaga's troops near Kyoto

1571   The Enryakuji is destroyed

1573   Takeda Shingen dies. Yoshiaki is deposed

1574   Nobunaga destroys the Ikkō settlement at Nagashima

1575   The battle at Nagashino. Takeda Katsuyori is defeated

1576   Work begins on Azuchi castle

1578   Uyesugi Kenshin dies

1579   Azuchi castle is completed. Persecution of the Hokke sect

1580   The fall of the Ishiyama Honganji

1581   Akechi and Hideyoshi are sent against Mōri

1582   The murder of Nobunaga by Akechi

But there were strategic as well as political reasons against action by the richest and most powerful barons. They were surrounded by rivals, and could not move in force towards Kyoto without first securing their position against attack from both front and rear. For example, the great daimyo Ōuchi Yoshioki had for a time left his fief and done well in Kyoto after the decline of Hosokawa. But in order to establish a central power in the capital, Ōuchi needed first to subdue the forces in his rear (Ōtomo, Shimazu, and others) as well as those who stood between him and the capital (Amako, Hosokawa, and many smaller warrior houses). In such conditions a march from the West to Kyoto was an almost impossible enterprise, and indeed he was forced to return home to protect his interests there.

Similar difficulties held good against an approach from the Kantō, where Uyesugi, or Hōjō, or Takeda, or even Satomi might have had designs upon the Home Provinces, but could accomplish them only after conquering various near and distant rivals. During the first half of the sixteenth century these barons were, in fact, busy fighting one another with no decisive result; their history was against them, and so was their geography.

This was not, however, true of Imagawa of Suruga, who besides being a powerful daimyo familiar with Court life was master of a domain not difficult to defend against attack from the east. There was seemingly no threat from the west: Imagawa was Constable of Tōtōmi and Mikawa as well as of Suruga, and he had no reason to apprehend a formidable resistance in Owari and beyond. Behind him was Hōjō, firmly established in his fortress at Odawara but too preoccupied with a watch upon Asakura, Takeda, Uyesugi, and other enemies to threaten Suruga. Consequently it was in a hopeful mood that Imagawa led a considerable array towards Owari in 1560, there to encounter a small force under the command of Oda Nobunaga, a young man of twenty-seven, who had for some years been preparing for this event.

The pedigree of the Oda family is uncertain, and need not detain us long, but there is a special historical interest in tracing the steps by which they rose from obscurity and reached the modest position to which Nobunaga succeeded as a youth, since it was he who set in motion forces that were to change and dominate the constitution of the state from late mediaeval to modern times.

The Oda family were minor vassals of Shiba Yoshimasa, Constable of Echizen about 1400. Yoshimasa's son was made Constable of Owari as well, but being qualified for high office in the Bakufu, he resided in Kyoto and, as was common in his day, left deputies to act for him, Asakura in Echizen and Oda in Owari. Thus Nobunaga's forebears belonged to that class of official gentry which figured prominently in the fluctuations of power so frequent in the fifteenth century.

In due course Oda the Deputy became more powerful, or at least more influential, in Owari than Shiba the Constable. Nobunaga's father was not the Deputy, but only an assistant to the head of the family, who held that office. It was a poor position, but he gradually improved his standing and even began to expand his own modest estates eastward and westward. This was about 1530. About 1535 he gave evidence of wealth and influence by making a handsome contribution to a fund for the repair of the Imperial Palace. When he died in 1551 he had become an important figure in the province, and his name was known in Kyoto at the Court.

His heir Nobunaga found his own position difficult, for he was young —under twenty—and untried. Some of his relatives refused to follow him, but by a great effort he managed to collect a small force of about one thousand men, composed mainly of ashigaru and low-grade fighting men. His next move was to suppress members of the Oda family who were hostile to him. In 1556 he disposed of a rival branch which held the small stronghold of Kiyosu. He then had to deal with his younger brother, who had the support of some of his late father's retainers. In this conflict his brother was killed, and by 1559 Nobunaga had over-come all serious opposition in Owari. Thus, as some historians put it, by a continuous process of "gekokujō" he made himself master of the whole province and put the Constable to flight. Later in 1559 he visited Kyoto, where he was received with favour by the Ashikaga Shōgun Yoshiteru.

2. Okehazama

Late at night on June 21, 1560, at the fortress of Kiyosu where he was now established, Nobunaga received news that Imagawa, with a force reckoned at 25,000 or more, was moving into Owari from Suruga on his way to the capital. The next morning news arrived that one of Imagawa's commanders had captured a fort called Marune. The commander, Matsudaira Motoyasu, stormed the fort at dawn and sent the heads of seven captives for inspection to Imagawa, who was much elated by this pleasant sight and ordered Matsudaira to rest his men and horses. More news came, reporting the capture of another fort, later in the morning, and Nobunaga's adviser pressed him to stand a siege at Kiyosu. He refused, saying that only a strong offensive policy could make up for the superior numbers of the enemy, and calmly ordered a counterattack. It is doubtful whether Nobunaga's total force at that time was much in excess of 3,000, but he may have recruited some support from robber bands, which were common in Owari.

His scouts had reported that the main body of Imagawa's army was resting after its successes, at a place called Dengaku-hazama. This was country over which he had roved as a boy, and he knew it well. Hazama means a gorge or defile, and it was in such a narrow position, unfavourable to manoeuvre, that Imagawa had bivouacked in the forenoon of June 22. People in the vicinity, hearing of his successes, came with food and drink for celebration. Officers and men relaxed until just after midday, when they were taken unawares by a violent rainstorm and a high wind. The whole camp was in confusion, and when the sky cleared, Imagawa's men saw a large force appearing from behind a hill that formed one wall of the defile. At first they thought that this was a revolt within their own army—evidence that their morale was poor. Their few muskets were drenched and useless; their bows, spears, and swords were deep in mud. Before they could sort out their weapons, Nobunaga had fallen upon them, and they fled in panic, plunging through the wet rice fields. Nobunaga himself made for Imagawa's command post, and in the mêlée Imagawa's head was cut off by one of Nobunaga's followers.

The battle of Okehazama,[1] although a small-scale engagement, is of great importance in Japanese history, for if Nobunaga had been defeated, Imagawa might well have reached Kyoto and established himself there, with what results one can only vaguely speculate. The battle is of importance in another respect, for the officer named Matsudaira, who captured Marune, was a rear-vassal of Imagawa, later known as Tokugawa Ieyasu and one day to be master of all Japan.

3. Mino Subdued

After this trial of strength events moved with a seeming inevitability in favour of Nobunaga. Tokugawa Ieyasu, the former Matsudaira, made a pact with Nobunaga in 1561, carrying with him his influence in the province of Mikawa. Nobunaga had a firm belief in the importance of political marriages, and his next step was to make friends with Takeda Shingen of Kai, by promising his daughter in marriage to Shingen's son. The young Imagawa, faced with a combination of three provinces (Owari, Mikawa, and Kai), lost heart and took refuge with the Hōjō family in the fortress of Odawara; and so the name of his family vanishes from the chronicles.

Peace along the eastern seaboard was assured, at least for a time, by the alliance of these three warlords and by an understanding with the Hōjō rulers in Sagami, whose desire was to keep order there. Nobunaga could therefore face towards Kyoto with some confidence. A glance at the map (p. xvi) shows that he was separated from Yamashiro and the capital by only two provinces, Mino and Ōmi, where there were possible antagonists, strong if not formidable. In northern Ōmi there was the family of Asai to be reckoned with, and Nobunaga formed

---

[1] Perhaps the most curious (if the least important) fact about the battle known as the battle of Okehazama is that it was not fought there but in the aforementioned contiguous defile called Dengaku-hazama.

an alliance with them in 1564 by sending his younger sister (O-Ichi) to be the wife of the chieftain, Asai Nagamasa.

The lord of Mino was not so easy to deal with. He was one Saitō Dōsan, the son of a tradesman called Naraya who lived at Yamazaki, near Kyoto. Dōsan had made a fortune as an oil merchant in Mino and had risen to high estate. Nobunaga had been at odds with him for some time and had tried his policy of matrimonial alliance by marrying Dōsan's own daughter. But in 1566 Dōsan was killed by his son, who with certain warriors in western Mino offered strong opposition to Nobunaga.

In the end, however, Nobunaga succeeded in subduing Mino by his good fortune in reducing the Saitō stronghold of Inabayama, which looked down on the Mino plain below. Nobunaga had overcome the antagonism of warriors in western Mino by promising rewards, so Saitō was without their support. But victory was due in large measure to the skill and judgment of one of Nobunaga's junior commanders, Kinoshita Tōkichirō, known as Hideyoshi. At Inabayama, as at Okehazama, the skilful use of topographical features played an important part in the success of Nobunaga's forces. For the strategy here, devised by Hideyoshi, was to build a stronghold facing Inabayama at Sunomata, in a commanding position near the confluence of the Kizu and Nagara rivers, on the border of Owari and Mino. (The work of building at Sunomata was done by a band of adventurers under the direction of a local robber baron named Hachisuka.) From this position of strength Nobunaga was able to storm and take the castle without great difficulty, a success that his late father-in-law had wisely predicted.

Upon the reduction of Mino in the last weeks of 1567, Nobunaga received a secret message from the Emperor Ōgimachi, congratulating him on his exceptional military prowess. It seems that His Majesty desired the restoration of imperial property which had been confiscated by his enemies. Earlier in the year the refugee Yoshiaki, the younger brother of the late Shōgun Yoshiteru (who had been killed in 1565 by rebellious vassals of Hosokawa), had requested Nobunaga's help in restoring the Ashikaga Bakufu. Later (in 1568) Yoshiaki was brought to Nobunaga from Asakura's estate in Echizen, where he had taken shelter. These two requests formed the authority for Nobunaga's further action. His motto now, engraved on his seal, was "Rule the Empire by Force." He took up residence in Inabayama castle, and renamed the castle town, calling it Gifu, with a classical reference to a situation in early Chinese history which he felt he had repeated.

It was now abundantly clear that Nobunaga aimed at governing the whole country. There remained but one obstacle on the path to Kyoto, an opposition force in the province of Ise, where the descendants of Kitabatake Chikafusa were flourishing and influential. The Kitabatake forces threatened to move into Ōmi and Yamashiro, and were in touch with the Miyoshi family in Kyoto and the Rokkaku in Ōmi. But Nobunaga soon drove them from the field. The Rokkaku checked him briefly, but he took their strongholds and swept them aside. The fall of the castle called Mizukuri crowned his effort. He sent for Yoshiaki, whom he had left in Gifu, and on November 9, 1568, entered Kyoto in panoply. Yoshiaki was named the fifteenth Ashikaga Shōgun on December 28.

4. *Nobunaga in Kyoto*

Although Nobunaga's adversaries in Kyoto (Hatakeyama, Hosokawa, Miyoshi, and Matsunaga) had fled, his reception in the city was cool. The experienced citizens thought of him as one more robber baron intent upon pillage. The fact that he brought Yoshiaki with him moderated their fears, although a number of Court nobles sent their families and their possessions to relatives in the country, having suffered from the rapacity of the warriors who had just left the city. But to the general surprise Nobunaga's troops were under strict discipline, and orders were issued under his seal ensuring the safety of the citizens.

This made a good impression upon the Court and the nobles, who turned to Nobunaga and begged him to order the return of their confiscated property. Nobunaga thought it prudent to conciliate them, and ordered certain of his officers to arrange for restitution. But his position was still somewhat uncertain, and his first care was necessarily to increase and improve his military strength. He had one important advantage in holding the great alluvial plain which comprised the two provinces of Owari and Mino, and next to them was the rich province of Ōmi. Here again geography was in his favour: these rich lands were farmed by a number of independent warriors of the ji-samurai type and were not under the control of any great chieftain. If he could get these men on his side, he was in a strong position for holding his own against attack from the west; and (an important asset) he could control the life of the capital, whose citizens could not survive more than a few weeks if supplies of food from the adjacent provinces were cut off.

His rear was tolerably secure against attack, thanks to Ieyasu, who had dealt with possible hostile combinations in the East by coming to terms with Takeda Shingen and by occupying the former Imagawa territory. Yoshiaki's appointment as Shōgun in 1568 was also a defensive measure, since it could be used to invest Nobunaga's action with legitimacy and therefore to give pause to warriors disposed to attack him.

The relations between Nobunaga and Yoshiaki were difficult. Their first difference of opinion took place when, soon after his installation, Yoshiaki offered a magnificent Nō performance to Nobunaga as a sign of gratitude. The programme consisted of thirteen items, and at the end of the fifth Nobunaga left in a bad temper, saying that the country was not yet at peace and he had no leisure for such entertainments. Next day he went back to his castle at Gifu. Yoshiaki offered him great appointments, but he would accept no subordinate position. As the legend on his seal made clear, he meant to govern the country by military power. He saw that the Muromachi Bakufu was almost defunct. He was willing to show it outward signs of respect, but he had no intention of obeying it.

Seal and two ciphers of Oda Nobunaga

Nor had he time or patience for political intrigue. From the end of 1568 he was busy in subduing or pacifying the provinces adjacent to Yamashiro. Towards the end of 1569 he rode into the capital at the head of a large force to announce the subjugation of Ise, and no doubt also to intimidate the Shōgun. In January 1570 he wrote a "vermilion letter," that is, a document under his official seal, to his representatives in Kyoto (his general Akechi and his servant, the Shingon monk Asayama Nichijō) to say that he had given Yoshiaki five articles which he must obey.

These all imposed conditions inconsistent with the dignity of the Shōgun, since they left him only his ceremonial powers. Nobunaga had a feeling for magnificence, and he did not grudge Yoshiaki any of the splendours of his office. In fact, he took a great interest in the building of a new palace for the Shōgun, now shouting directions from a place on the scaffolding, now striding about the garden in his tiger-skin cloak showing workmen where to place this bush or that stone.

Nobunaga's attitude towards the Emperor was one of great respect, even reverence, and he indulged his passion for building on a large scale when he pressed on the work of a new Imperial Palace. This was a very costly undertaking, as we know from the literary remains of Nichijō. The point is of some interest, because it contradicts the view of certain early Meiji historians who describe the Palace at this time as a broken-down place in which intruders peered at the lodgings of the ladies-in-waiting and paid a few coppers for a script of verses by some indigent prince. The truth is that immense sums, to which Nobunaga himself contributed handsomely, were being spent at this time upon rebuilding the Palace. In 1569 Nichijō had told the builders that they were spending too much; by that date the work had already cost 10,000 kan, and was far from complete. It was finished at the end of 1571.

Yoshiaki did not obey Nobunaga's rule that he must keep clear of politics, but continued to strike bargains with such important monasteries as the Hōryūji and the Daitokuji and tried to gain favour by mediating between hostile barons, notably between Ōtomo and Mōri, and even between Hōjō, Takeda, and Uyesugi, a most delicate operation in which there was little prospect of success. Yoshiaki's endeavours did little beyond angering Nobunaga, but their scope shows clearly that the office of Shōgun was not entirely empty and useless even now. Despite their lack of solid physical power, both the Emperor and the Shōgun had a remarkable influence derived from the prestige of their high offices. A long tradition was still at work. In their weakest days the Court and the Bakufu were still occasionally able to arrange peace between great warlords who were anxious to stop fighting but prevented by pride from saying so publicly. In such a predicament it was convenient for the parties to submit to persuasion from Kyoto, thus achieving their object while gaining merit as loyal subjects of the Throne or vassals of the Shōgun.

The further relations between Nobunaga and Yoshiaki will be discussed below; it is enough here to notice that by 1573 the Shōgun had shown himself so insubordinate that Nobunaga deposed him. Yoshiaki retained his title but not his office, and he wandered from place to place in search of support until his death in 1597. Thus there was no Sei-i Tai-Shōgun from 1573 until 1603, when the post was filled by Ieyasu.

The year 1570 was a difficult one for Nobunaga, and it is not surprising that he grew impatient with Yoshiaki and went his own way regardless of objections from any quarter. Early in 1570 he invited a number of powerful daimyos to Kyoto to discuss the affairs of the nation and advise the Emperor and the Shōgun. This was merely a device to test the warlords. Among those who did not reply was Asakura Yoshikage of Echizen, a very successful upstart ruler with whom Yoshiaki had taken refuge during his exile. His silence gave Nobunaga an excuse for attacking him, and at the end of May 1570 Nobunaga left Kyoto at the head of an army of 30,000 men. Northern Ōmi was held by Asai Nagamasa, whose wife was a younger sister of Nobunaga, and he relied upon this family connexion for a safe passage through Ōmi to Wakasa on his way to Echizen. But to his surprise Asai had responded to an appeal from Asakura, and now threatened to cut across his line of retreat. There was nothing for it but to retreat at once. While his enemies were in consultation, Nobunaga divided his force into separate divisions, which made their way back to Kyoto along byroads. Then on July 22, having reformed his army and obtained valuable reinforcements from Ieyasu, he marched out, and on July 30 he joined battle with the united forces of Asai and Asakura at a place called Anegawa in northern Ōmi. The fighting was developing in favour of Asai when Ieyasu delivered a powerful attack on the enemy's flank. The battle ended in the total defeat of Asai and Asakura. More than half of their officers and men died in action; the rest fled in disorder towards their respective homes.

Nobunaga's new army was now toughened by experience, and it seemed that he could proceed to a further extension of his authority with fair assurance. He had trouble with some unreconciled elements in the Home Provinces, who formed leagues and engaged in guerrilla operations, always on the lookout for an opportunity to take Kyoto by surprise. But a far more dangerous enemy was the great Ishiyama Honganji,[2] the cathedral of the Ikkō or Single-minded sect, which was becoming very powerful throughout the country and indeed already rivalled the great barons in its wealth, its military strength, and the influence its leaders exerted on its members. The great wealth of the Honganji came chiefly from the contributions of the Monto, the sectarians, who poured out money for the central treasury in a constant stream. The strong conviction of these fanatic believers, mostly peasants and other poor people, constituted a force which Nobunaga was obliged to resist with all his might, since it was his strongest single rival for sovereign power in the state.

5. Nobunaga's Strategic Problems

The rest of this chapter must be devoted to a study of the strategic problems that now faced Nobunaga. They were problems of political as well as military strategy, but at this juncture—in the latter half of 1570—military considerations were uppermost.

A plain record of marches and battles makes tiresome reading, but the process of unification was, in its earlier phases at least, a military rather than a political process, because it consisted in the destruction of obstacles to unity. The nature of the unity ultimately reached was influenced by the methods used to achieve it, and therefore the military problems that faced Nobunaga deserve attention for their political interest.

Nobunaga's defeat of Asai and Asakura had relieved the pressure on him from the north, but it was not decisive. There had been frequent and successful Ikkō risings in Kaga and Echizen, and the threat there had not been entirely removed. By itself it was not important, but it might be used by powerful warlords in the East and North. In the East, Uyesugi Kenshin of Echigo, Takeda Shingen of Kai, and Hōjō Ujiyasu, who dominated the southern portion of the Kantō, had so far

---

[2] The Ishiyama Honganji was a cathedral and stronghold established in 1496 at Ōsaka in an almost impregnable position facing west to the shore of Ōsaka Bay. It was difficult to approach by land, being almost surrounded by waterways; but it could be supplied with reinforcements and provisions by sea. Ishiyama is the name of the slight eminence on which the main buildings were erected.

右信長御影
為御報恩相
當柱一周忌之
辰横之三州
高橋長興寺
与語久三郎
正勝奇進之
天正十一年六月日

14

15

not made any durable agreements, but they had to be watched. In the North there was no solid force, only a number of barons (Satake, Yūki, Date, Nambu, and a few others) whose domains were backward economically and weak politically, since the rulers could not control the very independent rural gentry. These provinces presented no imminent threat.

In the western provinces the strongest ruler was Mōri Motonari, a remarkable man who (having displaced the Ōuchi family) controlled with a firm hand the western part of the main island and part of northern Kyūshū. Apart from formidable land forces, he had at his command a number of warships with experienced crews. Opposed to Mōri were the powerful Ōtomo and Ryūzōji in northern Kyūshū, and Shimazu in the south, governing Satsuma, Ōsumi, and Hyūga as a unit. These western barons had lately gained a new importance from their association with Portuguese traders and might have been dangerous to Nobunaga if they had been able to agree among themselves, but they seem to have thought chiefly of trade and of battles with their neighbours. Remote and preoccupied as they were, they caused no anxiety to Nobunaga.

In the central provinces between Mōri and Nobunaga were a number of newly prominent families with histories much like Mōri's. Amako, Ukita, Urakami, Hatano, and others, having long been subservient to such warlords as Akamatsu, Yamana, and Hosokawa, had recently driven their former masters from the land and now were busy consolidating their power. On the whole Nobunaga had no pressing danger to fear from the central and western provinces. His most menacing antagonists were nearer home.

At this time his immediate concern was to protect Kyoto. Here he was threatened by the powerful Enryakuji, north of the city. If he should make a move to the north, however, Miyoshi and Matsunaga and Saitō, whom he had driven out of Mino, were likely to occupy the the capital in his absence. They had built forts near Ōsaka and were a new source of anxiety. On the other hand, if he attacked them he would bring out the armed strength of the Ishiyama Honganji, the most dangerous of all the forces by which he was threatened.

For not only was the Ishiyama Honganji the cathedral of the Ikkō sect, it was a great fortified place. There was a garrison composed of believers from each section of Ōsaka and from the sect's provincial congregations in Kaga and Echizen and elsewhere. They were always on patrol, and were several hundred in number, easily multiplied by more than ten times over on the ringing of an alarm bell. The Honganji was considered as impregnable. Moreover, several provincial warlords had thought it prudent to establish friendly relations with this formidable body, among them being Asakura in Echizen, Asai in Ōmi, and Mōri in the West, and they were emulated by a number of kokujin here and there.

The threat of combination between such barons and the Ikkō sectarians was one which Nobunaga could not disregard. He knew he must come to a reckoning with the Ikkō; and an opportunity was soon offered. In November 1570 the Honganji sent help to the Miyoshi faction in Kyoto, which was active again, stirring up trouble in the city. Nobunaga sent a punitive force to put down the disturbance, whereupon the Ikkō troops were reinforced by soldier-monks from Negoro in Kii, and by a body of musketeers said to have numbered 3,000. Their assault was vigorous, and Nobunaga's force was obliged to withdraw with the loss of a large number of men. He saw that his most powerful enemy, the greatest obstacle in the way of unity, was not the old regime but the new militant church, the Honganji and the Ikkō leaguers upon whom it could call in all parts of the country.

At this point Asai and Asakura, who had recovered from their punishment at Nobunaga's hands, were joined by the soldier-monks of the Enryakuji, whose excuse for action was Nobunaga's refusal to help them to regain lands which his generals had confiscated. In addition to these troubles Nobunaga was faced with hostile movements in Ōmi and Ise, fostered by the Honganji. His position was so dangerous that he had to shorten his line and concentrate on the defence of Kyoto and Gifu. The Emperor intervened on his behalf, and there was a truce, but it did not last long.

Nobunaga now decided that in order to break through the net he must completely destroy the Enryakuji. Early in October 1571 he stormed Hiyeizan. The fighting monks were taken by surprise and subdued without much trouble. All the great buildings were destroyed by fire. The Komponchūdō, the pagodas, the numerous shrines and chapels with their precious contents, all went up in flames. Nobunaga's soldiery killed indiscriminately; monks, laymen, women, and children were captured and beheaded. As one writer said: "The whole mountainside was a great slaughterhouse, and the sight was one of unbearable horror."

At about this time the Ikkō leaguers in the Kiso River delta at Nagashima erupted against Nobunaga's forces there, and put up a very strong resistance in a ring of protected villages. Nobunaga went to supervise the attack but had to withdraw, pursued by the Ikkō men, who inflicted some losses upon his troops. This defeat seems to have brought Nobunaga's hatred of the sectarians to a high pitch, and he resolved to destroy them.

Apart from the Honganji, probably the most dangerous of his enemies at this time was Takeda Shingen of Kai. Takeda had for a time been nominally allied with Nobunaga against Uyesugi Kenshin and the Hōjō family, but this arrangement came to an end on the death of Hōjō Ujiyasu, a month after the destruction of Hiyeizan. The death of Ujiyasu upset the delicate balance of power, and the new Hōjō leader decided to break with Kenshin and come to terms with Takeda. Thus Takeda felt free to make his long-intended drive to the capital.

This adventure is at first sight of little interest, but its background is important. Takeda had been in touch with the treacherous Shōgun Yoshiaki since 1570, and he was related by marriage to the Chief Abbot Kōsa of the Ishiyama Honganji. He now took the lead in an alliance against Nobunaga and planned to move on Kyoto. The immediate obstacles to his design were his old enemy Uyesugi Kenshin in Echigo and Tokugawa Ieyasu on the eastern seaboard. This was a strong combination, and of course Nobunaga had also to be reckoned with, as a third party in a strong defensive alliance. Takeda therefore sought help from the Honganji and persuaded the Abbot Kōsa to cause the Monto in Kaga to rise against Uyesugi.[8]

This last move was a check to Nobunaga and obliged him to change his plans. Meanwhile, at the end of November 1572 Takeda began his offensive by marching westward with an army of 30,000 men. He reached Ōmi in January 1573, and joined battle with Nobunaga and Ieyasu at Mikata-gahara, along the lower reaches of the Tenryūgawa in Tōtōmi. Takeda was successful, and Ieyasu barely escaped with his life to Hamamatsu. Nobunaga, also in a difficult position, was driven to seek a diplomatic solution. In the name of the Shōgun Yoshiaki, he proposed a truce between Takeda and Kenshin. If Takeda refused, he could be accused of disobeying an order of the Shōgun. But Takeda replied that he would accept the mediation of Asakura, not of Nobunaga.

Nobunaga next tried for an agreement between himself and Takeda, again alleging orders from the Shōgun, but this device also failed. Takeda refused and complained to Yoshiaki of Nobunaga's misdeeds in a paper of five articles, to which Nobunaga retorted with seven articles of his own. After this documentary battle, another trial of strength was unavoidable. But Nobunaga's position was still awkward, for Yoshiaki was working against him, collecting funds and stirring up resentment. In March 1573 Nobunaga drew up a charge of seventeen articles against Yoshiaki, who then called upon Takeda, Asakura, Asai, and the powerful Ikkō league in Etchū to demolish Nobunaga. This was more than Nobunaga could stand, and he attacked Yoshiaki in his Nijō palace. Yoshiaki fled and took refuge with his friends.

Thus a final encounter between Nobunaga and Takeda was certain. But at this juncture news came that Takeda Shingen, wounded in a new attack upon Ieyasu, had died a few weeks later. This was a stroke of good fortune for Nobunaga and discouraging for Yoshiaki, who, however, thought fit to make one more effort. In June 1573 he called upon Matsunaga (who had murdered the Shōgun Yoshiteru, Yoshiaki's brother), Asakura, the Honganji, and other possible allies for help against Nobunaga. At the Abbot Kōsa's instance he asked Mōri for

---

[8] In the history books Takeda and his enemy Uyesugi have a high reputation as commanders in the military chronicles. They certainly enjoyed battles, but neither displayed any remarkable strategical gift. They fumbled their opportunities and they seem to have learned little from their frequent mistakes.

supplies. At the same time he wrote for help to Shingen's successor, Takeda Katsuyori.

But Nobunaga's preparations were better. He descended upon Kyoto, crossing Lake Biwa in boats he had secretly got ready, took Yoshiaki by surprise, and drove him out of the city. By August 1573 Nobunaga's position in the Home Provinces and the adjacent provinces was firm. In September he had his final reckoning with Asakura in Echizen and Asai in Ōmi, routing their armies, destroying their castles, and driving them to suicide. He awarded their lands to Hideyoshi, who built a castle at Nagahama in Ōmi and was thus established as a warrior of the first rank.

Before the investment of his castle Asai had sent his wife (Nobunaga's sister) and her three daughters to Nobunaga's headquarters. This lady, named O-Ichi, was said to be a great beauty. She later married a general who was killed, or died by his own hand, in an attack by Hideyoshi. She refused to escape and died with him. The daughters were taken care of by Hideyoshi, and the eldest, called Chacha during her childhood, later became his mistress and was well-known as his favourite, Yodogimi.

Drawing of O-Ichi, Nobunaga's sister and the wife of Asai Nagamasa, after a portrait in the Jimyō-in, Kōyasan

At the New Year celebration in 1574 Nobunaga is said to have received as a gift a lacquer box containing the heads of three defeated enemies, which he inspected with glee. This may be true, but his mind at this time was fixed not upon past victims but upon destroying the Ikkō sect.

Before delivering his final assault on the Honganji, however, Nobunaga thought it wise to secure himself against an attack which Takeda Katsuyori was obviously meditating and also to break up the Ikkō leagues in Ise and in the province of Kaga. He also had to take measures to prevent hostile action by Uyesugi Kenshin.

The order in which he undertook these tasks was determined partly by the movements of his adversaries. Several times since 1570 he had dealt with risings by a stubborn Ikkō league in a settlement called Nagashima whose five strongholds were situated in strong positions in the delta of the Kiso River. The risings were incited by Nobunaga's enemies and were never permanently put down. In July 1574 Nobunaga sent a strong force to Nagashima to settle the issue. His troops met with fierce resistance, but three redoubts at last gave way before enveloping attacks repeated day after day. From the seaward side the remaining defenders were under the pressure of a force of pirates from Ise, who bombarded them with large-calibre muskets and broke down their look-out towers. By the end of August they were short of food, and some were dying of hunger. They offered to surrender, but Nobunaga was implacable. He put a stout stockade round the two strongholds which still held out, Nakaye and Nagashima, and in which there were crammed some 20,000 people, thus cutting off the defenders from any chance of escape. He then set fire to the strongholds from all sides, and those within were burned to death. In October 1574, after this act of vengeance for his former defeats, Nobunaga returned in triumph to Gifu.

Meanwhile attack and defence at the Honganji perimeter went on intermittently through 1574 and into 1575. Help continued to arrive from Ikkō congregations far and near, including gold, rice, barley, oil, and clothing from the church in Echizen, the Honseiji.

Early in 1575 Nobunaga decided that he must finish the subjugation of Echizen, which was now dominated by the sectarians. But in June of that year he was obliged to modify his plans and move eastward to help Ieyasu withstand an attack by Takeda Katsuyori. The ensuing battle, fought at a place called Nagashino in the province of Mikawa, marks a new era in the history of warfare in Japan.

Takeda opened the attack with the old-style order of battle: four waves of mounted warriors charged one after another against the defences erected by Nobunaga. They were all destroyed before they reached his front line. Nobunaga had set up wooden palisades in a zig-zag pattern, of a height which the horses could not overleap. Takeda's cavaliers were brought up short against this obstacle and were shot down from behind it by some 3,000 foot soldiers armed with muskets. Every successive charge of the Takeda warriors was repulsed with heavy losses, while the defenders suffered hardly a scratch.

The muskets were still rudimentary weapons, muzzle-loaded and fired by a tinder, effective up to about eighty yards. The firing process was so slow that the musketeers were divided into three sections, firing in rotation. Takeda Shingen and Uyesugi Kenshin had used muskets in their battles at Kawanakajima not long after the weapons first appeared in Japan, and Takeda had ordered materials for the manufacture of muskets in 1572; but neither he nor Kenshin had fully understood the power of this new weapon. By contrast, the Ikkō leaders had quickly perceived the superiority of firearms to swords and spears. The Ishiyama Honganji soon developed a real arsenal, where muskets were made in quantity. The Ikkō settlements at Negoro and Saiga had similar workshops, and it was at Negoro that some of the best-known gunsmiths learned their craft. Sakai was also an important centre for the manufacture and sale of firearms and ammunition for sale to any purchaser.

The defeat of Takeda at Nagashino in June 1575 greatly improved Nobunaga's strategic position. The only threat remaining to the north was the military strength of Uyesugi Kenshin, alone or combined with the leaguers in Kaga. Nobunaga, using a strong force in a short, sharp campaign, broke the leaguers, and swept on to Tsuruga, subduing Echizen and later the whole of Kaga. He thus came close to Kenshin's domain, but refrained from attacking him, being anxious to avoid a major engagement. Meanwhile Kenshin was active. In the fall of 1575 he established a link with the Ishiyama Honganji, with armed monks in Kii, and with Mōri in Yamaguchi. He began to move south in October 1577, but was held up by bad weather and decided to wait until the snow melted in the spring. When spring came, he died of a haemorrhage at the age of forty-eight.

6. *The Fall of the Honganji*

While Nobunaga was dealing with his northern adversaries, Yoshiaki, the deposed and fugitive Shōgun, had been steadily plotting against him. From Tomo, in Bingo province, he despatched letters (dated in April 1575) appealing for help to be given by Mōri to the defenders of the Honganji.[4] But Mōri was for the moment reluctant to move, and the Abbot Kōsa, in urgent need of supplies, made peaceful overtures to Nobunaga, who knew that Kōsa was only playing for time.

Both Nobunaga and Mōri were fully aware of the importance of controlling traffic through the Inland Sea. Here the advantage lay with Mōri, who had a strong naval force at his command, composed of experienced privateers. In the summer of 1575 he ordered his captains to proceed with supplies to the relief of the Honganji. Nobunaga also had war vessels, some three hundred in number. They were stationed at the head of Ōsaka Bay, defending the estuary of the Kizu River. Here there was a brisk engagement, in which firearms were used on both sides. The Mōri ships won the fight, and had little trouble in getting the needed supplies into the fortress. This was in August 1575. At this point Yoshiaki and Mōri pressed Kenshin and Takeda to move. A letter from Mōri to Kenshin is preserved, from which it appears that Mōri's design was to make a frontal attack in great force upon Nobunaga, while

---

[4] Mōri Motonari had died in 1571. He was succeeded by his grandson Terumoto, who worked in harmony with his kinsmen and advisers Kikkawa and Kobayakawa. It was to these men that Yoshiaki's letters were addressed.

Kenshin, Takeda, and Ikkō armies descended upon him from the east. Mōri's letter is very specific. It is dated in September 1575, refers to his sea victory with satisfaction, and makes plans for the downfall of Nobunaga. It need hardly be said that the anxiety of these great warriors to support the Honganji was not due to a desire to protect Buddhists or Buddhism.

Neither Takeda nor Kenshin answered Mōri's call, and the fighting ceased for a time. Indeed, all was so peaceful that early in 1576 Nobunaga began work on his new castle at Azuchi, on the edge of Lake Biwa. While supervising the foundations there, he laid his plans for an attack which should destroy the power of the Ikkō sect.

The interrupted struggle was resumed in June. Nobunaga led a force of 3,000 against the Honganji, which mustered 15,000 troops. Nobunaga was at the head of a body of ashigaru, which was checked and withdrew when Nobunaga was slightly wounded in the leg. He then decided to change his tactics, and to attack the inland strong-points which formed the eastern outer defences of the Honganji.

In March 1577 he left his castle and assembled his generals in Kyoto. With them he led a very large force into Izumi by way of Yahata, Uji, and the province of Kawachi. Divided into two armies, they swept through Izumi, thrusting aside all resistance from local warriors, and entering Kii province delivered a strong attack on Saiga. There the Ikkō leaguers put up a stubborn resistance, but they could not withstand assaults which continued day and night, and at length they surrendered. During this operation Nobunaga detached a strong force to attack the monastery of Negoro. They set fire to the buildings, and the defenders were forced to come out and surrender.

Thus the whole of the province of Kii was subdued in less than a month. The soldier-monks of Negoro and the sectaries of Saiga were set free on binding themselves not to support the Honganji in any way. In April Nobunaga returned to Kyoto in good order, having cut off the garrison's source of supplies from the east and south. The news of his successes filled Mōri Terumoto with alarm. He wrote to Uyesugi Kenshin saying that now nothing could stop Nobunaga but an attack in full force from east and west in combination.

At the Honganji, the besieged garrison fell into a state of despondency on learning of the fall of Saiga. The Abbot Kōsa sent summonses to pastors and congregations throughout the country, exhorting them to stand fast and to send supplies and reinforcements to succour the defenders of the cathedral and the fortress. Only thus, he said (in a letter addressed to believers in Sagami and Musashi during the summer of 1577), could the Law of the Buddha be restored.

Mōri could do nothing at this time without help from Kenshin, and Kenshin, as we have seen, was slow to move in the fall of 1577 and was dead the following spring. The isolation of the Honganji was thus almost complete. Nobunaga ordered Kōsa to evacuate the fortress and leave Ōsaka. Kōsa consulted his colleagues and associates in long-drawn-out discussions, all the while imploring Mōri for help. Meanwhile his outposts were falling one after another, and his supplies were nearly exhausted. In April 1580 an Imperial Messenger was sent with a Letter of Advice from the Throne, and the fortress surrendered a few weeks later.[5]

Thus ended eleven years of bitter fighting. It will be noticed that the intervention of the Emperor was effective, because it gave "face" to both sides and prevented indiscriminate slaughter. The incident is also of interest because it contradicts statements that the sovereign was neglected, the Court penniless, and the Palace falling to pieces for want of repairs. It was, of course, Nobunaga who suggested to His Majesty Ōgimachi that he despatch an imperial missive to Kōsa.

It might be supposed that after the fall of the Honganji Nobunaga would rest a while from his campaigning; but in 1581 he decided on one more great battle. He and Ieyasu and Hōjō led an immense force to attack Takeda Katsuyori. The chronicles say that a total of nearly 180,000 men marched from different points against some 20,000 men assembled with difficulty by Katsuyori. The vanguard from Gifu entered Kōfu, the capital of the Takeda domains, without meeting any opposition. Katsuyori fled to Temmokusan, where he was captured and killed in April 1582. This was the end of the Takeda family, in its twenty-eighth generation.

Why Nobunaga used so much force against so weak an enemy is not clear. Takeda Shingen had caused him much trouble in the past and at times had defeated him in battle. He may have thought it wise to occupy, if only for a short time, the four provinces which Takeda had ruled. Moreover, it was necessary for him to reward his generals by gifts of territory. In this way he disposed of Kai and Shinano, while Ieyasu received Suruga, and a trusted general named Takigawa was awarded a part of Kōtsuke, where he could keep an eye on the Hōjō family and their activities in the Kantō. Part of Nobunaga's statecraft was devoted to the distribution of territory among his wartime friends and allies.

He probably took an especial pleasure in carving up the Takeda lands, for he appears to have had a violent, almost insane, hatred of both Shingen and Katsuyori. He even treated the monks of the Eirinji (the church which held Shingen's remains) with appalling cruelty, roasting them to death in a great bonfire. Ieyasu, on the other hand, paid respect to the corpse of Katsuyori and sheltered some of his adherents from Nobunaga's vengeance.

---

[5] Kōsa left the fortress in charge of his son in May 1580 and sought without success to raise a relieving force in Kii. It was actually the son who had to surrender the place and march out.

CHAPTER XVIII

CHRISTIANITY AND BUDDHISM
UNDER NOBUNAGA

1. *Missionaries in the Capital*

WHEN Francis Xavier left Kagoshima in 1550 and made his painful way to Kyoto, his purpose was to see the "King of Japan." At that time Kyoto was little more than a scene of desolation. There was no powerful ruler to whom he could appeal, and he was obliged to return to Yamaguchi, where he was protected by Ōuchi Yoshitaka and allowed to preach the gospel. He was then invited to Funai by Ōtomo Sōrin (later Francisco), the lord of Bungo, who also gave him protection and who became an ardent supporter of Christianity, for reasons political rather than religious.

Xavier, on his return to Goa in 1552 with an envoy from Bungo to the Portuguese Viceroy of the Indies, reported favourably on the prospects of mission work in Japan and spoke highly of the character of the Japanese people. He urged the despatch of missionaries without delay, and good men were sent. In western Japan they had much success, partly because they were favoured by rulers who wished to attract Portuguese ships and partly because the poor and oppressed country folk listened gladly to a gospel which offered them a prospect of bliss. But, although the missions in Kyūshū flourished, the directors in Goa were convinced that they must extend their labours to the capital, for it was the policy of the Jesuits to seek the support of the ruling classes wherever they went. They knew that in the long run they must depend upon the good will of the temporal power. Consequently, the leading missionaries in Japan were, as one of them put it, "at pains to see the King, because in Japan everything depends upon the rulers."

In 1559 there were only six Fathers in Japan, but one of them, Father Gaspar Vilela, was sent from the province of Bungo to the capital at the earliest opportunity. After some difficulties he was cordially received by the Shōgun Ashikaga Yoshiteru, who in 1560 issued orders that the missionaries were to be well treated and not taxed or otherwise hampered in their work.

It is not clear why Yoshiteru should have been so friendly. He may have received word from Ōtomo, but it seems more likely that it was because Vilela, in the early days of his sojourn in Kyoto, had made a good impression upon a number of warriors and had converted Miyoshi Chōkei, who was then acting as a kind of guardian to the Shōgun. Whatever the reason, the protection afforded by Yoshiteru was of great value. It enabled Vilela to preach freely and to move about the city with his companion, Brother Lorenzo, who was a Japanese of humble origin, a blind musician. Vilela soon became known in the country round Kyoto and as far afield as Sakai and Nara. The number of his converts grew fast, particularly among military men, who swarmed over the region south of the capital at this time, the Miyoshi and Matsunaga factions being engaged in their usual enterprises of conspiracy and slaughter.

Vilela was so successful that he appealed to Goa for assistance, but then violent turmoil broke out in Kyoto, and he was unable to carry on his mission or to protect his church and his converts. Late in 1560 he felt obliged to move for a time to Sakai, where he was safe from attack but found the prosperous merchants indifferent to his gospel. The Shō-gun had fled from Kyoto at the same time as Vilela; but although order was restored before long and the Shōgun returned to the city, Vilela was to remain in Sakai reluctantly for two years, returning to Kyoto in 1563. During these years Buddhist monks pressed for the expulsion of all missionaries from Japan and threatened violence, but the Shōgun's chief minister, Matsunaga Hisahide, silenced them.

Within a few years after Vilela's arrival in Kyoto several small Christian churches had been built at a distance from the city. In 1564, Vilela was joined by Luis Frois and another Father sent by the authorities in Goa in response to Vilela's request. At this time there were about twelve Fathers in Japan, most of them in Bungo, where the number of converts was very great.

Frois, who was ordered to Kyoto after nine years in Malacca, is an important figure in the history of the Jesuit mission to Japan. His letters provide highly reliable evidence on events from 1549 to 1578, and he remained in Japan until his death in 1587. He was active in Kyoto when Nobunaga was at the height of his power, and he was on friendly terms with many important persons. Vilela had been received several times by Yoshiteru; and he and Frois were both present at a New Year audience in 1565, where Yoshiteru sat in state, acknowledging the obeisances of some of the important guests by a slight movement of his fan. In the summer of 1565 this unfortunate Shōgun was murdered with his mother and his wife by Matsunaga and the Miyoshi faction, who had so terrified the Shōgun's friends and adherents that his funeral was attended only by a few monks from the Shōkokuji. The great Zen prelates kept away. Frois, in a letter written soon after these foul deeds, relates how Yoshiteru's younger brother Yoshiaki escaped and was finally rescued by "Nobunaga, the King of Owari, who raised a great army to subjugate the rebels."

Shortly after Yoshiteru's death an edict was issued by the Emperor (under pressure from the Buddhist sects) ordering the expulsion of all missionaries. Vilela and Frois escaped from the tumult with the help of a Japanese convert, and made their way to Sakai, a good observation point and a centre of news from all parts of the country.

The edict was a great blow to the Jesuits, and Vilela returned to Kyūshū, but Frois continued his work from Sakai and was respected by his converts. Their faith seems to have been firm and comforting, for (we are told) when Frois on Christmas Day of 1567 invited men from both of the armies then at war to celebrate the festival together in amity, they came gladly and left saying "We are brothers in Christ," but they resumed the slaughter in the morning.

In the early years of Vilela's mission a number of warriors in the Home Provinces had adopted the Christian faith. Some were ordinary bushi, others men of rank. Among the more prominent of Vilela's converts was a daimyo of good standing in Settsu, Takayama by name. He is said to have been converted after losing in a debate to which he had challenged Vilela. He took Vilela to his castle and there was baptised with his wife and children. He was given the baptismal name of Dario, and his eldest son, then ten years old, was christened Justo. When the boy grew up he was known by his title as Ukon (an honorary rank in the Imperial Bodyguards), and in the Jesuit writings, where he is constantly praised for his great services to the missionary cause, he is always referred to as Ucondono.

Takayama Dario had an elder brother named Wada Koremasa, a chieftain in Ōmi, who had rendered valuable services to Nobunaga in his campaigns in the Home Provinces; and Takayama, anxious to assist the missionaries, urged Wada to use his influence with Nobunaga and ask for the recall of the Fathers to Kyoto. As a result of this suggestion, one day in the late spring of 1569 Frois was taken to see Nobunaga, who had not long before entered the city with Yoshiaki. Yoshiaki also was indebted to Wada—to Vatadono, as the Jesuits called him—for aid and comfort during his years of wandering.[1]

The interview took place on a hot day, on a bridge across the moat at the entrance to the Nijō castle, which was then under construction. Nobunaga was there superintending the work, of which he was very proud; he wore a tiger-skin tunic and was surrounded by a great number of armed men. Frois was held in conversation by Nobunaga, then in an amiable and talkative mood. He asked Frois questions about his purpose in coming to Japan and was pleased with his replies, which were respectful but firm and included some derogatory observations upon Buddhist monks which were much to Nobunaga's taste. Wada was ordered to guide Frois round the building, and on their return Nobunaga dismissed him with kind words.

Shortly after this meeting Wada took Frois to an audience with the new Shōgun, Yoshiaki, and soon thereafter Frois received a license to

[1] The date of this interview is sometimes given as in the summer of 1568, but this is impossible, since Nobunaga did not enter Kyoto with Yoshiaki until the fall. Frois wrote describing the interview in June or July 1569, and he certainly would not have waited a year before reporting an event of such importance.

preach his doctrine in Japan. This favour aroused great antagonism among hostile Buddhist monks, who tried to have the license rescinded and the missionaries expelled. Wada was alarmed because they had appealed to the Emperor, and he arranged another interview with Nobunaga, who again received Frois in a friendly manner. On being asked to protect the Christians against the Buddhists, Nobunaga enquired what was the reason for this hostility, and Frois replied that it was because the missionaries exposed the sins of the monks. As the discussion proceeded, a certain Nichijō Shōnin—a monk of obscure origin and dubious character who was useful to Nobunaga as a secretary and as a go-between in many kinds of transactions—lost his temper, and when Frois spoke of the soul picked up a sword and threatened to cut off the head of the poor blind Brother Lorenzo, to see whether there were such a thing as a living spirit. He was seized and restrained by Hideyoshi, who was standing by; and the debate that ensued ended to the Jesuit's advantage.

Nobunaga's favours to Christian missions continued throughout the rest of his life, which was then to last another thirteen years; and despite the opposition and intrigues of the Buddhists, the Jesuits' work continued to prosper. Indeed one of the reasons for their success was the contempt in which certain sects of Buddhism were held by the ruling class. In seeking for an explanation of the growing number of conversions to Christianity, not only in the poor western provinces but also in the capital city and the surrounding provinces, which were the most advanced in all Japan, one must take into account the degradation of almost every sect of Japanese Buddhism in the late middle ages.

Ten years after the first visit of Frois to Nobunaga, Takayama Ukon succeeded to his father's land and his castle of Takatsuki. The number of baptised Christians in his fief had risen to 8,000, a third of its total population. The total number of Christians in central Japan at this time was about 15,000, and there were many handsome churches in the larger towns. More missionaries were sent for, and were received by Nobunaga when they arrived—among the most prominent being Francisco Cabral, the Vice-Provincial, Organtino Gnecchi (who made a strong impression), and in 1581 Alexander Valignano, a tall man whose stature astonished Nobunaga and whose Negro servant amused him. Valignano spent some weeks with Nobunaga at Azuchi, the great castle which Nobunaga had built between 1576 and 1579.

Thus the prospects of evangelization in Japan were very fair. In Kyoto and its environs the Christians were for the most part men of good standing, well educated, and devout. Seminaries were founded for the education of youths of good family; and one of these was visited by Nobunaga, who was pleased with what he saw and with music played on European instruments by the pupils.

The condition of the mission work in the country as a whole was surveyed by the Visitor-General Valignano in 1582. He concluded that there were 150,000 Christians in Japan at that time, and 200 churches, mostly small; of the converts by far the greater number were in western Japan, even allowing for central Japan a larger number than the 15,000 cited above. No doubt the number of converts included some who thought it fashionable to take up the new creed, or to adopt foreign habits such as carrying a rosary, or to wear an article of foreign dress, just as their remote ancestors had once copied Chinese fashions. But even allowing for these, the labour of the missionaries must have been stupendous, especially when one recalls that there were at first only two or three Fathers and a handful of brothers and other helpers; and that even in 1580 there were not more than twenty Fathers in the whole of Japan, and about thirty helpers, seminarists, and catechists, most of whom were Japanese.

It is usually held that Nobunaga hated religion, a view which his slaughter of the monks of Hiyeizan and his cruel treatment of the Ikkō leaguers at Nagashima would seem to justify. But what he hated was the churchmen's interference in political matters and their use of military strength. He had no animosity towards religion in general and thought it right that monasteries should be places of worship and homes of learning.

It is this attitude which accounts for his favours to Christian missionaries. He saw that they were men of high character and strong purpose whom he need not fear. One of the most important passages in the history of the Jesuits in Japan is the fortunate sequence of events that brought Frois into Nobunaga's presence.

2. Nobunaga and the Buddhist Sects

When Nobunaga was developing a castle town at Azuchi, he thought it necessary to provide it with certain religious institutions. This was a common practice, as can be seen from plans of mediaeval castle towns, which show a liberal allowance of sacred buildings, some for the samurai, some for the townspeople. He therefore persuaded, or rather obliged, Jōdo (Pure Land) monasteries in the vicinity to move into the new city, where he built for them the Jōgon-In. This was richly endowed as the presiding church of the sect in Ōmi and Iga provinces. His reasons for favouring the Jōdo monks can only be guessed, but he doubtless thought of the sect as mild and manageable in contrast to the Hokke (Lotus) sect founded by Nichiren, which had a long tradition of militancy.[2]

---

[2] The early tradition of Buddhism in Japan had been one of comparative harmony in the relations between different branches of the Church, all doctrines being regarded as different versions of one truth. But this tradition was broken by Nichiren (1222–82), a quarrelsome saint and a master of vituperation. In Nobunaga's time the Hokke sect had not mended its manners, but remained subversive and antagonistic to the civil authority; and it was natural that Nobunaga should keep a suspicious eye upon its leaders.

In 1579 it happened that a Jōdo monk from the eastern provinces was preaching in the castle town when he was heckled by a monk of the Hokke sect. Their argument was on the point of exploding into violence when Nobunaga intervened and ordered the parties to come to terms. The Hokke monk insisted upon a debate to decide the point at issue. Nobunaga agreed to this proposal and ordered a learned Zen abbot from the Nanzenji to be the judge, and to preside over a discussion in the Jōgon-In. The subsequent events were recorded in some detail in an account which throws light upon Nobunaga's policy in matters of religion and also upon the general condition of sectarian strife in the sixteenth century.

The parties assembled in the oratory of the Jōgon-In on a day in June 1579, and commenced the argument. The Jōdo leader said: "Among the eight points in your doctrine, is there or is there not the Buddha-calling?" To this the Nichiren leader replied: "There is." The argument continued, becoming more and more heated until it developed into an exchange of insults. But the Jōdo assertions were overcome by the Hokke reasoning, and Teian, the Jōdo spokesman, got red in the face and lost his self-control. It was late, and Nobunaga had no intention of letting the Nichiren people enjoy a victory. He had long ago determined to break the power of the Hokke sect, and the judge (a deaf old man of eighty-four) seems to have thought it prudent to declare in favour of the Jōdo party. Helpless in the face of this monstrously unfair decision, the Hokke leaders were obliged to give way. They subscribed to an oath in which they swore by all the gods in Japan and all the holy writ of the Tripitaka that they had been overcome in argument with the Jōdo sect, that they would never in future attack another religious teaching, and that they accepted the punishment of some of their colleagues. Murai, the Commissioner of Police (Shoshi-dai) in Kyoto, was ordered to announce this news publicly both within and beyond the capital.

Thus the Jōdo sect triumphed, as Nobunaga had doubtless intended from the beginning, for his magistrates had surrounded the meeting place with more than a thousand armed men, who, when the Jōdo men cried "Victory," attacked the followers of Nichiren with great brutality. The Jōdo spokesmen were handsomely rewarded. The matter did not end there, for subsequently the lay members of the Hokke party, who were evidently men of good standing, were sought out and executed as dangerous rebels. This grim story confirms the view that Nobunaga feared the political influence of the Buddhist Church. His treatment of the great monastic complex at Kōyasan is another example of his drastic method of dealing with sectarian opposition.

Kōyasan was so remote in position among the high hills of Yamato and (unlike Hiyeizan) so aloof from secular affairs that it was an almost independent ecclesiastical state. But during the civil wars of the late middle ages, its wide domains became a refuge for soldiers escaping from defeat and for criminals evading punishment. The laws of Japan did not recognize a right of sanctuary, but in general fugitives were fairly safe in the mountainous region south from Yoshino to Kumano and east over the lonely Odaigahara to the coast of Ise.[3]

After Nobunaga's subjugation of his enemies in the Home Provinces, notably in Yamashiro, remnants of the defeated forces of Miyoshi, Matsunaga, Hosokawa, and others found their way to Kōyasan, where according to custom they were given asylum, and—in suitable cases— even encouraged to enter holy orders. This state of affairs was displeasing to Nobunaga, especially when he learned that officers of Araki Murashige, whom he had defeated in 1581, were being sheltered in the monastery. He sent officials to demand the surrender of these men, and his envoys were forcibly ejected by the monks. This action infuriated Nobunaga, since he regarded it as an offence against his government to harbour rebels and criminals. He at once ordered all mendicant friars from Kōyasan to be seized and executed, and shortly afterwards he appointed his third son, Nobutaka, to the command of an army which was to proceed in six divisions by six routes to chastise the monks.

As the forces moved upon the holy place, the monks were at odds, some wishing to resist by prayer, some being in favour of armed force. The Court at Kyoto was alarmed, fearing that Kōya would suffer the fate of the Enryakuji, and the Emperor sent a special messenger to Nobunaga deploring his policy. Here we see an interesting testimony to the power of the Throne in certain circumstances, for Nobunaga accepted the remonstrance and stopped military operations, contenting himself for the time with ordering his officers in Yamato and Kawachi to keep a close watch on the monastery and its superior clergy. He then became preoccupied by the problems arising from his campaigns against Takeda in the East and Mōri in the West, so that Kōyasan escaped his further attention and by a stroke of good fortune survived as a sacred institution of imposing size and quality. It might not have survived for long if Nobunaga had not died in 1582.

3. Japanese Christians

It is sometimes suggested that the daimyos and the warriors who adopted the Christian faith were moved only by a desire for material gain, thinking that as Christians they could get a greater share in the Portuguese trade or could more easily secure weapons and other supplies of advantage to their military efforts. This is an altogether too simple explanation of the remarkable success of the missionaries. Perhaps some

[3] Nearly fifty years ago I was hospitably entertained on my way over Odaigahara by a band of hunters and woodcutters, kindly men who had committed offences in Ōsaka and thought it wise to leave the city.

western daimyos accepted baptism on political grounds, but often members of their families proved firm in their faith to the point of martyrdom. The Japanese warriors who went into battle wearing the Cross as an emblem on their helmets, and shouting as a war cry "Jesu" or "Santa Maria" or "Sant' Iago," were inspired by a strong faith, which may have been superstitious but was none the less genuine. All the history of war in Japan shows the belief of their class in a guardian deity, and the transfer of their allegiance from Hachiman to a new tutelary power should not be difficult to understand.

Seals of four Christian daimyos: Hosokawa Tadaoki, Kuroda Yoshitaka, Ōtomo Sōrin (Francisco), and Mōri Terumoto

The conversion of great numbers of peasants and artisans is even simpler to explain. Some were ordered to become Christians by their masters, but as a rule they were willing converts, finding solace in Christian doctrine, material help in the form of charitable gifts, medical care in the Jesuit infirmaries, and a new status and feeling of well-being in the little Christian schools and the churches where they attended Mass. That the faith of these simple people was very deep-rooted is proved by their steadfast behaviour under persecution in a later period.

Among the merchants the Jesuits had comparatively little success, for men of this class were (in the words of Father Vilela) proud and avaricious and addicted to pleasures. Since in addition the priests inveighed against usury and commercial trickery, traders in the towns rarely attended their churches.

It is a curious fact that the opening of diplomatic intercourse between Japan and European states was brought about by the Fathers in Kyūshū, for early in 1582, by arrangement of the Jesuits in Japan with their Society at home, a mission of four well-born Japanese youths was sent to the King of Spain and the Pope by the Christian daimyos Ōtomo, Arima, and Ōmura. The four boys, accompanied by Valignano, left Nagasaki harbour in a Portuguese ship for Macao, where they stayed for some months of study while waiting for the monsoon. At the end of 1582 they sailed for Malacca, and thence, after a voyage not free from dangers and hardships, they reached Goa, where Valignano left them.

Leaving Cochin in the company of three other Portuguese vessels, they sailed round the Cape of Good Hope and at last reached Lisbon three years after their departure from Japan. They were well received wherever they stopped on their way to Madrid, and at their destination they were welcomed gracefully by Philip II, the most powerful monarch in Europe, then ruling both Spain and Portugal. Soon afterwards they left Spain in a Spanish ship for Italy, where they went first to Florence and thence proceeded to Rome.

The Pope, Gregory XIII, insisted upon a brilliant ceremony, against the wishes of the Jesuits. Wearing Japanese costume, the young men rode on fine horses in a splendid procession to the Vatican. They were received in the Sala Regia, where they kissed the Pope's foot and were embraced by him with affectionate greetings. From the point of view of the Jesuits the mission was a great success, for their Society was granted a monopoly of evangelisation in Japan, and was promised a handsome annual subsidy. The envoys' stay in Rome was somewhat prolonged owing to the death of Gregory and the election of Sixtus. They returned to Japan in the summer of 1590, having been absent for over eight years.

In those years the Christian daimyos Ōtomo Sōrin and Ōmura Sumitada had died and the position of the Christians in general had deteriorated. The wind of persecution had begun to blow.

CHAPTER XIX

NOBUNAGA'S LAST YEARS

1. Civil Government

IT WILL be recalled that early in the sixteenth century the successful warlords began to pay close attention to the civil administration of their territories, hoping thereby to increase their military strength and improve their economic condition. The House Laws of their families nearly all contain provisions relating to monetary matters, to trade and communications, and in general to the development of material resources. The administrative acts of Hōjō Sōun, Asakura Toshikage, Takeda Shingen, and Uyesugi Kenshin are good examples of this trend, which was followed by Nobunaga first on a provincial and then on a national scale.

When Nobunaga marched westward from Mikawa in 1567, his first concern was to consolidate his military position by overcoming local opposition and by occupying strongholds of strategic importance, notably the castle at Gifu in Owari, his own native province. But he also began at that time to plan the economic development of Owari and Mino, which together formed the Nōbi plain, one of the three great alluvial plains of Japan.

His first step was to break local trade monopolies by declaring free markets in the leading towns. This was not a new idea, for local magnates had from time to time forbidden sales monopolies in their domains; for instance in 1549 Rokkaku had closed a paper merchants' guild in Mino under penalty of confiscation, and had declared a free market in its place.

Nobunaga first declared free trade in the town of Kano, in a notification which provided for free markets (*rakuichi*) and open guilds (*rakuza*) and for penalties in case of dishonest practices. These were the preliminary steps towards freedom of trade, and since Kano was the castle town below his fortress of Gifu, and therefore under his full control, the prevention of closed markets was simple. To abolish occupational and mercantile guilds elsewhere was a more difficult task, however, since it ran contrary to the interests of powerful institutions or persons then outside his jurisdiction. But Nobunaga could bide his time: the policy was laid down, and its execution would proceed by stages.

Upon his entry into Kyoto in 1568, Nobunaga lost no time in developing new policies for civil administration, although his military problems must have been pressing. One of his first steps was to issue a set of elaborate currency regulations, whose aggregate effect was to forbid barter transactions using rice as a unit of exchange; to order sales and purchases of more than specified quantities of certain goods to be made in silver or gold; and to fix the ratio of value between copper, silver, and gold. This edict, issued in 1569, was preceded by a public notice announcing the official rate of exchange between copper coins of varying degrees of pure copper content, and forbidding the use of "bad coin" (*akusen*), that is to say, counterfeit money.[1]

Other problems of civil administration to which Nobunaga turned his attention were the abolition of barriers within the territories which he occupied and the construction and repair of roads and bridges. In 1574 he issued special orders concerning the upkeep of roads and bridges in his own province of Owari, which were to be regularly inspected. He also ordered pine and willow trees to be planted along the roadsides, and fixed the width of main and secondary roads. This was by order under his vermilion seal in 1575.

The general trend of Nobunaga's ideas on civil administration is clearly indicated in the steps he took to develop a prosperous castle town beneath his great fortress on Azuchiyama. The construction of this great castle was symbolic of the ambition of Nobunaga, and an emblem of his power. Begun in 1576 and not completed until 1579, it was an immense structure with a soaring keep, and it dominated the country from the shore of Lake Biwa. It was in Ōmi province, but it frowned upon Kyoto, and it was a warning and a barrier to attackers from the eastern provinces.

The transport of the great stone blocks of which the castle was composed required an exceptional effort, and it was accomplished by a small army of men, straining at the ropes of oxcarts and encouraged by music. Contemporary paintings show them as they haul and sweat, while perched on the cart is a kind of master of ceremonies with a small orchestra composed of ladies of the town. Stones were brought by the thousands from nearby quarries and then selected. The transport of the heaviest of these to the summit was done by great numbers of men working day and night to lever them up by inches.

The purpose of this great structure was to watch over the approaches to the capital, and in particular to guard it against threats from Uyesugi and other likely invaders from the north. Experience had shown that a fortress inside the capital city was a danger, not an advantage, since the risk of conflagrations was constant and unavoidable. The city itself, apart from its inflammability, was far too sprawling and vulnerable to serve as a military base. It is evident that Nobunaga found these factors of such importance that he contemplated making Azuchi the capital from which he would rule the whole country.

He pressed on with the foundation of a big castle town while the

[1] It is interesting to learn that the text of this notice is preserved in the archives of the Tennōji monastery, where it was originally displayed on a notice board within the precincts.

main edifice was still under construction, but he met with difficulties at first because his military subordinates and the civilians in his service were slow to occupy the houses which he had got ready for them. Those which his generals were to occupy were enclosed by stone walls and prepared for defence as if they were independent forts, while those of the civilians—the townspeople in general—were some distance away, near the lake shore. It was two or three years before residents settled in numbers, but by about 1582 the population of the castle town was of the order of 5,000.

In order to ensure the prosperity of the town Nobunaga had to provide attractive conditions for the tradesmen and the artisans who settled there. Accordingly, in the summer of 1577, while the castle was still under construction, he issued a municipal charter, of which the main provisions were as follows: (1) the town was to be a free market, and no tax whatever should be levied on sales or purchases; (2) merchants proceeding along the central highroad (Nakasendō) were not to pass through the town without stopping, but must take lodging there; (3) except in case of war or other great emergency no levy for building or transport should be imposed upon the residents; (4) if a moratorium (tokusei) was declared within the province, it should not apply to debts owing to residents of the town.

In general the regulations were devised to attract money and trade to the town, and this was a significant departure from the restrictive practices of mediaeval commerce. But it need not be supposed that Nobunaga had anticipated the doctrine of Adam Smith. Other warlords had already taken similar measures to remove obstacles to trade; and his aim, like theirs, was political rather than economic. Freedom of buying and selling was not an end but a means; those who proclaimed it sought to abolish all controls but their own. The roads were to be improved not so much for the comfort of travellers as for the easy transport of soldiers and war material; markets were to be free in order to stimulate a flow of commodities from other parts of the country. In general the castle town was looked upon by the warlords as a reservoir of money, materials, and technical skill which would be essential in time of war.

Nobunaga saw these things clearly, and in a larger framework than other rulers. He thought always in terms of unifying factors, while he added gradually to his powers and spread them over an increasing range. By the beginning of 1578 he had so consolidated his military dominance that his New Year celebration was attended by warriors great and small from eleven provinces—Yamashiro, Yamato, Kawachi, Izu, Settsu, Etchū, Echizen, Owari, Mino, Ōmi, and Ise.[2] All these came to express their loyalty to him.

---

[2] The castle building was not completed, but he could show them some of the apartments and their lavish decorations.

2. *Nobunaga's Political Power*

The military successes of Nobunaga are a matter of record and serve to explain the degree of political power which he came to have. But the steps by which he established himself as a leader after his early and extremely fortunate victory at Okehazama are not easy to define, and deserve some study. How did he, with the aid of Hideyoshi, gather the political as well as the military support which enabled him to complete the first phase of unification?

There are differences of opinion on these points among Japanese historians, but it seems to be agreed that a large measure of his early success was due to his connexion with the province of Owari. It was in Owari that he had been born, and it was from Owari that he proceeded to establish his authority in the other provinces of the rich central region, moving his base from Gifu to Mino and Ōmi and then to the capital.

To control this region was to possess the granary of the Home Provinces and to dominate the approaches to Kyoto from the east and north. The wealth of the area depended of course upon its natural advantages of rich soil and abundant water, but also upon the composition of its farming population, for the farmlands were in the hands not of oppressive landlords but of a class of independent cultivators well organized in their villages. These men, the ji-samurai, were of modest military origin. Hideyoshi himself was of the lower rank in that class, and Nobunaga, though related to a family of somewhat higher rank, was on the same social level as most of the rural gentry of Owari. It was among men of his own class that Nobunaga found his earliest support.

Details of the methods by which fighting men were enlisted do not appear to be available, but it is clear that foot soldiers were recruited in great numbers, principally no doubt from the lower stratum of the farming population (i.e., the farmhands and domestic servants, men of the ashigaru type as distinct from the ji-samurai). What inducements or rewards were offered to these men is hard to say, but they must have been valuable if the size of the forces raised by Nobunaga and Hideyoshi is correctly reported. Actually, the hope of reward may have been inducement enough. We know, for example, that Hideyoshi was given all the domains of Asai, whom he defeated, and Hideyoshi's soldiers must have profited by a share in those spoils.

Nobunaga's military successes won him political support in other parts of Japan, and he was on the point of further extending his political influence when he met his death; but he certainly had seen the importance of a strong and competent civil administration. His policy at Azuchi may be regarded as an expression of this view, for while the castle was an emblem of military strength, the castle town was a centre from which he hoped to extend his political influence. This task he bequeathed to Hideyoshi, who opened his administrative career by proclaiming a land policy designed to put agriculture under central government control. Here also, it may be observed, Hideyoshi's work was facilitated by his familiarity with rural life in Owari.

3. Nobunaga and Sakai

The history of Sakai to the middle sixteenth century has been traced in earlier chapters, and it is now appropriate to refer to its later growth, since it figures prominently in the history of domestic and foreign trade and the rise of a class of wealthy merchants.

The geographic position of Sakai accounts for both its prosperity and its misfortunes, for its wealth was derived from its seaborne trade and its troubles arose from its proximity to the great whirlpool of political and military currents which always threatened but never entirely submerged the capital city. Time after time this emporium was squeezed like a sponge by warlords in need of funds; but in spite of this drain, or because of it, the Sakai merchants doubled and redoubled their efforts and built up such financial power that the warlords began to perceive in their dim way how foolish it would be to destroy so plentiful a source of wealth. So, gradually, Sakai was taken out of the area of hostilities at the request of its citizens, and thereafter any general who happened to be operating in its vicinity would take care not to let his soldiers loose, but to keep them outside under discipline.

The city government was in the hands of a Council of Thirty-six (known as the Ego-shū), which was by no means a democratic body but an almost despotic organ composed of the richest merchants. This kind of self-government was not unusual at this time. It was to be seen in Hakata, Ōminato, and other important centres of trade. The Council, and the influential citizens of Sakai in general, exercised some authority in other than municipal matters, even to the point of arbitrating between such quarrelsome warlords as Matsunaga and the Miyoshis, who were plaguing the Home Provinces about 1560–65. Sakai in this period was sometimes described as a free city, especially by the Jesuit missionaries, who went so far as to compare it to Venice.

After entering Kyoto with the Shōgun Yoshiaki in 1568, Nobunaga was short of funds, and he imposed a war tax on the Honganji of 5,000 kan and on Sakai of 20,000 kan. The Honganji paid but Sakai refused, and the Council began to strengthen the city's defences by making the moat deeper, erecting lookout towers, and scattering obstacles in appropriate places. However, the Council were not unanimous in their determination to resist, and when Nobunaga threatened to invade the city as a punishment for harbouring his enemies, they gave way and apologized with a payment of 20,000 kan. Nobunaga, who had meanwhile been given jurisdiction over the city by Yoshiaki, in 1569 appointed one of his captains as its Deputy Governor.

It may be wondered why Nobunaga confined himself to threats and took no more drastic step. One reason, no doubt, was that he knew from a reliable informant that there was already a pro-Nobunaga party in Sakai, and that he would get the best results by working through them. His informant was a very rich Sakai merchant named Matsui Yūkan, whom Nobunaga had known for some time and had come to trust. He followed Matsui's advice, and rewarded him for his help with important and lucrative official appointments, making him his Deputy in Sakai.

But Nobunaga had other reasons for his moderation. Sakai was at that time the principal source of supply of firearms, ammunition, and other military requisites, such as armour and helmets protected by thin iron plates. Matsui himself was probably an important contractor for the supply of war material. It would have been foolish therefore for Nobunaga, or any warlord in the middle of his campaigns, to interfere by force in the highly specialized business of supplying and transporting the materials on which their lives depended.

Nobunaga and Matsui shared a taste for articles prized by tea masters for their beauty or their rarity. In one book it is stated that in 1568, when Nobunaga was campaigning in Settsu, he was visited in his camp by Matsui, who presented him with a celebrated "Matsushima" tea jar, which was known by name to all connoisseurs.

Father Vilela, writing in 1568, said of Sakai (where he had taken refuge from the devastation of Kyoto), "In the whole of Japan there is no place so safe as Sakai. Here, whatever is happening beyond the city, there is no disorder. Victor and vanquished live peacefully together, and men walk the streets in peace. But a stone's throw from the city there is killing and wounding."

Sakai retained its immunity for some years to come, but after its capitulation to Nobunaga in 1569 it was no longer a free city.

4. Nobunaga's Last Campaigns

Nobunaga was a warrior first and last and he enjoyed military displays. In the spring of 1581 he arranged a grand review of troops, ostensibly for the entertainment of the Emperor Ōgimachi but in reality for his own satisfaction and to impress the public mind with his power and glory. His generals with mounted escorts rode at the head of troops from their respective territories, Niwa with the men of Settsu and Wakasa, Akechi with men from Yamato and northern Yamashiro, and the sons of Nobunaga leading men from his own provinces of Owari, Mino, and Ise. All had been ordered to appear in full dress, wearing the most brilliant colours; and a crowd said to have numbered more than 100,000 watched the 20,000 horsemen as they galloped by.

It will be noticed that all the warriors in this great army were from the provinces around the capital. Ieyasu was still engaged with Takeda in the East, and the West was still dominated by Mōri Terumoto, who rivalled Nobunaga in the size of his armies and in the wealth of his possessions. He had conspired against Nobunaga with the Shōgun Yoshiaki, and had aroused Nobunaga's anger by his help to the besieged Honganji.

Nobunaga naturally wished to settle accounts with Mōri, and as far back as 1575 (when his ships had been defeated by Mōri in Ōsaka Bay) he had ordered Hideyoshi to plan a campaign to thwart Mōri's ambition. Hideyoshi had consulted Akechi Mitsuhide, a general of the same standing as himself. These two men, although of relatively humble origin, had impressed Nobunaga as being clearly more gifted than their colleagues Shibata, Niwa, and Sakuma, and other leading vassals.

In 1575 Akechi had set about "pacifying" the province of Tamba, as a preliminary to advancing against Mōri. He met with great difficulties, and for several years made little progress. Meanwhile, parallel with Akechi's slow advance along the Sanindō (the highway north of the central mountain range), Hideyoshi had been moving along the Sanyōdō (the southern highway), and in 1578 he met with stubborn resistance from Mōri kinsmen at the head of 60,000 men. He was obliged to call for reinforcements, but even with this support his position was dangerous. It was relieved only when Ukita, one of Mōri's allies, turned his coat, attacking the Mōri army from the rear and obliging it to retreat.

The subsequent fighting included some remarkable feats by Hideyoshi in reducing fortresses that were thought to be impregnable. In 1580 he moved north from Himeji castle, an important point in Harima where the Sanyōdō and two other highways meet. After passing through Tajima he was checked by the fortress at Tottori, a mountain stronghold on the Inaba coast. He made no attempt to assault it but invested it very closely by ringing it with strong-points at intervals of about 500 yards, using a force of 20,000 combatants. His purpose was of course to starve out the garrison, and he had already taken the precaution of buying up all the rice in Inaba at several times the market price. The garrison was soon starved out. The emaciated men and women who tried to escape were shot down by musketeers, and the governor of the fortress surrendered and took his own life.

In 1581 Hideyoshi returned briefly to report to Nobunaga at Azuchi, and discussed with him the invasion of Bitchū province. He rejoined his army and in April 1582 marched into Bitchū, where he attempted to arrange the surrender of Takamatsu castle by a handsome bribe. This failed, and Hideyoshi now showed his skill by resorting to a remarkable engineering device. Takamatsu stood only a few feet above sea level, and partly on marshy ground. Hideyoshi built an elaborate structure of dykes and channels contained by great timbers, and proceeded to flood the castle by diverting river water and rain water (it was the rainy season) in such quantities that it began to be submerged. He also erected towers on barges, and from these his gunners kept up a steady fire. This danger brought hurried reinforcements from Mōri, and Hideyoshi sent a call for help to Nobunaga.

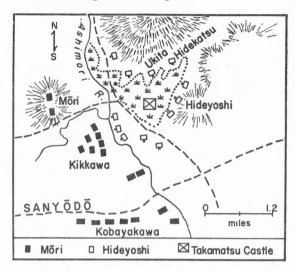

Hideyoshi's Siege of Takamatsu Castle

Meanwhile Ieyasu, having dealt the death blow to the last of the Takedas of Kai, had returned to Kyoto, where he was granted the province of Suruga as a reward for his services. This was at the beginning of June 1582, and it was at this time that Hideyoshi's appeal reached Nobunaga, with news that Mōri had mobilized all his forces. Nobunaga at once ordered his leading generals to proceed westward, and announced that he would take command of the whole expedition. While preparations were being made, Ieyasu went off for a short holiday in Sakai, at Nobunaga's suggestion, while Akechi Mitsuhide started for his province of Tamba, to mobilize his own contingent there.

Nobunaga himself left Azuchi for Kyoto in the middle of June to arrange matters there before departure. As was his habit he lodged at the Honnōji, a monastery on the avenue called Nishi-Tōin, protected by a moat. A few days later (June 21) the Honnōji was surrounded at dawn and attacked by a strong force of Akechi Mitsuhide's men. Nobunaga had no reason to suspect treachery by Akechi and was taken by surprise. He and his retinue resisted vigorously, but he was overborne and (according to one story) rushed into an adjacent room and committed suicide behind its closed door. The Honnōji went up in flames and his body was not recovered. He was in his forty-ninth year.

During the morning a detachment of Akechi's soldiers attacked the Nijō palace stronghold, which was occupied by adherents of Nobunaga.

Some of them climbed up to the roof of the Konoye mansion and shot down into the Nijō courtyard, with firearms and bows.

Later in the day Akechi marched upon Azuchi castle, which he captured without trouble. He treated the Jesuit fathers well, partly because he hoped to get assistance from Takayama, the Ucondono of the missionary letters. He did no damage to the fortress, but a week or so later it was in flames, perhaps lit (as some said) by Nobunaga's son in a fit of rage, but more probably by a rabble of townspeople who were looting and destroying, mad with excitement.

Having taken but not occupied Azuchi, Akechi hesitated. He had not made up his mind what to do next—a dangerous condition for any enemy of Hideyoshi; and meanwhile disorder was mounting in the adjoining provinces. He knew that he must soon meet an attack from Hideyoshi or Ieyasu or both, but he chose to negotiate with possible allies and made no firm military decisions.

The Jesuit letters give some interesting descriptions of the exciting events of those days. They are in general remarkably accurate, but they are of course only hearsay accounts. It is therefore worth while to look at some of the evidence furnished by persons directly concerned in the sequels of the Akechi affair. The most useful source is the diary of Yoshida Kanemi, a high Shintō dignitary at Court. He was a descendant of Kanetomo, the founder of Yoshida Shintō, and was related to Akechi by marriage. After recording the death of Nobunaga, he describes the scene in the Nijō palace and the panic of the ladies as they fled to escape the swarm of rough soldiers searching for Nobutada, whom they found and killed. A few days later he was ordered by the Court to go to Azuchi and request Akechi to restore order and safety in Kyoto. He made the journey, was admitted to the castle after some delay, and was well received by Akechi, then busy distributing gifts from Nobunaga's treasure. Akechi gave great sums to likely supporters, and on his return to the capital he visited Kanemi to arrange the presentation of several sums of 500 pieces of silver to the Court and similar amounts to the Five Zen Monasteries (Gozan). Kanemi himself received fifty pieces for his services, and later, when it was apparent that Akechi had failed, was rebuked for his dealings with a rebel.

The news of Nobunaga's death had reached Hideyoshi by swift courier late at night on June 22. He kept the news secret and opened pourparlers with Mōri, reaching an agreement by which Hideyoshi was to receive the surrender of Takamatsu castle and the three provinces of Bitchū, Mimasaka, and Hōki, which were already in his actual possession. This was a reasonable solution, which Mōri's advisers recommended that he accept. On the following day Hideyoshi took over the castle, raised camp, and marched at great speed day and night through wind and rain back to Himeji, which he reached late on June 24—a journey of 70 miles. After a short rest he raised as great a force as possible, and on June 30 he attacked Akechi near the key position of Yamazaki, southwest of the capital.[3] There Akechi was completely and finally defeated, and was killed as he fled through the fields.

5. Nobunaga's Character

Opinions differ about the character of Nobunaga. The Jesuit missionaries, though inclined to overlook his faults out of gratitude for his favours, wrote of him with qualified praise, dwelling upon his courage and determination and his great military skill but condemning his pride and his tyranny. His courage and his iron will are beyond question, but it may be argued that in a strict sense he had no exceptional military talent. He bungled some of his campaigns and at times used unnecessarily large numbers against weak adversaries. Indeed, part of the credit for his greatest victories is due to the planning of Ieyasu and Hideyoshi.

Nobunaga was fortune's child in the time and place of his activity, for in the progress westward from Okehazama to Kyoto he met no first-class opponent and he was favoured by the geographical situation of his own province of Owari. But it must be said that he took full advantage of his opportunities, for he had a restless energy of mind as well as body, and he was not bound by tradition. The record of his innovations is impressive. As a youth he learned the use of firearms, and by 1575 or thereabouts he had substantial control of their manufacture in the Home Provinces. In 1582 he was collecting metal and melting down temple bells for use in his foundries. He also promoted the manufacture of gunpowder, and encouraged the importation of saltpetre and of lead for bullets. It is supposed that one of the reasons for his protection of the missionaries was a desire to ensure the arrival of those essential articles in Portuguese ships.

Although Hideyoshi was more fertile in individual stratagems, it was Nobunaga who led the way in introducing the new patterns of warfare in which the foot soldier armed with a matchlock displaced the mounted man carrying a bow and a sword. The battle of Nagashino in 1575 showed the deadly efficacy of firearms. Nobunaga also experimented in the building of warships with iron-plate armour, and he encouraged the manufacture of large-bore artillery, which was used with success at Nagashima.

He paid special attention to the discipline of his troops, a matter of growing importance as hand-to-hand fighting was superseded by mass

---

[3] There is an interesting account of the battle of Yamazaki in a long letter addressed by Hideyoshi to Nobutaka's adviser Saitō Gemba, in which he mentions the part played in the action by Takayama Ukon and other commanders.

infantry movements. He developed the ashigaru as a regular trained foot soldier, and he fostered esprit de corps among his men by dressing them in smart uniforms which made a strong impression upon spectators.

The methods of fighting which Nobunaga used were utterly ruthless in a ruthless age. He would follow up every victory in the field by a merciless pursuit and slaughter of fugitives. He burned to death the survivors of Nagashima. He ordered his generals to pursue into every corner of Echizen the Ikkō men, women, and children who had fled before his armies, and he went so far as to write to the Shoshi-dai in Kyoto saying that the streets of the capital of Echizen were so crammed with corpses that there was no room for more, and fugitives must now be searched out and exterminated "yama yama, tani tani," "on every hill, in every valley." The total of those massacred in this campaign alone is said to have exceeded 20,000.

Nobunaga's gifts as an administrator and his grasp of economic problems cannot be denied, though he often applied his talents to base uses. Most judgments of his character are highly unfavourable, and he is severely condemned by Arai Hakuseki in *Dokushi Yoron*. A modern historian, the learned and kind-hearted Tsuji Zennosuke, has tried with but little success to find favourable aspects of Nobunaga.

If his virtues are open to doubt, his vices are unquestionable. He never showed a sign of compassion. His vindictive ruthlessness is apparent from the beginning of his career, when he killed his brother, to his last years, which were filled with wanton slaughter. He became the master of twenty provinces at a terrible cost. He was a cruel and callous brute.

CHAPTER XX

HIDEYOSHI'S RISE TO POWER

1. *First Steps*

BY JULY 1, 1582, Hideyoshi was in a very favourable situation. He had just avenged Nobunaga's death and was at the head of a victorious army. It was natural and easy for him to take the political initiative, since Ieyasu and other generals were not on the spot; and it is characteristic of his promptitude that, while turning over in his mind certain problems of civil administration, he at once invited Shibata, Niwa, Ikeda, and others of similar rank to attend a council in the Oda castle at Kiyosu in Owari, in order to decide upon a successor to Nobunaga and the division of his estate. There Nobunaga's second and third sons (Nobukatsu and Nobutaka) began to quarrel, and the discussion floundered until Hideyoshi, with his usual practical wisdom, went into an adjoining room and came back holding in his arms the infant grandson of Nobunaga, Sambōshi, who was at once declared the heir.[1] In his youth Hideyoshi had learned a great deal about simple human relations, and he could put it to good use, being in that respect far different from the cold and stubborn Nobunaga.

The provinces which had been under the direct rule of Nobunaga were divided among the generals, Hideyoshi retaining Harima and taking Yamashiro, Kawachi, and Tamba as well. He made a special arrangement to conciliate Shibata, allotting to him the important castle of Nagahama in Ōmi, within easy reach of Kyoto. With regard to civil government it was agreed that the four leading generals should act together, forming a council. Thus in effect the battle of Yamazaki had made Hideyoshi the master of the country, ready to complete the task of unification. Of course he had to meet opposition from his colleagues. The quadripartite council was bound to be dissolved by jealousies, and Nobunaga's sons could not be counted upon for loyalty.

Early in 1583 Nobutaka was discovered to be conspiring against Hideyoshi, who dislodged him from Gifu castle but treated him generously, and soon allowed him to return to Gifu. Takigawa in Ise had next to be suppressed, and then in late April Shibata Katsuiye (now showing his true colours) marched a force through the snows of Echizen into Ōmi, where early in May he was faced by Hideyoshi at a place called Shizugatake, close by the northern shore of Lake Biwa. At this time

---

[1] Sambōshi, later called Oda Hidenobu, was the son of Nobutada, Nobunaga's first-born.

1582 Death of Oda Nobunaga. Hideyoshi defeats Akechi at Yamazaki

1583 Hideyoshi's victory at Shizugatake. Land survey begins

1584 Hideyoshi and Ieyasu in conflict in Owari. Arrival of Spanish galleon in Hirado

1585 Hideyoshi becomes Regent. Shikoku and northern provinces subdued

1586 Hideyoshi becomes Chancellor

1587 Kyūshū subdued. Entertainment of the Emperor at the Jūrakudai (Mansion of Pleasure). Hideyoshi's edict expelling the Jesuits

1588 Hideyoshi's Sword Hunt

1590 Ōsaka castle completed. The fall of Odawara. Ieyasu enfeoffed in the Kantō

1592 Hideyoshi resigns as Kampaku in favour of Hidetsugu. Invasion of Korea

1593 Ming ambassadors arrive in Japan to negotiate withdrawal from Korea. Hideyori is born. The arrival of the Franciscans

1594 Fushimi palace completed

1595 Hidetsugu commits suicide. Persecution of his family by Hideyoshi

1596 Hideyori is made Regent

1597 Second invasion of Korea. First persecution of the Christians

1598 Land survey completed. Hideyoshi dies and a Council of Regency is formed under Ieyasu. Evacuation of Korea

1599 Death of Maeda Toshiiye. Ishida attempts to assassinate Ieyasu

1600 Battle of Sekigahara. Arrival of William Adams in Kyūshū

1603 Ieyasu appointed Shōgun

1605 Ieyasu resigns as Shōgun in favour of his son Hidetada

1609 Dutch ships arrive at Hirado

1614 Ieyasu issues an edict suppressing Christianity

1615 The fall of Ōsaka castle. Death of Hideyori and the destruction of the house of Toyotomi. Promulgation of the *Buke Sho-Hatto*. Foundation of the Tokugawa Bakufu

1616 Death of Ieyasu

Nobutaka, who had broken faith again—there must have been an evil strain in the Oda family—tried to create a diversion by attacking the castle at Ōgaki; and while Hideyoshi was absent from his base helping to meet this threat, Katsuiye moved against Hideyoshi's forward position in Ōmi, and put the defenders to flight. Among the defenders was Takayama Ukon, the Christian general who was a friend of the Jesuits in Kyoto. Hideyoshi, with one of those rapid strokes of which he was a master, galloped with a handful of young aides-de-camp from Ōgaki back to Shizugatake to face Katsuiye, covering a distance of nearly fifty miles in six hours by night. On the following day at dawn he and his officers led a determined assault upon Katsuiye's vanguard under Sakuma Morimasa and pressed him back into Echizen. Three days later they had taken Katsuiye's main castle at Kita-no-shō (the modern Fukui); and Katsuiye, after setting fire to the keep, stabbed his wife[2] and other members of his household, and then cut his own belly in full view of the armies.

Hideyoshi now had no difficulty in taking the adjoining provinces of Kaga, Noto, and Etchū, which he divided among Maeda Toshiiye and other generals as a reward for their services. He then returned to Azuchi to distribute further rewards and punishments. Oda Nobukatsu was ordered to rebuke his younger brother Nobutaka and oblige him to surrender Gifu castle. This was done, and Nobutaka was confined in a monastery in Owari, where he committed suicide.

After Shizugatake Hideyoshi had no important military operations to perform. The remnants of Akechi's army had been swept up by Takayama Ukon and his colleagues, and Hideyoshi received from one of his commanders the welcome gift of Akechi's head, which had been long sought. This dreadful trophy was sent to the Honnōji, or rather the ruins of the Honnōji, for public display.

Hideyoshi was now undisputed master. To calm popular fears he announced that the laws of Nobunaga would not be changed; and to show that he had no further warlike designs he opened his castle at Himeji and distributed among his comrades the silver, gold, and rice which had been stored there against wartime needs.

The action at Shizugatake, though an easy victory for Hideyoshi, must be regarded as one of the decisive battles in Japanese history. The fighting in Echizen and the last hours of Shibata Katsuiye are described in rather florid language and in much detail by Frois,[3] who was fortunately a very copious source of news (some of his material was no doubt furnished by Takayama Ukon). But the most interesting and presumably the most credible account of the important events of May 1583 is to be found in a letter written by Hideyoshi at Sakamoto early in July

[2] She was Oda Nobunaga's sister, O-Ichi.
[3] See Murdoch, I, 194, for an example.

in answer to an enquiry from Kobayakawa, the chief counsellor of the Mōri family, with whom he had negotiated from time to time. Without wasting words, Hideyoshi traces the main features of the campaign and gives a graphic, not to say grisly, account of the last hours of Shibata Katsuiye. He ends with an outline of his own future policy.

The tone of this letter is one of great self-confidence. Perhaps its most striking passage is one in which, discussing the last phase of the attack on Shibata's castle, he says: "I saw that if we should let Shibata get his breath, the thing would be long-drawn-out. I thought to myself: This is the time to decide who shall govern Japan ["Nihon no osamuru mono wa kono toki ni sōrō"], and therefore it will not be wrong for Chikuzen [i.e., Hideyoshi] to send men to die in battle here. So I made up my mind."

After his victory at Shizugatake Hideyoshi's position was much strengthened. At the end of 1582 he had been given a modest Court rank by the Emperor, and now his progress was carefully watched. He had under his control after a year's effort as many as thirty provinces, twenty of these being provinces which it had taken Nobunaga twenty years to subdue.[4] He had rivals and enemies, of course, but no immediately dangerous antagonist. His first care was to ensure the solid support of his own party, and here he was confronted with a difficulty, since his former comrade-in-arms Tokugawa Ieyasu showed signs of dissatisfaction. By 1584 the breach between the two had so widened that Ieyasu, yielding to pressure from Nobukatsu, Nobunaga's second son, took arms against Hideyoshi in two engagements in Owari, at Komakiyama and later at Nagakute. In each of these Ieyasu gained the advantage, but both men were too sensible to waste strength on a foolish quarrel, and Hideyoshi was not too proud to come to terms. Ieyasu was cautious at first and would not respond to Hideyoshi's overtures for some time; but at last, after the armies had glared at one another for some months, they made peace. This was early in 1585.

It will have been noticed that Ieyasu took no part in the events following Nobunaga's murder. He was not present at Hideyoshi's council at Kiyosu, and in the following years he appears on the scene only to take arms against Hideyoshi in 1584. His withdrawal from problems of national importance was deliberate. He was in Sakai, sightseeing and enjoying the tea ceremony and other pastimes in company with his friend Anayama Baisetsu, when news of Nobunaga's death was brought to him secretly. Without disclosing the news, he left Sakai quietly at

[4] Yamashiro, Yamato, Kawachi, Izumi, Settsu, Ōmi, Wakasa, Echizen, Kaga, Noto, Etchū, Tamba, Tango, Tajima, Inaba, Hōki, Harima, Bizen, Bitchū, Mimasaka, Awa, Iga, Ise, Shima, Owari, Mikawa, Tōtōmi, Suruga, Kai, Hida, Mino, Shinano, Kōtsuke. (Mikawa, Tōtōmi, and Suruga were strictly speaking Ieyasu's own provinces.)

night with a small escort, and made a rapid journey across Iga and Ise through country infested by bandits. He was fortunate in reaching the coast unharmed, for Baisetsu, who followed him, was killed.

From Ise Ieyasu took ship and crossed the bay to Mikawa, where he entered his castle at Okazaki. He had mobilized his forces and was preparing to march to Kyoto when he heard from Hideyoshi that Akechi had been defeated and that no help was now required. Though he no doubt felt that Hideyoshi had stolen a march on him, he readily turned his energies to improving his own position in the provinces to the east of Owari, extending his influence in particular to the province of Kai.

Once the danger of a permanent breach with Ieyasu was removed, Hideyoshi could proceed to carry out his plans, which were bold and far-reaching. One of his first steps was to begin the construction of a great castle at Ōsaka, which he regarded as the best site for a fortress to command the approaches to Kyoto from the west. His general intention was to reduce the number of small castles throughout the country, leaving only the strongholds of the great territorial lords whom he had invested with power, and thereby depriving the stubborn rural gentry, who stood in his way, of bases from which they could conduct subversive movements. He also paid attention to the distribution of the lands which he awarded to his generals, making sure that they left their former provinces and moved to areas where they had no traditional authority.[5] Thus Ikeda Nobuteru, who held the existing Ōsaka castle, surrendered it to Hideyoshi and moved to Gifu in exchange.

Hideyoshi's first statement of his policy of reducing the number of castles (*shirowari*) and redistributing fiefs (*kuniwake*) occurs in a surprising context. It is in a letter which he wrote while in Sakamoto to a girl called Mā, a daughter of Maeda Toshiiye, chosen to become when nubile a concubine of Hideyoshi. He tells her that he is looking into the occupation of land in Ōmi province. As soon as his hands are free, he will occupy and garrison Ōsaka castle and destroy most of the castles in each province, in order to prevent uprisings and ensure peace. Since Mā was in her thirteenth year, this information was doubtless intended for her father, and sent to her because Hideyoshi did not want to make a public announcement.

Gifu and Ōgaki were of little strategic value to Hideyoshi, since Ōmi was now more important than Owari as a base for overseeing the capital, and Sakamoto served that purpose well enough. The work on Ōsaka castle was begun in the autumn of 1583, at a time when Hideyoshi was much occupied with military problems, but he found time to institute certain administrative measures to which in the past he had given care-

[5] A detailed listing of Hideyoshi's redistribution of fiefs will be found in Appendix III.

ful thought. His first and probably his most important step was to order a survey of all farm land in Japan.

2. Hideyoshi's Land Survey

The system of land tenure lay at the heart of the national economy, and it was bound to come to the attention of successful warlords as they developed the administration of their domains. As a preliminary step to whatever fiscal policy they meant to adopt, it was necessary for them to learn the dimensions and the product of the farm land under their rule. For this purpose an accurate survey was needed, showing areas, crops, and such other particulars as the terms of ownership or tenancy. Surveys of this kind had been made in their own domains by Imagawa, Hōjō, and others as early as about 1530, and a more thorough investigation was made by Nobunaga in 1580 in the province of Yamato. The *Tamon-In Nikki*, the journal of a branch of the Nara Kōfukuji, reports with alarm under dates in that year a visit by two of Nobunaga's leading generals, Akechi Mitsuhide and Takigawa Kazumasu, who ordered the preparation of a list of all Church lands in the province, with full details of area, revenue, and ownership. The monks worked hard at this task for weeks, since nearly all the land in Yamato had for centuries furnished revenue to the monasteries. Akechi and Takigawa stayed in or near Nara for several weeks, with 10,000 men at their call; and at the end of the year the scribes wrote in the monastery's journal that the whole province was in a ferment, that such things had never happened before, and that the tortures of hell must be like the misery they and their brethren were suffering.

But the Yamato landlords came to little real harm at this time. They duly filed their returns—which were called *sashidashi*, "documents put forward"—but rights in land, especially in the ancient province of Yamato, were so various and so involved that Nobunaga's representatives could not decide what action to take next and let the matter drop.

Hideyoshi's survey was far more thoroughgoing. In 1582, immediately after the council at Kiyosu, he ordered all manors in Yamashiro to send in returns, choosing Yamashiro as the very home of the great manorial lords whose influence in the capital he was bent on destroying. But his plan did not stop there. He found that many of the returns furnished were inaccurate, either by design or for want of exact particulars, whereupon he decided upon a complete land survey in every province, to be carried out under the supervision of his own officials. It was to begin in 1583, in the province of Ōmi. It is characteristic of the wide spread of Hideyoshi's activities that this work was undertaken at a time when he was engaged in military operations of vital importance.

The work continued year by year until 1598, when all provinces had been surveyed, though not completely. The method of survey was changed as experience dictated, but its essential feature was a record by locality of the dimensions and yield of every rice field in Japan. The method employed was not finally determined until 1594. The calculation of area was made by means of a measuring rod of 6.3 feet (*shaku*) in length, the smallest unit of area being the square of that length. Following this measure, the yield was calculated in terms of a fixed quantity of unhulled rice to be harvested from one unit of area, allowance being made for different grades of soil and other variables.

The major classification of land (wet fields) for this purpose was carefully decided as follows (omitting subdivisions within a class according to quality): first-class fields, 1.5 koku (7.5 bushels) per unit of area; second-class fields, 1.3 koku; third-class fields, 1.1 koku. There were similar classes for dry fields. In both cases these grades varied somewhat by province. There was a general tendency to increase the burden on the cultivator and to be more rigorous in collection. But the surveyors usually took into account such circumstances as the distance which the grain had to be transported, local difficulties of cultivation owing to topographic or other causes, soil variations, and the upkeep of irrigation channels. The area of a survey was usually a single village, but it sometimes included a group of small villages.

On the face of it the survey was bound to be beneficial in so far as it cut through the dreadful tangle of rights and obligations and customary practices that constituted the shōen, and stated the position of the cultivator in exact terms. But this benefit is clear only if a long view is taken, and farmers and landowners do not see political action in a broad perspective. In practice, the working of the survey can be described only in a long and complicated story of obstruction and evasion, of trickery and bribery on the part of the rural population, from the small holder to the prosperous farmer. For this Hideyoshi and his advisers were in part to blame, because the first step they took when they fixed the standards of measurement was to reduce the unit of area without changing the rate of tax, so that the government in effect raised the tax by as much as one-fifth. There were certain compensations for this loss, since the general security of rural life was improved under the strict rule of Hideyoshi, but this gave little comfort to the taxpayer.

The truth is that the Japanese peasant in the sixteenth century wanted no change, for he had never been so prosperous. Any cadastral survey was bound to be a threat to him, since it would reveal the true area of his land, which he had never reported, or disclose the amount of tax which he had evaded by false returns. Consequently resistance to the survey was at times intense. Perhaps an extreme case was the scheme of a village headman who hid the report drawn up by the surveyors and substituted one which he had prepared to his own great advantage. Other objectors absconded without paying any tax, and refused to return.

But such devices were in the long run ineffective, for Hideyoshi's main purpose was to make the actual cultivator the permanent tenant of his land and to hold him and no other person responsible for the payment of tax on its product. This was to impose a unified system of land tenure and land tax throughout the country, and Hideyoshi's officials proceeded to put such a system into operation. But in practice they used their discretion and applied the new rules with some regard for local circumstances. In backward areas it was impossible to rely upon peasants who were ignorant and unorganized.

The more advanced peasants in the Home Provinces were so stubborn in their resistance that the surveyors sometimes confined themselves to the survey and made no serious attempt to enforce the rules. The main purpose of Hideyoshi's land policy was achieved once he established the principle that the actual cultivator and no other person was responsible for the tax on the yield of a specified area of land registered in his name. By this measure alone he brought the agriculture of the whole country under his control, created a new peasant class with uniform rights and duties which they could not escape, and diminished, if he did not destroy, the independence of the rural gentry. The cultivator's right was unitary and could not be divided or shared with others.

The over-all result of this policy was to make a great number of semi-independent peasants into fully independent small farmers. The richer farmers tried to circumvent these rules by private agreements with the small cultivators, and in this they met with a fair measure of success. But nothing could prevent Hideyoshi from achieving the main purpose of the survey, which was to bring the farming population (some eight-tenths of the total population of Japan) under his discipline, to tie them to the soil, and to leave the small holders after payment of tax with little more than was needed for their bare subsistence.

The ferocity of Hideyoshi's edicts shows at once the difficulty of changing the ingrained habits of the peasants and the strong measures to which the surveying officers were urged to resort. In 1584 Hideyoshi threatened to crucify the men, women, and children of villages in which false returns were made. Perhaps this was not a serious threat; but in 1590 he issued instructions (which are on record) to Asano Nagamasa, who was responsible for the survey in Dewa and Mutsu, ordering him to make it very clear to the rural gentry as well as to the peasants that if any landowner should resist inspection, he and his family would all be executed; and that if the peasants grumbled, whole villages would be put to the sword. The survey should miss nothing. It should be made to reach "to the recesses of the mountains and by sea as far as can be reached by oars."[6]

---

[6] The text reads, "yama no oku, umi wa rokai no tsuzuki sōrō made." The severity of these orders was due to a widespread revolt of farmers in Dewa, who had killed surveying officers and in general had resisted so violently that Uyesugi had been obliged to send a large force to suppress them.

Although the new system of tenure was in many ways burdensome, it had certain advantages for the peasant. He had only one master, and although he was strictly speaking not the owner but the permanent tenant of his land, he could not be disturbed and he knew exactly what tax he had to pay. Of his total crop he paid a fixed proportion. This varied from time to time and place to place, but the basic rate was laid down in 1586 by Hideyoshi as "two to the Prince and one to the People" ("nikō ichimin"). In practice, and allowing for changing conditions of harvest due to weather and other circumstances, the average was four to the Prince and six to the People ("shikō rokumin"). Since there were no surtaxes or other impositions, a division of five to five was not unduly onerous, though it must be said that the tendency was always to reduce the proportion taken by the peasant.

By 1598—it was the year of Hideyoshi's death—all provinces had been surveyed. A complete register (with sketch maps) of all cultivated land in the country was made in three copies, one for the Emperor, one for Hideyoshi, and one for distribution in parts to the territorial lords concerned. Thereafter transactions in land were described not in terms of area but in terms of the product, the number of koku assigned to the land in the register. Consequently, when a grant of land was made by Hideyoshi (or his successors) to a vassal, it was stated in terms of koku, and a daimyo of that period was described as having a revenue of, say, 10,000 koku (the lowest figure) up to over 1,000,000 koku (which was the estate of the Maeda family and very few others). When Hideyoshi accepted the submission of Mōri Terumoto in 1591, he gave him a certificate with a list of provinces granted to him, and attached a copy of the survey register showing a total revenue of 1,205,000 koku. The provinces were seven western provinces on the mainland and parts of two others. In return Mōri swore fidelity to Hideyoshi, promising military aid to the value of about two-thirds of his total revenue if he should be called upon. The amount earmarked for military aid was sufficient to equip and provide a contingent of 50,000 men for the expedition against Korea.[7]

In this way the various daimyos submitted to Hideyoshi, entering into a vassalage which was to form the new feudalism of the seventeenth century.

3. Hideyoshi's Military Problems: Kyūshū

While the great land survey was in progress, Hideyoshi was steadily pursuing his military policy, which was of course designed to bring the whole of Japan under his control. He still had to make sure of the whole of Kyūshū, Shikoku, and the Kantō provinces ruled by the Hōjō family, whose base was at Odawara. But he could afford to take these piecemeal, since in his central position he was almost invulnerable.

[7] It will be seen from the roster quoted in a later chapter that Mōri Terumoto led a contingent of 30,000 men to Korea.

His first task was to complete the subjugation of the provinces of Kii and Izumi, where there were still some unreconciled elements. He disposed of these in 1585, when he destroyed the monasteries of Negoro and Kogawa in Kii and obtained the submission of Kōyasan. Finally he chastised the settlement of Saiga, which had sided with the Honganji against Nobunaga. He then went on to subdue the island of Shikoku, which was not a difficult task; and he might well have stopped there, since he was now supreme in all territory west of a line Owari-Mino-Hida-Etchū as far as and including Mōri's territory in Chōshū (Nagato).

However, while Hideyoshi was occupied with pacifying Kii and Shikoku, Shimazu of Satsuma was increasing his influence in Kyūshū. In 1584 Ōtomo and Ryūzōji had appealed to Hideyoshi for help against Shimazu. Hideyoshi was unable to respond at that time, but in 1585, soon after being appointed Kampaku, he tried to influence Shimazu by ordering him in the name of the Emperor to make peace with Ōtomo. In reply Shimazu, whose family had been great warriors since Yoritomo's day, laughed at the idea of Hideyoshi, an upstart, being appointed to the high office of Kampaku, and said that His Majesty must have made a hasty choice.[8]

But it was also hasty to elect to withstand Hideyoshi, who forthwith took the necessary preliminary steps to equip a great army for a campaign against Shimazu. Such an expedition was bound to be extremely costly, and Hideyoshi had to raise funds from the rich merchants of Sakai, Hakata, and other centres of trade. He met with a ready response from some of the wealthiest, who were inclined to welcome the prospect of new markets in western Japan and then perhaps on the continent.

While leisurely preparations were being made, Shimazu's offensive strength was growing fast, and Ōtomo implored Hideyoshi to act quickly. He made a journey to Ōsaka in April 1586 to visit Hideyoshi in his castle there. He was hospitably received, shown round the castle, and entertained at a tea ceremony arranged by the great tea master Sen no Rikyū. He explained the situation in Kyūshū to Hideyoshi, by whom he was assured that if Shimazu proved obdurate a great expedition would be sent against him.

The state of affairs in Kyūshū was of course well known to Hideyoshi,

---

[8] Being of humble birth—his father was an ashigaru in service to a warrior family in Owari—Hideyoshi was only slowly promoted, though his merits were soon recognized by Nobunaga. Until about 1575 his rank was below that of senior commanders like Shibata, who in turn was outranked by Ieyasu. After that, from about 1582, Hideyoshi was gradually promoted and became the general officer commanding all troops in the central provinces, with the title Chūgoku Tandai. After Nobunaga's death his progress was rapid. He was made Nai-daijin in 1584, Kampaku (Regent) in 1585, and Dajō-daijin (Chancellor) in 1586, when the family name of Toyotomi was conferred upon him. He was sensitive about his ancestry and asserted that he was a Fujiwara, but nobody believed this.

The appellation of Taikō by which he was popularly known was the style used by a Regent on retiring from office.

who had kept intelligence agents there for some time past. He knew of the constant strife between the three great families of Shimazu, Ryū-zōji, and Ōtomo, and he was well aware of Shimazu's recent depredations. At the beginning of 1587 Shimazu Yoshihisa, then the head of the clan, sent a letter to Hideyoshi in which he justified his conduct by saying that he had taken arms in self-defence. Hideyoshi was not impressed by such excuses. Some months before he had issued mobilization orders to his own troops, and in February the summons went to thirty-seven provinces, instructing them to set their armies in motion on the way to Kyūshū, where rebels must be suppressed.

The size of the army was immense: it is said to have been composed of over 200,000 men. Provisions for 300,000 were carried, and the number of pack horses was 20,000.[9] The vanguard was to leave at once, and Hideyoshi would advance in April. The vanguard, under Hideyoshi's half-brother Hidenaga, left early in March as arranged, proceeding part by land and part by sea. Hideyoshi left Ōsaka on April 8 and led the main body along the shore of the Inland Sea, calling on the way at Itsukushima for worship of the goddess Benten, and arriving in Shimonoseki at the end of the month. He then crossed the Straits and passed through Chikuzen and Chikugo on the way to deal with Satsuma forces in Higo. Meanwhile Hidenaga had already been joined by Kobayakawa and Kikkawa, who had been sent by Mōri to relieve Ōtomo at Hideyoshi's request. Hidenaga moved from Bungo into Hyūga, pressing the Satsuma forces back as he advanced.

The Satsuma armies, though fighting with great courage, had not the discipline or the skill in manoeuvre of Hideyoshi's best troops, nor were they well equipped with firearms. They continued to fall back. The campaign was complicated and difficult, but in the end the combined pressure of Hideyoshi and Hidenaga was irresistible. All Satsuma's forces had to give way. By the end of May Hideyoshi had reached Yatsushiro, more than half way to Kagoshima from the Straits of Shimonoseki. Here the warlords from the islands—Matsuura, Arima, Gotō, and others—came to submit. Their warships crowded the offing and their battle flags were flown, to show that they would join the expedition against Satsuma. Hidenaga was ready to advance, and Hideyoshi drove on southward into Satsuma, to a point north of the Sendai River, where a desperate action was fought on June 6. The Satsuma forces were attacked from all sides, routed, and put to flight.

A week later an emissary from Shimazu arrived at Hideyoshi's camp and asked for a truce, which was granted. The emissary was Ijuin, a leading vassal of the Shimazu house, who had shaved his head and taken his vows, and appeared before Hideyoshi in monastic garb.

---

[9] These figures may be exaggerated, but a total of 200,000 men is not improbable. The *Tamon-In Nikki* gives a total of 25,000 men with 3,000 horses, but this must refer to the vanguard only, as it left Ōsaka.

At this point, where in similar circumstances Nobunaga would have been ready to slaughter all his captives, Hideyoshi displayed the shrewd political sense, not to say the magnanimity, which distinguished him from other great leaders of his time. He could afford to be lenient, for he had overwhelming strength at his command: his own army (which with the addition of Ryūzōji's men numbered close to 200,000), Hidenaga's 70,000 troops, the Mōri contingent, and numerous local levies under the command of warriors who had been injured or insulted by Satsuma chieftains and who were ready at command to harass the flanks and the rear of Satsuma columns on the move. In addition to the great force approaching close to Kagoshima (the Satsuma capital) from the north, a strong seaborne force was coming up the gulf to attack the city from the south.

But Hideyoshi did not give the word to attack. He saw clearly that no good purpose would be served by slaughtering thousands of Satsuma warriors and leaving a legacy of hatred among the survivors. He treated Yoshihisa's son Iehisa with civility and suggested that he should go to Kagoshima and persuade his father and his brother, Yoshihiro, to surrender. Iehisa departed but soon returned to Hideyoshi's headquarters, reporting that his mission had failed. Thereupon, in Iehisa's presence, Hideyoshi's generals clamoured for a final attack which would destroy Satsuma (their speeches may have been arranged beforehand so as to impress Iehisa). But Hideyoshi spoke again and said that he had no wish to take extreme measures. He wanted a peaceful solution, he said, and one could be reached with advantage to Satsuma if Shimazu would submit; for he had confidence in the pride of the Shimazu family, who, once they declared allegiance, would never break their word of honour. Yoshihisa was persuaded and went to Hideyoshi's camp as a hostage while Yoshihiro and Iehisa gratefully accepted the liberal terms offered by Hideyoshi.

Those terms provided that Shimazu should keep all Satsuma and Ōsumi and the southern half of Hyūga. The power of Shimazu was limited to those provinces, and the remainder of Kyūshū was placed under the governance of three of Hideyoshi's best commanders, Katō, Konishi, and Kuroda. Ōtomo and Ryūzōji were confirmed in their original holdings. The Mōri family was also rewarded by great fiefs in northern Kyūshū, while Kobayakawa was given Chikuzen, a rich prize.

Hideyoshi's triumphal return was impressive. He reached Hakata on July 12, and stayed there for some days. He made his headquarters at the Hachiman shrine of Hakozaki, and his generals camped at Hakozaki, Sumiyoshi, Tatara, and other places, covering a space of about fifty square miles. His naval force was anchored in Hakata Bay, with innumerable pennants flying in the breeze. The master Sen no Rikyū prepared fragrant tea in a pine grove on the shore. Hideyoshi gave orders for the rebuilding of the town of Hakata, which had been ruined in the battles of Ryūzōji and Ōtomo, and then on August 4 he took ship at Kokura for Shimonoseki, proceeding thence by land to Itsukushima, where he worshipped and offered to the gods a performance of sacred dances. Then he took ship again and returned to Ōsaka, to be greeted with congratulations from the Throne and welcomed by a great crowd of Court nobles, officials, monks, and citizens.

Hideyoshi's calm confidence in this great enterprise is revealed in his letters from Kyūshū to his wife, then in Ōsaka castle. In August 1586 he had written to Ōtomo Sōrin informing him of his intention to attack Shimazu and had suggested certain steps to be taken by Ōtomo in concert with Mōri. He had already decided on his own plan of campaign. Less than a year later, in July 1587, he wrote to his wife to tell her that he had defeated his enemy and was on his way from Satsuma into Higo. She should set her mind at rest, he continues, for he will reach Hakata early next month and that is halfway back to Ōsaka. He will be at home at latest by the first week of August. He then tells her of his future intentions. "I am exacting hostages even from Iki and Tsushima, and ordering them to come to the camp. I have also sent word by fast ship to Kōrai [Korea] ordering them to appear and submit to the Emperor. I told them that if they do not appear I will punish them next year. And I will also get China in my grasp."

He ends this bold statement by confessing that he is a little afraid of what his wife will think of him when he returns. He is showing signs of age—he was then fifty-one—and has grey hairs which he cannot pluck out. Then in his next letter he describes the conditions imposed upon Satsuma, the names of the hostages, which include all the Shimazu leaders other than Yoshihisa, who has to send his only daughter, a child of fourteen, to live in Kyoto.

A large number of Hideyoshi's notes and letters have been preserved, and of these twenty or more furnish valuable historical evidence. Their chief interest, however, is in the aspects of his character which they reveal. In this they are exceptional, for private correspondence in Japan is generally reserved and discreet and does not disclose intimate feelings.

Hideyoshi was not an ignorant man, but his education was imperfect because of the circumstances of his parents. He wrote most of his letters in kana, but his choice of words is good and he expresses himself clearly, in a colloquial style. His letters to his wife and his mother show the gentle and affectionate side of his character, while in writing to his colleagues and subordinates he spares no pains in explaining his own attitude and in attempting to understand theirs. Among his best-known letters are those to his wife cited above, his long memorandum sent to Kobayakawa describing the battle of Shizugatake and its sequels, and his letters written while he was besieging Odawara castle. But all are worth careful study.

4. *Hideyoshi's Military Problems: the Kantō*

After the victory over Shimazu there remained no serious threat to Hideyoshi's design of unification. It is true that the Hōjō family still ruled in the Kantō from their base at Odawara, but they did not actually menace Hideyoshi and they had as their western neighbour the powerful Ieyasu. In the North there were a number of warrior families who might one day prove troublesome, but for the present they could be neglected.

If there was a weakness in Hideyoshi's position, it was the influence of Ieyasu along the eastern seaboard, especially in Mikawa, Tōtōmi, and Suruga (and later in Kai and Shinano), an influence which he had been patiently developing for some years past. The battles of Komakiyama and Nagakute, though not decisive, showed at least that Ieyasu considered himself Hideyoshi's equal. Their peace agreement had been slightly favourable to Ieyasu, since it provided that the Ōmandokoro (Hideyoshi's mother) should remain as a hostage with Ieyasu, who was to marry Hideyoshi's younger sister. However, Hideyoshi's successes in other parts of Japan combined with his rapid rise in Court rank and office to give him an important advantage, for as Regent and Chancellor he took precedence over Ieyasu almost as a lord outranks a vassal. Fortunately this position was not abused by either. Ieyasu showed no sign of discontent, and Hideyoshi treated him with special consideration.

Ieyasu had not been asked to take part in the Kyūshū expedition because it was one of his duties to keep an eye on the Hōjō family, and no doubt he was glad to be relieved of the expense of sending an army from the East as far as Kyūshū. But in 1590 he was obliged to undertake another and probably no less arduous duty, by sharing in the reduction of the eight eastern provinces and Izu.

This considerable and highly fertile area—it included the great alluvial plain of the Kantō—was well protected against attack by its position behind a great mountain barrier. Hideyoshi had made peaceful overtures towards Hōjō Ujimasa not long after returning from Kyūshū, but in reply had received defiant messages. He therefore began to think of leading an expedition to the East on the same scale as the invasion of Kyūshū. Here Ieyasu's position was awkward, for his fief stood between Hideyoshi and the Kantō, and Ujimasa's son Ujinao was his son-in-law. When he failed to bring about a compromise between the Hōjō family and Hideyoshi, he was under suspicion on both sides; and he therefore felt obliged to pursue the campaign with exceptional vigour, to avoid Hideyoshi's displeasure.

Kanemi, a contemporary diarist at home in Court circles, records that late one evening in December, 1589, he received a summons to go to Hideyoshi's palace. A council meeting was held to discuss action against Hōjō Ujimasa, who had broken a promise to go to Kyoto and submit. Hideyoshi was angry, and it was decided that Ujimasa must be punished. Late at night the draft of a communication to Hōjō was prepared. The text of this draft is on record. It recites Hideyoshi's efforts to negotiate a settlement and contains some rather complacent statements of Hideyoshi's own virtues. It ends by saying that in the light of the Hōjō refusal to obey the commands of heaven, Ujimasa must be destroyed.[10]

Having despatched this ultimatum, Hideyoshi at once ordered the mobilization of a great force, probably exceeding 200,000 men. The Hōjō leaders had sent out their order in the summer of 1587 and had conscripted all able-bodied men, including those in the service of monasteries and shrines. But their numbers were limited and their army included a large proportion of old-fashioned warriors, in contrast to the up-to-date professional soldiers of Hideyoshi. It is doubtful whether Hōjō could muster as many as 50,000 first-class fighting men.

Hideyoshi's great army moved early in April 1590. Its departure is described by Kanemi in his diary. The Emperor and Court nobles watched Asano's division as it marched out. It was a brilliant sight. Asano and his son dismounted to show the columns their way. First came 1,500 horse, then another detachment of some 3,000. Next was Ukita's division, and others followed that day and the next. The streets were thronged by many thousands of spectators. On April 5, the day set for Hideyoshi's departure, the weather was fine. He paid respects at the Palace and rode off at ten o'clock in the morning. There never was such a splendid display of arms and armour. There were pack horses carrying gold and silver, and spare mounts led by grooms and wearing brightly coloured horse-cloths of brocade. Neither tongue nor pen could describe these wonders. The number of men is said to have been 20,000.[11] Hideyoshi gave a linked-verse party on the night before leaving the capital.

Before setting forth, Hideyoshi had given orders to Ieyasu, who was to advance along the Tōkaidō, and to Sanada Masayuki, the holder of Numata castle, who was to take the central mountain road (Nakasendō)

[10] It uses one of Hideyoshi's favourite locutions, "kubi hanerubeshi," which might be translated "Off with his head."

[11] This may refer only to the divisions leaving Kyoto, or it may be a mistake for 200,000. The student of Japanese military history is always faced with the problem of numbers, since most chroniclers are either ignorant of arithmetic or indifferent to it. The size of Hideyoshi's expeditionary force to besiege Odawara, however, is not difficult to estimate in round numbers. His mobilization order went to five areas—the Home Provinces; the central provinces (Chūgoku); the northern provinces; the great military bases at Ōsaka and Kiyosu (in Owari) and the country between them; and Ieyasu's five provinces (Tōtōmi, Mikawa, Suruga, Kai, Shinano). If the contribution of these areas was of an average size of 40,000 men, the total of 200,000 for Hideyoshi and Ieyasu combined would not be excessive.

across country. The Hakone Pass, by which Ieyasu and Hideyoshi had to approach Odawara, presented difficulties to the command of a great army, especially in the transport of an immense quantity of supplies.

Hideyoshi had no intention of wasting men in frontal assaults on Odawara. Unlike Nobunaga, he always preferred a strategy which reduced casualties, as is shown by his sieges of Takamatsu and other heavily protected castles. He was prepared to sit before Odawara for a long time, and knowing that he could not depend upon a regular flow of goods in great quantities over the high passes, he set up an elaborate system of transport by sea. A large fleet of vessels, some carrying troops, others provisions, was provided by Mōri and Ōtomo and the freebooters under their control. The Hōjō also had ships patrolling off the Izu coast, but they were no match for the opposing fleet, which was armed with thousands of muskets and cannon.

Hideyoshi's determination to reduce Odawara by hunger or thirst is shown by the scale of his measures for the transport and storage of food and munitions of war. He was lavish in all his actions, and here he came near to extravagance. His chief supply officer stored in Shimizu 200,000 koku of rice, bought up with gold pieces, as well as great quantities of millet and fodder. A long row of storehouses was prepared in Ejiri, and in addition to the large transport vessels he procured from Ōminato several hundred first-class lighters for moving freight.

His strategy is described in his own words in a letter to his wife written from his encampment on May 16, 1590. He says that he now has the enemy caught like birds in a cage. He himself is in no danger, and she may set her mind at rest. He is longing to see his young son (Tsurumatsu, an infant born to his favourite, Yodogimi), but he must resign himself to staying at the front until he has accomplished his purpose of bringing peace to the empire ("tenka odayaka ni mōshitsuku beshi").

He is prepared for a long siege. He has the enemy closely surrounded within a double fosse; not a man can escape. Once he has starved Odawara out, he will be master all the way to Mutsu in the North, and that means one-third of all Japan. He has gold and provisions in plenty for a long siege, and he hopes to be able to return for a visit before the end of the year. Meanwhile he wishes her to send his favourite, Yodogimi, to Odawara.

Apart from his own family feeling, which was very strong, Hideyoshi knew that the inactivity of a long siege was a source of danger, for mettlesome warriors were likely to quarrel and forget the requirements of discipline. He therefore decided to make their sojourn in camp more agreeable. They were to send for their wives, and, to please those ladies, merchants and shopkeepers were brought from all parts of the country with a great choice of articles for sale. To relieve the taedium vitae for all ranks musicians and dancers were brought from the capital, and a number of courtesans came with them. To these were added girls from the surrounding countryside, and all these entertainers were installed in suitable apartments.

The Hōjō leaders had at first intended to fight in open country, making use of the network of castles built since Sōun's time, but a council of war held before Hideyoshi's arrival had decided in favour of standing a siege. This made it easy for Hideyoshi's generals to capture the more important citadels and thus to spell the complete ruin of the Hōjō family. It was not long before the defence of Odawara began to weaken, partly with the pressure of the besiegers and partly from internal weakness. There was treachery within the fortress, for Hideyoshi had bribed one of Ujimasa's leading counsellors.

Although Hideyoshi had been prepared for a much longer siege, the defenders must have given up hope when they found that their fortresses had been taken and some of their warriors had surrendered in the field. On August 4 Ujimasa offered unconditional submission, and a few days later Hideyoshi entered Odawara. He demanded the suicide of Ujimasa and his brother Ujiteru, but Ujinao was spared because he was the son-in-law of Ieyasu. Ujinao had offered to commit suicide on behalf of the others, but (according to contemporary letters) Hideyoshi refused to accept this sacrifice and insisted on "the Law," by which Ujimasa and others were doomed. In a letter written soon after the surrender, Hideyoshi told his wife that the heads of Ujimasa and Ujiteru had been sent to Kyoto for exposure. Ujinao was sent to Kōyasan, and later was granted a small fief of a few thousand koku. Ujinori (also a brother of Ujimasa), who had held out in Nirayama castle, was treated generously by Hideyoshi and given a small fief.

The way was now clear to the northern provinces, where there were a dozen or more barons, none of whom had great strength except Date, who was gradually extending his influence. He was sent for by Hideyoshi and scolded, but allowed to keep his territories on submission to the Kampaku. By the end of 1590 Hideyoshi was master of the whole country, as he had predicted. The task of unification, in a military sense at least, had been accomplished, and Hideyoshi proceeded with his plans for creating a political and economic unity. An interesting example of his methods is provided by his treatment of Dewa and Mutsu. No sooner had Date and the other northern barons submitted to him than he ordered the land survey to be thoroughly carried out in both regions.

He had already begun to turn his attention to administrative problems, but there were still some military questions to settle. He had to think of future security in the East and the North. There were certain territorial adjustments to be made, and some "cleaning up" operations were desirable in the northwest. Gamō Ujisato, one of his greatest generals, was allotted a great tract in Aizu, a lonely region from which he could keep watch on Uyesugi and the Kantō provinces adjacent.

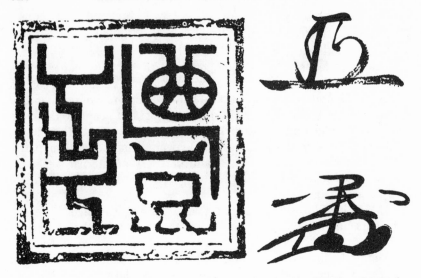

LEFT: *Hideyoshi's great seal.* RIGHT: *Ieyasu's cipher (top) and Hideyoshi's cipher.*

Next and most important was the disposal of the eight Kantō provinces themselves. This had already been decided in Hideyoshi's mind while he was sitting before Odawara. They were offered to Ieyasu in exchange for his former holdings. Ieyasu readily accepted, and by September 1 he had entered the castle at Yedo. His former provinces were divided among trusted vassals of Hideyoshi. This was a satisfactory arrangement, since Hideyoshi was glad to have Ieyasu at a distance, and Ieyasu for his part held the provinces celebrated as the home of the Kantō bushi, the hard-fighting eastern warriors. There were disadvantages in the somewhat remote position of the Kantō provinces, but they had been well governed by the Hōjō family, who had promoted industrial development and had looked after agriculture in the Kantō plain, by far the most extensive of the alluvial basins of Japan.[12]

It is pertinent to state here in political terms the result of Hideyoshi's military successes. In a general way they may be said to have brought order out of a protracted confusion that had attended and followed the war between the northern and southern Courts. During this period the provincial Governors became independent warrior chieftains, usually recognizing as suzerain one of their order but submitting only reluctantly to his commands. For a brief time the Ashikaga Shōguns had exercised that suzerainty, but in an imperfect and diminishing way, and as they gradually lost their power, the country was plunged into a series

[12] Ieyasu received only six of the eight Kantō provinces, since Awa and Hitachi remained in the hands of former holders. But he had also the rich province of Izu, west of the Hakone barrier.

of desperate and indecisive civil wars. It was not until the late sixteenth century that Nobunaga and then Hideyoshi were able to put an end to the prevailing anarchy. Hideyoshi achieved by force of arms and careful planning what none of the Ashikaga Shōguns could bring about, the restoration of a feudal system of government and a strict feudal discipline.

The most recalcitrant barons submitted to him and became his vassals. He confirmed them in their fiefs and allowed them to enjoy their revenues. By the closing years of the sixteenth century he had established a new feudal hierarchy, more stable and more rigidly organized than the system developed by Yoritomo, which had begun to collapse soon after the Mongol invasions. The process was to be completed by Ieyasu, but it could not have begun without the military successes of Nobunaga and Hideyoshi, nor could those successes have been achieved without their military talents; nor (it can be argued) without the use of firearms, which were introduced to Japan at a critical stage in her history.

CHAPTER XXI

HIDEYOSHI'S POLITICAL AIMS

1. *Hideyoshi and Nobunaga*

THERE is no general agreement among Japanese historians today on the nature of the political ideas and intentions of Nobunaga and Hideyoshi. The facts are not in dispute, since the actions of both men are amply documented by the texts of their edicts and a great deal of contemporary correspondence; but discussion tends to drift into a conflict of theories based largely upon comparison with the history of European feudalism. It is true that there are here some instructive analogies and contrasts, but discourse in this field may be left to specialists and we had better confine ourselves to following the main lines of political development in a convenient order.

It is clear that both Nobunaga and Hideyoshi aimed at absolute rule over a unified system, but unification is not merely a question of military force followed by edicts. It has to be accomplished by careful planning, executed by functionaries practised in the arts of government and administration. Mere tyranny will not succeed, and that both rulers understood this is clear from their fiscal practices. The collection of funds was of such importance to them that they found it prudent to make use of the richest merchants (especially those of Sakai, Hyōgo, and Hakata), who could finance great projects and were therefore accorded a great deal of freedom, which they were usually discreet enough not to abuse. While they flourished as individuals, the pressure of Nobunaga and Hideyoshi prevented their cities from acquiring the degree of independence enjoyed by the free cities of Europe.

Nobunaga had already begun to organize both rural and urban communities according to his ideas before he became master of almost the whole country. But his temperament and his early death prevented him from carrying out his designs in anything approaching a liberal fashion. (It will be remembered that his motto, carved on his seals, was "Govern the Empire by Military Force.") Hideyoshi, however, being a man with an active and wide-ranging mind, had been thinking about problems of government for many years; and when after Odawara he became truly the master of all Japan, he set about organizing the human and material resources of the country with determination, it is true, but also with patience and with very specific ends in view.

2. *The Organization of Government*

Hideyoshi had issued orders in 1583 for a national land survey, which as we have seen continued for more than a decade. The purpose of this measure, apart from ascertaining the total yield of farm lands, was to impose uniformity upon the structure of rural society throughout Japan. The peasant was to have no privilege other than security of tenure, and he was to obey a national and not a local or customary law.

The regulation of commerce was, of its nature, not so easy to achieve, but it will have been seen that although both Nobunaga and Hideyoshi favoured freedom of trade to the extent of throwing open closed markets and closed guilds, they both assumed arbitrary powers of control over economic affairs. Both can be charged with suppressing the rise of an independent urban class of tradesmen and artisans, which during the middle ages had been growing in importance and strength. Thus while encouraging agriculture and industry, they circumscribed the freedom of farmers and industrial workers. One of the most striking examples of this reactionary trend (for despite their constructive efforts both Nobunaga and Hideyoshi were in a true sense reactionaries) was their attitude towards the growing free cities of Japan. Sakai and Hakata lost their independence. Nobunaga assumed jurisdiction over Sakai and treated the rich city as if it were a fief governed by his Deputy (Matsui Yūkan). Hideyoshi instituted a number of industrial monopolies, in gold and silver mines, for instance, which became state enterprises in the sense that they provided him with much needed revenue.

A further step in the direction of absolute rule was Hideyoshi's policy of demolishing castles and fortresses, while shifting daimyos in order to prevent the development of centres of opposition to his government.

The purpose of Hideyoshi's great land survey (Taikō no Kenchi, it was called) was, apart from its direct fiscal advantage, to create a subservient peasantry, and to render impossible the agrarian risings which had plagued his predecessors.[1] It was followed in 1588 by a measure known as the Taikō's Sword Hunt (Taikō no Katanagari). The Sword Hunt was a measure of disarmament by confiscation that Nobunaga had earlier applied to members of leagues which had engaged in agrarian or sectarian risings. The measure had the double advantage from the ruler's point of view of preventing riots and distinguishing the peasant from the soldier, since throughout the middle ages farmers and townspeople alike had carried swords for defence or even only for display.

Hideyoshi's Sword Hunt was more comprehensive in its scope. It was, like Nobunaga's, designed to distinguish the soldier from the civilian, but it was also employed to confiscate the weapons carried by soldier-monks of the great monasteries of Kōyasan and Tōnomine. The direct cause of Hideyoshi's order was, it is thought, a violent rising of well-to-do and well-armed farmers in Higo in 1587.

The reason given for the order of 1588 was to disarm "peasants who

---

[1] It may give a useful idea of the dimensions of the land survey to set forth an estimate of the total area of cultivated land at different periods:

Mid-Heian (ca. A.D. 900):   862,000 chō (of 2½ acres)
Early Muromachi (ca. A.D. 1350):   946,000 chō
Register of A.D. 1600:   1,500,000 chō (producing 15 million koku)

keep needless weapons, do not pay their taxes, and plot risings against landlords. They are now to collect all their weapons and armour and then turn them in to the owner, tenant, or deputy of the respective estates."[2] The metal thus obtained was to be melted down and turned into nails and bolts for the Great Image of the Buddha which was to be installed in a new Hōkōji monastery in Kyoto. The peasants were told that such offerings would assure them of salvation in this world and the next.

Following the Sword Hunt came the announcement of a census of population at the end of 1590. This, it will be remembered, was very soon after Hideyoshi's return from Odawara, when he had completed the pacification of the whole of Japan. His first step was to order the expulsion of *rōnin* (vagrants) from villages in which they did no farm work and performed no military service. The land survey had brought such persons to the notice of the census-takers. The order was first enforced in 1590 in the province of Ōmi, and in September of the following year it was extended to the whole country by a notice which laid down rules for a census of houses. In every village a list was to be made of all houses and their occupants. All persons who had entered a village from another village or another province after the fall of Odawara (September 1590) were to be expelled. This order was known as the Hitoharai or Expulsion Edict.

The register thus compiled, together with the land register, served to bind the peasant firmly to the soil; and from the point of view of the authorities, these registers provided a convenient basis for conscripting labour to work on the construction of roads, dykes, and drains—the corvée in general. At the end of 1591 an even more drastic rule was issued, to the effect that any person in military service of whatever rank who newly entered a village after the fall of Odawara must at once be expelled. If that order were disobeyed, the whole township or village would be punished. Further, if any farmer should abandon his land and take employment as a day labourer or as a tradesman, the whole village would pay the penalty.

It may be asked what was the purpose of this extremely harsh legislation. The answer is twofold. In general Hideyoshi was determined to separate the peasants from all other classes, and in particular to distinguish them from the military class at every social level. According to one view it was desired to build a reservoir of manpower for use in a great overseas adventure which Hideyoshi was already preparing—the invasion of Korea (due to take place in 1592). Partly, no doubt, in preparation for this event, an effort was also made at this time to suppress piracy. Shipmasters, crews, and fishermen were obliged to take an oath that they would not engage in piracy, and it was made known

---

[2] The exact words of the first clause of the order issued on August 29, 1588, are: "The farmers (*hyakushō*) in all provinces are strictly forbidden to keep swords, side-arms, daggers, spears, guns, or any other military equipment."

that the daimyos in whose territory they were based would be punished for failure to prevent piratical behaviour.

There is disagreement among Japanese historians concerning the true purpose and the effect of the land survey and registration. It used to be regarded on the whole favourably, as a rational measure of land reform, but recent scholars look at it in a different light and enquire what change registration brought about in the life of the peasant and in the general structure of society, and who benefitted by that change. They do not all reach the same conclusions, probably because each concentrates upon a different aspect of an epoch-making enterprise. There can be no doubt, however, that the survey was intended to strengthen the new feudalism which had been steadily developing since Nobunaga's day. It was to abolish the last vestiges of the shōen system, and to establish the position of the actual cultivator as tenant and taxpayer, so that the ruler held in his hand the food supply of the nation.[3]

3. Rural Life

Hideyoshi's private letters and his public orders repeatedly stated that the land survey and other investigations must be carried out to the letter in the remotest corners of all the sixty-odd provinces; but there is good reason to believe that the well-to-do farmers stubbornly and often successfully resisted orders which called upon them to split up their families into a number of independent units. This offended the strong family tradition in rural society, the tradition which Hideyoshi was seeking to break down, because it was easier to deal with and to coerce an individual than a united family.

Village life, with its ancient customs and its natural solidarity, was difficult to change, and therefore Hideyoshi's sweeping reforms aroused resentment and at least passive resistance. This was particularly true of some of the larger villages, which were highly organized and on the whole prosperous. It is difficult to give a description of villages holding good for all parts of the country, for there were very wide variations in size and character; but the following outline may serve to illustrate conditions with which the land surveyors and the census takers had to deal at the close of the sixteenth century.

A typical village of the late middle ages in Japan in the Home Provinces or adjacent regions would consist of the dwellings of one or more well-to-do farmers native to the locality, of their adult sons, and of farm workers of various grades, comprehensively styled *hikan* or *nago*, who were theoretically independent cultivators of small plots of land, but who almost invariably did farm work for larger proprietors.

[3] Thus the actual cultivator of a plot or plots of land was now an independent unit, treated separately from his parents and his other relatives.

For a variety of views on this subject see the essays of Araki Moriaki, Endō Shinnosuke, and Miyagawa Mitsuru on Taikō no Kenchi. A list will be found in Thomas C. Smith's *Agrarian Origins of Modern Japan,* a valuable work dealing principally with conditions after 1600.

The well-to-do farmers were known as *dogō*, a term which implies that they were important members of rural society, long settled on the land which they farmed. They were for the most part members of the warrior class, and their appellation (ji-samurai) is sometimes translated as "yeoman farmer" or "country squire." This is only an approximation, but it gives a general idea of their social status. It was men of this standing who formed the nucleus of the power which Nobunaga and Hideyoshi acquired in the early stages of their careers.

The dogō might hold land yielding 50 koku or more, and for its cultivation he would need more labour than his family alone could furnish. He depended mainly upon the hikan or nago, supplemented in some cases by hereditary servants. The nago for their part usually held only very small plots, yielding about one koku; and since a koku of rice represents the consumption of one adult for one year, it was essential for the support of a nago and his family to earn more by working for the holder of larger areas of land.

Consequently the larger houses in a village were the dwellings of the dogō and his family and families of similar position, usually kinsmen in some degree. The cultivated fields would generally but not always be close to the farm dwellings. The composition of a village may be represented diagrammatically as shown below:

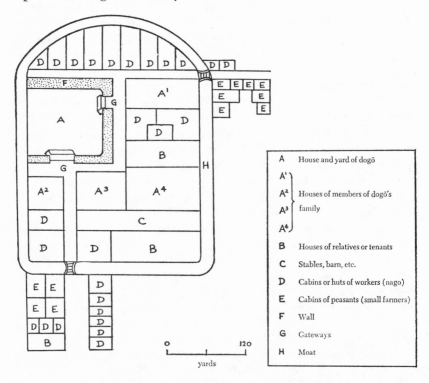

A	House and yard of dogō
A¹	
A²	Houses of members of dogō's
A³	family
A⁴	
B	Houses of relatives or tenants
C	Stables, barn, etc.
D	Cabins or huts of workers (nago)
E	Cabins of peasants (small farmers)
F	Wall
G	Gateways
H	Moat

Plan of a village in northern Yamashiro, based on a diagram in Nihon no Rekishi, Vol. 7 (Yomiuri Shimbunsha, 1959)

The village was sometimes surrounded by a moat, and the *yashiki* (the homestead of the dogō) was usually surrounded by a wall. The village illustrated is planned on the lines of a small fort, showing that the headman was a warrior as well as a farmer, that is to say a man of the ji-samurai or kokujin class. He would naturally assume leadership in the village; but after Hideyoshi's land survey, he had to decide whether to continue his profession as a warrior or to become a farmer.

It should be made clear that in either case he continued to receive his share of the crop inscribed in the register. He would of course have to pay to the nago or the outside workers a share of the yield of the plots which they cultivated for him. The intention of the survey and the register was not to confiscate land, but to ensure that the yield of each separate plot was recorded, and that the actual cultivator was made responsible for the payment of tax thereupon. The revenue of the landlord was not diminished by the fact of registration, but the lower grades of farm worker were able to resist pressure from landlords and gradually acquired independence as owners of minimal pieces of land. Registration did not bring this result about at once, and in remote parts of the country it was long delayed.

4. *Administrative Organs*

As the authority of Nobunaga and Hideyoshi was extended in scope, it became important to develop an organization capable of carrying out their governmental plans. When Nobunaga came into power, he inherited part of the administrative system built up by the Ashikaga Shōguns, and some of the offices and titles of the Muromachi Bakufu (such as Kanrei, Shoshi-dai, and Tandai) were retained in use. But new conditions and new rules needed new officers for their supervision, and often makeshift devices had to be adopted, for Nobunaga as he conquered new provinces had no time to decide upon a considered scheme in detail. He was thus obliged to rely provisionally upon a form of military government adapted to the new circumstances but leaving room for adjustment.

In his early days of power he was obliged to depend upon his comrades-in-arms—such generals as Niwa and Shibata and others of their rank—to fill the chief administrative posts. But soon after he was established in Kyoto he appointed a Commission of Five to govern the capital and the Home Provinces. The men appointed were Asano Nagamasa, Maeda Geni, Mashida Nagamori, Natsuka Masaiye,[4] and Ishida Mitsunari; and it is interesting to note that they were all by origin members of the small rural gentry of Ōmi and Owari, men who had supported Nobunaga in his progress to power and who were now his vassals.

Maeda Geni (he was also known as the Abbot Tokuzen-In, for he

---

[4] Mashida and Natsuka are preferred readings, instead of Masuda and Nagatsuka.

was in holy orders) was picked out by Nobunaga as a man of great ability, and Hideyoshi also had great faith in him. He was given the post of Shoshi-dai, which was equivalent to Commissioner for the Metropolitan Area, and at the same time he dealt with religious matters and was a judge in civil suits. Natsuka, who had a good head for figures and the power of rapid decision, was given charge of financial matters. Mashida, a man of upright character, was made Commissioner for Public Works. Ishida, a capable administrator, was made Chief of Police and Commissioner for Sakai, and he also dealt with trade questions in general. He served several terms as Commissioner for Hideyoshi's land survey, and applied its provisions to the letter in his own domains.

These men were used by Hideyoshi to give effect to his major decisions. The most important among them was Asano Nagamasa, who took a leading part in devising the land survey, which was a truly remarkable undertaking in both design and execution. Nagamasa was in fact something like a Prime Minister to Hideyoshi, presiding over a small cabinet. He was the senior of the five Commissioners, and was especially trusted by Hideyoshi with most confidential matters, since his wife was a younger sister of Yodogimi, Hideyoshi's favourite.

Hideyoshi's administrative arrangements were of a more permanent nature than those of Nobunaga, whose methods were of a somewhat hand-to-mouth character. He was a dictator in a hurry, whereas Hideyoshi, though despotic, had a gift for organization which served him in good stead in his political as well as his military life. In this respect he was superior to Nobunaga, who did not live long enough to develop his capacity to the fullest.

Hideyoshi, however, did not delegate full powers to his Commissioners, but continued to take an active interest in details of administration. He was inclined to use his authority as Commander-in-Chief to issue edicts and orders of a military character in civil affairs. His council of Five Commissioners thus tended to be a committee of specialists rather than a deliberative body deciding high policy.[5] Such a body was formed by the Five Elders (Go-Tairō) appointed by Hideyoshi towards the end of his life, mainly in order to prevent changes in the system of government which he had created in the interests of the Toyotomi family. The Tairō were Ieyasu, Ukita, Mōri, Maeda, and Kobayakawa. Their names show that they were appointed as the only men strong enough to deal with any difficult situation arising after Hideyoshi's death. The Tairō are reported to have been assisted by certain

[5] Some authorities are of opinion that Hideyoshi did not at this time create special organs for the execution of policy. There were, they suggest, no doubt a number of commissioners (bugyō) performing traditional functions and of senior feudatories giving advice; but as integral parts of the machinery of government the Go-Bugyō and Go-Tairō date from shortly before Hideyoshi's death, and they were appointed for the special purpose of guiding and protecting Hideyori during his minority. In ordinary circumstances Hideyoshi would lay down policy and give orders for its execution by officers of his choice.

junior advisers (Chūrō), whose duty was to mediate between the Tairō in cases of disagreement. But they seem to have been ineffective in that difficult situation.

Still lower in the administrative scale were the Deputies (Daikan), who governed territories under the direct jurisdiction of Hideyoshi (and of Nobunaga before him). The appointment of Matsui Yūkan as Daikan of Sakai, acting on behalf of Nobunaga, has already been mentioned. The habit of appointing rich merchants to such posts was continued by Hideyoshi, though they were placed under the direction of the Five Commissioners after 1595.

The area of territories under Hideyoshi's direct jurisdiction was very great. They were worth about two million koku at that time, and were scattered throughout the country. It was part of the function of the Daikan of one of those territories to keep an eye upon neighbouring daimyos.

Not much is known about the subordinate functionaries who worked under the Commissioners and other highly placed officers of state, but there are occasional sidelights in contemporary records. An interesting piece of evidence is furnished in the reminiscences of one Tamaki Yoshi-yasu, a kinsman of Mōri, who describes his experiences as a superintendent of land surveys in five provinces in five successive years.[6] (His first appointment was in Iyo in 1583, when he was thirty years of age.) He explains his procedure; he begins by climbing to a high point where he can get a general view of the farm land, its water supply, its different soils, its topographical features. He dwells on the hardships of the peasant who cannot grow enough rice for his own consumption, ekes it out with leaves and grass, and suffers from cold and damp for want of warm clothing. Tamaki may have been exceptional in his justice and compassion, but it is clear from the results of the survey and census, and from public works completed on a grand scale under Hideyoshi's rule, that there was no lack of talent available for the execution of important projects at what we may term a civil service level.

But there was a fundamental weakness in the despotic rule of Nobu-naga and, to a lesser degree perhaps, of Hideyoshi. Neither of them in their work of unification seems to have thought of developing a comprehensive system of civil and criminal law for the whole country, nor did they at any time declare that the Jōei Formulary and its many amendments were either obsolete or in operation. They were prompt to issue ad hoc rules, ordinances, and laws, but had little interest in legal principles. They governed by edict. Hideyoshi's Sword Hunt is a striking example of the dictator's attitude. He did not attempt to lay down rules and penalties limiting the use of swords and spears, but only to lessen the danger of revolt by depriving the most numerous class in the country of all weapons.

---

[6] His notebook, *Mi no Kagami,* is full of interesting things.

His attitude towards offences by both civil and military persons is well displayed by his order of 1597 establishing organs for self-government at a rather low level. These were the Five-man Group (Goningumi) of samurai and the Ten-man Group (Jūnin-gumi) of peasants. Their function was to preserve order in town and country. The members of each group were sworn to reveal any offence committed by one of their number, from petty theft to murder. Under the doctrine of joint responsibility they were punished for the crimes of others which they failed to report; and members of the group who were expelled had their little fingers cut off. The Ten-man Group had to keep a careful watch on village life, and prevent breaches of the rules governing cultivation and tax. Such duties as these inevitably lapsed at times into spying and delation.

One of the most important functions of Hideyoshi's government was naturally the administration of its finances. Among the sources of revenue was the product of gold and silver mines throughout the country. For the development of those sources, daikan were appointed by Hideyoshi, or in some cases the daimyo in whose territory the mines were situated was charged with their supervision and development, remitting a fixed percentage of their profit to the central government. Hideyoshi also obtained revenue from taxes levied in Sakai and from miscellaneous imposts.

Hideyoshi's currency policy was carried out by Natsuka Masaiye, who also took part in directing the land survey and the census. But there was no question of a regular financial office framing estimates of revenue and expenditure. Indeed, in contrast to the detailed administration of such measures as the land registration and the census, the reliance of Hideyoshi upon private enterprise is at first sight quite astonishing. It is well illustrated by the history of Konishi Yukinaga, one of Hideyoshi's favourites.

This Konishi belonged to a family which since the close of the fifteenth century had been active in the trade with Ming China, particularly in importing medicines. Yukinaga's father was Konishi Ryūsa, an influential Sakai merchant whom Hideyoshi appointed his Commissioner in Sakai and entrusted with the management of his funds. In other words Ryūsa became a kind of Treasury official. He evidently had a talent for organization, for during the Kyūshū campaign of 1587 he was in charge of the commissariat. He is said to have collected supplies for 300,000 men and 20,000 horses, bringing them to Hyōgo and Amagasaki and thence arranging transport to Shimonoseki by way of the Inland Sea.

His son Yukinaga was also well acquainted with maritime affairs, and was for that reason given command of a naval force in the Inland Sea. His services in this position were much appreciated by Hideyoshi, and he figures in later history as one of Hideyoshi's trusted general officers. Like his father, Yukinaga was a Christian convert, frequently mentioned in the Jesuit letters under the name of Don Augustino.

In such ways, it will be seen, Hideyoshi made use of rich men in very responsible work, both military and civil. He also employed persons with special qualifications as commissioners in charge of important public works, in building, irrigation, the construction of roads and bridges, and similar undertakings requiring technical knowledge and skill. These men as a rule were not permanent officials but were appointed for special duty. There was, for instance, a commissioner of works for rebuilding the Palace, Asayama Nichijō, a monk who had served from time to time under Nobunaga. There were also commissioners (bugyō) charged with the provision of building material on a very large scale for houses, fortifications, harbour facilities, and other such enterprises. These were government contractors rather than officials. The building of Hideyoshi's great castle at Ōsaka called for great quantities of material and it testifies to good direction and technical skill of a high order.

The financing of such great undertakings no doubt depended upon the cooperation of the richest merchants of Sakai and other trade centres, but the provision of currency presented a new problem, since the volume of monetary transactions increased throughout the country, thanks not only to the purchase of supplies for great armies but also to a general growth of industrial and commercial activity.

Following upon Nobunaga's currency orders of 1569, which had forbidden barter and laid down valuations for copper coins of various origins, an increasing number of copper coins was struck in Japan; but these were, it seems, not officially minted until Hideyoshi's time, when after about 1585 copper, silver, and gold coins were issued. They were known as Tenshō coins, from the name of the Tenshō era (1573–91).

The sudden increase in the production of silver which made this change possible was due in part to improved methods of smelting, but the most important cause was probably a realization among the warlords that they must develop the material resources of their fiefs—a kind of activity which was no doubt stimulated by wealthy investors from the cities. Nobunaga and Hideyoshi both paid great attention to the development of gold and silver mining, especially in the provinces under their direct jurisdiction (which were virtually their private property), and both collected in their castles very great reserves of gold and silver bullion.

Copper coins were good enough for small transactions of a retail kind, but a more portable currency was needed for such expenditure as the purchase of great quantities of supplies required by the expeditionary forces which in the latter half of the sixteenth century were marching up and down and across Japan. For such purposes payments were made in bullion, and to prevent fraudulent dealing the bullion

usually carried the mark of a goldsmith or a silversmith whose relia-
bility was known. Nobunaga had a store of such marked pieces in his
Azuchi castle, and Hideyoshi, as we have seen, carried great quantities
by pack horse to Odawara for commissariat purposes. Most of the daimyos held large stocks of gold and silver bullion and gold dust. The
demand for gold was so great that it was freely imported, while silver
was exported in large quantities during the latter half of the sixteenth
century. Apart from its function as a medium of exchange, gold was
very freely used for ornamental purposes. Hideyoshi's great seal, for
example, was of gold, and an issue of large gold coins known as the
Tenshō Ōban is thought to have been ordered by Hideyoshi in preparation for his Kyūshū campaign.

5. Hideyoshi's Relations with the Throne

Nobunaga, following his father's example, had made a point of treat-
ing the Throne with respect and of rendering services to the imperial
family. At the request of the Emperor Ōgimachi, he had seen to the
reconstruction of the Palace (the Tsuchimikado-dairi) very soon after
his entry into the capital with Yoshiaki in 1568. Hideyoshi, although
perhaps less influenced by the national habit of veneration for the sovereign, continued Nobunaga's policy of care for the person of the Emperor and of generous contributions to the expenses of the Court. He
assigned definite revenues to the Imperial House after the Emperor Go-
Yōzei had condescended to be present at a great entertainment in 1588,
and he much prized the titles of Regent and Chancellor which he had
obtained in 1585 and 1586.

The emperor exercised no direct political power, but he was the
acknowledged fountain of honour and the symbol of national unity. He
did not stand at the head of a feudal system as did the kings of England
and France in the middle ages, but the de facto rulers to whom the vassals owed allegiance were always careful in great matters to act in the
name of the sovereign. If they had not done so, they would, it is true,
have laid themselves open to a charge of treason by their adversaries;
but apart from these considerations of prudence a genuine sentiment of
loyalty survived through the tumult of centuries.

Occasionally the emperors intervened in national affairs, but there
is little evidence to show that they ever took the initiative. There is one
instance in which the Emperor Ōgimachi seems to have taken a strong
line. That was in 1569, when he protested to Nobunaga against the
licensing of the Jesuit Father Frois to preach in the capital. But the
pressure here came from Buddhist quarters, and it was proper for the
Emperor at their request to protect an established national religion.
Nobunaga, it will be recalled, paid no attention to this move, being
well aware of its origin; for on most occasions of intervention by the

Emperor or in his name, it could safely be assumed that he was acting at the request of political or religious leaders for their own purposes.

His Majesty's fiat was often claimed as an excuse for some act which might otherwise be regarded as shameful, such as the surrender of the Ishiyama Honganji in 1580; but here too of course the Emperor acted in response to pressure. Nobunaga frequently asked the Emperor to approve action which he proposed to take, or to issue a commission to chastise some alleged enemy of the Throne. But these were well-worn practices and did not signify the free exercise of sovereign power. An emperor who was bold enough to defy the supreme warlords on whose bounty he depended might end his life in banishment, as Go-Toba and Go-Daigo had done. Yet it should not be supposed that imperial action, even when so circumscribed, was of little real importance. On the contrary, it served at times to ease political tensions or prevent the development of awkward situations, resembling in that respect the function of a constitutional monarch in Europe today.

Magnificence was Hideyoshi's policy as well as his pleasure. In 1587 he gave a giant open-air tea party at Kitano, to celebrate his victory in Kyūshū. People of all classes from warlord to peasant were invited by public notice boards set up in Kyoto, Ōsaka, and Sakai. They needed to bring only a mat to sit upon and a teacup. There was a show of art treasures, and for ten days there were plays and dances for the guests to watch and music for them to listen to.

This was a prodigious entertainment, but for political significance as well as lavish expenditure it does not match the occasion when Hideyoshi and his great vassals entertained the Emperor at Hideyoshi's new Kyoto mansion, the Jurakudai or Mansion of Pleasure, which was completed in 1587. This building was a characteristic expression of his taste. It occupied a great space almost equal in area to the Imperial Palace Enclosure, and it was surrounded by a moat and thick walls of great blocks of masonry fitted together like those in the castles of Azuchi and Ōsaka. From outside it looked like a fortress, but the inner apartments were richly decorated. Hideyoshi moved there from Ōsaka in the fall of 1587, and in the first month of 1588 he invited the newly enthroned Emperor Go-Yōzei to be his guest.

Maeda Geni studied precedents for the entertainment of royalty, and on the appointed day His Majesty was escorted to the Jūrakudai by Hideyoshi, who as Regent held the highest Court rank.[7] The procession was brilliant with colour; there were dozens of palanquins bearing Court ladies, mounted escorts, guards of honour, and innumerable men at arms. Following His Majesty's carriage and the great Court nobles there came Hideyoshi himself, followed in turn by his great generals

[7] Second grade of first rank. The first grade was always posthumous.

and their attendant officers. When the outriders at the head of the procession reached the Jūrakudai gateway, the rear guard had not yet emerged from the Palace enclosure.[8]

Upon arrival, the sovereign was waited on by the great daimyos, not in their military capacity but by virtue of their Court ranks, of which the highest were held by Taira (Oda) Nobukatsu and Minamoto (Tokugawa) Ieyasu.

The Emperor remained for five days at the aptly named Mansion of Pleasure, in most luxurious surroundings which (the secretary said) beggared description. The real purpose of the gathering, apart from a display of extravagance, was disclosed on the day after His Majesty's arrival. The daimyos who had been invited subscribed to a written oath. It was a simple document of only three articles, which ran as follows:

1. We who are assembled here weep tears of gratitude for the presence of His Majesty.
2. If any evil persons should attempt to confiscate Crown estates or the property of Court nobles [kuge], we will take action against them, and we bind ourselves and our descendants to carry out this undertaking.
3. We swear that we will obey the commands of the Regent [Hideyoshi] down to the smallest particular.

This oath was sworn in the Emperor's presence to all the Gods and Buddhas in the usual formula, ending in a comprehensive clause including "all the Gods, great and small, of the sixty and more provinces of Japan." It was subscribed by six men of the highest rank, including Ieyasu and Nobukatsu, and was followed by a similar document signed by more than twenty of the leading warlords.

On the following day (the third) there was a great poetry meeting to which the Emperor contributed, and so did the retired Ōgimachi, in a verse declaring that all was well in the world and there was no cloud in the sky. This was in the month of May, when Kyoto is a city of balmy airs and light mists.

In the spring of the following year, Hideyoshi invited some of the principal Court nobles and the most important daimyos (beginning with Ieyasu) to attend him in the great inner gallery of the Jūrakudai. There he had arranged a great display of gold and silver pieces heaped upon trays, to the total value of 365,000 ryō (1 ryō being equal to 15 grammes), which he distributed among the nobles and generals (including Ieyasu) who were his guests.

It will be seen from the events just recited that Hideyoshi did not regard himself as a candidate for the office of Shōgun, but as a warrior who was, as well as Commander-in-Chief, the Regent ruling on behalf

---

[8] All these particulars and much more can be found in a record kept by Hideyoshi's secretary, Kusunoki Masatora. It may be noted that part of the escort consisted of samurai wearing not helmets but the ceremonial cap called *tori-ebōshi*.

of the Emperor. This is a point which should not be overlooked in considering the importance of the Throne in Japanese political history. When Hideyoshi resigned the office of Regent in 1592, he gave a Paper of Advice to Hidetsugu, who succeeded him. In one of its five articles he enjoined the new Regent to serve the Throne with great care.

6. Hideyoshi and Buddhism

Hideyoshi's policy in matters of religion differed from that of Nobunaga, who had gone to extremes of violence in suppressing what he deemed to be subversive activities of the great Buddhist sects. No doubt the Enryakuji and Kōyasan and the Ikkō fraternities had learned their lesson and did not stand in need of correction from Hideyoshi. They had been weakened by constant attacks and had lost much of their revenue. Most of the monks had abandoned their military habits, turning to study and pious works. This was a state of affairs which Hideyoshi thought it sensible to encourage and to turn to his own advantage. He did, however, choose to take a strong line with certain religious bodies. In his battle with Ieyasu at Komakiyama in 1584, he had met with opposition from Ikkō remnants including monks who had escaped from Negoro. He did not forget this clerical insolence, and in revenge he attacked Negoro early in 1585, quickly reducing the place to ashes. Here he was no less ruthless than Nobunaga had been on Hiyeizan. At about this time he subdued the soldier-monks of Kumano by a display of force; and against the ancient and revered Kōyasan he achieved a success which Nobunaga could never obtain. His method was simple and effective, for by a mere threat of force, by confiscating weapons in his Sword Hunt and by impounding Kōyasan revenues in the course of his land survey, he frightened the monks into submission and then gained their esteem by returning their estates. By using the same method during the course of the survey in other parts of Japan, he was able to reorganize monastic holdings throughout the country and thus to bring all monasteries and shrines under his regulation in secular matters.

His treatment of the Tendai sect was discreet, for without suggesting that Nobunaga had been wrong in destroying the Enryakuji he approved of an appeal for subscriptions put out by a prince abbot newly appointed after Nobunaga's death. The appeal was for funds needed to restore the Komponchūdō, the Hie shrine, and other historic edifices on the Mountain.

The Hokke sect had been almost ruined by Nobunaga after the deplorable debate at Azuchi, but it was now licensed to spread its gospel by Hideyoshi, who wished to be impartial between religious denominations. His most active support of a religious body, however, was accorded to the Ikkō sect, but not on religious grounds. The Abbot Kōsa, though ejected from the Ishiyama Honganji, had not abandoned his resolve to restore the central cathedral of the Single-minded believers.

EXEMPLVM
BINARVM EPI-
STOLARVM A P. OR-
GANTINO BRIXIANO SOCIETA-
TIS IESV E MEACO IAPONIAE AD
Reuerendum in CHRISTO P. CLAVDI-
VM AQVAVIVAM Præpositum Generalem
datarum, de proxima spe vniuersæ Iaponiæ
ad CHRISTI Ecclesiam adiun-
gendæ.

EXEMPLVM PRIORIS
EPISTOLAE, A P. ORGANTINO
BRIXIANO Societatis IESV Meaco
IAPONIAE datæ.

PAX CHRISTI.

VAE res non mediocriter hoc an-
no M. D. XCIV. nos afflixerun. t
primum diuturna P. Visitatoris, &
Reuerendiss. Episcopi, quem iam
in Chinam peruenisse ex litteris
Manilianorum cognouimus, absentia : dein-
de, quod nauis, quæ solet quotannis huc ex India appellere , & omnium harum Societatis
domorum, maximè autem Collegij, Nouitia-
tus, & Seminarij necessariam annonan. aduehere,
hæc

A page from a little volume of Jesuit letters—Relationes—from India and Japan. It was published in Rome in 1598. The Latin text of the letters from Japan is a translation from the original Italian of the author, Father Organtino, who was then living in Kyoto and was favoured by Hideyoshi (known in these letters as Quambacundono). The letters, written in 1594 and 1595, are addressed to Claudius Aquaviva, the general of the society. In the letter from which this illustration is taken Father Organtino writes with satisfaction of the progress made by the Jesuits and of the peace and tranquility brought by Hideyoshi. The illustration is the same size as the original.

He sought every opportunity of gaining the support of the secular arm as soon as Nobunaga was dead. He had cleverly gained the approval of Hideyoshi by sending sectaries to create disturbances in the rear of Shibata Katsuiye, Hideyoshi's antagonist in 1583; and in 1587, out of gratitude for past favours, Kōsa sent messengers to Kyūshū with instructions to the Ikkō leaders there to act as guides to Hideyoshi's army in Satsuma. As a result of these actions Hideyoshi treated Kōsa generously, and in 1589 granted him the land at Ōtani in Kyoto on which the shrine of the patriarch Shinran had once stood.[9]

Hideyoshi's own beliefs are not known. He carried on his person a small sacred charm, and he prayed for members of his family; but his only public act of piety was the building and dedication of a great Buddha image and a spacious fabric to contain it. This was an immense undertaking, which was begun in 1586 and involved the transport of large quantities of timber from nearly all the forest lands in central and western Japan. What moved him to this effort is not clear, but it is supposed that he wished to erect some permanent memorial to his own greatness. If that is so his purpose was not achieved, for both image and building were overthrown by an earthquake in 1596.

It has been suggested on the basis of one of the Jesuit letters that the reason for erecting this colossus was to dispose of a vast quantity of condemned copper coins. But this view must be mistaken, for the image was made of wood, and not of bronze as was the usual practice. Wood was chosen because of the technical difficulties of casting great sections of metal and the length of time required for its completion. The wooden framework required a large quantity of iron nails and bolts, and these by Hideyoshi's orders were to be made from the swords and other weapons of the militant clergy confiscated in the Taikō's Sword Hunt. An expert was brought from Ming China to assist the Japanese supervisors in the construction of the supporting framework and the shaped parts, which when they were in place were to be coated with lacquer. The lacquer was especially prepared in Sakai by Imai Sōkyū.

The work of preparing the site (which was in the Higashiyama district), collecting and moving the materials, and erecting the building is said to have required the labour of 50,000 men, working over a period of five or six years. This may well be, since there were few mechanical devices to replace manpower. One account says that some of Hideyoshi's generals and other officers took part, pulling on ropes and singing the lumberman's chanty as they hauled the great timbers, while others played the flute or beat the drum. Hideyoshi himself, according to one account, changed to a hempen jacket and lent a hand.

After the earthquake of 1596 a new building was erected under the

[9] This shrine was later (1591) transferred to Rokujō, the site of the present Nishi Honganji.

orders of Hideyori, and a new image installed, this time of bronze and much smaller than the first. There followed repeated disasters, and the image was now of wood and now of bronze. The surviving colossus, which is of wood, was erected in 1801; it is a monstrosity of which there is nothing more to be said.

7. Hideyoshi and Christianity

Under Nobunaga's protection the growth of Christianity in Japan was remarkable. It can be argued that he gave his protection because he wanted to ensure a continuance of foreign trade, and this was no doubt a factor in his decision; but he was a man of foresight and he must have balanced advantages and objections carefully before he made up his mind to treat the Jesuits well. He was influenced, we may be sure, by the character of the missionaries—their evident good breeding, their learning, and their unselfish devotion to their faith.

Hideyoshi took a somewhat different line. He was not interested in religion, but he treated the Jesuit Father Gnecchi Organtino in a friendly way when asked to give permission for a church and a house near to the new Ōsaka castle; indeed, he even selected a site for them. Takayama Ukon, the Christian general who was a trusted member of Hideyoshi's entourage, helped the mission to build the church, which was opened for worship on Christmas Day of 1583, not long after the completion of the castle. Hideyoshi raised no objection to the conversion of his subordinates, and a number of persons close to him, including some Court ladies, became Christians, some of them under the earnest persuasion of Takayama. There were other Christians in important posts, among them Konishi Yukinaga, Ukita of Bizen, and Kuroda, all officers who had served Hideyoshi well.

On several occasions in 1584 and 1585, when in Ōsaka between campaigns, Hideyoshi was on amiable and seemingly frank terms with the Jesuit leaders, and enjoyed conversation with them in his leisure moments. In 1586 the Vice-Provincial Gasper Coelho went up from western Japan (he had been in Nagasaki, then almost a Portuguese town) to visit congregations in the Kyoto area. He called at the Ōsaka castle in great style early in May, accompanied by Frois and other Fathers and a number of Japanese catechists. They were received ceremoniously by Hideyoshi and some of his great barons. Then, after the barons had withdrawn, Hideyoshi joined the guests and talked freely with them, paying especial attention to Father Frois, who spoke Japanese well and had known Hideyoshi in his early days. They talked of old times. It was an intimate occasion, and according to the Jesuit records Hideyoshi spoke without reserve to the Vice-Provincial, encouraging him to believe that he would make Japan a Christian country once he had conquered China.

He told Coelho that he meant to invade Korea with 2,000 vessels and

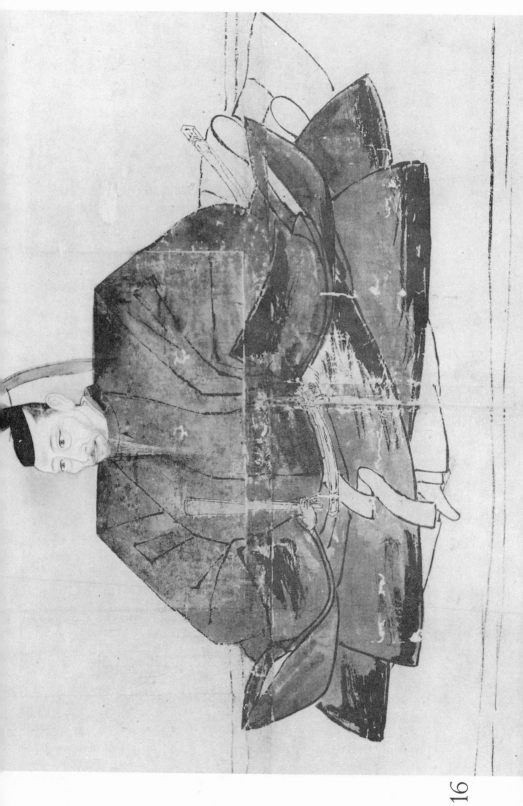

16

17

18

19

20

wished Coelho, when the time came, to purchase for him two well-armed Portuguese ships. Not long after this he granted certain privileges and exemptions to the Christians which were even better than they had dared to hope. He must have known by then that the number of Christians in Japan was between 150,000 and 200,000. The seminaries were training young men to spread the gospel year after year, and although most of the converts were in the western provinces, there were 10,000 in the capital and surrounding country. The outlook was bright indeed.

In the summer of 1587 on the way back from his successes in Kyūshū, Hideyoshi invited Coelho to visit him at his headquarters near Hakata, where he was considering plans for the rebuilding of the city, then much damaged during the fighting. He set aside a piece of land for a church. He also went aboard a small but well-armed Portuguese ship to see the Father, and showed himself most affable and interested. Then, in the middle of the night, only a few hours after Hideyoshi had left the Portuguese ship, an urgent message reached Coelho, accusing the Jesuits of various offences and demanding a reply. Coelho did his best, but Hideyoshi paid no regard to his defence, and on the following day an edict was issued banning Christianity and ordering the Fathers to leave the country within twenty days. The date of this edict appears to have been July 25, 1587, but there is some difficulty in establishing the exact course of events at this juncture, since the available documentary sources are not in agreement. The differences, however, are not important and the main facts are clear.

Hideyoshi had made up his mind to get rid of the missionaries. In one of his statements he charged them with the same kind of treasonable activity as that of the Ikkō sectarians: with encouraging daimyos to force their people to give up their old religion; with selling Japanese as slaves to China, Korea, and other parts of Asia; with killing animals (horses and oxen) for food; and with destroying Buddhist and Shintō buildings. There was more than a grain of truth in some of these accusations, for the Portuguese traders did buy slaves, and the Jesuits, or their converts, sometimes smashed Buddhist images and damaged Buddhist shrines. But it is most unlikely that these were the reasons which suddenly induced Hideyoshi to take such very drastic measures.

Various explanations have been offered but none of them is convincing. One Church historian suggested that Hideyoshi had been drinking some strong wine presented to him by Coelho, and had acted in a rage. Another guess is that owing to Christian influence the young girls of the countryside would not submit to him. There may be some truth in this, since he was excessively amorous by nature and was usually well served by procurers. But it is highly improbable. It is far more likely that he had been brooding for some time on the question of his relations with foreign countries, and that something he had seen or heard while in Hakata had touched off accumulated suspicions. It is known that he had an adviser, half pimp and half physician, one Seiyaku-In, who detested the Jesuits and who no doubt played some part in disturbing Hideyoshi's mind.

Whatever the immediate cause of Hideyoshi's action, it is certain that he acted for a considered purpose, though perhaps stimulated by momentary anger. He already had the Buddhist sects well under control, but in Kyūshū he found that, far from being oppressed, the Jesuits were in a very strong position, for it was they who controlled some of the leading rulers. It happened that both Ōtomo Sōrin and Ōmura Sumitada, the two most important "Christian daimyos" in Kyūshū, had died only a little while before the end of his campaign; and he may well have thought that this was a suitable occasion for action to accord with his own plan for a unified despotic rule over the whole of Japan. He was well informed of the activities of the Portuguese—both priests and laymen—in Nagasaki, a city which had become as it were a foreign possession, and he had probably already been told of the slave trade in which some Portuguese sea captains were deeply engaged. This defiance of Japanese sovereignty provided him with a reason for immediate action in accordance with a long-decided policy. But for some resistance in the Kantō he was now master of all Japan, and he may have felt that he could not embark on an invasion of Korea with full confidence until he had dealt with all possible agents of opposition at home.

The expulsion order of course alarmed the missionaries, who were wise enough to give every appearance of obeying its terms. Coelho, as soon as he learned the text of the edict (a copy was sent to him), protested that it was quite impossible to leave the country at once since there were no ships ready to take him and his colleagues. He assembled most of the missionaries in Hirado to take passage in a Portuguese vessel which was presently due to leave; but not all of them sailed away. Indeed most of them, perhaps a hundred in all, remained and went into hiding in Ōmura and Arima, seaport towns in Hizen province, where by judicious bribery they were able to stay and resume their pastoral work. Hideyoshi's officers were not scrupulous in enforcing the edict, and trade continued undisturbed. Nagasaki remained ostensibly part of the Ōmura fief, but in reality it was governed by the Jesuits until 1590, when it was brought under Hideyoshi's direct control.

While bearing heavily upon the missionaries, Hideyoshi took care to assure the merchants that they were still welcome. The last of the five articles in his expulsion edict states clearly that so long as they do not hinder the teaching of Buddhism, merchants from Christian countries may come and go freely, for purposes of trade. From other clauses in the edict he seems not to have denied individual freedom of belief, but to have objected to wholesale conversions at the instance of a daimyo or a great landlord. The memorandum of July 24 under his seal uses the phrase "kokoro shidai," which means "according to a man's own heart—his private sentiments."

On his return to Kyoto in 1587, Hideyoshi was faced with problems of more immediate concern than the treatment of Christian missions. He had to proceed with his positive measures of unification, which included currency reform, the confiscation of weapons, social legislation distinguishing the soldier from the peasant, and the subjugation of the eastern and northern provinces, beginning with the siege of Odawara. This occupied him until the year 1590, when his mind was filled with preparations for his invasion of Korea. He was now concerned not with persecuting missionaries but with continuing and increasing his foreign trade. Consequently the missionaries in Kyūshū were little disturbed and indeed made such good progress that, within a limited area it is true, they strengthened and deepened the faith of thousands. Their converts were mainly peasants and workmen living poorly in a war-ridden country and thirsty for some consoling faith. But important personages were also on the side of the Jesuits—Konishi, the Admiral, and a few other men of high rank. Among the most steadfast Christians were the wives and daughters of believers. The student of Japanese history, accustomed to a picture of Japanese feminine character as gentle and subservient, in time discovers that among all the martyrs none displayed a more stubborn courage than the women.

Hideyoshi did not withdraw his expulsion edict; but in 1590 he agreed to receive a mission from the Viceroy of the Indies, with which Valignano was to be associated. The mission was received in Kyoto in March 1591. It included as well as Valignano and several priests the four young ambassadors who had gone to Rome from Kyūshū eight years before and had just returned. With them came a number of Portuguese of good standing from Nagasaki and other ports. Valignano himself had been appointed to represent the Viceroy, and Hideyoshi treated him well, though he warned him not to ask for the withdrawal of the expulsion edict or for any other favours to the missionaries.

The edict had not prevented Japanese Christians in high places from continuing in the faith and encouraging new converts. Hideyoshi seems to have tolerated the presence in Kyoto of Organtino and other Fathers, and he took no steps against a number of missionaries whom Valignano had brought with him to Japan, beyond detaining them in Nagasaki as hostages—a measure which pleased both parties. When Valignano left Japan in October 1592 with a reply to the Viceroy's letter, there were more than a hundred Jesuits working under cover in Japan. They were of course most active in Kyūshū, but progress was made in the metropolitan region as well.

The citizens of Kyoto had always been enthusiastic followers of fashion, and after the appearance in the streets of Portuguese captains and merchants in their finest clothes, the city was seized by a mania for foreign dress and foreign manners. The beaux and belles of the city wore crucifixes, carried rosaries, and used Portuguese words. The arrival of goods from Europe as well as from China and the Indies was impatiently awaited, and the continuance of the Portuguese trade became a matter of importance to modish people. Even Hideyoshi, accustomed to the sombre Jesuit frock, was impressed by the gallant array of the Portuguese laymen. For more serious reasons of policy Hideyoshi was anxious not to cut off the supply of goods brought by Portuguese ships, since in the autumn of 1592 he had moved to Nagoya in the province of Hizen and had established there his headquarters for the Korean campaign.

This alarmed the missionaries, since they were now at the mercy of press gangs searching the towns and villages of northern Kyūshū for able-bodied men and provisions needed by the invading armies. The Jesuits were therefore in great danger, often on the run; but their enemies were petty officials looking for profit and willing to take bribes. They also could depend upon their influential converts for protection, and thus despite all perils and obstacles their numbers increased and their labours were fruitful. Hideyoshi, though he might from time to time issue some unpleasant order, was no longer disposed to order a root-and-branch persecution. Accordingly, the number of Jesuits in Japan did not diminish but increased after 1592. The report of the Society for the years 1595–96 shows that there were fifty Fathers in China and more than one hundred and forty in Japan. This was a remarkable situation, for Hideyoshi had licensed only ten priests in Nagasaki for the spiritual needs of Portuguese only, while Organtino was allowed to remain in Kyoto without church or office. Looking back to the night of Hideyoshi's thunderbolt, which struck the poor Coelho in Hakata in 1587, the position was scarcely credible. Now, according to the Jesuit reports, there were 300,000 Christians in Japan, and of these more than 60,000 had been baptised after the expulsion edict.

Nor were the converts only humble peasants. In the list of distinguished names occur: Gracia Hosokawa, daughter of Akechi Mitsuhide; Maria, sister of Hideyoshi's consort Yodogimi; Magdalen, the companion of Hideyoshi's wife; the sons of Maeda Geni; Sō, the hereditary Tandai of Tsushima; Mōri of Chikugo; Gamō Ujisato of Aizu; and that grandson of Nobunaga, Sambōshi, who as an infant had been presented by Hideyoshi to the council at Kiyosu. Most of them were members of the flock of the aged Organtino. Of all these Jesuit movements Hideyoshi was aware, but he took no steps to check them. The missionaries were on the whole too discreet to flaunt their triumphs and Hideyoshi was fully occupied with both domestic and continental projects. He could bide his time.

While the Jesuits were reaping their harvest and the Portuguese traders were enjoying a profitable commerce in Far Eastern waters, the Spanish conquistadores, whose main interest was in the development of a colonial empire on the American continent, developed a kind of outpost at Manila, on the island of Luzon in the Philippines. The Spanish sea captains based on Manila began to look with envy on the monopoly enjoyed by Portuguese ships in the Japanese trade, and the missionaries based on Manila, who were Franciscans, Dominicans, and Augustinians, resented the monopoly enjoyed by the Jesuits in Japan, which rested upon a papal brief of 1585.

Although Hideyoshi had granted freedom of trade to the Portuguese, he regretted having to make an exception to his own rule of absolute control over all matters, whether secular or sacred, in Japan. But the alliance between the Jesuits and the Portuguese traders was very strong. On one occasion in 1591, after he had brought Nagasaki under his direct rule, he ordered his commissioners there to force a Portuguese vessel to hand over its freight of gold at a reduced price. The Portuguese merchant replied that he could do no such thing without the intervention of the Jesuits. Angered by this disobedience, Hideyoshi pressed on with plans for bringing Japan's foreign trade under his own control. But he soon found that he could not force other countries to do business on terms laid down by him, and no doubt he held a grudge against both merchants and priests on that account.

CHAPTER XXII

THE INVASION OF KOREA

1. *The First Steps*

THE ORDER to attack Korea was issued on April 24, 1592. It set in motion the spearhead of an invading force of close on 200,000 men, while a reserve of about 100,000 was stationed in the vicinity of Nagoya, in Hizen province, where Hideyoshi had his headquarters.

Preparations had been made on a scale commensurate to the gigantic military effort which he contemplated. The continuous warfare of the past century, and particularly of the five decades after the rise of Nobunaga, had given military leaders much experience in mobilizing, supplying, and transporting great bodies of men and proportionate quantities of equipment and provisions. New methods of fighting and new weapons had added to the needs of an army in the field, which as late as Yoshimitsu's day, after two invasions and fifty years of civil war, had been relatively simple. No change of importance had taken place until the rise of Nobunaga and the extended use of firearms.

Hideyoshi's organization of supplies for his campaigns was always carefully thought out and efficiently executed, as may be seen from his conduct of the expedition to Kyūshū and the preparation for the siege of Odawara, which no doubt provided valuable lessons to his staff officers.

The base at Nagoya was under construction from the early autumn of 1591. This was to be the General Headquarters of the whole army. A special issue of gold and silver coins was minted, and provisions for 480,000 men were made ready. Troops and weapons as well as transport and other services were furnished by all daimyos in proportion to their revenue. Ships and crews were requisitioned on a similar basis from maritime provinces, as were the implements and labour required for moving cargo. Plans were drawn up in great detail, and by all accounts the execution of those plans was a feat of organization equal if not superior to any contemporary military achievement in Europe.

An analysis of the composition of the invasion force, showing the names of the commanders and the numbers of men engaged, is given in the archives of the Mōri family. It is an authentic and reliable source, which may be summarized as follows:

The main body consisted of seven contingents which were to form the first wave of attack. They were assembled on the island of Tsushima awaiting orders to embark. The commanders of the various units, together with their approximate strengths as listed by Mōri, are given in tabular form opposite.

I.	Konishi Yukinaga	7,000	
	Sō	5,000	
	Matsuura	3,000	
	Arima	2,000	
	Ōmura	1,000	
	Gotō	700	18,700
II.	Katō Kiyomasa	10,000	
	Nabeshima	12,000	
	Sagara	800	22,800
III.	Kuroda Nagamasa	5,000	
	Ōtomo Yoshimasa	6,000	11,000
IV.	Shimazu Yoshihiro	10,000	
	Mōri Yoshimasa	2,000	
	Others	2,000	14,000
V.	Fukushima	4,800	
	Toda	3,900	
	Chōsokabe	3,000	
	Ikoma	5,500	
	Ikushima	700	
	Hachisuka	7,200	25,000 (sic)
VI.	Kobayakawa	10,000	
	Tachibana, Tsukushi, and others	5,700	15,700
VII.	Mōri Terumoto	30,000	30,000
	TOTAL		137,200

In addition there were reserves on the islands of Tsushima and Iki: 10,000 men under Ukita on Tsushima, and 11,500 men under Hidekatsu and Hosokawa on Iki. Thus the grand total of the striking force was 158,700. Combatant forces stationed at Nagoya included contingents furnished by Ieyasu, Uyesugi, Gamō, and other important daimyos. Their total strength was of the order of 75,000.

It will be seen from the above figures (which are in substantial agreement with other accounts) that the total number of men mobilized by Hideyoshi was in round numbers 225,000. This does not include a naval force of about 9,000 men.

The order of battle required that the first seven contingents should invade Korea and occupy the whole country. This was to make the way clear for an attack upon China.

2. The Landing at Pusan and the Drive to Seoul

The signal to move was given at the end of April 1592, and the van, which consisted of the first three contingents, with a total strength of 52,500, began to embark from Tsushima, where they had been awaiting orders. The contingent commanded by Konishi Yukinaga, consisting of 18,000 men, reached Pusan on May 23 in 700 vessels which crowded the harbour. Konishi was followed two days later by Katō Kiyomasa with

22,000 men and Kuroda Nagamasa with 11,000; both these commanders were much chagrined at having been outstripped by Konishi.

Before following the movements of the invasion forces after their landing at Pusan, it is important for a student of this highly organized campaign to understand that it began with an amazing blunder. The Japanese naval force, which was supposed to convoy the ships carrying the contingents of Konishi and Katō, did not reach Nagoya from the Inland Sea (where it had assembled) until Konishi was on the point of leaving Tsushima. They did not sail from Nagoya until Konishi had been fighting on Korean soil for several days and the contingents of Katō, Kuroda, Kobayakawa, and others had already landed at or near Pusan and were moving inland.

Why the Korean navy failed to take advantage of this opportunity to destroy most of the invasion fleet is not clear. The weather appears to have been favourable and the enemy ships should have been easy to detect. It seems that the Korean government was still discussing policy and had issued no orders to Yi, the Korean Admiral. The Court supposed that the Japanese demand for a passage to China through Korean territory was an empty threat and certainly made no special preparations to prevent a landing. It was extremely fortunate for the Japanese army that Admiral Yi did not get among their transports.

The first three divisions to land captured the fortress at Pusan in a few hours. They broke a feeble defence by Korean soldiers, taking 8,000 heads and holding a few score prisoners. They then advanced day by day for about a month, encountering very little resistance. Konishi's contingent took the lead and moved with exceptional speed towards Seoul, marching about 275 miles in under twenty days. The second and third contingents followed close behind, and Seoul was occupied by Japanese forces on June 12, 1592. Konishi and Katō had competed for the capture of the city, but the decisive action was taken by Konishi, after Katō had tried to forestall him by racing along one of the three main roads leading north from Pusan.

By June 16 the third contingent from Pusan, 11,000 men under Kuroda, with some reinforcement from Shimazu's contingent, had reached Seoul by the western highroad, having as they advanced inflicted great loss and damage upon the Korean defenders. Almost at the same time Ukita, with the eighth contingent of 10,000 from Tsushima, arrived in Seoul and assumed the post of Commander-in-Chief.

Meanwhile the remainder of the invasion force (the fourth, fifth, sixth, and seventh contingents) had landed and were awaiting orders at Pusan, where the Japanese fleet was anchored. This naval force was strong in numbers, but it was no match for the Koreans. It was composed largely of craft manned by pirates who were under the control of daimyos of provinces bordering on the Inland Sea. Some larger vessels had been especially provided, but their commanders and crews had no experience of naval warfare and were useful only in transport work. They were not familiar with the tides and currents in the narrow channels south and west of the Korean peninsula and were therefore at a great disadvantage in action against Korean ships, which were better built and more skilfully handled. The Japanese navy, which was essential to the success of the invasion, was not able to obtain command of the sea and indeed was time after time roughly handled by Korean warships.

The Japanese fleet which brought the second part of the striking force to Pusan on June 7 was attacked by Admiral Yi as it lay at anchor off the island of Okpo, and it lost two or three score ships. Such attacks were repeated time after time by the Koreans. In one of them a Japanese squadron carrying several hundred fighting men was destroyed, and its commander, the pirate-admiral Kurushima, was driven to commit suicide. The failure of the navy placed the Japanese invasion force of 150,000 men in great danger, and its commanders were extremely fortunate to escape the grave results which might have followed a breach in their supply lines from Japan.

It was not for want of foreknowledge that the Japanese seamen suffered such reverses. The order of battle signed by Hideyoshi in April dwells on the importance of getting troops safely across the Korea Strait and enjoins the greatest precaution. "The loss of one man or one horse through bad judgment will be regarded as a grave offence."

The armies moving northward from the captured city of Seoul could not be expected to keep up the pace of Konishi's dash. When the later contingents (fourth to seventh) had landed at Pusan, they received their orders from Hideyoshi. Ukita, as Commander-in-Chief, was to remain at the headquarters in Seoul and hold the metropolitan province (Keikidō or Kyunggwai). Konishi was to take the northern border province (Heiandō or Pyönan), south of the Yalu; Katō the northern border province south of the Tumen; while the remaining five contingents under Kuroda, Shimazu, Fukushima, Kobayakawa, and Mōri were to occupy the central and southern provinces.

The Japanese army commanders in each province set about imposing upon the Korean inhabitants a new system of civil government akin to the feudal organization of Japan. They began a land survey and a redistribution of territories. Efforts were made to teach the Japanese language and Japanese customs to the inhabitants, and in general by good treatment and conciliatory propaganda to persuade them to consider themselves as part of Japan, an idea which was to be revived some centuries later when the military party in Japan conceived the notion of a Greater East Asia Co-Prosperity Sphere.

The King of Korea, with his princes and ministers, had fled before Konishi and Katō, leaving the city to be looted by its long-suffering citizens before the invaders arrived. The Korean general entrusted with the defence of Seoul made a feeble pretence of holding the line of the Han River, on which the capital stands, but he rapidly withdrew, and the King moved farther north to the city of Pyönyang, an early capital, on the Tadong River. It was then decided by the Korean commanders to hold a line along the Imjin River to the north, and before long a numerous force was massed along its course.

Meanwhile, the panic which had overtaken the Korean soldiers as Konishi and Katō pushed forward from the south had subsided, and in some areas was replaced by an aggressive spirit. In Kangwun province Shimazu's division had some hard fighting, and even in the metropolitan province Ukita's best troops took a beating from Korean levies under an enterprising general who was subsequently executed by royal command for cowardice falsely alleged by a jealous rival. This instance may be taken as a symbol of the state of affairs in Korea. The people showed courage and endurance; the government was weak and foolish. Yet despite their handicaps the Koreans were able from time to time to offer strong resistance to Japanese pressure. When Katō Kiyomasa, acting upon orders from Hideyoshi, passed into Hamgyung province in early July 1592, he was faced by some of the best fighting men in Korea. The province lay on the right flank of an army advancing north towards the Yalu, and it was therefore essential to hold it for the safety of Konishi's force. But Katō met with great difficulties and was obliged to struggle hard through the cold winter months of 1592–93. He did, however, at one point succeed in crossing the Tumen and entering Manchuria.

Konishi's task was easier. He had parted from Katō on July 9 and continued along the westernmost of the three highways to the north. He reached the Tadong River on July 15, and across the stream in front of him lay the city of Pyönyang, where the King had taken refuge. It was a strong city in a strong position. Konishi had his own contingent of about 18,000 men, and he was soon joined by the third contingent of 11,000 under Kuroda. The Tadong was a difficult river, but a blunder by the Korean defenders revealed the position of the fords. The Japanese crossed in great numbers and overwhelmed the defence of the city, which soon fell into Konishi's hands. Having seized the granaries and other stores, he sat down with Kuroda to await further orders from the high command. The King fled north to Wiju, on the left bank of the Yalu, and from there he sent messengers to China begging for assistance.

Fortune had not so far favoured the Korean arms, but the passage of Japanese armies had encouraged the growth of a resistance movement which by now was gathering momentum. The regular forces were led by miserable officers and were almost useless, but the farmers showed a strong fighting spirit in defence of their fields and their crops. In most provinces they began to harass the Japanese forces by determined guerrilla tactics, cutting off small detachments and keeping the main bodies on the alert by their rapid movements. In open country almost everywhere the Japanese were now on the defensive, and on one occasion at least they failed in an attack upon a Korean fort defended by local levies, although they outnumbered the garrison.

While the troops under Kuroda, Hosokawa, and Mōri were suffering reverses or at best holding their own against Korean irregulars, the Japanese generals in the north—Konishi in particular—were awaiting an order to advance into China. The King of Korea had sent repeated appeals for help to the Chinese government, until at last a Chinese force was sent to drive the Japanese back from Pyŏnyang. It was trapped and cut to pieces by the Japanese defenders, thanks to whom the complacent Chinese military authorities learned a useful lesson: they now saw that they must prepare for a serious military effort on a large scale; and orders were issued to equip and mobilize a formidable host. It is doubtful whether Hideyoshi had anticipated such a strong reaction from the Chinese, but Konishi evidently foresaw serious trouble. The Chinese, in order to test the temper of the Japanese command, sent a high officer to negotiate a peace or a truce with him, and after a brief meeting before the Japanese lines, it was agreed that the Chinese envoy should return to Peking to discuss terms while the two armies observed an armistice for fifty days.

Konishi no doubt welcomed a standstill, since he was anxious about his rear and his right flank, especially in view of reports coming in from the south telling him of Japanese naval disasters and of the Korean resistance movement, which was now developing offensive tactics in the southern provinces. The news of naval defeats was especially alarming, since if supplies from Japan were cut off, the Japanese armies would be forced to live on the country. Korean guerrilla attacks would then make it very difficult for the Japanese to depend upon Korean fields and granaries for food. Yet Konishi's appeals for supplies to the base at Nagoya were neglected.

Meanwhile the guerrilla bands were coalescing into disciplined forces under experienced commanders at a time when some of the Japanese contingents were beginning to show a loss of martial spirit. Letters sent home from the battlefront hint that many of the warriors were tiring of the dangers and discomforts of a campaigner's life, harassed as they were by a shortage of supplies, by sickness (due, they thought, to Korean water), and by the tensions of guerrilla fighting. The loss of strength from all causes was said to have reached one-third of the total by the beginning of 1593.

It was at this time that, the armistice having expired, a new Chinese army crossed the Yalu and marched on to Pyŏnyang, reaching the city early in February. Konishi with only about 20,000 troops stood up to the attack of a far stronger force (over 50,000 at the lowest estimate); but at last he had to withdraw along a prepared line of strong-points on the road to Seoul. His withdrawal obliged Katō Kiyomasa to follow suit, by fighting his way towards Konishi's columns. The next stage was of necessity a concentration of all available Japanese troops for the defence of Seoul against the Chinese, who had the advantage of some effective artillery pieces and a strong cavalry division.

Seoul was stubbornly defended by Katō and Konishi. They not only withstood a great Chinese army, but even counterattacked and put it to flight in a fierce action outside the city. Katō and Konishi were aware, however, that this energy in attack could not be long sustained. They suggested a meeting to discuss peace, and they agreed to the Chinese terms, which required them to evacuate Seoul. The Japanese forces moved south on May 9, 1593—almost a year after their landing at Pusan. One valiant Japanese officer said of the struggle on the outskirts of Seoul in the Han River bed that this river was more dreadful than the River of Hell ("sanzu no kawa").

The retreating Japanese were not seriously pursued by the Chinese, who soon returned to China, leaving only a small garrison to protect the King in Seoul. In his discussion with the Chinese emissary She Wei-ching, Konishi had agreed to three conditions laid down by the Chinese government, of which the substance was that Hideyoshi should be named King of Japan by the Emperor of China, that peace would then follow between the two countries, and that Korea was not a party to this agreement.

Hideyoshi gave a firm reply to the Ming envoys who arrived in Nagoya in June with these proposals. The Emperor was to send a daughter to become an Imperial Consort in Japan; the licensed trade between the two countries was to be resumed, by private as well as by national vessels; and this agreement was to be confirmed on oath by ministers of the two states. A further set of conditions provided that upon conclusion of a peace agreement between Japan and China the four northern provinces and the capital of Korea should be returned to the King; Korean princes should be sent to Japan as hostages; and the high officers of state in Korea should swear that Korea would never rebel against Japan. These conditions of course implied that the southern provinces should belong to Japan.

For the ruler of a country whose armies had been hurriedly withdrawn to avoid defeat Hideyoshi displayed a superb assurance. But he could not depend upon the support of all his generals. There was a split among the army leaders, Konishi and his party being against Hideyoshi's demands while Katō supported them. The internal situation was therefore not without danger. It might even be said that Hideyoshi's unification policy was at stake, since although men like Konishi and Ishida Mitsunari stood for feudal discipline, some of the more powerful daimyos, including Ieyasu, Shimazu, Date, and Mōri, wanted to develop within their domains a high degree of independence which Hideyoshi was not willing to accord.

However, there was no immediate clash, for Konishi had cleverly persuaded the Chinese negotiator Shên to come to Japan with a mission from China whose leaders were disposed to accept conditions which Konishi and She had agreed upon beforehand.

After numerous misunderstandings and delays an embassy from China was escorted from Pusan by Konishi and reached Kyoto in December 1596. There they were to perform the ceremony of investiture by which Hideyoshi would be made King of Japan and presented with a crown and royal robes. The members of the Chinese mission had no knowledge of the peace terms proposed by Hideyoshi, and when they read out the letter from the Chinese Court to the assembled company, Hideyoshi, who had been expecting a submissive and not a patronizing message, burst into a violent rage and abused the Ming envoys. Later in the day he told them that he would forthwith issue orders for a war against China.

It was then inevitable that the breach between Konishi and Katō should widen, one standing for a negotiated peace and the other for a renewal of offensive operations in Korea. Meanwhile Hideyoshi's own behavior was erratic and by all diplomatic standards improper. Having first insulted the Chinese ambassadors, he sent them parting presents, followed by a statement of his grievances carried by swift courier to overtake them on their way back to Korea.

While arguments between the peace party and the war party continued, the remaining Japanese forces were gradually being withdrawn from Korea. All that was left was a strong rear guard concentrated in the Pusan area. But then on March 19, 1597, new orders were issued by Hideyoshi. He carried out his threat to attack China and mobilized a new invasion force of close upon 100,000 men, principally from Kyūshū and the western provinces. With the troops already in Korea the total was of the order of 150,000—about the size of the first invasion force of 1592.

All these were first-class fighting men, but there was little sign of the cheerful optimism that had inspired the invaders of 1592. Katō, Shimazu, Konishi—all had suffered in bitter conflicts and the outlook was grim. The Koreans had taken up Hideyoshi's challenge. In response to their appeal a new Chinese army had crossed the Yalu and in January 1598 was making its way south from Seoul, incorporating additions of Korean and Chinese troops as it advanced. Following in reverse the road taken by Katō Kiyomasa in 1592, this army arrived before the position now held by Kiyomasa at Yolsan, a strategically situated coast town known to the Japanese as Urusan. Here there took place one of the severest battles of the war.

The Japanese garrison was closely besieged and on the point of starvation when relief came from Kuroda and other commanders, who not only raised the siege but forced the Chinese to a hurried retreat.

But in the spring the Chinese returned to the attack in such force that Konishi saw no hope of holding an extended front and advised a concentration before Pusan. Hideyoshi—in one of those rages that were becoming frequent—recalled more than half of the army and left the defence to about 60,000 men, mostly Satsuma warriors under Shimazu commanders. They were indomitable fighters and they withstood repeated onslaughts throughout the summer of 1598. By the end of October they had turned the tables on the Chinese and Korean forces, slaughtering them by the thousand. They are said to have taken 38,000 heads,[1] and shortly after this Konishi administered what proved to be the coup de grâce to the Chinese. Very soon a standstill agreement was reached, facilitated no doubt by the news of Hideyoshi's death (on September 18), which came to the Japanese in Korea during the last days of October.

The evacuation was soon completed; Konishi, together with Sō Yoshitomo (the daimyo of Tsushima, who was trusted by the Koreans), had earlier reopened peace talks with the Chinese command. These were not pursued after the Chinese army had returned home, but discussions were now opened with the Koreans, on the initiative of Sō.

This mild climax to an enterprise conceived and commenced on a heroic scale provokes many questions. Why did Hideyoshi undertake it? What was his true purpose? Why did he fail? These problems must be examined in the light of his political situation at the end of the Odawara campaign in 1590, and also in the light of his character as an individual.

But before turning to these matters it is convenient to point out here a serious defect in Hideyoshi's planning, which perhaps lost him the war and certainly made it more costly, namely, the failure to provide a strong naval force. We have seen that in the order of battle the importance of naval protection of transport was recognized; but no care had been taken to ensure the efficiency of Japanese warships and their commanders.

It was not until after severe defeats at the hands of the Korean Admiral Yi that steps were taken to improve the Japanese navy. The Koreans' advantage was due to the superior design of their ships, but also to skilful handling of their fleets as a whole, which included a planned use of artillery. It was impossible for the Japanese to send a striking force direct by sea to reinforce Konishi in Pyönyang or on the Yalu, and the movement of supplies from Japan to Pusan was hazardous.

Consequently after the first withdrawal from Korea the Japanese command began to pay attention to the development of naval strength, and the discipline of the pirate-admirals' squadrons was improved to

[1] Visitors to Kyoto used to be shown the Mimizuka or Ear Tomb, which contained, it was said, the ears of those 38,000, sliced off, suitably pickled, and sent to Kyoto as evidence of victory.

such a degree that they defeated a strong Korean fleet in 1597. Part of the credit for this victory should go to the Korean Admiral, who was frequently drunk, and part to Konishi, who at this time was holding a naval command. These engagements showed the Japanese leaders the importance of sea power, and the lesson was driven home when Admiral Yi returned to command of the Korean fleet, reorganized it, and threatened the security of Japanese land forces which were making their way south. After these experiences the Japanese military leaders paid attention to building and maintaining a naval force. One of their urgent requirements in the seventeenth century was a supply of good sea-going vessels, well armed. This fact is a key to Japanese foreign policy for some time after 1600.

3. Hideyoshi's Political Situation after 1590

Although Hideyoshi's power of organization was exceptional, there was a flaw in the execution of his policy of unification. It is not difficult for a powerful ruler with almost unlimited force at his command to produce an appearance of unity, and this was achieved by Hideyoshi in so far as he had brought his warlords to obedience and imposed his will upon the population in general. But his success in forcing an agrarian society into a single pattern by means of the land registration and the census and the Sword Hunt was obtained at the cost of much discontent in the country. The small landowners of the ji-samurai class—the very class which had furnished the strength of Nobunaga—found themselves deprived of much, sometimes all, of their land by the new registration policy, and formed a new class of masterless warriors or vagrants (rōnin) generally obliged to take service in a castle town under a chieftain who gave them a stipend. The well-to-do peasants also resented the reduction of their holdings and the ruthless collection of tax. They also formed a class of discontented people, numerous but powerless. Nor was every daimyo satisfied with his position.

This situation must have seemed critical to Hideyoshi's advisers, though they do not appear to have devised any remedy. But it is suggested that Hideyoshi's decision to invade Korea with an immense force was inspired by the need of some great undertaking to distract attention from popular grievances, use all available manpower, and stimulate production. This is no doubt too simple an explanation of a complex phenomenon; but it is true that the end of the civil wars had caused unemployment and distress in many trades and had in particular deprived the rich merchants and army contractors (goyō-shōnin) of much profitable business. Some Japanese historians are of opinion that these people played an important part in stimulating overseas adventure. They were thought of as an up-to-date version of the Wakō, the Japanese "free traders" of the fifteenth century. This is no doubt true of many contractors, but not of all, for several leading merchants of Sakai and

Hakata opposed the conquest of foreign territory. They thought that legitimate trade was more lucrative, and they were not averse to a little pressure short of war to open markets on the continent or in the islands to the south—the Philippines and the East Indies, for example. A resumption of regular trade was certainly one of the aims of the projected attack upon China.

But it must be remembered that years before 1590 Hideyoshi had often said (and so had Nobunaga before him) that he meant to subdue China when he had settled domestic affairs to his own satisfaction. On such occasions he had given no hint of any purpose other than the satisfaction of his own pride and ambition. He belonged to the class of great conquerors—like Tamerlaine or Jinghis Khan—but he did not understand that Japan could not match the resources of a great continental power like China. He was too accustomed to victories at home.

CHAPTER XXIII

HIDEYOSHI'S LAST YEARS

1. *Domestic Affairs*

THE SO-CALLED war upon Korea was in fact the first phase in a war against China, and it ended in defeat. When in his rage Hideyoshi ordered a renewed attack in 1597 he must surely have been suffering a disturbance of the mind. His hasty conduct was in striking contrast to the calm and patient efficiency which he had hitherto displayed in matters of vital importance, such as his handling of the Kyūshū campaign against Shimazu and his dealings with the Kantō warlords. The history of his last years seems to confirm this supposition.

Some of his letters from Nagoya to his mother and his wife reveal an immense self-confidence. In a letter of tender enquiry about his aged mother's health, dated July 14, 1592, he tells her that Seoul will soon fall, and that by the autumn he will be able to receive her presents in the capital of China. In the same vein and by the same opportunity he wrote to his wife, adding that he was thinking of crossing over to Korea himself, and taking command there of the expedition to China. This news alarmed the members of his family then in Kyoto, who begged the Court to restrain him. The Emperor Go-Yōzei accordingly sent a gentle rebuke to Nagoya. This was supported by the great generals, notably Tokugawa Ieyasu and Maeda Toshiiye, who thought that "the Taikō must have been possessed by a fox," a proverbial expression for erratic behaviour. He gave way and postponed his journey to Korea until the following spring so as to avoid winter storms at sea. Anxious about his mother's health, he decided to pay a rapid visit to Ōsaka, and on August 30 he crossed to Shimonoseki and hastened eastward. But on that very day his mother had died, and when he reached Ōsaka he is said to have fainted with grief on learning the news. His affection for his mother was one of his strongest feelings. When she was ill in 1588, this great despot humbly approached the heavenly powers, begging the divinities worshipped at the great shrines to spare her "for three years, or two years, or if that is not to be then only for thirty days."

An interesting letter written at the end of 1592 is addressed to Maeda Geni, who had remained in Kyotō in charge of domestic affairs under Hidetsugu. Hideyoshi orders Maeda to hurry to Nagoya for consultation about certain details of construction of the Fushimi palace, apparently anxious for its stability in view of the frequency of earthquakes by which the Home Provinces and the eastern seaboard had lately been plagued. There can be little doubt that Hideyoshi (then under sixty) was contemplating a life of retirement after the conquest of China.

For some time he had been giving much thought to the question of succession, since his only son, Tsurumatsu, had died in infancy two years before, and he saw little likelihood of another child. He had been obliged, therefore, though with misgiving, to choose his nephew Hidetsugu as his heir, and early in 1592 he installed Hidetsugu in the Jūrakudai. While Hideyoshi was occupied with foreign affairs, Hidetsugu as Regent took advantage of his absence in Nagoya to lead a disreputable life; and his reputation grew progressively worse. Hideyoshi was aware of this and said playfully that he wished he could appoint one of his favourite nieces to the highest office.

Although early in 1592 he had handed over the Jūrakudai to Hidetsugu, whom he expected to succeed him, in September 1593 while he was in Nagoya his mistress Yodogimi (then in Ōsaka) gave birth to a son, who was called Hiroi and later given the name of Hideyori. He had always intended that his heir should live in the castle at Ōsaka, and this was his main reason for building at Fushimi, some distance from the centre of Kyoto. He wanted his new palace to be solid without and elegant within, and while it was being built he remarked that he wished his apartments and their decoration to be "in a style pleasing to Rikyū." This was an odd statement, since Rikyū, his adviser on aesthetic matters, had been forced by Hideyoshi to commit suicide almost a year before. Now Hideyoshi regretted his own senseless cruelty, an intemperate act of which he would not have been guilty in his prime.

On February 10, 1593, while still at Nagoya, he writes to members of his family, for instance to his elder sister Tomo's husband, expressing an almost grandmotherly concern for their health, recommending baths at hot springs and a carefree life. Shortly after this—in April—to vary the monotony of life at headquarters while awaiting developments in Korea, he took an interest in Nō plays and dances, receiving instruction from an actor who had been invited to Nagoya for the New Year festivities. Hideyoshi worked hard, and in a letter to his wife he tells her that he has learned by heart ten plays. In another note he says that he will cross over to Korea in the course of the month (April?). Envoys from China have come to ask pardon and are at Pusan waiting for a fair wind.

All this time he was turning over in his mind the question of adoption, since he was not satisfied with Hidetsugu. He had also adopted Hidetoshi, another nephew.[1] Hideyoshi's wife took little interest in this

---

[1] Hideyoshi's family tree, so far as it is known, is as follows:

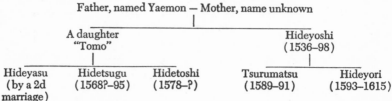

Father, named Yaemon — Mother, name unknown

A daughter "Tomo"   Hideyoshi (1536–98)

Hideyasu (by a 2d marriage)   Hidetsugu (1568?–95)   Hidetoshi (1578–?)   Tsurumatsu (1589–91)   Hideyori (1593–1615)

young man and was severely rebuked by Hideyoshi on that account in a letter saying: "You are childless. You should treat him as your child." Hidetoshi was sent for and arrived at Nagoya in the spring of 1593, where he made a good impression on the Taikō, who said that upon his own retirement the young man would make an excellent Deputy.

But very soon after this the picture changes, for Hideyoshi writes to his wife at the end of June telling her that the envoys from the Ming Court have arrived and that he has laid down conditions of peace. He writes as if he were a victor imposing terms on a vanquished enemy and says that if the Chinese will carry out their promises he will forgive them and return home in triumph. This, it will be recalled, was after Konishi had been driven out of Pyönyang and a disastrous defeat had been averted by Kobayakawa's skill.

Later in the year he writes of good news that has reached him of the birth to Yodogimi of a son, the unexpected "Hiroi," "the foundling," who has come to replace the lost Tsurumatsu. He affects not to be delighted.[2] He cannot leave Nagoya yet, as there is still work to do; but he expects to reach Ōsaka by the end of October. He writes in similar terms to "Fuku," the mother of Hideiye and the wife of his favourite general Ukita. The messenger, he adds, will describe the great Nō performance which had been arranged for the entertainment of the Ming ambassadors.

Returning to Ōsaka, he busied himself in pressing on the completion of the Fushimi palace and moving between Kyoto and Ōsaka castle, where Yodogimi was lodged. His jealous love of the infant Hideyori was extreme. He lavished passionate kisses on him and decreed that nobody but himself should touch the child's lips. This inordinate private affection was in startling contrast to his public behaviour.

As a general rule he had always been careful to avoid the sacrifice of men in battle if he could attain his ends by patience; but as he grew to supreme power his despotism led him to extremes of cruelty. His treatment of forced labour used on his unending building of fortresses and palaces was ruthless enough, although probably not unusual by the standard of the times; but in his later years his pursuit of vengeance upon those who displeased him was unspeakably harsh, especially when his family affairs were concerned. He was disappointed in his relatives and in the sons whom he adopted. Hidenaga, his step-brother, served him well, but died at the age of fifty. His nephew Hideyasu died young, and Hidetsugu, who had shown early promise and was considered as his heir after the death of Tsurumatsu, caused him anxiety. Imparting advice to this young man before his appointment as Regent, Hideyoshi had

---

[2] To avoid hubris. He does not want to tempt the Gods to destroy what he most cherishes. For the same reason the name Hiroi is a pretence that the child is not really his, but just found as it were by accident; Tsurumatsu had similarly been named at birth "Sute," which means "thrown away" or "abandoned."

written: "You should follow my example, except in three things—addiction to tea, a love of falconry, and a craze for women."

It seems that the pleasures of high office went to Hidetsugu's head. He lived a vicious life, performed no useful function, and was so brutal that he was known as Sasshō Kampaku, the Murdering Regent. The Jesuit missionaries knew him well, for he was by way of being friendly to the Christians; but they were obliged to admit that he had one serious fault—he liked killing people.[3] He is said to have had concubines by the dozen and to have sunk deep in dissipation, and to have plotted the capture of Ōsaka castle by corrupting its guardians.

At first Hideyoshi paid no attention to these scandalous tales, but he became alarmed when the situation in Korea brought into the open a serious division of opinion among the leading daimyos. As we have seen, there was a forward party standing for a renewed offensive and a moderate party in favour of diplomatic negotiation. An open breach between these two factions or groups would endanger the whole structure of government which Hideyoshi had erected on the foundation laid by Nobunaga. He therefore took action against Hidetsugu in August 1595, banishing him to Kōyasan and sending after him an order to commit suicide.

But this punishment was not enough in Hideyoshi's view. He was fanatically determined to destroy all possible claimants to the office of Regent in succession to Hidetsugu. Accordingly he pursued the members of Hidetsugu's household with a cruelty which by any standard must be called barbarous. Hidetsugu's three small children and more than thirty women in his service were dragged the length of the city and stabbed to death in front of a gibbet upon which Hidetsugu's head was exposed. That night at street corners there appeared broadsides warning the house of Toyotomi of the doom, the evil karma, that Hideyoshi's crime would bring to its members. On the following day several citizens were arrested for an offence of this kind and subjected to lingering torture for three days until they died. The Jūrakudai and other places where Hidetsugu had lived were destroyed.

Immediately after these events, Hideyoshi summoned the great barons—Tokugawa, Maeda, Mōri, and others—together with lesser daimyos like Ishida Mitsunari, and required them to subscribe to a written oath that they would give full support to Hideyori and would in all matters obey the laws and orders of the Taikō. This was in 1595 and the procedure was repeated in 1596, when Hideyori at the age of three was installed as Regent.

[3] This was the language used by Frois, who besides being a master of laudatory epithets seems to have had a gift of understatement when the sins of great personages were concerned. He said of Hidetsugu that "he had one weakness, namely a passionate delight in killing."

Reflecting upon these and similar events at this juncture, it is hard to suppress a feeling that Hideyoshi was losing his judgment. His affection for Hideyori had reached the point of mania. He could not bear the thought that the great feudatories might not submit to his son. It was no doubt some fear of this kind that caused his violent rage against Hidetsugu and the murder of Hidetsugu's children. It was presumably at his order that Hidetsugu's son and heir, an innocent child, was buried at the execution ground deep under the corpses of a score of other victims, and covered by a great mound. Only a morbid fear could explain such inhuman precautions.

These tragic events took place at a time when he was meeting with disappointment in other directions. His contemptuous attitude towards the ambassador of the Ming Emperor, which had led him into the blunder of a second invasion of Korea, served only to make him a little ridiculous in Chinese eyes. His brave men in Korea were driven to the sea, and in June 1596 a missive from the Chinese Court taunted him with wasting the few years that remained to him. He was then over sixty.

There was truth in the Chinese gibe, for at the end of the year 1595 he had been taken ill, though it must be admitted that he seems to have regained his spirits when he ordered the second invasion. This was a period in his life when he was much given to entertainments such as flower-viewing excursions on a grand scale. He took particular pleasure in the precincts of the Daigoji (still beautiful in modern times), where he planted many varieties of flowering cherry. In April of 1598 he gave a great party there. It was very exclusive, unlike the popular parties of his early days: a wide area was shut off and surrounded by armed men, so that the guests should not be disturbed by intruding citizens.

This was his last great entertainment. A screen painting of the period depicts him walking with uncertain steps, accompanied by richly dressed ladies, as he enjoys for the last time the natural and the artificial beauties surrounding him. In June 1598 he was taken ill again and grew weaker day by day. As he lay in bed in his Fushimi palace he suffered occasional fits of delirium. Once he ordered some of his attendants to be beaten to death, saying that this was the way to get rid of bad people. After that he rallied a little, and went out on the battlements to see the work in hand. On July 20 he wrote a letter to a lady who has not been identified—possibly the wife of the general Ukita—in which he said: "This is ten thousand times more important than an ordinary letter. I am anxious about your illness and write for that reason. I have been unable to eat for fifteen days and am in distress. Yesterday I went out to see the building work, but I felt worse and am growing gradually weaker. Take good care of yourself, and as soon as you feel a little better come to see me. I am waiting for you."

Halfway through the month of August he saw that he could not last much longer and he began anxiously to turn over in his mind the future of his son and heir Hideyori. It was then that he decided to use the Five Elders (Go-Tairō) and Five Commissioners (Go-Bugyō), not as part of the administrative machine but for the purpose of ensuring the continuance and the stability of the Regency which he had founded. Ou August 15 the five great feudatories (Tokugawa, Maeda, Mōri, Uyesugi, and Ukita) met in Maeda's house and there exchanged written oaths by which they swore to be loyal to Hideyori as they were to Hideyoshi, to obey Hideyoshi's laws, and not to engage in plots and conflicts for their own private ends. After this a number of similar oaths were signed and exchanged between other individuals or groups of daimyos, so that by the end of August or early in September all the powerful leaders from Ieyasu downwards in rank had committed themselves to support the house of Toyotomi and its rule by Hideyori when he should come of age.

The testamentary commands which they promised to obey are recorded in a memorandum drawn up by Hideyoshi's physician. Its date is not certain, but it was probably not completed until just after Hideyoshi's death. It must have been put in hand at the end of August after Hideyoshi from his sickbed had announced his wishes to a company including the leading feudatories, his wife, Yodogimi, and other members of his household. Its terms are as follows:

*

1. Tokugawa Ieyasu is asked out of his wisdom and experience to be the young Hideyori's guardian, to treat him as a grandson, and should he think fit, to see to his appointment as Regent to succeed Hideyoshi himself. This task to be performed by the Council of Five Elders (Go-Tairō).
2. Maeda Toshiiye to be a guardian of the child and to provide him with suitable companions.
3. Tokugawa Ietada to assist his father Ieyasu and to spare him unnecessary labour.
4. Maeda Toshinaga to assist his father, Toshiiye, and later to be one of the Five Elders; to give advice without prejudice; and to be rewarded for these services by gifts (including a valuable tea jar) and a stipend of 100,000 koku.
5. Ukita (Hideyoshi's favorite general) to be counted upon for loyal service to Hideyori.
6. Uyesugi Kagekatsu and Mōri Terumoto to be kept informed and consulted.
7. The Tairō to punish any breach of the law, by whomever committed. Greatest respect must be paid to Hideyori, however much he may give offence.
8. The Tairō to supervise monetary transactions and to be ready to render an account to Hideyori when he comes of age.

9. No step to be taken without the approval of Ieyasu and Maeda Toshiiye.
10. Ieyasu to stay in Fushimi in general control. He may inspect any castle and must always have access to the keep.
11. Hideyori to reside at Ōsaka, and Toshiiye to be governor of the castle.

*

It was on this occasion that Hideyoshi rose painfully from his bed and flung his arms around Toshiiye, imploring him to take care of Hideyori. He was still so obsessed with the desire to bind the great feudatories that he repeated his request for assurances from them. On September 5 Ieyasu took an oath, followed a few days later by the Five Tairō, swearing that they would obey the Taikō's injunctions in every particular.[4] That evening—September 11—he gave them his last message. He begged them to do all they could for the upbringing of Hideyori. Again and again he said, "I implore the Five to do what I ask." He wrote this in a farewell in simple words, in the kana script. "I depend upon you for everything. I have no other thoughts to leave behind. It is sad to part from you" ("nagorioshiku sōrō").

From this time his condition suddenly grew worse. His mind wandered and he babbled not of green fields but of the distribution of fiefs. He lingered for a few days and died on September 18 in his sixty-third year.

2. Hideyoshi's Character

It is usually agreed that Hideyoshi is the greatest man in the history of Japan. Yet while opinion on his military and political achievement is almost unanimous, there are various readings of his character. Judged by the written record of his life, he was without doubt a man of frank and open temperament, clever, ingenious, shrewd but without guile. He enjoyed friendly relations with people of all ranks. Affable and familiar, he was indeed impatient of social distinctions and tiresome etiquette. He was of an affectionate nature, with a strong feeling of duty to his family and his friends.

His gifts as a soldier were eminent. He combined patience with a power of rapid decision in crucial situations. In his early days he said that he disliked killing and wounding, and it is true that he would never waste the lives of his soldiers if he could find other ways of gaining the object. Nor did he as a rule slaughter his defeated enemies, for he was free from the cold hatred which led Nobunaga to such cruel revenge.

---

[4] Ieyasu's oath was sworn to the Five Commissioners (Bugyō), who were of lower rank than the Tairō. They were: Maeda Geni, Asano, Mashida, Ishida, and Natsuka. They in turn swore to the Five Tairō so that the whole government was committed.

He planned his campaigns with care and foresight, and he applied the same gifts to administrative problems. His experience of life first as a country lad of humble origin and then as a minor officer in Nobunaga's army was of great value to him in his maturity, for he knew hardship and understood the feelings of the peasantry. By the standard of his times he was a gifted and successful ruler until the last few years of his life, when he seems to have lost virtue. The contrast between his skilful and prudent conduct at the height of his powers and the excesses of his last years leads one to suspect that he was suffering from some mental deterioration. His pride and ambition had become insatiable after his successes in Kyūshū and the Kantō. His monster projects in building and entertainments betrayed a touch of mania. His domestic troubles were not of a kind to yield to forcible solution, and caused him constant distress. He lost his infant son Tsurumatsu, his wife was barren, and his relations with women, other than his casual bedfellows, afforded him perhaps more anxiety than pleasure. He wanted but did not inspire affection.

His frequent rages, which led him into errors of judgment, were so unlike his usual calm in difficult situations that they came near to madness. His treatment of Sen no Rikyū was unpardonable and sprang from a burst of ungoverned temper. His treatment of Hidetsugu's family was as insane as Hidetsugu's conduct. It was a mad vengeance for mad crimes. One begins to wonder whether there was an unfortunate strain in Hideyoshi's parentage, transmitted perhaps by his sister to her sons Hidetsugu and Hidetoshi, who were to say the least unbalanced. Her brother Hideyoshi was a genius who showed signs of derangement as his health failed.

A study of the character of men like Hideyoshi must raise in a reader's mind the question of their guilt, for their lives were stained by cruelty. They must be judged by the standards of the historian's own time, since he cannot know with certainty the thoughts and feelings of people in antiquity. He can say in a general way that cruelty was prevalent in mediaeval society everywhere, West or East, and that human life was less prized than it is today. He is bound to observe that the fiendish repertory of torture differs only in slight particulars between Japan and China on the one hand and European countries on the other; and it is doubtful whether at the beginning of the seventeenth century (which may be taken as the end of the middle ages) there was in Europe any true relaxation of the barbarous practices of earlier times. In England and Scotland torture was still common, chiefly as a means of extracting evidence but also, despite some ordinances against it, as punishment for criminal and political offences.

In mediaeval Japan the law was silent on such matters, for its rulers were despots whom no tribunal could control or even condemn. It is indeed probably vain to attempt comparison between mediaeval Japan and mediaeval Europe in matters of conscience, since they are separated by great differences of tradition, both secular and religious. Perhaps more is to be learned by looking for analogies not in mediaeval society but in the Roman Empire (after Augustus) during the first century of the Christian era.

The gap in time between the two societies is, of course, immense; but they are both essentially military societies, and in some material respects Rome was more advanced than mediaeval Japan; so that a comparison between them is not without point. There are interesting resemblances in both political forms and public behaviour. The ruler of the Roman Empire was a general, an Imperator; the ruler of Japan was a commander-in-chief, a Shōgun; and they exercised similar powers. Both were despots, both governed by terror. In their oppressive rule both went to extremes of cruelty, resorting constantly to private assassination, to mass murder, and to tortures of unspeakable atrocity. Yet an unprejudiced student is bound to admit that Hideyoshi and Nobunaga before him, brutal and ruthless as they often were, could not match the infamies of Tiberius, Caligula, and Nero. Nobunaga and Hideyoshi were greedy and almost illiterate. The Caesars of the Julian house were of noble birth and well educated, yet most of them were unable to control their cruel passions. They had not even the minimal excuse of Nobunaga and Hideyoshi, who were of modest origin and driven by ambition. And it should be remembered that Hideyoshi, by contrast with Nobunaga, was until his last years not addicted to slaughter for its own sake, and was inclined to be patient with offenders.

3. Foreign Affairs

(a) Relations with Portugal and Spain

Readers of Asian history sometimes derive amusement from the traditional Chinese view that China was the centre of the civilized world and all other countries its tributaries. But the ineffable assumption of Rome that for purposes of conquest, trade, and evangelism Portugal and Spain could divide the world between them is no less entertaining.

Soon after Albuquerque had reached the Moluccas (1512) Portuguese ships began to sail in Chinese waters and before long developed an important trade with China. The Pope had granted to Portugal a monopoly of maritime trade east of the Red Sea and as far as seventeen degrees east of the Moluccas. This monopoly of trade carried with it a monopoly of Christian propaganda, since none but missionaries approved by the Portuguese could find passage in their ships. Consequently for half a century after the discovery of Japan by Portuguese mariners in 1542, only Jesuits preached in Japan and only Portuguese ships traded to Japanese ports.

This Portuguese monopoly, derived from a special relation between the Society of Jesus and the Portuguese state, was confirmed after 1580, when Spain and Portugal were united under the rule of Philip II. It was observed, though only reluctantly, by the Spanish traders and the Christian missionaries in Manila, who were at that time the only European people who could have competed with the Portuguese in eastern Asia. The monopoly of missionary work in Japan held by the Society of Jesus was very specific, for it was granted by Pope Gregory XIII in 1585. It was, however, bitterly resented by the members of other orders—Franciscans, Dominicans, and Augustinians—who were then preaching the gospel in the Philippines. They were well informed of the successes of the Jesuits in Japan and desperately anxious to gather a harvest in that field, partly out of jealousy and partly out of a conviction that they could repair the damage that had been done by the Jesuits, whose errors they chose to regard as the true cause of Hideyoshi's persecution in 1587.

The Spanish traders in the Philippines also resented the Portuguese hold on trade with Japan, which was a state monopoly in the sense that the voyages of Portuguese ships from Lisbon to Japan were licensed by the Portuguese government. This was a very lucrative trade, since it was the only means by which the Japanese could obtain in quantity the Chinese articles—notably gold, raw silk, and silk textiles—which were deemed essential to their economy.

The ease with which the Portuguese made their great profits naturally stimulated Japanese merchants to look for a share, either by partnership with foreigners or by finding other markets. It is true that Japanese ships could trade at their own risk with China, but their voyages were not licensed by the Chinese nor could they be sure of freedom from piratical attacks, which the armed Portuguese merchantmen could repulse with ease. Consequently they turned their attention to Southeast Asia, and voyaged in waters once familiar to the Wakō, the privateers of the fifteenth century. From Malaya and Indonesia they extended their range to Luzon, where they traded with the native inhabitants as early as 1567, that is to say two or three years before the Spanish colony there was founded. There were small settlements of Japanese at several points along the coast, and in 1583 there was a sea fight between Spanish and Japanese ships at the mouth of the Kagayan River. By that time certain Sakai merchants were interested in the Manila trade, among them being Konishi Ryūsa, Yukinaga's father, and the less respectable Harada Kiuyemon with his assistant Harada Magoshichirō.

It was the Manila trade which gradually broke the Portuguese monopoly of trade with Japan. The Spanish sea captains and the Spanish officials were dissatisfied with their share of Asian commerce, since they were in effect limited to the regular voyages between Manila and Acapulco and some dealings with Macao. There had already been occasional contact between the Spanish sea captains and the government of the Philippines and the Japanese authorities. In 1584 a Spanish galleon sailing from Manila for Macao was driven by stress of weather to take shelter in the harbour of Hirado. At that time the port of Hirado was losing its trade to Nagasaki, where the Jesuits were firmly established and where Portuguese ships entered regularly.

The daimyo of Hirado, Matsuura Shigenobu, resented the Portuguese monopoly. He welcomed the Spanish ship, offered facilities for trade between Manila and his own fief, and said that he would welcome missionaries who were not Jesuits. But at this time there was ill-feeling against the Japanese among the Spanish residents in Luzon, because certain Japanese adventurers had been behind a rising of native tribesmen near Manila. The Japanese traders who travelled between Japan and the Islands naturally fell under suspicion—among them Harada Kiuyemon and Magoshichirō. These men together with one Hasegawa, an intriguing soldier who had Hideyoshi's ear, planned an attack on Manila by a force of several thousand men. But Hideyoshi would not allow the use of such numbers while he was organizing the invasion of Korea, and nothing came of their designs.

In 1591 Hideyoshi sent by the hand of Harada to the Spanish Governor Gomez Perez de Marinas at Manila a vainglorious letter, in which Hideyoshi said that after conquering Korea and China he would turn his attention to the Philippine Islands. He advised the Governor to submit and send tribute. In response to this threat Marinas sent a small mission, headed by a Franciscan, Father Juan Cobos, carrying a temporizing reply. Cobos made his way to Hirado, where Hideyoshi was occupied in supervising the Korean campaign, but his message gave no satisfaction. At Harada's suggestion a larger mission left Manila for Japan in May 1593. It was led by Father Pedro Baptista and included three other Franciscans. By assuming the function of official envoys, they had disingenuously overcome the ban on the entry of Christian missionaries. The letter of the Governor which they carried was noncommittal. It said that he must transmit Hideyoshi's letter to the King of Spain and that he was anxious to open trade with Japan.

The four Franciscans thereupon offered to remain as hostages and asked for permission to reside and preach in the Home Provinces. This was granted and they began to preach and to build, quite undeterred by the Papal brief of 1585. They soon had a church in Kyoto and a convent in Ōsaka and were joined by a few more Franciscans. They tried, though without success, to establish themselves in Nagasaki. There were naturally frequent and bitter disputes between the two orders. The anger of the Jesuits was easy to account for, since they were under Hideyoshi's ban and tolerated only in Nagasaki, while the Franciscans were breaking his laws at every turn. The patient tact of the Jesuits was outrivalled by the reckless ardour of the Franciscans.

Hideyoshi took no steps against the Franciscans, despite their flagrant breaches of his law, until 1596, which was after the first with-drawal from Korea. He might not have interfered even then, since he could easily rid the country of missionaries at a moment's notice; but the question of relations with Spain was brought to his mind by a strange incident, the wreck on the coast of Tosa of a galleon, the *San Felipe*, on its way from Manila to Acapulco.

There was a great deal of trouble over the treatment of the vessel and its extremely valuable cargo. The full story is long and complicated, but here it is sufficient to say that by some sharp practice the ship was broken up and the cargo confiscated to the great profit of the lord of Tosa and of Hideyoshi himself. The Spanish captain (or the pilot) went to Ōsaka to seek redress from Hideyoshi, and according to one story he was indiscreet enough to use threatening language, boasting that the long arm of the King of Spain would soon reach Japan, where the Chris-tians would rise in his favour. But there is no valid evidence to support this story, which seems to have originated in a subsequent quarrel be-tween the Jesuits and the Franciscans, each intent on slandering the other in an endeavour to explain Hideyoshi's sudden and vicious punish-ment of the Christian missions.

In January 1597 Hideyoshi issued an order for the execution of Baptista with six other Franciscans and nineteen Japanese followers. He sentenced them to torture and death in very plain terms. They were then in Kyoto, and by his orders, having first been mutilated, they were led in a pitiful cavalcade to city after city, to be shown as a warning to the people. They reached Nagasaki in February and there were cruci-fied upside down as common criminals.

It is difficult to understand why Hideyoshi went to such extremes, for his action had been far less violent in 1587, when he expelled the Jesuits but made no attempt to punish them. The story of the indiscreet Spanish captain may be dismissed as a fiction, if only on the ground that Hideyoshi was already well aware of the connexion between the sacred and the secular power in Spain and Portugal. The whole affair of the *San Felipe* had doubtless brought the matter to his notice in a very striking fashion. It was seized upon by his advisers, men belonging to a growing class of merchants who saw great profits in overseas adven-tures. They were in close relations with persons like Hasegawa, who belonged to the war party and stood for expansion and aggression. Hide-yoshi may also have been advised by Seiyaku-In Zensō, a onetime Hi-yeizan monk who had set up as a physician and seems to have gained his trust while exciting the hatred of the Jesuits (by whom he is called Jacuin).

But it is no less likely that Hideyoshi was surprised by a sudden re-vival of enthusiasm for the Christian faith, which had been concealed or inconspicuous after 1587, when the Jesuits had withdrawn from the capital, leaving only the aged Organtino, for whom Hideyoshi felt affection. The picture of the revival is surprising. Apart from the numerous converts made by the Franciscans with their vigorous propaganda, the Jesuits were encouraged by the timely visit of Martinez, who came as Bishop of Japan with letters from the Viceroy of the Indies. Martinez was received amiably by Hideyoshi, and spent some time administering the sacrament to converts, who came from long distances to Ōsaka and Fushimi. He was not interfered with, nor were there any Portuguese Jesuits in the group executed on February 5, 1597. Other than the Franciscans there were three Japanese Jesuit brothers and sixteen Japanese attendants of the Franciscans.

From his subsequent actions it is clear that Hideyoshi had made up his mind to eradicate Christianity from Japan. He revised the Edict of 1587, so as to make it more effective, and although he allowed Organtino to remain in Kyoto, he issued orders forbidding further conversions and generally proscribing the Christian faith. But he took no further punitive steps after the execution of the twenty-six; in fact he seems to have relaxed his efforts. This change of temper needs some explanation, and it may perhaps be found in certain previous events.

One significant fact is the favour accorded by Hidetsugu to Baptista and the other Franciscans after their arrival in 1594. It was he who ordered Maeda Geni to see to the building of a seminary and a church, which was completed in September and in which Maeda's son was baptised. In the following year Hideyoshi ordered the death of Hidetsugu and his family. The arrival of the *San Felipe* in 1596 may have drawn Hideyoshi's special attention to the presence of the Franciscans and the ruse they had adopted to gain entry into Japan. It is easy to imagine a scene in which Hasegawa and his friends warned him of the real nature of Baptista's mission. This was the year in which Hideyoshi was already showing symptoms of mental disturbance by his frequent outbursts of rage. Is it not probable that his vindictive treatment of the Franciscans was of this origin?

The punishment of the twenty-six martyrs did not put an end to the anti-Christian intrigues of Seiyaku-In and his friends. Having denounced the Franciscans, they turned to spying and plotting against the Jesuits, who were quietly continuing their work, especially their pastoral duties. The Deputy Governor of Nagasaki forbade all Christian services or meetings in the town, and obliged Bishop Martinez to leave the country. Presently an order came from Kyoto instructing Terazawa, the Governor, to expel all Jesuits from Japan, except a very small number to meet the religious needs of Portuguese residents.

To obey this order would have been to abandon all hope of spreading Christianity in Japan, and the Jesuits resorted to various expedients to evade it. They went into hiding, and in October 1597 a number of their lay compatriots disguised as priests showed themselves on the deck of a departing vessel. By such devices a large number of Jesuits avoided deportation, probably as many as one hundred out of a total of one hundred and twenty-five. They had many Japanese friends who would take the risk of helping them, especially in Kyoto where influential officials like Maeda Geni and Ishida Mitsunari gave them protection.

In Nagasaki they had to rely upon one or two friendly officials, chief among them being Terazawa, who (it is alleged) had been secretly baptised. But early in 1598, when it was rumoured that Hideyoshi was about to visit Kyūshū again, Terazawa's Deputy had to make a show of severity. He destroyed a number of churches in the surrounding country and warned the Fathers that they must embark without delay. In August 1598 the new Bishop who had succeeded Martinez found that Terazawa was hiding a number of Jesuits until they could take passage to Macao; but apart from these a large number were in hiding in the fiefs of Christian daimyos and had no intention of leaving.

Early in September Father Juan Rodriguez (once an interpreter for Hideyoshi), having recently arrived as a passenger in a Portuguese vessel, proceeded to Fushimi with the customary presents. On being told of this visit, Hideyoshi sent for the Father as an old friend and received him with generous gifts and kind words. This was only a few days before the Taikō's death.

Thus ends the story of Hideyoshi's relations with Portuguese and Spanish missionaries and through them with the colonial governments established at Goa and Manila. A survey of his treatment of the Christian missionaries shows him to have been lenient in circumstances which might have called for very harsh measures even from a less despotic ruler. His angry punishment of the Franciscans was inexcusable, though it can be urged that the three leaders had deliberately flouted his law by a piece of trickery. On other occasions he had turned a blind eye to the disobedience of the Jesuits, as for example when after his outburst of temper in 1587, though he frightened poor Coelho, he did not pursue the missionaries who continued their work discreetly.

It is easy to overestimate the influence of Christian doctrine among people of high rank in Japan, yet certainly Hideyoshi trusted a number of converts, and gave them high commands. Konishi Yukinaga was a good general, who did great things in Korea and even disagreed with Hideyoshi at times. Few other senior generals were Christians, but many had Christian relatives or reposed trust in subordinates who were earnest believers.

It is natural for Western writers to pay special attention to the growth of Christianity in Japan, but from a strictly historical point of view the activity of the missionaries is only an episode in the country's history. That it is an important episode nobody will deny, and the surprising success of the Jesuit fathers is of peculiar interest for students of cultural adaptation. It would, however, be difficult to show that Christian propaganda during the sixteenth century exerted any notable and enduring influence upon the social and political evolution of Japan.

The total number of Japanese Christians at the end of the sixteenth century—estimated by the leading Jesuits at nearly 300,000—is a remarkable figure, testifying to years of patient endeavour by the Fathers and their helpers. It must also be said that it does great credit to the Japanese Christians, for with their traditional loyalty they held to the faith in times of danger.

That these results were obtained under the rule of two despots, Nobunaga and Hideyoshi, speaks well for the good sense of those tyrants. It should be added that some of the success of Christian teaching was due to the degenerate condition of the great Buddhist sects, and it is important to understand that the freedom enjoyed by the Jesuits was partly due to the desire of Japanese leaders to retain and encourage the import trade which was in the hands of Portuguese sea captains and merchants.

(b) The Indies

Hideyoshi's reception of an embassy from the Portuguese Viceroy of the Indies in 1590 has already been described, and it will be recalled that he treated Valignano and his companions in a simple, friendly way, warning Valignano to keep his Jesuit followers in order, so as not to make strong measures necessary. It seems that he resented the mission, which was evidently a diplomatic protest against his treatment of the missionaries; but he kept his good humour and even agreed with Maeda to allow the Fathers who had come with Valignano to remain in Nagasaki.

In 1591 he addressed to the Viceroy a letter in which, after preliminary compliments, he set forth his view of the nature of the Japanese state, and his own functions as its ruler. The country, he says, consists of over sixty separate regions or kingdoms which for years had been disturbed and had known little peace. By training himself to acquire the necessary virtues he has been able to subject them all to his laws and to govern the land in peace. The virtues to which he refers are benevolence, prudence, and strength. By means of these qualities he has pacified the warriors and treated the peasants with compassion. By his system of rewards and punishments he has been enabled to establish security and to unify the country. Now men come from foreign lands to pay him homage.

He is planning to subdue China shortly, and then he will be nearer to India and communication will be easier. Regarding his attitude to the Jesuits he says that Japan is "the country of the Gods," and any teaching which is contrary to its ancient beliefs is against the stability of its government and the welfare of its people. He ends by saying that he desires trade and will ensure the safety of Portuguese ships and merchants bringing cargoes to Japan.

There is some doubt whether the text recorded in contemporary accounts is identical with the message sent to Goa.[5] It is supposed that the draft which was shown to Valignano contained objectionable passages and was amended at his suggestion. Maeda Geni is said to have persuaded Hideyoshi to agree to some changes and to include a clause permitting ten Jesuits to reside in Nagasaki.

Hideyoshi certainly took no pains to conceal his predatory intentions. He said more than once that he would go on to Southeast Asia and India and Persia after conquering China. He seems to have had no clear idea of the magnitude of countries which he proposed to swallow. Even Korea turned out to be much greater in extent than his generals had supposed.

While he was indulging his megalomania by such unsubstantial visions, truly great movements were afoot on the other side of the globe. A few years before his inefficient admirals had bungled the invasion of Korea, the clash of two great navies in Atlantic waters had diminished the sea power of Spain and had broken the Portuguese monopoly of voyages from Europe to the Indian Ocean and beyond. By the time of Hideyoshi's death Dutch and English vessels were trading in the Indian Ocean, and planning voyages to China and Japan. The English East India Company was formed in the year 1600, and in that year a Dutch vessel, the *Liefde,* was wrecked on the shore of Bungo. Her pilot was an Englishman named William Adams, who was well treated by Ieyasu. Ieyasu was a man of foresight, who knew that Japan needed good ships; and Adams had useful knowledge.

The early successes of Portugal and Spain were due to advances in the science of navigation, to improvements in naval architecture, and to the development of firearms for use at sea. The fire-power of the Spanish and English fleets in 1588 was something of which the Japanese were quite unaware. They were in general backward in naval architecture, possibly because the Inland Sea was so convenient for pirates that they felt no pressing need for powerful and speedy vessels such as Francis Drake had used in his raids on Spanish ships and cities.

(c) The Luchu Islands and Formosa

In 1584 an adventurer named Kamei Shigenori asked Hideyoshi for permission to invade the Luchu Islands. Hideyoshi, always ready to claim new territory, granted this request and named Kamei Lord of the Luchus (Ryūkyū no Kami) by handing him a fan on which he had written that title. Nothing came of this buffoonery, but in 1590 Hideyoshi wrote to the King of the Luchu Islands proposing an agreement on the

---

[5] The text is that of the Tomioka papers.

ground that Japan and the Islands, though distant from one another, were really members of one family.

The Islands were in fact tributary to China, although they had at times sent tribute to Japan. They were important to Japan because the Ming government allowed no direct trade with Japan, and the Luchus served a very important purpose as an entrepôt in oceanic trade.

One of the curiosities of diplomacy is a letter addressed by Hideyoshi in 1593 to a country named Takasago or Takakuni, ordering it to submit and send tribute. Takasago was a name given to Formosa by the Japanese; but there was no government to receive Hideyoshi's order. The letter has been preserved in the Maeda family, because the messenger, Harada Magoshichirō, could not deliver it and carried it back to Japan.

CHAPTER XXIV

AZUCHI-MOMOYAMA

M O M O Y A M A is a name given in recent times to rising ground south of the city of Kyoto in the district called Fushimi. Japanese writers distinguish a period in the history of Japanese art which they call Momoyama, although Fushimi might be more correct.

A prelude to the Momoyama phase is the period called Azuchi, after the stronghold built by Nobunaga on the southwestern shore of Lake Biwa. Azuchi and Momoyama together cover only a short space of time, from 1579, when Azuchi castle was completed, to 1598, when the Sambō-In of the Daigoji was dedicated. Into those two decades many great events were crowded, and the chief new visible feature of this period was its architecture, notably the great fortresses and palaces which Nobunaga and Hideyoshi built.

These edifices express in a striking way the character of the age, which is heroic in its temper. Hideyoshi's great buildings exhibit a grandeur and an elegance which represent this trend at its zenith, but for its origin we must look back a century or more. The first clear signs are the castles built by successful warlords in the late fifteenth century, notably Hōjō Sōun's castle at Odawara, Ōta Dōkan's castle at Yedo, and Asakura Toshikage's castle at Ichijōgatani in Echizen. Previous fortresses had been designed strictly for military purposes, but these new castles, in addition to strong defence works, contained spacious and well-furnished living quarters.

The fashion spread as successful warriors established themselves as rulers of provinces, and by Nobunaga's day the ideal castle was no longer a grim and uncomfortable fort, but rather a great mansion protected by bastions and surrounded by a moat. Its purpose was to impress rivals by its elegant interior as well as to frighten them by its strength. Nobunaga, it will be remembered, succeeded in his final domination of Owari by occupying the castle of Kiyosu, which was strategically placed on the edge of the Home Provinces. But as soon as he had mastered Yamashiro he moved to the capital, where he built the Honnōji, a protected monastery-residence in the heart of the city. Also at this time he built the great castle at Azuchi, which was by the standards of the time immense in size, powerful in its defences, and luxurious in its richly decorated apartments. The keep (Tenshukaku), which in the older fortresses had been the heart of the defence, was here a seven-storeyed building containing the audience hall, the private chambers, and the offices proper to a royal palace, as well as military stores and a treasury.

It will be seen that a great change had taken place since the days of the Ashikaga Shōguns. The buildings for which Yoshimitsu and Yoshimasa are most celebrated, the Kinkaku and the Ginkaku, far from being fortresses were villas in the tradition of the Byōdō-In, with a certain monastic flavour. Yoshimitsu's Hana no Gosho (1378) was a palace built for the Shōgun, to serve as the centre of the Bakufu. It was designed to impress the city by its beauty rather than its strength. Yoshimasa's buildings were of an even more modest character, country retreats suitable for aesthetic enjoyment.

The contrast between the Higashiyama style of the fifteenth century and the Momoyama style of a century or so later is most marked in decoration as distinct from architectural design; but in size also the late-sixteenth-century castles and palaces were greater and more impressive. Although Azuchi was the most imposing edifice of its day, the Ōsaka castle built by Hideyoshi was of even greater dimensions. Azuchi, however, set the style of paying great attention to external and internal ornament as distinct from features of military importance.

Little remains of these buildings today, but there are some respectable literary sources from which it is clear that the seven storeys of the Azuchi keep were designed mainly for use as a residence, and its splendours intended to impress all beholders. The purpose of its decoration was to contribute to the prestige of Nobunaga, and the result was to develop a school of art particularly suited to the age. It began with a somewhat vulgar display, but fortunately the taste of the artists soon asserted itself, and what is called Momoyama art came to include many masterpieces. Here, however, we are concerned not with critical appraisal, but with the arts as an expression of the spirit of the times.

The writer of the biography of Nobunaga known as *Shinchōkōki* tells us that at the New Year festival of 1578 Nobunaga received at Azuchi the congratulations of the great and small barons who owed him allegiance. After the ceremony he led them through the public and private apartments of the still unfinished castle and showed them the works of art with which it was adorned. Most of these were pictures in brilliant colours, of the kind known as *damiye*, by Kanō Eitoku (1543–90) and his pupils. They were painted on walls, panels, sliding doors (*fusuma*), and movable screens (*byōbu*). Each of the seven storeys of the keep was decorated with works on a separate theme. There were landscapes, rocks and trees, birds and flowers, animals real and mythical, and human figures, all depicted on a grand scale. Nobunaga's biographer names these objects with enthusiasm. He rejoices in profusion. In his descriptions there is no hint of the restraint that had governed the taste of Yoshimasa and his côterie when they planned their gardens and pavilions. The ideals of Momoyama were remote from those of Higashiyama.

This is clearly a new age of catholic taste in the arts and their application. Individual pieces did not entirely depart from an earlier tradition, but in general their bold attack and their brilliant colour brought about a new phase in the decorative arts. There is nothing new in the themes of Momoyama paintings or in the skill of a high order which they displayed, for even their bright colours were derived from the century-old Yamato school. What is new about the paintings is their size and number. Never before had so many works of contemporary art been displayed in one place. This emphasis upon size and quantity and the predominance of heroic subjects are expressions, if not of the character of the age, at least of the ambition of its leaders.

A striking feature of the decorative arts of Momoyama is the free use of gold. In the Muromachi period the demand for gold appears to have increased rapidly as relations with China were renewed, and by Nobunaga's day the trade with China consisted largely of imports of gold against exports of silver from Japan. Domestic production of gold was also increased. Gold was used for minting coins, but not in great quantities. Gold bullion was also in use as a medium of exchange, and the new dictators, first Nobunaga and then Hideyoshi, used gold freely and ostentatiously to impress the world with their magnificence. It was a common habit of both to show guests the beauties of their living rooms and audience chambers, and then to take them to see the piles of gold and precious objects in their treasure vaults.

Apart from these hoards, gold was used in very great quantities for decoration of all kinds. Hideyoshi's tea-room in the castle at Ōsaka was small, but the ceiling and walls were all coated with gold leaf or dust, as were the frames of the sliding windows (shōji). Even the shelves were of gold lacquer, while all the utensils (except the teaspoon and the ladle of bamboo) were of pure gold. Even the roof tiles of the castle keep were covered with gold paint. Never was there a display so boastful, so remote from the severe canons of the aesthetics of Yoshimasa's day. Perhaps the most degraded level of taste was reached by Nobunaga, who gave a drinking party in his Gifu castle to celebrate his defeat of three enemies in 1570. The heads of his victims were taken from a black lacquer box by Nobunaga, and displayed to the company. Each head was covered by a thin mask of gold leaf to which colour had been applied.

Such deplorable lapses should not divert attention from the fact that Azuchi was the birthplace of Momoyama art. In Hideyoshi's time a series of great buildings followed in a natural evolution from Nobunaga's stronghold and were decorated upon similar lines. As a leading Japanese art historian has pointed out, it is a curious anomaly that Nobunaga, by destroying almost all the great monasteries, struck a blow at the traditional arts and founded a new tradition, for hitherto the chief patrons of the painter and the builder had been the great religious bodies, in particular the Buddhist Church. Now, by Nobunaga's actions, all the arts were free from the dictates of religion and could find inspiration in profane as well as sacred sources. The essence of Momoyama art can be seen already in the paintings of Azuchi; and Kanō Eitoku, followed by his adopted son Sanraku, painted most of the great pictures for Hideyoshi's palaces. Among the most celebrated of these is Eitoku's "Lions at Play" ("Karashishi"), a six-fold screen about twenty feet in length and

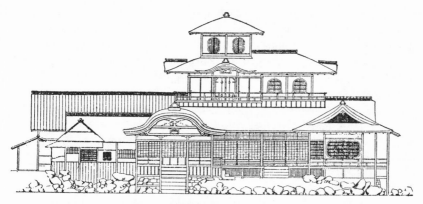

*Front elevation of the Hiunkaku, a pavilion at the Honganji, illustrating an aspect of
Momoyama architecture*

eight feet in height—dimensions in just proportion to the spacious room
in which it stood. This screen is now an Imperial treasure, and perhaps
as well as any work of art it reveals the taste of the day. Its colours are
brilliant on a background of gold. It is full of life and energy.

There were also fine painters outside the Kanō school, notably Kai-
hoku Yūshō and Hasegawa Tōhaku. Some of these were masters of ink
painting (*sumiye*), and their work, though without colour, displayed the
characteristic vigour of the Momoyama brush, while not departing from
a classical tradition.

In architecture nothing remains from Nobunaga's day, but there are
several important relics from Hideyoshi's palaces and other buildings of
his time. Among them are the beautiful gate (Karamon) of the Daitokuji, which exhibits brilliant design and superb craftsmanship; the Hiunkaku, an elegant small building at the Nishi Honganji; and the Sambō-In
of the Daigoji, which was a favourite resort of Hideyoshi and the scene
of his last great entertainment in 1598.

These are of great interest to art historians as specimens of Momoyama standards of taste and technical skill. They speak for a delicacy of
treatment which is in striking contrast to the imposing mass of the buildings to which they belong; and since they are in the native tradition of
fine workmanship, they can scarcely be looked upon as peculiar to Momoyama. The great edifices, however, do stand for a new order, for they
are fitting expressions of a bold, ambitious, and lively era.[1]

---

[1] Hideyoshi had a passion for building. His most important monuments are:

Ōsaka castle. A rebuilding of the Ishiyama Honganji. Work was begun in 1583.
It was an enormous undertaking employing tens of thousands of men. When it was
completed in 1590, it was the greatest and strongest castle in Japan.

The Jūrakudai. The "Mansion of Pleasure" was built as Hideyoshi's residence
from 1587.

Fushimi castle. Fushimi was built after Hideyoshi retired as Kampaku in 1591.
He transferred the Jūrakudai to Hidetsugu, and Fushimi was meant to be his own

It is scarcely necessary to add that the trend towards conspicuous expenditure was favoured, if it was not caused, by a rapid growth in the production of commodities of all kinds throughout the country in the sixteenth century. Foodstuffs were plentiful, the output of mines was being raised by improved methods, and the expansion of trade was hastened by the efforts of rich merchants in their prosperous cities.

Some writers have discerned in the artistic movements treated in this chapter a parallel to the European Renaissance; but the comparison is far-fetched since the great energy displayed by Momoyama culture was inspired by the material concepts of feudal society and was lacking in humanistic elements.

---

retreat. Work was begun in 1592 or a little earlier and completed at the end of 1594. During its construction from 20,000 to 30,000 men were always at work. They were furnished by twenty or more provinces.

Fushimi looked like a castle from outside, but it was a luxurious palace, similar to the Jūrakudai.

CHAPTER XXV

TOKUGAWA IEYASU

1. *His Early Life*

FOR SOME twenty years after the death of Hideyoshi, Ieyasu was the greatest figure in Japanese life; and after his own death in 1616 his memory dominated the political scene for the greater part of the seventeenth century. It is therefore of importance to study his character as it developed under the stress of events, both military and political, while first Nobunaga and then Hideyoshi ruled the country.

Ieyasu was the eldest son of a small warrior chieftain named Matsudaira, whose lands lay between the domains of the powerful Imagawa lords of Suruga and the Oda family, influential in Owari. This was a difficult situation, and it threw a shadow over the early years of Ieyasu. In 1547, when he was in his sixth year, he was sent to live in the Imagawa household as a hostage, but on the way to Sumpu, the capital of Suruga, he was seized by an agent of Oda Nobuhide (Nobunaga's father) and taken to Atsuta, where he was kept as a hostage for two years. During that time his father died, and the prospects of Ieyasu, at that time known by his boyhood name of Takechiyo, were very poor, as were those of the whole Matsudaira family. But a truce between Oda and Imagawa allowed him some freedom and he returned home, only to be seized again, this time by the Imagawa family, who took him to Sumpu as a hostage.

In 1560, during the battle of Okehazama, Takechiyo (now bearing the adult name Motoyasu), still a hostage, marched with a wing of the Imagawa army, but thanks to the utter defeat of Imagawa Yoshimoto at the hands of Nobunaga he was freed from a bondage which had lasted thirteen years in all. He was able to return to his home (Okazaki) in Mikawa, where he was welcomed by Matsudaira followers.

2. *Relations with Nobunaga and Hideyoshi*

In 1561 Motoyasu cut loose from the Imagawa family and joined hands with Nobunaga. He took the name Ieyasu; and while protecting Nobunaga's rear from assault he set about strengthening his own position in Mikawa province. He proved so useful an ally that Nobunaga gave his daughter Tokuhime in betrothal to Ieyasu's eldest son, Nobuyasu. Within a few years Ieyasu was able to overcome some strong opposition from Monto sectarians and rural gentry in his province, and by 1567 he had made himself master of Mikawa, completely ousting the remnants of Imagawa authority. His merit was recognized by the Court, and he was allowed to use the family name of Tokugawa in 1566.

A distinguishing feature of his campaign against the sectarians was his treatment of the rural gentry who had assisted them. Nobunaga in similar circumstances had put to death all who opposed him in Echizen and Kaga, but Ieyasu, while confiscating the land of his most stubborn enemies, was generous to those who showed a disposition to join him. Once firmly established in Mikawa (he moved to Hamamatsu castle in 1570), and while steadily supporting Nobunaga's policy of unification, he began to plan an extension of his own power along the eastern seaboard. This is an important point to remember in considering the subsequent activities of Ieyasu. He never lost sight of his objective in the eastern provinces, though he never neglected his duty to Nobunaga. His struggle with Takeda Shingen and Takeda Katsuyori was essential if he was to remove danger threatening his flank should he move eastward in force. He regarded himself as an ally rather than a subordinate of Nobunaga and considered that he was serving the cause of unification by extending his power eastward.

Ieyasu has been blamed for not hurrying to punish the assassins of Nobunaga, but he was in Sakai when the news reached him, and had the greatest difficulty in escaping with a small following. His first care, naturally, was to ensure the safety of his own provinces. Arriving home after a perilous journey across Iga, he spent the next ten days consolidating his position in Kai and Shinano. It was only then that he began to move westward, to be told by Hideyoshi that his help was not required.[1] If he was disappointed he showed no sign. After camping for a week at Narumi to watch the turn of events he returned to his own affairs.

Thereafter he was a good but by no means obsequious partner of Hideyoshi, who as Regent and Chancellor could give him orders but (especially after the trials of strength at Komakiyama and Nagakute) respected his judgment and did not press him for military aid. It would have been wasteful to send an expedition from Mikawa to Kyūshū, and Ieyasu seems to have hesitated even before joining the siege of Odawara. He had no intention whatever of taking part in the invasion of Korea. He sent a token force to Nagoya, but declined to go there himself, saying that he was happier hunting in his own domain.

Although Ieyasu preserved a high degree of independence, he showed little sign of wishing to rival Hideyoshi as a national leader, let alone to overthrow him. He was quick to resist any threat to his own territory, but he extended his strength eastward, away from the capital. No doubt he was fully conscious of his own powers, for he was experienced and successful as a soldier and as an administrator; but he was cautious and knew how to bide his time. He was respected by the great warlords, and those who were present when Hideyoshi spoke his

---

[1] Akechi had been defeated thirteen days after the murder of Nobunaga, while Ieyasu was absent in Kai.

last testamentary wishes could not but agree with the dying man's praise of Ieyasu's wisdom and experience.

It was natural that Hideyoshi should wish to appoint a Council of Regency, to ensure the succession of his beloved Hideyori. In his passionate desire to protect the future of the child, he exacted from Ieyasu and his colleagues solemn undertakings designed to prevent them from taking action in their own interests, the common feudal practices of holding hostages and arranging political marriages. Such steps might have worked if Hideyori's minority was to be very brief; but the boy was only five years old, and in the intervening years there must be great risks of disagreement, risks which Hideyoshi would have foreseen if his mind had been working clearly. But he saw the future only in terms of perpetuating his family. He left no wish or order respecting the urgent questions that were sure to confront the Council of Regency immediately after his death.

It is important to take note of these circumstances, since it is frequently stated that Ieyasu had no intention of carrying out Hideyoshi's wishes. It is of course possible that he agreed to Hideyoshi's requests well knowing that the future could not be settled by mere word of mouth, but wishing to ease the last moments of his dying comrade. But it is no less likely that he accepted Hideyoshi's charge because he could not foresee the turn of events in the next few years. Whether he was prepared to support Hideyori or intended to promote his own ambitions, the immediate problem before him was simple. He must at all costs maintain the unity which Hideyoshi had achieved. It was a unity depending upon a somewhat precarious balance of power rather than upon a permanent superiority of the great feudatories of whom he was the leader. His first step therefore must be to consolidate his own strength, without any particular reference to the claims of Hideyori.

A survey of the distribution of power in Japan at the close of the sixteenth century can best be made by examining a list of the most important daimyos and assessing their military strength in terms of their revenue.

First come the great barons, members of the Council of Regency formed by Hideyoshi on his deathbed. Their names, and their annual revenues in round numbers, were as follows:

Daimyo	Revenue in koku
Tokugawa Ieyasu	2,500,000
Mōri Terumoto	1,200,000
Uyesugi Kagekatsu	1,200,000
Maeda Toshiiye	800,000
Ukita Hideiye	500,000
TOTAL	6,200,000

The total assessed revenue of all fiefs in Japan was somewhat above 20,000,000 koku, and therefore the members of the Council together held in terms of economic strength almost one-third of the national total. It is true that the military strength of the great daimyos did not necessarily correspond to the amount of their revenue. Strategic position was in some cases an important factor. Thus Mōri Terumoto, holding nine provinces at the western end of the main island, was clearly more powerful in a military sense than Uyesugi Kagekatsu, whose great domains in the Aizu region were cut off from the central provinces by geographical as well as political obstacles. Maeda Toshiiye, with less than Uyesugi's million koku, was far more powerful because from his domains in Etchū and Kaga he could easily move into the Home Provinces. It was because of the loyal services of Toshiiye that he was enfeoffed in this important region in 1583. A close friendship developed between him and Hideyoshi, who (it will be remembered) entrusted him with the guardianship of the precious Hideyori.

At a lower level of rank and wealth came the Five Commissioners (Go-Bugyō), who did not decide questions of high policy but as heads of executive organs carried out orders of the members of the Council. These were Asano Nagamasa, Maeda Geni, Mashida Nagamori, Ishida Mitsunari, and Natsuka Masaiye. They had been rewarded by the Taikō with fiefs of moderate value, but their total revenue was less than one million koku. Neither singly nor together could they venture to challenge their masters. So long as the members of the Council and their subordinates preserved unity, there was little chance of a successful revolt against them by other great warlords who were, so far, uncommitted. Among these Date in Sendai and Kobayakawa in Chikuzen together held over one million koku and were almost certain to favour Ieyasu and the other members of the Council of Regency in case of civil war. But there were several powerful daimyos who, while ostensibly neutral, tended to be hostile to Ieyasu. The most eminent of these were Shimazu in Satsuma, Satake in Hitachi, Nabeshima in Hizen, Katō Kiyomasa in Higo, and Chōsokabe in Shikoku. Their total revenue was somewhat less than two million koku. They could be dangerous if they worked together with other enemies, but from them alone Ieyasu had little to fear. With ordinary care the succession of Hideyori could be ensured, if that was what Ieyasu desired.

But the equilibrium which had been brought about by Hideyoshi when he subdued the Hōjō family in the Kantō was by no means stable. The truth is that Hideyoshi failed in his domestic policy, for instead of buttressing his power by building up an efficient system of government, he left the conduct of national affairs to the haphazard judgment of his subordinate officers, and depending upon his own prestige at home, he spent all his energies upon his fantastic plans of overseas conquest. It has been suggested that one of his motives in planning the invasion of Korea and China was to acquire territory which would satisfy the ambitions of his great feudatories and of the independent warlords like Shimazu and Mōri. There is not much evidence for this view, but he was right in supposing that these men would not long remain satisfied in subordinate positions. Before he took to his death-bed there was already dissension among his closest coadjutors, for as we have noticed there were two points of view and two parties disagreeing about the withdrawal of Japanese forces from Korea.

Indeed it was this issue which brought about the first breach within the government after Hideyoshi's death. At the end of the year 1598, not long after the formation of the Council of Regency, the Commissioners Asano and Ishida were sent to arrange the withdrawal of Japanese troops from the Korean peninsula. They met with strong opposition from some of the generals, who felt that their position was still strong, since they had lately inflicted severe defeats upon Chinese and Korean forces and were well able to hold their positions in the southern provinces of Korea. However, once the party which favoured withdrawal had made a move to the ports, the others were bound to follow them. When they returned to Japan both parties found support. Among the Commissioners there was a difference of opinion between Ishida, who stood firmly for total evacuation, and Asano, who favoured the belligerent view. The quarrel threatened to develop into a more serious conflict, since powerful interests were involved, Satsuma standing for retreat and daimyos like Nabeshima and Katō Kiyomasa firmly against it.

The Council hastened to patch up an agreement early in 1599; but there were other rifts in the structure of the Regency; Ieyasu had an implacable enemy in Ishida Mitsunari (1560–1600), a man of great talent and consuming ambition, who had held a subordinate post as Commissioner, had been a favourite of Hideyoshi, and had achieved a position in official circles to which his rank did not entitle him. He was a master of intrigue who knew that he could profit by confusion, and it was doubtless owing to his covert stimulation that the members of the Council and the Commissioners brought charges against Ieyasu, alleging that he was deliberately breaking his vow to Hideyoshi by arranging marriages for political ends.

There was some truth in this accusation, but the marriages of Ieyasu's children could not fail to have some political influence. The truth is that if Ieyasu had strictly carried out the negative policy laid down by Hideyoshi, he would have lost authority himself and encouraged dissension which could scarcely be of advantage to Hideyori and the house of Toyotomi. Ieyasu therefore held to his own intentions, and the two parties—the aggrieved Regents in Ōsaka and Ieyasu in Fushimi—were on the verge of a serious clash. Warlike preparations were made on both sides; but once again a peaceful agreement was reached. The Commissioners, headed by Ishida Mitsunari, admitted their error and professed repentance.

Mitsunari's intrigue now took another course. His method was to stimulate grievances against Ieyasu, and he schemed to cause a quarrel between Ieyasu and Maeda Toshiiye, Hideyori's guardian, who was genuinely devoted to the cause of his ward. But a trial of strength between these two could lead only to the discomfiture of both, since it would split the great feudatories into two factions and end in disaster. Fortunately both Ieyasu and Toshiiye were men of wisdom, who could see beneath the surface of events. They came to an agreement thanks to the good offices of Hosokawa Tadaoki, a man of good sense who quickly saw through the stratagems of Ishida Mitsunari. Toshiiye went to Fushimi to visit Ieyasu in March 1599, and Ieyasu paid a return call at Ōsaka a few days later. Toshiiye was then in poor health, worn out by years of battle. He died in May in his sixty-first year and his adherents passed into the service of Ieyasu, to the chagrin of Mitsunari, who had supposed that he could profit by a lasting antagonism between two members of the Council of Regency.

Toshiiye's prestige was great, and in wisdom he was a match for Ieyasu. After his death there was nobody to restrain Ieyasu, who soon showed signs of autocratic intent and thereby aroused the suspicion and hostility of those who were or professed to be loyal to Hideyoshi's memory. Mitsunari was encouraged by this turn of events to approach some of the great daimyos, suggesting that they should combine against Ieyasu, who for his part was far too shrewd not to anticipate Mitsunari's stratagems. He had, moreover, on his own side such solid supporters as Katō Kiyomasa and Fukushima Masanori, who like most generals looked down upon civilian intriguers.

But the unity of the Council of Regency was impaired, since there were now two parties in the state. Of the members of the Council after Toshiiye's death, Mōri was not dependable and Uyesugi in Aizu was known to have great ambitions which Mitsunari took care to encourage. Ukita also was of doubtful loyalty.

The prospects of successful revolt against Ieyasu seemed good, but Mitsunari was impatient, and made two attempts to assassinate him. The first was early in 1599 when Ieyasu went to Ōsaka castle with Hideyori; the second was three months later when he called upon the ailing Maeda Toshiiye. Mitsunari's designs were discovered by Katō and certain other generals, who planned to kill him. Mitsunari, however, escaped to Fushimi, where he sought Ieyasu's protection. The angry generals pursued him, but Ieyasu persuaded them that it was best to keep this fugitive conspirator in confinement. He was therefore sent to his own stronghold at Sawayama (Hikone) in Ōmi province and ordered to keep out of mischief.

It is not clear why Ieyasu was so lenient, but he probably felt that Mitsunari could be useful. His next step was to dispose of Mitsunari's fellow Commissioners. From Fushimi he ejected Maeda Geni and Natsuka Masaiye, its wardens according to the wish of Hideyoshi, and appointed his son Hideyasu in their place, while he himself moved to Ōsaka castle, which had been the stronghold of Hideyoshi and the seat of government.

Maeda Toshiiye's place on the Council of Regency was filled by his son Toshinaga, who returned to his fief. Of the remaining members (Uyesugi Kagekatsu, Mōri Terumoto, and Ukita Hideiye), Uyesugi, without resigning, returned to his fief in Aizu, where he had lately been transferred. Thus the active membership of the Council was in the hands of Ieyasu, Terumoto, and Hideiye, but in fact the power of decision rested with Ieyasu alone. He made some pretence of consulting the Tairō, but in practice he depended more upon the support of generals, whom he rewarded with valuable fiefs. He also resorted again to the system of hostages, notably by holding Hideyoshi's widow, the Kita Mandokoro, as a protection against reprisals by her relatives.

In this and in other ways he was not keeping his promises to Hideyoshi, but he can scarcely be blamed for failing to keep the Council of Regency in being. He was obliged, if only in self-defence, to take steps against the gathering conspiracies with which he was faced. He left Mitsunari alone for some time, because he knew that the danger to his own position lay not in Mitsunari's plots but in the ambitions of the great daimyos. These men needed no urging from conspirators, for it was part of the tradition of their class that power passed from hand to hand, that every warlord should take what he could seize. All feudal history in Japan is a record of the rise and fall of great houses. There was no such thing as stability in the country at large or in the lordships of which it was composed until Hideyoshi's day, when an uneasy peace or rather a truce was reached, and lasted through the Korean war until the evacuation.

3. Sekigahara

The first open revolt against Ieyasu was planned by Uyesugi Kagekatsu. He had been preparing for action for some months when in May 1600 the watchful Ieyasu summoned him to Ōsaka to explain his conduct. On receiving an insolent reply, Ieyasu devised a plan of campaign under which he would lead an army of 50,000 direct against Uyesugi from the south, while three other armies would approach from west, north, and east. Ieyasu left Ōsaka on July 26 and on the following day he stopped at Fushimi, where the warden was an old comrade, Torii Mototada. The two veterans spent the night in reminiscent talk and parted at daybreak, both knowing that the castle would presently be attacked and Torii would die in its defence.

Ieyasu did not hurry into battle. He made a leisurely journey along the Tōkaidō, arriving in Yedo on August 10. There he remained until September 1, when he moved north and established his headquarters at Oyama in Shimotsuke. His deliberate progress at this time was due to his desire to watch the development of Mitsunari's plans. The campaign against Uyesugi was of minor importance, for after some early reverses Date and Mogami, who had approached Aizu from the northeast, were able to hold Uyesugi and to keep him on the defensive.

Soon after his arrival at Oyama Ieyasu received word, not unexpected, that Mitsunari's plots had ripened and were bearing fruit. He had left his Sawayama castle and was in full revolt at the head of a powerful combination. This was a situation for which Ieyasu was fully prepared, for he had never intended to pursue the campaign in Aizu. It was a blind to deceive Mitsunari.

We may be sure that Ieyasu was well informed of his enemy's activities. On September 8, at the end of a siege of ten days, a strong force under Mitsunari had succeeded in capturing Fushimi castle after desperate fighting in which the warden Torii lost his life. It was now Mitsunari's intention to assemble all possible supporters of his cause, which he represented as the cause of Hideyori, and to press forward through Mino into Owari and thence to attack Ieyasu in Mikawa. This design was based upon the bold but mistaken assumption that Ieyasu would be pinned down by Uyesugi and unable to use his full strength against another enemy.

With these ends in view Mitsunari moved to Gifu, where he was well received by Oda Hidenobu. He thence marched on to Ōgaki, entering the castle on September 18. But meeting opposition from hostile warriors in Tango, Ise, and Ōmi, he was obliged to detach a considerable force from his main body to deal with their interference. At the same time a number of important daimyos on whom he had depended were reluctant to challenge Ieyasu, and refused to move. Among them was Mōri Terumoto, who had Hideyori in his charge and would not stir. In the absence of a great general Mitsunari had to take command of the Western army himself. He had courage and some experience of warfare, but he was not fit to lead an ill-assorted force against a brilliant and practised captain like Ieyasu.

On September 11 Ieyasu had retired to his castle at Yedo and from there he directed a powerful movement against the West. He sent a strong force along the Tōkaidō, and he ordered his son Hidetada with 30,000 men to sweep along the Nakasendō. Both forces were to converge upon Mino, where Ieyasu would join them.

The object of Ieyasu's strategy was to strike a heavy blow at the enemy in Mino, before they could establish themselves firmly in that province. The importance of this area had been amply proved by Nobunaga's successes some thirty years earlier, for his stronghold at Kiyosu had been the base for operations which by 1568 gave him command

of the Home Provinces. Ieyasu's advance force under Fukushima, Hosokawa, and other trusted officers moved rapidly along the Tōkaidō, and
all its units assembled at their rendezvous at Kiyosu on September 21.
Thus the two armies faced one another across the distance of about
seventeen miles that separated Gifu from Kiyosu.

On September 26 Fukushima and his fellow commanders received
Ieyasu's order to advance. Within the next few days they crossed the
Kiso River and captured the citadel of Gifu. By October 1 they were
firmly established on high ground overlooking the town, and there they
awaited the arrival of Ieyasu. He meanwhile had been carefully watching the state of affairs from Yedo, and it was not until he had satisfied
himself of the loyalty and the military competence of Fukushima and
his comrades that he decided to commit his own army. He did not leave
for the front until October 7, and arrived at Kiyosu on October 17 with
more than 30,000 troops. He moved to high ground near Akasaka (about
two miles northwest of Ōgaki) on October 20.

While these movements were taking place, Mitsunari, who was not
without military training, had been desperately collecting allies from
every likely quarter. By the end of September he had with him Shimazu,
Ukita, and Konishi. Within the next twenty days Mōri Hidemoto, Chōsokabe, and Natsuka arrived with 30,000 men and camped near the
Tokugawa advanced position. Shortly after this Kobayakawa arrived
with 8,000 men, and took up a position on high ground near Sekigahara.
In numbers, therefore, the total strength arrayed against Ieyasu was
imposing, but he had good reason to doubt the loyalty of some of Mitsunari's supporters.

Early in the evening of October 20, while Ieyasu was holding a
council with his generals near Akasaka, a large contingent of the Western army marched towards the village of Sekigahara. They were caught
in a blinding rainstorm, and struggling in the darkness they reached
their destination only just before dawn on the following day. Despite
these hardships, however, they and the Western divisions in general
succeeded in establishing themselves in strength in positions which
Ieyasu would have to destroy by frontal attack if he was to make his
way to Ōsaka. They were in an almost impregnable situation, but they
had one weakness of which Ieyasu was aware. They had traitors in
their ranks.

While the Western army was taking up its positions on the morning
of October 20 and Ieyasu's forces were deploying north of the Nakasendō, the fog was so thick that Fukushima's vanguard collided with
Ukita's rearguard. Then as the fog lifted and targets became visible a
general engagement developed. There was heavy fighting all along
the line and the advantage was slightly with the Western army. At this
point, according to Mitsunari's battle plan, Kobayakawa was to rush
down the slope and fall upon Ieyasu's rear. But he made no move until
Ieyasu forced him to declare himself. Then he showed his colour by

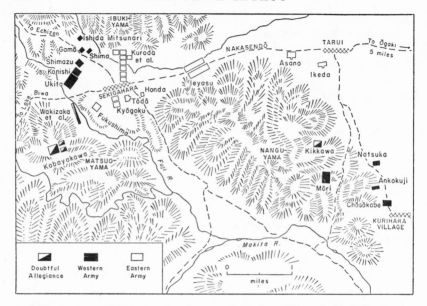

The positions of the contending forces at Sekigahara before the battle began

attacking formations of the Western army, which began to collapse under pressure from superior numbers. The battle was lost when Kobayakawa routed first Konishi and then Ukita, whose divisions together were ten thousand strong. Mitsunari then fled, and the next to leave the battlefield was Shimazu, who extricated himself after frightful losses and escaped with Ukita to Ōsaka, where they took ship for Satsuma.

The defeat of the Western army was overwhelming. It is true that Ieyasu's triumph was due in part to treachery among his enemies, and it is sometimes suggested that he took an excessive risk when he attacked a superior force holding strong defensive positions. But Ieyasu was not a rash commander. He was a military genius who had gained experience in decades of hard campaigning.[2] He was a skilful reader of men's minds, his political judgment was bold but sound, and he knew when to take a calculated risk.

Since many of the warriors who figured in the battle of Sekigahara became eminent, it is useful to record their family names, some of which recur in subsequent history.

Mitsunari had begun to form an army as soon as he learned that Ieyasu had moved eastward in August 1600. He visited Ōsaka, where he obtained promises of support from Ōtani Yoshitaka, Ankokuji Ekei, Maeda Geni, Natsuka Masaiye, and Mashida Nagamori, who are interesting but subordinate figures. In the name of Hideyori, Mitsunari appealed to all the great daimyos who were not committed to Ieyasu. When he attacked Fushimi he had the support, if not the active assist-

---

[2] He is said to have fought over fifty battles.

ance, of Mōri Terumoto and Mōri Hidemoto, Ukita Hideiye, Konishi Yukinaga, Shimazu Yoshihiro, Kobayakawa Hideaki, Chōsokabe Morichika, and Wakizaka Yasuharu.

While adding to the military strength arrayed against Ieyasu, Mitsunari attempted to influence some of Ieyasu's supporters by taking hostages from their families. He reached a pinnacle of evil behaviour when his henchmen seized Hosokawa's wife, a Christian convert known as Gracia, who resisted arrest and was killed by one of Mitsunari's swordsmen.

On Ieyasu's side in this civil war were Asano Yukinaga, Fukushima Masanori, Hachisuka Yoshishige, Kuroda Nagamasa, Hosokawa Tadaoki, Ikuma Kazumasa, Nakamura Kazutaka, Horio Tadauji, Katō Yoshiakira, Tanaka Yoshimasa, Yamanouchi Kazutoyo, Tōdō Takatora, Kyōgoku Takatomo, Tsutsui Sadatsugu, and Terazawa Hirotaka. Many of these were men who owed their position to the favour of Hideyoshi. They were not vassals of Ieyasu, but chose to fight on his side.

The number of men fighting at Sekigahara is not known exactly, but it was of the order of at least 80,000 on each side. Not all of those present were engaged, since the battlefield was a defile in which there was not room for the deployment of large bodies of men. Moreover, a number of Mitsunari's supporters, either through treachery or through bad management, did not come into action at all. These are said to have amounted to 30,000. On Ieyasu's side all troops present were fully engaged, but Hidetada's army of 38,000, which was to have arrived by the Nakasendō, was delayed by an error of judgment on Hidetada's part and to Ieyasu's great chagrin did not reach the battlefield.[3]

On October 21 Ieyasu spent the night in camp, having first ordered Kobayakawa and other commanders who had deserted Mitsunari to pursue him and to take his castle. The castle was taken, but Mitsunari had fled and was not captured until a week later. He was executed on November 6 with Konishi Yukinaga and a favourite of Mōri who had fought at Sekigahara, the monk Ankokuji. Konishi had been pressed to commit suicide by his friends, but refused because of his Christian faith.[4]

4. Ōsaka

After Sekigahara Ieyasu lost no time in starting for his permanent headquarters. He stopped briefly in Ōtsu to get news of the situation

---

[3] Further details concerning the battle of Sekigahara will be found in Appendix II.

[4] Among the important original documents exhibited at Waseda University in December 1959 is an order dated October 25, 1600, from Ieyasu to Tanaka Yoshimasa, one of his generals at Sekigahara, of whose loyalty he was uncertain. As a precaution the order was transmitted to Tanaka by a trusted officer close to Ieyasu, Murakoshi by name, with a covering letter also under Ieyasu's cipher and of the same date. Tanaka was firmly enjoined to use all his skill and strength in seeking out and arresting Ukita Hideiye, Ishida Mitsunari, and Shimazu Yoshihiro. Konishi Yukinaga, hiding in the hills of Mino, was also to be captured.

These letters, written in Kusatsu (where Ieyasu had arrived on the fourth day in Ōsaka, where the castle was occupied by Mōri Terumoto in his capacity as a member of the Council of Regency in charge of Hideyori. It was not certain that Ieyasu could enter the city without using force, for a number of Mitsunari's generals had brought their contingents from Sekigahara without loss and in good condition. Indeed one of the most surprising features of the battle was the number of Mitsunari's troops that did not enter into action.

In Ōsaka Mōri Hidemoto and some of his comrades were in favour of resisting Ieyasu, but Mōri Terumoto was against prolonging hostilities. He was well satisfied with his present position. He hoped to retain his great domains by submitting to Ieyasu, and therefore was easily persuaded to hand over the castle to Ieyasu, who entered it on November 1, and thus took his place as master of the empire. He had some scattered resistance to overcome by force or persuasion, particularly in Kyūshū and in Uyesugi country, but the main theatre of events was in the central and eastern provinces. There his purpose was to establish his authority as quickly as possible, by developing a well-organized and effective system of government which would command obedience throughout the country.

His first step in this direction was to reward the daimyos who had fought for him and to punish those who had resisted. There were in Japan 214 fiefs of 10,000 koku or more. Ieyasu confiscated the fiefs of ninety families with a total revenue of about 4,300,000 koku, and reduced four fiefs by 2,215,000 koku, so that he had at his disposal for retention or for distribution not less than 6,500,000 koku. The fiefs which he drastically reduced were those of Mōri, Satake, Uyesugi, and Akita, and the amount of reduction, it will be seen, was more than one-half of the amount derived from the confiscation of ninety fiefs.[5]

The greater part of the revenue thus acquired was retained by the Tokugawa family, and was added to the revenue from the extensive and rich provinces under Ieyasu's rule in the East. He also added to his wealth by acquiring rights in forests, mines, harbours, and important commercial centres. At the same time he rewarded daimyos who had fought on his side with fiefs in his own former domains, particularly along the Tōkaidō and the Tōsandō, where it was important for him to have reliable adherents. Here and elsewhere throughout the country they were established as independent daimyos and constituted the bulwark of the house of Tokugawa. They numbered about sixty at that time.

Ieyasu's next problem was to give a so-to-speak constitutional form to his control over the whole country, and for that purpose he determined to restore the Bakufu, which Nobunaga had flouted and Hideyoshi had ignored if not destroyed. He was appointed Shōgun by the

after the battle), show the importance he attached to punishing his enemies. Although Ukita escaped with Shimazu from the battlefield, he was condemned to death; but on an appeal from Shimazu his sentence was commuted to banishment.

[5] For a detailed list of Ieyasu's rewards and confiscations see Appendix III.

Emperor in 1603, but he took no advantage of the office for some time. He was indeed careful to avoid the impression that he intended to displace Hideyori, and he took pains to keep upon good terms with Yodo-gimi, who regarded herself as the custodian of the line of Toyotomi. Whatever may have been his ultimate intentions, Ieyasu could not afford to give his enemies and rivals an excuse for rising against him. There were still generals in or near Ōsaka who would rise to protect Hideyori. They included not only those who, like Mōri Hidemoto, had lately marched their troops intact from Sekigahara, but also many warriors who had fought for Ieyasu against Mitsunari but remained loyal to the memory of Hideyoshi. Fukushima, Asano, Kuroda, and Katō, among many others, were in this category. They might well have turned against Ieyasu if they had been offended by his actions, and in that case they would have been joined by daimyos hostile to the Tokugawa, especially those in western Japan and Kyūshū.

Ieyasu therefore proceeded with caution. He had decided soon after entering Ōsaka in 1600 to make his capital at Yedo, the stronghold of his own great domains in the Kantō. Here was to be the centre of his military power, and within the next few years he took steps to strengthen Yedo castle and to protect it by a screen of fortresses at key points in the surrounding country. He did not reside at Yedo for some time after 1603, leaving the place in charge of Hidetada, his eldest son. He himself had much to do elsewhere. He settled for a time at Sumpu (Shizuoka), where he had spent the years of his youth as a hostage.

Ieyasu was still careful not to raise the delicate issue of Hideyori's future. He was a man who preferred the substance to the shadow, and for several years after Sekigahara he devoted his main effort to strengthening his own position by the careful placing of his vassals, by repairing strongholds, and most important of all by increasing his own revenues and capital possessions. He paid close attention to developing domestic industries and foreign trade. This was a time when Spanish, Dutch, and English traders began to display some interest in trade with Japan, and they were encouraged by Ieyasu, who was impressed by the importance of maritime traffic and wished to promote shipbuilding in Japan.

Before leaving for a visit to Yedo in 1603 Ieyasu had allotted to Hideyori fiefs of a total value of about 650,000 koku, a rather modest amount for so important a person. Before this he had placed strong garrisons in fortresses dominating Kyoto. He had gone out of his way to make friendly gestures of loyalty to the Throne, and on the site once occupied by Nobunaga's Kyoto stronghold he had built the Nijō castle, which was to be the headquarters of the Shoshi-dai, the Shōgun's deputy in the capital, whose principal duties were to serve as a channel of communication between the Court and the Shōgun, and at the same time to keep a watch upon the daimyos of the western provinces.

After 1603 Ieyasu's influence increased rapidly, and Hideyori's position was weakened by the deaths of such faithful supporters as Asano Nagamasa, Katō Kiyomasa, and Maeda Toshinaga. In 1611 Ieyasu began to bring pressure to bear upon Hideyori; by 1614 he had made up his mind to destroy the house of Toyotomi. Although his old adherents could no longer stand behind him, Hideyori had offers of military aid from a new source. Masterless warriors—rōnin as they were called—poured into Ōsaka by the thousand from all parts of Japan, and entered the castle as its defenders. These men were for the most part warriors who had lost their property or their occupation thanks to Ieyasu's drastic redistribution of fiefs.

Ieyasu welcomed this challenge. He was waiting for an excuse to attack Hideyori, and at the end of 1614 a force of 70,000 men under Hidetada surrounded the castle. There had been affairs of outposts and skirmishes during November, but Hidetada's army did not arrive before the castle until December 10. Although the attacking forces (now augmented by the levies of Ieyasu's great feudatories) far outnumbered the garrison of about 90,000, during the early part of January they made no headway, but suffered some reverses. They continued to attack, but with caution enjoined by Ieyasu, who was anxious to avoid a costly siege of an almost impregnable fortress. He knew that its only weakness was dissension among its occupants, and he was soon ready with peace proposals. These were accepted, but Ieyasu broke the spirit, if not the terms, of the agreement. Though what is called the Winter Siege (Fuyu no Jin) was thus brought to an end on January 21, 1615, Hidetada at once set to work on the following day, filling up the outer moat and pulling down the outer ramparts. He then proceeded to fill up the inner moat also, so that by February 16 the outer ring of defences had been totally demolished, whereupon he returned to Fushimi.

In May the siege was resumed. Ieyasu had promised safety to Hideyori, but naturally his word was not believed after his previous falsehoods. In the Summer Siege (Natsu no Jin) immense numbers of men were brought up to surround the castle. There may have been as many as 100,000 defenders, and almost twice as many in the attacking force. Struggles of a desperate kind continued day after day until June 2, when the defenders decided to fight a pitched battle outside the fortifications. This began on the following day and lasted until the late afternoon, when Tokugawa forces entered the inner defence zone of the castle.

That evening Hideyori's wife (who was Hidetada's daughter) sent a message asking Hidetada and Ieyasu to spare her husband and his mother, Yodogimi. No reply came. On June 4 Hideyori committed suicide and Yodogimi was killed by a retainer to save her from capture. On moral grounds the conduct of Ieyasu was unforgivable, for he had basely broken oath after oath; but he had destroyed the house of Toyotomi, and was supreme in Japan. In contrast to the fleeting dominance of Nobunaga and Hideyoshi, the Tokugawa family was to govern the country for two hundred and fifty years.

CHAPTER XXVI

THE FIRST YEARS OF THE TOKUGAWA BAKUFU

1. *Ieyasu's Politics*

IEYASU died on the first of June, 1616, in his seventy-fifth year. Although he had devoted much of his time since the death of Hideyoshi to urgent military problems and had fought two vital campaigns to ensure his supremacy, he had by no means neglected questions of civil government during the last fifteen years of his life. Indeed, in 1605, only two years after his appointment as Shōgun, he resigned the office in favour of his son Hidetada in order to be free to pay full attention to the political structure which was to sustain the power of the house of Tokugawa. His resignation and the succession of Hidetada were also intended to give public notice that the office was to be hereditary in the Tokugawa family. Himself a triumphant warrior, Ieyasu was determined that his family should hold what he had won, and that there should be an end to civil war. It was his purpose to devise a system which would hold in check the ambitions of the most powerful barons, who, though they had submitted to him after Sekigahara, were of uncertain loyalty.

It is important to understand that although the victory at Sekigahara gave Ieyasu a commanding position, in the interval between the defeat of Ishida Mitsunari and the fall of Ōsaka he had much opposition to overcome, particularly among the proud feudatories in western Japan. There was no open revolt requiring military measures of suppression, but there was a degree of covert hostility which he must somehow reduce. The situation called for skilful political treatment. The task was no less important than battles and sieges, and in its performance Ieyasu displayed a talent equal to his gifts as a soldier.

The most dangerous of the western barons was Shimazu, the lord of Satsuma, Ōsumi, and part of Hyūga, whose resources combined with his remote situation made him almost invulnerable. Immediately after Sekigahara it had been proposed to attack him, and preparations were made by Katō Kiyomasa, then firmly established in northern Higo; but Ieyasu preferred negotiations to force, and early in 1602 Shimazu Tadatsune submitted to the Shōgun at Fushimi castle, where he was well received and honoured. Other peripheral lords, such as Uyesugi and Satake in the North, were impressed by this example and abandoned any projects of revolt that they may have had in mind.

Ieyasu, for his part, moved with circumspection, taking care, as we have seen, not to offend the feelings of those of his supporters who owed a debt to Hideyori as the son and heir of Hideyoshi. West of the Home Provinces and north of the Kantō Ieyasu exercised no direct authority, and he was therefore obliged to proceed gradually and cautiously with his plans for limiting the power of the great barons in those regions.

The basis of Ieyasu's civil policy was to distribute fiefs in such a way that his most trusted vassals occupied domains from which they could keep watch and ward upon barons whose allegiance was doubtful. The dependable vassals were known as Fudai, or hereditary lieges of the house of Tokugawa, in contrast to the Tozama, the "Outside Lords," with whom Ieyasu had no hereditary tie. Most of the Fudai daimyos held fiefs of about 50,000 koku or less, with the exception of Matsudaira Tadayoshi (Ieyasu's fifth son) at Kiyosu, who had 500,000 koku, and Ii Naomasa at Hikone with 100,000. They were all placed at strategic points from Kyoto eastward along the Tōkaidō and the Nakasendō to Yedo.

In the Tozama, powerful lords who had been neutral or had adhered to Ieyasu after Sekigahara, he had little trust. He treated them with formal respect, but they were carefully watched and given little opportunity to plan combinations against the Bakufu. They were frequently called upon to perform tasks that put them to great expense, as for example when they were given the unwelcome privilege of building or repairing citadels, supposedly in the interest of the nation. Among those who suffered from such impositions in the decade after Sekigahara were Katō, Asano, Kuroda, Ikeda, Nabeshima, Hosokawa, and Shimazu, all of whom were required to furnish labour and materials for fortresses to protect strategic points between Fushimi and Yedo. For these services they might receive a small payment in gold from Ieyasu, by way of *douceur* and not of reimbursement.[1]

Ieyasu took all possible steps to thwart alliances and agreements among the Tozama, imposing limits on the size of their castles and on the capacity of the transport craft used by the barons in coastal provinces. Where possible he reduced their freedom of movement by appointing Fudai vassals to neighbouring fiefs. An interesting example of this method is the action taken by Ieyasu to guard against expansion by powerful Tozama in the northern provinces, men such as Date, Gamō, Mogami, Uyesugi, and Satake. He placed Fudai vassals at Mito, Utsu·nomiya, and other key points in the northern Kantō, thus preventing egress by a possible league of Date and his neighbours. In pursuit of this policy of surveillance, the Fudai daimyos were moved about so

[1] Among the works of this nature carried out between 1602 and 1615 were the building and repair of a number of castles—Nijō, Fushimi, Hikone, Yedo, Suruga, Nagoya, Kameyama, and Takata—as well as repairs to the Imperial Palace. The drain on the finances of the Tozama was very heavy. They grumbled but did not dare to resist.

often that they complained bitterly of the transfer from province to province, the *kunigae*, as it was called.

Although Ieyasu paid unremitting attention to civil affairs, he made no attempt to organize a coherent system of government. He dealt with problems as they arose, and his methods had a military flavour. He was determined to secure obedience, and it was his method to give direct orders rather than to govern by legislation. He did, it is true, issue a code to guide the behaviour of the military class, but not until the end of his career. It was a collection of rules known as Buke Sho-Hatto, or Ordinances for the Military Houses, and it was promulgated (with a spoken commentary) to an assembly of vassals in Fushimi castle in August 1615. It had been compiled at the instance of Ieyasu by a group of scholars, both monks and laymen; and its principal clauses were designed to limit the power of the great feudatories, who were told that they must not enlarge or repair their castles without permission from the Bakufu, that they must not bring men from other fiefs into their domains, that their marriages must be approved by the Shōgun, and that they must at once denounce any subversive activity by their neighbours.

The issuing of this document was little more than a formality or a matter of record, since Ieyasu had already achieved his purpose of subjecting the Tozama by the methods just described, and by increasingly harsh treatment as his earlier forms of pressure succeeded. But even more effective than direct coercion was the great addition to his own strength that resulted from his economic enterprises. He was immensely wealthy, as the Christian missionaries frequently reported in their letters home. After Sekigahara he had vastly enlarged the scope of Tokugawa property rights by taking into his direct jurisdiction the cities of Yedo, Kyoto, Ōsaka, Nagasaki, Yamada, and Nara. These he placed under the control of officials appointed to further his interests. He also assumed ownership of certain gold and silver mines, relying upon one Ōkubo Nagayasu as his agent in the development of workings in Sado, Iwami, Ikuno, and other valuable sources of mineral supply. After the establishment of a mint at Fushimi in 1601 he profited by the minting of gold and silver coinage for circulation throughout the country. But perhaps his greatest interest was in foreign trade, which he desired to promote not only as a source of revenue for himself but also on grounds of national policy. The foreign trade of Japan had for too long been in the hands of the Portuguese.

2. *Ieyasu's Foreign Policy*

After the invasion of Korea official relations between Japan and China had come to an end, but imports from China were still essential to the Japanese economy or, to put it more correctly, to the economy of the ruling class, who could not dispense with the silks and other luxuries to which they had become accustomed during the period of licensed trade. Fortunately for them the Portuguese, who were allowed to trade with China, could meet Japanese needs by the regular supply of Chinese goods carried in their trading vessels from Macao to Japan.

At the same time Japanese junks were sailing to distant ports in Southeast Asia in search of profitable merchandise. The close of the sixteenth century saw a great increase in the size of Japanese communities living abroad. There had been Japanese bodyguards of kings in Burma, Siam, and Cambodia since about 1550, but by 1600 there were Japanese settlements in most parts of the Far East. There was a strong company of Japanese soldiers in the Portuguese garrison of Malacca as well as a small colony in Macao; and the number of Japanese residents in the Philippine Islands had reached several thousand by 1605.

This was the beginning of an age of expansion by Japan, and the needs of the country could be satisfied only by a growth of foreign trade. The Portuguese were therefore necessary to Japan, and their position remained strong until a new and ruthless competitor appeared in Far Eastern waters. Ieyasu resented the Portuguese monopoly. He had already, very soon after the death of Hideyoshi, shown a willingness to trade with the Philippines. He had even sent word to the Spanish Governor in Manila offering to open ports in eastern Japan to Spanish ships, and asking him to send capable shipbuilders for employment in Japanese shipyards.

There can be little doubt that Ieyasu had been impressed by the failure of the Japanese naval forces in the invasion of Korea, and saw the value of well-armed vessels like those of the Portuguese. The Spanish Governor, however, was dilatory, and when at last he sent ships to Japan they carried no naval architect but, to the annoyance of Ieyasu, many missionaries and few serious traders. Meanwhile a curious train of events had brought to Japan a man who knew a great deal about ships and shipbuilding. This was one William Adams, an Englishman from Kent, the Pilot-Major or Chief Navigator carried in a Dutch ship, the *Liefde*, which was the flagship of a squadron of five vessels sent from Rotterdam by way of the Straits of Magellan for the purpose of competing with Spanish or Portuguese traders. They were well-armed vessels, and they had orders to destroy their rivals' ships and trading stations if they saw fit. This was a time when Dutch mariners were on the move in every ocean, and it is interesting to note that a Dutch vessel reached Japan a few years before Hudson discovered the island of Manhattan.

The Dutch squadron had encountered great storms on the voyage from Chile, and the *Liefde* was crippled. When she was towed into a harbour in Kyūshū, there were only a score of her crew alive, and these (according to Adams) were denounced by Jesuit missionaries and barely escaped crucifixion as pirates. Fortunately Ieyasu had heard of their arrival, and had sent for Adams, who reached Ōsaka in May 1600. The guns and ammunition of the *Liefde* were removed and taken to Ōsaka. According to a Portuguese chronicler the cannon were used by Ieyasu at Sekigahara, but this is improbable. They were, however, certainly used in the siege of Ōsaka castle in 1615, by which time imported guns were being supplied by the Dutch and English trading posts in Hirado, and ordnance cast in Japan was also coming into use.

After a year's delay Adams was taken into employment by Ieyasu and built some small ships for him,[2] as well as explaining matters of navigation and describing conditions in European countries. Five years later he asked for permission to return to his home, but was not allowed to leave Japan, though in other ways he was generously treated. Meanwhile the Dutch East India Company had established several trading posts in the Far East. But they were not satisfied with peaceful mercantile competition. Their ships had orders to attack and destroy all Portuguese ships and possessions, orders which were carried out with considerable but not invariable success after the year 1601. By 1605 Ieyasu, disappointed by the poor response of Manila to his overtures, had invited the Dutch to trade with Japan. In 1609 (the year in which Hudson discovered the island of Manhattan) two Dutch ships, which had been cruising south of Japan in search of the annual Portuguese carrack from Macao to Kyūshū, arrived at Hirado and there established a trading post. They were followed four years later by an agent of the English East India Company.

The ensuing rivalry between Portuguese and Dutch traders was advantageous to Ieyasu. He made concessions impartially to both missionaries and merchants, because his mind was set on a rapid development of Japan's foreign and domestic trade. He did, however, take some steps to show the Portuguese that their monopoly of commerce and evangelism had come to an end, and to punish them for their cruel treatment of certain riotous Japanese seamen in Macao.[3] The truth was that he was glad to see the Portuguese in trouble, since as a result he no longer had to defer to the Jesuits in the interest of trade.

Thus for a while he treated all foreigners with equal consideration, giving no preference to Portuguese, Spanish, or Dutch. What he wanted from them was a flow of foreign goods and foreign knowledge. His relations with Adams show that he hoped to develop a strong merchant marine and to procure powerful weapons. His discussions with the Governor-General of the Philippines (Don Rodrigo Vivero y Velasco)

---

[2] One was of more than 100 tons. She was lent by Ieyasu to a Spanish dignitary in 1610 and sailed to California as the *San Buenaventura*.

[3] The punishment took the form of the destruction of the Portuguese vessel *Madre de Deus* in 1610, and the death of most of her crew. A full account of this atrocity is given in "The Affair of the *Madre de Deus*," by C. R. Boxer, in *Proceedings of the Japan Society*, London, 1929.

show that he wanted skilled miners who could teach his people efficient smelting processes. He regarded these matters as most important.

This favourable treatment of foreigners lasted through the year 1611, when suddenly the Tokugawa government reversed its policy and began to prohibit the preaching and practice of the Christian faith. The reasons for this change are still the subject of controversy, but they were clearly political rather than religious. Ieyasu was determined to get rid of all missionaries, and on January 27, 1614, he issued an edict suppressing Christianity in Japan. The churches in Kyoto were destroyed and the missionaries taken into custody. Some Japanese Christians of high rank were arrested and sent into exile, among them being the "Christian daimyo" Takayama Ukon, who died in Manila a year later. A few poor Japanese believers were punished for refusing to abjure their faith, and some were imprisoned; but the edict was really directed not against the common people but against members of the military class, because their Christian beliefs were thought to be inconsistent with loyalty to their overlords. During Ieyasu's lifetime no foreign missionary was put to death, though many flouted his decree.

3. *Administrative Methods*

Ieyasu, as we have seen, made no attempt to create a systematic government, but met his administrative problems as they arose, without feeling the need of a complex machinery of ministries and boards. Indeed it was said of the Tokugawa government that it resembled the conduct of village affairs by a headman and his elders. This is true of the early stages under Ieyasu and Hidetada, but after their day a very elaborate and rigid system of civil government was developed.

The business of national government was conducted by Ieyasu on the same general lines as the regulation of a fief by a powerful daimyo. He gave orders to his subordinates, who carried them out to the best of their ability. It was characteristic of the early stage of the Tokugawa Bakufu that there was no clear division of functions, for although Ieyasu depended upon his trusted vassals, the Fudai, to carry out his plans, he also depended upon various people of lower standing who happened to come to his notice. He made use of monks and Confucian scholars to draft the Buke Sho-Hatto, and he was in close touch with prominent merchants and other men who had special knowledge or experience. They were usually gifted persons, and they took the place of regular functionaries.

An interesting example of Ieyasu's method of choice is the case of Ōkubo Nagayasu, already mentioned as his agent in the development of mines. Nagayasu was a man of humble origin, who had been a sangaku performer in Takeda's province of Kai and had found his way to Mikawa, where he was employed by Ieyasu's principal vassal, Ōkubo Tadachika, a man fond of sangaku performances. Nagayasu attracted the attention of Ieyasu, whose service he entered at a time when gold and silver mines at Iwabuchi in Mikawa were being developed. Nagayasu displayed such talents that at Ieyasu's suggestion he was allowed to take the surname of Ōkubo and given the title of Iwami no Kami. There is no doubt that his efforts added immense sums to Ieyasu's wealth.

Another man of humble origin whom Ieyasu employed on important business was one Honda Masanobu, a falconer by trade. He and his son Masazumi carried out confidential missions of a diplomatic nature; but in general such men held no specific appointment, being used only as occasion demanded.

It should be remembered that each daimyo was responsible for the government of his own fief, and hence that the functions of a central government were of limited scope. It was only in special circumstances that the Bakufu interfered in the domestic affairs of a vassal's domain so long as the issue of loyalty was not at stake. The lands and cities under the direct jurisdiction of the Tokugawa family were administered as if they were Tokugawa property, and the officers appointed to them were Tokugawa servants. Thus the national administrative functions were of a general rather than a particular nature, and did not seem to require the service of trained specialists. It is in this context that the provisions of the Buke Sho-Hatto assume an interest and importance not at first sight apparent. They are not a code of law but a statement of the principles which should govern the conduct of the feudatories.

The keynote is in the first article, which enjoins the practice of the military arts combined with the pursuit of learning. Since Ieyasu was determined to put an end to civil war, it was natural that he should envisage a peaceful society subject to his governance; yet he could not tolerate a decline in the military spirit of the members of the warrior class, and therefore he was obliged to encourage swordsmanship, archery, and equestrian skill. The second article forbids licentious habits, and other articles call for frugality among the vassals and their dependants.

The remaining orders and prohibitions deal mainly with the internal affairs of the several fiefs. Their holders are not to give shelter to fugitives from justice; they are not to take into their service men accused of treason or under suspicion of grave offences; and they must not employ or provide residence for men from other fiefs.

It will be seen that the purpose of these rules was to exercise some measure of control over the Tozama, who, though not entirely independent, were too powerful to submit to close supervision by the Bakufu. The Fudai daimyos were on a different footing, since they could be made to obey the Shōgun's orders on pain of being deprived of their fiefs. There was no administrative machinery to impose the Shōgun's will upon the greatest feudatories. There was only the threat of force, and to this the first Tokugawa Shōguns were unwilling to resort.

It will be seen that some of the provisions of the Buke Sho-Hatto are reminiscent of the Kemmu Shikimoku, especially of those clauses which called for simple and frugal habits. It is known that Ieyasu considered the Shikimoku and other documents of a like nature before giving instructions to the scholars who drafted the Buke Sho-Hatto. The document of 1615 was more than once revised, and a study of its changes throws light on the later development of Tokugawa institutions.

Not all of its provisions were obeyed, but its purpose was achieved in so far as it was intended to usher in an era of peace. From 1615 for two hundred and fifty years Japan was at peace under the rule of the Tokugawa Shōguns.

APPENDIXES

KYOTO TOPOGRAPHY

Kyoto was laid out symmetrically on the lines of the diagram which can be found in *A History of Japan to 1334*, p. 472. The diagram, however, shows only an abridgement of the street plan of the eastern half. The western half was never fully developed and gradually shrank until by the thirteenth century it was almost deserted except for a few streets in the northern section adjacent to the Daidairi or Great Palace Enclosure. The tendency was to expand north and east, but there are no satisfactory maps of the capital during the middle ages—after A.D. 1200—and information is to be found only in scattered references in documentary sources which are not always reliable. It is known, however, that by 1200 many of the main streets running from west to east had been continued across the Kamo River and extended the city in a somewhat irregular fashion as far as Higashiyama.

But the most interesting change was an expansion of the city to the north, where there were several streets running east and west from points north of the Great Palace Enclosure. These were, starting from Ichijō: Musha no Kōji, Ima no Kōji, Kita no Kōji (Imadegawa), Itsutsuji, and Bishamon-ōji. To the west they extended to Kitano and to the east they continued across the river. This development was gradual, but it must have been nearly complete during the thirteenth century, since Go-Toba had a residence bordering on Itsutsuji in 1220.

Largely owing to fires and other disasters the Great Palace Enclosure gradually fell into disuse, and the sovereigns occupied palaces outside, usually in the northern part of the city between Ichijō and Nijō. Only the Dajōkan, the office of the Chancellor (Dajō Daijin), was kept in repair; and it was used for the coronation ceremonies of successive emperors from Go-Toba (1187) to Go-Tsuchimikado (1442).

When the Emperor Go-Daigo returned to the capital from exile in 1333, he stayed for a time in a palace at Reizei-Madenokōji. In the following year, according to the *Taiheiki*, he ordered the rebuilding of the Great Palace Enclosure, but this was never undertaken. In 1336, when he was a prisoner of Takauji, he was staying in the Kazan-In, a Fujiwara mansion, until his escape to Yoshino in January 1337. Takauji meanwhile supported the senior line, and the new Emperor Kōmyō was moved to the Tsuchimikado Palace, which covered a large area between Ōgimachi and Tsuchimikado and Higashi-Tōin and Takakura. The Tominokōji Dairi, which had been the Imperial Palace since 1315, was destroyed by Hosokawa Jōzen's troops when Takauji attacked the capital in 1336, after Minatogawa.

When Takauji first established himself in Kyoto in the year of Kōmyō's enthronement, he resided at Nijō-Takakura with his son Yoshiakira. This was the Ashikaga Bakufu during Takauji's lifetime. Other Ashikaga houses at that time were the residences of his brother Tadayoshi and Shiba Yoshimasa, who was appointed military governor of the city, with the title of Buyei.

Tadayoshi's house was at Sanjō-Bōmon, a point just east of Higashi-Tōin and between Nijō and Sanjō. It was destroyed by fire and rebuilt more than once; and after Takauji's death it was taken over by Yoshiakira in 1364, when it became the Bakufu headquarters. It remained in Ashikaga hands until the collapse of the family. It covered with its grounds about two and one-half acres.

Shiba Yoshimasa, who was appointed Buyei when Takauji became Sei-i Tai-Shōgun in 1338, occupied a residence and offices near the junction of Muromachi and Ōimikado, covering an area of about 300 yards square. It was destroyed during the Ōnin War, being in a sector held by Yamana Sōzen, but it was rebuilt and remained in Ashikaga hands until 1573, when it was seized by Nobunaga. In 1579 it was repaired and enlarged.

It was not until 1377, when Yoshimitsu commenced building the Muromachi-dono (popularly known as Hana no Gosho or the Palace of Flowers), that the Bakufu could correctly be styled the Muromachi Bakufu. The Muromachi-dono was situated between Muromachi and Karasumaru, facing Imadegawa, thus being an extension of the city north of Ichijō (see map, p. 224). The work was completed in 1378, and the building became the headquarters of the Ashikaga Shōguns. It was enlarged by taking in land north of Imadegawa. It was surrounded by a moat. Yoshimitsu lived there until 1395, when he moved to his Kitayama villa.

In 1457 Yoshimasa built a palace known as Kami Gosho, which was the residence during the Ōnin War of the Emperor Go-Tsuchimikado and the retired Emperor Go-Hanazono. It was destroyed by fire in 1476.

Monasteries

Important monasteries built in or near Kyoto by the Ashikaga Shōguns were as follows:

TŌJI-IN (等持院). A monastery of the Rinzai sect of Zen, founded in 1342. It was the burial place of Takauji, who was buried there in 1358. Situated northwest of the city, beyond Kitano, it became the mortuary of the Ashikaga Shōguns. It was destroyed by fire, but was rebuilt by Yoshimasa in 1457. It contains effigies of all the Ashikaga Shōguns.

TŌJIJI (等持寺). This building may be regarded as a memorial to Takauji, for it was his Nijō-Takakura residence converted into a Zen monastery after his death in 1358. It was founded at the desire of Musō Kokushi and was favoured by Yoshimitsu as the first of the Ten Chapels (Jissetsu) of Zen Buddhism. Gidō was its first incumbent, in 1380. It was destroyed by fire during the Ōnin War, and not rebuilt.

TENRYŪJI (天龍寺). This famous Zen monastery was founded by Takauji at the behest of Musō Kokushi, and was dedicated to the repose of the soul of Go-Daigo. It was completed in 1345 and its buildings and precincts together covered an area of nearly 100 acres. It was situated northeast of Arashiyama, near the village of Saga, where the Kameyama-dono had once stood. It was the greatest monastery west of the capital, and was most richly endowed. It was destroyed by fire time after time, and was restored on a small scale by gifts from Hideyoshi.

MYŌSHINJI (妙心寺). Hanazono lived in the Hagiwara-dono, which was a family residence; but in 1335, after taking the tonsure, he converted part of the premises into a small Zen chapel, called the Myōshinji in honour of his director Myōchō, who later became Daitō Kokushi. To this chapel Hanazono would withdraw for Zen sessions, and he spent much of his time there in study and meditation until his death in 1348. It was not until 1350 that the Myōshinji was enlarged to its later dimensions. The monastery lies to the west of the city, to the north of Hanazono on the way to Saga. It was destroyed during the Ōnin War and rebuilt in 1473. It covers a large area and possesses valuable works of art and documents of historical importance.

SHŌKOKUJI (相國寺). This monastery of the Rinzai Zen sect was founded by Yoshimitsu, and situated north of Itsutsuji and east of Karasumaru. It was completed in 1392 and dedicated in the following year. Destroyed by fire in 1394, it was at once rebuilt, only to be destroyed again in 1425. A new building was erected, but not completed until 1466. The next year, 1467, saw the outbreak of the Ōnin War, when the Shōkokuji became the camp of the army of the East and was the scene of most desperate fighting. The buildings were destroyed during a fierce battle in the autumn of 1467.

ROKUONJI (鹿苑寺). After Yoshimitsu's death the Kitayama palace, which he built in 1397 on the site of an old Saionji villa, was dedicated as a Zen monastery, called Rokuonji after his posthumous name Rokuon-In. Of all its numerous buildings nothing remains but the celebrated Kinkaku or Golden Pavilion, which escaped damage during the Ōnin War only to be destroyed by an incendiary in 1950 (it has recently been rebuilt). The wide Kitayama domain lay west of the Kamiya River and reached to the skirts of Kinugasa-yama. Its eastern boundary was not far from Nishijin, the encampment of Yamana's army during the Ōnin War.

JISHŌJI (慈照寺) is the name given to the palatial villa of the Shōgun Yoshimasa at the foot of Higashiyama. It was dedicated as a Zen monastery after his death in 1490, when he received the posthumous name of Jishō-In. Of the numerous buildings of which the Higashiyama retreat consisted only the Ginkaku or Silver Pavilion remains, standing in the garden designed by Sōami.

APPENDIX II

SEKIGAHARA: MEN AND WEAPONS

The records of the campaign which ended in Ieyasu's victory at Sekigahara give a remarkably good picture of the nature of warfare in Japan at the end of the sixteenth century.

1. Numbers

The number of men engaged cannot be known exactly, but a reliable estimate can be formed by taking the revenue of each commander and allowing the provision of three men for each 100 koku. A recorded specimen of this reckoning is as follows:

TROOPS FURNISHED AGAINST UYESUGI AND SATAKE

Fief	Revenue in koku	Strength of contingent
Yūki	101,000	3,030
Gamō	180,000	5,400
Satomi	90,000	2,700
Soma	60,000	1,800
Sano	39,000	1,170
Hiraiwa	33,000	990
Mizutani	25,000	750
Ogasawara	20,000	600
Yamakawa	20,000	600
Minagawa	13,000	390
Matsudaira	5,000	150
TOTAL (number of men)		18,000

By this method, the total number of men engaged in the campaign may be estimated as follows:

THE EASTERN ARMIES UNDER IEYASU

The force under Hidetada proceeding westward along the Nakasendō	38,000
Forces engaged at Sekigahara, including 30,000 men under Ieyasu's direct command and the several contingents of Fukushima, Kuroda, and other generals............	74,000
Troops stationed on Nangu Hill and at Ōgaki...........	26,000
TOTAL........	138,000

THE WESTERN ARMIES UNDER ISHIDA

Troops mustered at Sekigahara, of which more than half were contributed by Ukita, Kobayakawa, and Mōri Hideaki	82,000
Forces engaged in siege operations or covering Ōgaki	13,000
TOTAL........	95,000

It will be seen that over 230,000 men were in the field in the year 1600.

It is evident that during the almost incessant wars of the sixteenth century Japanese generals had gained such experience that they were able to handle great bodies of men with considerable skill. In their wars of position they moved large forces by night, as is clear from accounts of Sekigahara, which show that both armies marched through storm and darkness to their positions during the night before the battle.

The provision of supplies for such great numbers was difficult, and commissariat plans broke down at times, largely for want of adequate means of transport, since there were few wheeled vehicles and the use of pack horses was not efficient for operations on a large scale. Armies were often obliged to live on the country by confiscating standing crops or rice just harvested. Before Sekigahara Ishida Mitsunari wrote to one of his generals from Ōgaki, saying: "Here we have plenty of food as we are surrounded by harvested fields." This was in October 1600, a good season for campaigning.

In the battle of Sekigahara, while the contending forces were about equally matched in numbers, the advantage lay with Ieyasu principally because his was a single command, whereas Mitsunari was obliged to discuss his plans with an ill-assorted council of commanders who were his equals. Before they could reach agreement Ieyasu was able to force them into a defile so narrow that free manoeuvre was difficult. Ieyasu, like Hideyoshi before him, owed his success to experience in sole command of large armies.

2. Weapons

There are no exact records of the arms carried by the troops engaged at Sekigahara, but a general idea can be gained from the composition of a reinforcement sent to Ieyasu by Date Masamune in October 1600. Of a total of 3,000 men, 420 were mounted, probably carrying swords, 1,200 carried firearms, 850 carried spears, and 200 carried bows; there are no particulars for 330 men.

A similar contingent of some 2,000 men from another quarter included 270 mounted men, 700 men carrying firearms, 550 carrying spears, and 250 carrying bows; there are no particulars for the rest. These and other records show that by 1600 the most important weapons were firearms, followed by spears and next by bows. The sword came last.

The firearms were called *teppō*, and weapons under this general name were classified not by calibre but by the weight of the shot fired, which ranged from about half an ounce to four ounces. Cannon at that time were not efficient. They fired a shot of not more than two or three pounds, their range was short, and they were unreliable. After Sekigahara guns were obtained from the English and Dutch traders and were used with good effect at the siege of Ōsaka castle.

The spear played an important part in the fighting at Sekigahara. Spears were usually about ten feet long, though a few were even longer. The *naginata* or halberd, a spear with a broad blade, was little used, being regarded as old-fashioned and clumsy.

Archers were in action at Sekigahara, though not in great numbers. The principal use of the bow was for sharp-shooting by skilled marksmen, and it was especially useful for picking off enemies during a siege. The Satsuma warriors were rather old-fashioned, and Shimazu Toyohisa carried a bow as he rode into the fight at Sekigahara.

As for the sword, most combatants carried one, or a pair (one long and one short), in addition to their principal weapon, whether musket, spear, or bow, and whether they were mounted or on foot.

APPENDIX III

FIEFS AND REVENUES

1. Fiefs and Revenue under Hideyoshi, 1598

The total number of fiefs in 1598 was 204, and their total revenue was 18,723,200 koku. Small estates of under 10,000 koku are not included in this total. There were certain holdings (called *azukarichi*) outside feudal tenancy,

on which there is no exact information. The following list gives the names
and revenues in koku of the principal barons.

Tokugawa Ieyasu	2,557,000
Mōri Terumoto	1,205,000
Uyesugi Kagekatsu	1,200,000
Maeda Toshiiye	835,000
Date Masamune	580,000
Ukita Hideiye	574,000
Shimazu Tadatsune	555,000
Satake Yoshinobu	545,700
Kobayakawa Hideaki	522,500
Nabeshima Naoshige	357,000
Hori Hideharu	300,000
Katō Kiyomasa	250,000
Mogami Yoshimitsu	240,000
Chōsokabe Morichika	222,000
Asano Nagamasa	218,000
Maeda Toshimasa	215,000
Mashida Nagamori	200,000
Fukushima Masanori	200,000
Miyabe Nagayasu	200,000
Konishi Yukinaga	200,000
Ishida Mitsunari	194,000
Akita Sanehide	190,000
Gamō Hideyuki	180,000
Kuroda Nagamasa	180,000
Hachisuka Iemasa	177,000
Nagaoka Tadaoki	170,000
Ikeda Terumasa	152,000
Ikoma Chikayo	150,000
Nakamura Kazuuji	145,000
Oda Hidenobu	135,000
Tachibana Muneshige	132,000
Mōri Hidekane	130,000
Mori Tadamasa	127,000
Tamba Nagashige	125,000
Horio Yoshiaki	120,000
Yūki Hideyasu	101,000

There were 5 fiefs with revenues of 100,000 koku; 3 with 90,000; 4 with
80,000; 3 with 70,000; 12 with 60,000; 9 with 50,000; 7 with 40,000; 20 with
30,000; 37 with 20,000; and 68 with 10,000.

2. Fiefs and Revenues under Ieyasu, 1602

After Sekigahara, Ieyasu confiscated the fiefs of his principal enemies and
reduced those of families who had displeased him by giving little or no support or whom, like Uyesugi, it would have been imprudent to press too hard.
The following lists show the principal members of each category.

(a) Fiefs Confiscated

There were 90 fiefs confiscated, with revenues totalling 4,307,000 koku;
of these, 78 fiefs were under 100,000 koku (with revenues totalling 1,880,000
koku). Those of 100,000 koku or above are as follows:

Ukita Hideiye	574,000
Chōsokabe Morichika	222,000
Maeda Toshimasa	215,000
Mashida Nagamori	200,000
Miyabe Nagayasu	200,000
Konishi Yukinaga	200,000
Ishida Mitsunari	194,000
Oda Hidenobu	135,000
Tachibana Muneshige	132,000
Mōri Hidekane	130,000
Tamba Nagashige	125,000
Iwashiro Sadataka	100,000

(b) Fiefs Reduced

Four fiefs were diminished from 3,140,700 koku to 924,800 koku.

Mōri	from 1,205,000	by	836,000	to 369,000
Uyesugi	from 1,200,000	by	900,000	to 300,000
Satake	from 545,700	by	339,900	to 205,800
Akita	from 190,000	by	140,000	to 50,000
			2,215,900	924,800

3. Redistribution of Fiefs under Ieyasu

The total (in koku) available for redistribution was 6,522,900—4,307,000 from confiscations; 2,215,900 from reductions. Of the 204 fiefs under Hideyoshi, Ieyasu left 69 unchanged, diminished 4, and rearranged the remainder into 115 fiefs with which he rewarded the families who had stood by him. The following lists show major holdings that were left unchanged or increased.

(a) Fiefs Unchanged (over 100,000 koku)

Shimazu	605,000
Nabeshima	357,000
Hori Hideharu	300,000
Mōri Tadamasu	120,000
Nambu Toshinao	100,000
Honda Tadakatsu	100,000
Sakakibara Yasumasa	100,000
	1,682,000
62 fiefs under 100,000 koku	1,747,000
TOTAL (69 fiefs)	3,429,000

(b) Fiefs Increased

Holder of fief	Addition to fief	Total value in koku
Maeda Toshinaga	360,000	1,195,000
Yūki Hideyasu	650,000	751,000
Date Masamune	25,000	605,000
Gamō Hideyuki	420,000	600,000
Kobayakawa Hideaki	51,000	574,000
Mogami Yoshimitsu	330,000	570,000
Kuroda Nagamasa	343,000	523,000
Matsudaira Tadayoshi	420,000	520,000
Ikeda Terumasa	368,000	520,000

Katō Kiyomasa	270,000	520,000
Fukushima Masanori	298,000	498,000
Asano Yukinaga	178,000	395,000
Nagaoka Tadaoki	139,000	369,000
Tanaka Yoshimasa	225,000	325,000
Horio Tadauji	70,000	240,000
Tōdō Takatora	120,000	203,000
Yamanouchi Kazutoyo	134,000	202,000
Katō Kamei	100,000	200,000
Hachisuka Iemasa	10,000	187,000
Ii Naomasa	60,000	180,000
Nakamura Kazutada	30,000	175,000
Ikoma Kazumasa	23,000	173,000
Takeda Nobuyoshi	110,000	150,000
Kyōgoku Takatomo	23,000	123,000
Terazawa Hirotaka	40,000	120,000
Satomi Yoshiyasu	30,000	120,000
Sanada Nobuyuki	88,000	115,000
Okudaira Nobumasa	20,000	100,000
Torii Tadamasa	60,000	100,000
Okudaira Iemasa (new fief)	100,000	100,000
	TOTAL	10,453,000
85 fiefs under 100,000 koku		1,746,000
Total value of 115 fiefs:		12,199,000

(c) Total Number of Fiefs in Japan in 1602

There were 188 fiefs with a combined value of 16,552,000 koku, plus the estates of Ieyasu (which were valued at 2,557,000 koku in 1598), bringing the total value of estates over 10,000 koku in Japan to 19,109,000. These figures, however, do not include the holdings of the imperial family or of religious establishments.

THE PRINCIPAL HIGHWAYS OF JAPAN

The principal highways of mediaeval Japan were the Tōkaidō (東海道), the Sanyōdō (山陽道), the Nakasendō (仲仙道), and the Kōshū-kaidō (甲州街道) (see maps, pp. xviii, xix).

The Tōkaidō ran from Kyoto through Ōtsu, Kusatsu, Yokkaichi, Kuwana, Narumi, Okazaki, and Hamamatsu, and then near the coast line of Mikawa, Tōtōmi, Suruga, and Sagami provinces, passing through Fuchū, Ejiri, Hakone, Odawara, Totsuka, Yoshida (eight miles to the west of Kamakura), and Kanagawa to Yedo. The total length of the Tōkaidō was 127 ri, or about 310 miles.

The Sanyōdō ran from Kyoto to Fushimi, Yodo, and Yamazaki, and thence through Hyōgo along the shore of the Inland Sea to Hagi, near the Straits of Shimonoseki (Akamagaseki). Its total length was 145 ri, or about 350 miles. The name Sanyō indicates that the road ran on the sunny (yō) side, i.e., south of the central mountain chain. By contrast the less important Sanindō ran along the shady (in) side of the mountains, i.e., to the north.

The Nakasendō or central mountain road followed the same line as the Tōkaidō from Kyoto to Kusatsu, and then passed through Sekigahara and Tarui and across Mino into Shinano by way of Shimosuwa, Kutsukake, and Karuizawa. Then bending southeastward, it passed through Kōtsuke and Musashi (and the towns Kumagai, Kōnosu, Okegawa, and Koshigaya) to its terminus at Yedo. The total distance from Kyoto to Yedo by way of the Nakasendō was 135 ri or about 330 miles.

The Kōshū-kaidō left Yedo and ran in a westerly direction through Fuchū and Hachiōji, and continued across the mountain range that includes Komagatake and Yatsugatake, reaching its terminal point at Lake Suwa in Shinano. Here the traveller could turn south to follow the Kisogawa or north to enter Echigo by way of Nagano. Kōshū is the name of a region which included Kai province. The road passed through mountain country, often at a high level. Its length from Yedo to Kōfu was about 76 miles, and from Kōfu to Suwa 44 miles.

BIBLIOGRAPHICAL NOTE

For the guidance of Western students standard works by Japanese scholars are indispensable. The general histories which I have found most useful are Vols. 6 and 8 in the series *Sōgō Nihonshi Taikei*, entitled respectively *Nambokuchō* and *Azuchi-Momoyama*. Both are detailed and very accurate. A more recent series is *Nihon no Rekishi*, published by the Yomiuri newspaper in twelve monthly volumes since February 1959. The treatment is somewhat popular and not without a journalistic flavour, but the contributors are all historians of good standing and the work is accurate as to facts and interesting in its interpretations.

As for works on special periods or topics, the mass of new historical writing in Japan today is overwhelming, and it would be idle to attempt to furnish a selective list. For some years after 1945 many of the new historians displayed such ideological prejudice that I preferred as a rule to follow the pre-war veterans, among whom were several writers of commanding stature. More recently, however, Japanese historiography has entered upon a new phase. Historical studies have made great strides, as one may infer from statistics of the membership of historical societies. The Historical Society (Shigakukai) now has three thousand members as compared with three hundred a few years ago; and the number of other responsible associations for the promotion of historical research has increased more than tenfold.

The reasons for this rapid growth are manifold. Chief among them, no doubt, was the new freedom of expression guaranteed by the Constitution of 1946. In the reconstruction period an awakened interest in social and economic history led to a real advance in those studies and was accompanied by a great activity in the collection and examination of regional and local records, which in a number of instances has brought about a revision of accepted views. A copious publication in recent years of new source materials in carefully edited texts has been of the greatest value to scholars.

It is obvious that a Western student attempting to trace for Western readers the course of Japanese history over a period of several centuries cannot rely upon digests of a multitude of studies by Japanese specialists. Of course he must in a general way be familiar with the trend of their work, but if his own recital is to have any style and unity he must take care lest it become a shapeless mosaic of fact and opinion drawn from other people's historical writings. For this reason, as well as for a necessary economy of effort, I have confined myself principally to the works on separate topics which are listed below after the essential primary sources.

PRIMARY SOURCES

1. *Collections*

Of the collection of source materials called *Dai Nihon Shiryō*, now under compilation by the Historiographical Institute (*Shiryō Hensanjo*) of Tokyo University, the sections concerned with the period covered by the present work are as follows:

Section VI: volumes 1–32 are completed, and cover the years 1333–70.
Section VII deals with the Ōnin War, 1467–77.
Section VIII: volumes 2–21 are completed, covering 1479–88.

Section IX: volumes 1–13 are completed, covering 1508–21.
Section X: volumes 1–9 are completed, covering 1568–72.
Section XI will cover 1582–1603 when complete.
Section XII: volume 1 treats the beginning of the Tokugawa Bakufu. The periods 1488–1508 and 1522–57 are not yet treated.

Students unfamiliar with the use of these truly excellent compilations will find that *Dai Nihon Shiryō* presents extracts from primary historical sources in day-to-day order. Use of this material is facilitated by reference to a general survey of historical material called *Shiryō Sōran* (史料綜覽), which records events day by day and serves as an index to the source material set forth in *Dai Nihon Shiryō*. Thus, for example, with these two guides it is possible to follow the daily progress of the Ōnin War and changes in the contemporary political scene.

For standard historical texts (including some secondary material) the collection called *Shiseki Shūran* (集覽) is very useful, and at times more convenient than the monumental *Gunsho Ruijū*.

A convenient guide to key passages in basic documents is the three-volume *Kokushi Shiryō-Shū* (國史資料集), which gives excerpts concerning leading events in chronological order. Vol. 3 (466 pp.) includes the Sengoku and Azuchi-Momoyama periods. It was published in wartime and paper and type are poor, but it is handy enough and at times saves a search in the vast collections.

Parallel to *Dai Nihon Shiryō* is *Dai Nihon Komonjo* (古文書), of which the section called "Iewake" is devoted to family histories classified according to families whose records are used. This series is especially useful for study of the Sengoku period, when all the great families and many small ones were striving for power. It includes Court nobles and religious bodies as well as warrior houses.

Apart from these standard collections there are separate volumes of regional, provincial, and local history, now being issued in great numbers. I have not consulted any of these directly but they are freely used and cited by recent specialists in economic and social history.

2. Single works

(a) Nambokuchō (1331–92)

For the period from the accession of Go-Daigo in 1318 to the reign of Go-Murakami in 1367 the best single authority is the classic *Taiheiki*. It presents the loyalist view, but in contrast to the *Heike Monogatari* it is an impartial work, and even at times critical, since it enters into the case of both parties in the dynastic war. Its authorship is unknown, but its general attitude is quite clear. A contemporary attack on the *Taiheiki* for its partiality is to be found in *Nan-Taiheiki*, written by Imagawa Sadayo (Ryōshun), who alleges that the *Taiheiki* is prejudiced, mistaken, and untruthful, especially with reference to the exploits of the Imagawa family.

The most useful edition of the *Taiheiki* is *Sankō Taiheiki* (参考), which collates several versions.

Baishō-ron (梅松論), the work of an unknown author written ca. 1349, centres upon Ashikaga Takauji and deals with the rise of the warrior government until the death of Nitta Yoshisada at Kanagasaki in 1338. It is an important record and should be read in conjunction with the *Taiheiki*.

In addition to these it is useful to consult *Horyaku Kan-ki* (保暦間記), by an unknown author who evidently played a part in the conflict between the two Courts. It is written in the style of the military romances, but it is a critical work and contains useful material on the military society. It begins with the Hōgen Revolt in 1156 and ends with Go-Daigo's death in 1339. It is described by Arai Hakuseki as biassed, but he was a man of very decided opinions himself.

The *Jinnō Shōtōki* (神皇正統記) is valuable for Chikafusa's version of events in which he took part. His letters to Yūki Chikatomo have been questioned, but are now thought to be genuine.

Kusunoki Chūmonki (注文記) is an interesting statement of Kusunoki's order of battle before he withdrew to Chihaya. It is in *Gunsho Ruijū*, ZZ3.

Kaei Sandaiki (花宮三代記) is a chronicle of the times of the first three Ashikaga Shōguns. In *Gunsho Ruijū* ("Zatsubu"), vol. 12.

Entairyaku (園太暦) is the journal of Tōin Kinkata during the years 1311–54. It is a valuable source, and gives interesting detail for the years 1334 onward. In four volumes, published by Taiyōsha.

Hanazono Tennō Shinki (宸記) is the Emperor Hanazono's journal, covering the years 1310 to 1332. In two volumes of *Shiryō Taisei* (史料大成). Vol. 2 also contains fragments of the diary of the Emperor Fushimi, from 1287 to 1311.

Kemmu Nenkanki (建武) contains the celebrated lampoons known as the "Nijōkawara-rakugaki," satirizing Kyoto life in 1334.

Chinyōki (椿葉記) deals with the dynastic issue. In *Gunsho Ruijū*; and see also a study of this work in *Rekishi to Chiri*, Vol. 31, no. 4.

(b) Sengoku Jidai (1392–1568)

Among the most important documentary sources for this period are several diaries, listed below:

Kammon Gyoki (看聞御記), the journal of Prince Fushimi Sadashige (Go-Sukō In), which covers the years 1416–48. It is in Supplements 3 and 4 of *Zoku Gunsho Ruijū*.

Manzai Jugō Nikki (満済准后) is the journal of the Abbot Manzai of the Sambō-In, trusted adviser to the Shōguns Yoshimitsu and Yoshinori. It is in Supplements 1 and 2 of *Zoku Gunsho Ruijū*, and covers the years 1411–35.

Onryōken Nichiroku (蔭凉軒日錄) is a journal kept in the Rokuon-In of the Shōkokuji by a secretary directly appointed by the Shōgun. His office was styled the Onryōken. The extant portions of this journal cover the years 1435–66 and 1484–93. (There is a continuation called *Rokuon Nichiroku* for the years 1552–72.) The secretary was in close touch with the Shōgun. He supervised the monks of the Five Monasteries, and was privy to most important decisions of the Bakufu. The journal therefore furnishes precious material on political, economic, and artistic matters. The text is in Vols. 133–37 of *Dai Nihon Bukkyō Zensho*.

Ōnin-ki, *Ōnin Ryakki*, and *Ōnin Bekki* are reliable contemporary accounts of the Ōnin War, differing very little, and probably all three are versions of one original. See *Gunsho Ruijū*, in the battle section ("Kassenbu").

Daijō-In Jisha Zōjiki (大乗院寺社雑事記) is perhaps the most important single source for the political and economic history of the years from 1450 to 1527, a period of great activity and change before, during, and after the Ōnin War. It consists of the diary of Jinson, Abbot of the Daijō-In of the Nara Kōfukuji, and similar records kept by other functionaries of the monastery. This valuable collection was published in twelve volumes by Sankyō Shoin, from 1931 to 1937.

Shōdan Jiyō (樵談治要) is an essay by Ichijō Kanera on steps to be taken to restore order in the state after the Ōnin War and the disturbances which followed. It is written from the Court noble's point of view. In *Gunsho Ruijū* ("Zatsubu").

Myōbōjiki (妙法寺記) is the journal of a monastery in the province of Kai, giving brief but interesting data on the Takeda and Hōjō families and on rural economy. It has an account of a famine in Shinano in 1473. See Vol. XI of *Zoku Shiseki Shūran*.

Kūge Nikkushū (空華日工集) is the journal of the celebrated Zen patriarch Gidō. An account of Gidō's life together with the text of the journal and a good index is in a valuable work by Professor Tsuji Zennosuke entitled 空華日用工夫略集, published by Taiyōsha in 1939.

Sanetaka-Kō Ki (実隆公記) is the journal of Prince Sanjōnishi Sanetaka. A study of Sanetaka, based upon this journal, is to be found in *Higashiyama jidai ni okeru ichi shinshin* (縉紳) *no seikatsu*, by Hara Katsurō, 1941.

Tokitsugu Kyō Ki (言繼卿記) is another source of information on the life of a Court noble in the Sengoku period. Yamashina Tokitsugu held high office at Court and was responsible for the finances of the imperial family. He appealed for help to powerful barons throughout the country, and it is said that he persuaded Nobunaga to repair the Palace. His diary covers his career from his twenty-seventh to his seventy-sixth year (1576), and is a good source on conditions in the capital and in Yamashiro, where his estates were situated. The text is quoted by Okuno Takahiro in a work entitled *Tokitsugu Kyō Ki*. See *Dai Nihon Shiryō*, Section X, Vol. 6.

Kanemi Kyō Ki (彙見卿記) is the diary of Yoshida Kanemi, a Court noble holding hereditary office in the Shintō hierarchy who was in close touch with the Palace and with Nobunaga's entourage. He describes the sectarian debate at Azuchi and the sequels of the Honnōji murder.

Kahō or Family Laws. Those of Hōjō Sōun, Ōuchi, Takeda, Chōsokabe, and Asakura are in *Gunsho Ruijū*, Vol. 17. Those of Imagawa are in *Shiseki Shūran*, Vol. 11. Other family records are in *Dai Nihon Komonjo*, "Iewake." Interesting because of the part played by the Uyesugi family in feudal politics are *Kenshin Kaki* (謙信家記) in *Zoku Gunsho Ruijū* ("Kassenbu"), and *Uyesugi Kafu* (上杉家譜) in *Shiseki Shūran, Bekki*.

Teikin Ōrai (庭訓往來), manuals of instruction in the form of letters which provide useful information on daily life—arts and crafts, trade and travel, etc. Examples are in *Zoku Gunsho Ruijū*, Vol. 13.

Tamon-In Nikki (多聞院日記) is a journal kept in the Kōfukuji. It gives useful data for the latter half of the fifteenth century and most of the sixteenth. The great Nara monasteries took care to be well informed of events in the capital, and they received frequent reports on conditions in the provinces from their estates.

(c) Azuchi-Momoyama (1555–1600)

Several of the works mentioned under (b) above, such as the diaries of Kanemi and Tokitsugu, run into the following period, which is covered by Sections X and XI of *Dai Nihon Shiryō*. *Tamon-In Nikki* gives useful references to Nobunaga's relations with the Imperial Court, his siege of the Honganji (1576–78), and the campaigns of Hideyoshi until 1587. *Kanemi Kyō Ki* contains valuable entries until 1587, which is the date of Hideyoshi's great Kitano tea party. *Tokitsugu Kyō Ki* stops at 1576, but there is a continuation by Tokitsugu's son to 1601. *Rokuon Nichiroku* (鹿苑日錄), as we have mentioned, is the continuation of the Onryōken journal, and has useful information on events in Kyoto from 1552 to 1572.

The standard lives of Nobunaga and Hideyoshi are *Shinchō Kōki* (信長 公記) and *Taikō Ki* (太閤記), both of which are in *Shiseki Shūran* and, unlike the popular biographies, are reliable.

Sōtan Nikki (宗湛日記) is the diary of a rich Hakata merchant named Kamiya Sōjin, who was an enthusiastic adept in the tea ceremony. He describes a great tea gathering in 1587 at Ōsaka castle to which he was invited by Hideyoshi together with the celebrated Rikyū and other adepts from Sakai. These and other documents show what changes in their social standing came to the rich merchants at this time. Another great tea party was the monster entertainment at Kitano. This was a more popular affair, also described by Yoshida Kanemi in his diary. He records the presence of Sōyeki, Sōgyū, and Sokyū, tea masters who were at the head of different groups. These and similar records are to be found in the series entitled *Chadō Koten Zenshū*.

Most of these diaries express the metropolitan point of view, but for important general trends the archives of the great families are indispensable. Most of these are easily consulted in the section "Iewake" of the *Dai Nihon Komonjo* series, and among them of particular interest are the records of Mōri, Kobayakawa, Kikkawa, Uyesugi, Asano, Hosokawa, Yoshida, and Ōtomo. The Mōri archives, for example, contain a letter from Hideyoshi describing his campaigns; and at times the best text of one of Hideyoshi's edicts or laws can be found in the archives of one of the great families to whom they were notified. Thus the text of the edict announcing Hideyoshi's Sword Hunt is to be found in the Kobayakawa archives.

The archives of the great religious foundations are valuable at times for political as well as religious history. A good example is the *Kōyasan Monjo* (高野山), also in the *Dai Nihon Komonjo*, "Iewake"; and another is *Honganji Monjo*, in the same series.

An interesting work is *O Yudono no Uye no Nikki* (御湯殿上日記), a journal kept from 1477 to 1820 in the Imperial Palace. The extant portions cover this long period but the published parts are from 1477 to 1687. They are in a supplement of ten volumes to *Gunsho Ruijū*. There is a close study of the text in Vols. 15 and 16 of the Proceedings of the Japan Academy (學士院紀要). The work is a confidential diary of Court affairs kept by ladies serving in the inner apartments of the Palace. Though concerned with the intimate life of the Court, it contains frequent references to relations with the Bakufu and important barons. It owes its value partly to the fact that after the Ōnin War many Court nobles and officials left the capital and no longer kept diaries. It is written mainly in the kana script.

Zenrin Kokuhō Ki (善隣國宝記) is not strictly speaking a primary source, but it is a record of the foreign relations of Japan during the Muromachi period, put together by a monk, Zuikei, before 1473. He had access to diplomatic papers regarding relations with China. In *Zoku Gunsho Ruijū*.

An important study of Tokugawa documents is in course of completion by Dr. Kōya Nakamura. So far three volumes of this monumental work have been published, and there is more to follow. Vol. I (782 pp.) contains documents for 1556–90; Vol. II (832 pp.) ends with enfeoffments and confiscations after Sekigahara. I regret that I received these volumes too late to make full use of them. Published by Nihon Gakujutsu Shinkōkai, Tokyo, 1958–60.

SECONDARY SOURCES

Apart from historical dictionaries and other works of reference the following list includes the principal single works consulted during the preparation of this volume.

Nambokuchō (南北朝). By Uozumi Sōgorō in *Sōgō Nihonshi Taikei.*

Nambokuchō Jidaishi (南北朝時代史). By Kume Kunitake, in *Waseda* series (1907).

Nambokuchō Jidaishi. By Tanaka Yoshinari. An early work by the first Director of the Historical Compilation Institute. Last edition, 1922.

Ashikaga Jidaishi (足利時代史). Tanaka Yoshinari (1923).

Yoshino-Muromachi Bunkashi. In *Nihon Bunkashi Taikei,* Vol. VII.

Nihon Rekishi Koza (日本歴史講座). Vol. III of a series published by the Tokyo University Press, 1957. It is compiled by the Rekishigaku Kenkyūkai, and contains essays by good authorities on political, social, and economic matters through the middle ages to the Momoyama period. The last essay deals with the material foundations of the Tokugawa Bakufu. A valuable work, it gives a useful reading list on the last pages.

Kantō Chūshin Ashikaga Jidai no Kenkyū (關東中心足利時代). A valuable work (out of print) by Watanabe Yosuke, which shows the difficulties of the Ashikaga Bakufu in Kyoto in controlling the warriors in Eastern Japan. Tokyo, Yūzankaku, 1926.

Muromachi Jidaishi. By Watanabe Yosuke, in *Waseda* series (1907).

Muromachi Jidaishi. By Naganuma Kenkai, in *Dai Nihonshi Kōza,* Vol. 5.

Ashikaga Takauji (足利尊氏). A biography, by Takayanagi Mitsutoshi (1956).

Kitabatake Chikafusa (北畠親房). By Nakamura Naokatsu (Kyoto, 1920). A useful, if somewhat romantic, life of Chikafusa, with an appendix on Akiiye. It pays attention to the political background. By the same author is *Chikafusa Den.* (Tokyo, 1937).

Musō Kokushi (夢窓國師). By Tamamura Takezō, Kyoto, 1958.

Musō Kokushi. By Professor Nishida Naojirō. Published by the Tenryūji in 1950, for the 600th anniversary of Musō's death. Out of print.

Rekishi to Jimbutsu. Biographical essays by Miura Hiroyuki, including studies of Kusunoki Masashige. Tokyo, 1916.

Sengoku Jidaishi Ron (戰國時代史論). Fourteen essays by Watanabe Yosuke and others. This is an early work (1910) and is out of print. But it contains excellent material by the best scholars of the day.

Chūsei Shakai (中世社會). Seven chapters on mediaeval society in Japan, including an essay on the Shugo-daimyos by Satō Shinichi and a useful study of new trends by Toyoda Takeshi, who also contributes an introduction to the volume and an essay on the formation of the domains of the Shugo-daimyos and the growth of towns.

Chūsei Shakai no Kenkyū. An authoritative work by Matsumoto Shimpachirō. It contains a close analysis of political and economic aspects of society during the late Kamakura and Nambokuchō periods. It deals with developments in rural life leading to the collapse of the shōen and with the agrarian riots.

Chūsei Nihon Shōgyōshi no Kenkyū (中世日本商業史). By Toyoda Takeshi. A fascinating study of the history of commerce in mediaeval Japan, in which the evidence is most skilfully presented. New edition in *Iwanami Kōza,* Tokyo, 1957.

Buke Jidai Shakai no Kenkyū. A collection of essays by Makino Shinnosuke, written between 1913 and 1930 on legal, economic, and religious aspects of the feudal regimes in Japan. There are interesting sections on land tenure, with data on Hideyoshi's Land Survey, on social changes, on ecclesiastical matters, and on the character of the Abbot Jinson and his journal (*Jisha Zōjiki*).

Sakai (堺). The history of the town from its origin to the times of Hideyoshi. By Toyoda Takeshi in *Nihon Rekishi Shinsho*, 1957.

Nihon no Kaizoku. "On Japanese Pirates." By Naganuma Kenkai. *Nihon Rekishi Shinsho,* 1955.

Ikkō Ikki (一向一揆). An account of the relations of the Shin sect of Amidism and the feudal society, with special reference to sectarian riots. By Kasahara Kazuo, in *Nihon Rekishi Shinsho,* 1955.

Nihon no Hōken Toshi (日本の封建都市). "The Feudal Town in Japan," by a leading authority, Toyoda Takeshi. *Iwanami Zensho,* No. 160, 1952.

Nobunaga to Hideyoshi. By Okuno Takahiro in *Nihon Rekishi Shinsho,* 1955.

Nobunaga, Hideyoshi, Ieyasu. A pleasant work by a great scholar, Tsuji Zennosuke. Tokyo, 1943.

Taikō no Tegami (太閤の手紙). Text and commentaries on Hideyoshi's letters, by Kuwada Tadachika. A convenient and reliable work. Tokyo, Bungei Shunjū Shinsha, 1959.

Chūsei ni okeru Shaji to Shakai to no Kankei. A study of the place of shrines and monasteries in mediaeval society, by Hiraizumi Kiyoshi. Tokyo, 1926.

Nihon Shōnin Shi (Chūsei Hen) (日本商人史). A history of traders in Japan from early times through the middle ages. The fruit of long research by Toyoda Takeshi. Tokyo, 1950.

Bakufu Ron (幕府論). A good short essay (42 pp.) on the nature of the Bakufu in the Kamakura and Muromachi periods, by Satō Shinichi. In *Shin Rekishi Kōza,* Vol. 3.

Muromachi Bakufu Seiji. A study of Bakufu government by Uozumi Sōgorō, in *Iwanami Kōza, Nihon no Rekishi,* Vol. 2.

Honnōji no Hen (本能寺の変・山崎の戰). An account of the murder of Nobunaga and its sequels, including the battle of Yamazaki, by Takayanagi Mitsutoshi (1958). One of a series of eight volumes on battles in mediaeval Japan in course of publication by Shunjū-sha (春秋社).

Nihon Senshi (日本戰史). This is the standard military history of Japan, compiled by the Japanese General Staff. In the present work it has been drawn upon for details of Okehazama and Sekigahara, and consulted on points in the siege of Ōsaka castle. Its documentation of Sekigahara is especially rich.

Nihon Senshi no Kenkyū. A short study of the history of warfare in Japan by General Hayashi Yasokichi and Major Hashibe Yokichi. It contains discussions of Kusunoki's campaigns and descriptions of battles fought by Nobunaga and Hideyoshi, together with accounts of Kawanakajima, Sekigahara, and the siege of Ōsaka castle. Kaikōsha, 1937.

Azuchi-Momoyama Jidaishi Ron. A collection of twelve lectures by leading scholars under the auspices of the Rekishichirigakkai, published in Tokyo, 1915.

Gokaidō Saiken (五街道細見). A detailed account of the main highways, by Kishii Ryōei, with an excellent map. Tokyo, 1959.

Ekirin-bon Setsuyōshū. A facsimile published by the Koten Kankō-Kai (易林本節用集). A useful guide to pronunciation in mediaeval Japan.

Nōmin Kaihō no Shiteki Kōsatsu. A compilation by *Shakai Keizaishi Gakki.* A study of peasant emancipation by six writers, including two essays on agrarian movements in Europe.

Fukusō to Kojitsu. A study of costume by Suzuki Keizō. Kyoto, 1950.

Official Relations between China and Japan, 1368–1549. By Wang Yi-ting. In Harvard-Yenching Institute Studies, Vol. 9.

Money Economy in Mediaeval Japan. By Delmer Brown. Far Eastern Association Monograph, No. 1, 1951.

L'Est et l'Ouest. By Joüon des Longrais. A valuable comparative study of feudal institutions. Tokyo, Maison Franco-Japonaise, 1958.

Okinawa. By George H. Kerr. A history of the people of the Ryūkyū archipelago. Tokyo, 1958.

Kyoto, The Old Capital of Japan. By R. Ponsonby-Fane. A description of the city from 974 to 1809. Kyoto, 1956.

The Affair of the Madre de Deus. By C. R. Boxer. London, Japan Society, 1929.

Fidalgos in the Far East (1550–1770). By C. R. Boxer. The Hague, 1948.

Jan Compagnie in Japan, 1600–1850. By C. R. Boxer. The Hague, 1950.

GLOSSARY

BŌMON (坊門). Entrance into a section of one of the avenues in Kyoto.

CHIGYŌ (知行). Property rights in land exercised by a person in direct control. The term is used loosely to stand for "fief."

DAINAGON (大納言). A counsellor (Court Rank).

GENIN (下人). Domestic servants of noblemen, religious bodies, and warriors of the myōshu class. They were serfs.

GŌ (郷). In the Nara period, an administrative area comprising several villages. In the Muromachi period, a self-governing large village or group of villages.

HANZEI (半濟). A system of tax collecting by which a Constable or Deputy retained half the tax for his own military use and remitted the remainder to the manorial lord.

IKKI (一揆). An association of persons for joint action. A league. By extension, the action of such a league.

JI-SAMURAI (地侍). A member of the military class living in a country district where his family have been long settled. See KOKUJIN.

KANREI (管領). Government; a Governor or other high administrative officer.

KOKUJIN (國人). Landholders long settled and influential in a given locality. See JI-SAMURAI.

KUBŌ (公方). An honorific title for the Shōgun or his representative in the Kantō.

MANDOKORO (政所). The Household Office of a great family. The name was in mediaeval times applied to the mistress of a house, and came to mean a secondary wife. The true wife was called Kita Mandokoro.

MYŌSHU (名主). An owner of land in a shōen in his own name. A daimyo (大名) was a great landowner.

NYŪDŌ (入道). A person who has entered holy orders.

RŌNIN (牢人). Persons who have absconded and are vagrant. The term originally meant fugitive peasants, but later was applied to unemployed members of the warrior class.

SHIKIMOKU (式目). A formulary; a code of law.

SHUGO-DAIKAN (守護代官). The Deputy of a Constable-daimyo.

SHUGO-DAIMYO (守護大名). A Constable who has become a great landowner, by confiscations or similar means, in his province.

SHUGO-UKE (守護請). A system of taxation whereby a provincial Governor contracted to accept an agreed amount of tax from a manor, taking half for his own military expenditure and paying half to the lord of the manor.

SHITAJI (下地). Land furnishing revenue. Often used to denote the revenue, as is "shitaji chūbun," which means the division of revenue from a manor between the landlord and the steward.

SŌBYAKUSHŌ (総百姓). The whole body of farmers in a village. United farmers.

SŌJŌ (僧正). An ecclesiastical rank, best translated "abbot." A Daisōjō holds rank above a Sōjō, and may be styled High Abbot or Chief Abbot.

SŌSON (総村). All the villages (in a given area) combined for self government.

SŌRYŌ (総領). The whole estate, and by transfer of meaning, the inheritor of the whole estate.

TANDAI (探題). An Inspector; a high commissioner.

TANSEN (段錢). A tax on arable land at so much per unit of area—the *tan.* If paid in rice it was called *tammai.*

TOKUBUN (得分). Income or revenue.

TOKUSŌRYŌ (得宗領). A relic of the Kamakura period when the Hōjō Regents acquired estates throughout the country for the Hōjō family. Such estates were called Tokusō lands, after the style of the head of the Hōjō family, Tokimune.

YAZENI (矢錢). "Arrow money," a war tax.

INDEX